I remember my baby hair wit[h] ████ [b]raids
Frenchy's, Boudin in the parking ████
Shout-out to Willie D
I was in that Willie D video when I was about 14
Lookin' crazy
Shout-out to Pimp C
You know we used to sneak and listen to that UGK
Didn't do your girl, but your sister was alright, damn
In ya homeboy's Caddy last night man, haha
Hold up, Texas trill
H-town going down, man

BEYONCÉ, "Bow Down/I Been On" (2013)

HOUSTON
RAP
TAPES

NEW EDITION

An Oral History of Bayou City Hip-Hop

LANCE SCOTT WALKER

FOREWORD BY WILLIE D

UNIVERSITY OF TEXAS PRESS ✧ AUSTIN

Requests for permission to reproduce material
from this work should be sent to:
   Permissions
   University of Texas Press
   P.O. Box 7819
   Austin, TX 78713-7819
   utpress.utexas.edu/rp-form

The paper used in this book meets the minimum
requirements of ANSI/NISO Z39.48-1992 (R1997)
(Permanence of Paper). ∞

Library of Congress Cataloging-in-Publication Data
Names: Walker, Lance Scott, 1973- author. | Dennis,
   William James, 1966- writer of foreword.
Title: Houston rap tapes : an oral history of Bayou City
   hip-hop / Lance Scott Walker ; foreword by Willie D.
Description: New edition. | Austin : University of Texas
   Press, 2018.
Identifiers: LCCN 2018008702
   ISBN 978-1-4773-1717-4 (pbk. : alk. paper)
   ISBN 978-1-4773-1792-1 (library e-book)
   ISBN 978-1-4773-1793-8 (non-library e-book)
Subjects: LCSH: Rap musicians—Texas—Houston—
   Interviews. | Rap (Music)—Texas—Houston—
   History and criticism.
Classification: LCC ML3531 .W36 2018 |
   DDC 782.421649097641411—dc23
   LC record available at
   https://lccn.loc.gov/2018008702

doi:10.7560/317174

Contents

Foreword

WILLIE D

I can't stand writers, reporters, and so-called journalists who stick microphones in the face of people and don't know what they're talking about. That happens a lot in hip-hop, the whore of the music industry. Because it's so easy to get in—pun intended—many newcomers go for instant gratification. They would rather rape the game to get paid than to get to know it intimately and fall in love.

Fortunately for hip-hop enthusiasts and those interested in a unique narrative on H-town culture, authors Lance Scott Walker and Peter Beste aren't hip-hop rapists. They are homegrown Texans and passionate nurturers of the art, seeking to feed the urban spirit of the biggest city in the South to our hungry bellies with this opalescent collection of interviews conducted between 2005 and 2017 with numerous members of the Houston rap community. To read Al-B of the pioneering battle rap group Royal Flush recount early battle rap stories at the Rhinestone Wrangler nightclub alone is worth buying two books; one to have on hand and one as a replacement tucked away in a safe or wherever you hide your valuables. Because trust me, like a fool walking out of the bank with a moneybag, you will get jacked.

When I performed in Helsinki, Finland in 2007, I had no idea that DJ Screw was so popular there and that K-Rino was selling out clubs in the UK. Thanks to the easy accessibility of the internet, many artists from Houston who may not have enjoyed mainstream success are now seeping into the consciousness of hardcore rap fans.

What's beautiful about *Rap Tapes* is that the authors speak to everyone the same way. Whether they sold one million records or one, homage is given. It's important that the writers of hip-hop history reserve a space to document Scarface, Z-Ro, and Bun B among the best to ever do it. It is equally important to magnify the talents and contributions of their predecessors Romeo Poet, Raheem, and Ricky Royal, which is thankfully achieved.

The topics in *Rap Tapes* are as diverse and incendiary as the individuals who tell them. Readers are taken on a virtual ride through some of Houston's toughest neighborhoods like Fifth Ward, Third Ward, South Park, and the Southside. Issues of gentrification, crime, healthcare, drugs, and more are discussed in detail, no sugarcoating.

Houston Rap Tapes flows more like a bunch of fellows who haven't seen each other for ages, hanging out on the block reminiscing, rather than a calculated literary guide to Houston's history. Although the latter will get you a book deal, it is the firsthand knowledge shared by those who lived the stories and their own unique worldviews that will connect the book to an audience beyond Houston's city limits.

Poet José Saramago said, "Human vocabulary is still not capable and probably never will be of knowing, recognizing, and communicating everything that can be humanly experienced and felt." I agree, but in relation to much of the indiscreet answers and information from H-Town's rap community, *Houston Rap Tapes* brings us vicariously close.

For those who need convincing past this introduction, allow me to leave you with the immortal words of the homie Pimp C, "Y'all shoulda listened to Andre, bitch, we got somethin' to say!" ✖

Preface

LANCE SCOTT WALKER

In the process of compiling *Houston Rap*, the photo and oral history book to which this serves as companion, we had to leave a lot out. In fact, *most* of the material that photographer Peter Beste and I began gathering in 2004 and 2005 didn't make the cut. Peter shot thousands more photos than we could ever include, and I had to boil hour-long interviews down to a paragraph or just a few lines. The length of those quotes preserves the context for the most part, but nothing compares to the full text of the conversations.

And it's important stuff in those conversations. Plenty of Houston's rap history has been documented over the years, but even more of it only survives as unwritten stories. As Houston's landscape is further developed, and so much of its physical history is erased in favor of strip centers and condominiums, those stories work to keep that history alive. Gentrification may have rendered parts of some Houston neighborhoods unrecognizable, but the fabric of the communities who once resided there remains strong, spread out as it may be. Houston's like that.

It is an enormous city, the fourth largest in the nation and one of the fastest growing, with an infrastructure that divides it up into smaller cities that really are their own towns. The neighborhoods of Fifth Ward, Third Ward, and South Park and its surrounding Southside area are all known as the birthplace of Houston rappers, but aside from that, they really couldn't be more different. Their histories are unique, the vibe in the streets is different, and of course, so are the people.

Your city is only as big as the parts of it you allow yourself to see. These are perspectives from some of Houston's marginalized corners. In the culture, the slang, and the history, you see something revealed that is inimitably Houston, but there are neighborhoods like Fifth Ward, Third Ward, and South Park in a lot of American cities. The struggles laid out here and the feelings expressed may be unique to the individuals who tell the stories, but we can all relate. Through the years-long process of making these two books—doing photo shoots and interviews at backyard barbecues, in private living rooms, leaning against cars in the Texas sun, in corners of nightclubs, out under the street lights, or through countless late-night phone conversations—rap music took a backseat to the human element that opened up. The men and women interviewed here are known as rappers, producers, DJs, radio personalities, and the like, and we learn Houston's history through their own, but we also learn about their passions, regrets, memories, and hopes.

There is a long history of rap music in Houston, but no nostalgia. People grow apart and move on, but the momentum of rap in Houston has never died, regardless of its popularity elsewhere. There is a family element to it that reaches across the neighborhoods. Chalk it up to the insular atmosphere of Houston, as global a city as it may be. That's what makes it special. It is all at once a huge melting pot and its own planet. They may tear down a lot of buildings in Houston, but nobody forgets.

For this New Edition of *Houston Rap Tapes*, we have added 22 more interviews, and the book has been reorganized into sections that cover different eras and movements in Houston music history, with contributions from a wide range of photographers. Still, this isn't meant to be a complete look into Houston rap—more like a cross section—and the names you see here aren't all the most famous ones. But Houston's superstars had a lot of help building their communities, and some of the lesser-known characters have big stories they've just never been asked to tell. In that, we get Houston at street level. It is a city that has always had its own identity, characterized in part by its outsider status, and you see why when you hear from its artists. It's a long game in Houston, and you do it all from scratch. Mainstream attention may come and go, but the neighborhoods keep on living and breathing, and everybody sticks around. I hope these conversations shed some light on that world. ✖

FOUNDATION

The genesis of rap music in Houston, Texas arguably took place in the 1980s. That was when Houstonians could hear DJ Darryl Scott mixing hip-hop records into his funk sets in the clubs of Charles Bush and Ray Barnett on the Southside. Steve Fournier was breaking boundaries on the Northside, sneaking in more hip-hop than the club owners would allow at Boneshakers and Strut's Disco. R.P. Cola came up blasting rap records through the speakers of any underground nightspot that would let him on the turntables, even the strip clubs. Crowds around the city lit up when they heard hip-hop played in the clubs, and once the kids who were rapping in the streets got to performing in those clubs, they began to form groups and start making records themselves. To be sure, the '80s were when Houston defined itself as a creative nexus for the genre. But all of the folks who made that scene possible were already laying the groundwork in the late 1970s, when Houston was just *waiting* for something like hip-hop to come along.

The Bayou City had a vibrant music scene in the era before hip-hop. Plenty of the city's blues and zydeco artists were making their money playing gigs in Fifth Ward, Third Ward, Fourth Ward, and all over the Southside—the very same neighborhoods that later produced the young men and women who would embrace hip-hop and become DJs and MCs themselves. The music was changing, but the older generations had cut roads they were sure the younger generation would later follow (and they did) through Texas, Louisiana, and along the Chitlin Circuit through the South, building networks in any city or town that would have them. Hip-hop was something new, but as the poetry of the streets, it had everything in common with the music that came before it.

Darrell Veal moved south from New York and ended up living in Fifth Ward, where people got to know him as MC Wickett Crickett when they saw him freestyling in cafes and clubs around town—even on the bus—getting onstage with any funk or boogie band that would have him. Thelton Polk was out there rapping too. He went on to be called Sir Rap-A-Lot and then, after his brother James

Prince took that name to start his record label, Polk renamed himself K-9 and was drafted into the original Ghetto Boys.

Producer/writers like Mikki Bleu (John Kenneth Williams) and Mel Owens were at work in bands like Glass and Perfect Timin'. Mel recorded a rap 12-inch, "Don't Stand (Me Up)" in 1985, and Mikki would go on to produce the first Ghetto Boys single the following year. Before that, in 1984, Captain Jack released a 12-inch and Steve Cummings and his funk band Chance backed up Jazzie Redd on "Break Dancin'," two of Houston's earliest hip-hop singles. A couple of students—Colin Buckner and Robert Harkness—over at Texas Southern University (TSU) in Third Ward recorded what was likely the first, "Thumpin," under the name Brother's Disco in 1981.

TSU advanced the cause further a couple of years later with "Kidz Jamm," the Saturday morning radio program on which most Houstonians first heard their local rappers. Lester "Sir" Pace and Walter D were spinning records. Jazzie Redd, Prince Ezzy-E (a.k.a. O.G. Style), and MC Wickett Crickett would freestyle on the air. King T was there. KTSU Program Director Pam Collins kept them all in line.

The movie *Breakin'* came out in 1984, and that was where hip-hop began for a lot of folks. That meant things got busier for Big Steve and Captain Jack in the clubs. People were exchanging tapes of "Kidz Jamm" broadcasts. On Sunday afternoons, Darryl Scott was at MacGregor Park selling mixtapes, making money hand over fist until he was finally forced to open a shop—one of his many moves that would influence the generation that followed. ✖

MC Wickett Crickett (1959–2015)

One of the earliest advocates of rap music in Houston, Darrell Veal arrived in the city in the 1970s from New York and soon began hosting shows with live bands in Fifth Ward cafés. In the following decades, MC Wickett Crickett was there for every movement in Houston hip-hop. He only recorded one 12-inch, "Where U From / Can I Hit It," in 1996, but nevertheless forged a legacy that includes giving DJ Screw his first gig (as he did for countless other Houston artists). Wickett Crickett remained a visible and important part of Houston rap culture, MCing talent shows and weekly club nights all over the city until his death from lung cancer in November 2015. He was 56.

What year did you come to Houston?

Well, I was down here in the '70s on and off, but the rap era didn't start down here until '80 . . . '82, '83. It was something new to them. Because I was going to clubs, freestylin', hosting little shows, but they didn't know what it was. They had bands playing in clubs, people singin' . . . they used to have talent nights, and I used to get up there and win the prizes 'cuz I would freestyle . . . like the drummer would play a beat—I'd tell him to put a beat on—and I'd just freestyle about the people in the audience. They didn't know what that was, like being able to rhyme and talk about what people got on and what the next person is doin' and all of that. That was something new to them.

Was this before the Rhinestone Wrangler?

Yeah, that was *way* before the Rhinestone Wrangler.

What clubs were you in then—talking about late '70s, early '80s?

Well, back during that time they used to have a club called The Fresh Connection. It used to be off of Kelley . . . and what was that street . . . Los Angeles? I know it was off of Kelley and something. But it was before you get to Hirsch Road. They put up a bus station there now, but everybody in the '70s and the early '80s, that's where they used to go, to The Fresh Connection. It was right on the Northside. It was, like, real, real crunk. And then they had a club on the Southside called The Blue Ice. They had another little club, there was Turning Point I, Turning Point II. And they was all café clubs. The Fresh Connection came when the hip-hop scene came. But before the hip-hop scene, everything was like café clubs because you had bands playin' in clubs.

So it was kind of spread out. The club on the Southside—where was that? Ice . . .

That was Club Blue Ice. That was on the Southside. Turning Point I, Turning Point II, and there was another club—it's still there. I can't think of the name of it but it's on OST [Old Spanish Trail] and, what is that . . . that turns into Griggs . . . where it split up there? At Griggs and Calhoun. There was a little club right there. Can't think of it . . .

PHOTO: PETER BESTE

The Spot?

Right across from Church's Chicken. It's been there for ages. It's still there. And one of the dudes that I met, he was DJ Slick Rick down here. He now plays guitar for a dude named Mel Waiters, a professional blues cat. But he was like one of the first DJs I met that really helped me out a lot when I first came down here. It's right across from Church's on Griggs. Right there at Griggs and Calhoun, there's a little club right there. Been there for ages. It look like it's small, but go in and it's alright—it's a pretty nice size.

You're not talking about The Spot? That really long place next to King's?

Nah, it's not called The Spot. It's right across the street from Church's Chicken. On Griggs and Calhoun. I can't think of the name of it, but it's blue on the outside. . . . Oh, I know what the name of it is: the name of it is King Leo's. That's what it is. King Leo's.

So what was going on there? You were in there and people were freestyling . . .

I was the *only* one freestylin'. They had comedy nights. They would have comedy and bands playing in clubs. They didn't know nothing about the rap era. The era really hadn't got to them yet. The first thing they knew about rap down this way was "Rapper's Delight" and Kurtis Blow. But rap had been out. Rap had been out before then. You had rappers been out in New York who'd never even made it out this way.

Once it came in, did it creep in or did it explode?

It kind of exploded. It kind of exploded because people knew about it from "Rapper's Delight" and from Kurtis Blow. Kurtis Blow came with stories. "These Are The Breaks" was a story about what you go through every day in life. So, in the beginning, most of your songs was tellin' stories, and that's what rap was. In the beginning, hip-hop was fun music with stories about the government, with no money, no jobs, poverty, you know . . . "New York, New York / Big city of dreams / everything in New York ain't always what it seems / You might be fooled if you come from out of town / But I'm down by law and I know my way around / Too much, too many people . . ." Know what I'm saying—all the stories back then was true stories, and so rap in the beginning was telling people just what it was, but it wasn't so much violence. There was a lot of violence under rap, but it wasn't as violent as it was when the late '80s came in because when the late '80s came in, the world had been introduced to crack. But before that—before crack came—it was always drugs, but it was drugs that older people used. Like Quaaludes and mollies and trees. You know, in the '70s, a bag of weed—a ten-dollar bag of weed was called a "lid," and it was like a fat sandwich bag. You know, now a ten-dollar bag of weed ain't no more than like a little old small something, you know, I mean everything changed. Weed wasn't the problem. When crack came in, crack took over. 'Cuz crack was something that anybody could afford. You couldn't get no heroin . . . when [Laid Back] put the song out about heroin, that was the drug. Heroin was the drug, the white horse. That was about heroin because people that had a little money was shootin' heroin. That was like the tightest high you could get, was heroin. Everybody was gettin' strung out on needles. But then . . . a lot of people couldn't afford that fix, so they just broke it down to crack and made it where anybody could afford crack.

That hit Houston too . . . you're talking about '84, '85, '86 . . .

Yeah, but when it came to Houston, it was pure, and what happened was the Colombians that was comin' down here from Miami was bringin' it down here and makin' friends in the black neighborhoods with the blacks, and telling them that this was something that, once they got it started out there . . . because see, a lot of the early people that smoked it became dope fiends because they thought it was something they could handle. When they first started smoking it, they smoked it smashed up . . . you know, they smashed the rock up, and you could roll it in a joint with some weed. So they thought it was like something to enhance the weed in the beginning. And they called it "primos." Well, they felt like, "I'm smoking weed and this, I'm not gonna get hooked." But they didn't understand that they was steady getting hooked because it was a mellow drug. The crack in the beginning, it started off smellin' kinda sweet and mellow, but it was still cocaine. So then, the more you got hooked on it, the more you didn't want the weed. You wanted the pure cocaine. You need the whole high. And the crack in the beginning was pure crack. It wasn't cut. People didn't start cuttin' it until the '90s because they wanted to flip they money. So instead of them givin' 'em pure crack, they was goin' to them lil' shops, them lil' weed shops and novelty shops to buy some stuff called "Propane," recookin' they stuff and givin' 'em half coke and half blow.

What was it? Was it baking soda? What was that stuff?

No, it wasn't baking soda. It was like the same stuff you used for [a] toothache or somethin'. It was like to numb your gums . . . it was the same effect.

Novocaine.

Yeah. That was the same effect.

So they were using that because people would notice the difference a lot less because it was a numbing effect.

They wouldn't notice the difference because crack did the same thing.

So it wasn't really until the early '90s that people started to cut it. You're right in that people didn't really understand crack when it came out, especially how it snuck through, but it became the "epidemic" through the media and . . .

You had two types of people that had gotten involved with it. You had the people who was already on horse, and when they got it, it was because they couldn't afford the high stuff no more, so instead of trying to pay fifty dollars for a bag, you could take fifty dollars and buy a bunch of big rocks, and just cut 'em up and smoke rocks all day. So when they couldn't afford the heroin, the straight powder, they were buyin' crack, and the first crack was so pure when it came in that the thing was it kept you high, but it had you where you wanted to keep buyin' it. Heroin had a longer high, but heroin was more expensive.

Was heroin really popular in Houston in the early '80s, the mid-'80s?

Well, in the '70s, it was low, low, low key. But it wasn't as bad. Heroin was never really bad down here like it was in New York. You had pimps that came from Dallas and other places, and they would get they girls hooked on heroin or some shit. Normally pimps used that shit, but wasn't too many regular people messin' with that shit because the '70s was the era of the blues. Texas is more the blues people, and Louisiana was next door—they was into blues and zydeco. But see New York is like right there on the water where the drug trades was. You got New York, New Jersey, Mississippi, Manhattan . . . you know, Miami. You got all these people that's right there on the coast, so the drug is right there. For them, to get money this way . . . the East Coast was never bringin' drugs here. You know, they had their own problems. New Jersey, Detroit . . . all them areas wasn't too busy. The crack was right there. They was too busy killin' each other for turfs. The crack was already there.

All the crack that was coming into Houston in the 1980s was from Miami, wasn't it?

Yeah, the crack that came into Houston was from Miami. Colombians. Once the Colombians came down here and turned Houston onto it, and you had certain areas of people that had money, that got together and had millions, put all they money together and sent people to Miami to do the pickups. Well, in the early times, the laws didn't really know nothing about the interstate. You could ride all out of town. Crack wasn't really a big epidemic, and they wasn't really worried about . . . highway patrol was never really just stoppin' nobody to check they car for drugs or none of that. That scene didn't come in until after the rap era got real, real tough. After rap got tough, and rappers started rappin' about how they go up-and-down the highway doin' this, that, and the other . . . that's how the laws started figuring out, "Okay, so this how they movin' it." When they would see cars come in from out of town somewhere with different license plates, they might just take a chance just to stop and check 'em, just because they kind of looked halfway suspicious. The majority of the time they would come up with something, so the more they start catchin' people on the interstate, that made 'em start bein' more aware of how it's getting in. A lot of rappers shot theyself in the foot because they was telling too much in they rap songs, even how they was FedExin' stuff. You know, they got to the point where they was mailin' stuff to . . . they might mail it to an address, and wrap it and FedEx it straight to that person. They was all kinda ways it was goin' on. Greyhound buses or whatever. You know, it got in. Too many rappers started tellin' the stories about what they was doin', and that's how the cops started knowin' stuff. And that was coming through I-10. That was all coming through Louisiana, Mississippi . . . Yeah, I-10. I-10 was the problem. Anything going down I-10 was always . . . that was it. They told too many stories about I-10. I mean, you could

leave Houston and go all the way to Penn State. Three days to Penn State or whatever, I mean you always had people to take it. It just was that when people got busted on the interstate, they started givin' up too much information to make they case a little cheaper 'cuz actually it was like . . . the laws didn't want who they caught. They wanted who the *source* was. They were like, "We know you not the person. You're the person who he's makin' some money off of. We wanna know who you're gettin' it from. What's your contact?" So if the person didn't snitch, what they did was they took they cell phones and they just kept records of all the numbers that was in they phone. And they would, like, call these people back, or follow these people to take pictures of them, and they'd start sending out secret indictments. So you got like 20 people involved and different areas getting a secret indictment, and not knowing who's tellin' on who and they start all tellin' on each other.

So this is all like late '80s, early '90s . . . The I-10 Connect.

Just about every rapper. Dallas . . . even Dallas. Everybody knew. Because see, when Miami brought it in, Miami didn't stop in Louisiana. Miami people had a lot of people they deal with right here in Houston, Texas. 'Cuz Houston, Texas is so big that people down here was grindin', as to where you couldn't take a chance of takin' nothin' to New Orleans, because New Orleans was like the murder capital of the world. Plus, New Orleans—if you got caught with anything in New Orleans, you got 10 years. You got straight 10 years. They was up under the other law, whereas in Houston, if you got 10 years you mighta did five years instead of 10. That's how it was in that time—that was before they changed up everything. You know, when the crack came, that was during the time when the government had moved all the foreigners over here and gave them bank accounts and stuff. That's when all your Koreans came in, your Chinese, your Japanese . . . you know, because flea markets in the '70s was vegetables and grapes and stuff like that. Then flea markets turned into places to go get jewelry and clothes and all that other little stuff. Little clothes that was remade over, with a name like the real name, but it wasn't the real stuff.

Knockoffs.

Yeah, see the first flea markets was vegetables. Flea markets was groceries and vegetables. That's what flea markets was in the beginning. But when crack came, flea markets became places for the Koreans and all your little small vendors to set up in one big spot. And sell they merchandise.

How did crack change that, when crack came into Houston?

Crack changed the mentality. Crack changed the mentality of the whole era. Crack changed the era of goin' to school and getting a summer job . . . you know, before crack came, kids used to . . . couldn't *wait* 'til the summer come, so they could apply for a summer job, get a summer job workin' at AstroWorld or one of them parks, or one of them schools. But once crack came, you know, people dropped out of school because they parents was either on it, or . . . the daughter was goin' with somebody who was sellin' it, and he already had a car and was pickin' her up, takin' her to school. He givin' the mama money that the mama didn't have, the daddy wouldn't have. So he'd up and pay rent, and then the government started this . . . the government was all part of the whole thing. I mean, they knew . . . it was they crack, so they knew that it was gonna get moved. During that time, what they did was—to make sure that it got moved, they opened up a bunch of government projects. That way they would know just where they drugs was bein' moved at. That way, when they opened up the government projects, they knew that the girls' rent wasn't no more than five dollars or ten dollars. So common sense . . . if she got a kid and her rent ain't nothing but five dollars or ten dollars, and these cats here, if she halfway look like something, they gonna stay with her and move they issue 'cuz it's in a project area. So that way the laws ain't got to look all everywhere, they can look right in certain neighborhoods where the project apartments at, and they know that's just where the fiends and everything was at, 'cuz they rent wasn't nothin'. So they know if the cats got nice cars parked in them kind of places, they know that's where they stuff bein' moved at, so all they got to do is just target those projects, and target the stores in that area.

They know they either hangin' at the store, or they somewhere in the projects. So it's easier for them to bust these cats and get either the money back or some of the dope back. That's why people are screaming "recession" now, because there's no drugs! There's no bad money! And that's why the people that have money, the older people that got money in the banks, you know, your Walgreens and your McDonalds and Burger Kings, all this old money that's been around for ages . . . Sears and stuff, they money *been* in the bank. So it was okay for the banks to loan they money out, because they knew they money was gettin' flipped. Well now, all that old money, them people done said, "Don't loan my money out no more. Don't trust my money." So, these banks ain't got no money to loan out, and credit cards . . . ain't nothin' you can do, 'cuz you done issued all these credit cards to all these people that ain't got the money to pay it. So now they programs, saying, "If you're in credit card debt, call these here numbers," so they can let you pay it little by little, because they realize it's better to get some money out of 'em than none at all.

But it's still predatory.

Yeah, but you're still not gonna pay back all the money you owe, because they know you ain't got it.

Of course not.

And there's no drugs here. There's no bad money no more. That's why you can damn near get a new car for little to nothin' because there's no money. Import and export, all them other places that was over here was over here because the importing and exporting was good with the drugs, because the United States was tradin' guns to these foreign countries. So these foreign countries was makin' money over here. Your towels, your plates, shit by China, shit by Japan. Your foreign cars. You know, all that shit, you're tradin' with these places and at the same time you're steady sayin', "United States," when actually, you just got people over here so you could watch 'em. It had nothing to do with the United States. It had to do with, "If you keep an eye on 'em, you know just what's goin' on, 'cuz you got half of 'em over here."

Do you think the goal was to get crack into the hands of the African Americans of the baby boomer generation?

That's exactly what it was. What it was, see, that was my era. That was my era when crack came. So, when crack came during my era, it was given to black people, but it was given to black people to *move*. And what happened was they didn't really get worried about it until a lot of white kids started gettin' hooked on it, and they couldn't understand how it could be.

That's when it made it to the news.

It was supposed to have been just a black, hood thing. Once they started seein' a lot of white kids was just as bad hooked on crack, and you had white business people that was loanin' they Porsches and they Benz out to get crack—you know, and they couldn't understand how did that happen. It was because it was a cheap drug. Everybody took it as a game in the beginning. A little old rock like that? You looked at that little old rock and said, "Oh, this can't—this not gonna make me want more." But you didn't know the effect it would have on your body. Some people could smoke crack and it didn't do nothing to 'em, as to where other people smoke crack and it took 'em over. And see, the early crack was the pure crack, so once you got a taste of that pure crack when it first came out, you was always searchin' for that. So you could spend your money getting blow up, 'cuz you was gettin' a piece of the high. You wasn't gettin' the whole high that you got when the crack first came, so you had to continuously pay money as to where you're spending 20 to really get 10. You see, everybody wanna say that crack was put in the neighborhoods to mess up the black families or whatever, but that really wasn't what it was. It was because crack was brought over here by Colombians to black cats that was tryin' to be hustlers and make quick money. That's all that was.

They didn't care who they were selling it to.

Yeah. They didn't care who. When they first started out, it was really like smoke . . . before crack even came, people were smoking embalming fluid.

Wet.

Well, now they call it Sherm, but back then they was callin' it Angel Dust. People was rollin' it up in paper squares and hittin' it, and other people didn't know. They thought they was smokin' weed. In my era, they was callin' it Angel Dust. It's the same thing. When somebody used to get hooked, they didn't know what they was getting hooked on. They just thought it was pot that they could handle. "Ten dollars? I can get high for ten dollars? Oh come on." And see, when it first started out, a ten-dollar rock was like . . . big-sized when it first started. But once people started realizin' that they could cut that in half, and sell it for 10, then it became a money issue.

They were cutting it with all kinds of stuff! I talked to someone once who told me he was cutting embalming fluid with elephant tranquilizers, ether . . .

And that's what he was doin', and he probably was killin' people! You had other people that was mixin' it with Novocaine and Propane just to blow it up, but they wouldn't try to put all that extra shit in there, because they wanted the customer to keep comin' back and they was too afraid to get a murder case.

But what I'm saying is that, in every situation, you didn't really know what it was being cut with. Like if you were to go on the street and buy it, even 10, 20 years later . . . how do you really know what it's cut with? How do you even know what you're smoking?

You talking about the Sherm?

Or the Angel Dust, assuming that's pretty much the same thing.

Sherm and Angel Dust, yeah, that's the same thing. Well, you never know what that shit cut with, period. That's a murder case, 'cuz that's embalming fluid. I have a sister-in-law—as we speak, I got a sister-in-law just went to jail for that shit.

She was selling it?

Yep. She on a $30,000 bond right now! I mean, that's a major case. That Sherm is a major case. Drugs is what run the whole United States, and until another drug come out that . . . a lot of money is bein' moved again, the United States is gonna be at a standstill. Like it is right now. And that's why you're gonna hear more about jackin' and robbin', 'cuz these cats is used to gettin' up outside and makin' $500–$1,000 a day. And that's gone like the buffalos. That's why you don't even have a . . . like you used to have that *City Under Siege*? That's been gone. *City Under Siege* used to be comin', knockin', and kickin' doors and runnin' people down. That's been gone because they found out half the time, a lot of the laws that was bustin' people was putting the crack right back out there, givin' it to some people they knew to sell it in they area. So I mean, there was so much investigation that half the time they would take the money and the dope, and wouldn't return all the money that they took off of people or whatever. So you got corruption everywhere. That's gone. 'Cuz there ain't no dope corners like there used to be. The laws been known that. That's why they game is drivers license and insurance now.

Do you think there's a new drug on the horizon that's going to change the makeup of the United States in the way it's been changed before?

Nah, the drug era out of there. The only thing that was close to it was the X pills. Now, the X pills is cheap. People don't even get high like that no more. 'Cuz the music ain't the same. The music was what made you get more high. But now, all of the music is relaxed. It ain't no gangsters no mo'. All the gangsters you used to listen to ain't gangsters! They done played in movies and shit now. The laws and government let you know it wasn't no gangsters 'cuz they put 'em in the movies playin' cops.

Ice Cube, Ice-T.

There wasn't no more gangsters! So once the music changed, everybody's more mellowed out now. You know, ain't nobody on that old rough high. Because now people laid back. I mean, ain't

no more turfs to fight over. Ain't no more, "This mine, I'll sell my dope where I wanna sell it," or, "Screw the law," and all that. All that era gone! Ain't no more, "Go get your TEC-9 and shoot up the hood," and all that. All that's over with.

Lemme ask you this: you saw this because you were in Houston at this time, but in the early '80s when rap came into Houston, it was along the template of what was happening on the East Coast, with groups like Def IV and Royal Flush and even the early Ghetto Boys sounding like their New York contemporaries . . .

Well, Ghetto Boys was the first really gangster—if you check the era, Ghetto Boys themselves really, because they saw a lot of gangster stuff, so when they came out they was really gangster in the beginning, period. They was always gangster. Def IV was tryin' to be hip-hop. They was more or less hip-hop, because one of them came from New York anyway. And you know, Royal Flush was from the West Coast—one of them was from the West Coast. I mean, they were from different areas, but Ghetto Boys themselves were straight Fifth Ward gangsters from the dope era or whatever. That's why Scarface and all them, they told us stories of the dope era. Of what they saw. Of the gangster stuff. You know, they grew up among the dice shootin', the pimps . . . because Lyons Avenue and Liberty Road and all that is where the prostitutes used to walk 24/7. It was the lands of the pimps and players and hustlers. You know, the dice shooters, the card sharks, the early '70s to '79—all the way up to '79 and '80 was the blues and the cafés and the gyp joints and the pimps and the prostitutes. And the heroin. And the Quaaludes and the trees and the mollies. You know, the black mollies. That was all the early drugs back then.

What neighborhoods was all that being moved in?

Third Ward and Fifth Ward. Because see, Fifth Ward used to go all the way to Downtown.

And Third Ward encompasses Downtown. A lot of people don't realize that, but if you look at a map of those old political divisions . . .

Third Ward by Elgin. Because they had an old radio station that closed down that was really one of the first hip-hop stations, that was KYOK. And then you got KCOH, that's part of Third Ward right there over by Almeda. KCOH is still around. LaBranch was where KYOK used to be at. I can't think of the other street, but it was off of LaBranch. That was when the first rap concerts came to Houston. After they went out of business, then you had Love 94 came in. But then Love 94 got sued, because one of they DJs was makin' fun of Michael Jackson when he had that accident when his hair got burnt up. And they sued them . . . they sued Love 94 right off the air.

So what's the first rap concert you remember coming to Houston?

I did the first rap concert come to Houston. It was at AstroWorld. It was the Swatch Watch Fresh Fest.

Who was playing?

It was Run–D.M.C., Whodini, Fat Boys . . . that was the first actual rap concert. I was one of the hosts of that show. It was a tour. It was the first tour that ever came to Houston. It was called the Swatch Watch Fresh Fest.

When the Fat Boys had their own Swatch Watch— The Limelight. Was that '86, '87? That wasn't the tour the Geto Boys were on, though.

Nope. The Geto Boys came later. They was doin' something, but they never really did anything like that with them. When they did stuff, they did stuff like at JB's Entertainment Center on Scott Street. That's when they had Run–D.M.C. that came. They had that group that had that song out "What People Do For Money." They had a couple of little old rap shows came after that. You know, rap was still new, and the young people was into it, but a lot of the young people in Houston didn't have studios. Rap-A-Lot had the studio, then there was a group out called Jefferson Ink out the Southside. Wayne Jefferson and them put out the first Southside song and the first song on the Northside before

Rap-A-Lot. They had a song called "Bedrok." I can't remember the name of the band but the song was called "Bedrok." With Ricky Taylor and them. 'Cuz the same dude who did that with them was . . . he started them because he used to be with an R&B group in the '70s called Archie Bell & the Drells. Oh! The Glass band. That was the name of the them. The Glass band. And they had a song called "Bedrok."

So is this before "MacGregor Park?"

Yeah, that was before Rob did "MacGregor Park." He stayed behind Jones School. The man who put him out.

Robert Harlan?

Yeah, because I postered the show when they did it at JB's Entertainment Center.

He was the South Park Rapper, Robert Harlan, right?

It was a man, they had a studio at his house. It was a family, and they recorded that for Rob, the dude, the man that did it was a man named Robert. He let his family—they used to throw stuff—they had a big concert comin' up they threw at JB's Entertainment Center. But Rob and them, they did it at his house, at the studio they had in his house. And they had some band perform. During that time Rap-A-Lot was doin' stuff, Lil' J was a good friend of mine. At that time, J came over there to check the show out just to see what it was all about. That's when Rob had that song "MacGregor Park." We was goin' to MacGregor Park on Sundays. But then after the law start trippin', they took it all the way to the Northside, and everybody start goin' to Deussen Park on Sundays.

Where's that?

Deussen Park? Way north. It's way on the Northside. That's when Slick Rick's song ["La-Di-Da-Di"] was popular.

I ask because *Houston Rap* is a commentary on the neighborhoods where rap came from in Houston—Fifth Ward, Third Ward, South Park . . .

Acres Homes, all the neighborhoods. You gotta understand—all black neighborhoods. And then, there were drugs in Spring Branch because the Hispanics that stayed over there sold drugs, and the white kids was gettin' it. So crack was everywhere. You had certain areas where, like . . . you know the area of Westheimer where most of the white people stay? Wasn't no drugs over there because there was no low income over there. Wasn't nothing really over there. If anybody was sellin' drugs over there it was big stuff, it was weight. But most of your low-income areas is where the drugs at. Anywhere that was a neighborhood that was a lot of blacks or a lot of Hispanics, that's where your drugs was at. The lower income. You know, so that's all neighborhoods. Fourth Ward, Third Ward, Fifth Ward, South Park, Sunnyside. The whole Northside—Acres Homes, Trinity Gardens, Fifth Ward, Kashmere Gardens. South Park, Sunnyside, Hiram Clarke, Mo City, every neighborhood. I mean it was fast money! You know, once crack came in, you stop calling your "girlfriend" your "girlfriend." Your girlfriend became your "gal," you didn't hold hands, you didn't dress alike no more. Y'all didn't go out to the clubs together no mo'. 'Cuz everything was like, "Oh, you handcuffin'." So, people start goin' with these slangs they was hearin' on the East and the West Coast, and they forgot how they live down here, more or less start changing they culture. And, you know, the respect went out the air. There wasn't no mo' respect no mo'. Once fast money came, you didn't have to respect nobody. That's the way they took it. It's like, "I got my own money. I ain't gotta yes sir, no sir you, I ain't gotta wait on you to get your paycheck to buy me somethin'. I'll go make it for myself. I don't have to come in when you tell me to come in. I'm payin' half the bills."

And it wasn't even about your girlfriend—it was just about the way you lived.

No, what I'm sayin' is . . . even girls, period. When crack came in, fast money came in, so if you was a square cat, waitin' to use your mama car for the prom or somebody rentin' you a car . . . but here go the dude that's young, and he walkin' around with $2,000 or $3,000 in his pocket, and a car, and everybody ridin' with him at lunchtime, and he get to take who he want to the prom. The girls goin' with the dudes with the money, so they done broke up with they square boyfriends and they out there wantin' to be seen. So it's whoever has the money. You know, getting a baby durin' the early '80s was gettin' a baby because you knew that you could get your apartment, you could get out of mama's house, get your own apartment, and your rent wasn't no more than fifteen dollars or twenty dollars, back then. So you wasn't trippin' on havin' no baby. Plus, if you had a baby for a dude that was a big dope dealer, he had to take care of you, and your kid. Your rent wasn't nothin', so he was spoilin' you. Buyin' you clothes and everything. 'Cuz he didn't have to pay no rent. He could stay right there.

Was rent really that cheap back then?

Yeah, fifteen dollars to twenty dollars.

For a month was fifteen dollars or twenty dollars?

Yeah. Government apartment. The most you might've paid . . . you mighta had somebody had to pay forty dollars or fifty dollars for a whole month. Plus you get stamps, so your refrigerator stayin' full. If the dude ain't gotta pay no rent, and he a big dope dealer, he stayin' there with the girl, and that rent only forty dollars or fifty dollars, he's makin' a killin'.

How do you think that era translates to today, when we're talking about a huge recession and the economic landscape in Houston?

Because it's already done spoiled everybody. It's already spoiled everybody. Once the fast money came in, the respect left. People stopped respectin' one another. It was like everybody respected one another, you went to work, spoke to your neighbors, you bust your butt to get a car. Once the crack came in, you could get a car quick as hell. You ain't got to bust your butt no more. Wasn't no "wait 'til the end of the week" to get paid. You made a $1,000 a day almost. When you makin' that kind of money, you know, you got it in your head you could have any woman you want. And back durin' that time, women wasn't tryin' to be with no one dude unless he was the dude that had all the money. So, if he had all the money, that's who she was tryin' to be with, else she end up with his potnah. So, when crack was the thing, that's how it was back then. Girls was with whoever had the money. But now, ain't no bunch of dope dealers no mo', so you got a bunch of strippers. They gotta get it for theyself. The dope dealers gone to jail. The rap thang changed. Dudes start rappin' . . . talking 'bout money over broads. That wasn't the word, but they start sayin' that 'cuz they start realizing that they was goin' to jail behind women. They start seein' how broads was breakin' up with them and goin' with they potnahs and shit. So boys started havin' it in for women, they start callin' . . . boy, they was hatin' women. So that's how all the good women got stuck out, 'cuz all of the players was messin' it up for them. So once that happened, the gay scene just came right on in. There wasn't no mo' hidin' it. You used to didn't see a bunch of girls cutting their hair like dudes and dressin' like dudes . . . but once the crack thang had came in, it was like, "It doesn't matter who have money." You had the gay girls dressin' like dudes. They had the money.

Was that in one part of Houston in particular?

Nope. That was all—that was everywhere. And it's—now it's a common thang. The only thing that's bad about it, is there's kids startin' as far as middle school already lookin' like that. You got girls in middle school that cut they hair and lookin' like dudes in middle school tryin' to go with girls. I mean how can you, at the age of 13 or 14, already know you wanna be with a woman? So, when parents are not parents no mo', they don't have . . . they can't say, "You can't do this," or, "You can't do that," because they didn't have the money, the jobs. They didn't have the jobs or the money, and these kids goin' to school wanna dress like what they see everybody else. And you can't tell 'em nothin' 'cuz you smoke crack or you done . . . bought 'em

a bunch of stuff for Christmas and then, Christmas night, while they asleep, you sold all the stuff to get your high or whatever. You know how many families, how many kids woke up with nothin' Christmas morning? After they seen a bunch of toys? Under the tree? And they had to live with knowin' they parents smoked all they toys up that night? You know how many families went through that? Just imagine that feelin'—you a little kid and your mama got the money. The check came, or the dope man bought everything, but then, during the night, they went round to other people, and other people's kids got the toys you had under your tree 'cuz your parents smoke. So now that everybody's spoiled, they don't know nothin' about the "bust they ass and get a job." They too spoiled, stayin' up all night, makin' money and goin' to the after hours, you know, strippers in Houston . . . goin' to school, gettin' a good education, get a job. All they know now is "sex sells," because that's how America portray everything. Hell, I mean . . . look how your calendars is set up. You got *Sports Illustrated* . . . women get in clubs where everything is catered to sex. That's how America is.

Our definitions of that have morphed over the years, but more than being morphed, they've been forced.

But it started with, you know, them contradictin' theyself with sayin' . . . like, it started with that "freedom of speech" situation. You gotta understand—if you tell America that they got the freedom of speech, so then, once you say that they got the freedom of speech, then that mean they can put out these movies that's . . . everything they doin' is torturin' and killin' women . . . it's like, "Hey, movies is just actin'." But at the same time, you got people that's lookin' at it that's *feelin'* that shit! So you got people that sits and watch that stuff, and they live for the fame, and they look at it like, "Well, one day, they gonna put a movie out about me." So they sittin' up there lookin' at these movies, thinkin' about how much money that's grossin' from these people goin' these—horror movies gross more than any other movies! Than love movies or whatever. They got more people goin' to see Jason and stuff like that than any other movie! So once America see that everybody takin' everything for granted, that's why nobody really worry about . . . I seen somebody's kids got snatched right in McDonald's around a lot of people, and nobody even noticed what happened. Everybody just so comfortable with what's goin' on. People used to be like, "No, don't go there . . . you don't know that man." Now, everybody's just so into they own self that . . . to get snatched right up! Right up under your nose!

And that's the manifestation of the lack of respect you were talking about . . .

Once people realize that America has always showed you a side that it wanted you to see, that's it. But until people understand that all you can do is get what you can get out of it and try to make the best for you. See, they had a chance, like . . . anybody that came up through the crack era, and didn't get a crack case, and made a bunch of money, and put it up and invested it right? They were the lucky ones. But you had some people thought it was gonna be like that forever. And now they spoiled. And the government knows if you finish school, if you went to college, what you should be grossin' a year. And so, it's fittin' to get so critical that . . . we headed deeper and deeper into the computer age. The more advanced you see the cell phones, the more advanced you see the video games, people don't really see what's happenin' right round they heads. They steady tryin' to get it to where it won't even be no money on the streets no mo'. Everything'll be just like that card that women use to go get groceries or what- ever. You won't even have to worry about currency and people gettin' to the bank. They steady tryin' to find ways to advance shit. Just like they made money where it was a strip in it. Okay, some people tryin' to duplicate that. They realize that. So then they made it to where there was another face in there. But that was hard, that was hard for them to do that. People always find ways to duplicate or get around somethin'. That's just America. You got real Rolexes and you got fake Rolexes. [Laughs] And they both look just alike, except when you turn a real Rolex over, it got serial numbers and stuff on it. Each time you buy a Rolex, when you buy it, it have a serial number and everything. Fake Rolex don't have nothin' on the back of it. Everything. They have a way to do it. Gucci. Anything. They always gonna have the remake so they can make they money off of it, so the dealers can get paid. Everything is a hustle.

DJ Steve Fournier

RHINESTONE WRANGLER

When Rhinestone Wrangler opened near the Astro-dome in the mid-1980s, it was Houston's first all-rap venue. The Southside nightclub was the work of Steve Fournier, who had moved to Texas with his family in the 1960s from Chicago and fallen in love with hip-hop as the genre came to life, flying across the country as a young DJ to buy up rap records and bring them back to play in Houston clubs. In 1985, Fournier formed The Rap Pool of America to distribute new releases to fellow DJs, while his Rap Attack Contests at the Rhinestone provided the arena for a scene that would birth Rap-A-Lot Records artists Royal Flush, Romeo Poet, Willie D, and the early Ghetto Boys.

PHOTO: UNIVERSITY OF HOUSTON LIBRARIES SPECIAL COLLECTIONS

Seems like in the early days, it wasn't even about records. '84, '85, there were a few records that had come out in Houston. Nothing on Rap-A-Lot, obviously. But seems like early on you had to be a battle rapper.

There wasn't a lot of rap records out of Houston at *all*, and maybe just a tape at the time if I can remember correctly. And I knew—because I had been to New York back-and-forth and LA and everywhere else—that they needed to battle against each other to get somewhere. They need to get better. You know, that was not the focus here. We were just the *buyers* at the time. We were just the buyers of the music. We weren't the focus, and the only way to make us the focus was for the guys to *practice*, just like you would practice playing basketball or anything else every day, to get better. And so I said, "You know, if they battle each other, then before you knew it, people would be comin' from Louisiana, Oklahoma," their cousins would be comin' from LA and New York to visit their cousins in Houston, and they'd jump in there because they just thought . . . they were from New York, and wore the right clothes, and they could rap! But the people in Houston were already so hip to the game that they could care less! They could care less what you looked like. It was just—could you rap or not? We always did the rap contest first. Always. And everybody had to rap to the same beat. What-ever beat was picked, that's the one. And thank God that was just about the time people start . . . because then you're talking about five years into rap, and the record companies started putting out instrumental versions. So that was good! If they didn't have the instrumental, it was up to the DJ to keep playing the most instrumental part of it, whatever we played. But we didn't have many to pick from, so we already knew which ones had the longest instrumental part in there. And then if it wasn't that, if we didn't take a rap song, we'd just take something that was like funk, which was just like before rap. We picked a funk tune that had a long breakdown they could rap to, James Brown or Jimmy "Bo" Horne or whoever it was.

What nights did you do it?

We were open five nights a week. We were open Wednesday, Thursday, Friday, Saturday, Sunday, and every single night all we played was rap. That's it! There was no exception. The only exception I made was for a slow song. That was it. If some R&B song was *so* Number One on the chart for *so* long that the people would give it a break, then we would put it in there. But when I got the spot at the Rhinestone Wrangler, the deal that I made with the club owner, he said, "I will let you play all the rap you want, as much as you want, all the time if you want. I don't care. I'm a businessman—make money." And that's how it got that way! He was a little old—he wasn't much bigger than me. I'm bigger now because I've gained weight, but he wasn't much bigger than me. He was a little, old, short Greek guy, and all the ladies loved him because he was a good-looking guy. But he looked at it strictly— that was the first time a club owner in a long time had looked at it strictly as a business. "I'ma open the door at this time, I'm gonna shut it at this time, I'm gonna count my money, and I'm gonna go home 'til the next day." It was just a pure business to him. He didn't care what I played, how nasty it was, how X-rated. He didn't care. It was just, "How many people in the door, and how much liquor did we sell?" And that was it!

How did you two find each other?

He found me at Boneshakers. He said, "You need to come over here when you get ready to leave," 'cuz by that time Boneshakers's owner had made enough money that he was done with the one in Houston. He just kept the one he had by his house in Louisiana. There was another Boneshakers in Alexandria, Louisiana. He just kept it rolling there, and he would bring us there like once a month, sometimes twice a month if we could get away. He would bring me there with my other guy I was playing with to boost up the crowd a little bit and bring the newest music for the DJs he had to play for the next two or three weeks. He knew it was closing and he came to me and he said, "Man, look, I got this place over here by the Astrodome. It's a round little mini-dome, and I want you to come over here and see it." I looked at it, and it was set up for like a Las Vegas in-the-round dinner club. I mean it was set up for Dean Martin, Tony Bennett or something. That's the kind of place it looked like. It had two or three levels—imagine a circle, a big place, and it had two or three levels, and the pit was where they danced—but you could see that's where they had a raised stage before, and that's where the performers performed. He bought it and he wanted to change the whole concept, so I looked at it and I said, "Well, first of all, I'm gonna give you an honest answer—all these mirrors all the way around this place?" I said, "You need to take 'em down, come in here and sheetrock these walls, paint the walls. All these nice tables on the first and second landing? Take 'em out, keep 'em on the third landing." And I said, "Just put a standup bar rail, you know, like a rail with a little 10-inch piece of wood on it, a bar rail, on these other levels *because* that's what the people that are gonna come here are gonna do. Your mirror wouldn't last but a couple of weekends and it'd be gone." So he did that, and I said, "Always keep on staff your handyman." I said, "Where's your handyman?" I met him and I said, "Look, you're gonna work almost every day. You're gonna come in and check this place, and the two days you want off, you pick 'em, because the other days you're gonna be in here fixin' the holes, fixin' the sheetrock, fixin' the bathroom. It's just part of the club business when you're dealing with a young crowd." And he was business-minded enough to understand exactly what I was talking about. This is what I loved about *my* end of the business—that every other club owner in town was so stupid to the fact of how much money we were makin' in that club. Because their attitude was,

"Oh, I'm not handlin' all those young people in my place. They're just gonna tear it up." And then you would say, "Well, lemme ask you—what's your best night?" "Oh, you know, Friday and Saturday night's my best nights, man." That's what the older clubs would say. "Oh yeah? How many people does your place hold?" "Oh man, I got it right there about 400 people." "Oh that's great! Friday, Saturday night! Oh man. You sell some liquor?" "Oh my god we sell some liquor!" "Okay," I said, "Well okay, how much do you charge at the door?" Uh-oh! Problem! "What do you mean you don't charge at the door?" "We can't charge at the door because the old people come in and say they spend too much at the bar." "Oh! Okay—so how much do you make at the bar?" And this is where this part comes in: "On Friday night we make about eight grand." "Well that's great! And how about Saturday?" "Oh, about the same." "Oh, that's great! About 16 grand! And how much liquor do you have to buy on Monday?" "Oh, about eight grand worth of liquor!" "Okay! I got you. And you still have to pay your waitresses and stuff, DJ too?" "Yeah!" And they'd be smilin' like they made money! In Texas, there is no admission tax law. *There is no admission tax law.* There is no tax on admission! They said, "We'd never want your young crowd. They don't drink worth a shit!" "Nah, man, I don't blame ya." And all the time we'd be laughing our way all the way back to the club. Why? Because we would make—back *then*—our club was big, so we'd have 1,400–1,500 people almost every night we were open. Back *then* at eight dollars a pop, *and* we *still* made money at the bar!

Because you got a cut of the bar too on those nights?

No, no, no. The deal that I had with him, and this was the deal I always had with anybody I worked with—I would figure out what my family needed to live, and then anything else I did in the music industry was gravy. So I would tell them, "Okay, I need to make X many dollars a week if there's one person in this place or if there's 2,000 people a night. I'm *never* going to come to you and ask you for another penny. I'll *never* ask you for another cent. I'll just be happy for you that you're makin' money just as long as every Monday morning when

we meet, and you give me the money to go to the radio station, my check is there. You'll *never* hear a word out of me. The first time my check ain't there, I'll never be back again." And that's how I always did it. That's how I always did it. I was more about the security of it. I wanted that money there rain, shine, snow, whatever. I wanted it there. On the same token, I didn't mind that he was makin' so much money when it was packed. Fine! More power to him! He put up all the money for the club. He put up a couple hundred thousand dollars to bankroll that club—*I* didn't! I wasn't gonna do that until I got my own place down the road. But he did. It was strange that the club owners in town that had the small clubs never ever figured it out. Never *tried* to figure it out. All they could do is drive by my club and see thousands of cars in the parking lot, on the feeders of the freeway, and go, "My god, they got a lot of people." But they never would go into it! I say, "How many cops you got?" "Oh, we only have one officer that works the club." I said, "I have five." "Yeah. We'll pay him $100 a night. That's $500." "Yeah, that's $500!" But you don't understand, the money we were making, we see the big picture. We didn't worry about the officers gettin' theirs or the fire guy getting his, we don't care about that, because we see the bigger picture.

So going to the Rhinestone Wrangler, you had totally free reign to play whatever you wanted. Does that mean that at Strut's and at Bone-shakers you couldn't exactly play everything you wanted?

No, I couldn't. But there wasn't that much rap out!

Strut's was on Aldine? That was the first one?

Yeah—that was the first one. That was the first club that rap was ever played in the state of *Texas*, because Houston was the first place. That was the first place, and the very first song that I ever played on a turntable, was T-Ski Valley "Catch The Beat." That was the very first song ever played in a Houston club. And so from there, another one came, then another one came, then all of the sudden Kurtis Blow came out with "The Breaks," and "Christmas Rap." That's the first rapper that ever played in the city of Houston. I brought him to Strut's Disco.

What year was that? '81?

No . . . it's better for me to remember by what year did "The Breaks" come out, or "Christmas Rap." "The Breaks" came out in about '80? I was only able to play the rap that I could find, or that I heard from the tapes I kept gettin' from my good friend by that time, Red Alert. Kool DJ Red Alert. He would slide me those tapes so I could hear, and then I would call him and say, "That song. That's the song. I need that song." And he'd send it to me. He'd make sure I got it. And then the other rap show in New York was across town, his, like, rival, Mr. Magic? I met him a couple of times. Me and him didn't kick it off, but then I think he knew that me and Red Alert were becoming better friends, and he heard from the people that traveled to Houston that, "Steve's friends with Red Alert in New York, and we listen to him on the radio, and that's how we get some of that music down here quick." They would come here, and they would go, "We're from New York." Yeah, "I don't have shit down here!" But at that time there were only about 12 or 13 rap records out, so it surprised him when out of the 12 or 13 they were listening to on the mixtapes back home, that I had 10 of them. That would just blow their mind. They just couldn't figure it out. "How does that happen? This is Houston, Texas!" And of course, everybody who came to Houston, Texas *then* said, "Oh, man, I've never been to Houston. They got horses and cowboys?" And then they get off the plane and see, "Damn, this is a big ol' city!" It's just like everywhere else, man.

"The Breaks" came out in 1980, but that Christmas song came out in '79.

Alright, so "The Breaks." It was when "The Breaks" got hot. That must have been '80, because what happened was, after "Christmas Rappin'" everybody knew him, and then when they come out with that new song, the record label called me, and whoever was the management for them at that time—whoever it was that called me—their agent said, 'We're coming through this way, do you wanna have him come through there?" And I said, "What's the price?" And she told me, and I said, "Well, give me a second, give me a couple of hours, I'll call you back." And I told the club owner, "Look, you got a chance to be the first in the whole city, the first in the whole state, to play the first rap act ever to come through." And by that time, he wasn't that hip to rap at all, but he knew enough to know what "Christmas Rappin'" was. He heard that, right? And she said how much it was, and I told him, and he said, "Let's go for it." That's just how it happened, man. And it was out of the 1,100 people we had there—whatever it was, it was packed—I believe there must have been at least a hundred DJs from all of the state that *just* started DJing. Remember—this is only like a year and a half, two years out. You had two turntables goin' and all that, and they came there to watch Kurtis Blow's DJ more than they did *him*. Their mouths were dropping to the floor, because they'd never *seen* nobody scratch before! They hadn't seen nobody with little tape on their records before where to stop it. They never seen any of that. And so they were just all freaked out. I had seen it because I had been to New York for battles that had picked up, the spinoffs and stuff. So at Strut's was the first place it got played—then Boneshakers was the place where there was more to play, but the owner there was like, "Nah, we're not gonna give you *that* much rope." So we kept it half and half, and then when it was closing down there was obviously a lot more rap out. So I wind up playing more, and the owner would say nothing but he didn't like the fact that—he could figure out that I was playing a whole lot more rap than I was doing anything else. And then when he closed, that's when this guy approached me. That brings you to Rhinestone. And he knew my biggest pet peeve. He knew, because like a good businessman, he would come in there!

The guy from Rhinestone would come into Boneshakers.

Right, because he wanted to *know*. He would drive by. This is what he told me: On the way home he would drive by the place, and *could not* believe *how* many cars were in the parking lot and on the feeder of I-45. And all he thought about as a businessman is *money*! His club is makin' money. And so he came in the club, and hung out and watched, and he approached the DJ booth a couple of times just to say hello, if I needed a beer or something. And I just thought he was a guy sittin' there hangin' out, you know, gettin' away from his wife or whatever. But then when it came time that the word was out it was about to *close*, he called me, and he said, "Look, man, come to the club." And that's how it went down. I was so happy, because he could have probably paid me nothing, but I would be able to play all the rap I could possibly find throughout the country. And he never went back on his word, man. He never went back on his word. Ever.

So how long did Strut's last, then?

Two and a half years. The longevity of a club in Houston with max profit and everything is about two years. A couple of years is about the max profitability, where you make your maximum money in the club business, and then all of the sudden the third year it starts to go down, and the fourth year usually you're gone. There's a couple of clubs in Houston where the club owner has the place because his father owned the club, passed it on to him, and his father's died, so he owns the *whole* building, *every* seat, every machine, and has owned it forever already. You know, it's paid for itself over many times. And for those people who have those clubs, it's just an easy living, because that's the business they grew up in. They could change it once every year. They still own the building! It's still there! One week it could be a country club and the next week it could be a gay club—it could be whatever! They owned the club! To where our club owners went in sayin', "Oh, no. I'm not gonna buy *that* deep into it. I'll do a lease with ya, for two or three years, but I'm not gonna *buy* this place." Which to me was always a smarter way to go anyway. You know you're not gonna be here forever. This is your life, you want to make your money, you wanna bank your money, and then you wanna go do something else. And that's what most people do in *any* business. So, I understood that. And I was *young*! So I honestly don't know where I learned a sense of understanding what they were

talking about, because my father died when I was about nine years old, and he was a hardworking man—*hard*. Hard, hardworking man, and my mother took care of all of us because she was a good Catholic woman. There were six children, so her job was big enough just tryin' to keep us all fed. So I guess I just had to! I had to learn how to fend for myself. I had to learn in a *hurry*. In a hurry I had to learn how to do business and all of that.

In the clubs you kind of learn on the fly, right? You kind of learn from . . .

The people that taught me—the people that really taught me the club business in Houston was two gentlemen—Ray Barnett and Charles Bush. They're the ones that taught me the club business. And because during the Rhinestone era Charles Bush and Ray Barnett owned older clubs, they came around. They were both black club owners that owned all the hot spots for adults.

Cinder Club, Screamin' Eagle.

What's the other one called . . .

The piano place.

Yeah, the piano place . . . Baby Grand! Those were the clubs in South Park, and I mean they were dope clubs when they owned them. They had pizzazz. I mean a place that you wanna take your wife out to. They were top of the line clubs, and they didn't own just one or two. Ray Barnett was the *king* of the Southside. He had six clubs goin' at one time. And then Charles Bush had north *and* south. He had about eight! Eight clubs goin' at one time. I remember the guys who would come around and pick up his money. I remember they didn't even—this was before concealed weapon laws. I mean, they would just come in the back door with their AKs on their side, and the other one with a gun in his hand, 9mm in his hand, go into the office, collect the money. They didn't believe in the trucks to come get your money and all that. No, no. They didn't want *no* official people to know what kind of money they were makin'.

"We'll count it."

Their job was to bring it to the main office, and they *would*. Those people were so loyal to Charles and Ray Barnett. So incredibly loyal. I mean, the closest thing it could be is the mafia—but not the mafia. But I mean with that loyalty, with these guys—because I'm sure those guys got paid *very* well to go pick up their money every night. And to risk their lives every Monday night for some guy who was tryin' to figure out exactly what time they're tryin' to go where first or whatever, so you know, they taught me the business. At the Rhinestone they seen that, and they would always try to pull me away, "Man, we'll double. Whatever he's payin' you, we'll double it, man. Come to the spot for us." I was like, "I ain't like that, man. The man came to me, and I gotta be loyal to him. Just like your people are loyal to you. I gotta be loyal to this man." And then when the business started to *close*, then they came and got me. They said, "Aw, man! You *got* to come this way *now*." [Laughs] So I say, "Gimme the biggest place you got," and they brought me to the biggest places they had, and one of the biggest places, that was when Earl Campbell was the shit with the Oilers. He had a club called Tyler Rose, and it was beautiful. It was gorgeous. And he goes, "This is the eighth club I got." He goes, "This the club I want you to flip. I want you to flip it. I'm gonna close it down." People from the other clubs will say he was a smart man. He already had other clubs. He was already building another club, to get it ready, because he knew exactly what he was going to do. The trick in the club business is when you know your club is going down, you go down the street and start building another one. Just start building it. And then the night you want everybody to come to your club for a grand opening, you mysteriously have sewer problems in your club, and it's not open. So everybody has to go to the brand new club. And then your other club just . . . never opens again. This is how the business is, so he knew what to do there, and he gave me that place, and we called it Spuds.

Where were the Tyler Rose and Spuds? Were those on the southwest side?

Yeah, that was on that West Bellfort and Airport area, and it was on the corner lot, and aw, man, *packed* them in there. People on that side of town were so *glad* to have a club like that over there that just played rap all day where they were just goin' crazy, man. They would go crazy.

And what happened to the Rhinestone? Do you think it just ran its course?

No! He closed it because—for two reasons—he had made his money, he'd done made his money, and the law was startin' to get on us good. I mean, they were like, "Aw, this is . . . this is a problem. No one came up this two or three square blocks because they're scared to death. Y'all got all the gangsters, all the drug dealers, everybody's over here." So when the laws start comin', he done made his money, you know, more than he thought he was gonna make. So he was just . . . he didn't wanna deal with it. He was not that kind of guy. He didn't want that conflict. His image was squeaky clean, he didn't have no problems with the law, and so he just wanted to keep it like that. And by the time they closed, we're talkin' '87? There was *so* much more rap out. So much more at that time, and it made it a lot easier for other club owners to understand that obviously it's not going anywhere. It's not a fad. So I guess we'll jump in, you know?

Did he have anything to do with Rhinestone Rangler, the second one that opened up on the Northside, or that was all Lil' J?

That was Lil' J. Lil' J—they say, "Man, it wasn't even a question." I think when I did that, I went over there, and that was about a year, a little bit more, because of the same situation, because the drug stuff—the gangs was getting really bad, and we were right next to a Jewish Community Center, and it didn't work. The place was upside down. By that time, Charles Bush was so happy because he used to do this to me, to give you an example. He'd say, "Look, man, Steve, come down on a Monday." Because that was the big thing—always on Monday you went and met the club owner, and he'd give you the money for the radio. For me, anyway. He'd say, "Okay, this is how much we're gonna spend on the radio. Go buy the spots and make your commercials." So I would go voice the commercial, make the commercial—*think* of the commercial, whatever, at the same time. But, at that time you also had the meeting with all the clubs, so they had this big meeting table, like when you go to a record company—big meeting table, with about 20 chairs all around this big huge table. All the managers had to be there Monday. I said, "Alright, man, I'll sit in there." Because I knew what was gonna happen, and I knew what he was up to. He had all those managers and assistant managers in there, all these people who had 10 or 12 years in all these clubs, and he totally fucked with them! Remember, the money comes in on Sunday. He stays up all night and counts his money. He has the money machines and everything. He's counted the money in nice neat stacks, and he had it in brown paper bags, and he had took this bag and dumped it on the middle of the table. And so you're talking about like seven other clubs. So that may have been about 50 or 60 grand. You know, all nice, neat stacks. He goes, "This is what all y'all made me. All you clubs together, that's what you made me. Now, I got to buy the liquor, I got to pay y'all, I got to pay the 'lectric, I got to pay the janitors *out of that money*." And then he went to the other end of the table. And I said, "Oh, don't do this." He brought a grocery sack and dumped it on the table, and it was about six times more than their stack, and he goes, "This is what *this* young man did for me this week-end. *This* is what this young man did for me. I got to pay but a *little* bit for liquor, and *this* is what he did." And then I told him, I said, "I ain't never comin' to another one of your meetings again, man." I said, "You set me up like that." Because of course, they were lookin' at me goin', "That motherfucker!" And I looked at them all and said, "Look, I did not know this was gonna happen, man. Don't . . ." And he goes, "No, Steve—they need to know!" Then the rest of the conversation was, "So what y'all need to worry about is that I'm gonna send Steve to flip one of your clubs. Y'all need to get out there and hustle! And make me some money!" It was just a way to get them energy again. You know, clean their club again, paint outside again—do *something* to bring in some money. That's all it was. And he was very big about—he would have been perfect for the show with Jon Taffer or whatever it is, *Bar Rescue*. He would have been perfect, because his clubs were—you can eat off the floors in his restrooms in *every* one of his clubs. Charles Bush made a *big* deal about that. He would walk through a club and just *walk* it and look through *every*thing. Because he had owned the clubs! And those people, one decade of people would come, and then the next decade . . . they would know his clubs! "Oh, that's a Charles Bush club. You know it's gonna be classy." You know it's gonna be classy. The air conditioners are gonna work, and you *know* it's gonna be clean. You *know* it. And so that was a big deal. Ray Barnett on the other side was kinda the opposite. His thing was, "I serve good drinks." That was his thing. His restrooms may not have been that clean, the air conditioner might nota worked all the time, but *you were gonna get a good drink!* That was their big thing. So they're kinda opposite, but they were about the same age, and they grow—somebody had to teach them, and whoever that was before them, I don't know. Somebody taught them, then they taught me the business, taught me how to make money and taught me the ins and outs of it and what really counted, what didn't. You know, there's one book for the liquor board and then there's one book for you! One book for liquor, one book for you! And how the liquor board's figured out—because they couldn't have the admission tax law. All they really figured out was about how many people you had in the club. They used to figure that out by how much liquor you sell. And so they go, "Well, you only made $2,000 at the bar, or $2,500. You could only have had a couple hundred people in there." And then all these rumors and all this legend goes out there about young people don't drink helped us out *tremendously*. You say, "Hey, we got a young club! People don't drink!" "You're right! Okay. Next." No question. So even if we did have a good night at the bar, we knew to put down bad.

Do you know if Charles Bush is still alive?

He is. Ray Barnett died in 2012, but Charles Bush is still alive. I don't think he has anything to do with the club business anymore. I think he lives up in Dallas. The last time I seen him it was so many years ago. It had to be eight years ago. He was in the airport, and he said, "Steve." I turned around, and I was so happy to see him, because I hadn't seen him in so long, we sat there and talked for at least an hour. I couldn't even remember when my flight was or whatever. We were just so glad to see each other. And I found out that he had went and somehow wiggled his way with the City Council of Houston—he wasn't on the City Council, but he got a real good friend—he was *real* good friends with all of them, and they gave him a contract to have these little booths in the airport at Intercontinental. You know, like the food booths and shit? Yeah! And you don't just *get* those contracts, but he got a couple of 'em! He said, "Yeah, I got a couple in Dallas." Actually, that's how he retired. He knew all the right people, man. They all grew up in his clubs. One way or another, somebody came through his clubs at the time, and they all remembered him, and he always made sure that he did whatever he was gonna have to do. Like for example, Charles Bush had quite a bit of money most of the time—cash flow. That's a better word for it. He had a lot of cash flow all the time, so say some kid's mother passed, and they didn't have no way to bury her. He'd be the first one to go give the kid 10 grand and say, "Go bury your mama." All that kind of stuff throughout the city left an impression on people's mind forever. Even if people would knock him, and say, "Oh, he's just a gangster. He just did the drug business undercover," whatever. Half of that mighta been true, but not *all* of it. The thing is they respected him because he *always* helped. He always helped people, and that was a big deal. A big deal.

I've never known anybody who knew where he was.

That's it, and I think purposely. He did it for so long—like 40 years or something—he just was so fed up with everything, he just wanted to get away. His kids were grown, Charles Jr. did a couple of clubs for a while and it just wasn't his thing at all. Ray Barnett's son Kerry. It was his thing, but too much his thing, and he couldn't stay out of trouble for nothin'! For nothin'. I mean he—Kerry Barnett was livin' the true gangster life. I mean he was to the T. His dad took his clubs back! "Give me my club back! Give it back. Just get out of here!" Him

and his dad didn't—I know he misses his dad, but they didn't get along at all. Only because he'd say, "Steve! Why is my kid in trouble? *Why* is he always in trouble? Why can't he just make a living and go on about his life?"

At the Rhinestone, that was you, Big Steve, and R.P. Cola? All three of you were involved?

I was involved, and then they needed to get a manager to run it. That's where Big Steve came from. And I needed a DJ to help *me* because I was starting to get so deeply involved in the *industry* during the day that by the time nighttime came I was gettin' wore out! I mean it was just like nonstop, and that's when I said, "Well, let's go get R.P.! He's my friend! Let's go get him." And we got him, and that's how it went down exactly. And then R.P.—it ended up being . . . it was just natural. It was never *said*, but it was always like, "Well, you just spin—go ahead, I'll be the MC. You just spin the music." Because I was bringing music into the club anyway, so R.P. and them couldn't wait 'til I got there, because I always had the music! The new music for them. And it was never said! It was just me and R.P. were friends, and I said, "No, you go ahead—spin the music and I'll just MC the whole night and get the crowd hype and do the rap contest," and whatever else crazy thing we were doin' at the time.

You met R.P. from the other clubs?

I *think* I met him because he came from out of town and he came to Boneshakers when we were open, and he just started at some club. He always used to come to our club because we had all the people, and when they closed their club down, on that night he was all, "I'm just gonna go over here and play around." He would always come to the Boneshakers. And I think that's how we got to be friends. And then I mentioned about R.P. and I think Big Steve mentioned about R.P., and that was it. That's just how it happened. And Big Steve was good at what he did. At what *he* did, and that was—all I can say about Big Steve is he was good at what he did, and that was bullshit, bullshit, bullshit, bullshit and manage the club. Oh man. The *king*.

And still doing it!

Yeah he's still doing it! I know the game he's still playing because I seen him a while back. We just laughed. I said, "Man, you're still playin' the same game." He'd go to any of these strip clubs now, and say, "What's your worst night?" "Man, my worst night is Friday night. It sucks." "Give us Friday night. You ain't got to pay us *nothin'*, and you can make all the money at the bar you want. All we want is the door. You don't have to pay for commercials, security, nothin'. Just sit back and make money at your bar." And these topless club owners will say, "What the hell—why not?" And Steve'll run with it! Steve will run with it as long as he can—a year, a year and a couple months—and when it goes down, he'll go to another topless club owner, "Hey man—what's the worst night you got?" He's been doin' that for a hundred years.

That's why his clubs move around town all the time.

All the time. He doesn't have to think about it. If all you had to do was go around and bullshit people all weekend, drive around, and work one night a week—what a life! What a life, man! He's got it, you know? That's what he wants to do, and he's happy doin' that so more power to him. And he brings Captain Jack with him wherever he goes, because Jack needs to work too! He's like every other human being—you got to work! And so wherever Steve goes, Jack goes. They're like a team. And R.P. works at topless clubs, so his name is so historic with topless clubs ever since back then that he can go get a job at any topless club anytime he wants. He just walks in the door and they give him a job. So he's set. He likes doin' that, Steve and them like doin' that, and so good for them. I have no hard feelings against them at all. Good for them.

When the three of you got together, when that arrangement came around, was that because the Rap Attack Contests had already started? Had you already started doing them or did that come about naturally, the battles would happen like that?

No, no. I just started them! I just told Steve and R.P. that we were gonna start doin' a rap contest. And then after the rap contest the guys still wanted to battle, and that's how the rankin' started. That's what the people *really* wanted to see.

Was the cappin'.

Yeah, the cappin' part. The rappin' part was for the rappers to battle each other to get better. To hear people from different parts of Louisiana or Oklahoma or wherever they came from. They just wanted to get better at it. The cappin' part—that's what everybody wanted to see. That's what everybody would miss work for the next morning, just to stay up Sunday night and see that.

That was always Sunday nights.

Yeah, and everybody would be late on Monday morning. Everybody. They'd get on the radio the next morning—the DJ's would call 'em, "You on your way to work?" "Yeah man . . . I was at the Rhinestone last night . . . awww, man . . ." I don't think so much—not in a bad way—but I don't think that Big Steve and R.P. was as much excited about it as I was. I mean, they did it. They liked it, they had fun! But I was the one who pushed it like, "I wanna do this! I'm gonna do this." But they had things in the club they did too that I probably liked but I wasn't jumpin' up-and-down for, either. This was my baby, and I was just havin' a ball with it. Because, you know, bein' the MC in the club, I was onstage doin' all that stuff, and *I* was havin' a good time too! It was a lot of fun, man. It was a fun time.

So the Rap Attack Contest was somethin' different. That wasn't the cappin' contest. The cappin' contest . . .

Came after. First it was the Rap Attack Contest—rappin', and after the winner was chosen, I'd say, "Who's gonna stay for the cappin' part of it?" And *everybody* wanted to stay. And believe it or [not], more people came around the stage after that! As soon as they knew the cappin' part was comin'.

Was the winner of the Rap Attack Contest automatically in the cappin' contest?

Not automatically. He didn't have to be. He won a hundred bucks, or whatever we were givin' away that night. I think it was usually a hundred bucks. So he won a hundred bucks, but he was the king! Of the Rap Attack. So he had to come back next week to defend his title! And the one that won the most was—once Willie D got goin', that was it. No one ever beat him, man. No one ever beat him. He won it like 12, 13 times in a row. No one could knock him off.

Who was the first one to win—do you remember?

No—I remember the regular characters like it was *Saturday Night Live*. There was Classy C . . .

Romeo Poet.

Romeo Poet, Royal Flush, and his whole gang. Rick and all them. People from out of town came in, Willie D came in . . . some guys from the Northside came in. There was so many. There was enough to where every Sunday night in the Rap Attack Contest there was at least seven or eight people battlin' each other. And then for the cappin' contest, there was at least six of 'em that stayed around and did *that*. But as that got more popular, oh man—there was about 10 people used to sign up! So I would say the first 10 people get to be in it. You know, whoever signs up. And there was a big board at the front door entrance on Sunday: IF YOU'RE GOING TO GET IN THE RAP ATTACK BATTLE OR THE CAPPIN' BATTLE, YOU MUST SIGN UP NOW. In big letters: IMMEDIATELY. If you're not signed up—no matter . . . they would come up to me, "Get me in! Get me in!" "No man—that's the deal. That is the deal. Sorry! You'll have to wait 'til next week." "But I came all the way from . . ." "I'm sorry, man. I'm not gonna do that to anybody because word's gonna get around, and that's it. That's not how we *do* it." But like I said, R.P. liked it, but it was sort of like my baby, and he knew I had a ball doin' it so they just went along with it, and then the more popular it got, they just sat back and laughed too!

And had you been much of an MC before that? Were you mostly just spinning before, or were you talking to the crowd a bunch before the Rhinestone?

No, because back then there was no such thing as an MC. When rap first started, the MC was basically the rapper, and so us DJs had to spin the music and had the old fashion microphone in the middle. You know, you were talking at the same time, so you're playing with the crowd as you were spinning, and that's what made you a popular DJ. People liked to have a good time and hear the DJ say stupid stuff and all that. They used to love it, and so I just learned by myself. I just learned what to say and what not to say. I was definitely growin' with the music. I grew up! As the music grew up, I grew up, and people thought the way I did it was just the way it was supposed to be done because no one did it before, I guess. But I used to have a good time with it. When I was at Boneshakers, I used to have another DJ, DJin' with me, because you gotta understand, these clubs that we had, no one in the city of Houston had ever been used to crowds nightly of 1,100–1,200 people—on Easter, 2,500 people. No one could imagine that, so one person could not possibly do those jobs. So there was always two DJs. I would spin for an hour, they would spin for an hour. It was never a jealousy thing. It was never an ego thing. It was whatever felt right that night, and that was the cool thing about it, because we were passionate about what we did, and that's biggest number one. People ask me over and over no matter if I go to book signings or wherever you go—"What's the biggest pet peeve about DJs today?" They are not passionate about what they do. They are *not passionate* about what they do, and it's not their fault. It's the way they were raised, it's the age they are, it's the decade they were brought into. Instant success. They want everything instantly—instantly. Now. Now. Now. It's gotta be right now. And that's not how *we* learned the business. For all the good DJs around, it took time. Pay your dues! Sit in them clubs when there ain't a motherfucker in there but *you*, and the owner's sayin' the only way you're gonna get paid is if you keep spinnin' that music like this place is full. Get paid nothing to do that, and do it for a long time, and that means you got passion for what you do. DJs now—you talk to them, they don't even believe you could get away with the things we did as DJs. And that's not like an old guy going, "Oh, you kids don't know." It's a *fact*. Why do you think you can have a club that's only open one night a week? Why do you think that is? It's because y'all don't know what you're doing! If you knew what you were doing, you'd have a club that was there for at least two years that was open three or four nights a week, makin' *you* money all the time. Y'all destroyed the club scene! It's not no one else. You don't know the days of carryin' five or six crates of records upstairs. You don't even know carrying five or six bags of CDs no more! All you know is the computer. Plug it into the mixer and that's it. That's it. You don't know how to talk, you're scared to get on the microphone, you don't even *wanna* talk on the microphone. It's not a show no more, so you get one night a week. If you're lucky. That's what you *get*. Our deal was we had to come with it every night. You had to get on the microphone and act like a nut. You had to play the music all the time. You ask some of these DJs, "How many times you play a song a night?" "Aw, man—maybe I'll play it twice. Maybe." And I go, "Well, how many times the *people* wanna hear it?" "Oh, they wanna hear it three times an hour." "Oh . . . so who's the customer? The people, right? So what difference does it make? Where is there a bible, where is it written in stone? Where's the police officer? Where's the DJ police? There is no such thing! They're your customers! If they wanna hear it every 30 minutes, *play it* every 30 minutes. You gotta be here for five hours, so what damn difference does it make? Play it every 30 minutes, make everybody happy, go home happy." And they're just astonished! They're like, "You can do that?" "Why not?" Why not. There's been many nights in the club, where the club was packed, and you're talkin' about 800 or 900 people on the dance floor, jammin' away, havin' a good time. Lights going on, fog goin' on, they're just havin' a great time. Just about the end of the record, I'd get on the microphone, pick up the needle, and say, "Wait a motherfuckin' minute! We're gonna play this thing *one more motherfuckin'*

time," and start it all over again. And they *loved* it. If you're not in control of your crowd, it's your fault. That's the differences about being passionate about what you do and just, "I'm here for five hours, I'ma turn the computer on and have a drink." I used to *make* people call the radio station. I'd have them have the radio station number memorized by the end of the night. 'Cuz I'd say it on the microphone, "You call 'em and ask 'em to play this record right here." I'd go to the radio station with money to buy my commercial spot, program director would say, "You little—get your ass in here! I've got my phone lines *jammed up* about this song!" And I purposely would bring the record up there, "You mean this one right here?" "Aw, man—where can I get a copy of that record?" "Well, y'all didn't wanna play it for the young man when he came up here and *asked* you to play it for him. So I had to play it at my club all week long for you to play it? Man, I should be sittin' in your seat." That's what I used to tell program directors. "I should be sittin' in your seat, makin' the money you're makin'."

Was there a different prize for winning the cappin' contest?

Pride. The prize was your pride. That's it—that no one beat you. And I purposely did it like that, because I didn't want anyone that was from out of town or that knew better to think that in Houston, Texas, that's what rappin' was about. No, the first part what was rappin' was about. This was for fun. There was no money involved. It was just fun, and it really kept it separate like that, and that's what made it last for so long.

People would really come from Louisiana and Oklahoma and get in those contests?

Everywhere! New York, LA, if they were in town visiting their cousins, they would go, "Man, I gotta go to this *spot* you keep tellin' me about!" And of course they'd see it and go, "Aw, man, I can rap like that!" "Get in it! Go ahead!" Shit, they'd get up there and let Willie D or one of them get ahold of 'em. It was over.

Darryl Scott

THIRD WARD

Known throughout Houston lore as the DJ who originated the slowdown approach that DJ Screw would later adapt into a new genre, D. Scott was the hottest mixtape artist in the city in the 1980s. At night he was spinning records in the clubs of legendary Houston nightlife mavens Charles Bush and Ray Barnett, while on Sunday afternoons he was a fixture with his sound system at the huge MacGregor Park parties that spawned the LA Rapper's 1985 single of the same name, selling mixtapes out of the trunk of his car until he ran out every week. Scott opened Blast Records & Tapes in 1984 and is lauded by many in Houston's scene as a tutor and mentor.

When was it that you first started DJing?

Probably in 1975.

What were kids listening to in those days? What were you spinning?

It was more R&B, but rap was on its way in. I was DJing before Sugarhill Gang came out. I was one of the first to introduce it to the city. I was already doin' Kool Moe Dee with Doug E. Fresh and all of them . . . Treacherous Three. I was playing rap before Sugarhill Gang came out but it really, it blew up once the Sugarhill Gang hit the airwaves. I was playing some of that, some Fatback with King Tim—that had some rap in it first. Also quite a few other little things that I was playing at the time, before Sugarhill Gang came out. Even before they came out with the label I was gettin' a lot of stuff out of New York that was rap-oriented.

White label stuff? People just sending you singles?

Yeah, pretty much. I would go down to New York, matter of fact, and go into the stores and listen, test it, try it, and buy it.

So where were you spinning back then? Where were the hot clubs? This had to be before the Rhinestone Wrangler, right?

Yeah, yeah, this was before the Rhinestone Wrangler. At that time we was doin' like Superskate—that was a skating rink—and there was J.B.'s Entertainment Center on Scott. That was more of a club type of scene. Especially for the teens at that time.

And really that same generation of kids ended up as the first wave of Houston rappers, right?

Of course. I was young at that time, when I was DJing. I was like 13, 14. I was already gettin' into the clubs. The clubs—Big Apple New York, The Screamin' Eagle, all of those guys—they hired me illegally. I wasn't even supposed to be in the club! I would sneak into those clubs. Grand Central Station, Fantasia 5000. All of those clubs I was DJing early, early—way before I was at a legal drinkin' age.

Were those all on the Southside of Houston?

Pretty much, yeah. Pretty much. I started a little dance out at a skating rink—Superskate, which was

COURTESY OF DARRYL SCOTT

So that's who did that track. That track came out earlier than "Car Freak," earlier than the Real Chill single "Rockin' It," so who was the artist?

It was Robert Harlan. Known as the "South Park Rapper."

But this had to have been too early for these to have been purely hip-hop parties. You had to have been spinning some funk, soul, . . . maybe disco?

No disco. I was more funk.

More from the funk and R&B side?

Yeah, we was doin' more Gap Band. We was doin' things like Cameo, like Bar-Kays . . .

Rufus Thomas? Stuff bleeding over from the late Stax Records era?

Nah . . . not Rufus Thomas. They wasn't feelin' that too much. Ray Parker, Jr. you know, anything that had that funk. Lakeside. A lot of Parliament, Funkadelic, Brothers Johnson. And then when Juno came out with "Rappin About Rappin [Uh-Uh-Uh]," Junie [Morrison]. They was onto that pretty much, but it was more that funk type of sound. Every once in a while, you know, a little Earth, Wind & Fire. I would also introduce them to some Thomas Dolby, "She Blinded Me With Science." There were some things that I just kind of . . . I cultivated them. Phil Collins, I cultivated them with some Phil. Some Genesis.

He was mixed in with Earth, Wind & Fire too at that point. Early '80s. "Easy Lover."

Yeah. And they was just really being introduced to something different other than just the black funk artists. I would play the white funk artists, matter of fact came out with a black rock classic that had most of those songs on there that everybody . . . Peter Frampton. They loved "Benny And The Jets," things of that nature. You wouldn't hear a whole lot of that in black clubs, but I would play it. I would break the audience of just being caught in that same old redundancy.

the Northside. I had a huge Northside following. They would come out here when we were doing the MacGregor Park thing—that's what really got the MacGregor Park thing crunk again is that I would announce, I would be out there spinning, outside at the park, and that's what got the Northside coming over here. And then the Southside, you know, got wind of it, and then they started overcrowdin' it, and it just got too jam-packed, and I got blamed for the riot.

This is what year? This is the late '70s?

Yeah, late '70s. '78, '79.

Okay, so rap music in its early form—Spoonie Gee, the Sugarhill Gang, Treacherous Three—was being heard in Houston around this time, or was making its way into Houston around this time, but was there anybody in Houston actually rapping?

Oh, yeah. We had the South Park Rapper—which was Robert—did the song "MacGregor Park . . ."

When do you feel like rap really took root in Houston, really seeped in?

During the Sugarhill era, that's when Grandmaster Flash and them started comin' out, back to back, Kurtis Blow started comin' out with more things, then Treacherous Three, then the Fat Boys—we just had a handful of rap songs we could play. Mostly it was R&B and funk, but the more rap that came out, the more we were playing things, the "Happy Birthdays" and Freedom. "Genius Of Love," Tom Tom Club. When they started droppin' Dr. Jekyll and Mr. Hyde . . . those things started coming out, that's when rap kinda really took over from that point, and that's when the older folks would say, "Aw, it's just a fad," and it never stopped and just kept growin' and growin' and growin'.

Seems like most of the early rappers from Houston tag Run—D.M.C. as a starting point for them, but everything you reference precedes them by years.

Actually, I used to rap. I was rappin' before Sugarhill Gang came out, and that's when it really hit when Sugarhill Gang came out because they thought that was me. My rap was right off in that area. I would rap to my intro song that I always got everybody crunk with, which was called "Get Up And Dance," by Freedom. When it would get to that break I'd say my little short rap that I'd put in there, and they was very familiar with that. Once Sugarhill Gang came out with the entire record then they were . . . oh man . . . they was just really crunk. From that point it was like, "Man! You came out with a record? You came out with a record?" And it was like, "Nooooo." This other guy, Thelton, which was the brother of Lil' James—where James got the name Rap-A-Lot from.

From Sir Rap-A-Lot? Right? K-9.

That was it. K-9. Thelton was rappin', too. He would get on the mic at the skating rink and rap. Right after I started rapping, he wanted to, and he'd find him something that had a break in it, and he would start rappin'. So that became a weekly thing as well, but that was before the Sugarhill Gang had hit the scene.

So this was '79, '80?

Somewhere off in that area because I was still playin' some Treacherous Three and some "Put The Boogie In Your Body" and things like that. Orange Crush.

"The New Rap Language," right?

I wasn't playing that one, but I was able to find some stuff before they signed to a major label. I found some stuff on some grey label.

Do you remember K-9's transition into one of the original Ghetto Boys?

Oh yeah, actually I was a part of that. Lil' James would come over and sit and wait for me while I was out doing my thing that I do—I was playing tennis a lot at that time—he would come out and wait on me because he knew that I knew what was going to move the crowd. And he wanted to make sure he got my approval on the thing. And he was the one that let me know that he was about to get ready to form the group and the record company.

Seems like he always looked at it from a business perspective.

He made sure he got with the top DJs to make sure that they put their ear on things before he decided that he would invest his money and time in it. "Do you think it's going to be something that could move, something you would play and that people would purchase?" He was doing his research.

When do you remember R.P. Cola coming around? More like mid-'80s?

It was around in that area. "Cabbage Patch" and all of those things, those guys . . . you know, they was looking and paying attention to what other DJs was doing, and they started rappin'. Then Captain Jack came out with "Jack It Up."

Seems like early on, before the time of "Car Freak," that Miami bass would have been popular in the cars?

Not a whole lot. Trust me. During that time everybody had my tapes in their vehicles. And I wasn't putting . . . there was some Roger Troutman, some Bar-Kays, and some Cameo with some rap also mixed in there. When I came out with the tape with Sugarhill Gang and Freedom and all of those things on there—"Be Bop Rock" and those things on there—they wasn't playing any Luke because I wasn't putting any Luke on my tapes. And everybody that knew music, it was just one of those things—if you didn't have a D. Scott tape in your deck, you wasn't doin' nothing. You wasn't makin' no noise.

Captain Jack

LOUISIANA

A stalwart of the Houston club scene who has been promoting and hosting since the 1970s, Jack also released one of Houston's first hip-hop records—the vocoder-drenched 1984 electro single "Jack It Up." He followed that with the 1987 Rap-A-Lot 12-inch "Sexy Girls," (produced by Mikki Bleu), but otherwise kept to nightlife rather than recording, continuing to stay relevant through the eras. When Houston rap broke nationally in the mid-2000s, Jack was the one on the mic Sunday Nights at Club Konnections (along with Big Steve of Rhinestone Wrangler fame), which was then such a huge part of Houston rap nightlife, cross-promoting between the nightclubs and the strip clubs.

So how long has that been going on—that kind of relationship between the clubs, especially the hip-hop and the dance clubs in Houston, with the kind of after hours thing with the strip clubs?

First thing about strip clubs—strip clubs really have kind of taken over things. And stuff was goin' like that in Miami, and now it done kinda made its way to Houston, you know?

The party just sort of continues there. I guess if you were to trace it back and to say there was any stigma attached to a strip club, it seems like it's kind of gone in Houston, huh?

Yeah, yeah. You're right. I mean, you still got the strip club action, but it's always late night. You still got your regular strip clubs. People go to Treasures and The Men's Club and stuff like that. Especially on the black scene, you know, the after hours thing has really, really taken off.

How long's it been like that? I mean, you've been doing this for decades, really. Was there an after hours scene back in the day? You started promoting clubs and stuff in the '70s, right?

There wasn't much after hours going on. There was probably one or two places that did that, and those were private clubs.

Talk about the growth of that, from the early days of the after hours in the private clubs to now, the way it works now.

You know what? Back in the day, there was one after hours spot . . . I'm tryin' to think what was the name of that club . . . I remember there was a club called the Red Room that used to stay open after hours off of Dixie Drive. And they used to sell what they called "near beer."

I remember that!

You remember that? Yeah, "near beer." It only had a little small percentage of alcohol in it. But they would be open, they'd stay open 'til like four or five in the morning, and people would leave all the other clubs and fall off in there, man and pack that place out. And that was the only place I knew to go for after hours. Now, before that, before I got off into the DJ scene—and that was before I got off into the DJ scene—I'm actually talking about

PHOTO: PETER BESTE

the '70s, really, because I've been around longer than dirt. But there was another place—there was another club that we used to go and hang out at that was right there close to Downtown, off the edge of Montrose, close by the freeway . . . As you get ready to get on the freeway, the club was at Smith Street . . . They didn't even have a DJ. They had everything on reel-to-reel. They had all the music on reel-to-reel! But they had the hits on there! Everything was recorded, and there was a guy, when that reel would run out, he'd go in there and flip it around or put another one on, and that thing would play for like three hours. Yeah! It would play for like three hours, and you know, you couldn't request nothing, you had to just jam it, but they had the hits on it! And people would pack that place out, and party up in there. But see, those clubs—back then, those clubs . . . it's so different today. You know, none of the strip clubs was doin' nothing like that. I mean, you couldn't go to—you didn't have any clubs where you could go and party and then you could watch strippers and all that kinda stuff. All the strip clubs had to close at two

o'clock. Back then. The only place you could go that stayed open all night was a place over in Third Ward on Wichita called The Big House. And The Big House was all-nude, but you had to have a membership. You go there, they stay open all night long. Now, you could go there, but that really wasn't a party place. That was a place where you could go and watch women come out, strip down naked, do all kinds of tricks with the vagina and all that kind of stuff, and they [had] a room—a little hallway in the back, they would line up five . . . about 10 or 12 girls, you could go back there and pick you one, take her upstairs, and do what you wanna do.

And that was an after hours place?

Well, no—that place actually, I don't know if that place ever closed!

New Orleans style.

Yeah! I think that place was a 24-hour place, because that place was pretty much . . . that place was kind of like a strip club whorehouse. That's all they did in there was prostitution. I mean, you'd go in there, they had rooms upstairs, you go up there and do your thing. But you had to have a membership. Anybody couldn't just walk off in there. They had a little slot door, you'd look through that slot door, and you could see out that slot door and they could see who's out there, and they ask you to show your membership card. Raise up the membership card, and then they come in there and the guy check your membership card out, check your ID out, and, "Go ahead." And in order for you to get a membership, you had to come with somebody that already had a membership. You could not just walk up there as a stranger. You might be undercover.

You might be a cop.

So if I'm gonna get in there, I gotta go in there with Lance because Lance got a membership, and he gon' say, "C'mon, Jack, I'ma take you over here to this spot, man, my spot, man. You gonna have to buy a membership, but you can get one 'cuz you with me." And that's the way it worked.

So that place was around for how long?

It was around for a long time. I guess that place hung around . . . I discovered it in 1974. In 1974 I discovered that place, because a friend of mine from Louisiana—he used to work for Hostess Bread Company. And he stayed right across from me, and me and a cousin of mine, we all went together, and he took us over to that place, and we all got memberships, and then we went back again and again and again!

So when did strip clubs in Houston start staying open all night?

It ain't been that long . . . Oh, I know! I'll tell you exactly when they started. I'll tell you exactly when they started, Lance: When they changed that law from . . . where the ladies could be topless, and they turned the clubs into bikini clubs, and a lot of the BYOB clubs started opening. So, by them being BYOB, they had no restrictions on how long they could stay open versus a regular strip club that has a liquor license. The clubs that have a liquor license, they supposed to close at two o'clock. Or, if they're gonna stay open late, of course they can do that with an extra late-night permit and have to put up the liquor. But, they also take the risk of . . . if anybody is drinking after two o'clock, they'll lose their liquor license. Whereas a BYOB club, you can bring in your liquor off the street. And, of course a lot of these after hour clubs that got these BYOB— even though they BYOB, they still find a way to try to sell a little alcohol illegally up in they joint.

Pam Collins

TEXAS SOUTHERN UNIVERSITY

Former KTSU "Kidz Jamm" Program Director Pam Collins was tasked with wrangling a new kind of music onto the air as the genre was coming to life when she took over at the Texas Southern University radio station in the early 1980s. The crew she would oversee created the most influential radio show in Houston hip-hop history—"Kidz Jamm"—and many of the voices and talents from that show went on to important work in hip-hop at large as rappers, DJs, producers, and people working behind the scenes. This interview occurred on a Saturday morning at exactly the time "Kidz Jamm" would have broadcast during Pam's time at KTSU.

Funny you call me at this time—"Kidz Jamm" would be on the air right about now back in the day, wouldn't it?

COURTESY OF PAM COLLINS

Yes, it would be! Now that you mention it. [Laughs] Hadn't quite thought about it like that in a long time.

When did it start?

If I'm thinking correctly, it was maybe like '84. I took over as program director about '82 . . . no, it had to be '81, and I was program director for about five years, so maybe by the second year or so that I was director, so it had to be '82 when we first started "Kidz Jamm." '82 . . . somewhere right around there.

How did the idea come around?

Well, I was program director at the radio station and the general manager at the time, who was Charles Porter, Sr.—Charles had young kids in his family, and he wanted something to keep them *occupied*. So basically, to be quite frank with you, it wasn't my idea. I didn't particularly care for kids to be on the air. I didn't want to have anything to do with it. It was something that was handed to me and said, "Hey, we need . . . we gonna do this." So I kind of backdoored into doing "Kidz Jamm," but once I got handed the pad, it was like, "Okay, well since we're gonna do it, I gotta be responsible . . ." because my whole thing being—you have to realize, at that time there were five paid staffers at KTSU. Everybody else that was on the air were volunteers, and so I didn't really wanna deal with kids who were fickle and finicky. I wanted someone—I had adults that were on the air on the weekends, because you know I'm workin' through the week, you know, working long hours . . . the *last* thing I wanna do is come to the station on the weekends, okay?

And deal with kids.

And deal with kids! At that time, I had to be about 25. You know, I'm tryin' to get my groove on on the weekend! But what happened was since we had some kids that were coming in, once we started, I realized that they had some talent. There were particular ones that had talent, and once I started working with them, I worked with them as adults. I didn't babysit, because I wasn't *about* babysitting. It was like, "Okay, it's going to be this way, this way, this way. If you don't like it, leave." So I was very tough on them, I was very hard on them. But what it did to them is it made them understand, and they became very astute with the way of radio.

And who were the first ones? It was Stacey—that was his daughter, right?

Charles, Jr. was there, Stacey was his daughter—it was a bunch of kids at that time. Lester Pace was doing [it] . . . Michael . . . I think his last name was Moore. I'm trying to remember. Darryl [Scott] . . . it was a *lot* of them. And so what I ended up doing was that different ones that had different skills, I broke them up into different segments. Some did public affairs, some did news, some did sports, some did this, some did that . . . whatever they excelled in, or were interested in, we could use, and so, collectively, they were a unit. And that's basically how it started. Now, the *music*—so far as . . . to be quite frank with you, at that time, you have to realize, rap was just coming into the scene. I come from a jazz background, so I really didn't care for rap, the beginnings of it. Certain ones I liked, but the main thing for me was that there would be no profanity, and for sure there's not gonna be nothing about no "bitch this and ho that, and blah blah . . ." That was the connotation that was coming with some of the music. So, I had a very negative concept about rap to begin with, and I was very, very, very strict about, "Don't bring anything in here that, for one, has misogynistic

overtones or has any profanity. Because I'm *listening*, now. I might not *be* here, but I'm listening! I'm *always* listening!" But basically, rap had to grow on me, dear. I'm from a whole different train of thought so far as much was concerned. Hip-hop I was a little bit more embracive of, because hip-hop came with a message a lot of the time. But rap . . . okay, I'm not from the street, I don't have street experiences, so you . . . you're really not talking my language. But some of the beats I liked, and some of the music . . . what I *did* like about the whole rap thing was that artists who were sampling and using music . . . for one thing, they didn't have any musicianship—for me—*but*, they were entrepreneurs, and I applauded the fact that they went outside of the record industry mold and began to *create* and make things *happen* musically—whether I thought it was music or not. They're stepping outside the box, and I don't have a problem with working with someone who's bringing fresh new concepts and ideas into the situation. The compromise was that, "Look, you're going to have to have a message. You're not just going to have anything that goes out over the air. And it's going to be controlled. Otherwise, you got problems with *me*." From the very beginning, they all understood that, and I think that kind of shaped and molded what was going on within the whole concept of "Kidz Jamm."

And then how did it develop over the first couple of years? Did it kind of stick to that mold, or did you see it really growing in new ways?

Well, it started off with that mold, and that was the true core. I did not censor them musically about what they played. There was one incident that I can remember particularly. At that time, you have to realize that in the control room, a bunch of kids, a bunch of chaos around, and I had a red light on top of the control board. That was my direct line, and when they saw that red light go off, they *knew* who was on the other line—being *me*. So, when that red light went off, it was like, "Okay, something . . . you've done something, right? You're in trouble." But I happened to be . . . it was a Saturday, I was out doing something, I can't remember, at the cleaners . . . somewhere around the area, and I'm listening, and something was played that had some offensive lyrics. I did a U-turn in the middle of the street, I mean, I did a zero to 90 back to the station, and I popped up—and at that time, KTSU was located just before you . . . if you come down Wheeler and about to access the . . . I think the PE building is there now, but there was a street Wheeler went across and all the way through, and before you got to the railroad tracks, to the left was a two-story house, and that's where the station was. I rolled up in there and the music was going, and they didn't see me. And I popped in, they were doing their thing, and I walked in on them—which I never did, really—when they were on the air. Walked in, walked in the control booth, and I said, "Change the record. Right now."

The record was still on?

The music was still on! The song was still on. "Change the record." And he changed the record, right? I said, "Give me the record." And I broke it in front of them. Told him, "Get up. Get out." Everybody stood like there like . . . *agh*!

Don't mess with Pam!

Well, no . . . that was my style. I'm not gonna babysit you. I'ma tell you *one* time. And that's the way I dealt with them. As adults.

Jazzie Redd

FOURTH WARD

Although usually identified as being from Houston's Fourth Ward due to his long association with the late rapper O.G. Style, Jazzie Redd is actually from Beaumont, and spent time out in California as his career unfolded. But his start was on the radio—on "Kidz Jamm"—and even though he went on to record a couple of albums and several singles, most people know him from hearing his voice on the air. That's also because he's back on the radio again—now in his hometown of Beaumont. This interview was conducted at the end of one of his nightly radio shows. In fact, the conversation began before Redd's radio show was even finished.

You're on the air tonight—is that every night?

Yes, sir. Yeah! I've been on the air for 11 years over here. Hang on one second, I'm gettin' ready to sign off right quick, hold on for me . . . *Aw yeah!* Tell me where you been, I say we fell off the zone here in the Golden Triangle, the big station Magic 102.5, "Jazzie Redd Hour." Matter of fact, gettin' ready to get up out the door, man, yeah, the clock on the wall say, 'That's all, y'all . . .' I'ma wrap it up, put it away, call it a day. Thank you for tunin' in, I'll catch you back here tomorrow, man, same time, five o'clock in the P.M. it's goin' down in the BM because Jazzie Redd will be on your air. See that's what I'm talkin' about—hang it tight! Do what I do. I'll catch you then. Friday make sure you're down at five o'clock and tune back in because I got some big winners, Beyoncé tomorrow night at NRG Stadium in Houston, so a lot of things happenin'

for you. Of course, you know the big thing is to always build for ya, and I'll build for ya too. C'mon back, five o'clock, I'll see you then, right here on the big station Magic 102.5. Boys and girls, all ages, I gotta go!

[Music: *"The time has come . . ."*]

Yes sir.

You were already in swing by '85, right? You made your record in '84.

Yeah, yeah, we were up and running, and I did—what was that "Top Secret?" That was me and O.G. Style, Eric Woods. He was Prince Ezzy-E at the time.

But even earlier than that you did the record with that group, Chance.

I was one of the first rappers in Houston to come out with actual record! With Chance, man, we did that "Break Dancin" song.

That and Captain Jack's record came out the same year, but I think yours is the first proper rap record where you're really rapping.

Yeah, Jack was mostly just doin' his DJ stuff on the record and everything. It wasn't really *rap* rap. But the "Break Dancin" record with Roger Cummings and his brother Steve and the Chance band and I was the official real rap, because you know they was singin' and they knew I had the rap on there

PHOTO: PETER BESTE

and it was all the old . . . you know, when break dancin' was big and all that, so they wanted to do a song coverin' the break dancin' and all that. I thought it was cool that they asked me to do that because I was on "Kidz Jamm" and they knew I was rappin' and I thought that was real cool.

So you were on "Kidz Jamm," but were you performing in any clubs or anything like that?

No, I wasn't performin' yet. I was just rappin'. That's what I did when I first came in on "Kidz Jamm." Wickett Crickett, he was already—he wasn't a part of "Kidz Jamm," but he knew Lester [Pace] and he would be up there all the time, and I knew Crickett, since I was in, like, maybe 10th or 11th grade I been knowin' Crickett. He used to go with a girl—one of my homeboys, his sister—who we went to school with. We stayed in the same projects together. He used to date her. And Crickett was from Fifth Ward. He used to come across the track, come over to Second Ward and see her, and that's how I met Crickett. We always rapped and Crickett

brought me to "Kidz Jamm" and I met Lester and everybody, and shit, man, we started rappin'. Me and Lester hit it off because he was rappin' so we had a little group together called The Double Trouble. And then my role on "Kidz Jamm" when I first came in was the "Master Rapper." Every Saturday, I'd do a rap. Each week I'd do a new rap, and so that's how I got real big as far as people knowin' who I am on "Kidz Jamm," rappin' every Saturday.

So by the time you did that record with Chance, you were already on "Kidz Jamm."

Yeah, 'cuz that record came out in, you said like '84 with the Chance band? You know what? I had just got on "Kidz Jamm" around that time because I graduated high school in '83. I had just got on "Kidz Jamm" right after that so it was right in there.

"Kidz Jamm" couldn't have been on long before you started, right?

I think they were on maybe like a year or so, so if I'm thinking right "Kidz Jamm" was already on, Lester, they was already there, doin' "Kidz Jamm" before I came so it had to be on like a year before I came in the picture.

Was D. Scott involved when you started?

We were doin' our thing pretty much around the time Darryl was doin' his Blast Tapes. He had Blast Records & Tapes, you know, you got a Blast 15, whatever number you got, you got the baddest one. "Gimme that Blast 78" or whatever. He started makin' his tapes. This was after we were at "Kidz Jamm" and all that. He was a little after us, but he always mixin' and doin' stuff over at the park. Yellowstone and all that, just sellin' the tapes out there. We used to hang out at the park, and Lester will tell you about Screw—that we were screwin' records before Screw even started doin' anything he was doin'. We'd *been* screwing records down. We used to do that on "Kidz Jamm." We would take a record we used to play on 45 and we'll put it on 33, slow it down. "Fresh Is The Word," we used to screw that record, have it goin' real slow, and me and King T. King T will tell you about all that too because he was there with us. He was like 14, 15 years old. He grew up with me, he lived with me and my mom for years. I kinda raised him, he was kinda like a little brother to me. We used to call ourselves "DJ Screw and MC Bone." I was MC Bone, he was DJ Screw.

King T called himself DJ Screw, huh?

Yeah. He was DJ Screw for—he was always DJ Terry T—it was just somethin' we was just playin' around with, we was called The Screw and The Bone. We was just kinda playin' around with somethin', but that wasn't his official name. It was just a little thing we came up with for a short period of time.

Did you go to California at the same time as King T?

I went to California in '87, '88. King T had left. When they flew me back to LA, that's when he had his record deal and put out "Payback . . ." and all them early songs, "Better Bring A Gun" and all that. When he first got on I was his Houston DJ and I was his MC, so back then he was usin' all my raps. He wasn't a rapper. He was a DJ, but he was usin' all my raps, man, because B-2 Omega—Pierre Maddox, Born 2Wice—told me, "Man, that nigga Terry T, he stealin' all your raps!" I'm like, "What? What raps?" And he played "Payback . . ." and all that stuff. But he gave me credit for it so all that was cool. That's when I did "Dope Fiend" and all that stuff, started writin' for King T and all that. I was in LA workin' with Quality Records, distributed through Capitol. That's how I got clearance for a lot of the songs I did, writin' for King T.

Didn't you and Lester have a song?

Me and Lester got a song called "This Is My Bass." We was a group—I told you we had the Double Trouble group—we played that on the air and the guy, my boy from school, he had it and sent it to me. "This Is My Bass!" Boy we was jammin'! Talkin' 'bout rap, real rappin'. That's what we was doin' in them days.

This was a song that you produced?

Yeah, this was some shit we did on drum machine. King T did the beat, we had the drum machine, man, we *lived* in the radio station. We used to spend nights in there! We *slept* in the studio.

RHINESTONE

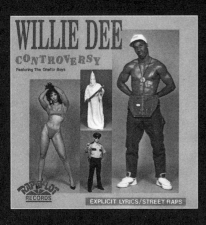

As hip-hop moved into the mainstream in the early 1980s, its cultural elements of MCing, turntablism, breakdancing, and graffiti spread across the city of Houston. But it wasn't until the Rhinestone Wrangler nightclub came along in the mid-'80s that Houston finally had a *home* for hip-hop, where the genre wasn't just accepted, but was the only music being played.

There were other spots playing hip-hop during that era—Rainbow Skate Rink, Gucci, The Palladium—but the Rhinestone, an in-the-round nightclub in a nondescript strip mall just west of the Astrodome, became the breeding ground where DJ Steve Fournier's Rap Attack Contests fostered a generation of talent into bold, fearless young artists, some of whom went on to vibrant careers. Willie D, Ricky Royal, Romeo Poet, Raheem, and K-9 (a.k.a. Sir Rap-A-Lot) were in the house. A few went on to form the first incarnation of The Ghetto Boys, while others would end up in the later Geto Boys. Others still would move on and leave rap music altogether, having made a permanent impression on anyone who stayed up late enough on a Sunday night to see those rap battles last until the small hours of the morning. Royal Flush, Born 2wice, Def IV, College Boyz. A lot of history was made in that club, and the crowds were a big part of the reason why.

In the late '80s, the Rhinestone finally closed and a second version called Rhinestone Rangler opened on the Northside, bringing in more national acts like N.W.A., Sir Mix-A-Lot, and De La Soul. The Rangler also acted as a defacto home for James Prince's burgeoning Rap-A-Lot label, which would release a flurry of records from its flagship act The Ghetto Boys as the decade closed out. That was when gangsta rap took root, when The Ghetto Boys became Geto Boys, and the voices behind the mics were now those of the iconic Willie D, Scarface, and Bushwick Bill. DJ Ready Red was still in the group, but everything else was changing. The music got darker. Darryl Scott had begun to slow things down. The myriad elements that would put the city on the map were already becoming evident.

The last three interviews in this section are the new ones—Scarface, Def Jam Blaster, and Sire Jukebox—and each overlaps the other because they all worked together and were present in the era of the Rhinestone Wrangler. Def Jam Blaster recorded a couple of tracks with Mr. 3-2 around the time of the Rhinestone—a record that was finally released just a few short months after 3-2's murder in late 2016—and he talked about that experience. Scarface talked about Darryl Scott and DJ Screw. Sire Jukebox talked about the pain in his life after The Ghetto Boys. There were no mobile phones in the mid-1980s. Surprisingly few pictures or videos exist of the Rhinestone Wrangler era. All we have are the stories. No one has forgotten. ✖

DJ Ready Red

This East Coast transplant found himself working as DJ/producer with Rap-A-Lot Records upon his arrival in Houston in 1987 and became a member of the original Ghetto Boys, helping craft their early sound (which is why the early Ghetto Boys sounded like they were from the East Coast). Red began his tenure with the group after their debut 12-inch "Car Freak" and stayed up until their 1991 platinum album *We Can't Be Stopped*, on which his is the first voice you hear in "Rebel Rap Family." Ready Red also did production on Willie D's classic 1989 album *Controversy*. Back in his hometown of Trenton, New Jersey, Red is still an active DJ.

You got to Houston before Johnny C, didn't you?

I got to Houston about three months before him, yeah. March of '87.

Was he planning on coming out also?

Not at all. It wasn't even in the cards. Not for that right there. After I got there, my commitment was serious. See, back on the East Coast, this is serious. This is a way of life. With hip-hop . . . it's more than just . . . it's the cartel. Everything combined together. And when I got there, one by one, except for Jukebox—he stayed down, and Raheem—he wanted to go solo. He'd *been* wantin' to go solo. He was like Houston's LL Cool J. He was gifted with lyrical skills. And K-9 was in and out of jail all the time. So the commitment wasn't there, man. Jukebox wanted to bring one of his friends named Rapping Lee into the mix. And I said, "Uh . . . Lil' J,

hey man, I got an MC back home named Johnny C." And he heard Johnny C on a demo tape that I had. Next thing you know, Johnny C was catchin' a plane on down.

Raheem said the same thing, that his commitment wasn't to Ghetto Boys. More like he accidentally ended up in Ghetto Boys.

That's how J would just pair people together. See, there has to be some type of group. You just can't put three or four people together and say, "Okay, you got a group." That's why they don't last long. That's why there's not a lot of longevity in a lot of groups that I see, man, because they mismatch, they misplace, and everybody can't get along sometimes. So you know, that's how that goes. Crews, from like the original hip-hop . . . your Grandmaster Flashes, Soulsonic Forces, Crash Crew, Cold Crush Brothers . . . those guys were all together before they even thought of makin' records. So that's why they went side to side and could shine like one. Flash could make the Furious Five sound like one because the vibe had been there for years. They knew each other's strengths and weaknesses.

So what do you think it was about the different styles of rap that made up Ghetto Boys at that time that made it work?

Well, at that time we were still reachin' for what we were tryin' to do. We were tryin' to be commercial. We did what we heard Run and them doin', what

KOOL DJ RED ALERT AND DJ READY RED. PHOTO: COLLINS LEYSATH

anymore, and I just stayed to reap the benefit from what I put in for the past two years. I lost a whole family behind that album, man. So I figured I'd stay for one more album and see what was goin' on. Then after the *Grip It! On That Other Level* album started sellin', Rick Rubin got involved, so I said, "Finally! Rick Rubin, man . . . LL Cool J, Public Enemy, Run–D.M.C., so maybe things will start to get right here."

It's a different game.

Yeah! I was surprised, and I felt honored even bein' in his presence, man. Because Rick is the man. I'm just gonna say straight up—he's the man.

How long was he with you guys on the group level? Was he a presence that was around a lot?

Well, Rick Rubin . . . he came over to my apartment that I had on the Northside of Houston, and what had happened was . . . he was like, "Okay, I'm gonna change this around, here's your new name . . ." Instead of the G-H-E-T-T-O name, he came with the G-E-T-O. And when you look at it, it's more commercially acceptable, you know what I'm sayin'? Plus, with him being a Jewish guy—ghetto actually refers—it's a Jewish term. So we kinda changed that around. And then took it from there. But as far as what *he* changed around, he took what I had and he just knew how to engineer it, man, to the point where it just brought it all up. I couldn't believe that was some of the stuff that I actually had off the first album. So it all worked out pretty good, man. But yeah, he put his touches—on the mugshot album? He put his touches on that.

So that started changing the way that you thought about beats from there on out? Like when you started making beats after that, after he'd been in there?

You know, actually, I kinda got my props, because after they saw that he didn't really change none of my structures or anything—he just mixed it. Then they started seein' me in a different light as a beatmaker. Because I never presented—I'm not a Dre beatmaker. I wish I could make beats like Dr.

we heard the Fat Boys doin'. We was tryin' to be commercial, acceptable, until we found out that that wasn't gonna happen from a Houston-based rap group. So after we did an album called *Making Trouble*, then we did a series of 12-inches. Johnny C did "Be Down," and then that kind of put a split in there because due to the market then and everything that was goin' on . . . if you compare the *Making Trouble* album to the first N.W.A. album, you'll see there's a very close . . . similar concept-wise. They were touchin' on their type of gangsterism, we was touchin' on our type of gangsterism on there but then the next album's just totally off the chart, know what I'm sayin'? Just totally off to the left. We're talkin' about drug dealin', slayin', havin' sex with headless corpses and all this other crazy stuff, man.

On *Grip It! On That Other Level* . . .

Yeah. On *Grip It* . . . Johnny C, Jukebox, and myself, we did a whole 'nother album that got shelved because the personnel all quit. Johnny C went solo, Jukebox didn't believe in what we were doing

Dre. I'm a DJ first of all. You know what my thing is? I keep two records on time for my MCs. I can do the live show. How I even got into beatmaking was because there was a record called "Flash Is On The Beatbox," and I heard Grandmaster Flash could do the beatbox, and that's my number one idolized, groupie worship hero, you know what I'm sayin'? So I just naturally got the progression and then started wanting to make beats, because Grandmaster Flash was makin' the beats. So that's not really been one of my strong fortés, but I did bring something to the table.

Was this when you were still in Jersey, with the Mighty MCs, wasn't it called?

I was just starting to mess around with a Roland 626. A friend of ours—you know, me and Johnny C, we both come up under funk, and Jazzy Bradley was a funk musician in Trenton that kinda put us underneath [his] wing. And we would go down in the basement and stay for hours while they would rehearse. So we got to be around musicians. And then one time I wanted to duplicate a beat by James Brown, before sampling James Brown had got popular, maybe like three years before sampling got popular. This would be 1984. I asked him, I said, "Hey, can you play this beat?" And he was tryin' to do it on a Roland TR-707, and he couldn't quite do it. Now, he tells me that I said the beat was whack that he made for me, and he said, "Could I do better?" I said I probably could if I knew how to program. He went in his closet and pulled out this dusty Roland TR-626 and said, "Here. Here you go. Here's the book. Come back." I came back about a week later, had the beat matched perfect. That was before sequencing was coming out, and like I say, my thing was just running on time. I was running the turntable along with the beat machine, so I guess I was preparin' myself for the next step, doing production as far as the sampling. And as a DJ, you can take all the little phrases and elements and everything like that, and just, you know, kind of put it all together.

So were you working with those same tools whenever you got to Houston?

Actually, when I left in January of '87, I packed 50 of the most [popular] records that I could think to—things that I knew I could make a living with as a DJ at that time—and a Roland 909 drum machine, and I just would program the 909. When I hooked up with Rap-A-Lot, we went out and we found a TR-808, a little sound mixer, and got some 400s, and none of that is sequenced. On the *Making Trouble* album that was all bein' tracked, when I'm runnin' the records and everything together.

And J put you to work—you had an apartment above his car lot, is that right, over on North Shepherd?

This is what had happened: We was all livin' in a Fifth Ward house, and there was maybe five or six people in there. And, the car lot would stay locked up at night. Now, as a musician, I'm not just gonna let equipment be in there for the takin', you know what I'm sayin'? So one day, I said, "I do not wanna sleep with five or six people in this house, this wild and crazy." I said, "Man, do you mind if I stay with the equipment in the room?" He says, "Yeah, but lemme give you somethin'." So he gave me a Mossberg shotgun and said, "Here, you watch the lot for me." And that's how I started staying up at the car lot.

Being there with your equipment, you probably started getting a lot more involved with it.

I got a *lot* more involved with it. Shit, I'm the type that—I sleep with the equipment, man. Even at my grandmother's when I was young, my grandmother would come into the room, I had headphones wrapped all around me because I'd be sleeping with the drum machine, or I'd be asleep at the turntables. She'd say, "Go to sleep!" And I never still, at this time, still sleep at night. I'm always more creative durin' the nighttime process. Something about when you're burning that midnight oil in there at night and you see that sun come up. I was a vampire for years, man. I got a rhyme: "I stayed in my room for days at a time / when I cut the beats and the MCs rhyme." And I'd just stay up in the room, man, and just try to get it right. Get down with your mouth and walk all around with the newest products and the tape. That's how you got your juice back in the day. Up in the lab, as they call it.

What struck you about the rap scene in Houston when you first saw it? Like when you first got down to Houston, going to the club and seeing what was going on, what struck you?

They had this thing called "cappin'," which, I was goin' in there . . . 'cuz I'm not a pretty bad MC. Sub-par, right? Back in the day, you know, I could rap. From bein' a DJ, you just pick up on it. So I say, "This is a different region of the United States—let's see what they do first." Man, they came out there, started talkin' about mamas, "suck this," "suck that," and that's one thing on the East Coast that you ain't gettin' involved with back in the day, you know what I'm sayin'? And there was one guy who stood out, name was Willie D. And he was goin' against a guy named Romeo Poet and the Royal Flush. And Willie D could fit any MC's lyrics at that time, but he made them cap rhymes. Like he used to do Dana Dane "Nightmares" and he would come up with something that he'd say, "There's a rat on the couch / and it said 'gimme five' / and his mama look like a hoe / that's why she dyin'," and all this other type stuff, man. And he would win week after week after week after week. They called it "cappin'." So I got used to the structure even though my hip-hop is not necessarily your hip-hop. And when it spread from more than just the Tri-State area—New Jersey, Connecticut, New York—and it started comin' on down to Pennsylvania, Delaware, Virginia, and it started goin' Midwest, everybody took what they could take, and developed it. But hip-hop, to me, has always been national, all over. It's just that it's not from the original—where it was created at. But if you gotta do something . . . like everybody was always doin' block parties. There was always DJs in every state that you go to, and they always had people on the mic that was good. They were actually doin' hip-hop but they didn't know that was the term for it. Houston always had its place with the rap. Since the "Rapper's Delight" came out, man, that was just goin' on everywhere, so there was always people from different regions goin' down to

different places that were always there. There's a lot of people from New York there, and the group that I went out with was from Chicago, was DJ Lonnie Mac. You had Burgermeister who was from New York, Vicious Lee, John B from Brooklyn . . . that was my circle. As a matter of fact, I was with them before I became a Ghetto Boy, because we decided to go with Rap-A-Lot as the Def IV.

I was gonna say that sounds like the guys that were in Def IV, which were signed to Rap-A-Lot after you guys, right?

Which . . . yes sir, so I told them, "Look guys, let me see what I can do." Because after he—J asked, "Who did the beats?" Well, that was me. And my brother John B, he came up there with me, and J was more interested in the beats. So I said, "Look, we gonna do this. Let me get in the door, and when there's an opening, I'll call you," you know what I'm sayin'? And after we got established, J said, "Well, is there anybody else . . .?" I said, "Well, the group I was with, J, the Def IV." You got the Royal Flush, you got . . . "I Know How To [Play 'Em!]" . . .

What was her name—the female rapper—Choice.

Yeah, Choice. You had Nate . . . what was his name . . . his DJ, Boss, just passed away.

O.G. Style.

The Coughee Brothaz—the Odd [Squad]—you know, so we always looked out for everybody that we possibly could, man. The bottom line—if you was on Rap-A-Lot, and you was a Ghetto Boy, your future was secured.

So when did you guys start touring? I know you were going out and hitting all of the South, working your way up to Chicago. When was that?

You talkin' about seriously touring or just—well, our first tour that I remember was right after *Making Trouble* dropped. Harry-O, Michael Harris . . . Death Row Records . . . he was a friend of Little J, and he was from LA. He got us on the Fat Boys's "Wipeout" tour. The Fat Boys, Salt-n-Pepa, and Dana

Dane. We started off with Ice-T in LA, then we went to . . . it was Phoenix, it was Tucson, and it was Oakland, California—that's where I met Cameron, The Holy Ghost Kid. And we started talking at that time, and that was my first big tour that I ever had been on myself. I don't like that, and our record wasn't even released yet, but, you know, Harry-O was a mover back in them days, man, and he made it work. He made the promoters respect us, give us a lot of good time onstage when we were an unknown act, you know?

How were you received? How were the crowds?

We were received pretty good, man! We were received pretty good considering they never heard our sound, man. We were received pretty good for what it was worth at that time. I mean, we learned a lot. And if you been in this game for years . . . making records is a science. So when we . . . we said, "Okay," said, "You know what? We need to change this up." He said it to me like this, and I said, "Why am I hearin' 25 records bein' played on the radio a day with the funky drummer beat?" Because I was like this—pretty much, once somebody else did somethin' with it, it was like, "Oh, I don't wanna use that record. Somebody else did something with it." Why do you think the record is being played? Because they sound similar. Or they have that beat that's unleashed there. Okay, how can I attack this where it's the beat, but it does not sound like everybody else, but you hear that familiarity in there? So I said, "Okay, I'm gonna unlearn what I have learned." A lot of my philosophy, man, comes from Bruce Lee influence and stuff. That was my first idol, you know what I'm sayin'? Hip-hop, to me, is a martial art. It's always evolving, always changing. That's the style of Jeet Kune Do, which is always intercepting, and contracting. Contracting, expanding, contracting, expanding, you know? And I said, "Okay, I'll attack this. I'll use what I need, strip it down, and bring it back up." So then, once I started knowin' the game . . . my beats got a little bit better, overall the tracks got a little bit better, and they started bein' acceptable and played. That came off of *Grip It! On Another Level* . . . I think, as an artist, every record is expected to do better because you know a little bit more. So

the succession of records got us a little bit better than where we were.

Well *Grip It . . .* marked a change also in the lyricism because that's really when Geto Boys started to get a little bit darker, right?

Yes. That's when—after, I was tellin' you we had made the album that got shelved. And Willie D became a member of the group. Then we got Scarface and made Bill a rapper, and we started just talking about a little bit more of the dark side.

And that's what turned Jukebox off. He left because of that.

Yeah. Actually, Jukebox wrote the "Mind Of A Lunatic," man.

He did!

He did, you know, and lemme tell you something, man: A lot of people—well, I can speak for our group, man—we all come from good, decent backgrounds, you know what I'm sayin'? We just know how to get dirty when we need to. Jukebox was very talented, he was good in school, but he wanted to find something . . . when you are being something that you're actually not—Jukebox had his doubts, man, and he saw a parallel of sittin' with the thieves, and thinkin', "I gotta fuck somebody before the weekend?" That started taking a toll on him, man. It started changing him, man, so he left because of that, and Bill just picked up the parts, you know, and kept goin' on. It was always going to be Geto Boys, just like there was numerous Temptations changes and New Edition lineups and all that. That's just how it happens sometimes.

What do you think brought about that change? What do you think brought the Geto Boys over into that darker kind of territory?

Lil' J wasn't impressed with the last album that we did with Jukebox, Johnny C, and myself, man. It was very commercial, and he didn't think that he would take a gamble on that album, man. He said, "Go back and see what's happenin', but I'm not putting that album out." When you tell an artist that, and you done put your heart and soul into something, you know—you really gotta take a look and examine what's goin' on, you know, what's happenin'. So everybody just kind of broke camp, and I was there with just Bushwick Bill. And I had started working on Willie D's *Controversy* album, and so did Johnny C and Jukebox. If you listen to Willie D's *Controversy*, "Do It Like A G.O." is on there, with Johnny C and Jukebox rappin'. So it was just me and Bill, and next thing you know this guy Scarface was comin' over my house and K-9, who was out of jail now, was havin' a battle over at my apartment. And that's how all that came together.

Who was K-9 battling?

He was battling Brad Jordan, who would later be known as Scarface. [Thelton Polk, a.k.a. K-9] was an original member of the Ghetto Boys. After he saw what we were doin', and there was a chance for him to come back into the group, then he wanted to battle K-9. Well, Brad Jordan done blew him out the water, man.

He was DJ Akshen at that point, right?

Yes, he was DJ Akshen at that point, yeah.

What did you think of him? Was that the first time you'd met him?

Brad was brilliant, man. You know, this little guy just kept bumpin' me—you ever go somewhere and this guy just always is there? Like, "Aw, man, I can rap, man." I was like, "Yeah, yeah," you know. And I would hear him, I'd say, "You know what?" I kept givin' him my card. I said, "Look, I don't wanna hear you outside the club. I wanna hear you where I got you in an environment where I can record you." But I was always busy. And finally, you know, every time I did hear him, he did drop some bombs, you know. So that's when, to me, if you listen to the "Seek And Destroy?" Brad had that type of delivery, man, where he could have been the next Rakim, the next Kool G Rap, the next Big Daddy Kane. Because out of all them tracks that I like Brad rappin' on *Grip It! On That Other Level*,

I like the "Seek And Destroy" over the "Scarface," because that song, to me, at that time—well, I'm from the element where you got true MCs, not rappers. I'm an old-schooler. The four elements, you know. That's how I live now—by the four elements. Well, actually, the most popular of the four has always been DJing and MCing. You know? That's what you had to do to record yourself—a DJ or an MC. You had to have some skills on the wheels or you had to have some skills on that mic. That's the element that I came up. The ones that I saw comin' up before me, the original pioneers of this craft—the Kool Hercs, your Bambaataas, your Flashes, your Theodores, your Red Alerts, you know what I'm sayin', Hollywoods, all these cats—those are the ones that you're patterning yourself after. Every martial artist that came after Bruce Lee—who do you think the guiding light was?

They look up to him.

They wanted to inspire themselves, you know. I feel that you never become better than those before you, because that's theirs. You just take it to the next level. But the basic pattern and foundation has already been set for you. So therefore, the blueprint is pretty easy. If I can read all the notes that you left behind, and I had a structure of your foundation already, of course I can add on to it because now I'm deep into the foundation of it. I get to see what's goin' on, so I can strip, rebuild, strip, rebuild, bring it down. Good stuff, man. So yeah, you always gotta give homage, man. Every time I put the headphones on, cue up the record, I'm doin' an homage to all the DJs from the past who came up with that. So it's like—they're always going to be a part of you, because that's what they do. That's them.

I know you like "Seek And Destroy" better, but I wanna talk about the "Scarface" track because of the effect that it had on Houston, and the kind of game-changing that a lot of people look back on—I talked to K-Rino about that and he said, "That was the first time I really thought we could do this, like a local act could do this," when that song broke.

Now, first of all, Brad had something out with Lil' Troy at that time called "Mr. Scarface." I heard the record, heard some of the elements being dropped in there, and I said, "Well I can remake that." But a couple years before he thought about that, I've already started doin' my *Scarface* the movie samples. And I said, "You know what? If I employ these with that, and remix this and put that with this, and tell him to call himself 'Scarface,' I think we might have something here." So the only thing I did, man, was pretty much remix that and put "Scarface" on there. John Bido had helped Brad along with that album for Lil' Troy, you know. And . . . that was my involvement, but yeah, when that came, it was more than just "Scarface." It was the "Gangsta Of Love," it was "Let A Ho Be A Ho," "Read These Nikes," but I'm just talkin' about just as far as DJ Akshen. To me, that was his best flow as an MC on there, where he's just lettin' it go and just cuttin' it up, man, you know, just flowin' off the top.

On the "Scarface" track, you mean?

Overall, I like the whole album. I'm very proud of *Grip It! On That Other Level* . . . I'm very proud of that because finally, we started goin' all over. We started goin' all over—all over the country. Four guys from Fifth Ward. There was only six of us. There was our road manager Keith . . . it was our roadie Steve, and it was the four of us, man. We went to Chicago, Detroit, LA, all over the country, man. And people said, "Man, we ain't think y'all was gonna come." They told us this in East St. Louis, man, "I ain't gonna mention names, but some of these groups, man, they be scared to come, but y'all came, man. Y'all came, man!"

"Man, we're Geto Boys—we're not afraid of anywhere."

Yeah! You know what? Because we went there, and we had a relation because we always kept ourselves accessible. They seen how we came to they town, and we came as guests, you know what I'm sayin'? We never tried to take over. That's why—if you go places, man, cats ain't tryin' to start nothin'. But if you go there with the wrong attitude, you know what I'm sayin', that's when beef starts.

I always tell friends, "Now how this guy get killed? Because he was tryin' to do a little something extra." People just ain't gonna—you know, sometimes it happens . . . you might just be in the wrong place at the wrong time, but to get killed, and this happen to you, man, it's because there was an opportunity for it to happen because you pissed a couple of people off.

A lot of times it is just the little things.

It's the little things, you know. We had some little—some little troubles, man. Sometimes, man, we can't help it, man, if the girls was on us. We can't help it if the "Gangsta Of Love," we didn't know that that would be a signature . . . "Ooh, can you do me like y'all do in that song?" You know what I'm sayin'? Me and Bill, we was roommates, and we couldn't believe how much play we got off that song, man. Memphis was good to us, man. We had Tony Presley, who was second cousin to Elvis, man, he gave us an exclusive tour of Graceland, man. That was very cool, man. We met Isaac Hayes through that.

You guys were in—you were just like in a van or what?

Yeah we were in a van, man! We weren't tryin' to kick it high post back then, man. We did a van, shuttle bus, weekend gigs, you know what I'm sayin'?

Were y'all playing in front of a lot of people every night or was it small clubs?

It would be anywhere from 150 people to 2,000 to 3,000 people, man, in them small venues at that time. We could fill up a club or what I called the renovated movie theaters. We used to be down at the . . . Maceba Theater in Houston? That used to be in Third Ward somewhere, man. We filled that up one time. Yeah, and it'd be astonishing, man, that they would just come in there to see us, man. It was like, wow. You know what blew my mind? You know how you see the Michael Jackson tour sales they be showin' you, man, and you be like damn! Well, one time, man, the guy from Chicago picked us up, and we was goin' to the elevated 'L' station, and there was a record shop—the 'L's are just elevated platforms—and there was a massive traffic jam, and it looked like a block party in the streets of Chicago. And we was like, "Man, who is these people here to see?" He said, "Man, that's the people who have come out for the in-store." There were thousands upon thousands of people in the street in Chicago, man. Just for us. And I was like, "Wow!"

This is for *Grip It! On That Other Level*—that's on that tour?

Yeah, this is for the *Grip It . . .*, man, we would go to Chicago every week, man! The promoter at that time—we was workin' with the late DJ Pink House. He was a very popular house DJ at that time, and man, we was goin' every week. We played Harvey, Illinois, we played the North Side of Chicago, the South Side of Chicago, the East Side of Chicago, West Side of Chicago, Gary, Indiana—we just was in the Midwest a whole lot, man, and always loved, man. Always loved. That's one thing that we always showed, man. We always would chill, never a problem, man. Never had any problems, you know.

How much changed, then, once *We Can't Be Stopped* came out?

Well, you know what? That's where I kinda left, man. After the Rick Rubin thing . . .

So you didn't do that tour, then, for *We Can't Be Stopped*—did you work on that record?

I worked on that record. I didn't receive any credit, but I'm the first one you hear on it. "As the year 2000 reached into the free world / a band of lethal assassins . . ." And my friend, I tell you what—see how the sound changes on the next album. I didn't get any credit, man, but I'm gonna let it go.

So you left why?

I left because, hey man, I'm tired of this funky arithmetic, man. It just got to the point, man, where I shouldn't have to be onstage worryin' about my

lights being cut off, and yet you buyin' $100,000 Mercedes and all this and all that. And yet, you know, we still struggling. So it was just the kind of point where it was like, "You know what? Forget it man." I walked away. Some people say I walked away from a gold mine, but I actually have no regrets, man. Twenty years later I have no regrets for leavin' that because it's still goin' on. Still goin' on, and I still can't believe that some people still allow themselves not to have anything, you know?

How do you mean? Because of the arithmetic, you mean the pay?

The pay, not handling to . . . even some groups from the '60s, man, went gold and platinum, and they still get a nice, nice royalty check. They still get nice publishing checks that they can live off the rest of their lives, things like that. I don't see none of that. So I really don't know what's goin' on now, and I really don't care because I'm not involved in it, but I say, man, as an artist, take care of your business. That way you can feed your family, man.

Do you still keep in touch with Willie?

Me and Willie D, man, we talk like we never left a beat, man. I talked to Face the other day. He was up in New York. He had gave me a call. He was doin' the Hip-Hop Honors. I used to stay in touch with Bill. I haven't talked to Bill in a while. Last time I talked to Bill he was workin' on his gospel album.

Isn't that crazy?

Well, Bill was a Bible college student, man, when he had first came down to Houston, man, with his sister.

He was in Kansas City or something like that, right?

I'm not sure where he had came from. He was with his bigger brother Chris at that time, but then he got sent to Houston. I kept bein' in the club and something kept like rubbing my leg lower than me. You know, you in the club, you not used to something that low? I was like, "Aw, it's this cat right here." Well, that kinda—me and him kinda hit it off instantly, man. Bill's a b-boy, you know what I'm sayin'? I was a breakdance DJ, so I'd put the breaks on, and Bill could just cut it up, man. He was like my Larry Love, man.

When he and Willie started working on lyrics for him to transition to become an MC, did that happen in the studio, or what was the scenario with that?

Me and Bill would always hang out all day smokin' weed, man. And I would always try to get him to rap and do some things, you know. He was like, "Red, man, I can't rap . . ." So I taught him some rhymes that he could rap, but he was like readin' it off the paper. "Bill, instead of you dancin', man, you need to rap." He took to it instantly. He had a unique voice at the time. It was different, you know.

Willie told me a story—I guess it was you guys in the studio, and he took Bill aside and sat down and they had a conversation, and he wanted to talk to him about writing his first rap, and he wrote his first rap with him, which was "Size Ain't Shit." You know, he just kind of got his story down and everything.

Oh, yeah. Well, Willie D at that time was the true backbone as far as the lyrical content. The only one that he didn't write for was Face . . . see, Willie was the only true representation of Fifth Ward. We're all transplants.

Willie was born and raised.

Yeah, see we all fit in, but that's like the Godfather of the Dirty South, man . . . That's why they try to get with Willie D, because they all pretty much done bit his sound and style, man.

Willie D

FIFTH WARD

Originally signed as a solo artist to Rap-A-Lot, Will is one of the most famous rappers from the South and is as known for his solo records (his debut, *Controversy*, is widely praised as a Southern classic) as he is for his work with the group that put Houston on the map, Geto Boys. A man of many talents, formerly a political radio talk show host, a professional boxer, and real estate mogul, Willie is as active as ever of late, writing and making music as a solo artist and touring with Geto Boys—even penning an advice column for a while. Interview conducted along with Peter Beste at Willie's Houston home after he whipped us both at pool.

PHOTO: PETER BESTE

How were the shows in Europe?

Those things were sold out before I even got there. Man, it was crazy. It was like all these kids screamin', and man, they ain't know the words to songs, they was just, "Willie D! Willie D!"

You're gonna start doing more overseas shit now, huh?

I'm already settin' it up. I'm already on it, man.

Where's your next stop?

I don't know yet. We're just talking to some booking agents and promoters, just putting a team together right now.

That's the tricky part.

Yeah, so it's just a matter of . . . it's all just a matter of going places where people know their market, you know what I mean?

You'd do well in London.

Germany too. I've been hearing about Germany for a long time. You know, how they're crazy about Geto Boys out there. Wherever Geto Boys work, I could work, you know? And we've never been there. So it's a matter of going to those markets.

Where's the furthest the Geto Boys ever went on tour? Tokyo, right?

They went to Tokyo without me. That was when I left the group. But that was just for a couple of dates and that was it. That was way back in . . . shit, that was '92 or '93. It's a whole 'nother world now. To go out there and see that, man . . . kids walkin' up to me givin' me "Rodney King" cassettes, 12-inches of "Bald Headed Hoes." Givin' me that. I'm like, "Where y'all get that shit from?" Ebay.

Fifty bucks.

Hell yeah. They pay.

And that's the only chance they'll get to see someone like you perform.

They got a hip-hop movement out there. They got some rappers out there, but they can't touch us. They're nowhere near the quality of US rappers.

They didn't grow up on it in the same way.

Well . . . I think they been on it for a long time. They've had it, for years and years. I mean, there was kids walkin' up telling me that they been listenin' to me since they was in the kindergarten. You know, so they've been on it, they just didn't look at it like, "This is something we wanna do." I guess it wasn't any type of structure. Nothing in place that they could go and say, "Okay, this DJ spinnin' rap music, or this guy is starting a record label, I'ma get on this." I don't think they looked at it like that. I think it was more of a cult movement in the beginning, and now it's starting to really grow. First of all, hip-hop is in every corner of the world. But it's really starting to grow to where you have people starting to form record labels more often, and you got DJs that's just totally dedicated 100 percent to the cause. It just blew my mind, man. It just really opened . . . because, you know, I've been traveling, but to do business. You know, to do real estate and traveling . . . vacation, like that. I never do shows.

I saw the photos. The ones from Finland.

See, that guy knows his market. The show was sold out probably a week before I got there. It's a club. They sold tickets. Sold out. They knew what they were doing.

K-Rino did well out there too.

That's another thing. I know if K-Rino did well out there, then I know I can go out there and do something. They had to turn away like 300 kids, man. That was in the cold too. It was cold! I mean like *cold* cold. I mean like 10 degrees! They were standing out in the cold. It was kinda unorganized, though, 'cuz some of the kids I heard, they was complaining that they had tickets already and they was in the cold for two hours. But then, they still had like another 300 kids that could not get in.

You'll have to go back again sometime.

Oh, I'll be back next year. From now on, Finland is on the list of cities to do. Another thing is that all of those countries are so close by that you can hit a country and hit two cities in each country. Like Norway would be good because the median income in Norway is $38,000. See, they don't think rappers know this kind of shit. But yeah, they got money in Norway. Everybody got money in Norway. They got something. Not necessarily everybody rich, but everybody got something. Ain't nobody really starving in Norway.

You thought about buying land out there?

I hadn't really thought about it, nah. You know, the opportunities I take, man . . . the opportunities are more like people that I know say, "Hey, this is what's going on . . ." and they're inside on the deal. They know what's going on. They know. Because, man, if you don't really just fuckin' all the way know, if you ain't in the loop, if whoever you dealin' with is not all the way in the loop, and you trust that person that's in that loop . . . you can get your head knocked off.

There's a lot of stuff that can get in the way of a perfectly good-looking piece of land. Environmental assessments, that sort of thing . . .

Yeah, exactly. They got some environmental issues in Fifth Ward too. That's where all those chemical plants were and shit. A lot of those plants that were in Fifth Ward are shut down, been shut down for years.

What kind of plants?

I know one of them . . . one of the plants, one of the big issues out there is . . . what's the name of it . . . that damn company? It was some type of petroleum company. They were takin' they shit and dumpin' it in the ditches and shit.

In Fifth Ward?

Yeah. That was just basically dumping that shit in the drainage.

These were processing plants, then? For oil companies?

Some of them, like Enron, Exxon, and a couple of other companies was in on the shit.

So when did they shut those down?

That's been shut down for years. I don't even know exactly when, but it's been years and years.

'80s, '90s?

If it was the '90s, it was early '90s.

How did that affect Fifth Ward?

Man, there's a lot of motherfuckers runnin' around with cancer or dead, but man . . . When you're poor, *what can you do*? I mean, most poor people don't wanna do nothing. Most poor people don't even know they *can* do something. A lot of poor people don't even know that that's the reason why they dying. They just think, "Oh shit. I'm dyin'." That's for real, and that's poor *all over the world*.

That just happens to be *our* poor. But that's all over the world, man. You don't know. You don't even know that you have recourse. You don't know. And people ain't been educated on fightin' back unless it's some street shit, like fighting your neighbors or beating up . . . fighting your family members, killing your best friend. And nobody like . . . fightin' the government, the city. "What the fuck you mean, fight the *city*? You mean like . . . Houston against *me*?"

When did you first start rapping?

First started rapping . . . I was listening to Run–D.M.C. in Fifth Ward in the bottom. My hood. You know what? I think you got a picture of the bottom . . . you remember those apartments I told you I used to live in, Kennedy Apartments? That's where I first started rapping.

'83, '84, something like that?

'83, '84. I can't pinpoint it exactly, but it was '83, '84.

You got good really quick then, didn't you?

I had to. A friend of mine . . . we used to hang out in the park and sing. Not rap—*sing*. Sing old '70s songs, like Motown hits and stuff. And when I say "the park," I mean either at the park in the neighborhood or in the middle of the apartments was a little park.

Courtyard?

Yeah. We'd hang out there and we'd sing. One day we was listening to the radio and Run–D.M.C. comes on, and my buddy says, "Ah, man, we can do that, man. That's Run–D.M.C." I like to describe Run–D.M.C. as basically complex. 'Cuz their rhymes are like . . . the words wasn't really . . . there was no real complexity in the words, but the way they put it together and made it . . . they were able to achieve their own identity through the way they put it together. Everybody couldn't just put it together the way they put it together. But, you know . . . I wasn't smart enough to know that at the time. All I knew was that they were rapping using very basic words and very basic verbage, and I'm like, "Shit . . . well okay, I think I can do that." So he goes in his house, I go in my house, and we agree to come out in an hour with our raps. He came out in an hour. I came out in an hour. He said his rap, and everybody started laughin'. I said my rap, and everybody goes, "Ohhh . . ." And I only had like eight bars.

What was it about?

I can't even remember. Shit was probably just being braggadocios, though, because that's what happened back then . . . you just brag on yourself. You the best, ain't nobody else nothing. They're sucker MCs, you're the greatest. That kind of thing. So . . . their reaction encouraged me to write more, so I started writing a little more, and then I started getting in contests and challenging people. People would come up to me or come around the neighborhood, and we'd battle and stuff like that. So I'm knockin' everybody down and I'm getting more encouraged along the way. In the meantime, I got an amateur boxing career going on, but this rap thing was something that everybody could see me do. With boxing, you know . . . I'd go train and it's just you and the other fighters and the coaches, and then when we'd go fight in the tournaments or whatever, we'd go to Pasadena or Austin or whatever . . . nobody else around you, your peers don't really get to see you, to get to see you perform. With this, this rap . . . I could be on the spot and I can impress my buddies, see a chick I wanna holla at, I'ma rap in front of her. Everybody was lovin' it, so that eight bars turned into a verse and that verse turned into a song, and then after I wrote that song I started competing in contests, and then I went on and started writing more and more and just goin' on and on and on. So it was a snowball effect like that. Originally, I never wanted to be in a group because I always hear about how all these groups break up and all this conflict in the groups and stuff, so I never really wanted to be in a group. So when I originally signed with Rap-A-Lot, I signed as a solo artist. Myself and Lil' J, we had the same barber, and my barber used to tell me all the time about this dude. We both from Fifth Ward and we

got the same barber. We didn't know each other personally. So I would see him in and out of the barbershop, but I never spoke to him. And he never spoke to me. I knew what he was tryin' to do. He knew what I was doin'. To be honest, I think both of us some arrogant motherfuckers and neither one of us wanted to take the first step. But my barber used to tell me all the time, "Man, there's this guy, man . . . why don't you and Lil' J get together, man . . . you make the music, he got the money, man. You got the talent, y'all put it together and put out an album, man. Y'all sell a million copies, and they'll make a movie about it and put me in it." That's how it all got started.

Who was your main competition on the other side of town?

Man, to be honest there wasn't no main competition on the other side of town. It was like . . . Willie D. It was Willie D . . . my main competition was Romeo Poet. Romeo Poet, man . . .

He was from Fifth Ward too, right?

I think Romeo is from Fifth Ward.

I think that's what K said. He said he would see him all the time at the Wrangler.

Romeo Poet manages Popeye's.

In Houston?

Yeah. I don't know which one, but he was managin' even way back then.

You know anybody that would know where that was?

I could probably track him down, make some calls. I mean there ain't nothin' but six degrees of separation. So I could probably track him down if I just made some calls and calls and calls, but I could track him down. You need to meet Romeo, man. Romeo kept the pressure on me to be good. He made me better. That was my nemesis. Romeo Poet and Royal Flush. In fact, Royal Flush . . . the first talent show I ever got into, or battle for the mic I ever got into, it was with Royal Flush. They were the big shit in town. It was Royal Flush and it was against Romeo Poet.

Royal Flush the group?

Yeah, who Rap-A-Lot eventually signed. Well, at some point Royal Flush and Romeo Poet—they joined forces. And so I was against them. It was me against them, and I held my own. I mean I really . . . Rhinestone Wrangler, which was the just the absolute . . . probably the greatest club ever, ever in Houston, had a hell of a run. They used to be about five . . . I'd say four nights a week jam-packed. Beautiful . . . I mean beautiful girls. Fat chick couldn't . . . fat chick nowhere to be found. This was a bad place. This place was off Main on Murworth. Right there by the Astrodome. They had a club called Grammo's. It became Grammo's years later. Man, that was the club of clubs, period. That was the king. If you want a blueprint for clubs, and to be successful . . . figure that out. But we used to battle at the Rhinestone Wrangler. The last 13 weeks in a row the Wrangler was open, I won every week. I won so much, people stopped comin'. I mean the competition stopped comin', not the people. People was losin' they jobs. People would come up to me and tell me they lost they job because they stayed at the contest. They wanted to see the contest. The contest would start around two-thirty, three o'clock. This was back when the clubs was closin' at five in the morning. You could sell liquor all night.

What year was that?

It was like '87, '88. [Laughs] That was the days, man. Vanilla Ice came there. I smoked him about four times. He came there. He used to come every now and then. Like, that's why when I see people talk about . . . when I hear people talk about Vanilla Ice, and they talk about how cocky and arrogant he is? He was like that before he started makin' records. I mean he'd come up onstage tryin' to look all tough, and he would rap, he would talk all that shit. And it was a two-part contest—the first part was just where you show your lyrical skills off.

If you were fortunate enough to be voted into the finals, then you battled where you did rank-rappin'. You'd talk about everybody . . . each other mama, talk about what a person got on, talk down, that kind of thing. Diss rappin'. So that's what we did. And they used to cheer for Vanilla Ice to make him get in the finals. He always was in the finals 'cuz they wanted to see me wreck on this white boy. And I would bust his ass every single time. I didn't discriminate. I fucked him up like I fucked everybody else up.

Do you remember the most exciting battle you had there?

I remember sayin' when I was battlin' Romeo Poet one night, I said, "You come on this stage and act like you so damn def . . ." Nah, I said . . . I said, "I see your girl right there . . ." His girl was in the audience . . . "I know you love her to def / but that baby she had / that ain't yours by yourself!" Everybody like . . . the whole club just went fuckin' crazy. But yeah, I remember that specifically.

Where else was everybody battling around that time?

That was really the only place where we really did real battle raps as far as like a venue, where we actually did battle raps. Rhinestone was the place. No other place, period. As far as contests and stuff, I used to go to Joe's. I used to get in contests at Joe's on Jensen and Bennington.

Is that still considered Fifth Ward?

Nah, that's Trinity Gardens. Yeah, so . . . basically, schools, you know, anywhere there was a talent show, I'd go.

What are the boundaries of Fifth Ward?

Ah shit, man, you talking about . . . Clinton . . . you got Clinton. A lot of people actually consider Harrisburg to be the boundary.

The southern boundary?

Yeah, the southern boundary. Harrisburg, then I would say the northern boundary would be . . .

Cavalcade?

Cavalcade, it would be Cavalcade. The eastern boundary would be . . .

It goes as far as Wayside?

Not Lockwood . . . What's the other one . . . uh . . . nah, we ain't that far. It's like . . . not that far—you're kinda familiar with this shit! Not quite to Wayside, though. Not really quite to Wayside 'cuz when you get down that far you're really at Settegast, so it's not really a main street, it's just like past, just right past Lockwood. And I'd say west is North Main.

We were gonna take a ride through there . . .

They ain't gonna fuck with you. Y'all some crime analysts. CSI. Forensic specialists. Forensic photographers or some shit.

Right. Duncan Funeral Home is right there!

See, that's a big misperception. White people always think they gonna get fucked up in Fifth Ward. All you gotta do is just go out in that motherfucker like you . . . you gonna get fucked up if you walk out there lookin' like you a dope fiend walkin' the street. But you roll up in that motherfucker with some cameras and shit? They gonna be like, shit . . . One motherfucker actually get the nerve to ask you what you doin', though. "Whatchu doin' there, man? You with the magazine?"

What else should we see in Fifth Ward?

Y'all go take a picture of Wheatley High School. That's important. Take a picture of Wheatley. The old Wheatley.

Who went there?

Barbara Jordan, Mickey Leland. Shit . . . my grandmother, my mama, daddy. E'rebody went to that

motherfucker. I didn't. I went to Forest Brook. It's on the Northside, on Tidwell between Homestead and Wayside.

That's where G-Dash is from.

Yeah, well, we went to school together. They had basketball games there. Exhibition basketball games. Like Swishahouse against Rap-A-Lot.

I went to one of those. Over at TSU.

Yeah, so you got . . . Wheatley, they just built a new Wheatley. You can see the old Wheatley right next door to it. Right across the street from it is an elementary where I went to school.

Tell us an interesting old fight story.

I'm day one born and brought Fifth Ward. That's what's on my birth certificate. When I was six we moved to Settegast, and then we kinda moved around Kashmere Gardens and all of that. Different places on the Northside. And then when I was 15 we moved back to Fifth Ward. So, when we moved back, we moved into the bottom. That's the southern part of Fifth Ward. It's the part closest to Clinton, where the Kennedy Place Apartments is. That's where we moved to. It was brand new apartments. Upscale projects. So I get out there, you know, e'rebody wanna test you and shit. So one dude, you know, he a bully and shit. We playin' basketball so, you know, he tryin' to handle me real rough, foulin' on purpose and shit like that. So finally I just . . . at the time I was probably was 150 pounds or something. And I know he was at least 230, maybe 240. And he tryin' to be all rough and shit. I see that he wanna fight, so next time he go up for a rebound I just pick him up and dump him while he in the air and I start whoopin' his ass. After I whooped his ass, I stretched him out and his buddy kinda break it up or whatever. And I go to my house and . . . I don't run—I didn't run—I *walked* to the house. And I'm inside of the house and a whole mob of people come to my house and he come knock on the door, "T's son, come on out! Tell your son come on out!" So . . . I'm fittin' to come out with a closet pole to fight 'em. And my mama make me put the closet pole down. You know, she's like, "Nah, you gonna fight 'em. You gonna go, you gonna whoop his ass!" And I'm like, damn . . . I already got away. I whipped this motherfucker's ass already. And she gonna make me go back and fight this motherfucker some more? This motherfucker big, know what I'm sayin'? So I'm thinking, "Okay, fuck, I ain't got no choice." So I go outside. He put his chin up. When he get close . . . just close enough up on me, I jab him with the left and catch him with the right, pick him up, do the same thing to him again. I started chokin' him, and I started chokin' him 'til e'rebody just asked me to let him up. "Let him up! Let him up!" I just kept squeezin' 'cuz I knew they was on his side, so I was tryin' to squeeze the life outta his ass. So my mama said, "Alright, you let him up now. You whooped his ass. You let him up." Man, my mom was fuckin' gangsta. My mama cut up a white man in the '60s. My mama was . . . my mama was not no fuckin' joke.

So that had a big effect on your upbringing.

Nah, I ain't see her cut the man up.

I mean that your mama was hard.

Hell yeah. She hard on me. Too hard on me. But you know, my mama was a gangsta, man. She gangsta for real. She'll fuck you up. She was dangerous. For real.

No one fucked with you after that, huh?

Nah, nah, I still had a couple more fights. See, the thing about Fifth Ward . . . a motherfucker don't *believe* you can whoop his ass. And even if he were to believe that you could whoop his ass, nobody's gonna live the shit down. Nobody gonna let you live it down, they gonna always fuck with you about it. So, that's when your pride come in. So, either you gonna whoop his ass a second time, or he gonna whoop your ass, or y'all gonna end up with somebody killin' somebody. That's why there's so much killin' in Fifth Ward, 'cuz of that pride over nothing. A lot of it is . . . a lot of it to me is like bullshit, you know . . .

Empty pride.

Yeah, empty pride. Almost like you proud of the wrong shit, you know what I'm sayin'? So you know, you fight a dude once . . . I'm tellin' you, most of the fights I had in Fifth Ward, I had to fight a dude twice. And you can't really ever get comfortable fightin' nobody. I mean, I'll whoop his ass once, and I'll whoop it again, but you never know when that motherfucker gonna pull out somethin'. You don't know if he gonna pull out somethin', somebody else gonna pull out somethin'. People fight dirty in the hood. Nobody fight fair.

They just wanna win. They don't care how.

They wanna win. A lot of the time you don't think about the consequences 'til you layin' on the ground bleedin', you know, or your eyes flickerin', or you sittin' behind bars. You know, like, "Damn, I killed him. Had to kill him. Or I coulda killed him, but I didn't have to kill him like that. I coulda made a self-defense case for myself. But I just went out and walked up to him in front of e'rebody . . . POW! POW! POW!" A buddy of mine named Rocky, he robbed . . . well, we'll put it like this . . . they *say* he robbed the neighborhood club, right? The owner shoots him, up by his eye, fucked him up real bad, right? Not by his eye . . . by his neck, fucked him up real bad. So about a week later, two weeks later, he was out in the neighborhood sittin' on a bench, he's like, "Yeah, Willie, I'ma kill that motherfucker, man. I'ma kill him. He ain't have to shoot me. I ain't robbin' a motherfucker!" He robbin' somebody, and he say, "He didn't have to shoot me." So, yeah, dude shoot him. And he sittin' on the bench, he telling anybody that would listen, he say, "I'ma kill that motherfucker. I'ma kill him." Probably about three weeks later, he catch him at the corner store, or across the street from the corner store. So, the difference between me and some of these guys is that . . . I just didn't get caught, you know? I just did not get caught. Or I left early. I ain't return to the scene. 'Cuz I coulda easily been in jail, or been one of those dudes dead too. That's why . . . I never could understand why . . . you know how people say, "Don't return to the scene of the crime?" You know how they say that? Fuck not *return* to the scene—*leave* the scene of the crime! You know, we got dudes in the hood that fight each other, try to kill each other, beat the shit out each other and then'll stay there, and let somebody leave and go do whatever. It's like, "I don't give a fuck. Let 'em go get somethin'." It's like most of 'em don't even be thinkin'—they don't be thinkin' that, "Oh, he gonna come back with a gun and he gonna kill me." They be thinkin' . . . "Oh, I'm just gonna kick somebody's ass." You know, in the black community a lot of times, historically we've been raised to settle conflicts with fists and guns, and more so than guns, just fists. It's just, you know . . . whoever strongest, that's the one that's gonna win, you know. Whoever is physically strongest.

Not necessarily who's right.

Exactly. It's like whoever is physically strongest, that's the guy that everybody look up to, and so you think just because you strong and you got muscles and shit, you gonna fuck somebody up. And so you sittin' here just like, "Ah, I don't give a fuck. I ain't goin' home." 'Cuz you tryin' to . . . you *proud*, and you don't want anybody to feel like you leavin'. So, you gonna sit there, he gonna go home and get somethin', and you gonna let him come back, he gonna kill you, and he'll be out of jail in five years. Or less. He might not even go to jail because they gonna say it was self-defense. 'Cuz don't nobody give a fuck about two niggas in the hood. They got more important motherfuckin' shit to worry about than two motherfuckin' niggas over here killin' each other. And then, both of them probably had criminal records anyway so they don't give a fuck. That's the way I look at it, man, is that you gotta . . . another reason that I'm still here is that I love the shit out of *me*. I love life. When you don't value life and you don't think about bein' 60, 70 years old, grey hair and grandchildren and shit, you most likely ain't gonna see those kinda days. 'Cuz you livin' day to day, just goin' through the motions. You ain't thinkin' long-term. You thinkin' livin' in the now. So you gonna end up goin' to the penitentiary for a bunch of years, and you gonna end up in a grave. You gonna catch an early grave. That's what's gonna happen. So, when I started

really thinkin' about it, I say, "Okay, motherfuckers is dyin' around me. All around me motherfuckers is gettin' killed for real." Okay. I got to get the fuck . . . first of all, get the fuck up out of here, and then also . . . I gotta learn to stop frequenting places where motherfuckers get killed. Somebody else gonna get killed, yeah. Man, there's clubs in the neighborhood that's been closed and opened for years . . . between killings! And people still go to the club! Somebody get killed, maybe once every two months, sometimes once every other week, then it cool off and a couple more people get killed. But the places stay open. Any respectable club, anywhere else, where they payin' taxes, shit like that, payin' liquor taxes, shit like that . . . they'da been closed down by now. That's too much heat from the government. They'll shut that shit down. But in the hood it's just . . . bring your own bottle . . . to them it's like a little quicksand contraption. You know, fuck it. Let 'em kill each other.

Ricky Royal

GREENSPOINT

He was known as "Gangsta Ric" long before he got to Houston in the early '80s, settling on the Northside and pulling together a group of high school rappers who would collectively become known as Royal Flush. Among them, Ricardo Royal (as he is also known) was the biggest voice that would surface during the battle rap era at the Rhinestone Wrangler. After that scene ran its course, Royal Flush went on to release a 12-inch and two albums on Rap-A-Lot. "I Never Made 20" is his best-known work with Royal Flush. After his time in Houston, Rick entered another phase of his career as a radio host in Dallas, where he still produces and makes music.

COURTESY OF RICARDO ROYAL

When did you come to Houston for the first time? Did you come from the East Coast or from the West Coast? I know you lived on both.

I came to H-Town in '80, '81 and did the eighth grade . . . and then my mama moved me back to the East Coast, to New Jersey. That's where I was born at. Shit, she moved me back to the East Coast, I did the ninth grade there, then I came back to Texas. And I came back to Texas to stay.

And you went to Aldine.

Yeah. I went to Hogg Middle School at first. In Studewood. Then we moved to the Third Ward area, and then I moved back to the East Coast, but when I came back, my mama had moved from the Third Ward area to the Aldine area. Greenspoint. What they call Greenspoint now. It's called Greenspoint now, but when I moved there, it was real, real nice and shit. It was like a suburban area. We turned that shit out. Between me and my niggas, by the time we got finished with Greenspoint, that shit was called *Gunspoint*.

What happened? What do you think was the biggest change there?

We changed it by some of the activities we was involved in! We started, you know, we started fuckin' around sellin' drugs and carjackin' and all that kind of shit. Doin' some boostin'. Boostin' clothes outta Greenspoint Mall . . . We were selling drugs in Greenspoint and The Villages of

Greenbriar. That was our stomping grounds—Villages of Greenbriar. Off of Imperial and Greens Road?

Greens Road is just north of the mall, right?

Yeah, but I'm talkin' about . . . Villages of Greenbriar was where a lot of us lived at, and those apartments—it's a real big-ass apartment. As a matter of fact, it almost takes up half of Imperial. In between Imperial and Seminar . . . in between Greens Road and Seminar. Real big apartments. Big enough for us to congregate and get together and cause havoc on the rest of Greenspoint, 'cuz there was a lot of us. When I first moved there, there wasn't no black people lived in Greenspoint.

At that point, was music a part of your life? Were you listening to music—were you into stuff?

Hell yeah! From day one, brother. Day one I been fuckin' with music in terms of either listenin' to music heavy or bein' in a dance group. I started off in dance groups when I was young, playing drums and shit. I played drums, led the choir when I was about 8 years old, and then they put me on drums because I asked too many questions about other shit. I guess they didn't like that. They took my ass out the front of the choir and put me in the back of that bitch. I ain't even know how to play no drums! They ain't want me talkin' at all. I asked the preacher, I said, "If Adam and Eve was the first two people here, how did the rest of us get here? After they had Cain and Abel, and Cain killed Abel, there was only three people left. How'd the rest of us get here?" And that motherfucker ain't had no answer for me. Nobody ever had an answer for me—although there is an answer. Nobody wants to admit that shit. Cain and Abraham was fuckin' Eve! And made a bunch of kids. Wasn't no rules! Wasn't nothin' wrong with it. It's just a good feelin' goin' on! Know what I'm talking about?

Was no Bible.

And the Bible was written by *men*, so how can you really believe everything? I'm just more realistic about shit than a lot of other people are. And I'm

logical. You gotta make some logical shit for me. You can't just tell me some cartoon, clownin' ass shit. Not gonna get it.

So you were already playing instruments early on.

Yeah, I started playing drums at eight, but I wouldn't consider myself a musician on the drums because I didn't know how to play. I'm hittin' the tom and the snare, but I didn't fuck with that foot pedal. I ain't know how to do that shit! But I actually taught myself how to play drums later on in life.

Like on a full kit?

Yeah, like you sit in front of a drum set. And same thing with the bass guitar. I ain't gonna say I'm a bass guitar *player*, but I taught myself how to play. I've always been good at that type shit, like anything I see that wanna fuck with, I jump on it and I get it. Except for rap, believe it or not. Rap was one of my most difficult things to learn how to do.

Why was that?

Because I didn't know what the fuck I was doing. I used to be the drummer for my brother's rap group. My brother had a rap group—him and my cousins and a neighbor—and I said, "Shit, I wanna learn how to rap! I wanna do me a rap." So I did this rap, I came up with this rap: "Like the Pittsburgh Steelers without Bradshaw / like 7-Up without the crazy straw / like water without the fall." But when I went to say the rap to the group, my fuckin' mouth . . . I was like, "Like Terry Bradshaw without the straw / like a crazy straw without the straw / like a straw without Terry Bradshaw." And them niggas was like, "Nigga, get the fuck out of here!" And my brother—he the leader of the group—he stuttered and shit! This nigga like, "Ain't w . . . w . . . w . . . ain't we tell you to play the drums?!" Ain't that a bitch? And I promise you my niggas, when I tell you, that that was the beginning of gangsta rap, because I went and wrote a rap. I said, "Fuck me tryin' to put a rap in my head," just come off my head with it. I went and sat down and intricately put together a rap in my head, and I talked about every last one of them. I went down the line, like, "Fuck you, Rob / your head looks like a doorknob / fuck you, Trent / you ain't about shit / fuck you, John / you ain't got it goin' on / and if any one of y'all niggas don't like this rap / after I finish, we can all go scrap / as a matter of fact, I'll bust y'all niggas in the list / with my motherfuckin' fist / and after I get done / y'all can kiss my dick / matter of fact, nigga—I quit!"

How old were you then?

Shit . . . like 10! I was like 10 years old, and I slammed my motherfuckin' drumsticks down and left the room. Like, "Fuck y'all." That's how gangsta rap got started, because I never ever changed the way that I rapped. Like, that's how I started, and I never ever changed my concept, my subject matter, my attitude about it, and at the same time, since all them niggas shitted on me, I became a rap terrorist. I started hatin' rappers.

That's what made you a battle rapper.

Well that's what made me a *vicious* battle rapper. Battle rappin' . . . back in the day, they would be battle rappin', they did all that MC shit. See, I never was a MC rapper. I didn't rap hip-hop. I wouldn't talk about my microphone, my flow, the DJ, the beat, the track—my rhyme's got this, my flow got that—none of that shit! Everything was about fightin', fuckin', fightin' some more, gettin' girls . . . talkin' about niggas real bad, but real shit about them too. Wasn't nothin' funny about it. It was on some real shit. I was really a terrorist, and I brought that style of rap to H-Town.

So how old were you when you started hustling?

Hmm . . . technically, 11. Because . . . put it like this—I used to serve fiends in my daddy's trap. My daddy and my stepmama had a trap, in Atlantic City, New Jersey. The fiends would come to the crib, I'd go upstairs and let 'em know who down there, he tell me . . . they give me what I need to give 'em, and the fiends . . . the custos would give me the money, I'd take it back up to pops, and that would be it. And then one day, my stepmother . . .

she began to give me money for it. She broke it down to me, "Since you really helpin' us out . . ." 'Cuz they don't have to come down them long-ass steps to serve 'em. I served 'em. So I would get twenty dollars off every $100.

That's a lot of money at that age.

Hell yeah, nigga! I went to buy me some damn . . . motherfuckin' silver . . . silver was real cheap at that time. Buy me some silver—necklace with dice on it and shit. Some rings and shit—four finger ring—get me a big nameplate, hang that shit around my neck, get me some motherfuckin' wrist-bands, headbands. Nice little Adidas sweatsuit, some Adidas shoes and shit. Yeah. I was ready, and all that came from sellin' drugs and livin' in a trap. I was livin' in the trap with my people.

So that was in Jersey. You came back to Houston after that.

I came back to Houston really for . . . that was in Jersey before I actually moved to California. I moved to California after that. I was like 10, 11 . . . I take that back. I was 10 when I was doin' that shit, because when I moved to California, I was in between 10 and 11. Moved to Los Angeles, California right into the bloodiest motherfuckin' neighborhood on the planet. Called The Jungle. Right next to Baldwin Hills. Baldwin Hills is a rich black neighborhood in LA, but on the other side of the street is The Jungle. You seen the movie *Training Day*? The Blood neighborhood? That's the neighborhood I was raised in.

And so you were there how long—a year or two?

Nah—three? But my most important years. My developing years. I'd say from 10, 11 to 13. So almost four years, but shoot—I became a little man in that motherfucker too. If you know anything about Los Angeles, and the neighborhood life, your ass grow up quick. And I grew up real fast, bro. When I say I grew up fast, I grew up fast. I mean, I had done things in Atlantic City . . . I was always a hood nigga. I ain't gonna sit here and act like I was just some goody two-shoes, good little dude.

I was always a hood nigga. They called me "Rick Royal" in the projects in Atlantic City, and called me "Slick Rick" in school and shit like that, but when I got to LA, they started callin' me "Gangsta Ric." And that's the name they gave me. It wasn't even a nickname. It was a label. Which ain't cool, because if you think about it, you know, you label somebody, my nigga, it's almost like you tellin' them what they gonna be when they grow up. I almost was left without a shot, without a chance to be anything else. At least, as far as my psyche was concerned, I was already feelin' like, you know, "This is what it is." But at the same time, my mama ain't like that shit. She saw people start callin' me Gangsta Ric, and then . . . my mom had converted to Islam, so most of my family in California was Muslims. But me, personally, I was torn. Between Islam and gangbangin'. I gave up Islam about the third week into it? I wasn't with that shit no more. When they finally made me realize there wasn't no Christmas—we don't celebrate Christmas as Muslims? Oh, I quit the Muslims!

That was it.

I wasn't with that shit no more! I was like, "Hell nah! They call me Kareem—y'all can call me whatever y'all want to. I'm in the Bloods now, 'cuz ain't no Christmas!" You mean to tell me I'm comin' outside on Christmas, my niggas . . . kids got new bikes, new sneakers and shit . . . new clothes, new toys and shit, and I'm just this motherfucker waitin' on Kwanzaa, and then we ain't even gonna get no toys on Kwanzaa? Nah, fuck the Muslims. I mean, no disrespect, know what I'm sayin'? I mean, I ain't ridin' on 'em like that, I'm just sayin' I didn't wanna be a Muslim no more. I was a kid! You can't take Christmas away from a 10, 11-year-old kid. I been *waitin'* on Christmas! You waitin' on Christmas all year long. If there's not anything you're going to be happy about this year, if you have a fucked up birthday, then you know Christmas gonna be good.

So when you went to Houston, you kind of had this persona already.

When I got to Houston, my nigga, I was a gangbangin', bloody-ass little thug, criminal-minded killer. And that's real talk. My juvenile record is worse than a lot of niggas' shit in they whole life. I'm talkin' about I been arrested for attempted murder twice in LA, gang allegation charges, shit like that. Expelled from school for tryin' to kill a nigga. Tryin' to kill a nigga named Charles Lockett. And this was my boy too, but when I was on my way to school one morning . . . let me put it like this: I was cool with Charles Lockett. I ain't have no problem with Charles Lockett, but when I was on my way to school one morning, at Audubon Junior High School in LA, and I see my Blood brothers runnin' down the street away from our school. I'm like, "What's goin' on?" They're like, "Kareem, catch him!" They was runnin' after Charles Lockett. At that point, if my niggas chasin' you—if *they chasin'* you, you did somethin'. Without a hesitation, I whipped out my switchblade, which was a big-ass switchblade. I had like a seven, eight, nine-inch switchblade in my back pocket. And when I tell you, man, I swung this knife at this nigga, at his abdominal area, like his ribcage or whatever . . . I might have killed him if I'd hit him. I should have known right then and there he was goin' to the pros in football. Because I missed him! He jumped back, and I missed him, so I got his shirt. And that was probably the best moment of his life and my life, 'cuz I'd have went straight to jail for murder. The way I swung at him—I swung with all my might. I don't know if you've ever seen somebody do this shit—swing at a baseball, miss it and turn all the way around?

Fall down . . .

I ain't *fall*, but you know what I'm talkin' about—swing to hit the ball, miss it, and your whole body turns around because you swung so hard. That's how hard I swung the knife at him. But I missed him, 'cuz he jumped back. He jumped *away* from it, and got away. And then he ran back to the school, and went and got the dean and security, and they came out and met me in front of the school. I had threw the knife down up under my foot and put some . . . I think it was some Newports or some Kools . . . a cigarette pack on top of it in a little paper bag. And they was like, "Where the gun at? Where the knife at?" I said, "I don't know what y'all talkin' about." Because I couldn't believe he went in the school and told on me. I didn't even know snitchin' was a part of the game. And they grabbed the knife, arrested me, expelled me . . . after that I was out to get kicked out of every damn junior high school in—I went on a junior high school *tour* in LA I went to Jefferson Junior High School, I went to Mount Vernon . . . and Mount Vernon was where I first saw a group called Royal Flush, which—I stole they name when I got to Texas. It was a pop-lock group. And they name was Royal Flush. They had Playboy bunnies on the back of they jackets. With some blue khaki jackets. In LA, we used to call anything with that twill material . . . khaki supposed to be a color. We ain't give a shit. All that shit was khaki to us. Fuck the color. If you got some Dickies, they're khaki. That's a real LA nigga for you there, that understands that terminology. So I was in the Valley, tryin' to shoot at Crip niggas and shit, 'cuz these shot-callers, they give you assignments to do. So we skipped school, we'd all get on the bus, ridin' on what they call the RTZ all the way out to the Valley, and as soon as I whipped the gun out, and started bustin' at these niggas, out of nowhere, undercover cops just ran out and swarmed our ass. I'm talkin' about the dudes must have been waitin' on us or some shit. I don't know who put together this damn plan, but they let these niggas know we was comin'. Because them niggas was waitin' on us. We seen the Crip niggas by the gate at this school, like behind a fence. We started hittin' them niggas up, so I pulled a gun out, and the cops started chasin' us, and here I am with my first real, real serious—I been chased by cops before in Atlantic City, but not like this. I'm runnin' with a gun in my hand. And I threw the gun—I was fast as fuck, though. I threw the gun—I was runnin' in a mountain area. I threw the gun way down the other side of that fuckin' mountain. But that cop—I'll never forget that shit. This some real shit, Lance—this fucked me up for the rest of my life—that cop *never stopped chasin' me*, my nigga. I'm fast! *Dogs* stop chasin' me. This motherfucker was on his mission, man! Like this motherfucker was really runnin' after me! And that nigga caught me too. Nigga ended up catchin' me after I took his ass on a long-ass ride. He caught me—I remember that nigga put his foot on my face,

and I was on the ground—that's how he caught me, because I tripped over all these rocks and shit. And this motherfucker put his foot all on my face and shit—my face was right next to some shit. Some hard-ass shit. Like a dog or somebody had came and shitted out there. A mountain lion, I don't know. I kept tellin' him, "Man, get my face away from this shit!" That nigga ain't give a fuck. He kept puttin' his foot on my face, tellin' me, "Shut up. Shut up." I'm like, "That's some mean-ass shit right there!" Literally!

So it scarred you as far as your interactions with the cops.

You know, that just let me know them niggas is really about they business. Like, "Motherfucker, you supposed to *been* stopped chasin' me." I guess he could see me, because I ran in this big mountain area with all these big-ass hills and shit. But them niggas ain't find that gun, though!

They didn't?

Hell no, them niggas ain't find that gun.

So you went to jail?

Hell yeah. My mama came and got me, my mama and my uncle came and got me. My uncle was cool. I had an uncle named Ricky. He was cool until that day. I guess he was mad 'cuz my mama had to come get me. And the whole time we on the elevator . . . let me tell you something too, bro . . . I don't give a fuck about no damn cops, I don't give a fuck about no jail. Just don't let my mama get here. Please, lock me up! Put me somewhere! I'm down for the jail bid—don't let my *mama* get to me, 'cuz she gonna fuck me up! I was more scared of my mama than I ever would be about a cop.

What was the biggest thing that changed for you when you got to Houston?

Well, I gotta admit, man—Houston changed me because Houston had an identity at that time. And niggas had some pride about theyself. Niggas wasn't fittin' to let nobody come in that motherfucker and turn they ass out. You best believe I came from LA with that Blood shit. I'm at Hogg Middle School, the whole school red, so I'm thinkin', you know—we already here! I'm good! I'm ready to get it in! And these niggas was like, "We don't know what you talkin' about—Blood? We don't do that shit around here." And everybody in Texas was sayin', "'*cuz*" and "*dawg*." That's LA gang words. You say dawg, you a Blood. You say 'cuz, you a Crip. So, that wasn't no big deal to niggas. Niggas wasn't tryin' to hear that gangbangin' shit. I was an outcast. I was an alien to these niggas. They wasn't hearin' that shit. "We playas and hustlas. We ain't on that motherfuckin' gangbangin' shit." I respected Houston for that shit too. Because I couldn't get niggas in the Bloods and shit at that point. So that changed me a whole lot. I always was athletic. Always into sports. I played football my whole life. My dream in life was to go to the NFL. That was my first love, and realistically, technically, really still is my first love—football. So I concentrated on football.

And you started Royal Flush in high school?

Well, I didn't start it—what it was, was that all the rappers at Aldine decided to make a group. And I always felt like they did that shit to stop me from terrorizin' everybody. 'Cuz I was on some battle rap shit. So I guess they figured if we be a group, I guess we can all get along.

Do you remember what year that was?

Shit . . . I got to Aldine, like, '82. That was my freshman year, '82. It was me, a dude named Class C, Tricky T— that's Tim Johnson, Donald Stewart—he was Cowboy. 'Cuz that nigga had that voice. He sounded like Cowboy from the Furious Five. And a guy named Ernest Polk—his name was Sergio. A whole lot of dudes in the group. The Royal Flush group was really a gang that had rappers in it. James Miller, Mac White, Spud . . . a nigga named Earl. We had so many members in Royal Flush . . . and anybody from Willow Run neighborhood, Acres Homes . . . Greenspoint, the Aldine area . . . all them niggas . . . if you knew us, you was just a part of Royal Flush. That's how we started off. There

was a few niggas in the group that were rappers. At Aldine, we just used to be in rap contests all the time, tearin' niggas heads off. We'd go to different schools and . . . matter of fact, we used to skip school, and hear about a talent show at another school, and skip school, and go make they talent show and beat everybody ass.

Do you remember when you went to those talent shows—did you ever see anybody who later on became a real rapper?

Not really. Not at that point, but we used to come back to school, because, of course, schools—we in the same district, so of course the schools would know. They had somebody waitin' for our ass when we got back. And we'd be on detention and shit. Everybody in one classroom—all the rappers in one classroom, in detention and shit the whole damn day. To rap, we would pull some extreme shit. The first time I ever boosted some clothes was because of rap. We needed some uniforms, so went to Montgomery Ward's and got these black and red sweat suits and shit. So here's the plan: Everybody pick out they size and shit, go in the dressing room, put your shit on, and then put some clothes back on. Over the top of it. And in some cases, some niggas wasn't able to do that, so they had to put the sweat suit over the top of they clothes. So everybody had they uniform, and there's about 10, 11, 12 of us . . . we give each other the nod, it's time to go. We walked out that door—this was before they put them tags on clothes—we all walked out of that motherfucker, went out the door . . . because Montgomery Ward's actually had an exit door that went out to the parkin' lot. We went out that motherfucker, the exit door, and I'm talkin' about we sprintin'. I'm talkin' about like we some Kenyans. In the Olympics and shit. We runnin' our ass off for a long time! Because we had to run back to Greenspoint, know what I'm talkin' about? I'm talkin' about all of us. Ain't one of us get caught. We all played football, ran track, and played basketball. That motherfucker wasn't about to catch us. And then the next day, we went to Northline Mall and got our names put on the motherfuckers.

Romeo Poet

NORTHSIDE

One of Houston's earliest known rap artists, his name always comes up when the conversation turns to the legendary Rap Attack Contests held at the Rhinestone Wrangler in the mid-to-late '80s. Briefly a member of Royal Flush, he was one of few rappers to give Willie D a run for his money in those contests. Romeo never released a record of his own in Houston back in the day, but he recorded a few songs with the group Southern Funk Playas in 1997 alongside Big 50, Rite Choice, and the late Big T (famous for singing the chorus on Lil' Troy's 1999 hit "Wanna Be A Baller"). He now resides in Dallas, where he owns several restaurants and makes reggae records.

ROMEO POET AND WILLIE D. PHOTO: MATT SONZALA

When did you start rapping?

I started back in 1985, man. Forest Brook High School. Forest Brook is on the Northside, off of Tidwell.

North of Fifth Ward. Homestead area? Is that where you're from?

Homestead, yes. Scenic Woods.

What was it like back then, the neighborhood?

The neighborhood . . . Forest Brook was a lot different than it is today. You know, it was more . . . like I say, with the music, with the hip-hop scene, that's when the whole neighborhood was actually starting to change. From, you know, bein' involved in a lot of other crazy stuff like gangs and all that? When the hip-hop era came along, it was like the . . . the Renaissance. A change in everybody. That's when Run–D.M.C.'s music was just coming out, and a matter of fact, man, Willie D was at the same high school. We was over at Forest Brook, and that's actually how we had met each other, is that we used to battle on The Brook. It's like a little passageway, a little bridge that goes across the school, that connects both sides of the cafeteria with the building. And we used to meet on The Brook and battle. During lunchtime. That's how it actually started off, before we got into the . . . the big scene of the clubs and all that.

Yeah. So he was already rapping at that time too. Were y'all in the same grade?

Yeah. Same grade. Seniors. From that point, I mean, the high school, the next level came and we left the high school. I was the first one to go to the Rhinestone Wrangler. I'm sure you probably hear Steve Fournier's name a lot, right?

Oh, yeah. Big time. He was already DJing at the Wrangler at that point?

Yes, he was DJing at the Rhinestone Wrangler. Him and Big Steve.

Wow. And so—how long had the Wrangler been open at that point?

The Wrangler—when I started goin' there (mid-'80s), it was already open, so I think maybe like a year or so. Like a year or so.

And their format—was it all rap, or what else would they play?

No, it wasn't close to rap. That's what the crazy thing was. In fact, there was very little rap. And the thing was—this was the crazy part: It started off like a talent show, where . . . at the end of the night, like two o'clock in the morning when they stop sellin' drinks? They used to have this thing called the . . . "The Rap Attack Contest." This is how it all started, and we used to go there and compete on Wednesday nights. As a matter of fact, though, when I heard about it, before Willie D went, I was the first one to go. You probably heard of Royal Flush, right?

Of course.

Royal Flush was the group that used to rule the Rhinestone Wrangler when it came to hip-hop. So, a couple of friends would tell me, "Hey man, you good at rappin', but you need to really see how good you are. You need to go to the Rhine-stone Wrangler, enter the Rap Attack Contest. On Wednesday nights." The Rap Attack Contest was—well, first, you would do something that you

actually made up, and then at the end, the crowd would pick out the best rappers and you had to battle against each other, freestyle. Off the top of their head. And that's how it all got started. So I started off battling the Royal Flush.

The whole group?

I used to battle the whole group, and I won for like probably like three months straight, man! Every Wednesday I won for like three months straight. And after that we all became pretty close. I ended up joinin' the group Royal Flush.

You did, really?

I joined the group Royal Flush, yes. So me and Rick [Royal], you know, to this day we're real close. But, we started off battling each other, and we battled so much, we became good friends. And the reason they asked me to battle, Rick said . . . he just shared this with me like about a year ago. He said, "Man, you want to know why we really asked you to join the Royal Flush, man?" He said, "Because nobody had the guts enough to get on the stage and rhyme against us." He said, "You was such a small dude, I said, 'Man, this guy got some balls.' And you were out there, and you was just freestylin' and talkin' all that noise to guys that are three times bigger than you, man." I was really small, man. And he said, "That's what made us ask you to join the Flush, man." 'Cuz he say, "This little dude got heart, man." So that's how I ended up joinin' the Royal Flush. But from the Royal Flush, Willie D came on the scene right after that. That's when Willie D came along, and he started battlin' against the Royal Flush. And he came and won like probably a month straight. You know how crowds are—once you been winnin' for so long, somebody new come along, something fresh and new? Willie D came in with the . . . with the Fifth Ward style, you know? And that's when we started battlin' each other. So it kinda went back-and-forth, and the Rhinestone was like . . . sometimes I would do my solo against Willie D, sometimes he would battle against the Flush, and it was just back-and-forth, man. But the Rhinestone Wrangler was the birthplace of it all.

So that was like '84, '85, something like that it opened up?

'85, '86. Mmhmm.

So if their format wasn't rap, what were they playing?

Well, they were playing a little rap, but let me tell you what the craziest thing about it was: When they first started doin' the Rap Attack, they hadn't been introduced to people usin' profanity and under-ground language. They were playin' like the clean rap version. So when we get to the rap contest, Big Steve was the manager of the club, Steve Fournier was the DJ. But he was the only DJ that had guts enough to actually let us get up there and do it. Because, you know, he would actually *like* it. Big Steve used to say, "Y'all can rap, but no cussin'." But he come to find that, that's what actually drew the crowd to the Rhinestone Wrangler, was the Rap Attack Contest. People would come from every-where—all over town, north, south, east, and west— just to hear the Rap Attack Contest. But when we first started off, Big Steve would say, "Y'all can rap, but no cursin'." Whenever we cursed, he used to turn the microphones off. Every time we used profanity. But it got so big, man. When the people started comin', that's actually what made that club, man. What actually set the whole hip-hop scene in Houston is because the Rap Attack Contests. People started coming from all around just to see it. You know, people come from out of town, every-body in Houston say, "You gotta go the Rhinestone, hear the Rap Attack Contest."

That was Steve Fournier's thing? He was putting that on?

That was Steve Fournier, exactly.

Did you know him at that point? Before?

I never knew Steve Fournier until I went to the—in fact, I was underage. I couldn't even get in. The only reason they would let me in was because I could rap, you know? Because you had to be 21

then. I couldn't even get in the club. I was, like, 18. Just making 18. And like I say, Steve Fournier . . . I used to get ready to go to the club, I used to call him in advance and say, "Tell Steve to come to the door." He would be the one to come get us in the club.

He would just come walk you in.

Exactly.

So who else was showing up to those, then, if Royal Flush was coming in there beating every-body, who was it?

A female rapper by the name of Cinderella. She was known. Lester "Sir" Pace—he a DJ personality.

"Kidz Jamm."

Lester "Sir" Pace, Wickett Crickett . . . Big Mello. Of course, Big Mello wasn't out on the scene, but they used to just be there, hangin' around. Jazzie Redd . . .

Ezzy-E—O.G. Style? He would come out then, huh?

Ezzy-E, Jukebox from the Ghetto Boys, they used to be there. All the original Ghetto Boys, they used to hang out there. Lil' James used to be in the club. As a matter of fact, that's how me and James got real close back then.

Because he was always at the club, huh?

Lil' James used to be at the club, yes. Lil' James from Rap-A-Lot . . . Casanova IV, well that's like— Lonnie Mac was a DJ personality. You know, a lot of people knew Lonnie Mac too.

He just died, didn't he? A couple years ago.

Exactly. He just died a couple years ago. He used to have a group called Def IV.

Oh, he was in Def IV. That's right. Tell me what you remember about Lonnie Mac.

Lonnie was one of the cats from New York who actually started bringing New York flavor to Houston. He was one of the pioneers of that. Him, the Royal Flush—of course they were from Jersey. Rick Royal was from New Jersey. East Orange, New Jersey. Lonnie Mac—he's the first one who start bringin'—when people start bringin' the 1200 Turntables? Remember when they didn't have them down here? He was one of the guys that used to be exportin' 'em from New York down to Houston.

Oh, you couldn't buy them in Houston, huh?

Exactly. You couldn't get 'em in Houston. So he was the first—one of the first guys to bring the 1200 Turntables here.

How would you get yourself psyched up when you go in and you start battling? That freestyling, was that—were you writing rhymes at that point, or were you a freestyler, that was your thing?

You know, to be honest, the coldest thing about it is because I was freestylin' for the longest, but I never got into the act of competin' against people until, like I say, some friends of mine, we used to go to the skatin' rink all the time, and they'd say, "Hey, man," they'd say, "I'm tired of doin' all this little boy stuff. We need to go to where the grown folks hang at, man." They say, "You say you're a rapper, you need to go ahead and try your skills out at the Rhinestone, man." They say, "There's a group named Royal Flush and stuff, man. That's how you can tell how good you are." You know, everybody in my neighborhood, man, used to say, "Romeo Poet, man? I don't think nobody can beat this guy rhymin'." So, that night when I went up to the Rhinestone that was my first time actually just battlin' somebody, you know? And that's how my battlin' skills actually started, right then and there. I used to be in the neighborhood doin' it, you know, in front of a lot of friends, you know, but in front of crowds? That's the first time it started, at the Rhinestone Wrangler, and I went against the Royal Flush. I used to wear like python boots and Polo shirts, so I was freestylin' about stuff like that, right? And we just started rankin' on people. You know, we used to talk about . . . you know,

nowadays you can't do it, but we used to talk about anything, about people's moms, what they had on, everything, man. It was anything goes.

Anything somebody was wearing was fair game.

Anything they were wearin', talk about their family, talk about anything, you know. The good thing about it is, though, it would never turn out violent, you know? It's not like just—if anything, people would be afraid to come up front, because they knew, "Hey, these guys will talk about me tonight, if I be up here." Oh, we would talk about people in the crowd, people on the stage, just anything, you know?

All good-natured.

It was all good-natured, and people used to get— like I say, people came in from . . . as a matter of fact, Northside, Southside, they didn't mix too much back in the day. And that's what started the different sides of town mixing, because people started comin' from all over when they heard about the rap contest, what was goin' on. So people from the north, south, east, and west, two o'clock in the morning, whether they were workin' or what, everybody knew when you get off of work, or whatever you're doin', when they stop sellin' alcohol, two o'clock in the morning, the Rap Attack Contest starts. The club would stay open 'til like five.

Wow—so it would last hours then?

Yeah—after hours. It used to be between two and five thirty in the morning. It was all rap, and that's what people were coming to see, whether they go to school the next morning, or they had to be at work the next morning . . . people used to come and pack that club. And guess what? It wasn't on a weekend. It was in the middle of the week.

Willie D said people used to lose their jobs because they were staying there so late.

Exactly. They sure did. I knew a lot of people lost their jobs, people failed school, everything.

How many people do you think that club fit?

Oh—Rhinestone? Capacity probably was . . . capacity was probably like up to 800 people I would say, but that club used to be so packed, man, there was every bit of—there used to be over a thousand people in that club, easily. I mean, people parked all on the median, in front of the club.

Do you remember the first time that you heard a Houston record being played in there? Did that ever happen while it was still in that location?

The first time I heard a Houston record, I think it was the Royal Flush. You know what? As a matter of fact, I take that back. You know who it was? It was . . . what's his name . . . Raheem! Raheem, the album, that's a first time I heard a Houston record played was Raheem. I turned on the radio . . . "I turn on the radio / to hear the rappers go / to try to beat me / and neither will they grow." That song there. That song that he did off a mix of a Curtis Mayfield song.

I talked to him too. I talked to him about those days because he had that first major label deal, but then he did—he was mixed up with Lil' J back then too.

Right, exactly. And the crazy thing, too, is that another thing to add to it—you probably think that when Scarface came out, he was originally with Rap-A-Lot, right?

Nah, he was with Lil' Troy.

Lil' Troy—so, me and Lil' Troy, we go way back too, because me and Lil' Troy was actually down with the same label, before all this happened too.

Oh, really?

I kinda had a chance to rub elbows with everybody. Yeah, Lil' Troy, when he had Short Stop on the Southside? I was actually rollin' with Lil' Troy then too. So, me and Lil' Troy, we got ties that go way back, me and E.S.G., we go way back—because we were kind of like, affiliated with all the same

people, you know? Slim . . . Slim is actually the one who used to work with Perrion Records, the label that E.S.G. was first on, Perrion? That's the first label that Steve Caldwell . . . that's before he actually signed a nationwide deal, the major distribution deal, though. It was Perrion.

And that was a Houston label?

That was a Houston label, yeah.

So was R.P. Cola already on the scene at this time?

Oh—yes, R.P. Cola was at Rhinestone. I can't leave him out. You're right.

So Steve was spinning during the rap . . .

Steve [Fournier] was the main DJ, yeah, and R.P. was there as well, but Steve was like the main one, and R.P. was his partner.

Were there other clubs around town or was the Rhinestone that main one that was . . .

There was other clubs, but the only club we ever went to was Rhinestone. Yeah, there was a lot of clubs around, but, you know—that was my first time ever even going to a club. Shit, I was 18 years old, man, so I mean . . . first of all, I couldn't get in any other clubs, and that was my first time even going to a club, when I went to the Rhinestone Wrangler. And then only reason I got in it was because, like I say, I could rap. And it was part of the entertainment part. They knew that the Rap Attack Contest—I'd show up for that. I used to not get there until like 11 o'clock, 12 o'clock. I'd show up right before the Rap Attack Contest. One o'clock, you know.

Perrion Records—did you release a record with them?

No I did not—as a matter of fact, see . . . this is the thing with me, guy, and this is why I saw I just like . . . for some reason, my thing was always I was on the side. I was watching a lot of artists make a lot of mistakes, first of all. And me, myself . . . versus just sayin', "Okay, I wanna go sign with this label—they wanna put my album and this label in." I was always like a student of the game, man. Had the skills, but just always just . . . I would just sit back waitin' patiently, man. But I used to see a lot of people make mistakes, you know. The only person that I really was going to sign with was Lil' James from Rap-A-Lot. James, he did the thing he did, first with Royal Flush . . . Royal Flush came out as a group first. And I didn't sign with Royal Flush. Back then, that's when I was seeing . . . I saw a lot of people get burned, and signing—that's when they was just like, rappers was just signing just to get a contract, just to say, "I have a record out." And I always—I was one of the guys that always said, I didn't wanna just be in that position, sayin' I had a record out. You know, rappers were gettin' robbed blind back then. Everybody was sayin', "I got a record, I got a record out." But you know, until recently, probably like maybe, what . . . 10 years ago? You just started hearin' about rappers in Houston gettin' major, major deals, you know? But back then, that's the only reason why I didn't sign with Rap-A-Lot, because Royal Flush was the first group that committed to sign with them. And by that time, you know, we had broke up—Royal Flush. We didn't break up on bad terms, but I said, "Hey, you know what? I'm not ready to sign with a label yet." They went on and signed with Lil' James.

That just wasn't the path you wanted to go down.

That just wasn't the path I wanted to go, and I guess, you know, things happen for a reason.

Elite Al-B

GREENSPOINT

An early figure on the scene in Houston, Al-B was part of one of the city's very first rap groups in the Northside posse Royal Flush. He was around for the Rap Attack Contests at the Rhinestone Wrangler and appears on the Royal Flush album *Uh Oh*, on which the group worked with Houston super-producers Cliff Blodget, Karl Stephenson, and, of course, James Smith—or as they were starting to call him around Houston during the time of the Rhinestone, James Prince. *Uh Oh* and an

accompanying single were released on Rap-A-Lot. In 1991, Royal Flush put out a follow up record, *976-DOPE*, on the Dallas label Yo! Records. Al-B now lives in Alabama.

You met Pimp C early on. When did you last see him?

I had seen him like three months before he passed. He was in Birmingham, and I had come down for the show, and that was my first time seeing him after he'd got home. And dude was like, "We gonna chop it up. Let me go out and do this show." But by that time . . . I'm teaching now, so we didn't get to actually chop it up the rest of the night, but we had a long, two-hour talk before he performed that night. And we ain't even talk about nothin' but God, man. We sat up there and just chopped it up about God. Not religion, but just God in general. God and music. And that's all we chopped it up about.

Yeah, was there something on his mind, something that brought it up? Coming out of the pen like that?

Actually, it was everything. It was like, basically . . . I believe in the Hebrew Israelites, and I believe in the history of black people in the Bible, and he and I were just, really just choppin' it up about that. And he was like . . . because he never shared his personal religious beliefs on his music. I think only one song that he's every really done that, and people really don't be payin' attention to it, but

PHOTO: ALLAN BUSH

that's what it was basically about. Me and him was conversatin', and our conversation was the same. I guess in his mind, he was like, "Damn, you believe what I believe." His last words to me before "I'll see you later" was, "Man, I always knew me and you was kindred spirits, and I always knew we was like brothers, and we was cool and everything." Not like best friends, but we just was . . . respectful of each other, like to the ultimate. No matter what kind of crowd he was in, this dude always like, "These are the niggas right here that opened the door for me and Bun to step through it." I mean, I don't care what state he was in. If I was around, he always did shit like that. He was like, "I always knew we was kindred spirits, man. But now I know why."

When you came back to Houston and joined up with Royal Flush, were the Rap Attack Contests still going on at the Rhinestone?

Yeah, they was goin' on, but they was kinda fallin' off by then. That was—like I said, around '86, '87? 'Cuz we'd go to the Rhinestone, but we'd also go to the Northside. We'd got to a bunch of different clubs, and we was just like . . . the rap battles started becoming . . . not passé, but the same people was winnin' all the time. It was either Willie D or Rick. Willie D or the Royal Flush. One time, this dude—you know the dude that's on "Weeds," Romany? The dude that played . . . the dude that grew the weed for the girl . . .

On that TV show, "Weeds?"

Yeah. The black dude that grew the weed? He was from Houston too. He was in a group called The College Boyz. They was on MCA Records. Some-times, jokers like that would pop in—not a joker, I'm not disrespectin' my man, 'cuz my man was talented. I ain't even gonna say that. But they'd pop in and get into the rap battles, right? But the finale was always Willie D versus the Royal Flush. Whether it was Willie D versus Class C, or Willie D versus Rick. That's all it was! All the time. At some point, the battles had to kinda . . . you know, run they course because the level of competition wasn't there. Like nobody was really consistent. Nobody else was really consistent at that.

Not every rapper can do it.

Yeah, but back then, though, other battlers . . . people used to, like, be talkin' about skill and this, that, and the third and how everything flowed, all that? Nah. A Rhinestone Wrangler battle wasn't like that. Rhinestone Wrangler battle was like "Def Jam Comedy" on rap. Russell Simmons packaged "Def Jam Comedy," and you just laugh your ass off all night? That's how the Rhinestone Wrangler battles was. Willie D versus the Royal Flush—who can talk about each other the worst and get the best response from the crowd. It was like . . . Rhinestone Wrangler was like "Def Jam Comedy" rappin' *8 Mile*. Like it was packed out like that, like for real—it was packed out like that, right? And these niggas would just be goin' back-and-forth, bustin' each other ass, like, who can drop the funniest shit, period. Because the whole way you won was strictly on the crowd's response. It wasn't who rapped the nicest, who was the flyest, who hit the most—it wasn't none of that. It was straight up, who can get the crowd to respond? That's how it was. Humor was injected in that. You can hear it in some of Willie's rhymes today!

Oh, yeah.

He a funny dude! He talkin' some real shit—he can talk some serious shit, but he a funny dude, you know what I'm sayin'?

And that was over on Murworth—that was on the Southside?

Yeah, yeah. Right in the shadow of the Astrodome, man. Right in the shadow of the Astrodome, The Rhinestone Wrangler, right down the street. Walk out the parkin' lot, look to the right, boom! Astro-dome right there.

And when you did the battles, was it on a stage or was it on a floor in the middle of people?

On the stage. Like it was just a stage, right? And the crowd—but you know, the Rhinestone always kept reinventing itself, so the stage would move. So, for six months the stage might be right here, and for six months it might be right there, or every two months they might switch the location of the stage, but wherever it was, whatever location the stage was in the club, when the battle went down, man, I'm tellin' you—everybody in the club, from the restroom attendant, the bartender, the waitresses, every patron was eyes on that stage. Every patron. The owner, everybody.

How long would it last?

Man, for fucking *ever*. 'Til whoever couldn't go no more . . . or somebody just got a laugh so damn hilarious that R.P. or Steve Fournier just said, "Stop the fuckin' music. That's it. It's over." But it was so dope, though. It was so dope because that kind of promoted that club in a lot of ways, man. Because people came every week for that battle, to see who was gonna win, who was gonna say what. Like the hardest dudes in the club, man—like the hardest street niggas in the club would be like . . . it would be just like they would forget they roles for a minute. Forget that they . . . forgettin' that they had issues. When they was in the Rhinestone, it was like a little vacation for a minute. "All right, now the door's open, we gotta go back out." Man, the Rhinestone Wrangler was a . . . I ain't ever seen a venue like that, ever. Like, as far as people-wise, that shit was a fire hazard every night. Every night it was open, like seriously, it was a fire hazard every night.

Like 800 people, something like that, right?

Yeah, fire hazard every night, dude. I'm not playin'. Seriously, it was packed like that. Every night. And then, like I said, when battles start playin' out, then attendance started slippin' and shit started goin' down. And then, you know, J Prince musta . . . I don't know what bugged J, but he wanted to be a record label. And then, you know, we started lookin' at shit a whole lot different then, you know what I'm sayin'?

Raheem

MISSOURI CITY

The first rapper from Houston with a major label record deal, Raheem actually started out as a Ghetto Boy, with "Car Freak" being his first recorded appearance. After that, a young Oscar Ceres inked a deal with A&M Records and released *The Vigilante* in 1988. Then he was thrown onto R&B tours to support it. "Dance Floor" was a hit, but he generally made an ill fit for the label and soon was dropped. His association with Rap-A-Lot continued years later, as J Prince welcomed him back into the fold with the release of *Invincible* in 1992. In the late '90s he was a member of Blac Monks alongside Mr. 3-2 before leaving Houston for the Northeast.

Take me back to the birth of rap music in Houston as everybody remembers it. Were you already rapping in '85, '86?

Yeah. And to be honest with you, I'm glad you said, "rap music as everybody knows it or remembers it," because rap music started *way* before the Ghetto Boys. Like O.G. Style and those guys, they may have not gotten deals, but those guys were involved in Houston rap years before Ghetto Boys formed. As a matter of fact, even though me and E [Prince Ezzy-E, a.k.a. O.G. Style] had our little beef on wax or whatever, I was like one of his biggest fans at one time because "Kidz Jamm" . . . 90.9 [FM] . . . Wickett Crickett, Lester "Sir" Pace, Walter D, Jazzie Redd. I looked up to all of those guys.

That's Fourth Ward right there too. Jazzie Redd.

Exactly. They kind of paved the way for Houston rap. They showed the artists down in Houston, you know, that it could be done. Because at that time New York was kinda runnin' rap, period, and they would freestyle over instrumentals and stuff like that on the air. So for me and any other artist at that time, it was an opportunity to come to the radio station, play our demo tapes, or just spit something live over the air on TSU radio.

So this was like '85?

Probably about '85, around that time. I definitely tip my hat to those guys for allowing us to build that courage as individuals comin' from down South. Because you know at that time nobody coming from down South was recognized as bein' a real rapper, you know what I mean? But they were that outlet.

Don't you think that was kind of the fuel for a lot of you guys, that rap was really owned by the East Coast, even though you had artists like the Wreckin' Cru out West. But the idea that rap wasn't supposed to come from anywhere else, and people were ignoring the South, didn't that give you guys that independent spirit?

It helped. It definitely helped. But at the same time you gotta realize that rap wasn't really bein' respected as an art form, *period*—East or West Coast. So we just wanted to get our foot in the door and just say that we were rappers. We weren't really trippin' on the fact that we were

PRINCE JOHNNY C AND RAHEEM. PHOTO: COLLINS LEYSATH

from the South or they were from New York. It was just about—we were good rappers, we were good writers, and we wanted to be in the circle, whoever was coming out and was hot at that time. It didn't matter where they were coming from. We just felt that we could compete and rap . . . you know, that's what it was. It was kind of like a lyrical contest sport. You had to battle. And so, that's kind of what brought most of those older artists into the game. As the business kicked in, it started turnin' into flash and money and things of that nature, but originally it was just about getting on and letting it be known that we were a force to be reckoned with, too. In terms of our lyrical content. We weren't trippin' on where cats were from or nothin' like that.

K-Rino told me a story about a battle that you and he tried to have that never happened. Maybe you came to his school and he got pulled back into school . . . I guess this would have been '86. Around the time Real Chill was starting. Do you remember that?

I do. [Laughs] But he killed Jukebox, though. I remember that. He tore Jukebox up.

That's exactly what he said. That he didn't get to battle you, but he tore Jukebox up in the parking lot of a skating rink.

Man, he ruin't Jukebox, ain't no ifs, ands, or buts about that. But you know, K-Rino—I got a lot of respect for that brother. I never really got an opportunity to hear him get down until real late because I left Houston, and, you know, I had a lot goin' on when I was down there. The last five years that I was there I was real busy.

You put out a couple of records in that time too, didn't you?

Hell yeah. Actually I did something with the Blac Monks in '98.

[Mr.] 3-2.

Yeah. Well, 3-2, Awol, Storm. So I had that poppin' off. And other things. I was going through some situations with Rap-A-Lot. I was actually tryin' to get another solo project out. I did some things with Scarface that he never released. There was a lot goin' on.

Tracing back to the beginning, when you were talking about "Kidz Jamm" and that era. Was Royal Flush formed at that time? Triple Threat, Def IV, those groups?

Yes, all those groups were formed . . . Royal Flush, they was like the kings of the Rhinestone Wrangler. The *original* Rhinestone Wrangler. They were like club rappers, and they had Rhinestone Wrangler sewed up. You couldn't come through there and really try to win no contest if the Flush was in there because the Flush, they were like the reigning kings.

Romeo Poet was there around that time.

Class C, all them cats.

So you would go in and battle at the Rhinestone too?

I was too young. I was 15 years old. I used to have problems gettin' in. But when I met NC Trahan, well, Lil' James and all those dudes—they used to get us in. And they would kinda hide us because we weren't supposed to be in there in the first place. So we never really got on the mic and did anything in terms of battling the Flush. Or Willie D, or any of those guys that got up on the mic, because they were old enough to be there.

When J was courting you guys to form a group, you and Jukebox and Thelton [K-9] . . .you guys were still in high school, right?

Me and Jukebox were still in high school. Thelton had graduated. Thelton was already out of school. But in actuality, I was never really supposed to be a Ghetto Boy. The reason I became a Ghetto Boy was because Jukebox didn't show up for a recording session on "Car Freak." And the part that he was sayin', I had written because we used to write everything together. So [J Prince] just said, "Yo, 'Heem, go in there and spit 'Box's part." So I said, "Aight," and I went in there, and I spit his part on "Car Freak." And because my voice was on the record, I took the picture and that's how I became a Ghetto Boy. *Making Trouble* was written after "Car Freak," that whole album . . . everything you hear Johnny C sayin' . . . not to take anything away from Johnny C's creativeness, because Johnny C is amazing to me. I mean my man got down. But everything you hear him sayin' on the *Making Trouble* album, I wrote. Basically I told J, I said, "Look, it's time for me to go solo. I wanna do my own thing." Because I came to him as a solo artist. I never intended to be a Ghetto Boy. And he said he understood, and Ready Red said he had a homeboy in New Jersey that was willin' to come down and get down. So when Johnny C came we basically just filled in for the parts that I wrote. I was cool with the Ghetto Boys, but I wanted to do my own thing, and the Ghetto Boy thing was J's creation, you know what I mean?

So you and Johnny C were never in Ghetto Boys at the same time, then.

Nah, nah.

Not even on *Making Trouble*?

Nah, I wasn't on *Making Trouble*. I wrote Johnny C's parts on *Making Trouble*, but I never recorded anything. And see, that in itself kind of had vibed me because I felt as if, you know, "Why not let him come in and do his own thing as opposed to havin' him rap what I wrote." And we did have a small confrontation about that because he was kinda thrown into a position where he had to do something, and me, I was kinda young and arrogant at the time, and I started . . . I mean, we had a brief battle. It wasn't nothin' major to get blown out of proportion or nothing. But once again it was competition, and I felt as if, you know, if you want to compete, compete with what you do. Don't try to compete with what I do.

So you left the Ghetto Boys to do what you were doing originally, to become a solo artist. So this like '87, somewhere in there?

Yeah, *Making Trouble* came out about a year, year and a half after "Car Freak."

So you were out starting to do solo shows then. At what point did A&M start courting you?

Okay . . . now I don't wanna step on J's little story, you know, but according to J, he put that together. That's not the way that went. He wanted them to do the *Making Trouble* album, and A&M said that they didn't want it. And Cliff Blodget had my album in the stash, and he said, "Well if you don't want this, check this out." And they played my album, and A&M said, "Okay, well we'll work with him." And that's the way that went. That was not the genius of Lil' J. Not to take anything away from him, because he had a plan, he stuck with it, he made it happen. I got all the respect in the world for the man, but that's just not the way that particular situation went down.

So Blodget produced your album too?

No . . . Karl Stephenson.

But Blodget produced the demo that got you signed?

Karl Stephenson produced it from the get. Basically what Cliff did was just present it to A&M Records when they said that they weren't ready for *Making Trouble*. And keep in mind that I'm not saying that *Making Trouble* wasn't good or that it wasn't put together well. It was just simply . . . they weren't ready for that gangsta stuff yet.

That's the interesting point about what you were doing versus the direction you went. The stuff you were doing was much more akin to the national audience at that point.

Well it was comin' from the mindset of a 15-year-old. It was straight hip-hop. It strayed more so toward some of the things that were happenin' then in music, and the Ghetto Boy thing was a bit different. It was new. N.W.A. hadn't come out yet so gangsta rap really hadn't been discovered, and A&M wasn't ready for that. A&M wasn't ready for *me*! They had me on tour with Jeffrey Osborne and Lester Williams! What's wrong with this picture here? I can't get up there and sing "Whoo Whoo Whoo" and have them old ladies throwin' they panties up on the stage. But, you know, that's all they had to work with. At the time it was R&B singers that they had on the label, and I just had to get in where I fit in, and it didn't work. Straight up, it didn't work. But I appreciate the opportunity to be with A&M, and I definitely appreciate the fact that Cliff Blodget thought highly enough of what I did at that time to even present that to 'em. Because I didn't even know he had a copy of it, to be honest with you, but he looked out for me. But they weren't ready for it. It didn't work. After I did that, I kinda went . . . you could say underground for a while . . . because I was still dealin' with a lot of teenage issues. You see a lot of people didn't realize . . . a lot of people thought I was 21, 22 at the time. You know, I'm 15, 16 years old. I'm meetin' my first girlfriend. I'm doing a lot of things teenagers do at that age. So I kinda went underground for a little while.

That was young.

Yeah, exactly. I'm a kid, pretty much. But I came back to J, I said, "Look, man, I got another album.

What can you do for me?" And he said, well, "Yo, lemme hear what you got." And so I presented the *Invincible* album, and he was like, "Yeah! This is hot! I could feel this." And he put it out, and when he put it out, it did what it did, and to this day I don't know what it did.

Backing up for a second . . . you being on the national stage, you were the first visible Houston artist because you were the first major label artist. How were you treated in that national spotlight as the first Houston artist?

I was hated by the rappers, and I was loved by the chicks, and that's pretty much it. Accordin' to J, though, I hadn't arrived. I hadn't really broken any ground. And that was his quest for more. One thing about J—you could never do enough. You just had to constantly be doin' more. Which was good, to a certain extent. At that time, I don't think I was focused on the things he was focused on.

Here's the other side of that question: how were you seen in Houston, being its first export?

Hmmm . . . well at that time, like I said, rap still hadn't reached its peak yet, and so I didn't get any preferential treatment or anything like that, if that's what you're askin'. But the rappers hated me. Everybody from the Flush to the Ghetto Boys hated me.

So that was the case locally.

Yeah, that was the case locally. On the national scale I couldn't really tell you what the take on me was at that particular time because I was in the wrong arena, you know? I was on tour with Shanice Wilson and stuff like that. I wasn't around a rap audience.

That says a lot for J, then, to take you back after all of that. For him to say, "I still see something in this artist," especially seeing as you were hated by the rappers he even had on his own label.

Definitely, definitely. And for that, I got a lot of appreciation for him giving me that opportunity to do one more album because my creative process was still growing to a certain extent. When I did the "Dance Floor" album, I was still learnin' in terms of my writin' skills, in terms of the type of tracks that I felt like I needed . . . there was a lot that I was still goin' through. And I had an opportunity to show a little more on the *Invincible* album, but even after the *Invincible* album, I had more to give. But me and J, we just couldn't . . . for some reason we couldn't make it happen for a third time.

In between *The Vigilante* and *Invincible*, a lot changed in Houston. The tone changed to something a lot darker.

It did.

Was that reflective of Houston, or something else?

I think, and this is just my take on it—I just feel as if music at that point . . . everybody was tryin' to outdo everybody. If you're plannin' on killin' a person this way, well I got to kill 'em a little worse than you kill him, know what I mean? It had gotten a bit ridiculous to me, to be honest with you. It was like, "Come on, man . . ." Especially if I know you, and I know this really ain't your personality. A perfect example, though he my man . . . Ganksta N-I-P. I think Ganksta N-I-P was a bit over the top, you know what I'm sayin'?

You remember Darryl Scott from back in the day and the techniques he was developing?

I'm glad you mention Darryl Scott because Darryl Scott and I got a real deep history. Darryl Scott was one of the first individuals that ever made a beat for me so that I could take it up to "Kidz Jamm." Me and a couple other cats back in the day used to go to Blast Records all the time. We used to skip school and go over there. Darryl would let us hang out, buy us pizza, feed us, let us get down on his equipment and everything. So that's my man right there. I'm sorry I left him out.

That's my job.

[Laughs] Darryl Scott played a big part in keeping us motivated, keeping us focused, keeping us out of trouble. He gave us that safe haven to perfect our craft.

He was somebody you really looked up to at the time.

Absolutely. Not only that, he was ownin' his own record store, know what I'm sayin'? A black man ownin' his own business back then? You the *man*, dog! Plus he used to get all the fly chicks. Oh man . . . Darryl's shop was good.

Was he producing for people back then too?

He had a little drum machine, and all it took was a beat and some scratch and he gave us that. Word up. My first time goin' in actually E had a demo . . . I can't think of the name of the damn song . . .

When you say "E," who are you talking about?

Oh . . . O.G. Style. His original name was Prince Ezzy-E. So I called him "E." But O.G. Style, he had a demo tape that they used to play on TSU every week. The voice was on one side, and the beat was on the other side. So with Darryl I was like, "Man, I gotta get with E this time, I gotta get with E this week." And he was like, "Well come on in the back." And he hooked me up a stereo beat, man. I walked it up to Jazzie Redd and them, and they put me on, man, right then and there. And there was a lot of cats, man. There was this chick, man, called Queen Supreme, Lady C . . . man, just endless amounts of people that were gettin' down back then, that you know, faded into obscurity or just left it alone, you know . . . early.

I think if there would have been an industry in place in Houston at that point then they would have stuck around.

I agree. I agree.

J created that.

Yeah, he did! Absolutely. He the Godfather, man. Can't take nothing from him. He believed in his own dream. Also, he believed in all the time and effort me and Jukebox put into comin' over there rappin' for him, rappin' every opportunity we got, writin', perfectin' our stuff, havin' it memorized, bein' able to drop it on point. He saw something in that. He saw something in that and he said, "You know, I'm gonna give you cats a chance." And he did. He was one of the few dudes that kept his word. He said, "I'm gonna create this label, I'm gonna put you guys on wax, we gonna name the label Rap-A-Lot, after Sir Rap-A-Lot."

Thelton's name.

Well, we discussed it. We discussed it.

Thelton's his brother, right?

Yeah, yeah. That's his brother. Yeah, we sat down at the round table and we discussed it. That was one of the few times that J actually treated us like men as opposed to, you know, little school kids. "What you think we should call the record label? What you think we should call the group?" I said, "Hip-Hop Vigilantes." Whenever you talk to him, ask him about that. He was like, "Hell nah!" He was like "Hell nah—Hip-Hop Vigilantes?" I was like, "Yeah. Ghetto Boys?" You had the Beastie Boys, the Boogie Boys . . . "Man, ain't nothin' fly about that." And he was like, "Nah, Ghetto Boys, we gonna roll with that." I was like, "Aight." Here go his check. It's a wrap. But at the same time, I knew that I wanted to do my own thing, and he knew it too. When we recorded "Car Freak," I recorded my solo single—it was a song called "It's My Record"—that same particular day. It never came out. I guess J wasn't feelin' it at the time. But still, he paid that money, let me go in there and do my thing. I definitely got a lot of respect for J, man. He that individual that put me on. If it wasn't for J, wouldn't be no Raheem, no Geto Boys. J the man. No doubt.

Who do you still keep up with from back in the day? I know you talk to Ready Red . . .

I talk to Red. I talk to Bushwick. I really don't talk to anybody on a regular basis to be honest with you because all this distance. People down there doin' they thing. I talk to Willie D briefly probably about six months ago. I haven't talked to Face. Whenever I come across someone that may know them or what have you, they'll turn them on to my number or vice versa, and, you know what I mean, you conversate, and we talk about old times and what have you. And you know, I wish 'em luck. To keep on doin' what they doin', whatever it is they doin'. It's all love. It's definitely love. You know, my thing is, you know, I ain't got no hate for Houston or no dislike for Houston. My time was just up.

Willie's always good for a phone call too. He's good people.

Yeah, man. He one of the few people that still quote lines from "Dance Floor." I'm like, "Man, come on, you don't get off to that old stuff, man . . ." "I turn on the radio . . ." I'm like, "Look at this man . . ." But yeah, Willie D good people, man.

He's got all those memories.

Okay, well, you know, Willie D, he can definitely give you a little more insight in terms of the successful side of Houston and the rap scene. Because when I was doin' it there just wasn't no money involved, you know what I mean? It was just all work, and never really nothing we saw back off of it. For what reason, I don't know, you know, maybe money wasn't comin' in like that. Keep in mind, we did "Car Freak" and never even had a contract, so they was goin' through a learnin' process also. I definitely wasn't up on my business, 'cuz, you know, I'm like 15, 16 . . . give me a couple dollars and Pontiac 'Bird, let me go to the club, get in free, and I'm good. You know, back *then*! [Laughs]

A couple of free Sprites at the bar, and I'm good.

Man, I'm straight. I'm cool. Shit. So, I mean, I moved on, and I started seein', "Man, this band could be lucrative, for real, for real." And J started sayin' he was gonna do it, he doin' it, he got the homeboys out there, they got that platinum plaque, and of course I started waterin' at the mouth, I'm like . . . "Shit, what's good? Lemme do something!" He put me back down, but J kinda wanted my stuff to sell itself, you know, he didn't really wanna have to put a whole lot effort into it. You know that's kinda what happenend with *The Invincible*, not to mention that him and Cliff were goin' through a situation at that time that I kinda . . . or my *album* kinda got caught up in. It was probably just pretty much bad timing. Because anybody will tell you that that particular album, they still don't understand why that album didn't go. I still don't understand why it didn't go. But you know, I ain't got no hard feelings. It is what it is. Whatever happened . . . you know what I'm sayin'? I moved on. He moved on. It's all good.

As long as you made a good record, that's all that counts.

Exactly. I mean I did what I set out to do, and that was to let everybody know that at that time I was the reigning king, whether it be a battle, whether it be storytelling or whatever. On the mic—couldn't touch me at that time. But now, I'm gonna let these young boys have it. [Laughs] I kinda been layin' back, know what I mean. I mean I still do stuff but you know, I'm not as intense as I was back when I was younger.

Time and a place for everyone.

Exactly, and you know, because of that I can accept and respect other forms of music. And if it's garbage, I'm gonna let you know it's garbage. And there's a lot of garbage comin' out. There's a lot of garbage everywhere now because I'm on the East and I'm checkin' some of these cats out and I'm like, *nah*.

Tell me a story about Big Mike.

Just to give you some dialogue on my man Big Mike, man, I got outta jail one time, and me and Dr. Dre was at a club—what was that club—Club Riddims! And these niggas was . . . excuse my French . . . these niggas was gonna jump me or some shit, you know what I'm sayin'. They wanted to rumble with G, and I know G from back in the day. He was ridin' with Dre that night. And the police, they grab me, 'cuz you know, they don't know who the hell I am. They know Dre, they know G Riddim or what have you. The police, they grab me, and shit, man . . . Mike grabbed the cop and said, "Man, where the hell you goin' with him? Man, nigga that's Raheem!" That's Mike! That's that Mike mentality, man. That's my boy right there for life. He just always kept it real with his boys. He's one of the only cats that I can honestly say . . . success and all that, none of that changed him. That's Mike. That's it. That's a real brother right there, and I hate that things didn't go well on that *Til Death Do Us Part* album. But if you talk to Mike, tell him I ain't forgot. This nigga grabbed a cop and told him, "Yeah, where you goin' with him? Don't put the cuffs on . . . don't put the cuffs on him, that's Raheem."

What did the cop do?

They let me go! Straight up! Hell yeah. Motherfuckers let me go. I will never forget that shit. I was like, *damn*. But I was really fired up then. I really wanted to go to blows with G's motherfuckin' ass that night. I'm like, "Damn, motherfucker you from Houston too. Shit . . . the fuck is you ridin' with that LA nigga for?" But you know . . . I was beefin' over some crazy shit. Some shit I shouldn't have been beefin' over.

Tell me about the first time you met Bushwick.

Bill, he was aight.

What's an early story you remember about him?

When Bushwick Bill jumped up close to four feet off the ground and smacked the shit out this dude in my girlfriend's apartment. Shit . . . I don't really know what the hell happened. Ain't nothin' really gotta happen for Bill to jump on you and shit. Bill crazy as hell. But J had just inducted him into the Ghetto Boys and he was stayin' with me . . . well, he wasn't really stayin' with me, just stayin' overnight. But my man Shakim was like, "Yo, Bill about to fight this motherfucker out in the park." So I went outside, man, and I saw Bill jump up off the ground and smack the shit out this motherfucker. I was like, "Damn! This motherfucker got heart." Not to mention he was cuttin' motherfuckers all in the club and shit.

When he was a dancer?

Well, J wanted him to be a dancer at first, but he jumped off of that real quick. He didn't wanna be a gimmick, so they said, "Aight, we'll have somebody write something for you, and you'll be in the group, you'll be a rapper."

Willie D wrote his first raps, yeah?

I believe so. Bushwick Bill. That's my man right there. He's something else. You can't live with him, and you can't live without him.

Lil' Troy

DEAD END

A Southside drug dealer turned label owner in the late '80s, Troy is credited with bringing into the fold a young rapper named DJ Akshen, who would later become known as Scarface. But when a stint in jail interrupted things for Troy's Short Stop Records, Scarface signed to Rap-A-Lot. Troy emerged anew nearly a decade later with his 1999 hit "Wanna Be A Baller," featuring Big Hawk, Lil' Will, the newcomer Yungstar, and (posthumously) Fat Pat. Big T sang the hook, and Troy put the whole thing together. The album on which it appeared, *Sittin' Fat Down South*, has sold almost two million copies to date. Troy still produces records and works in Houston's strip club/after hours scene.

Last time we spoke we were talking about how different Houston is at night, how it's such a late-night town, and how some people don't go out until the small hours. When do you think that came about, that modern era of late-night life in Houston?

What it's like in Houston—it's a whole new world, you know what I'm sayin'? After two o'clock in the morning, it's a whole new lifestyle, a whole new set of people be out, with a whole different mentality and everything. But it still be a party scene all night, though, at the same time.

What do you think is different about the people who don't go out until super late?

Those self-employed people, most times, that stays out 'til five, six o'clock in the morning, that go out to the after hours. Most times they be self-employed people right there. They don't have a conventional job to go to at eight o'clock in the morning for eight hours a day. No. They have their own hours. And they party. It's a different type of music a lot of times. You hear the street, gutter stuff. You don't hear the stuff you hear on the radio every day.

It's almost like a different set of rules at that point.

Pretty much it is a different set of rules 'cuz you got different people in charge, you know? People that run the radio station during the daytime and now, early, they sleep. They don't live at that time of night.

Do you feel like there are phases in Houston where late night is really hot and then it'll taper off for a couple of years, or do you think it's a constant?

It's a constant. We've been doin' this after hours for a long time. It's just now startin' to catch on with the media and magazines and everybody, but this is what we normally do, you know what I'm sayin'? I used to not leave my house 'til after two o'clock in the morning to go out. 'Cuz the clubs we used to go to, we could smoke after four. But we didn't want to go there 'til after two o'clock. And after four o'clock in the morning, it's a free for all. All the main clubs close, then you have the after hours, so everybody from the main clubs will

COURTESY OF TROY BIRKLETT

Where was that?

Southside, southwest side. That was the main—Holmes Road, South Park. We kept after hours.

So the strip clubs weren't a catalyst, then. The strip clubs were just a part of it when they came along.

Yeah, 'cuz the strip clubs would stay open late and they was taboo. They wasn't goin' by the rules neither. So anytime you got an after hour club, you not actually goin' by the rules. Unless you got a Members Only. You got a Members Only, that way you could get away with all this drinkin' and everything in the club. See, you not supposed to sell liquor after two o'clock. You can't tell that's the case down here, though, 'cuz we have liquor all night, 'til six, seven, eight o'clock in the morning.

Do you think those after hours places were able to avoid the police because of where they were in town—on the Southside?

Nah, really, mainly, if you ain't cause a bunch of problems, and you ain't got a bunch of shootings and stuff like that, the police will let you make it. Laws—you ain't killin', a bunch of fightin' and shootin', they ain't gonna mess with you. They'll see a bunch of cars there, ain't gonna bother it. It's not a big disturbance.

Do you think the MacGregor Park era—the big parties with Darryl Scott DJing in the early '80s, do you think that was a jump-off point for the car culture we see today, or was it earlier than that?

It was earlier than that. When Martin Luther King Boulevard was South Park Boulevard, we all had cars and we would all meet up at MacGregor Park. But we was doin' that before MacGregor Park. See, MacGregor Park was sittin' right next to a rich neighborhood, and the white folks didn't want us in they neighborhood too much. So it was hard for us to go down there at first. They didn't want us down there—all the cars and all the noise ridin' up in the neighborhood. So we rode up-and-down MLK Boulevard. And down into the Dead End. We rode

come to the after hours, and it's still a big old party now. But it's different people runnin' the game. It's a different set of people that run the game at nighttime.

Have the strip clubs always been a component of that? They're not the only places open that late, but they're kind of a centerpiece in a lot of ways because they can be.

Nah, strip clubs—that ain't where after hours first start comin' from, from the strip clubs. Strip clubs didn't get popular bein' after hours. We always had after hour clubs down here. They wasn't no strip clubs, though. They was just regular after hours. We had a few strip clubs that was after hours, but our main thing has been after hours, period. It was called Members Only. You had to have a member's card to come in at night, and you'd drink free. You have a card, you pay somebody for a card when you come in, and you drink free. That comes from the Members Only clubs we was doin' at first.

from Bellfort and OST all the way down to Dead End. We rode up-and-down MLK.

MacGregor Park started getting really popular in '82, '83, right?

Ah, I think maybe after that. It was after that . . . '84, '85, yeah, 'cuz we was ridin' elbows then. We put on elbows in '84.

How different was the South Park of the early '80s from now?

Ah, man, there was so many live cars out and sippin' . . . everybody just partied and rollin' around them streets. We used to break 'em off. See, "break 'em off" came from us in South Park. We would break the street off and pull in front of you at the red light, right? We'd block the street off and let all the cars that's behind us come by. Breakin' 'em off.

Just pull into the intersection.

Yeah, we'd stop at a red light, and what I would do is I would pull up and block the cars coming from the east, and my other potnah would block the cars comin' from the west, and everybody's comin' from the south, ridin' straight on through, you feel what I'm sayin'? Right before the last car leaves, he'll let the cars comin' from the west, and I'll let the cars comin' from the east . . . they'd all take off. So we'd ride down the street with 40, 50 cars from the neighborhood, block every intersection that we goin' down! We didn't have to worry about no video cameras or nothing. There was no cameras at the red lights or nothing. So we would just come on through, and just block the street off all the way down, 30 or 40 cars deep. That's something you can't do nowadays. A lot of times you'll see the red line, the blue line, the gold line, they ridin' together, but you can't break 'em off in the streets like we used to 'cuz they got cameras almost everywhere now.

You'll get a ticket from the cameras now.

Yeah, and we had the original '84 elbows back then. The original. There wasn't no 22s and 20s and all that. Nah, there wasn't none of that.

So what were people driving back then? What were you driving?

I had a little Sable. A two-door coupe and a Sable, white with a blue top, blue inside, blue elbows. Before that I had a Nova with elbows and vogues on it. Back in the day we used to take the springs off our cars, during the MacGregor Park days, and we'd come down there just bouncin' up-and-down 'cuz we took the springs off. We just come through bouncin' up-and-down, and we had them LOC glasses on and put it on 97 Rock. We used to call them glasses "amp glasses" durin' the MacGregor Park days. They real, real dark. It's what them old people wear for cataracts when they can't see. That's what we used to wear. That was the style right there.

Why did people start wearing those?

We wore 'em for the glare, and we was cool! We would ride around, smoke our weed, and drink our liquor. There wasn't no syrup back then. This was before the syrup days.

Scarface

SOUTH ACRES

For Houstonians, Scarface is king. Whether or not he's actually their *favorite* artist, everyone is aware of the level to which Face brought the city. Universally respected and atop nearly everyone's list of great rappers from *anywhere*, Brad Jordan started out calling himself DJ Akshen in the mid-'80s, but by the time he met up with Willie D, Bushwick Bill, and DJ Ready Red to form the most famous incarnation of Geto Boys, they were calling him Scarface. Lil' Troy went to jail, Rap-A-Lot called, and Akshen became Scarface. That was when Houston music changed, because "Mr. Scarface" became the city's first local hit. But everybody talks to Scarface about Scarface, so we talked about DJ Screw, Darryl Scott, and fellow South Acres denizen, Big Floyd (Surround By Sound).

That whole scene with Floyd and everybody customizing cars was way before Screw, yeah?

How old would Screw be today if he was still alive?

46.

He'd be 46? Okay, so in 1985, Screw was 14 or 15 years old. I don't think nobody was makin' tapes back then but Darryl Scott. And then me. I was makin' tapes along with Darryl Scott, but I was just makin' 'em for Quincy.

When did you meet Screw? You met him before "Let Me Roll?"

Oh, I met him way before "Let Me Roll."

When he was at Quail Meadows or Broadway Square?

Broadway Square. I didn't never go to his house, though. I met Screw through Quincy. Quincy always had Screwtapes, right? And I didn't meet Screw face to face until shit . . . Brass Monkey days.

PHOTO: PETER BESTE

I remember Brass Monkey. I saw Bushwick perform there. So did you go to Screw's house on Greenstone?

Nope. I didn't never go to none of them places, man. I didn't go there. I didn't meet Screw until later. But I knew of him. We knew of each other. My brother Warren Lee was a big Screwhead. He had the Tahoe, the K5 Tahoe with all Screwtapes in it, smokin' weed, ridin' around.

And then that whole car culture caught up with what Screw was doing.

Naw, fuck no. Floyd was way before DJ Screw.

I'm saying that music helped turn even more people on to the car culture. I know a lot of people were getting their cars customized and making sure there was a tape player in there long after people were making tapes.

That's true, but I can't say Screw was the reason why niggas started puttin' stereos in they car and shit. I had mad shit in my car, and I wasn't a Screwhead.

What did you think hearing that music and seeing that culture unfold? I mean, I know you had your own thing going on, you were doing solo records, Geto Boys were doing lots of touring . . . you were in Atlanta later on in the '90s, right?

I did Def Jam South in '99.

How were you seeing that culture unfold from afar? Did you feel like people outside of Houston were aware of it?

Naw, nobody outside of Houston except the people that would come into the city really knew too much about it. You know, if you came into the city you took—if you was from New Orleans or somewhere, Louisiana—if you was from Louisiana or somethin' and you came to Houston and knew somebody was havin' Screwtapes, then you took somethin' *back*. You know, you went and got you some tapes. Shit didn't . . . and I really don't know the whole Screw culture because like I said, I was . . . I was Scarface, you know? I got my own shit I had to push on.

Do you remember Darryl Scott slowing down stuff on his tapes?

He did it first! He most definitely did the chopped up, slowed down—listen to his tapes, man! This ain't made up. The proof is in the tape. The proof you could hear when it came out. You can listen to the tape and hear him choppin' it up and slowin' it down too. Where was DJ Screw from, originally?

Well, he was born in Bastrop, but he was in Houston when he was a little kid, but then really he's from Smithville. When he discovered hip-hop he was out in Smithville. That's when *Breakin'* came out. So he identifies with Smithville. But I think he probably met D. Scott, late '80s, something like that.

Oh, so Darryl Scott *did* know Screw?

Oh yeah, because Screw was going over there buying tapes and eventually got his number and was calling him, asking him how to do it. D. Scott was doing tape stops and everything—remember those pause tapes?

Yeah.

You knew him pretty early on, right—D. Scott?

Oh, I knew Darryl Scott a long time. He used to be the DJ at SPN. We used to walk to SPN at St. Francis. That's a church, but there was always a dance on Friday nights.

And what was he spinning? The kind of funk stuff he was playing coming up, or he was playing some hip-hop?

Yeah he played hip-hop back then. Jazzy Jeff and all kinds of shit, man. Darryl Scott was a DJ. I think that Darryl Scott may be—you know how Screw is a lot of people's reason for gettin' into this shit? Well Darryl Scott may be the reason why I got into it. No question about it, 'cuz I heard a whole lot of rap comin' out of there, man, you feel me? There was a whole lot of rap comin' out of Darryl Scott's store. That shit was bangin'. It was mindblowin' to me.

Def Jam Blaster

MISSOURI CITY

William Ross (a.k.a. Def Jam Blaster) has been a headlining DJ at virtually every big event in Houston, including the Super Bowl, the NBA All-Star Weekend, and live performances involving everybody from Puff Daddy to Beyoncé. He has won numerous Houston radio awards and has worked locally with Billy Dee M.C., Willie D, Royal Flush, Big Mello, Raheem, and fellow radio persona Madd Hatta. He released a 12-inch in 1992 with his group NoDōz and produced tracks for Rakim, Mobb Deep, Wu-Tang Clan, and his childhood friend, Scarface. A record he and Mr. 3-2 put down to tape in the '80s was finally released in 2017 on The ARE's On The Good Foot label. This interview was conducted the week of Mr. 3-2's funeral.

COURTESY OF WILLIAM ROSS

Heavy week.

Yeah, I got two services to go to on Saturday. Two buddies.

Oh man. Somebody else you were close to?

Yeah, it's this guy I had a successful record label with doin' my mixtapes with in the '90s. He got hit by a drunk driver.

Never any easier when it's random.

Actually the car accident is much scarier. There's nothing you could have done knowingly. 3-2 was kinda livin' that life, man, so you know when they called and told me about him I was like, "Oh, okay. Alright. Shit." It wasn't like, "What? I can't believe it." I had unfortunately kinda known he was struggling for a while.

I knew he wasn't going to be around forever, but honestly I thought his heart was going to stop. I just didn't think for a second . . . well I knew he wasn't in good health.

Yeah, like you I didn't think it would be something violent. He wasn't really that kinda dude too much.

You guys go way back, don't you?

We were very good friends in high school and probably on up into right before the Blac Monks days. We were still pretty good friends durin' the Convicts days.

Was he the same guy in conversation with you that he was on the records?

Not to me, just kinda like Scarface. He was just a very talented writer. But you know, that was it. He was a regular middle-class guy like myself, like, and we were friends from high school—*from* school. You know, we rode to school together, we hung out at school and after school. He was just a regular dude, but he was just a good writer. Now again, once you get kinda after Convicts and Blac Monks, we weren't hanging out at all in that time frame. I think it was probably life started to imitate the art at that point. You know, start to become more like the stuff you been writin' about all this time.

But what about when y'all were starting out, did he have aspirations to—he wanted to be a writer, or he wanted to be a rapper, or what were his dreams?

He was definitely a rapper. I mean, we were a group. We recorded lots of songs, and our intention was to put out records. When I'm saying he was a good writer, when you get to hear some of this stuff from what we did, he's rappin' his ass off. You know, he's goin' hard just like the New York artists in the '80s, just rappin' about bein' the baddest rapper. That's how I know him. When I say he's a good writer that's what I'm referring to, but definitely was with the intention of, "Yeah, we're a group and we're putting out material." The stuff just never got released because we were signed to Short Stop, and when Lil' Troy went to jail—he went to jail right after we put out the Scarface 12-inch, so that just killed all the other projects. I think there were three groups that I remember, and one of 'em, I mean the Scarface 12-inch came out and then only one other project got released a little bit later. By the time that project got released, 3-2 had already signed with Rap-A-Lot, so our stuff was done as far as with Lil' Troy, any of the material that we had. It was mostly demos, what we were workin' on at my house, but we never even got to do anything with *that* stuff since he went to jail.

What was the group called?

Private Identity. It was just me and him.

You were producing and he was rapping.

That's it. Yep, the standard '80s DJ/producer. That was the formula.

And so the feel of that stuff was kinda your typical pre-gangsta rap sound?

Definitely the music . . . I was going to be more specific—I did two-thirds of the beat for that "Scarface" 12-inch, and it's all sampled. It's all sample-based, slightly up-tempo, you know, not really slow gangster stuff at all. This was all sampled, hard beats like some East Coast stuff that woulda been comin' out at that time. Samples and him just rappin' his ass off about bein' the best rapper or whatever, me doin' the beats and the cuts. This was pre-gangster, but I did some of his first gangster stuff too. It was still the same style *music*, but I remember that he started rappin' about different stuff. I wanna say one of the first songs he did like that I think was called "Massive Murder." I was like, "What's this title? What do you mean Massive Murder?" And then, when he came to my parent's house, where we always recorded stuff in my bedroom, and when he was doin' these lyrics I was like, "Oh, okay! Let me make sure I close the door." I was like, *wow!* All of the sudden he sounded *mad* on the record. I mean the opening line is "Goin' for the K-I-double-L / boy, you better bail / lyrics get hotter than heat in hell." I was like, "Oh, okay! We goin' hard!" It was still dope hip-hop, the subject matter was just a little different. I mean, it's got a Barry White sample—some good samples that we were usin' with DJ scratching in it—so it still was cool. That was just the direction we went in for a little while, from there until he eventually went to Rap-A-Lot and got with the Convicts.

What was the Barry White track you sampled?

I mean it was just "I'm Gonna Love You A Little More Baby," you know, just some random bar in there that I looped.

I'm a big fan, you know. He's from Galveston.

Yeah, yeah, I know! I know.

So did y'all do any shows? Do you remember what year it was? Was it around the time of . . .

We did a few. This is goin' from '87, '88 until maybe '91. We probably stopped doin' stuff in '91. Once he got with the Convicts, we stopped actually makin' music together. I actually made the show tapes for the Convicts, but I didn't make any more music for them. I had not yet worked out a deal with Rap-A-Lot. I eventually did work out a work for hire arrangement for them and then went on to do some work with other artists—Raheem, Willie D, and some other artists—but when he was doin' Convicts I hadn't worked any of that out yet, so I didn't do anything with the Convicts. But he and I were still cool.

You worked on that second Raheem record? The one that was on Rap-A-Lot?

The Invincible, yeah. I did that song, "Underground Jugglin'" and I think the outro, so I did three songs on there.

I think I pulled "Underground Jugglin'" for . . . I pulled a Screw mix of that to put on my radio show a couple of weeks ago.

Me and somebody were jokin' about one of the big things in that era of doin' music for a company was the credits. You know, you write 'em down and cross your fingers that they get 'em right, and they didn't get 'em right on the Raheem album. They left out a couple of names, and "Underground Jugglin'" is one of the ones I didn't get credit on there for. I got credit for the title song, you know, "The Invincible," but not for "Underground Jug-glin'," so, you know, it was just one of those things, you know, like, "I hope they get it right!" And they didn't. Because it was that—I don't know if you remember, but instead of just listing the names, they would use symbols, like instead of writing . . .

They'd have that little legend.

Right, like an asterisk or somethin', so they just messed up however it was they were doin' it, but it was no huge deal. Most of the people around the way knew that I did that song.

So there's going to be a reissue of the stuff you did with 3-2?

You know Russel Gonzalez, right? On The Goodfoot Records, they reissued the Scarface record, and on the heels of that, he was like, "Man, Blaster, I wanna put out some of the stuff you did with 3-2." So, early last week, everything got finalized, he sent off for the wax to get pressed, and a couple days later I get a phone call that 3-2 got killed. And I was like, "Man, the timing is just eerie that he sent that off to get pressed." Because you know, "Man, it's tough to talk to him, but I'ma reach out to him once this gets finalized and gets closer to gettin' it back, then I'll reach out to him and say, 'Hey, man, here's what's goin' on, you know, they're gonna write a little check, and I'm gonna split it with you.'" And then I get that phone call. I'm gonna still do that with his mom, you know, I'll see her later on in the week. But it's just terrible. I was lookin' forward to bein' able to call and tell him, "Hey man—got a little 45 comin' out, you know, kinda cool."

Get you a little money.

Yeah, you know, the money is peanuts, but still just to me it's cool that, hey, somebody likes somethin' we did almost 30 years ago. They wanted to put it out. So yeah, the stuff I'm describing to you, two of them will be comin' out, Russel will be puttin' those out I guess however many weeks it takes to get the wax done. But he'll have the whole treatment just like he did Scarface, I had a lot of cool pictures from back in high school doin' stuff and at shows or just at school, you know, posin'.

So when do you think the last time you talked to him was? Has it been years?

It's been about a year now. I had been on a mission to find him. I wanna say E.S.G. was able to track down his number for me, if I remember correctly, and you know, he's like, "Yeah, he's out there bad." I say, "I know." Because I had *seen* him. The last time I saw him in person was probably in the early 2000s. He came up to the radio station, like, five in the morning one day just totally out of it. I was like, "Dude—dude, what are you doin'?" I was like, "We can't let you in here." You know? "I'm sorry!" But then, like I said, a year ago I called him and, you know, talked to him during the day, and it was great! You know, "What's goin' on, what are you doin', tell me about your life." And he just told me everything. But then he would call me at, like, four in the morning, out of it, you know, fried out. And it got to the point where I couldn't take his calls anymore! It was a little painful, but I was just like, "Man, okay, I just have to completely not take his calls, because he's only calling me when he's fucked up now." And, you know, I can't talk to him like that. Because initially I wanted to go meet him out for lunch or somethin', and I've always been a really square dude, and I was just . . . I don't know what else comes along with that lifestyle you livin', so I'm just gonna chill. You know, I wanted to at least just talk to him on the phone, but *that* was even difficult. So we had a few conversations via phone where I was like, "Okay, now he's *only* callin' me when he's high. I can't talk to him like that." That was just the end of it.

And it was wet? That's what everybody says, that it was Sherm.

Yeah. Yeah, he couldn't shake that one.

Everybody's got that drunk uncle that calls them. You stop takin' those phone calls after a certain hour.

Yeah, and I hated it, man! Because I put so much time in tryin' to find him, you know, I was like, "Man, this is my friend—lemme find this dude." For no particular reason! Just because I hadn't talked to him in a long time.

And what did he say when you said, "Tell me what's going on with your life?" Where was he in life when you talked to him?

I mean, I don't . . . he was . . . I was like, "What do you do? How do you pay the bills?" He said he was working construction. He would work construction jobs. Somebody would call for a project, they'd put together a team and he'd be on a team, so he had spent the last couple of months, six months, whatever, doin' that kinda work. I was like, "Man, that's awesome! That's cool." So we just kinda caught up like that, you know, a regular homeboy conversation that you hadn't talked to in a while. He was like, "Man, we should try to put together some shows." But I was like, "I don't wanna get that deep into it. I'm just a DJ, doin' my stuff. Yeah, I made beats, but I'm not doin' that anymore." He was like, "Oh, okay, cool." You know, just kinda catching up.

I wonder if he was ever able to fully live off the music.

Yeah, I don't know.

You know, because nobody gets checks from Rap-A-Lot. Nobody gets checks from Rap-A-Lot, and as a matter of fact the further back you go, the further people have deviated from Rap-A-Lot, the more they'll talk about it.

Well Scarface is one big voice that will now talk about it.

He wrote about it in his book!

Yep.

I think everybody's been so scared of Prince forever, they just didn't wanna say anything.

Yeah, you just kinda avoid the topic, like, "Yeah, whatever—y'all know what it is." You don't need me to add onto it. But work for hire—I got my checks as a work for hire. I was always like . . . I genuinely don't have anything bad to say about them, but I was never signed as an artist to a contract. I was always like, "Okay, you did three tracks as a work for hire, here's a check." Cool! That's all I was supposed to get.

That's different though—nobody gets royalties is the whole thing. Maybe they got advances or something. But it is what it is. But when somebody does work that great over such a long period of time, you like to think that it catches up enough to pay for things, but I wonder if it ever did. It's too bad that the Death Row thing never worked out, you know?

Yeah, that was an interesting time period. I remember . . . I wish I could remember in more detail as far as the time frame, but I remember when he went to do that, and then he came back. It was like, "Okay, let's make some more songs." And for the first time ever, he gave me an idea for a sample to use. That wasn't his thing. He didn't know about breaks and samples and stuff, so he gives me this sample, he's like, "Do you have this record?" And I'm like, "Yeah, I got that! What's up?" And he was like, "Yeah, let's use that, put it over the 'Friends' beat." I was like, "He's comin' with ideas!" That never happened. So we make this song . . . you know, it's just us makin' songs, like, "One day we'll put out an album" type thing. But he was already startin' to affiliate with Rap-A-Lot. That would be the last song we did before he went straight into the Convicts. Whether he was going with the Convicts, whether he was joining the Geto Boys, we weren't sure which it was going to be. And then quite some time later, I hear the song come out on *The Chronic*, the same beat, and I said, "Okay, now, in retrospect, I don't remember if it was before or after the trip. I'm tryin' to give [Dr.] Dre the benefit of the doubt. Okay, 3-2 went out there and heard this from Dre, and he brought it back for himself." That's the way I put it in my head because, you know, there was nothin' I could do about it either way. And 'cuz I didn't come up with it. You know, 3-2 told it to me and I'm like, "He musta got this from Dre somehow." But it's the song, "A Nigga Witta Gun." The sample over the "Friends" beat is the exact song we made called "In The County." Obviously different lyrics with different people on the beat—but that kinda blew my

mind for a while. People in Mo City who had heard the song from us were like, "Man! What's up with this?" And here's all I could say, "You hear Snoop say, '3 and to the 2,' and somethin' about the Peter Man in the song." There's the connection. I can't say which way it happened, but they give him a subtle shout out in the song, both of them, so I say, you know, I'm thinkin' 3 got the idea from Dre and brought it back. That's the one song we did that I didn't completely come up with all by myself as far as the beat, so he must have heard that out there and just brought that idea back. So yeah, I wish it woulda gone somewhere too, and I can't imagine what went wrong, but with Rap-A-Lot and Lil' J there's no tellin' whether he just might have not wanted 'em to do it. They went out there but didn't want 'em to do it.

When I listen to Snoop . . . I hear an influence.

Lemme tell you what the influence was. Now, this is goin' back to the '80s. In high school, there was a group of guys, and Chris [3-2] hung out with 'em. I didn't. They were kinda the bad boys of the area, so I didn't hang out with 'em. I wasn't tryin' to be with that, but you know, Chris was kinda tryin' to be down with 'em, and he hung out with 'em, and so they *all* had this little way that they talked, and you know, Chris picked it up, so he would do it too. So that's where that, "I don't love 'em," "Hey, big baby," all of that was from them dudes. And when we heard that on the record, *every*body in Mo City was like, "Man, what the *fuck*? How did this get on *The Chronic* album, and why is Snoop doin' this? Who did that?" And I knew that they went out there and spent some time with Dre, so it's 100 percent that that's exactly where Snoop got a lot of that stuff, specifically that whole jumpin' into the high pitched voice all of the sudden. That's a very specific thing that these guys did in Missouri City, just one little group of dudes. And it quickly spread throughout Willowridge, but that was their little thing that they would do. They would just be talkin' normal and then all of the sudden, "I don't love 'em baby." You know, almost like a pimp voice or whatever. And so we were like, or at least those in the know, I was like, "He *had* to give them a shout-out on that song! He just took their whole thing.

He just took their *whole* thing. He had to acknowledge that." That would have been immoral not to acknowledge that you had just taken somebody's whole little slang thing from them, and they're not even on the record, you know?

And so those guys, that group that he was runnin' with, they weren't necessarily artists or anything, they didn't end up makin' . . .

No they weren't artists at all. They were just kinda, you know, thugs of the area.

But Chris took it and ran with it, because he developed a whole . . .

Well he was *with* them. I mean, he was with them, so it made sense that *he* was doin' it because he was part of the lil' group, the clique. These were dudes he started hangin' out with more so, so yeah. It was natural for him to talk like that all the time, although interestingly enough, he never did it on any of the songs. Even though we may have only done one or two more songs after that time, but apparently he must have been doin' it while he was out there with Dre and them.

That makes sense.

And again, I'm sayin' Snoop is the one doin' it and he gives them that . . . it's like "3 and to the 2 . . ." I mean he *says* their names in that song. In that same verse, you know, so it all comes full circle. I wish they would have gotten a chance to be a part of it more. But yeah, he definitely got that lil' thing directly from 3-2. Now, Big Mike wasn't doin' that. That was 3-2. That was a Mo City thing. So he got that directly from Chris. And I bet if somebody sat and talked to him, he'd probably tell you! I don't think it's the type of thing, an issue sayin', "Yeah, I got that from them boys back in the day!" But I tell you, it was a huge thing. That whole, "Deeez Nuuuts/Hold on," that's *all* 3-2. That shoulda just been him that did that whole skit. 'Cuz that's *exactly* what they would do. That was *exactly* their thing, man.

Do you remember how he got the name 3-2?

Yeah—it never occurred to me that everybody didn't know this, which is just naive on my part, but his name is . . . it's just his initials. The third letter and second letter of the alphabet. Chris Barriere. C-B. 3-2. That's it.

That's all it is!

If you write that somewhere that's gonna be like a mind-blowing fact for anybody that is a fan of his, because apparently that never came out. I just assumed everybody knew that and for some reason that it woulda come out at some point in an interview or a song or who knows, but somebody said something recently on Facebook when I typed that, people were like, "Oh shit I never knew that!" I was like, "Well, I guess that wasn't public information." But I always would have wondered what's the significance of those numbers. But that's it. 3-2. Always. He was always 3-2.

Sire Jukebox

THIRD WARD

Often referred to as "The Original Ghetto Boy," Jukebox was an early part of Ghetto Boys alongside DJ Ready Red, K-9 (a.k.a. Sir Rap-A-Lot), Prince Johnny C, and dancer Bushwick Bill. He missed the group's first recording session and was replaced on "Car Freak" by Raheem, who subsequently left Rap-A-Lot and went off on his own. Jukebox appears on the group's 1988 album *Making Trouble* alongside Prince Johnny C, Ready Red, and Bushwick Bill—who was not yet rapping. Both

GHETTO BOYS, RAHEEM, SIRE JUKEBOX, DJ READY RED.
PHOTO: CARLOS GARZA

Jukebox and Prince Johnny C left Ghetto Boys in 1989 when Willie D and Scarface came aboard and the name was changed to Geto Boys.

Would you compete often at The Rhinestone Wrangler?

Yeah, we competed quite a few times. But then once we started recording, my mind wasn't on trying to win at Rhinestone, we was trying to put out an album. We were trying to go nationwide, you know?

Was battle rap your thing, or were you wanting to make songs?

Battle rap, I came up battle rapping.

Seems like your destiny maybe was to move on from that and start writing.

That was our goal. I didn't go to the Rhinestone until I met NC Trahan and James—James Smith, 'cuz he was James Smith at the time. I didn't go to the Rhinestone because I was too young. But because of the influence they had in the city—Raheem was even younger than I, you know—we were able to get in the club.

Who was NC Trahan? Was he a hustler?

NC Trahan was a good man. He was like a big brother, father figure, he was a good man. I don't want to say . . . I just want you to know he was a good man.

And what happened? He was shot?

Yeah, he got killed by . . . the day Raheem shot his "Dance Floor" video, that night we were at the club—shit, I can't even remember the name—it might have been the Rhinestone Rangler on the Northside. I just know it was over on 45 and Parker. And he got killed. Somebody shot him in the face.

It was at the video shoot? Or just it happened to be that same day?

It was after the video shoot. The video was shot at Texas Southern University. And he got killed at the club.

Do they know who did it? Did they ever catch him?

Yeah, they know who did it.

Did they catch him, though?

They know who did it. They know who killed him. I think the guy may have did some prison time for it. Yeah, they know who did it. We knew who did it the same night.

But he was considered part of the Ghetto Boys, right? Kind of?

No, he wasn't considered part of the Ghetto Boys, he was . . . honestly, the birth of Rap-A-Lot was in his home, in his living room. He was just a good man, a great friend, and a good mentor, and he made sure Raheem and I did what we needed to do as far as school was concerned. He would furnish microphones and beat machines. He purchased them. Him and James Prince were very good friends, best friends. He was just an all around, just solid dude, you know? Reliable, dependable, trustworthy, he was really just a good dude.

Do you remember what his real name was?

NC Trahan. If it did stand for anything, I never knew it. On his obituary it said "NC Trahan."

I always hear his name in association with Ghetto Boys. Sounds like he was kind of another producer for you.

No, he wasn't a producer. He was more like a manager, or a mentor. We were a group of friends. Before anything else, when Rap-A-Lot was founded, the people who were there at the time, we were all friends. And it's a friendship, the bond, that they brought to Rap-A-Lot. You know, a lot of people don't know that before Raheem and I showed up, Rap-A-Lot wasn't even an idea. K-9 was there, Trahan was there already, and if I believe that—and I'll say Raheem believed this also—that if he and I don't go to Fifth Ward and meet James Prince, or Smith at the time, there would be no Rap-A-Lot Records. Because before we showed up, there's wasn't even no mention of it, no thought of it. K-9 was already there rapping, but they wasn't trying to establish a company with him. It took Raheem and I to be injected into the scenario for Rap-A-Lot to come to fruition.

So what was K-9's situation before, I mean was he—

He was rapping, he was J's brother.

How much did you know him? Did you know him aside from James Prince?

I didn't know him prior to me going to Fifth Ward in late 1985, I didn't know him. I met him around the same time I met James and NC.

So you just came together with all of those people at the same time?

Yeah.

That was in late 1985?

Yeah, late 1985, early '86.

And so how old were you then?

I was 14. I was in high school—10th, 11th grade. When we dropped "Car Freak" I was in the 10th grade. We dropped "Car Freak" in the summer of 1987.

And when did you record it? Not long before that?

Yeah, not long before that, it was . . . it all happened so . . . like bam, bam, bam! It just happened, you know? The producer was Mikki Bleu and Daryel Oliver, I believe at the time.

How well did you know Mikki Bleu?

We were looking for people who knew how to produce music, and he was one of the people that knew how to do it, and I established a pretty good relationship with him back then. Plus he was little older than us.

Yeah, he produced everybody. I was talking to Jazzie Redd earlier tonight, and when Mikki Bleu came up I said, "Well look up John Kenneth Williams." He said, "Naw, that's another guy." I said, "No, that's the same guy."

Yeah, he worked on "Car Freak."

Were you in the studio with him when he was doing that?

I was there for everything except the recording. I'm not on "Car Freak." I'm on the picture, but I'm not on the album. I missed the recording.

Right, that's right. Because Raheem . . . but are you on the B-side?

I'm not sure. I missed the recording. I think the B-side might be just the instrumentals.

But there was another 12-inch right after that, and you're on that, right?

Yeah, I'm on that, yeah. I'm on everything after "Car Freak" up until my departure in 1989.

Right, 'cuz you're on *Making Trouble*, and there's a couple singles, too, that y'all did. I have those. I have "Be Down" on the A-side and "My Musician" is on the B-side.

Yeah, exactly. Yeah, mm-hmm, and that's with Ready Red.

Then, "You Ain't Nothing" was a single.

Yeah, we had an album, Ghetto Boys—*Just Made A Jump In The Heights*—me, Johnny C, and Ready Red, that was never put out. We had a few songs on there that all three of us are of the opinion—if the album would have been put out at that time—that we had a few breakthrough songs on there, because *Making Trouble* was heavily influenced by J Prince. You know, we didn't have the creative liberty that we had with *Just Made A Jump In The Heights*. We were trying to appease J Prince, and we did what he told us to do, and that's basically him speaking through us. But on the *Just Made A Jump In The Heights* album, it was all us, and it was a lot of hip-hop, you know, because we really wasn't no gangsters. We were rappers. We wasn't no gangsters, you feel me? And so we were able to bring out more of who we were and our own identity and our own creativeness with *Just Made A Jump In The Heights*, and it was bit discouraging when the album wasn't put out.

It was a full album? It was a whole album's worth of stuff?

It's maybe 12 songs.

And did any of them—

I just know of one of them, "Must Be The Music," that was on a compilation CD, with a lot of other songs. That's the only song they put out on there.

Because this is whenever James wanted to make it more gangster, and you weren't feeling that, you didn't want to go in that direction.

No, what happened was, I don't know where people get this part of the story from, but we were at his house. He had a studio at his house, and I remember it was myself, Scarface, Willie D, James Prince, Cliff Blodget, Bushwick Bill, and his wife, Mary. We were writing, and they was trying to get Willie D to write for me. They were trying to get him to write for me all day long. And I just wasn't—I'm an MC in the truest sense of the word. I don't need nobody writing for me, and that's what made me leave the group. Regardless of what you hear, or what anybody tells you, what you've read, I left the group because of creative differences. I feel like at the time, I was just as good as everybody in the room. And I don't know what made them feel like Willie D needed to write for me. Not that I'm taking anything away from him or . . .

You just want to write for yourself.

Yeah, I was my own . . . I can do it myself.

So what did you do? Did you end up going and working on solo stuff when you left the Ghetto Boys?

I was lost. Because the Ghetto Boys was . . . I felt like they was mine. I'm the original Ghetto Boy. I, more than anybody else . . . I am the original Ghetto Boy. And so I was hurt, I was lost, and it came out in what I attempted to do, and that hurt and anger and loss caused me to make decisions that led me to go to prison for a very long time.

That took away all your whole creative outlet.

I tried to go back.

To the group?

I went and talked to James one time at Tuffley Park in Fifth Ward. It wasn't a good conversation.

He had a different vision in mind by that point?

Yeah, I believe he did. But it wasn't very long after I left that I had tried to go back. It's okay. It is what it is.

I guess that difference in vision is what direction you were feeling like they were going anyway that wasn't *your* direction.

Well, I believe he had bigger expectations and plans for me than I had for myself. I believe James did. You know, like I said, we were friends, and I was there before anyone. And I stayed there with the exception to Ready Red. I was the last of the originals there. Because the Ghetto Boys was going to be me, Willie D, and Scarface. And Bushwick didn't start rapping until I left and went to prison. If you notice on "Mind Of A Lunatic," on a *few* songs, Bushwick did raps and stuff that I wrote. So, it is what it is, you know?

And how long . . .

How long was I in prison?

Yeah.

12 years. I was in prison for 12 years.

Man, and that was how soon after?

I left the group in '89. I went to prison in '90.

So you were gone throughout the '90s and past 9/11.

Yeah, I went in, I got locked up June the 18th of 1990, and I came home June the 18th of 2002.

Where were you locked up?

In Tennessee Colony, Texas.

That's where Pharoah was, or he is. I wrote letters to him there for years. Did you know him?

Well, how long has he been there?

Late '90s, yeah, he was locked up like '97 or something like that.

I didn't know him, I did 10 and a half years over there. I may know him, I may not, but when I was on Beto, it was like the fourth worst prison in the nation. It was a terrible place.

As far as the conditions or the violence?

All of it. The conditions, the violence, the corruption, the . . . you know, you just found out who you were.

You found out who you were.

Yeah, when you dropped into the roughest situation you've ever seen, or ever imagined.

Did you write a lot while you were in there?

I wrote quite a bit. And then my mother passed while I was in prison, and I stopped writing. I lost something when my mother passed and the State of Texas didn't allow me to go to her funeral. I was mad at myself. I was mad at the system, and I had convinced myself that the system was trying to make me a monster. And I refused to let 'em do it. Yeah, I stopped writing. I would scribble some things down, but as far as a full song, I haven't done anything like that since October of 1997.

That was when your mother passed?

Yeah.

But you never picked it back up, you never started writing anything . . .

I have. A lot of people will ask me to do a feature, or do this or do that, and I'm contemplating maybe, hopefully. Me and Raheem been talking about it, honestly.

Where is he now?

He's around. He's really introverted.

Yeah. I talked to him. I interviewed him. Over the phone, I think he was in Philly whenever I talked to him.

This was recently?

No, it was like eight years ago.

Okay, yeah, he's even more private now. I spoke with him last week. He and I both feel like, for some reason people are trying to write us out of Houston. Ya know, it might be because when I came home I went to Rap-A-Lot, and J gave me a job, and he was gracious to me. But, we fell out on bad terms . . . and uh . . . that's all I'ma say about that.

Did you have any contact with him once you got out—have you seen him since?

Who, J Prince? Yeah, he gave me a job. I was with him almost every day during the job at Rap-A-Lot. He gave me a job at Rap-A-Lot.

How long did you work there?

I worked there from . . . I think the end of '03 'til maybe right after Z-Ro dropped *The Life Of Joseph McVey*, 'cuz I was on the road with Z-Ro on the *Life Of Joseph McVey* album. He put that out in 2004, so that's when I left Rap-A-Lot—in 2004.

Where did that tour go?

Like the Chitlin' Circuit, down south. You know, we did a lot of little places and lil' clubs and small venues, but everywhere he went he packed the house. He was much more popular back then if you ask me.

He's still hugely popular now. He gets all the money. In Houston, when he does shows he gets more money than anybody.

That's good for him. I'm happy for him.

What was your involvement in the label? Were you doing managing? Like tour managing?

I did, back then they had retail, I used to did retail. I established relationships with all the record companies and made sure they had everything they need in the store setups and posters and they had the product. If we wanted to do walk-throughs,

I had a list of every mom and pop store in the country, and I was the liaison for Rap-A-Lot and the mom and pop retail stores. I did some publishing. I designed publishing spreadsheets for 'em, did some accounting for 'em at the time. I went on the road, they had YukMouth and Dirty on the road together at one time. And then they had Z-Ro on the road, and I went on both of those tours with those guys.

Around the time of the Rhinestone Wrangler were you going to any of the record shops, Darryl Scott's place or anything like that?

Darryl Scott lived across the street from me. I knew his whole family. We grew up in Third Ward together in the Blodgett Street Apartments.

Where was that?

The Blodgett Street Apartments was between Canfield and Tierwester in Third Ward. The Texas Southern dormitories, they sit where the apartments used to be, and that's where Darryl Scott grew up, and I grew up over there. I remember when he first opened that . . . Darryl Scott when he used to put them tapes out and everything. I remember all that. I knew him very well.

Were you buying his tapes? Were you getting his mixes?

Yeah, I used to get his mixes.

Do you remember him slowing down some songs on his tapes?

I remember that.

Yeah . . . And Lester Pace?

Yeah, I remember that, but it wasn't as heavy as what Screw did. It was a lot different.

It was different texture, right? It's different sonically, like it doesn't have the same bottom end or something.

Right. Now what Screw did in hindsight was genius. In hindsight it was genius, and he's a legend because of it. It has solidified its place in the culture of a major city. The culture of the hip-hop of Houston is continuing to be heavily influenced by—more than any other sound—the DJ Screw sound. The hip-hop in Houston is engulfed in the DJ Screw sound, and that's a plus and a minus.

I've always thought of it as a gateway to get people interested in what's happening in Houston in general.

I just don't believe that—I think that up and coming artists should not be fearful of stepping outside the box. You don't have to be a member of the Screwed Up Click or a part of the Screwed Up culture to be great in Houston.

Yeah, oh, of course not.

We need up-and-coming artists who can appreciate being individuals. Kind of like Travis Scott or these young kids Donnie B Good, Freon Icy Cold, and Psyco Sid. We have some young guys who are not afraid to be themselves, and I believe that they are gonna inject greatness—another vein of greatness—back into Houston hip-hop because it's much needed. You know, the time of the comin' down, and comin' through and rollin' slow, and sippin' slow and throw it up—it's coming to an end.

Did you go on "Kidz Jamm?"

Yeah, I was on "Kidz Jamm" a couple of times. I remember being on "Kidz Jamm" with Jazzie Redd. I knew Redd pretty good. O.G. Style. Yeah, I was on "Kidz Jamm" a few times.

Did you freestyle, or did you bring lines that you'd written? Jazzie Redd said nobody was really freestyling.

I brought lines I had wrote.

So was that before Ghetto Boys?

It was, yeah, I was on there before Ghetto Boys and after Ghetto Boys. During, yeah, because we was at TSU like every day. We went to Yates, we would skip school and go to TSU like every day. We had they students rapping and doing whatever the hell mischievous teenage boys did in the 1980s.

You knew a bunch of people over there?

I knew a lot of people over there. Yeah, we opened up for . . . it was The Awesome Three and Jukebox. TSU had homecoming, and we were being managed by a group of girls from Alpha Kappa Alpha. They had homecoming, and me and the group I was in at the time, The Awesome Three and Jukebox, we opened up for the S.O.S. Band, and it was like the biggest thing in the world for us, you know?

Where was that? At TSU?

At Texas Southern, and this is before Ghetto Boys. So I was even younger and between me, it was myself, Rapping Lee, Diamond Tee, and a kid called himself Kid Bronski Fresh. We opened up for the S.O.S. Band, and I want to say it was '84, or '85, TSU had the S.O.S. Band come to their homecoming, and we opened up for them. It was at Texas Southern, at the Hannah Hall Auditorium.

You were rapping? You had a DJ? What was your set up?

No, we were just rapping.

And beatboxing?

At the time, I was beatboxing. I was beatboxing and rapping, and it was a pretty good show. It was a damn good show. I remember it, I remember it. We did good, 'cuz we was so accustomed to doing talent shows. We had our little performance down, and we did very good.

So you were doing talent shows at school, but was that your first show that was outside of that kind of realm, where you were in a big club?

The first big show was that show. 'Cuz the hall was packed! It was the first, our first big show.

And so that was, you think that was '85?

Yeah, it was '84, or '85.

That was your first big show, but did you do other shows and clubs around town?

No, not clubs, just talent shows. Yeah, we used to chase all the talent shows. I remember we did a show, The Awesome Three and the Jukebox, we did a show . . . somehow we hooked up with the Shriner's Hospital. We went and did a show in the hospital for the children at Shriner's. Those were the two that I remember most. So one of them was very big, and one of them was just meaningful. You know?

Was The Awesome Three and Jukebox still a group when you met James Prince?

I went to James with one of the guys, Rapping Lee. When I met James, I went back and told them. 'Cuz I was like, "Hey man, I done met this guy, and he's telling me he's going to help me make a record," and this and that, and they didn't have the faith that I did at the time in Prince. I just knew he was gonna do what he said he was gonna do. So I stayed on him, those two or three days, they didn't have my enthusiasm about the situation. And so Raheem was around at the time, and so when they said no, I told Raheem, "Hey, come on man, 'cuz . . . let's go, you come with me." And he came and there it is.

Because it was a different context, it was some kind of chemistry that you and Raheem had, or they just believed the two of you?

Raheem and I were friends, you know, we would just . . . he knew I was in The Awesome Three and when I left The Awesome Three, you know, it was just he and I, and we was the Hip-Hop Vigilantes.

Yeah, he told me that he suggested that name, and James was like, "Naw, hell nah." Were you there when that happened?

Yes, I was.

Of course, you were, 'cuz he said . . . Raheem said he set y'all around a table.

Yeah.

And he said, "What y'all want to call the group?" And he said, "Hip-Hop Vigilantes".

That's who we were. And that's why . . . and Raheem is so . . . he was a spitfire, and that's why he named the first album *The Vigilante*. He was like, "They not gonna take that from me. I'ma call this first album *The Vigilante*." And that's where that came from.

And that was his album with A&M, and then years later he comes back to Rap-A-Lot and makes a record. Which certainly says something about longevity of relationships with James Prince, for some folks, not for all folks, but, you know, some folks. And so that was interesting to see, his record that was *The Invincible*, that second album.

One of the surest signs that you get is how many other successful people that you create. You know, you know you're successful when you create a trail of successful people. People who can create the type of generational wealth that you created. People who can take care of their children and their grandchildren for generations. So if you've been in business for 30 years, and you haven't created any millionaires, you the only millionaire, it's something wrong. It's something wrong. Somebody's not being fair. It can't just be after 30 years, one millionaire or one person with the bulk of the wealth. You know what I'm saying, right?

It should be people that you're helping along and sometimes those people, you help them along and they end up moving faster than you, right?

And there's some people that you never forget.

Yeah, exactly, and you never forget that experience.

And I feel like Raheem and I are two of the people that he should have never forgot because our relationship was bigger than any of that. And I'm going to just leave that right there. And I don't . . . I used to be with him every day. At one time in my life, I considered him my best friend. He sold me to a certain quality of life that I may not have achieved without knowing him. But before I met James I was in school every day. And I'm not blaming him. I had my own free . . . I was in school every day, I went to school, I never played sports, I was a bookworm. I never knew what crime was until I met criminals. That's it.

You should still be making some money off of *Making Trouble*. I bet you haven't seen a check for that in as long as you can remember.

Never.

Scarface did call him out on some stuff—did you read his book?

I haven't read *Diary of a Madman*.

You should read it. He talks about when he went to Def Jam, and he couldn't believe how much money he was getting paid. He didn't realize that people made that kind of money because he'd never been paid that.

Big Mike tried to burn the building down.

And got locked up.

Yeah, he got locked up. I don't think it was for that, but . . . yeah, he tried to burn the place down behind his money. You can't, you know, you just . . . you can't do everybody bad. Everybody not going to accept it.

But you been working, you been welding, is that right?

No I'm a scaffold foreman, I'm a foreman for a scaffold division of a company. I work in the refinery.

Oh right, that's why you're in Texas City.

Yeah, I started out here, but I work for a refinery in Baytown.

How long you been out there, working in the refineries? Is that ever since you got back, or a couple years after?

Soon as I left Rap-A-Lot. When I left Rap-A-Lot I started working in the trench, since 2005.

Right on, and are you liking it?

It's not my dream job. It takes care of my family, so I love it. My children don't want for anything, and they the light of my life, light of my heart. So I'm able to take care of my family, even though I'm . . . like I said, it's not my dream job, but I'm doing what I have to.

But you're a foreman, you're managing how big of a team?

My crew, it's just me and eight guys. I used to be a general foreman for another company, and I had like 150 guys under me.

That's a lot to look after.

Yeah. I just gotta keep them safe and keep them motivated, and lead by example.

SOUTHSIDE

This chapter spans the 1990s and is named for the Southside. That's not because the Northside wasn't a huge part of the decade—they were—it's just that this was when the Southside started to shine, and a whole lot of people made that happen by putting out a whole lot of records. Rap-A-Lot had a flag up on the Northside and had even signed a few artists from the South—Scarface, Big Mike, Ganksta N-I-P, the late Big Mello—but it was when the Southside learned how to do it on their own that the real impact began to come from south of Downtown, hence this section being the largest in the book.

The Southside boasts whole platoons of rappers. South Park Coalition (S.P.C.), Screwed Up Click (S.U.C.), South Park Mexican's Dope House Records. Devin the Dude and his Odd Squad (eventually Coughee Brothaz) were mostly from the Southside. Grit Boys, Botany Boys. There are so many neighborhoods—virtually all of them in Third Ward, which encompasses Downtown, South Park, Sunnyside, Yellowstone, Herschelwood, Dead End, Cloverland, South Acres, and Hiram Clarke. The Southside goes as far out as Missouri City.

And there were places to buy those records on the Southside. Near MacGregor Park, Darryl Scott had Blast Records & Tapes, and Russell Washington opened up Bigtyme Recordz in nearby King's Flea Market. Stickhorse was carrying hip-hop records in multiple locations around the Southside. Soundwaves on South Main became a regular stop for new releases, and a growing amount of their stock was local music. People learned how to get records pressed. The CD format made it easier. Labels started popping up everywhere. Cartel Records, Suave House, Perrion, Evolution, Wreckshop.

There was a line drawn through the middle of the city in this era, a Northside/Southside beef that turned bloody for some before running its course near the end of the decade. The warring dissolved completely in the new millennium with some watershed collaborations between North and Southsiders, but not before a long exchange of recorded venom back-and-forth between the different sides of town. Southwest Wholesale worked with both sides, North and South, changing the game in Houston through production and distribution arrangements with a whole slew of artists and labels around the city. This system was the lifeline for many in H-Town, and it helped carve out careers for a lot of artists who may not have been able to make the same thing work elsewhere. Houston radio stations still weren't really playing Houston rap, but the fans supported it.

Between the ecosystem at Southwest and the numbers DJ Screw was doing, both with Screwtapes out of his house and his official releases that started coming out in the middle of the decade, there were a lot of records being sold by the Southside in the 1990s through a number of different movements. But a lot of those records were sold on the Northside, and there are interviews with Northsiders in this section (The ARE, KB Da Kidnappa) for that matter, because the things they're talking about tell the story of how the two sides connect.

Besides, what was happening on the Southside in the 1990s is what inspired an answer in the later part of the decade from the Northside, where they went just as hard and could relate to the slowed down sounds coming out of DJ Screw's house. On Screwtapes, people talked about their neighborhoods. It became a lot more important where you were from, and Houston began to further explain its geography through lyrics. The voices that would eventually come out of the Northside had been listening for years, and by then the Southside had set the tone. ✖

K-Rino

DEAD END

K-Rino originally broke through in 1986 with his group Real Chill, who cut an early Houston rap record with their 12-inch "Rockin' It." Eric Kaiser (K-Rino) then went on to form the South Park Coalition and became one of the most prolific recording artists in Houston history, releasing over three dozen albums, the majority of them since 2004, with countless more compilations and appearances at home and abroad. K-Rino is universally respected and nearly always mentioned in the same breath as the top two or three rappers in the city. He is a member of the groups 144 Elite and C.O.D. (Cummin Out Doggin). In fall 2016, K-Rino released seven albums on the same day.

Talk about Houston, even without the rap, just kind of Houston in general. Your thoughts on it. Your perspective on it. You've grown up here, you've lived in multiple neighborhoods in Houston.

Houston is a cool city because, number one: I like the weather. I like to play basketball, so it's the only place I know where I can shoot hoop year-round. A lot of people like to come down here and live down here because the cost of livin' is pretty cool compared to places like California or New York or places like that. It's an independent city. A lot of people do they own thing out here. We're not predominantly followers. We pretty much do our own thing in Houston. A few people tryin' to claim gangs and all that, but that ain't too prevalent out here to my knowledge. It's a cool city, man, and with the music scene bein' like it is now, there's a bigger spotlight on the city because the world's attention is on Houston now. So there's a good opportunity for anybody that wanna come down, whether it be music, real estate—you know, the real estate market is huge out here because there's so much land and space. It's a good place to live. I wouldn't live anywhere besides Houston. I'll go visit a lot of places, but I wouldn't trade just livin' in Houston for nowhere.

Do you think the recent blitz will ultimately be good or bad for Houston's independence, as far as hip-hop?

It depends on what the attention is centered around. If the attention is centered around—like we were speaking about off-camera—the garbage side of the industry, then it's bad. If it's centered around the true foundation of the hip-hop scene and where it came from and where it is now—that process almost like a child bein' brought into the world from conception to manhood—that's a good thing. Because I can remember when there wasn't a scene, when people laughed at us. People thought we was country. People said all we did down here was ride horses, rope cows and all that, nobody down here had no rap skills. You know, I had to battle cats on the East Coast just to prove that Houston had rap skills. So it's a good thing depending on what that attention is centered around. We don't wanna glorify no nonsense. A lot of cats, new cats that get in the game, they don't understand that. They come in, they glorify a buncha drugs and a buncha nonsense that's really not representative of what the game is about or

like, "Man, they ain't gonna support you if you from here—they gonna look at ya like, 'Ah, I know that fool. I ain't worried about him.'" When Face dropped the song "Scarface," if you go to the club and it come on and everybody singin' it word for word . . . that's what gave everybody motivation to be like, "Aight—I can do this too," you know? Because if he could make 'em feel his words and he could sell records, then I could do that too. Because I was the same way! I used to be like, "Man, they not gonna support—you gotta go out of town. You gotta leave and come back." But once I saw that, to me, that was the turning point of knowin' that the scene can blow up out here and people will support they own. The radio stations, they not gonna do it until the streets—until you blow up in the underground. Once you blew up in the underground and then the streets is followin' you, then they'll jump on the bandwagon, but initially you not gonna get that from the radio stations.

How much did things change for you once the Geto Boys started to break?

It just changed for me from a motivational stand-point. You know, we was still doin' the same things that we was doin', but we saw this guy go from the same level we was on to *this* level. So it was motivatin'. It was like, "Okay, he did it—we can do it too." And then it wasn't even a year or two later when the S.P.C. thing started takin' off and we started seein' firsthand within our own circle. So it was a blessin', man, 'cuz somebody got to be the first. Somebody got to be the person to get the ball rollin' and get things sparked up, and in my eyes it was Face and the Geto Boys that did that. Even though there mighta been cats that came a little bit before them, somebody still had to be the first, to lay that blueprint. And that's what they did.

what it was about in the beginning. Because in the '90s, everybody that you see that's a part of this deal that we're doing here right now, we focused on skills. We was known for that. I traveled, and I knew the things that attracted people to this city, to the artists in this city, and it was talent and skills. It wasn't about a buncha bubblegum rap back then.

You've said to me before that you feel the first time the people in Houston ever gave rap from Houston a real chance was when the Geto Boys released the track "Scarface." Do you think that set everything off on the right foot as far as where everything is now in Houston?

Yeah, I do because that was the first glimpse. For me, that was the first time I ever saw the locals supportin' somebody else that was local. 'Cuz it seemed like before then, that was something that people didn't view as being possible. Because everything had to come from New York, everything had to come from the West Coast. But then it was

You've been sober your whole life. You don't make a big point of it, but it's a fact. How do you feel about the whole culture of syrup, not so much with your clique but with the S.U.C. in particular—do you think it's been a positive thing or a negative one? It's definitely affected the music.

Well, it's a negative thing from the standpoint of that . . . it's not good for you to consume that. But, if I'ma criticize that, then I gotta criticize myself for my own vices. Because just because I might not do that, there's still something else that I might do. Behind closed doors, that might not fall into that particular category. It might be drugs for this cat, it might be . . . sellin' drugs for this cat, it might be stealin' for this cat, or whatever the case might be, so . . . I don't believe in glorifyin' none of the negative things. We do it, but I don't condone glorifyin' it. So I don't knock nobody for what they do. I might not agree with it, but we have to come into the knowledge of understandin' it like, "Okay, we do this, but we in the process of *growth*." As long as you're in this music business you're in the growth process. There's things I rapped about 10 years ago that I wouldn't say now. I listen back, and I'm like, "Man, I shouldn'ta did that." There's things that I did 10 years ago that I wouldn't do now. So . . . I'm gonna look at that person not necessarily for where he is and what he's sayin' now, but I'ma try to see the potential in that artist to grow. And it's whoever's job that may have already been through them stages and came out of 'em . . . if it's me or if it's anybody else . . . it's they job to incorporate that into they music and to chop it up with that person one on one. To try to bring them to that point. It's about just growin', man. I don't condone it, but I'm not gonna condemn them for that.

Do you think that where something like that is concerned, that it's a fine line between glorifying . . . and just telling the truth?

It is. But the thing is . . . the rap audience—they know how to distinguish that difference. Anybody with general intelligence knows how to distinguish the difference between the glorification and the realization. So if you look at a situation where you say, "Okay, this cat braggin' about how many keys he moved and how much dope he sold," you could tell, you know? Because it's gonna pretty much be in your face. But then you got another song that might say, "Well . . . I did what I had to do to survive . . . I didn't wanna do it. I had to stay alive. My mama was strugglin', my daddy . . ." whatever

the case might be. So you look at that from a standpoint of sayin', "Okay, this cat speakin' to the hearts and the minds of the dude who like, 'Man, I don't know no other way. I got to do it the way I'm doin' it.'" The audience knows the difference.

Do you think the whole culture of syrup drives Houston music or just mirrors it?

Nah, nah, it don't drive it, because Houston music was here before that came.

As far as the Screw sound, though.

Not even the Screw sound, because they started off just rippin' freestyles in Screw house. And that wasn't the basis of the lyrics back then. It was mixed in just like people used to say about us . . . they'd say, "Ah, man . . . S.P.C. . . . all they rap about is violence. All they rap about is killin' and this and that." So people would say that was the driving force behind what we did, but it wasn't. Because there's a lot of other things that we incorporated, a lot of knowledge that we gave in our music. We used to be offended that people would say that about us. So I would look at them as the same way. There's too many skilled artists in the S.U.C. There's a lot of artists in the S.U.C. that I love listenin' to, and all of 'em don't talk about that! What happens is, when you got these copycat rappers out here, just the regular run-of-the-mill cats out here that may hear somebody speak on a lil' somethin in a song, and then they try to run with it, and they glorify it. That's what spreads it out in the street like that—people not bein' true to who they are as an artist.

Skimming off the top.

Right. You know, you don't do it like that. Them guys are way deeper than just talkin' 'bout some syrup. And like I say, I can relate, because they used to try to put a brand on us. A reporter told me one time, a journalist for this magazine, "Why all y'all rap about is violence?" I'm like, "You don't listen to our music if that's what you think that's all we rap about." Because that ain't all we rap about.

What led you to form the South Park Coalition?

Well, it wasn't a calling or nothin'. I just wanted to put together an organization of local rappers and unify the city in a sense, because it was a lot of battling and hatred going on in those days. I just felt like we could be stronger if we came together. At the time I didn't know that it would grow like it did. I can't take all the credit for the growth because many other rappers and record labels had a hand in exposing the S.P.C. on a worldwide level.

Is it as powerful today as it was when it was formed . . . or more so?

No, it's nowhere near what it used to be. Our popularity started in 1991, when Ganksta N-I-P signed a deal with Rap-A-Lot Records. N-I-P is an S.P.C. member, and being on a major label like Rap-A-Lot gave him worldwide exposure. Other S.P.C. members were featured on his album, and that provided us with a platform to show the world who we were. We were really the first organized group of rap artists from the South. The S.P.C. consists of many solo artists and groups. We had the South on lock from the early to mid-'90s. I give Rap-A-Lot Records a lot of credit for making us popular as well. These days, our biggest support comes from overseas.

You started in '86?

It was '86 when I was just messin' with it. It was '87 when we really started piecing it together. It was me, but it wouldn't have been nothin' without the cats that was in it, you know what I'm sayin'? N-I-P wasn't even in it in the beginning, it was just dudes I went to school with, dudes like Rapper K and C-Rock, these old-school cats that a lot of people don't even know now. Me and N-I-P and all them used to battle back in the days. Me and N-I-P had this one strong battle that really, like, set everything straight, and we went so hard that everybody who was out there said, "Man, we can't really say who won. It was a tie," and me and him just got cool after that. And we've been like that ever since.

Where was that?

That was at a spot called The Battleground, it's on Bellfort and Martin Luther King. It's a Walgreens now, but it used to be just . . . it was raw over there.

It was the same building, though?

Nah, we wasn't inside. We was outside in the parking lot. But the Walgreens now wasn't there then. It's more beautified now. But it used to look real rough over there. See, he went to Jones High School, I went to Sterling. He didn't wanna battle me in my spot and I didn't wanna battle him in his spot so we just met in the middle. So that's the spot we decided on.

So this was '87—before the S.P.C.?

The S.P.C. was going on, but they wasn't a part of it then, but it was small. Like I said, it was really just cats that went to school with me. So once me and N-I-P battled, he brought his people, I brought my people. But when I got cool with him, his people became my people . . .

And your people became his people . . .

Right, exactly. We all came together. N-I-P, Murder One, A.C. Chill, Klondike Kat—they all went to school together. Me, Rapper K, C-Rock . . . all of us went to school together. So we just mashed our people together . . . me and N-I-P was the leaders. Once me and him got cool, everybody else got cool.

That was after Real Chill?

That was after Real Chill, yeah.

Before Real Chill, when you were in high school . . . what were you listening to?

When I came up, man, rap was new in Houston. I was listening to Run–D.M.C., all the mainstream stuff that was out then. EPMD was around . . . this was right before Boogie Down Productions and Public Enemy era . . .

And N.W.A.

Way before N.W.A., yeah. LL Cool J, Kool Moe Dee, that was what we was jammin' to back in the day, and that's the stuff that really molded us, that made us into the artists we was. I was talking to my partner Braindead tonight about how we was a product of the era that we came up in. That's what we rooted in. That's the type of stuff that we rap about. There was more versatility back then. You know, guys would make an album with . . . they wouldn't make an album with 15, 20 songs on it. They might make an album with 10 songs on it, and the topics was different. They would talk about different things on the songs.

Where did you get the name K-Rino from?

It's a name I done had since I was a young cat, before I even knew anything about rap. It didn't really have no significant meaning to it, but when I started rappin', I didn't have a name. I was just . . . a rapper. So I just took that name and used it as my name, but when I got, you know, smarter in the game, I was able to put an acronym to it: Killer Rhymes Intellectually Nullifying Opponents. I broke it down like that. I been K-Rino so long that it just stuck with me, and I kept it when I started flowin'.

Were other kids rapping when you first came out?

I'll put it like this: When I first started coming into the scene out here, it was around '85, '86, but the deal was that everybody was trying to be so much like Run–D.M.C., Fat Boys . . . whoever was hot at the time. And they'd have talent shows. Every school had a talent show, every club had a rap contest, and you would see the same cats in these contests everywhere you go, depending on what side of town you was on. And me and my boys, we used to go get in the contests just like everybody else, and it was just a competition, man. Boys would show up, all the rappers would be spread out in different parts of the club. Like, we might be over there to ourself, these cats might be over there to theyself. Just all through the club. But you knew who they was. Everybody knew who

was gonna be in the contest, but it didn't all come together 'til the DJ got on the mic and was saying, "Everybody in the rap contest, report to the DJ booth and choose your music." 'Cuz boys didn't have instrumentals. We didn't have keyboards and drum machines then. We was from the days where we used to have to walk up to the DJ booth and say, "Hey, man I wanna rap off that Ice-T." We had to rap off other people instrumentals, you know what I'm sayin'? So it was fun, man, because it was in its purest form, because we was just doin' it for the love. Nobody had records out. We was just doin' it for the competition and for the love. To be able to say, "I won a rap contest." You'd be lucky if the prize was fifty dollars. Or you *really* came up if there was a trophy involved. If one of the schools, the high schools, had a talent show then you might get a trophy. But for the most part, it was for the love, and then when the contest or the talent show was over, it didn't matter who won because boys gonna still be battlin' after, especially if you didn't win the contest. You feel like you got cheated, and "I'm better than him, so we gonna battle. We gonna let the streets decide." It was the fun days back then because it was in its purest form.

What were the other groups out there that were doing it?

I can tell ya, no doubt. On the Northside, it was Willie D. As far as battling goes, Willie D was the king. Willie D had the Northside sewed up. But it was also groups like Royal Flush—they was on Rap-A-Lot for a while. There was another cat named Romeo Poet. These was all on the Northside. Romeo Poet—he a legend, man. He never put a record out to my knowledge, but he was around from way back in the day. Him and Willie D used to have classic battles at this club called the Rhinestone Wrangler back in the day. They had classic battles, man. I mean, got in *fights*. Royal Flush. It was straight love because there wasn't no money involved, you know what I'm sayin'? All those cats were legends, man.

Were they battling with beats behind them, or was it a cappella?

It was a mixture of both, man. I can speak for myself, a lot of my battles that took place was just straight a cappella. And then you gotta think back to back in them days, you'd have a beatbox, be beatboxing for yourself. It was a mixture. Now, in the club situation, it could go either way. You might have a beat, but to my knowledge, to my remembrance it wasn't really too much just rappin' on a beat. The contest was for that, but when the battle started, it was just straight up me against you.

And people would crowd around, circle around you?

Yeah, no doubt, man. Back in them days, a battle could break out anywhere, man. In school . . . man, the hallway. My spot was the furthest corner of the hallway. You pack up in the corner, you got your dudes doin' the beatbox. We'd just tuck in the corner—he'd beatbox and I'm rappin', the crowd is gathered, facing us, with they back to everything else. It was packed, man, just packed, and then you might get a cat that wanna come in and get down. Sometimes we'd just have a flow session. Other times, somebody'd wanna challenge you. People used to come from different schools to rap with us people. So it was a mixture, man.

Who was running the Southside back then?

Back then . . . the Southside, I would have to say me, Klondike Kat, Ganksta N-I-P. Because there wasn't no music industry. Rap-A-Lot was just starting out, and they was doin' they thing.

That was around '86, '87, right?

I know the Ghetto Boys dropped that record "Car Freak," and I think all that stuff came out around '86, yeah. They came out right before us, right before Real Chill. So it might have been '86, or maybe early '87. I'm not sure. But before us you've got Wickett Crickett, O.G. Style, Lester "Sir" Pace, all the "Kidz Jamm" . . . Jazzie Redd. These was the dudes that we looked up to, so if I would have to say "run the Southside," I would have to say *they* was runnin' the Southside. Then we came along, street level, 'cuz I built my name up in the streets,

from battlin' and from rappin' in contests and talent shows.

So out of all that, who would you say was the first solid group from Houston?

The first Houston rap group that was really solid was the Geto Boys—the original Ghetto Boys and the current Geto Boys—because J Prince had the first legitimate record label. He did something that nobody ever thought to do, you know, by starting an independent label, manufacturing and doing it all on his own, getting a buzz in the streets successfully. Because the thing in Houston, the thing, period, was like, "Look, man, if you ain't from New York or LA, you ain't got a chance. You can't win." Because number one: you're not gonna get respected by the rest of the industry. And number two: the locals ain't gonna support you. That was the thing, man—the radio, the local radio station ain't gonna play ya. So nobody even conceived or believed that somebody from out here could come up like that. But Rap-A-Lot put it down. When the Ghetto Boys came out they had Jukebox, Johnny C, Bushwick . . . Ready Red . . . a lot of them was doin' they thing. But they was really the first group, and they was popular, you know what I'm sayin'? They had some good songs, man, and I started to see people accepting a Houston group. We came right behind them, and we got a lot of love behind them.

Who released "Rockin' It?"

My father. My old man, he supported me from day one, so when he found out I was tryin' to rap, he was like, "Man, what you wanna do?" And I said I'm trying to put a record out. And he was like, "Okay, well let's do a record." My old man, he was a hustler, so it wasn't no problem.

Bankrolled it.

The record dropped. No doubt. We made a lot of mistakes. We had the paper to really do a lot of things, but we didn't have the knowledge of the game to make the money work for us the way that it needed to make a success.

Do you think that knowledge even existed in Houston at that point, besides what J was doing?

It didn't exist in the rap industry, because there was a lot of groups that came along in Houston that had successful records maybe in R&B in the past. You had people like Archie Bell & the Drells, and Skipper Lee Frazier was the guy that was really backing them. And they had a big hit, a national hit. So he had plenty knowledge of the game, but that wasn't something that we knew. We didn't know exactly all of the right steps to take to push and market and promote a record the way it needed to be done because, like I said, the game was in such a primitive—just in its infancy at that time, and we was just doin' this, just walkin' in the blind, hittin' our leg on furniture on the way. We had to take a lot of bumps and bruises.

You point out mistakes on that end, but when you go back and listen to the record, do you feel like you had mistakes on that end too?

Well, you gotta understand that the whole of the project wasn't 100 percent from us. In other words, we had other people that had they hand in it, influencing us or advising us or telling us, "Do this, do this, do that." Because we did bring a couple of people in that had been involved in the business on different levels that would tell us, 'cuz we was kids. We was still in high school. So they'd bring this guy in and say, "Yeah, man. He's a producer." Or they'd bring this guy in and say, "He knows a lot about the business." So they would put a hand in and say, "We need to make songs like this, something marketable, this is something we can shop to the labels." So the mistakes on that level . . . I wouldn't put all the blame on us, because there was a lot of ideas and things that we wanted to do that we wasn't able to do, just like being on a major label now. The major label might take a certain amount of creative control from an artist. That's what we went through, even though we was independent. Our inexperience, and dealing with the cats that had experience—they didn't allow us . . . they wasn't just gonna say, "Here's the songs, now y'all do what y'all do." It was like, man, the

production, the concepts—they had a hand in all of that. It got to the point where they was really sayin', "Man, y'all should do this. Let's remake this. I did this beat. See if y'all can put this to that." Really, man, we was commercial back in them days.

Do you feel fortunate that you had a taste of that pretty early? I'd be willing to bet that it led you to where you are now.

Yeah, man. There's always been a part of me that's glad that we didn't just blow up like we was. 'Cuz if we did, I don't think that we'd be around now. Not saying we're just on a major level now, but because of the fact that that wasn't who we was then. So if we'd have came out like that, and had that stamp on us then, by the time I grew up and matured into the kind of artist that I wanted to be and that I am now, it'd have been a contradiction. It wouldn't have been accepted. You know, people hear that record now, and they say they still hear a lot of the present me in it, but they know that it's kinda still night and day.

You got it out of your system.

Yeah, you know, like I got it out of my system, but there's a learning process too. I had to go through that because I'd rather start off bad and then evolve into what I really wanna be and what I really am than to go in reverse order.

Was that some of the impetus behind forming the S.P.C. afterwards?

Well, the formation of the S.P.C. was just something that naturally came, man. I just wanted to have a group . . . a clique. I had a bunch of friends . . . I was a solo artist before the Real Chill thing came along, and I went back to that afterwards because that's what I really am at heart. But I always had partners that rapped. I always had friends that I was real cool with and ran with. We'd go to clubs together, we'd go battle together. We were already an organization, we just didn't have a name to it. So we'd been S.P.C., it just wasn't by that name, or any name.

Did everybody kind of feed off of each other at that point?

Once all the members was in place, then we definitely fed off each other. We made each other better, man. It's like, when you're dealing with that many tight rappers in each other's mitts all the time . . . we're making songs where all of us are on these songs, it's like that all the time. If we all in the room, and I look over there and I see N-I-P writin' his verse, the beat playin', Dope E. over there writin' his verse. Klondike Kat over there writin' his verse. A.C. over there writin' his verse. You know in your mind—you don't know what's on they paper, but you know in your mind, *mine can't be weak*. So you step your game up. There's a difference between me sitting in a room by myself writing a verse, because I don't feel no pressure. It was really righteous competition. We was competitive with each other, but not from a negative standpoint. It's like, "I don't wanna be the weakest one on this song."

Was it the same kind of competition you felt in the battles?

The battles were competition, but back in them days it wasn't friendly. It's like a war, man. You know, the object in a rap battle is to humiliate your opponent. I don't wanna just beat you, I wanna humiliate you. Like in a boxing match, you're trying to knock this dude out. You don't want him to ever . . . you want to be considered to be the best. You don't even want it to be close. So back in them days, it was real, genuine dislike. We didn't really like each other. That's how it was. But, that kind of competition, even through all that dislike, when you hear this person, you still have sense enough and respect enough to say, "Nah, this dude is good." You see what I'm sayin'? So you not gonna be like, "No, the dude can't rap." Respect comes out of it, especially when you done bumped heads three or four times. It's like Ali and Frazier. They didn't like each other. They fought three times. But after that third fight, they had respect for each other.

Even though they probably still disliked each other.

Yeah, they probably still disliked each other, but there was respect. And then what comes into it is, "I don't even dislike this person no more."

How did the club scene change in the late '80s, when Rap-A-Lot started releasing more records— were there a lot more people in Houston listening to rap and coming to the shows?

Well, people was listening to rap, but they was listening to rap from everywhere else. When the Geto Boys did they thing, that was the first taste that people in Houston actually wanted to hear an artist from they own city. When the Geto Boys had this song "Assassins," and they had this other song, an instrumental called "My Word." Man, that's all I used to hear. People ridin' down the street bumpin' their bottom 'cuz they had that bass in it. Then when Face signed with Rap-A-Lot, that single "Scarface" that he dropped?

When he was still Akshen, right?

Yeah, he was still called Akshen on that particular song. But the bottom line is, that song set Houston on fire. That's the first song that just . . . everybody and they mama was just lovin'. It would come on in the club, everybody was lovin' it. That's when I first started sayin', "Man, you know, we can do this from out here. 'Cuz Houston will accept you." The thought all them years was, "They ain't gonna support you out here." 'Cuz they was lookin' at you like, "Oh, I know that fool. He ain't nobody. He ain't anything. He ain't Run. He ain't LL." Face broke that barrier down.

This was like '89, before the Geto Boys broke nationally.

Right, right. That's really the song that set it off, that "Scarface" single. Then when Willie D came into the mix, and they dropped that *Grip It . . .* album, it was over after that. Because they had contrast. Face was this type of rapper, Willie D was totally different. Two different types of rappers in the same group. And contrast is what makes any great rap duo. Even though Bushwick was rappin' too. But in the forefront was Face and Willie D. If you look at any of the great rap duos in the history of rap, the two rappers are totally different. Whether it be Run and D.M.C., Pimp C and Bun B, 8Ball and MJG, Andre and Big Boi from Outkast, there's contrast there, and to me, that's the formula.

How long have you realized that?

Really, man, that didn't come to me until about a year or two ago. I might have been on the internet, and somebody made a post about the best duos. And as I was reading what they had, that's when it hit me, that the thing about this whole thing is that these two rappers are totally different in every group. Because if they both sound the same . . . you know, you gotta have something to distinguish one from the other. That's what draws interest from the fans, because they can be totally different, but there's still a chemistry there. That's what made us successful, it's just that it wasn't a duo. There was more of us. I don't rap like N-I-P, N-I-P don't rap like Kat, Kat don't sound like Dope E., Dope E. don't sound like Point Blank. Everybody was different, and that's what people would say was the main thing that attracted them to the S.P.C., because we would always do these click songs at the end of whoever album it was, and the point behind that was that every style would come in different. Everybody was bringin' something different to the table. But it was chemistry at the same time.

Was that coming into play when you were making *Worst Rapper Alive*?

Well, the thing is that I'm a solo artist, so that never really crosses my mind when I'm doing a project. By the time I did *Worst Rapper Alive* . . . see, I'm seasoned now, so it was just another album. But all my albums take on an identity of they own, they got their own personality to them, based on the mood I was in mentally or where I was mentally when I was creating them.

What do you think the best song you've ever done lyrically would be? What are you most proud of?

Lyrically, it's hard to say. Probably one song that jumps out is the song on *Fear No Evil* called "Two Pages." For just pure lyrical skills, that's one of my best. There ain't a hook. It's called "Two Pages" because it's just two pages of straight lyrics, start to finish, and I got another one like that on the *No Mercy* album called "Non-Stop." It's nonstop all the way through. Those two are pretty lyrical. I got one on *Worst Rapper Alive* called "Loaded," but to be honest with you, man, I couldn't say. I couldn't say. I'm working on a new album now, and I got a song on that's called "Four Minute Warning," and it's just four minutes of lyrics. I think that's the best one out of all of them.

Can we hear a verse?

I can give you a snippet. Just a little piece. I gotta make sure I say something . . . y'all can edit it. In the first few bars I say: My mother had an abortion / years before I spit a rhyme out / they threw me in the trash but two hours later I climbed out / with blood and afterbirth, I started on a blind route / civilians were threatened by the sight of a newborn baby with a lion's mouth / I calculate and repopulate / at age four I started removing my own organs just to see how they operate / I can make the apocalypse end with a preposterous spin / I'm an alien python that sheds rhinoceros skin / you choke and gag when the words are spoken fast / I smoke and blast paragraphs / my throat can last in a cast swallowing broken glass / I provide infinite homicide / making you die the death that every human in history ever died / I worship on the Sabbath / then put bodies in cabinets / spared the sinners and killed the saints 'cuz they was arrogant / what precedes the millimeter or 33s / I'm a self-producing species / your brain holds less intelligence than my feces . . . that's just a little bit of it. Just a little something, man. That's on the new one. I'm looking to finish that at the end of January.

What's it called?

Ah, right now I don't even have a title for it, man. I'm just gettin' all the tracks together. I got about 10 songs written. But it's gonna be alright.

Peter said he asked you a few months ago about *Worst Rapper Alive*, and you responded by saying that there was something about it that didn't make you like it as much as you did the last two. Now that it's out, do you feel any different?

Nah, I feel the same. I'll put it like this: My albums . . . I compete with myself when I make an album, when I write a song, because they all are going to be judged up against each other. But when you drop so many projects, people are always gonna have they favorites, you know, and say this one was better than this one. But for me, I have to make sure that in my mind, every one is better than the last one. Every one got to be better than the last one. So, I know it's a good album, but I felt like it could have been better. I felt like it could have been better just based on the standard or the level I'd been coming with based on the previous two before that, on *The Hit List* and on *Fear No Evil*. When I got to *Worst Rapper Alive*, I was like, "Well, I got a lot more songs now, but I don't feel like it's on the level that the other two was." Not saying it's far from it. If the other ones are considered an eight, then *Worst Rapper Alive* wouldn't be no less than a seven in my eyes, but I'm trying to make it a nine, know what I'm sayin'?

I've thought about that a lot, though—that when you think about records that are important to you in your life, you can sit there and argue that such and such album wasn't as good as the one that preceded it, but I've always thought that it's about where your life lines up with a particular piece of work, either as a listener or an artist. Is it the same as a lyricist, a rapper, that you can argue its merit based on where you were in yourself when you completed it?

It's like this basketball game we're watching. The deal is this here: When Dr. J came along, when he retired, it was like he set the standard. "There'll never be another Dr. J," this and that. Then Jordan come along, and go to another level. "Oh, there'll never be another Jordan." So really, it's about that era. People still tell me that *Danger Zone* is my best album. I dropped that in '95. So, they entitled to their opinion, but when somebody tell me that an album that's 10 years old or seven years old is better than something I recently dropped, that's a motivation to me, a challenge to me, 'cuz I'm like, "Nah, that's not how it's supposed to be." I don't even want the fans to consider that to be the case, to be like, "I don't feel no progression." For me, I'm like, "I'm elevatin'." So I can't allow people to listen to a 10-year-old album and say it's better than a two-month-old album. Even though there's still a compliment mixed in there, the best compliment someone can give you is to say, "Oh, his music is timeless. I can still listen to it today, and it's still as relevant as it was when he first dropped it." So that's cool too, but for me, I compete, man. I compete against myself. You can't never take a break as an artist. A lot of artists, they get in the game, they get a little success, they get a little fame or whatever, and then you start seeing they level dip off. They start dropping off 'cuz they get relaxed. But the bottom line is . . . whatever you establish yourself to be, and whatever bar you set for yourself, you got to always equal that or exceed that, because people might be hearing about you. You got a reputation. "Man this dude, K-Rino, man . . ." everybody tellin' them about this cat, he good, he this, he that. And then they hear you, and you not at your best. You took a break, took a day off on that particular verse. First impressions is lastin', you know? So I got to make sure that, like Michael Jordan said when he was talking about basketball . . . they asked him one time, "How come you play so hard, and y'all only playin' against the Clippers? The Clippers the worst team in the league." He said, "Because there might be somebody that's never seen me play before, and somebody been tellin' 'em about Michael Jordan." He got to be Jordan every time out. So, if I set a standard for myself, whatever it is, I got to live up to that standard every time I grab a pen or some paper and start writing a verse. Because I don't want that person hearing me for the first time to say, "He ain't all that, what everybody make him out to be." Because first impressions stick with people.

You spoke about there being some things about _Worst Rapper Alive_ that you didn't like as much as the ones before it. Do you feel like it can still be progressive, even if you don't like it as much?

Progressive to me?

Progressive to you. Everyone else is on the outside, and how a record ties into or affects their lives is different from how it affects the artist.

It would have to be considered progressive to me after a certain period of time, to where I could see the effects of the album or what impact the album might have had on the people. At first creation, I might say, "Well, nah, I didn't really take it to the next level like I thought I did." But then when the album hit the world and people start saying, "Well, this song changed my life in this way," and "We wanna use this song for this and that," or "This song really touched me here," or "Everybody's feelin' this," then in hindsight I can look back and say, "Okay, maybe I did elevate, and I just didn't perceive it."

Do you think it's because at that point, once you sort of separate yourself from it, you see it as an outsider? You're never gonna listen to it as a listener would . . .

I'm my own worst critic, man. I'll always be my own worst critic. But I write from the perspective of the outside lookin' in.

Because it's something that you wanna hear.

What it is . . . I put myself in the room with the person who went and bought the album, and they sittin' up in they room or they car listening to it. So when I write a certain line, I always envision in my mind how people is gonna react to it when they hear this line. Sometimes, you be like, "They gonna trip out when they hear this." Sometimes you be like, "Nah, that ain't good enough." So yeah, I step on the outside. You know, you gotta have an out-of-body experience because if you get too self-centered and too internal with what you're creatin', you start getting tunnel vision, and you'll fool

yourself. You gotta make sure that you're writin' for you, writin' from your heart, but at the same time, people are gonna be able to hear it and feel it.

But it's a unique middle ground that a lot of artists skip over and don't understand. Even putting that record on to hear as an outsider, you still created what you wanted to hear.

See, what you're doing is you're giving the people _you_, but on the same token you have to speak the language of the people, so you have to do it in a way to where they will relate. Like you say, it's a middle ground you gotta reach. You gotta be able to say, "Okay, this is me, without question this is me. But on the same token this is me presenting it in a way that you will understand me better." If that answers the questions.

So how do you collect stories? I asked you in another interview about your dreams, and how you reference those sometimes. Where do you draw from—do you go out into the world to try and absorb stuff, or does it all just sort of pop in?

It's a mixture, man. It depends on what kind of story it is. If it's a regular, down-to-earth hood story, it may be something that's based on actual events. If it's some type of mental, make-you-think type of story, then it might be something that was just inspired off of my own thought of what I needed to be projecting to people at the time. Like, people need to hear this, on this level. But with me, the stories all come about the same. Once I get the concept, the ending of the story comes first. The best way for me to write a story, I have to know how it's gonna end first. I don't make it up as I go along and then try to lock up on the ending. If I get the ending, I'm gone from there.

Is the beginning important?

The beginning is important, but the ending writes the beginning for me. It's like watching a movie. The most important part of a movie is that people wanna know how it's gonna end. That's why people watch it, whether it's a scary movie or whatever it is, it's gonna upset you if you dedicated two and a half hours to this movie and then the ending is boo-boo, you see what I'm saying? You're like, "Aw, that's it?" So, I make sure that the ending is gonna be strong, so that the ending creates the rest of the song for me. I can't explain it, but that's what happens.

How long do they gestate? You've got that notebook, and you write stuff in it all the time. Say you've got a notebook full of stuff—does any part of that find its way into your lyrics two or three years down the line, or is it a group that you get out with each album?

Nah, say I mighta wrote something in 2002, but I didn't use it in 2002, I used it in 2005, because when I wrote it in 2002, it didn't fit. It wasn't time for it yet. So, I might be on another concept in 2006 and say, "You know what?" And that line will pop in my head and say, "Yeah, this fits here," and you go back and you get it.

You still own it.

Exactly, and nobody's ever heard it. So yeah, that happens. Every rapper does that, though. Now, what you don't wanna do—you don't want to be the type of person that recycles lyrics that you done already exposed to the world. That's the challenge of it, to keep coming up with new, original lyrics and things that nobody has heard you say and do, because a lot of rappers, they recycle words, say the same stuff over and over again.

You also don't want to stitch together a bunch of stuff that doesn't work together just to have a track.

No doubt. The best songs are the ones where the lyrics just fall out of your brain. When you gotta just strain and make yourself come up with something, then it's time to put the pen down and relax and try again another day. But a lot of times, man, when you know you got a concept and it's on, it's clickin'—you gonna just be flowin' with the pen, just smoothly flowin'. People ask me, "Man, how long did it take you to write such and such?" And it might be a song that, when they hear it, it's

a complex song, so they feel like, "It musta took him weeks to write that." So they be surprised or they just take it as, "Oh, he just playin' around, he arrogant." Nah, man, I wrote that in an hour and a half. 'Cuz when you clickin', it just comes out.

Compared with where a lot of rappers aren't actually rapping about anything.

Yeah, it's true, man. I blame it a lot on the industry's influence on rap now. But I also put some responsibility on the rappers, you know. Because we know that there's certain songs that we should make that's supposed to be a benefit, supposed to be helpful to the listener, and we all guilty of not doin' that as much as we should. But at the same time, I grew up at a time when you could hear Public Enemy, KRS-One, X-Clan—you'd hear songs like that on the radio. You see these cats' videos all the time. Now, when young black kids that's listenin' to rap, when they started gettin' into this type of music and started becoming more conscious, the industry put they hand on it and was like, "Nah, we need to take they focus off of this, and put they focus on something that's not so militant." So now, you see the materialism. You see sex, drugs, murder. You see these type of things being pushed to the forefront to where that's all you see, and they have an influence on the kids that's goin' out buying it. True enough. I don't really knock the artists that are rappin' like that because I'd be a hypocrite to do that. I still make a lot of songs that ain't the most positive songs in the world. But I always say, at least give one or two, just to show the people that, "Hey, you know what? I have fun, I party, I talk about what I talk about, but let's be real. I do care about what's going on in my community." I don't glorify the negative parts of the hood. *Speak* on the negative parts of the hood, but offer solutions in your music if you can. Because some of them . . . you can't blame a rapper for talking about what he talking about if he don't know no better, or if he don't know the answers, you know? I can't expect a dude to offer a solution that he don't have. So I'm for all these cats out here, you know, I wish them all the best. But I wish that all of us, me included, would start being more responsible for what we say. Because you know, that's some serious blood on your hands, when you say things that have that kind of influence on people that's listenin' to it, and then they go out and may act on somethin' that you said. It happens, and people will say, "Man, you can't blame that on the . . ." No, you can't blame it entirely on us because it ain't our job to necessarily raise the children. That falls on the parents, but the kids is listenin' to rappers more than they listenin' to they parents these days! So, we got to help raise 'em, man. We got to.

DJ Domo

LA PORTE

Most folks became aware of DJ Domo when he picked up the vacancy in Geto Boys after DJ Ready Red left the group around the time of *We Can't Be Stopped*. But Domo was a staple of the scene by then. DJ Domination grew up in La Porte, a town on Galveston Bay a half hour southeast of Houston, where the Battle of San Jacinto went down. He made the drive at night in the late-'80s, coming into Houston to hear what was playing in the clubs, then coming back to play those clubs himself. When DJ Domo became Geto Boys' DJ, he also became Scarface's DJ, and soon he was with Devin the Dude and Coughee Brothaz, not just spinning but producing as well.

PHOTO: SAMA'AN ASHRAWI

How did you come to first work with Devin?

Shit . . . I first met Dev when the Odd Squad got signed to Rap-A-Lot. I was already DJing for Geto Boys by then. I was just DJing back then. I kinda met all of them—Dev and Jugg [Mugg] and Rob [Quest]—when they signed to Rap-A-Lot. And then as soon as we met up, we just started kickin' it. So I started goin' over to Rob's house. Rob really the one that kinda started me out doin' beats and shit. Watchin' him, watchin' Mike Dean. In the studio with Joe. Joe showed me a lot of shit. You know N.O. Joe? Joe produce a lot of Face shit. He does a lot of UGK.

Who was doing Devin's beats then? Just Rob?

Rob did all of the music. Rob pretty much did the music, and then in the studio, Mike Dean was there, Joe was there for certain songs. Everybody kinda touched together. I did cuts on the Odd Squad album. I wasn't doin' beats back then.

When did you start working with the Geto Boys?

I started fuckin' with Face first. There used to be a club out on 290 and Antoine called Amnesia, and me and my partner Wiz [M.D.] used to DJ out there and shit. Bushwick and Face lived out there, so they used to come through the club. So we just started kickin' it. I used to go over there, pick them up. We would just kick it. This was about '90.

When did you meet Willie D?

I first probably met Will right around that time. I never really hung out with Will around then, though, you know? I used to hang out with Bill and Face. Bill and Face and Ready Red sometimes. But back that far I never really hung out with Will. I used to see him and shit when I used to go do shows back then. When that first Geto Boys album, that *Grip It! On That Other Level* . . . that's pretty much when I would see Willie D, 'cuz he used to go do shows. I been seein' them since they put out that first "Car Freak" record, when it was a different lineup. I seen all of them 'cuz I was DJin' all them years. And they was from Houston, so naturally I'd go to the record store and I'd see all the records, so I'd know what's what, you know? So, since the first record they put out I been knowin' 'em. I used to be around before I started DJing for them because my partner Wiz . . . he produced, like, that old Def IV shit. You remember that? Some old Rap-A-Lot shit, the old Def IV. He produced one of their singles. This was way before Willie and all them got with Rap-A-Lot.

Were you working for Rap-A-Lot first?

No, no. I was DJing in clubs . . . I always was fuckin' with Face in the clubs and shit. It was like there was a point in time where Face was like, "You gonna be my DJ when my shit come out." So I was kinda goin' through his shit already, and there was just a turn of events, like when Bill got shot and everything. Right around this time was when Ready Red quit the group. He didn't wanna DJ for 'em no more. Everybody telling me, "Go DJ for the Geto Boys." Finally, I found them. I went to the mall one day, to the Galleria. Face's uncle was workin'. He worked at Footlocker. I see him and he's like, "Hey, gimme a ride over here by Brad [Scarface] house." So I took him over there, seen Brad he was like, "Come on DJ for us," and shit. So I went over to [John] Bido house . . . he had an apartment on the Southwest side. I go over to Bido's crib. They got another dude in there, my homie Marcus Love. They had Marcus in there DJin'. They tryin' to get him. Somebody else had brought Marcus through there. They goin' through the show or whatever.

That's all they got over there. They got two records. J Prince over there, J made the show. Just the two records, "This how the show go." So the dude over there, he going through it, steady fuckin' up, steady fuckin' up. So they was like, "Shit, let Domo try it." So I went over there and did that shit in one time. Didn't have to do it again. They was pretty much like . . . they was gonna take the other dude out first. They was like, "We gonna take dude out, and then you can come back on the next one." Willie, Bill, and Face was like, "Hell nah. We gotta fuck with Dom." I had my shit tight, know what I'm sayin'?

You'd already been around them for a long time.

Yeah, I'd been fuckin' with them already.

How long before you took over?

I was fuckin' with them for at least a year before I started DJin' for 'em.

You started spinning for them in '91, right? What were those tours like—the ones around the time "Mind Playing Tricks" broke?

The first tours was like the livest ones we ever went on. It was cool for the fact that it was at a crossroads in time where we had groups on the tour. Old school groups . . . Latifah was on there. MC Lyte . . . we had Public Enemy. Geto Boys and Public Enemy kinda co-headlined the whole thing. Some nights we would go last, some nights they would go last. Depends on where we was. Naughty by Nature was on there. Leaders of the New School. Ice-T was on some of 'em. Just the way the whole tour was set up. I still got it—it was a little book with an itinerary. Everything in there—where you goin', where you gonna stay, what time you gonna leave. What time you gonna get to the next city. What time the food gonna be served, what time you do your shit. Everything. Never been so organized since.

How did the Geto Boys fit into that tour? I mean, you were way different from anyone else on that tour.

It was some funny-ass shit, dude. I tell people, man . . . back then, tours were big. They had the whole stages and shit. Public Enemy . . . Naughty by Nature . . . they had big-ass stage props and shit. Then we get up there. This our backdrop right here—we got a little bitty-ass thing hangin' up by the ceiling and shit. Sittin' on a banquet table with the turntables.

Did people appreciate it?

Yeah, they used to love that shit! We used to go out there and jam. That was a big-ass show, dude. "Mind Playing Tricks," when that shit used to come on, people would lose they mind.

How long did that last? The energy, the popularity that that song brought?

Yeah, man, that song always . . . still to this day you put that song on . . . people go crazy. It's still a big song at the shows.

How were the Scarface tours compared to a Geto Boys tour?

It was kind of different . . . I mean, the crowd's kind of similar, you know what I'm sayin'? The people and the reactions and shit, as far as himself I mean . . . you're just dealin' with Face himself instead of havin' to deal with all three of them.

Maybe a little bit more relaxed?

Yeah, when it's all three of them, you got three motherfuckers sayin' three different things, and you gotta try to listen to everybody and still try to make the shit jam.

When did you first start DJing?

I first started DJing in '83, in my room, just bull-shittin'. I DJed my homeboy's birthday party. Rode down the street on my bike with a backpack full of records. Went over to his house, and he ain't have no equipment. He had one turntable, so I sat there and played the record, took it off, played another one. Played the record, took it off. We were still in junior high, you know? We were still havin' little parties and shit. The next year we had two turntables. The next year after that we had four speakers. That was in La Porte. That's where I'm from out there. Down 225, down near the water near Baytown. Not too far.

When did you first start playing out in the clubs?

I think the first club I DJed at probably was a club in Baytown. My homeboy Charles Bush . . . as a matter of fact had a club on OST. I first started DJing for Charles . . . man, as a matter of fact, on OST at Club Infinity we used to be live on the radio over there. I first played "Mind Playing Tricks" live on the air at that club. Live on the radio. Me and Steve Moye and Reggie Effekt used to DJ in there. We had four turntables set up.

That was like early '90s.

Had to be '91, something like that. Infinity. That club in Baytown was called Club Soda, something like that. I used to DJ at a couple other clubs that was live on the radio. I can't remember the name of the motherfuckers.

Rob Quest

THIRD WARD

As one-third of Devin the Dude's first group Odd Squad, producer and rapper Rob Quest has been on the perimeter of several movements in Houston since the late '80s, and he's been deep in every one of Devin's projects, including Coughee Brothaz, the group featuring fellow Odd Squad rapper Jugg Mugg, who has been a constant companion of Rob's over the years because he helps him get around. In 2017, Rob moved to California to work with Houston producer Mike Dean (Geto Boys, Rap-A-Lot, Kanye West, Travis Scott) and to try getting used to a big new city full of big new sounds.

You feeling it out there in LA?

I'm loving it, actually. It's going good. I'm knee-deep in the mix. I had a little setback last week, man, here's something I haven't done in a while, man—I injured myself. This is the first time in a long time that my blindness has come out of nowhere, man. It was all my fault. I was doing a little too much. I was kind of getting beside myself. You know, I'm real mobile for a blind person, so I don't use the cane a lot of times. I can kind of, you know, since I was able to see once upon a time it's easy for me to visualize and gain my bearings and kind of maneuver around without a cane a lot of times. So I was doing too much, and I fell—from an attic. One floor, maybe like 10 feet. I had a rotating fan in my hand. I was carrying it all downstairs because I didn't want to make another trip up-and-down the steps. You know how we multitask and grab everything so we won't have to come back? So I had my, like, backpack, water, my phone, a fucking fan, and . . . you know, I was maneuvering in the dark,

basically. With all of that stuff. Going down some steps. I misjudged where I was, and I fell, and I had to go to the hospital and everything, so I'm still trying to recuperate. But you know, I'm a warrior.

Yeah, well you're getting used to a whole different environment and everything, right?

Well, it only takes me one or two times to be somewhere and I know where I am. Like, literally I can maneuver without a cane. But this particular time, it didn't happen. So it humbled me, you know, because sometimes I get beside myself. I do so much without a cane—I'm not like the average blind person—but then I have to watch that. I forget sometimes, I am blind.

How old were you when you went blind?

I was like 18.

How did it happen?

Cataract and glaucoma was the main cause of it, but it started from a condition called sarcoidosis. And I don't know if you're familiar with sarcoidosis—it kind of made headlines when it ended up in Bernie Mac. That's what he died from. It affected his lung and brains but mine affected my kidneys and liver, so in essence what it did is enlarged and inflamed the liver and the kidneys, and the spleen. So in turn, of course, you know, your liver and your kidneys, when something goes wrong with that it can cause other problems in the body. Me—in my eyes.

ROB QUEST, DEVIN THE DUDE, JUGG MUGG. PHOTO: LANCE SCOTT WALKER

So that's connected to the organ issues you had a couple years ago?

Well, that's the . . . yeah, ultimately, my liver succumbed to the sarcoidosis.

Right, so you had the transplant.

So I got the transplant.

And how does that feel?

I mean . . . I don't really know. I haven't had any complications from it, so I'm gonna say great.

It fits, right?

Yeah. Oh, I'll tell you a funny story about that. So, you remember that old muffler commercial, used to have the Midas?

"The Midas touch?"

"We'll make it fit!" Remember that used to be like? Well, this is like we'll make it fit. Right? So, right before I got the transplant, my mom told me the story of what the doctor said: "Well, we saw the donor, it's a little large, it's a little big, but we'll make it fit." My mom—I remember mom cracking up because he sounded like the muffler dude: "We'll make it fit."

So you got that new muffler installed?

Yeah, like it ain't the right one, but we'll make that motherfucker fit. They was like, we'll make it fit. I'm like, damn, y'all gonna cram it in there or something? I already know you can just carve off a little bit.

Were you already producing when you were 18?

I had been dabbling. I wouldn't call it producing then. My electronic item was a toy, made by Mattel Electronics. It came out in, like, the mid-'80s, and it was called a Synsonics Drum, and what it was, was a little flat component with four gray pads on it. You had these, I want to say 16 little bitty buttons down at the bottom that had a repeat mode that you could hold down and play. So it was, in essence, so cool, you can just take, like, an audio jack and plug it to your line in or your phone box or something, you know, so it was like a beatbox. But it was more like just for fun, it was almost like some lunchroom table type shit going on. But producing didn't come in until the late '80s, when my mom bought me my first real piece of gear, which was an Ensoniq EPS keyboard, which is kind of like the little brother to the real famous ASR, Ensoniq ASR that a lot of producers deem classic. So no, I wasn't really producing. I wouldn't call it producing then, not quite.

Yeah, but I guess I'm more thinking about just sort of knowing your way around a machine by sight.

No I was always blind, you know, so it was always a thing, having to memorize what things were, I always had my mom or dad or somebody around me to really show me exactly what it was that I was doing, and it was just up to me to kind of memorize and kind of play around with it, get familiar with it, trial and error. And it wasn't just like all of a sudden I woke up blind, it was slowly but surely, I was losing my sight little by little. You know, I think it got to a point where it was like, okay, we have this surgery where you can regain all of your sight back or you could lose your sight, but eventually you're gonna lose your sight so what do you want to do? So I took a chance, you know what I mean. I was gonna eventually lose it, it had gotten to . . . I was, I think my last . . . right before I had the surgery, I think I was 20/2200. That was the lenses that were the Coke bottle type glasses then, almost binoculars. They call them monoculars. I was close anyway, so I was like, "Fuck these glasses, man, let me just go ahead and let's try it, let's see what happens."

And it didn't work—the surgery didn't work?

It didn't work. But I had already been prepared. Like, while I was at school, they were already teaching me braille, and I was just kind of learning to live and adapt to this lifestyle by then. I was already through it, yeah.

Did you already know what direction you were going as that was happening? Because it sounds like you're talking about many, many years that was taking place. Did you already know you were gonna make music?

No, not really. I was an aspiring drummer and dirt bike enthusiast, freestyle, skateboard, through, you know, seventh grade. I was playing punk rock, stuff like that.

Me too.

I was into Dead Kennedys, Black Flag, Oingo Boingo. BMX freestyle and that kind of stuff. So, you know, seventh, eighth grade, I was not thinking about making rap music. By then it was like, Run-D.M.C. first album probably was out.

What year were you born?

'71.

You're two years older than me so you would've been hearing all that stuff, like, '84, and I was hearing it probably like '86 because I'm younger. I got to middle school a couple years after you.

Yeah, yeah. I was into the MTV hair bands. Twisted Sister, Quiet Riot, all those . . . the interest in MTV was huge. Yeah, so I got to see all that. I got to see that. That was cool.

When did rap take over?

Rap kind of took over, kind of like I said, when I was really, 17, 18—when I was almost blind. I was, kind of was sedentary, a lot more in the house. I wasn't doing the freestyle bikes and skateboarding and playing drums. All that kind of stopped. So, now I'm in the house, listening to more music. Doing indoor type of stuff. Geeking out, reading books. That kind of thing. That's probably when the music took over. I'm going to say like '86, '87. I was pretty much going to the record store every couple weeks, buying albums, and just really absorbing a lot of music. Just buying records. I had cassettes and had a lot of music by then in my collection. It kind of evolved while I was the house.

Did you find that . . . were your ears evolving? Is that a thing? That's a real thing?

Most definitely. It was almost scary at first. Especially when I first lost my sight because now I'm hearing every fucking thing. It was just freaking me out. I'm hearing all outside. I'm hearing trains from miles away, people talking, and it's real weird at first. It's almost scary. I just remember just having to get used to fucking hearing so much. It's like, I don't want to hear all that actually. I almost wanted to block it out. Why am I hearing down the block?

I noticed that you kind of mix yourself whenever you're in a place where a bunch of people are talking. You don't talk very loud. You keep yourself down at a level. I don't know if the visual has

anything to do with it. But I just noticed that when I've had conversations with you, you talk only as loud as you need to.

Right. I'm not that loud dude anyway.

But is that because the only perception you have of that environment is what you're listening to at the same time that you're talking?

Well, I guess you could say that. Sometimes people tend to mix-up blindness. They want to talk extra loud.

Right! What is that?

They're confused. I'm blind, not deaf. I can hear real good.

When you did start getting into making beats, how do you organize? How do you organize a sound? I know your ear can identify sounds in all kinds of ways.

Right.

If you go, "Okay, I want to save this sound."

It is definitely different now that I've gone over to computer music. Computer generated music now is—the organization is tremendous. It's a lot better now. I'm able to organize and arrange things. I have my own little library inside my drum machine. People always be like, "How do you know where all the sounds are?" I can scroll with this jog wheel on my machine, right? I can spin and rotate it so many times. I'll be in a certain area of the alphabet and this giant list of things that I have. The sound base that I have. Then, once I load one up, I'll say, "Okay. I know what sound that is. I'm in this area." Patience. A lot of memorization. A lot of people ask me, do I count steps? I don't do that. You can almost set a visual, a mental picture, in your head, idea where something is. I do little, smart little blind tips. I make markers. I make notches on things. I tie rubber bands. I make knots. I do my own little subtle tricks to know where certain stuff is. It's like stuff you see out in public, if you look at little things. For instance, on your keyboard. Most

keyboards, universal keyboards for a computer, on the "F" and the "J" key there's a little dot on every keyboard you see. That's the home row keys. I know if I put my pointer finger on the "F" and a pointer finger on the "J" key, that's the home row keys. That's a little blind thing for blind people. That's just that little certain spot right there. I do little shit like that with everything.

A mixing board must be a pretty important tool for you too, right?

I do have a little mixing board. Once you know one mixing board, you damn near know them all because you have your levels. They're all pretty much organized the same way. Like with anything, once you show me something once or twice I'm pretty much there. It's just a matter of trial and error and kinda playing with it. I had an actual learning curve for my machine, but I pretty much kind of got it. There's still a few things that I don't use very often that I might still require some help on. But, for the most part, I can compose a song by myself.

I would imagine for those areas where you need help that once somebody kinda gets you familiar with what it is that's there, that kind of takes you to the next level, right?

As a matter of fact, my man, my partner that I'm working with out here, it's a Japanese producer who I'm out here living with. He just showed me some stuff recently. He had to figure out a way to kind of teach it to me because a lot of things everybody does with a mouse. There's actually keystrokes for everything that you can do with your mouse. A lot of people don't know there are actually keystrokes to those things that you can do to make the same thing happen that you do with the mouse. As he discovered, he showed me. "Okay, you don't need the mouse to try to place that fucking cursor in this certain spot. You do this keystroke. It'll take you right here to it." The Mac computer has a voiceover adaptability function—all Macs do—and it talks. It's basically the screen reader. When I navigate the arrow around, it's telling me where I am.

Just constant feedback then.

It's not one of those voice commanded computers. It's just telling me where I am, and it's up to me to do all the operations and the functions.

It's just there to kind of move you along wherever you are on the screen.

Now, the machine, it doesn't have any adaptability. Actually, I'm working with Native Instruments to try to open up the script for some type of audio or some kind of screen reader feedback, but I'm pretty much learning that just by memorizing the buttons and layout of the actual controller. It's just like if you had a remote control—your remote control to your TV—if you closed your eyes, you could probably work it. It's your remote control. You know at the top right corner, that's the power off button. I don't know where yours is. Where the two elongated up-and-down type switches are, that's the channel changer. If you was to feel it with your thumb, you could probably maneuver it with your eyes closed. Same thing.

How old were you when you met Devin and those guys? Did you meet Devin first, or did you know Jugg Mugg first?

I met Devin first. That had to be, I want to say in '88 or in '89. I met him at a talent contest at TSU. We met at the show. I thought that was pretty cool because his personality allows him to be really outgoing and to ask questions. I think what amused him is that I brought my drum machine to the auditions. You know, most people bring their cassette or CD. I don't know why I didn't bring a cassette or CD. I don't know. I just brought my actual musical equipment, which is unheard of. Could you imagine somebody doing a show, they bring in a fucking MPC? You'll be like, "Alright, I'm lit."

Well, it's meant for that, I guess.

I mean, it really is. Honestly, it is. And a lot of people do perform with their musical gear in there. But, you know, back then that was unheard of. That wasn't what people was doing.

So, that was in there cause what you had back then was an MPC by that point?

No, no, no. I had a, it's called a Yamaha RX7. Almost sound like a car—Mazda RX7. But it was a Yamaha drum machine. I had the song that I was going to perform, one of my many little programs that I had on there, and I brought it up and I hooked it up. I was like, "Yeah, I got this cord, can you get this speaker in?" And I played it out loud, and it kind of blew everybody away. Because they were like, "Oh, shit." They ended up afterwards to be like, "Yo, can you make me a beat?" You know, like I'm rocking over an instrumental, you know, somebody's instrumental. I think it was Roger Troutman's, "I Want To Be Your Man," instrumental. And Devin was like, "I want you to make a beat to it, like an 808. But some boom to it. So I can really rock it." And I was like, "Yeah, I'll do that." And then the rest is history.

Had you worked with anybody before? I mean, you were producing beats . . .

Oh no. No, I never worked with anybody before. My mom forced me to go to that contest. I had just been in the house.

So the first person who ever approached you about working together on anything was Devin the Dude?

That's right. He was called the Fat Square Twista.

Fat Square Twista, that was the name he was going by?

That was his name. Fat Square Twista. 'Cuz he rolled big old-ass joints.

So y'all already had that in common.

Well, no. I wasn't smoking. Remember, I was green. I was a kid losing his sight. I was just sitting house, so I'm real sedentary. Start kind of gaining weight. Start getting kind of fat, inactive. So I was green. I ain't drink beer. Ain't had sex. None of that kind of stuff. Real green. See, Devin, he was kind of in the hood, so he was almost like my big brother. He kind of coached me into dating and chicks, and introduced me to gear. I ain't saying he turned me out, but he was the older kid. He was like, "Yo"—I'll never forget it—"You want to get a forty?" And I was like, "What's a forty? Beer?" He was like, "You ain't had beer before?" And I was like, "Yeah, I think I sipped some beer before. My grandfather let me sip it." And he went and got a forty, and I remember he passed it to me, and I was like, "What you want me to do with this?" He's like, "Well, shit, hit the motherfucker." "Well, what about a cup?" He's like, "What do you need a cup for?" I was like, "Bro, uh?" He was like, "What, you been eating pussy?" "I ain't been eating pussy." He said, "Well, if you *have* been eating pussy, shit, the liquor going to kill it." So I was bugged out. He was just like, "We're going to drink behind each other, you know what I mean? We're going to share." I was like, "Get the fuck out of here." He was like, "Yeah, motherfucker—hit that bitch and pass it back to me." So I thought that was really kind of cool. That was like, my first blood brother inception, you know what I'm sayin'? We drank behind each other. So, I felt that was special.

He's the one who got me to smoke weed. Devin.

Get the—you know, guess who else started smoking weed?

Who's that?

Mike Dean.

From Devin you mean?

From our studio session! When he recorded us in '93 at Digital Services, Mike had not been smoking weed, bro. We brought that weed in there, smokin' that weed. He started back smoking weed.

He's a professional now.

He always tells us. He's like, "Bro, man, when y'all motherfuckers came in, bro, won't nobody smoking weed." 'Cuz you know we was smoking big by that time, and fucking, Mike Dean, for the first week or so, he was in there trying to cover his face up and

trying to record us. Devin was like, "Man, get some weed, man. You know you want to hit it." And then it's been on ever since. It's been on ever since. And Mike Dean is like, "Motherfuckers, hey, it's herb man. It's medicine."

Devin got me to smoke too!

Yeah, that's kind of how it was with me, man. I mean, for the longest I had tried to avoid it. I've drank with him, but for years I didn't smoke though. I didn't smoke. I was in high school too, so I was really kind of square and good kid almost. But, eventually I did. I succumbed. It was great. I don't regret it.

It's been endless source material for 25 years now.

Absolutely. I mean, the only reason I don't now is because of health reasons.

So that album came out, in '93? '94 I guess it came out, and you recorded it in '93.

Yeah, we recorded it, and we went through negotiations for like a year before we put it out.

And did you go out on the road? What followed that?

Those first years we toured. We had our first tour that year. We did the whole Midwest, and Scarface took us on tour too. We did a lot of southern states. We did two cities in Florida, Georgia, and Alabama. Face took us on a small tour. And then shortly after that, Dev started doing his solo stuff. So, you know, I went back to school. I was studying for a couple of years. I didn't finish, but, you know, we just kind of played the background. We decided collectively to let Dev do his solo thing. And so, you know, that's what we did, and I just kind of pretty much honed in on my craft, and you know, he took us along pretty much every step of the way.

Yeah, he really has. Was there a sense that that was going to happen, that kind of, like, let me go do this solo stuff and then I'm going to—

Well, yeah. That was the plan. It was like, okay, you know, we get it. You are the star. You have the charisma and the whatever it is that's cool that everybody loves. I never intended to ever be in the group, honestly. I was kind of told to be in the group. Because I just wanted to be the producer. But when we submitted our demo tape I was featured on a couple of songs, and J [Prince] thought it would be a novel idea for a blind person to be in a rap group. It was almost like, not a gimmick but, you know, like, hey, we can sell this, you know what I'm saying? So it wasn't until later I actually got serious about actually being an artist. Later, much later. I just wanted to do the music. I wanted to be the music guy.

Sounds like it's kind of the same gamble he took on Bushwick, but he really, he lucked out that the two of you weren't just gimmicks and you're good artists.

Yeah. And it was really cool that we were, like, really friends too. Most groups are not, you know. They're kind of just put together.

Geto Boys for sure were like that.

Right, right, right. So we actually was homeboys so none of the . . . you know, nothing really broke us apart. You almost couldn't have one of us without the rest of us there, you know? It was part of the source material.

And so you started coming back into the picture . . . Coughee Brothaz came around I guess kind of early, mid-2000s.

Mm-hmm. I was a big part of that.

But you also had some appearances. You did appear on some of Devin's solo records too, right?

All of them.

And were doing some producing too?

Yeah, pretty much all of them. Either producing or rapping. I was on all of them.

That's what I mean. It's like you had something to do with each one of them, but then when Coughee Brothaz came around, that was more like a showcase. It wasn't Odd Squad, but Odd Squad was part of Coughee Brothaz, so you were showcased a little bit more.

Odd Squad and the homeboys. That's right. Our crew almost became mostly made up with people that were into the music, not just weed smoking. Ultimately that's what it was at first—a lot of our pothead friends. Pothead, drug friends, but then we realized after a while damn near all of them was talented too. They produced and they sang and they rapped too.

I was going to say being around that must have made them sort of musical.

Yeah, well, we just started acquiring a lot of musical friends that happened to smoke weed and drink. And do the shit we do. So it was kind of like *collectively* we were there. It's like, we need to do like most groups do, you know, let's put out the rest of the crew. Let's present them. So that's why we kind of did the Coughee Brothaz. Everybody that's a part of it kind of all had their own story, how they kind of was brought along and how they was found or how they made a space for themselves or how we made a space for them inside the group. 14k is probably the most interesting.

Yeah, they're from . . . Where are they from—New Mexico?

New Mexico, yeah. They called on the phone from one of the albums where in the intro he gave his real phone number except for, like, two numbers, and they fucking called it. They figured out the number and really actually called him. We thought nobody would ever do no shit like that, but if you think about it, man, people do dial numbers, telephone numbers that people mention in songs.

I feel sorry for whoever has 867-5309.

Right, yeah. He left off two numbers. It was a six and zero. So basically they had to call 60 times before they got the number right and it was Devin. He fucking answered the phone. It was crazy.

And then so what did they say?

They was like "Is this Devin?" And he was like, "Yeah, this is Devin." And they just started rapping. They found a friend. One of them picked up the phone in the other room so they was basically on two phones. And he said they started just going at it, freestylin' for him on the phone, and he was like, "Who the fuck is this?" When they finished their spiel like, "Yo, this is blahs and blahs and blahs from New Mexico, man. We just wanted to rap for you, man, we're sorry." But what was crazy, that didn't really sell him yet. You know, that was cool, and he was like, "Wow, that was pretty good," but they actually showed up for a show, right? And they was like, "How much would it cost me to come down here and do a show in the city?" They gave the price, which he thought that was going to be, like, you know, "We ain't got enough for that." They came up with the money, sent the deposit, right? So we're like, "Damn—okay." They rented the van and everything, and we drove down. When we got there we were expecting to see, like, some grown men, and they were little fucking teenagers. They were like 17 years old, some teenagers. So basically we got booked by some teenagers, some kids. They paid and booked us to come do a show in their city and paid for it.

In New Mexico.

In New Mexico. So we was impressed. Like, "Damn, y'all motherfuckers doing it. Y'all some bad motherfuckers." They wasn't playing either. You know, along with their skills and their whole state, that was impressive for us. So I was like, "Y'all some bad motherfuckers."

Seems like Coughee Brothaz is a mindset above all else, huh?

Yeah, absolutely. So, you know, they live in Houston now. They got families and doing great and still doing their music and everything. They were kids. 16, 17 years old, bro. By then we was in our early— we was in our 20s back then.

That's one of the most interesting things about Coughee Brothaz, is how it's like this big collective that sort of expands and contracts and is different every show and every record, right?

Mm-hmm. Yeah, yeah. There is no set members. So usually when we say who all is part of the Coughee Brothaz, we always say Odd Squad and their friends. It's always going to be me, Devin, and Jugg. But, you know, it's just our crew. It might be different every time, you know. So we've basically just giving them a platform to present themselves, allowing them to be featured somewhere and get their voice heard.

And then maybe even develop stuff for themselves, I mean like Tony Mac and Smit-D. You've known those guys for a long time too, right?

I think Tony Mac's first appearance was on a record with Big Mike and Pimp C. I think that was his first, if I'm not mistaken.

Goes way back. So what are you working on out there in LA? Are you working with some artists in particular that you're going to be producing, or are you building up like—

I definitely got a catalog. Right now I'm just out here. Mike Dean is my main goal, to try to help me get some major plays. Travis Scott, Kanye, the sort of big records that I've been dying to get on. I just met up with a singer/songwriter out here that I just sent some music to. I'm out here trying to get my feet wet. I want to get label placements and do big things. My music has outgrown our little clique, know what I'm saying? I have more sound outside of the sound that you hear on Devin the Dude records. So I'm just out here trying to get more opportunities.

What's the other stuff like? You're saying that there's other sounds that you have—is it all hip-hop, or is it stuff that brings in other genres?

Right now I'm into making pop records. We doing R&B, we're doing a lot of trap, we're doing a lot of hip-hop. Doing even some reggae, some dance hall type stuff. That's what I mean. So I got records for everybody from Beyoncé to Future. And like I say, I want to be able to fill my credits and my resume up. I want to really dig. I want to be somebody that, when you say my name and hip-hop production, it'll ring bells like Timbaland or Pharell. That kind of thing, to see if I can be like that right here.

That's the way to do it, to dig yourself out of the previous environment and put yourself into a new one, because then you have to sink or swim and you don't have that same support network around you, and it's scary but it's worthwhile. You kind of have to do that when you want to take that next step.

That's right. So far I'm enjoying it, though. I'll put it like this: I'm already visualizing it in my head. I've seen it and, really, it's done. I'm just positioning myself to go ahead and make it to fruition. It's already done. Really everything that's happening is like I've seen it already. So I will be successful. It will be a big thing. Me and you are going to have this conversation, I don't know how long from now, but we're going to talk about this moment, about being at this stage, and how we were talking like this, now. "Did you ever think it'd be like this?" And the answer is *yes*.

N.O. Joe

NEW ORLEANS

As the producer of multiple gold and platinum-certified albums for artists as diverse as Ice Cube and Brian McKnight, Louisiana native Joseph Johnson has been heard throughout the music world whether folks have seen his name or not. But in Houston, his association with Rap-A-Lot Records (Geto Boys, Scarface, Big Mike, Devin the Dude) and UGK has helped define the Southern sound since the early 1990s, and in H-Town *everybody* knows Joe.

You were saying you had your guitar player in the studio tonight—were you making beats, playing along with him?

Well, those guys are professionals. I play a little, like, I used to play a little guitar, but I let them do what they do. Now, if I'm here by myself, I might be picking around with stuff, eatin' a sandwich. I put it like this here—me and Pimp C had a thing—we called ourselves "slugs," and the thing was we'd kinda pick around with stuff, slug my way through a bassline, or slug my way through a little guitar playin', you know, just to get the idea down, flush it out.

Just so that you can refine the notes and the rhythms.

Well, you know, if I have a bass player or a guitar player comin', I mean there's no need for it because they're gonna come in and they know what I want. You know Corey Funky Fingers? We been like—I actually brought the MPC to Houston. When I came here, everybody was like—I met Scarface in New Orleans—and he told me to come out and check out some stuff, and he wanted to let [J Prince] hear what he was talkin' about. He was like, "Aw man, N.O. Joe, man, this guy's got some stuff." I came down here, man, and I had that big ol' drum machine in my hand with that armrest on it. [Laughs] The guys were lookin' at me like, *"What the hell?"* I say, "Yeah, just step back, fellas. Gimme a little room." I mean, there was about maybe 15 people in a 9' × 10' room or somethin' like that. And I guess Face was tellin' them about me, and so I finally plugged my machine up and it was like, "What is that thing?" Now what I would *do* is prior to that I would take my keyboards and

I would play 'em inside my MPC, so you'll have keyboards and all of that stuff *within it*, because really I didn't wanna lug all of that stuff, you know? And so when I press play on there, dude, everybody in the room was like, "What the fuck! It sound like a record!" So I just start playin' beats all night, man, and I had about 10 people rappin' around me. DMG was one of 'em. You know, they were just amazed, like—"What is this thing?" That was my weapon of choice! Before then, the SP-1200, I kinda learned how to work that under Mannie Fresh. I used to go by his house, and I didn't have an SP-1200. He was the one that had all the equipment because they had a record deal. They was with RCA or somethin', and when we linked up, man, I was like, "Man, I need a drum machine! I got all my sounds cued up and everything." And he was like, "Just come on over to the crib, bro—you can use mine." And I got over there, man, and I started doin' beats. And I only had a limited time once I got over there because the machine would get hot. I'd have all of my tapes cued up and everything, and he would come back in there 30 minutes later, 45 minutes later, "Hey man, I gotta turn this off. I gotta get up out here. How many you have done?" And I was like, "I got seven." He was like, "You got seven songs done???" I was like, "Yeah, lemme finish the seventh one off, man, and I'll come back tomorrow."

It had enough room for you to do all that in there.

Yeah, I had it all on different floppies. I knew I had a limited amount of time so I had all my tapes cued up of what I wanted to sample, whatever drums I wanted to sample, I had everything ready. I just hit "play," hit "sample," boom—got that. Then I start programming. Song done. Next song, same thing.

Were you using the SP-1200 going into the MPC? To sample, right?

Yeah, to sample. And a friend of mine, Cokey, he actually turned me on—because he was like a geek on the drum machines and all of that stuff. We started off usin' a Yamaha RX5 or somethin' like that. And he actually brought the MPC60, and I was like, "What is that? That look complicated!" And so we just kinda sat down, he showed me

how to work it, and, man, I start doin' beats on it, and I never turned back to anything else because I found out that I could—like with the SP-1200, the thing I didn't like about that was you had to sync stuff up to it. Like you couldn't really MIDI until later, but with the MPC60, I could MIDI—remember the Roland D50? I could have like four different keyboards that I actually sequenced and quantized within the MPC. So a lot of people just used it as a sampler, but I had whatever I could get my hands on because that's what I could afford at the time. So that's been my weapon of choice. The first record I actually did here was on a song called "The Unseen" on the Geto Boys album.

How old were you?

19.

And you worked with Big Mike the same year?

No, Big Mike didn't come until after Geto Boys. So I did the whole *Till Death Do Us Part*. I did that whole album except the "Intro," "Outro," "Straight Gangsterism," and "Street Life." But every other song on there. That changed the face of Southern music. There's actually a live version of that album because when I came in, Mike Dean was just kinda learning to play guitar at the time. He already played keys, and I said, "Hey, you know, I wanna play a lot of this stuff live." Because we had some samples in there. So there was a whole live version of that album. Of course, the guys, they wanted a more rugged, sampled sound. But I still had my organs and stuff like that, so I had a sample of the organ in the ASR-10. I had a rack mount system, and I also had the sample on my MPC, and I got that organ sample from Sea Saint Studios, which was Allen Toussaint's studios. And that was my signature sound that I put in the songs! So the Southern rap stuff, the organ within the music, the hard drums, that's where it came from. Because, you know, I grew up in the church, and I always wanted to keep, like, a soulful feeling on the songs that I produce—still gangster enough that you go, *Oooh!*—but it's still so soulful that it touch your heart when you hear these certain sounds in it.

DJ Styles

THIRD WARD

Carlos "DJ Styles" Garza was one of the main producers (along with N.O. Joe and Mike Dean) behind the Odd Squad's 1994 debut, *Fadanuf Fa Erybody!!* That was the album that introduced Devin the Dude, Jugg Mugg, and Rob Quest to the world. Carlos was also a longtime employee at the South Main location of Soundwaves, where he transformed the shop's hip-hop section, working alongside a young DJ Premier (who went on to become half of the group Gang Starr). He has remained active in the city's hip-hop community over the years, amassing an archive of photographs and memorabilia from the early days of Houston hip-hop. In 2018, Carlos built a new studio on the southwest side, called Garza Sound Studio.

DJ STYLES AT RHINESTONE WRANGLER. COURTESY OF CARLOS GARZA

What were you producing before you got with Odd Squad? You were active in the '80s, right?

Well, this is how it kinda went down: I originally, like most people from that era—Sugarhill Gang—when I first heard that, that was the song like, "What was that?" I think I was in elementary school, and a friend of mine played that song for me on a tape recorder, he had brought a portable one to school. From that one song, it just opened up a whole—I just wanted more! I wanted to know what it was. I had never heard anything like that. But when I heard it, remember . . . I came from nothin' but Mexican music. You know, *corridos* and stuff like that, you know, straight up Mexican stuff. That's all I heard! That's all my dad played. I didn't really listen to the radio that much.

What kind of Mexican stuff? Like *norteño, conjunto, Tejano*?

Yeah, but no *Tejano*. My dad was heavy into the *corridos* from Mexico. He was actually friends with Cornelio Reyna. He grew up with him, and so I remember him playing that. The only black music that I do remember my dad played was Chubby Checker. And of course Elvis—he loved Elvis. In his record collection he had some big band stuff. I don't know if that was his, like he actually bought it, but it was in his collection. And a lot of Mexican music. You know, so goin' from that to this hip-hop stuff, it just blew me away, dude!

Jumped out at you.

Yeah, and from that day, man, I just wanted more and more. And that's kinda what got me going with the hip-hop stuff. So after that comes the breakdancing and the graffiti. Because ever since I heard that song, I would religiously listen to the radio because I wanted to hear that song again. I was listening to Lester Pace on KTSU.

"Kidz Jamm."

Yeah! And at the time, I didn't really know them. Later on, I met them, but it was Lester Pace, Luscious Ice, and King T. When they used to play out of that KTSU. That's kinda where it grew even *more*. And then from there, the next stage into hip-hop was when I saw *Beat Street* and *Breakin'*.

And *Krush Groove*!

That took it over the edge, man. I mean, if I was blown away by "Rapper's Delight," *Beat Street* . . . I loved *Breakin'*, but I think *Beat Street* . . . I can't remember which came first.

They came out like a month apart. *Breakin'* was actually first, but *Beat Street* was my favorite too.

I mean, I was done. My life was hip-hop after that. It was *every*thing to do with hip-hop.

All the elements [of hip-hop] were kinda still together then too.

Yeah! And of course rap was *it* then. That's all I was listening to, and then I got into the graffiti thing. I never really did tag anything big, but I did do a lot of graffiti. I did do a handful of things, but other guys that I met, this one guy named Bird who was from New York, when I saw his stuff, I was like, "Man, fuck this. I can't beat that." I would still do it, but there was no way, man.

What name did you use?

I think it was Pacemaster. Pace! That was my tag name/my breakin' name, so that's what I went by.

Were you ever "Pacemaster" as a producer?

No, no. The next thing that evolved from that was DJing. You know, because we had a DJ when I used to break. It was a group of us from my neighborhood. I grew up right there on Old Spanish Trail and 288, that neighborhood right there. And so the group of us from there were breakdancing all up-and-down OST, man. All those clubs—Turning Point, Club Escapade, I mean literally every club, dude. We'd go in there, they'd just throw money at us.

So what would you do? Did you have a scheduled performance, or would you just show up somewhere and break?

Nah! We would just show up and they were happy to see us, man. We would just tell the owner, "Hey—we wanna dance." And they'd give us 10 or 15 minutes. They *loved* it.

How many of you were there?

Actually, believe it or not . . . well, you probably will know. The only famous one, I guess, from Houston was Big Mello. He at one time was part of the group, I think when . . . it was me, my brother, Big Mello . . . it was like six or seven of us, total, along with the DJ . . . so seven or eight.

What was the name of the crew?

The Dynamic Crew.

And did Curtis go by "Big Mello" as a dancer?

Yeah! He was always Big Mello, or Mello. He always went by that. Man, that guy was multi-talented.

Yeah? How was his breakin'?

Well, he wasn't breakin', he was poppin'. So we would pop, break . . . actually, I was the *only* breakdancer. Everybody else was poppin' and lockin'. They were more like dancers. They weren't breakdancers. I was the only one that would, like, battle it out with everybody else! Everybody else would just dance. We had a great time, dude.

So what year are you talking about right there . . . '84, '85?

Yeah . . . '84?

That's really when breakin' was going nationwide.

I'll put it this way: whatever year *Beat Street* came out, it was heavy. I mean, it was only a handful of us. We all kind of knew each other, especially from that side of town, from the Southside, around '84, '85. Thank God they released that movie, because if it wasn't for *Beat Street*, man, who knows what we would have been doing, you know?

Exactly! But isn't that hip-hop in general, for you?

Yeah, but I guess what I'm sayin' is that *movie*, man, really was a tipping point. That thing was just so amazing to me, dude. I couldn't believe what I was seeing, and to find out that they had been doing it for *years* . . . that was like old-school! That was old for them. I think to this day I still have posters and books and all kinds of breakdancin' material, man. Just anything I could possibly get my hands on, man. I wanted it. Anything! I didn't care what it was. I was in love with it.

Didn't it kind of make you thirstier for it because it wasn't everywhere? I mean there was no chance of getting too much of it.

Well, it was so *new*.

And it trickled out.

Yeah! Like when we went to the clubs, they were totally blown away, like, "What are you kids *doing*?" So after that, man, you just do it once and they want you to come back. So literally that was how we made our money. That's how we bought boomboxes and outfits was we would dance every weekend. We would go out together and save our money and buy what we needed.

Were you DJing already at that point?

No, well I got to a point where I just stopped breakin'. We kinda broke up, and everybody went their own way.

Did you feel like it kind of died down in Houston? Was breakin' a short-lived thing in Houston?

It wasn't as hot. At least in my eyes. It could have been—it was funny because it was still happening. My friend—I just met him a year or two ago, but he was with this crew called Chaos, and he was explaining to me that *he* did a lot of the b-boy events around that time, in the late '80s and early '90s. These guys were traveling the US, and they would hold a lot of events. So when I was kind of, like, getting out of it, and getting into DJing, they were still doing it. But in my mind, you know, "Ah, they're not doin' it no more." When they actually were. But yeah, that's what made me . . . it didn't interest me as much anymore.

Kind of ran its course.

So I got into DJing, and the DJ that used to come with [Dynamic Crew] taught me how to DJ.

You were a hip-hop DJ from the beginning, then.

Yeah, and this was when I was in high school, so '86, '87. And once I get into something, man, I'm *in* it. I'm goin' all in. So as a DJ, what's your dream job? Working at a record store. And so that's when the production started, when I started working at Soundwaves. And that's when I went and purchased the SP-12. I don't know if you remember this, but they used to have a place on 59 called the Drum and Keyboard Shop.

Yeah, The Drum Keyboard Guitar Shop. Right off 59, with the big windows in front.

That's where I bought my first SP-12, and where I went from the DJing to production. Because for a long time, the person who really inspired me to do it was [DJ] Premier. After a while, that's where I met him. I met him at Soundwaves, and he let me hear his music that he had done with tapes. Like stop tapes. He had a little 4-track, and he would explain to me what he had done, and I was, like, fuckin' blown away, man. This dude is in his bedroom with records—not even a drum machine, just records. He's stacking all this music, and then he would have an MC rap over these arrangements that he would do with his turntables! It would just blow me away, man, and that's what made me wanna get even *more* into it, after being with him. And from there—to be honest with you, man, all my inspiration came from working at that record store. That's really what initiated everything. All the different people that I met there, all the different DJs, and of course wanting to know how this music was being done. And starting to find records, like breakbeats. I was up on it a little bit because the people that worked there, the older guys, like the owner, they were like, "Yeah, that's The Average White Band," or, "Earth, Wind & Fire." And in *my* eyes, I'm thinkin' it's original music! You know, back *then*. So when I would hear these samples, I was like, "Oh my God, that's where he fuckin' got that from!" You know, LL Cool J or whoever. It just fucking completely blew me away.

Matt Sonzala

AUSTIN

Matt grew up between Houston and Erie, Pennsylvania, understanding early in his visits to H-Town that there was something special going on musically. He interned at recording studios, got a job at the radio station, started promoting shows, and then got on the radio at Houston's KPFT, first with Rad Richard and then his own show "Damage Control" with DJ Chill. In the early 2000s, his *HoustonSoReal* blog (later renamed *AustinSurreal*) was a vital resource for people learning about Houston rap music. Matt also worked with South By Southwest for years and has been instrumental in expanding the careers of artists like Willie D, Devin the Dude, and K-Rino by helping them arrange headlining tours overseas.

MICHAEL '5000' WATTS AND MATT SONZALA.
COURTESY OF MATT SONZALA

When you first started going to rap clubs in Houston in the late '80s, what was the vibe?

I don't remember being shocked that nobody really noticed me. It wasn't nothin'. At first, I was like, "I can't go to this by myself," some dumb, white 17-year-old. Literally. 18-year-old . . . I don't even know if I can get in, you know? But they didn't give a fuck. Those type of clubs—it was just kinda wild. At first, I was totally nervous, like, "I can't go to some club like that by myself." And people would straight up tell me I better not go. It was pretty wild and stuff, but nobody gave me any shit, ever. I would just be there, pretty much by myself, too young to drink, stupid enough to think that it really was going to start at 10, standing around, by myself, literally, for four hours until the show would start at two—or after two—or not start at all. And those shows were 15 minutes at the most. I went to some shows that were legit, and there was a bunch of different artists on them. They were cool. I mean, Brand Nubian played The Palladium. A Tribe Called Quest played The Palladium. De La Soul played the Rhinestone Rangler before—that was before my time. I was still in Erie at the time. But I mean, De La Soul—Dante Ross was with them, they played the fuckin' Rhinestone Rangler, dude.

Who were the first rappers that you met?

Well, my big break was . . . I was at a school for audio engineering, and one of my teachers was Jeff Wells, who owned Sound Arts Studios, and at that school, it was really a bunch of fucking heavy metal dudes and . . . not, like, everybody, but mostly. And I liked heavy metal too. I liked punk rock and all that shit, but people were, like, shocked that I knew so much about hip-hop or whatever, and they would always make a point of that. And one of the teachers was like, "Yeah, you really like this stuff, huh? Well, you know, we've got the Geto Boys—they're going to be recording in my studio." And this is like six months before they recorded *We Can't Be Stopped*. And I was like, "What?" And he was like, "And I need an intern. If you want to intern." "Fuck yeah, I wanna intern!" And literally it took for fucking ever for them to start recording their album, but I started going out to Sound Arts, helping out. And like, I was interning there the whole time they did *We Can't Be Stopped*. Doug King's production in the front—he had a little studio in the front, and he did all the pre-production there—then they came and did all the vocals and mixing and stuff inside. I was there the whole time, so . . . I did *not* buddy-buddy up with everybody. In fact, Bushwick was the only one who would randomly remember me in places, like he'd say hello to me. Willie D and Scarface never remembered me or gave a fuck. J Prince, he was there every day. To this day, I was introduced to him for the millionth time at SXSW this year, and he was like, "Oh, nice to meet you." I've interviewed him, I've talked to him so many times, and some Rap-A-Lot guy was like, "J really wants to meet you, man. What you've built here at SXSW, man—he's really impressed."

Geto Boys were never in there together, then—no?

Never. No. I mean, rarely—one or two times, they were there because J had them to meet about something or whatever. Willie D, you know the whole, "We're gonna kick down the door," and all this. Willie D and me had a straight-up argument because nobody was there from the studio except me, and Jeff would say things like, "Make sure they stay in-line, man." I'm like, "What the fuck am I going to do?" And Willie D's like, "Man, we gotta break down the door! We need the sound realistic!" And other people in the studio were like, "Well,

we'll find a sound effect. We'll make it . . ." And he's like, "Man, we gotta kick this shit! We gonna break the motherfuckin' door down!" I'm like, "You can't break the door! I mean, these are studio doors, soundproof door, all this shit, this is going to throw off your recording to break this door down." "We'll pay for the door! We'll fix the motherfuckin' door! What the fuck, man? We'll pay for this!" And J Prince is just sittin' there. I'm like, "J, please . . . somebody say somethin'." Like, this dude's . . . I'm a fuckin' intern, I'm here, this dude—this was before cellphones too. I couldn't just call Jeff, "Hey, get over here." I'm like, "Dude, you can't just break the door down. If you wanna break the door down, give it a couple of hours until Jeff is here, and tell Jeff. And he can make that decision. I ain't makin' that decision, man!" He was like, "Man, what the fuck!" And he did not break the door down, but I was like, "Dude, come on . . ." Man, it was a fuckin' experience, dude. And that was around the time Bushwick shot himself. It was nuts. It was nuts. Ready Red was gone. I was always like, "Where the fuck is Ready Red?" Nobody really knew what was up.

He was in the process of quitting at that point, wasn't he?

Oh, he pretty much already had at that point. It was pretty obvious.

He's on the first track of that record.

Yeah, but that's it. He didn't really participate in much. Pre-production.

The record came out in July, but in May, when Bushwick shot himself, were they still working on the record? Were you still around them at that point?

I was definitely around, yeah. But I think the record was pretty much done, and they had released "Mind Playing Tricks," I think around then? And the "Mind Playing Tricks" video was shot out there too. I saw all that stuff firsthand.

Where did they shoot that?

Over on the Northwest side, by Sound Arts Studio. A lot of it was shot over there. Like, the main stuff—the nighttime and all that were all over there. I saw the vibe. They are crazy motherfuckers, straight up. They are genuinely crazy. It's not an act. They all have issues. Willie D is the most stable one out of all of them, and that's crazy.

When the tape was rolling, did you feel like you were really hearing something special?

Oh, yeah. Definitely. But I was more geeked out. I didn't know that that album was going to be as big as it was. They were already pretty big as far as controversies and stuff went. That was the record that put them over, like, more acceptably musically, and to be honest with you—no disrespect to anyone, but I felt like they were less aggressive on that album than they were on *Grip It! On That Other Level*. I felt like they slowed it down.

That's the way the music was going anyway.

It totally went that way. But I mean, all the upper echelons of Houston rap were there in some capacity, from those days. And the people who became architects of that stuff—Bido and those type of guys were all around, man. 3-2—he was always . . . put it this way—anywhere I ever went in those days, I saw 3-2. I didn't know him personally like that, but 3-2 was in every event. He was in the Convicts, he was just everywhere, man.

Did you work with the Geto Boys in any capacity again following that? Was there a continuation?

I never worked with them again. I never really worked with them. I mean, I'd see them around when I interned for the radio station—The Box, for the first two years The Box was around.

If you were trying to explain the fan bases in Houston to someone, the sides, how would you sum that up?

Well, the local stuff . . . what I always liked about Houston was that Houston people always supported . . . hip-hop-wise, they supported themselves—each other—completely. You know, like the Southside sound and the Northside sound, like the Southside and the Northside had their fans. They had real fan bases. They really did make the sounds of their streets, and the stuff that was happening in New York and all of that didn't really make a big difference to them. It wasn't really their thing. Until The Box and things like that became really commercial, and kind of lost that edge. For a lot of years, that shit was their thing, so a lot of the regular folks in the hood, they had their thing, straight-up. And then there were plenty of kids who also—you know, whether they liked the stuff in the hood or not, you know, they liked Gang Starr and they liked De La Soul. They liked hip-hop from other places. So I think there were some people who kind of were limited in their scope—both sides, I think, are actually limited in their scope—like there were a lot of kids who kind of rejected the local stuff because they felt like there was more out there or whatever. And then there were local people who rejected the other stuff because they didn't really give a shit about it. It was really way out of their realm, and that shit happened everywhere. You know, New York people didn't care about anything except for what they were doing. The West Coast made their own thing. And it's sad that some of that's kinda changed. As the perspective should have gotten wider, it's gotten more narrow, I think. With the commercial stuff—people just going for whatever. Back then it was such a new culture, it was kind of dynamic. So, like, the Houston stuff sounded like Houston, and it was what it was. Even though it had a West Coast influence, you know, the people in the hood—none of us had internet and cellphones and all that, so they just had what was happening around them. And there was some pretty dynamic stuff happening.

And there were two communities, really, connected to different things—the ones that would be turned on to something like Gang Starr, and then the guys who didn't give as much to the music but wanted to be creative in their lyrics and go hard. The more Southern guys. A different approach altogether.

Right. I mean, that's true. One thing I'll say is that the community into Gang Starr and all that was a much smaller community. There wasn't a big community at all, and as far as Run–D.M.C. and all that goes . . . well, take it even further—those guys in the hood who may or may not have been listening to Run–D.M.C., they were listening to Zapp, and Maze, and The Band. And the bayou stuff that came from Louisiana and all that. Talk to Wickett Crickett . . . In those days, there was definitely a big community of people who were really into old-school stuff. You know, all them Southside guys—K-Rino and all them told you, I'm sure, many times that they original hip-hop stuff was straight-up *dance*. You would go to the club to dance. You were dancing to bands. Not that there were no DJs, but before there was Ghetto Boys and all that shit, Houston was going out to see these funky bands.

Big Mike

SOUTH PARK

Born and raised in New Orleans, Mike moved to Houston as a teenager and started off as a solo artist before being drafted into the Rap-A-Lot group Convicts in the early '90s alongside Hiram Clarke rapper Mr. 3-2. The duo went to LA to work with Death Row Records' iconic producer Dr. Dre in the early '90s, but an album never materialized, and Mike took an offer to join Geto Boys when Willie D briefly left the group. After that he went on to a successful solo career, which was derailed for several years when he was imprisoned in 2000 on an arson conviction involving the Rap-A-Lot studio. Big Mike began making records again in 2005.

BIG MIKE AND GANKSTA N-I-P. PHOTO: ROWDY WILLIAMS

You got any Geto Boys tour stories?

One time, we was in St. Louis—and this was after the show, after we had performed—we all went out to a club in St. Louis, and Bushwick got into it with somebody at the club, some of the locals at the club. And we was jumpin' in the van to head back to the hotel, and the van got gunned down. We were all layin' down on the floor, all in the seats in the van, and they're just shootin' up the van, you know what I mean? That was one crazy incident that had happened. Fortunately, nobody got shot. Nobody got hurt or killed. We made it out there alive. But I do remember that one vividly.

What did Bushwick have to say about it afterwards?

[Laughs] I mean, what can you say, basically? Everybody at the time was pissed at him. I mean, you can't be out of town . . . we're on other guys' turf. You gotta respect that. We didn't find out what the argument was about. Everybody was jumpin' off, and we was like, "Let's go on and leave, it's time to go." It's not a knock on Bushwick or anything like that. You can't change what you did in the past. We was all a little wild, a little crazy, feeling ourselves a bit much.

And as far as he's concerned, he's 20 feet tall.

Yeah, yeah, that's Bill. But you know, I had a chance to see him recently throughout the years, a few years ago, and we had chopped it up. He's making his spiritual music and things like that. He's really changed a lot from what I can tell. But I understood him. It was a lot to deal with, with the pressure of dealing with the label and the sudden stardom and the pressure that comes with being an artist in the game, that roller-coaster ride. So I can kind of understand, because I was a little out of control at certain times, you know what I mean? But we live and learn from our mistakes, and they all add to make us a better person. If you learn from it.

You're sort of a Northside and Southside guy, aren't you?

Southside, man . . . not to take nothing away from the Northside, but the Southside is the ones that was making the noise first. And you know, in Houston, it's "*Southside*." That's what you hear about all the time. Because you had cats comin' out doin' they thing from the Northside, so the whole city was gettin' they shine, but for the most part, the Southside was the staple.

Well, you look at Houston, look at a map, and you see how many people came from that area.

That come from that area! Yeah, because on this side of town, we had everything . . . Six Flags, clubs . . . everything was on this side of town.

You had Carro's, Boomerang. . .

Carro's, Boomerang, 929, Jamaica Jamaica . . . everything was located on the Southside of town. And I just think we had that action at the time, everything was poppin' at that time. But like I say, that's not to take nothin' away from the Northside, it's just that that's where things was poppin' at the time.

And they happened in very different ways too. The Southside didn't really get their shine until Ganksta N-I-P signed with Rap-A-Lot and brought the S.P.C. with him. That's when people started finding out, really, about the Southside. People always divide the two, but they don't think about the fact that there's always been a connection.

And the Southside of Houston is synonymous with music, and that's just the way it is. It's not that I'm trying to claim a side . . . that's just how it happened. You look at the demographics and you look at the number of rappers that came up out of Houston, like you say, the majority come up out of the Southside! But the Northside's doin' they thing. You got Slim Thug and Boss Hogg Outlawz and a lot of other cats that's from the Northside that's really doin' they thing now, but they'll even tell you the Southside struck first.

But the Northside laid the blueprint, with Rap-A-Lot.

Yeah, Fifth Ward—some people consider that Northside, but as far as like the artists, the names, the trendsetting, everything was taking off from the Southside.

Do you go back to South Park ever now?

Yeah, yeah, yeah! I'm not just from around here, I'm from *down* here, you feel me? I be out there. I mean, that's where all my friends are, the people I grew up with, the people I went to school with. That's where I left it at, where I did my thing at. I'm always out there. My people, they see me. I'm out here. I don't be hanging out on the cut and things like that, you know what I mean? But I'm in and out the city. I'm just like a normal person, you know. I'm not sittin' up on high, you know what I'm sayin'?

The reason I ask is because there really is this sort of South Park mystique . . . there's something about South Park that really draws people there.

You know what it is, is that the rappers that was comin' out in Houston that was really makin' a big splash, Scarface, me, you know, we were all representing the Southside because that was the side of town that we're from. Not just South Park in particular, just the Southside, period. Now South Park, that's just a classic Houston neighborhood, you know what I mean? It's classic. It was like that before I even came down here. I understand it, but I don't know if I could just describe it fully, the whole mystique about it, but it's kind of like Uptown in New Orleans. It seems like it's just where the action is, you know what I'm sayin'? If you somebody visitin' Houston in the urban scene, in the urban music or whatnot, you wanna go ride through South Park. "Where the Southside at? Where South Park? Where Sunnyside? Where Third Ward? Where Yellowstone?" You wanna go ride through there.

What do we hear in your lyrics?

You can hear where I came from. You can hear my struggles throughout the years. You can hear my hopes for the future. You can hear my care for other people, not just necessarily in the black community or the inner city, but people in general struggling with something. My heart goes out to them because I have had the opportunity to struggle throughout the years with certain things. Coming up as a child, the oldest out of nine kids, with a single mother, watching her struggle to maintain a life for us. Being her helper, gettin' out there on my own. Being out in the streets, wanting to hustle, dealing with that struggle. Because it *is* a struggle. I'm not gonna glorify it. Yeah, I made good money and whatnot, but it was a struggle. It was a dangerous situation. It was an uncertain time for me. Me going to the penitentiary—that was a struggle that I had to deal with, but by the grace of God, it wasn't too hard on me. I was able to get out unscathed. The coming home, not getting the reception that I thought I would be getting, like when rappers go to the penitentiary and they come home . . .

That was 2004?

Yes, 2004.

How did you get back up on your feet?

You know what, it was just . . . it was my family, man. My family, they was bein' real patient with me.

Lez Moné

HIRAM CLARKE

Lez Moné released her one album, *Talkin' Shit*, in 1994, at a time when there were fewer female artists in the industry anywhere, especially in Houston. But she stood out because her flow was a brash, in-your-face brand of street rap that hit hard and coalesced with the energy of what was going on in H-Town. Lez is a longtime collaborator of fellow Hiram Clarke denizens Harvey Luv and the late Big Mello, and was part of the group Nuckleheadz along with RacQuel Gemini a.k.a. Sugar Sugar, appearing on 8ball & MJG's 1995 album *On Top Of The World*. For the past 14 years, she has worked as a real estate agent in Houston.

How did you get your start?

It wasn't easy! Especially at that time, when Houston—they weren't even lookin' at Houston as far as—they weren't even acknowledging Houston as far as the music industry goes and for rap especially. So it was very difficult, but I was able to break down a couple barriers and get in there and do quite a bit. I got my start from another Houston rapper—Big Mello. He passed some years ago, but Mello had signed with Rap-A-Lot, or he had a connection with Rap-A-Lot or something, and he introduced me to Lil' J . . . I call him Lil' J. I think they call him somethin' else now. James Prince or something. Yeah, so he introduced me to him, and at that time, I mean, Mello called me, he said, "Lez, I'm over here with Lil' J. He wants to hear you." So I went and met them where they were, Lance, and I rapped *live*, with no music, and Lil' J said, "You know what? I wanna sign this girl." And in a couple

of days he had presented me with a contract. So that was where it all started.

But the record didn't come out with Rap-A-Lot.

No, Lil' J presented me with a contract, and luckily at that time I had some ties with a music attorney who looked over the contract for me, and it just wasn't in my best interest to sign with Rap-A-Lot. So I stayed independent for a little while, and then I started working with a guy out of Dallas. I didn't *sign* with Rap-A-Lot, but that's how I got started—doin' that rappin' for Lil' J.

You had a really good attorney.

Yes, yes I did!

So at that point, how geared up were you to go professional at that point? Did you have songs, rhymes, verses, and you were ready to record an album?

Well, at that time, I was just getting started. And I think even just freestyled. Lemme tell you, I started out, Lance—I used to write poetry in high school, so I was very good at writing poetry, and then, I didn't know that *rap* was poetry. You know, I was young, and I just thought I was writin' poetry. I mean, poetry—it came easy to me. Like second nature. And then I found out, "Okay, well I can freestyle too!" Because it just *comes* to me. When I performed for Lil' J I didn't have *anything*—any songs written—I just had poetry that I had written. So

PHOTO: LESLIE HALL

when I went to perform for him, or just rap for him, I just went straight off the top of my head because again, I used to write poetry every day. It just came natural to me. But, I had no plans of being a rapper until Mello told me, "You know what? You can rap! You know, you can rap!" But before that, I didn't know at all.

Y'all grew up together?

We grew up together. Mello and I were very close. Harvey Luv, who is out of Hiram Clarke. We're very close, producer, yeah, Harvey Luv, Crazy C. He was actually from Missouri City, but we were all very cool. I mean, all of the rappers that were rappin' at that time were very close friends of mine. I had a lot of respect from those guys, and when I was with them, I was one of the guys. So I grew up with Mello, grew up with Harvey Luv and all of the others that were rappin' at that time.

And they ended up on your record too.

Yeah. Harvey Luv ended up producing—now, Harvey Luv *wrote*—wrote "Take Care Ya Bizness." A lot of people didn't know that, but he wrote the lyrics to that song, and Crazy C produced it. And as time went on, we ended up doing quite a bit of music together.

Were you doing a lot of shows before the album came out? You did do some tours after.

Oh, I did. I did a lot of shows before it came out, and after the project dropped I toured six states with Too Short, Craig Mack, Bone Thugs-N-Harmony, Scarface, Big Mike, and Spice1. We went on a tour of six states, so I was with those guys for six states, and lemme tell ya—talk about some stories to tell!

I bet! Those must have been pretty wild shows every night.

Well, what I learned from that tour—I used to think that *men* were the only ones that had groupies. This was the biggest memory that I had. I thought men were the only ones who had groupies. I found out that that's not true. I was the only female in that whole lineup. But I found out *men* can be groupies too! I didn't know that! Lord, have mercy! Oh my goodness, they would be at the *hotel*. I mean, the women would do that for the guys. They would come to the hotel, they would stand in line to get in the guys' rooms. You know, it was some really wild stuff. But there were also guys there that were doin' the same thing, tryin' to get with me! And I would run into the room and lock the door and Scarface would stand at the door with a gun! Crazy times.

What's a crazy story you remember from one of those shows, one of those tours?

Well, you know what, they kinda kept me kinda guarded pretty much. I was the only female. They didn't wanna be responsible for anything happening. They didn't want anything to happen to me anyway, but they kinda treated me like their sister. So I had a nanny who toured with me because at the time, my son was about two years old. They had a nanny with me for the tour, so I pretty much stayed—after the show I would go straight to the room, and getting through the lobby of the hotel and to my room I would just see some of the craziest things. And one of the *craziest* things I remember—this was a whole different tour—but I remember this girl, she had obviously gone to a concert where we performed, and Bushwick Bill, you know, he's what—three feet tall or somethin' like that? And this girl was like almost six feet tall, and she was crying and begging to go in Bushwick Bill's room. She was standing at the door crying and begging to go in there and be with him. And she was like six feet—I mean this girl was like a basketball player tall. And you know, you think Bushwick Bill didn't let her in—he sure did! He let her in and a couple hours later I guess whatever happened in that room, I was like, "Oh my god—really?"

Bushwick's like, "I'll make this work."

Yep! And he did. That's another thing—those girls, they didn't care that he was short. They cared nothin' about that. They just wanna be next to the star. They wanna be with the star just to say, "I was with the star."

So what happened after that? You didn't make another record, but it sounds like you made more music with Harvey Luv and everybody.

I did. I did not release anything after *Talkin' Shit*, but I recorded another project that was never released. Well, I think before that I did a *Freaknik* soundtrack. I did like four songs for this *Freaknik* documentary that some guys I know—the Daniel brothers—they filmed this documentary and released it on DVD, so I did four songs on that soundtrack. And so I did that and then from there, that's when I started recording—it was called *The Comeback*. Lez Moné—*The Comeback*. And man, I had some great songs on that album, but we never released it.

And then, so how long did you stay active, working and doing shows and everything?

I stayed active for a while. I didn't stop rapping until—I didn't *completely* stop until a little after 2000. But what I was doing was guest appearances on different things, but as far as recording something of my own, I didn't record after *The Comeback*.

And that was something that Harvey Luv had worked on?

Yeah, Harvey Luv worked on that. Jhiame produced on there.

Jhiame Bradshaw?

Yes, Jhiame produced on there, Harvey Luv, Grizz, Crazy C, and as far as artists go I had some features on there with E.S.G. Oh, they brought the fire! I'm tellin' you that would have been a great album if I could have gotten it released.

That's why I ask because it seems like you had more to say just based on how you said it.

Yes. I had matured in my delivery. I had matured in my message because I had traveled. I've been all over the country, and I'd seen so many things and had experienced so many things that I had so much to say on that particular album. But unfortunately, I tell you, if that would have come out, that would have been the one to take me over the top.

What do you think about Houston artists now? Are there still Houston artists you listen to? I'd imagine you still see plenty of them.

I do. I'm still a big fan of Houston rap. I'm a fan and a friend of Slim Thug. I listen to him. I still listen to Scarface, who is producing—got, I think, some new stuff coming out. He's got some new stuff coming out with N.O. Joe. So I still do listen to Houston rap, and I'm close friends with a lot of those guys. I mean, we have a long, long history. But lemme say this, Lance, because this is something I've always wanted to say: I'm a fan of Houston rap because I am a *product* of Houston rap, but I don't feel that Houston supports their own like they should. They didn't then, and they don't now. The radio station here and those who have the power at the radio station, they never have been strong supporters of us. I mean, we would go to other cities and states and that's the *only* artists we would hear on the radio. But when you come to Houston, we play everybody else's music and not our own. When we would travel to New Orleans, to Mississippi, or wherever we would go, *those* are the artists that we would hear on the radio! The artists from New Orleans would be playing on the radio in New Orleans! The guys from Mississippi would be playing on the radio in Mississippi. The guys in California would be playing on the radio in California. The guys in New York . . . But when you come to Houston, we didn't play our own artists' music. I felt very, very strongly about that, and I even voiced it on Madd Hatta's show one time when I was doin' a radio interview, and I still feel the same way. I mean, Houston's gotten better that we get a little bit more support than what *we* did, but it's nothing like it should be. We should have more artists coming out. We have a lot of talent in this city.

The ARE

GREENSPOINT

Russel Gonzalez is a founding member of K-Otix, who were at the center of a Houston scene that blossomed in the second half of the 1990s, and he has produced tracks for countless artists from far beyond that circle. Houston is his base, but in 2007 he started spending time in New York with famed hip-hop production duo Trackmasters, a partnership which resulted in him contributing to "Something About You (Love the World)" on LL Cool J's 2013 album *Authentic*. Over the years he has produced tracks for Phife of A Tribe Called Quest, Masta Ace, Keyshia Cole, Dallas production team Hydroponic Sound System, and Houston's own Kay of The Foundation. He is the founder of the On The Good Foot label.

When you and K-Otix got started, you weren't necessarily concerned with what was going on in the Houston market, were you?

Exactly. We had a great formula. We had a great fan base, and we were able to tour and sell records. The years that I was with them it was about making good music. There was not really an issue of "Oh, let's do a radio record," or "Let's put a singer on this hook," for this reason. We just kind of made music. And sometimes we would get a song that would just be a big one, and sometimes we would get a song that would just be an album cut, you know?

You guys came around what . . . '92, '93?

'93 was the year we were really getting together and recording stuff and passing out demos, and we went up to the local KTRU and KPFT and did the radio shows there and promoted ourselves, but it wasn't until like '96, '97 that we put out our first record.

What was your outlook on what was going on in Houston when you came out?

At that time, you know, we were kind of outsiders to a degree, but the underground level was pretty thriving still. We had a lot of groups that came up with us, and we were doing shows at little like . . . *dives*, you know? It seemed like a real scene. Kind of like this New York rap, jazzy, backpack hip-hop. I guess in the big picture we really weren't *that* big for Houston, but there was really a movement going on, and a lot of those groups over the years just kind of fell out. They either broke up or just went on about other business. But one of the things was that we kind of felt like outsiders but we were catering to the *world*. So it wasn't like we were going, "We need to make something that the radio here will play." We understood the politics behind it and it wasn't necessarily what we wanted to do, so rather than make a song that sounded like a Big Mello track or things like that, we chose to keep moving in the direction of A Tribe Called Quest. That always kept us separate, but even in those times, in the '90's, looking back—a lot of hip-hop, a lot of what was considered gangsta rap was still real sample-based. You go back and you listen to a Big Mello album, anything from the early '90s to the mid-'90s Rap-A-Lot, and it was straight samples. So it wasn't like we were separating

PHOTO: ADAM ISRAEL VALADEZ

ourselves on purpose. I think you had two different genres coming out of Houston, and one of them was just a little bit more dominant. From early on, since we were influenced by and really big fans of the East Coast movement like Das EFX and A Tribe Called Quest and things like that, that kind of stayed our focus. We wanted to appeal to the masses and not just Houston.

Seems like the only bridge between those two scenes was Odd Squad—seeing as they had sort of an East Coast aesthetic, and yet they were on Rap-A-Lot.

It's crazy because Odd Squad, because DJ Styles, he was one of the producers that was involved with Odd Squad, and his influence came out big time. He was more into music all around. He came up on Eric B. & Rakim, and he was into the East Coast stuff—Diamond D and all that. He recognized a lot of those jazz samples and things like that, so the difference in that is that you had Odd Squad, who was taking all kinds of samples and horns and almost like a golden era sound and using that stuff. And a lot of that came through from Carlos [DJ Styles] to where you had the other Rap-A-Lot stuff—that came through from Crazy C and Doug King and other producers like that—and *they* were

more influenced by the samples that were more kind of *gangsta*. You know, the Isaac Hayes and the stuff that sounded almost more like a West Coast . . . like *funk*, you know? And that's what gave Odd Squad such a standout sound. They were doing all kinds of shit, and their singles and stuff, all the way down the one "I Can't See It," I mean, that was a straight-up jazz sample. So that made a big difference, that was a big bridge, but what did stay the same was what Devin and Rob and all them were talking about. They were still talking about getting high and slangin' shit on the street. That's where it kind of coincided with artists like Big Mello and Big Mike and Geto Boys. You know what's crazy? Sometimes we'd perform at events in Houston—and our music was really East Coast, you know, straight boom-bap, you know? But it was still so universal because we would do events here in Houston—you remember that movie *Jason's Lyric*?

Filmed in Houston.

Right, it was filmed in Houston, and we performed at the block party for that. And this was early on. This was before our EP. And our shit sounded like straight Das EFX, Diamond D, all that. And we got up, and it was in the middle of the hood, you know? And dudes that would normally be Geto Boys fans and street thugs and whatever . . . they loved it. So it just kind of showed through that our sound was still universal—good music's good music. We did feel like outsiders to a degree, but we thrived off of that. We were comfortable with that—with being a little bit different. And I think we got attention for that.

I interviewed G-Dash from Swishahouse and asked him if he thought the music industry would set up camp here the way it has in Atlanta, and he paused. It made me realize just how internal Houston has been all these years, just how Houston-centric it has all been.

I've said this for years. And the reason Houston has been that way is because Houston is not that marketable. When you think about all the artists that come up, like every three to five years—you have a wave of artists. In the mid-'90s, you had major labels coming in and picking up artists like UGK. You had labels come through and pick up E.S.G.

Street Military got picked up by Wild Pitch.

Yeah. And then that died. Then three to four years, major labels came in and picked up Yungstar—Sony picked him up. The new wave came through. And then after that, they dropped them all, and then the new wave came through and it was Lil' Keke, Screwed Up Click, all them, you know? But the problem is that the labels don't know how to market the Houston stuff. They're not marketable. You can take somebody in New York or Atlanta, and these dudes, they can put them in Pepsi commercials, they can put 'em in movies. For some reason, they got that pizzazz. They got something about 'em. They got something about 'em that makes them different to where they get attention. You can't do Paul Wall like that. You can't put him in a Pepsi commercial. It just doesn't work. You can't. I've been trying to figure out what it is for years, because I've said that New York and Atlanta and even West Coast dudes, they have that pizzazz. And New York cats, they'll be put in commercials because they look crazy and they're not afraid to wear pink fur, you know? LA's got their own thing, but they got the pizzazz. They got the *gangsta* pizzazz, but something works. When it comes to Houston, Paul Wall and Chamillionaire, they don't *got* that pizzazz. All they got is their music, and that's *it*. And the problem is that their music only goes so far when you don't got pizzazz because labels just don't know what else to do but put a record out that sounds—whether it be good or not—sounds the same every album. And each song on the album pretty much talks about the same shit. So labels get these artists and they have a record out there and they make some sales and then they're like, "Okay . . . we don't know what else to do with you so you're on your own now."

And then they get dropped.

Usually there's one. Usually there's one out of the bunch that'll go a little further, but they might have

good success, and their label will get 'em on TRL. You know, they'll give 'em a little bit more push than the rest, but even those artists don't ever really explode like an Outkast, or a Three 6 Mafia with a TV show. They *just* can't get over that hump, and I've seen it coming up through the industry and coming up in retail. I've seen the wave, and I saw it, like I said, from mid-'90s, I saw how the labels would come through, they'd pick up about five different artists.

Sample pack.

Yeah, and then they'd be promoting them and blowing them up, and then after a year you wouldn't see them again. And then it would be like, it would be quiet for a little while, and then you'd have somebody else come through, and be making some noise on the street—Lil' Flip—and then all the labels run down here and grab up Lil' O, Lil' Flip, you know what I mean? And then only one ends up surviving for a second album. So it happens like that. It's weird, man. It's just something about Houston. These labels get these artists and they're just not marketable. I think it's just too one-dimensional.

Seems like it's intrinsic, though, just to stay in Houston. Never to leave.

Most of the artists here have a different mentality than the East Coast or West Coast. It's a lot slower. It lacks the entertainment side. You know, I've always said that New York and LA are the "entertainment world." That's where things really pop off and where things are able to happen, but Houston, as big as it is, it's just not an entertainment city. We try, but we just never can grasp it because we don't have the corporate part here, the money that comes through here—we just don't have it. That's really what might give people the mentality of . . . the "stay at home," mentality. "I'm just gonna sell out of my trunk to the people here in Houston." They never think to really get out and market themselves in other ways. But it's tough, man. It's really tough. The business, the way it is now . . . there's no more sellin' out the trunk like it used to be. Because you pull up into Carrington's and you got 10 people trying to sell their CDs outside in the parking lot. Before, you had a little bit more quality control—you had one dude that would show up, and he'd have a hot fuckin' record. But now you gotta compete with about five, 10 dudes out there trying to hustle their CDs, and more than half of them—nobody knows who the fuck they are.

Or it's a mixtape with somebody else's beats.

Uh-huh. So it's a different game nowadays but the mentality still stays the same. Houston people are always focused on Houston, and a lot of artists that really blew up and that did it more so on their own were artists that actually went out and did it somewhere else and brought it back home.

K-Otix

SUNNYSIDE/HIRAM CLARKE

Formed in 1992, Damien Randle and Micah Nickerson, along with their producer and DJ Russel Gonzalez (a.k.a. The ARE), comprised one of Houston's best-known underground hip-hop artists, working outside of the more popular traditions of southern gangsta rap. Throughout the '90s, K-Otix built a following in Houston but cast an even wider net with overseas tours and plenty of attention from outside of the city. They started releasing records in 1997, with one album and several 12-inches on the NYC-based Bronx Science Recordings. The ARE left K-Otix in 2004—at which point Damien and Mic started working as The Legendary K.O.—returning to reform the group for the 2016 LP *Legendary*.

Houston has always been sort of split between the gangsta rap side and the sort of underground, hip-hop side. Why do you think there's never really been any crossover?

Damien: Well that's a good question. You know, I grew up right in the middle of the whole S.U.C. movement, so a lot of the folks that I grew up with were involved with or really gravitated towards that. I don't think there's really a conscious effort to not work together. I think, from what I've seen, it's really based on what your influences are. I tend to say that the people who have what people consider the "underground" sound have been kind of influenced, you know, not only regionally but from the East Coast and the West Coast, and from different parts they kind of put it all together. Whereas I think a lot of folks in the South Park Coalition and, I'd say, the S.U.C. really drew their influences from people who were more homegrown. You're gettin' to the same place, but you're just taking a different road to get there. I think there just hasn't been a lot of crossover for the same reason why different sub-genres in rock haven't crossed over. I think there's a mutual respect for it, but I just think it just hasn't happened to a large degree, because it hasn't happened. I don't think there's been any conscious separation between the two.

Micah: I think that it depends on what you want as the outcome. As far as an underground artist, they may see gathering together with a more southern artist . . . see it as more like a sellout move or more of a "get money" type of maneuver, whereas a more southern artist might get with an underground artist to try to manipulate the artist, to get more of a hip-hop type of crowd for their audience. So I think it depends on the motive as well, and just to kind of bounce off what D said, I think the respect is definitely there because most of these artists know of each other. We know of Devin and Scarface and, you know, Slim Thug and whatnot, but the difference is as far as mixin' the style together . . . is there an audience for that? Will a syrup sippin', Screwtape listener listen to a more hip-hop audience and vice versa?

It's funny that you mention Devin because he's one artist you could really say is nestled between the two genres.

DAMIEN AND MIC. PHOTO: SERGIO SANTOS

what's goin' on over here?" A lot of them—Paul Wall, Slim Thug, Mike Jones—came to the forefront at that time, but at the same time a lot of our fan base around the world was like, "We already knew about you guys—how come they aren't including y'all in the same kind of talk?" I know a lot of people asked us if we felt sort of left out, and we didn't feel left out. We were still doing shows overseas at the time.

You guys really escaped the stigma of being the "Group That Did The 'George Bush Doesn't Care About Black People' Song." Was there a conscious effort to not allow it to become a novelty?

Micah: You know, when we first made the song, we just wanted to capture the moment. I think a lot of people from other parts of the country didn't really understand how it felt to be in that type of situation. So me and D were like, "Let's capture the moment, take a snapshot of this moment, to let other people, when they hear it, they can actually feel it." And I think when we made the song, we didn't really expect it to blow up like it did, and it kind of lit its own fire and kind of went a whole other direction, and the whole point of the topic was really to keep it serious, to kind of, you know, not overshadow the fact that it was a tragedy that happened. And that's why we didn't try to capitalize off of it.

Damien: Devin's a good example of that because he's one of those people that draws influences from a lot of places, and, you know, he's fortunate in that he has a very large international following too. And just to kind of piggyback off of what Mic said, the audience that you develop really plays a strong hand in the type of music that you make, and Devin's a good example of that I think because he makes music with more universal themes than a lot of other southern rappers, because his audience is a bit more diverse than what you might see from other regional acts.

Being that there is a sort of division there, did the H-town explosion of 2005 affect you guys at all?

Damien: It affected us, but not in the way that a lot of people feel. The thing is, we've been doing this since 1992, so we've had a pretty . . . you know, most of our audience is not in the Houston area. Most of our audience is in other parts of the country or international. We have a lot of European fans over there. So for us, we already had an audience in place that was checking us out. Then when 2005 came around, a lot of them were more or less like, "Oh, y'all been doing this already . . .

Damien: And the trap that a lot of artists fall into when they come across something like that . . . you gotta understand that for us, this was something that was written while Mic was at home and I was on my way home from work. Then we recorded it and put it out. So it's like he said—we wanted to capture the moment. This sounds like a cliché, but we honestly never knew it would spread like that. You know, we did it on Tuesday. By Thursday it was already all over the place and we started getting calls from people. It took us by surprise . . . and we didn't even have to say this—we're two grown intelligent dudes, and we know this: You can't turn yourself into a novelty. Truth be told, that's not really our song. We just kind of put down, in verse, what other people were going through, what other people were feelin', but we can't lay claim to the whole thing. So, we don't want to make too much out of it because we don't want to be known as, like you said, the "Guys That Did The George Bush Song." We didn't want people to expect us to do more George Bush songs and all of the sudden we become pigeonholed and this and that. We were two dudes that live next door to you or across the state from you that happened to be right in the middle of everything that was going on.

Craig (BBC) Long

FIRST WARD

Craig has been a visible face in Houston as an MC, b-boy (BBC: B-Boy Craig), promoter, artist, and clothing designer since the late 1980s. In the early '90s, he and I worked together in the art room at Mickey Phoenix's Calico Print, which around that time began collaborating with Houston graffiti artist GONZO247 and Aerosol Warfare. BBC has been a regular on the mic at Magic Bus, Power Tools, Club Waxx, Rhythm Room, his monthlies The Bench and The Scenario, and the massive Mixed Media events he hosted at the Museum of Fine Arts Houston from 2004 to 2011. Of late he is out promoting the #HHIFE (Hip Hop Is For Everyone) movement, welcoming everyone to hip-hop through celebrating the genre's diversity.

I just had a conversation with Raheem where we spoke of the old club the Rhinestone Wrangler and how he used to have to sneak in. Were you around back in those days?

Yeah, man, the Royal Flush crew, man, I used to go see those guys all the time. Southside, yo.

The Wrangler off of Murworth. He said those guys were the kings of that place.

It used to be packed, dog. And it's crazy how, like, hip-hop has changed, and especially in Houston. You know, you're talking about the age before computers, e-mail blasts, all that stuff. It was just like word of mouth, you know?

How did the energy level of those crowds compare to that of The Bench?

Well, back then the MC controlled the crowd in a different kind of way. Everybody was so in tune with what was going on. I mean, there was still competition, and it was respected competition, but it was like, when so and so would step into the area, you *knew* it, you know? But at the same time, it didn't feel so . . . *celebrity*. Everybody didn't feel so above you. Like, they were on the same level with you, but this was what they did. They

BBC AND JOE BELMAREZ. PHOTO: JOHN CRUZ

made paper, but they didn't have the entourage and bling. They dressed the same, but the energy was just different. Especially coming from . . . when you think about Raheem and all those cats, South Park Coalition, you could put somebody like Public Enemy in there . . . I guess they hit big in the late '80s, early '90s. But I think about, like, the South Park Coalition and all those cats—they were political, and *real* political. I'm gonna have to say they were way more political than Public Enemy. Man, they were *way* more political back then. They just all stood up different. When you talk about Raheem and such . . . after that stuff started to change. It got more lyrical.

Raheem said that it was a real weird time for him because he was the first major label artist from Houston, and he was being sent out on tour with Shanice Wilson, Lester Williams, Jeffrey Osborne, and he'd go out there doing "Short Shorts," and they just didn't know what to do with him. So he comes back to Houston to regroup, and it's becoming a different city.

It was weird because for him and for me, because you're coming up where hip-hop is peace, love, understanding, and having fun—the ideal four elements of hip-hop. You weren't really now pushing the fact that MCs, DJs, graffiti . . . Afrika Bambaataa said that hip-hop was a party. Where everybody gets together to get unified, love and just having fun.

So how did you get involved, then? How did you start out?

Well my thing is, you know, I've always been an artist. I found my niche, artistically, in this city. I came up watching my brothers . . . they'd have these parties at the house. You know, "grown folks" parties. Me, coming from a big family . . . I'm the youngest of 12, so of course I remember my brothers and sisters talking about going to the skating rink—Rainbow Skating Rink—that a lot of people on this side of town would go to. So I remember my brothers and them having these parties. And of course I would have to be "in bed" by a certain time. But I didn't want to go to sleep, man. I would basically just sneak. I would sneak as far

into the room—because we had a big old house—I would sneak as close to the room where the party was going on as I could. Just watching, you know. People. All night. Until I'd get caught. And have to got my room. And by "my room," I mean "our room." But it was just kind of crazy. After that we lived in this house with a garage, and my brothers made this "chill area" where they would come hang out after school, and I remember my little friends that lived next door to me would be like . . . I was in elementary school, man, and they had all these albums, these funk and soul albums, groups like . . . like the Ohio Players, or A Taste of Honey, with these women on the cover. Because you're talking about the 1970s when censorship was . . . you could probably cuss more back then than they can now, without getting shit for it. Censorship wasn't through the roof back then.

So you wanted to create, you wanted to be a part of something like that.

Yeah. Because it was basically me lookin' up to my brothers and stuff. They were into the whole funk, soul scene, and they already had the cool names and stuff. My brother Jerry, all his friends called him "Hollywood," like "Yo, Hollywood, what's up?" they called him Hollywood instead of Jerry. And my other brother was "Black." It didn't have nothin' to do with the fact that he was black, that was just his name. And it was this endless scenario where he could be someone other than who he was.

And you started doing that for yourself when?

Late '80s . . . you know, I started breakdancing, the whole graffiti thing . . . everything fell into place. Like I said, early on I was always an artist, so that came first, and I was just like, "Oh, man . . . look at all these colors and stuff," and it was just wild. I mean that's nuts, dude. So I started doin' a bit of graffiti. I did jackets and hats and stuff for people. As time went along, I mean I was definitely a black guy with two left feet. Not really much of a sportsman, I didn't play basketball, didn't dance very well, but that didn't matter. But I had real cool Michael Jackson Afro, and then I saw breakin' . . . not the movie, but *breakdancin'* for the first time and was like, "That's some crazy shit." And I couldn't dance, and I don't know if this makes any sense, but I couldn't dance—but I could break-dance. You know? It was a really weird scenario. So there was that, then the music, sometimes I would end up DJing. Never really took DJing a 100 percent serious. Breakin' and graffiti were my thing. And then I started rhyming, so I started MCing and hosting and stuff, and people would always ask me, "Man, you gonna put out an album?" But I was a straight freestyle cat. There's a lot of professional MCs that will tell you that they don't freestyle. If you don't freestyle, you should not mess with the mic no matter who you are. If you're a lyricist, you write lyrics. It's totally different than freestylin'. There's a lot of MCs that have got on the stage to freestyle and rhyme and have choked. That's just not what they do. So eventually, of course, I'm a b-boy. Everybody that's a b-boy, like . . . Lance Walker, if you're a b-boy, you'd be "B-Boy Lance Walker." That's what all the breakdancers were called. And of course originally that was "Bronx Boy" because breakin' originated in the Bronx, but once it got wider, they pretty much changed it from "Bronx Boy" to "Break Boy."

Because of DJ Kool Herc.

Right, which means boys dance to the breaks in the songs.

How is The Bench a culmination of all of those things leading up to now?

The Bench was a representation of all four elements of the culture. And now it's "The Bench Presents," where the name itself is synonymous with hip-hop. It's the culture. The b-boys, our showcasing writer, showcasing DJ, and I always have a *live* hip-hop act. That's the most important part because hip-hop has changed so much, and outside of Houston you don't realize that hip-hop acts in Houston aren't solely just Paul Walls or your Boss Hoggs or Geto Boys even, for that matter. I don't think groups like South Park Coalition get the recognition that they deserve, and they're the foundation of hip-hop here in Houston. They're like pillars. I mean, seriously—there wouldn't be a lot of this shit if it weren't for them.

Murder One

SOUTH PARK

Known as "Ronnie Love" back in the day, Murder One was a player in the battle rap contests of the late 1980s and an early member of the South Park Coalition. Now a veteran of multiple solo albums, he continues to make records and do shows around Houston to this day, often with longtime collaborators K-Rino, Point Blank, Cl'Che, and Klondike Kat.

We were talking about the competition between rappers in the beginning days in Houston. You guys were right there with the pack, weren't you?

During that era we were all compressed in one club, at the Rhinestone Wrangler. That's where every artist, any group, we had to compete against each other. And at that time it was the home of Willie D—because Willie D was a solo artist before he got to the Geto Boys situation, and he was one of the [artists] that Lil' J signed after the Geto Boys—before he even became a Geto Boy himself. So basically it was like every side—north, south, east, west—was tryin' to be the best rapper in town. There wasn't no beef or no, "You from the South, you from the North," or "You was on the mic longer." It was pure talent, and if you had talent you got credit for it. That was the type of era we was havin' at that time.

Seems like it really helped that there was just that one place for people to come to.

You know, we had clubs inside the hood where you could ride your bike to it, to compete or whatever, but that was like the major place at that time, was like in '87. There was other places beside that, but that was the place that . . . if you had a Run–D.M.C. or an LL Cool J in town, they had to go through that club first. It was a real venue. I mean it held a lot of people. I saw a lot of people based in New York. Basically, at that time there was more New York acts than anything else—besides the artists who was competing against each other.

Because most hip-hop was coming out of New York anyway.

In Houston, we made our own New York in many ways. We knew we wasn't too much getting accepted outside our area. So we made it what it is today.

What was South Park like before rap really took root there?

It was just DJs and mixin'. It was, "What school got a party goin' on?" That was what it was before we had rap clubs. The DJs controlled everything. Because without the DJs we wouldn't'ta knew the Run–D.M.C.s, the Kurtis Blows, all that. So at that time, before we got into it, to influence us to get into it was the DJs. At that time, who was hot in the business? Ice-T. Breakdancin'. That's all we knew right there—we had breakdancin' and the DJs. That controlled every party. And then the hip-hop came later.

The culture was already there.

PHOTO: PETER BESTE

Yeah, the culture was there. Once the DJs set the tone for the culture it was obvious that rap was gonna be not too far behind it. You had the DJs and the breakers. Only thing missing was the MCs. By the time "Sucker MCs" came out, everybody and they mama wanted to rap then! That was the hottest thing that I'd heard.

Not to mention that it gave you, the youth, something constructive to do . . .

Yeah, it gave us something to stay off the streets. Don't just go outside to sell drugs. At the time, I was playing football, N-I-P was a drum major, you know . . . people didn't know that. N-I-P was a drum major, I played football. It gave and it took away because I had two things I was doin'. I was rappin' and I was playin' ball. I took rap over ball 'cuz I had a stronger passion for that. If it wasn't for Darryl Scott, I don't think none of us woulda been into hip-hop.

So how did the streets change after that?

It was one big party! Like I said, we already had the DJs and the breakers. We just needed the MCs. And that's how it changed. Before the MCs you had boys would ride down the street beatin' down the block. Everybody had 808 drum machines, and we

all came out there. You had boys playin' loud music with bass—BOOM! Beastie Boys, Run–D.M.C., that's all you heard. Whodini. People like that. So for us . . . we were like, "We need to get played. We need some of that airtime that these cars are playin'." And that's what brought the MCs together. It was all lyrical. It wasn't all cosmetic like it is today. Everybody put a lot of makeup on they skills these days 'cuz they figure they have to do that. They don't have to do that.

It's interesting because even the early stuff you guys were doing was telling what was going on in the streets, even that early on . . .

And that's what you gonna get. In the '80s, we wasn't usin' profanity. That's the only difference.

Because you didn't feel like you could? Why?

Because everything that came out then . . . wasn't no profanity. If you didn't have lyrics, you didn't have anything. We'd depend on it back then. We would say, "Oh, that dude can really rap." It was more skills than anything else. And then in the era when N.W.A. and all them came, that's when the profanity got into the formula.

Do you feel like that helped it or hurt it?

I mean, you know, you got to change with time. So it benefited it because it kept the audience goin'. And anyone that wasn't cursin', had to do the cursin' to stay in the business.

But you feel like what was being said in the lyricism of that period was pretty representative of what was going on?

Yeah, like today, if you listen to a K-Rino album or my album, Geto Boys album . . . not just us, I mean you know there are still rappers out here with morals. You know, 'cuz people love the stories, and people love the passion of what they have been through or they are doing, and so you have somebody not glorify it, but at least let the world know, "This is what I'm doin' for mine."

So what do you think the next real movement will be in Houston?

It's goin' back to the '80s. The Murder Ones and K-Rinos and Street Militarys . . . we fittin' to get our chance again. Not meanin' we out of the picture, but the real rappin' comes back into play. Everybody wantin' real rap. We hear it all the time. Not knockin' what boys do, don't get me wrong, I don't want people sayin' that. That's not true. It's just that . . . how many times you can snap a finger? How many times you can do this dance? How can I indicate this kid that's growin' up in bad times right now . . . that's what they want? We got our kids listenin' now. We just not gangsta rappers. There's a meanin' behind everything. Me and K-Rino got this song on my album called "Conversations With God." We askin' God, "Why is this? Why is that?" You know, answers . . . questions that people wanna know . . . let's change. What can you tell me to change? For our community. There's a lot of positive stuff that went in.

I asked K about this, and he said, "You know, whether we like it or not, we're teaching them. We're teaching our youth."

We are.

Do you feel like they absorb it and appreciate, understand it for what it really is?

If we comin' real with it, they appreciate it. There's not a fan I'ma . . . snap my fingers and step with it . . . what they gonna get out that? I'm not knockin' it. Everybody got a way of talkin'. My English . . . I probably got the bad . . . the worsest English you could really use, but in my rap form, you understand everything I just put on the table. And people accept that. You have older people . . . right now I got people call me all the time 50, 40 . . . almost 60 years old . . . "Y'all keep doin' what y'all doin'. I got my 14-year-old son listenin', my 13-year-old son listenin' to it." Like, "Y'all keepin' it real . . . y'all tell it like it is," this and that. You know, that's why we do what we do. You can take money from me, you can take jobs from me, but you can't take the heart from me. When I got in this business, it was passion. I didn't think about the money. I thought about money when it got to 2000. I been in the music game 20 years now.

Point Blank

SOUTH PARK

Also known as The Bull, he came to Houston from Chicago in the early '90s and right away met up with Dope E. of The Terrorists, who would go on to produce for him countless times over the following decades. Point Blank also crossed paths with K-Rino early on, becoming a part of the South Park Coalition and going on to form a group called Wreckless Klan with Ice Lord and fellow S.P.C. member PSK-13. He eventually signed with Russell Washington's Bigtyme Recordz, which released his debut, *Prone To Bad Dreams*, in 1992, and now puts out records for himself and other artists on his own Money Fam label.

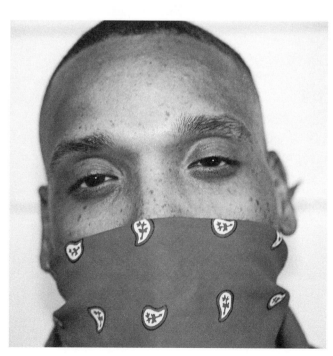

PHOTO: PETER BESTE

Were you rapping at all in Chicago? I guess that was a little young.

I mean, I was rappin' . . . my hood knew I knew how to rap. Anybody that came to my hood . . . I was a terror in my hood.

And when you moved to Houston, did you move right to the Southside?

When I moved to Houston, I got dropped right on in the Dead End off MLK. I used to stay in King Gates Apartments, but they don't call them King Gates no more. I went to Sterling High School, which—K-Rino attended Sterling High School. I got dropped in South Park. That's the first hood I entered, and . . . shit, I still rep it today to the fullest, you dig?

There's kind of a mythology. South Park is really kind of a magical place for a lot of people. Did you feel that right away?

It was real. You know, I was straight from the Chi, but . . . it was right with my agenda. I felt right at home.

Who did you meet first out of all those guys?

Dope E. [a.k.a.] Murdoq. He was the one I used to run into all the time. You know, tryin' to get in where I fit in. S.P.C. already had a flag up. I was straight from the Chi, gettin' it in, learning my way through. Me and Dope E. used to run into each other all the time. I was tryin' to get beats from him and shit. You know, he did beats for everybody at that time. And we just ran into each other all the time. We ended up moving into the same apartment complex. We both was in the same leasing office, gettin' our leases and keys to apartments, so it was just meant for me and Dope to fuck around.

And he produced some of the first stuff you were rapping on in Houston?

Yeah, *Prone To Bad Dreams*, my first album. Dope E. of The Terrorists produced all that. Him and Egypt E.

I got the tape. It's got a Houston side and Chi-Town side.

Yeah, no doubt. I was like fresh on deck. Pimp C did one track on that album, "Cut You In Half." And Dope E. did all the rest of it.

And what year was that? That was '91 . . . something like that?

Yeah, we probably was doin' the recordin' in '91, but it ain't come out 'til '92. And when I got locked up, when I got out of jail me and Dope E. hooked up. And he really did my whole record.

Were you with those guys early enough to where they were still doing battle raps? This was still in high school, with those guys?

Yeah, K-Rino was in high school. Like I said, I was in Sterling. You know, I saw K-Rino from afar. If you wanted to do some music, you had to know who K-Rino was. Hell, I went to Sterling High School, and that was the school he went to, so them niggas used to hook up in the bathroom all the time. I used to go in there and watch them niggas, but I never got involved in the battles or nothin'. I was just back observin', and watching K-Rino eat niggas' ass up in the bathroom. I even talked to him about this and let him know some of the days I went . . . when I didn't know him, when I wasn't friends with him. I knew who he was, but I wasn't introduced to him. But when I was going to that

school, everybody respected K-Rino. I used to go in the bathrooms when they went in the bathrooms. K-Rino used to wreck shit. He used to be at the talent shows, and I used to be at all that shit, but you know, nobody knew who I was at the time. I was an underdog on the rise.

There was stuff going on in the skate rinks and everything at that point, right?

Yeah, it definitely was going down, and Ganksta N-I-P, you know, he was the king of the swing. He was hot in the clubs. You got to hear about Ganksta N I P, know what I'm sayin'? South Park was really holding it down, you know, Scarface, Geto Boys . . . of course, you know, they at the top of the rankings, but the South Park Coalition was in the mix.

Do you remember the first time you heard N-I-P, or you saw N-I-P?

Well, like I said, I used to run into all of 'em from fuckin' with Dope E. But you know, me and N-I-P real encounters was in this club called 808. They used to call it Infinity. It was a hood club in South Park. It was really goin' down in that motherfucker back then. So me and N-I-P used to get it in, with me and N-I-P, man, we just connected. Me and N-I-P got down for a long time.

Is that who you started performing with early on, when you were doing shows?

I wasn't doin' no shows yet. I did go on tour with N-I-P, after we was already in the mix, already family. At the beginning, I used to go do little talent shows and contests up at that club. N-I-P used to rule at the club. When I got to the club, N-I-P ran all that shit. He would win everything and all that. So, he was kinda retired when I got there, as far as bein' in the contest, because he already was the king of that motherfucker. But I end up gettin' in it one night, and I end up winnin' that bitch. That was at Club 808.

808 was right over by King's, right?

Yeah, it was over in that area. Even Scarface used to be in this bathroom I'm talkin' about. That's just something we used to do. When we got to the club, some of the rappers, we'd end up in the bathroom together. I end up in there rappin' one time, and Scarface was in there listenin' to me rap. We all used to get up in that motherfucker and get down, in the bathroom, kickin' some hard-ass flows in the bathroom of the club.

So what year did you go on tour with N-I-P?

I went on tour with N-I-P when he was with Rap-A-Lot. On one of them albums—the album that got "Small Town Killas" on it. Whichever album that N-I-P dropped that got "Small Town Killas" on it (*Psychotic Genius*). Geto Boys had a tour. It was all Rap-A-Lot. Geto Boys, Scarface, 5th Ward Boyz, Ganksta N-I-P . . . and I think they had them dudes from Cali . . . Menace Clan.

After that record came out, and N-I-P had featured a lot of you guys on that record, that's how a lot of people found out about the South Park Coalition and brought in a new audience, right?

That's right. I still was fresh on deck in South Park. When I won my contests, and started gettin' my own crowd, my own thing, N-I-P came to me and told me he wanted me to be on this song called "Rough Brothers From South Park." He was already gettin' it in with his record. He told me he wanted me to be on that song, so I got on it.

And your album [*Prone To Bad Dreams*] came out after that or before that?

It was after that. I don't think I even had no record yet. I was plantin' my feet. I hadn't even met Bigtyme yet, to even have no record deal.

Is that the only record you did on Bigtyme?

Nah, I did *Prone To Bad Dreams*, *What is The World*, *In The Door*, *Bad News Travels Fast*, *Wreckless Klan*. I did a lot of albums on the Bigtyme label.

And you started your own label.

Yeah, I had stared Wreckless Entertainment, and I still currently got Wreckless Entertainment, but my current label now is Money Fam Ink. That's the new movement.

That's your label or the label that you're on?

Nah, it's my label, but at the end of the day . . . I got an artist named Money Fam Dre. That's where the Money Fam name even came from. So, at the end of the day, I'm leaving the cap hangin', but I gotta say, it's all our label, you dig what I'm sayin'? 'Cuz we a family. I ain't makin' no moves that don't nobody know about. I'm just like president of the shit, CEO of the shit, but it's all a family situation. It ain't nothin' happenin' without the other one.

Because it becomes a movement that way. You promote all the artists at once.

Money Fam is the movement. Money Fam Dre is from Texas City. Over the past year, I've just been workin' him in, just tryin' to introduce him to my fans and create him a market for his self, you know what I'm sayin'? I got a lot of artists, and I try and teach 'em to grind, man. That shit don't just come to you. You gotta . . . I show these niggas. I don't just talk. I get out here and *do*. Niggas gotta get out here and do what I do. I'm out here in the trenches in this shit . . . I'll travel all over the world. I don't give a fuck.

Does it take a lot to get the young guys to understand that?

I mean, I ain't got no bunch of energy, man. I got kids, and I take time to be teachin' my kids, but if there's somebody that I feel worth the knowledge I got to give 'em and worth the game I got to give 'em and show them to open their eyes to, then I'll give 'em that time if they askin' for it and they wanna do it. But a lot of people just want the fun. They want all the fun and shit what come with the situation, and this shit is hard work. This shit ain't easy, runnin' around gettin' motherfuckers to buy your music and all that shit. It ain't like they goin' in the store to get your music. They buy it because they see you out, representin', bein' a real individual. I go city to city, state to state, town to town whether they know I'm comin' or not. I done been way to Australia. Seven cities out the trunk, all in Australia.

Do you still tour a lot?

Yeah, I still tour a lot, man. I just did a show last night with Big Pokey in Houston. At a club called 6324 in the hood, at 610 and MLK at an after hours spot. It was that boy Knock's birthday, from Herschelwood Hardheadz. We all was up there 'til about five in the mornin' . . . I'm on the road, I'm headed toward East Texas. I just left Huntsville, now I'm workin' my way to Madisonville, and I'ma go through all the 'villes. Probably go through Dallas and get up on 20, go through Marshall . . . there ain't no tellin', man. Gonna make me a 360.

So what do you do, you have neighborhoods that you hit or you hit record stores? Where do you go?

I hit everything when I hit a city. If there's a record store exists, I'm at it. I'm in the hood, I'm wherever real niggas at. That's why you don't see me, because motherfuckers can't go where I go. If they say, "It's hot over there," that's where the fuck I'm at, because that's where I gotta be to get mine. Everybody can't go where I go. This travelin' shit dangerous. It's a dangerous job, brother. Can't no pussy-ass nigga do it.

Do you go mostly in Texas, or do you go Louisiana too?

I go Louisiana—all over, man. I got fans everywhere. I'm all in the streets of Alexandria, Lake Charles . . . I be all in the small towns . . . Crowley and Ennis . . . all over Louisiana I got love. I get a lot of money in The Boot.

What are the shows out there like, when you go out there and perform?

I ain't did no shows in The Boot, but the streets accept me. They been acceptin' me. My music classic out there in Louisiana, and they still buyin' my new shit. I ain't did no shows out there, but you know, I stay in the streets out there and keep myself in they face and stay relevant. I think they was playin' me in Lake Charles on the radio station. They was playin' "Make Doing Bad Look Good," "My Mind Went Blank," and shit like that. You never know where they playin' you at, man. But you know, I'm in the street with this shit.

What's your new album going to be called?

No Money, No Reason.

And when's it going to come out?

It'll come out soon as God want it to come out. When everything in order and everything where it need to be, blessings come running my way, and everything happen the way it need to be whenever it's meant. Whenever it's time. It's being worked on, it's being mixed, new things happening every day. Tour's all ready. If a situation come my way, I'm ready to get down, but I'ma put it out when the time is right, man.

Back in the day, early on, when *Prone To Bad Dreams* came out and everything like that, would you go do the shows in smaller towns like that, or would you just kind of stick around Houston? Aside from the tours.

I did whatever they had hooked up. I wasn't doin' what I'm doin' now. If I was doing what I'm doing now then, I'd be rich already.

So when did you start doing this, the approach where you're going to all of the small towns and everything?

After my last [stint in the penitentiary], after I got out and just started gettin' more serious, runnin' my own shit when I went to deal with Southwest [Wholesale] and just came back a different person.

2001 is when you got out?

Yeah.

How long were you locked up?

Almost three years. I got locked up soon as *Bad News Travels Fast* dropped! I was in jail, and I put a whole lot of work and money in that record. I got locked up, I didn't even see it released!

What did you get locked up for?

Shit . . . fuckin' around in the streets, man. Fuckin' with them drugs. Got caught with some Sherm, got caught with a couple of strats. I just was reckless back then, to be honest. I'm a different person now. You gotta watch what you do out here and how you do it. Got caught up with a drug case and pickin' up . . . I had caught a weed case in Baton Rouge, in Louisiana. I just was reckless, picking up felony cases everywhere, had to pay these motherfuckin' lawyers, takin' all my motherfuckin' money. And, you know, still ended up gettin' some time and shit like that. Had to wake up. You know, God just had to stop me for a minute.

And when you got out, you were a different person?

Yeah, no doubt. A whole new man with a whole new plan. Like I said, when I got out, I had stopped fuckin' with Southwest. I had stopped fuckin' with Robert Guillerman. When I did *Bad News Travels Fast*, I really was already—I had records out myself. Robert Guillerman wasn't givin' me the money I wanted 'cuz I guess he ain't feel like I was ready to just have the shit, so we pulled Russell [Washington] back in since Russell was the one puttin' my records out. I did it 'cuz I had more control, but it still had "Big Tyme WK" on that *Bad News Travels Fast* record. That really was all my action. Russell got pulled in, and I just . . . I end up lettin' it happen . . .

Did you take a hit when Southwest went down?

Hell yeah, I took a hit. I had about 75G's up there. And was fittin' to pick up 25. I mean, at the end of the day, every time I went up there to get some money, thinkin' it's gonna be one thing, it always be less. But at least, every month—every other month or whatever, you pick up 10, 5, whatever, you know . . . depends on who it is. The money varies. Plenty of people got big paper from up there. I used to pick up some nice checks from up there, but you got 8, 9, 15, 16, 17G's comin' in, then now when you still doin' what you doin'—that's a big-ass help, bro.

What sunk Southwest?

I don't know. I guess they got in over they heads with the shit they was doin'. Tryin' to cover that money and file bankruptcy on that shit. I don't even know what kind of corruption was goin' on up there. All I know is that it affected our whole southwest region. It ain't affect niggas like me, 'cuz I get out in the streets and they buyin' my shit. So, when they stop doin' that shit, I was still out here gettin' it in, and niggas had to get out and try to do what I was doin', to get money! But I was already used to doin' it. I already was out here doin' it, so the only thing I missed was gettin' them big checks every now and then.

Right, but you knew what you wanted to do anyway. You knew how you wanted go about it.

Exactly. I do the best I can with what I got, man. At the end of the day, you do the best you can with what you got, be thankful for what you get. Man, I've raised my kids doin' this shit. I live off the rap. I don't work no job and rap, I don't sell no dope and rap—I don't do *shit* I used to do and rap. Blood, sweat and tears, I'm out here gettin' money with this shit. Sometimes, we had the seats back, sleep in the motherfuckin' car—with money in our pockets. It's by choice, not by force. Tryin' to make every dollar we can. We travel around this motherfucker and rake every motherfuckin' city we go to, top to bottom. Then we go to the next one and do the same motherfuckin' thing. And so on and so on. Oklahoma, it don't fuckin' matter. Every-motherfuckin'-where. I might pop up any-motherfuckin'-where and blow a motherfuckin' mind. "Man, what you doin' here?" Gettin' it in.

Dope E.

SOUTH PARK

A.k.a. Murdoq, he is the founding member of The Terrorists, who released their debut album on Rap-A-Lot in 1992. He is an original member of the South Park Coalition and has produced albums' worth of material for Gangsta N-I-P, K-Rino, and Point Blank, to name a few. He now lives in Austin and still records under both of his aforementioned names.

You're someone to speak on the Illuminati.

No doubt, yeah. You know, it's . . . I mean, as far as the name and what they doin', you know that, again, that whole thing is funded with the people that have the paper, you know? They control the music, you know? They control the sports league, entertainment league. They perform at high levels, spending our money. And then again, all of that's a part—that's the reason why they are well-liked, you know? "Illuminati" is like the mature name or the latest name we have. I mean, really, once you go back you'll get to Bohemian Grove, you know? It's where over a thousand globalists hook up every so often, you know, three, four months or whatever. In Sonoma, California is, like, one of their places where they hook up and do they little meetings. But Bohemian Grove'll switch to . . . you know, as you continue to go back it'll switch to Skull and Bones, and Skull and Bones goes all the way back. Skull and Bones is the affiliation of the Illuminati. Like, it's all controlled by the same entity. And so that's, like, my research on it. It's not just this new group of people that's doing this or, you know, that's in the music business or whatever, the entertainment field, and controlling stuff, it's like . . .

Entertainment's just one small part of it.

Exactly. You know, they start recruiting back in high school. I remember myself—you know, me goin' to an all-white school, I remember drawing skulls, skullhead, skull and bones, and I remember takin' that to K-Rino. I remember this shit. I said, "You want some hard shit, some gangsta shit? This need to be the logo. It's gonna be South Park Coalition with that shit sittin' there." And he's like, "Uh . . . nah, nah." But we still said we didn't like the skull head and the bones—like, we didn't know why we didn't like 'em, we just based our teenaged opinions on shit. It's like they start recruiting then. That's why a lot of 'em, like I say, is highly prestigious. It's nothing little. You know, you got your little . . . I'm talkin' about the players that graduate from Princeton, that are known to go to Yale . . . it starts on the local level, it starts on the city level, all the way up to the Federal level. That's where the Federal—that's the "big boys," as they say—that's where the fascism starts to hit at, and that driving force is the Illuminati. That's the so-called name of it in entertainment. So that's just one small portion because the Jesuits—the Jesuits control the Illuminati! So it's like . . . where does it stop? It stops where your knowledge is. It stops where you think that it exists at and the name you learned it is. But it's a lot of names.

You're talking about it being in control of entertainment, and music being—especially rap music—being dumbed down to the point that it is, it's like saying, "Now I see that you're in control of this, *now* I see what you're doing with it."

Exactly. Like I said, man, we're talking about the latest, latest phase . . . like when you're a child. And we'll both agree as a child, that's the easiest time for you to get deceived. The easiest time. Because you hadn't went through any experience, you don't know anything . . . if my uncle—and I stayed with my uncle—nine years old, I was stayin' with him, and he was asleep in the back. And then somebody came off the street, "Hey man, your uncle there?" "Nah, he's asleep." "Okay, hey—go in there and get five pounds outta there. We had already talked about it. And bring them to me. I gotta take 'em to Louisiana, flip 'em, and bring 'em back. Don't wake him up." And I go in there and get them pounds and go give 'em to him. And I find out later he's all, "What happened to my pounds?" "Larry came by." He said, "No, don't do that shit!" And let's say . . . well, it doesn't matter—I was gonna say, "What if I'm 16 . . ." but it doesn't have to be like that. Let's just say I'm still nine and it happens again. "Okay, well shit . . . you're gonna have to wait 'til my uncle wake up, Larry. I can't do that no more. I got in trouble, man. That's not

right." See, you've been introduced to it. So all I'm saying is, is as a child, we're introduced to all these evil depictions and images that's perpetuated on television . . . you know, all over the radio. And how do I know? Because I remember my mother telling me to get out the room several times, or plug my ears when the radio's playing, or cover my eyes when the TV's going . . . and the separation between that is we're still being introduced to negative weight. Humans aren't responsible for a higher power as they bring negativity, and then they say, "Hey, you know, you have to, you know, take this television guide, this remote and program the certain stations." Now are you are responsible for that, watching your child. No, no we're not. Just take it off completely. Let's say they wanna stop drinking, but they don't pass the law and say, "Don't get caught drinkin' and driving." Just take it off the streets, man. Just take it out the stores, stop the distribution, shut the fuckin' companies down. But they stir it up to make it seem like responsible—so they're making us control their negativity that they are creating. Who am I saying, "they?" You could say "Illuminati," but I'm sayin', when I was a child. So did the Illuminati exist back then? That's why the name is just a new name or whatever, because when I was 4 or 5, I'm steady lookin' at "Sanford and Son," I'm lookin' at "Good Times," you know, I'm lookin' at these TV stations, sitcoms that I'm trusting, and I am getting my views from that, and I'm patterning my thoughts and my life and my actions after these TV shows that are on television. That is a fact. People don't wanna say that, but it's a fact.

Top Dog

SOUTH PARK

Best known in the Houston music world for his work with the South Park Coalition and his 2005 solo album *Slam Dunk'n Hoes*, Top Dog is a former pimp and current author, now having published several books under his real name, Alvando Ray. The first of those books, *Deep In The Mind Of A Pimp 2000*, was published the year after this interview.

Where were you in the mid-'80s? Were you in South Park?

Yeah. I was beatboxing and doin' a little rappin' over there, but I was more of a beatboxer than I was a rapper. I used to try and do a little rappin' too or whatever, but at the time, it seemed like I enjoyed beatboxing more.

You just felt like you were better at it?

Yeah, yeah. But then me and Mike-D, you know with S.U.C.? Back then we used to beatbox and rap together a lot. Back in middle school and then later on . . . because he was more of a rapper than he was a beatboxer, but, you know, he used to beatbox a bit too. Later on down the road he pretty much started pursuing his rap career, and you know, you got to a point where people wasn't really beatboxin' no more. But you know back then, that's pretty much what it was all about, rappin' and beatboxin'.

Back then, some of the stars were beatboxers. Buff Love, Doug E. Fresh . . .

Yeah, yeah. That's what we used to do back then.

So where were you . . . were you at the Rhinestone, or what?

Nah, I didn't start really goin' to clubs and stuff 'til later on and stuff. I missed a lot of the big concerts and stuff that used to come into town. Growin' up . . . I don't know . . . I was in the streets real hard and, you know . . . a lot of the concerts and different things, some of the things people were goin' to . . . I didn't go to a lot of that. Later on I started tryin' to hit up a lot of stuff or whatever, but I got in the streets kinda early.

What were the streets like in South Park for you at that young age?

Well, I was already gettin' high and stuff like that, in middle school, you know . . . so I got to high school, it wasn't really no big thing. Basically, I just intensified the high. Started doin' a little petty hustlin' and stuff like that . . . you know, more girls and stuff like that 'cuz you know, when I was 12 years old, that's when I first realized that I was a player. And then when I got 13, I tried to pimp my friend's ho . . . but you know, since then—I'd say within about the last year, year and a half, I've pretty much tried to change my life. Take a different course. You know, I've been thinkin' more about the spiritual than the natural. Because when I close my eyes for the final time, I wanna be confident in where I'm goin'. I don't wanna be

caught up in this, you know what I'm sayin'? But like you say, back in the mid-'80s or whatever, there was a lot of things . . . there was a lot of things bein' birthed and a lot of new things . . . people was breakdancin', poppin' and lockin', and you know, I tried to do a little bit of breakdancin', but it really wasn't my thing. Like I say, I was mainly a beatboxer, and you know, I was skippin' class a lot and gettin' in trouble . . . I really didn't think I was gonna graduate, to go to high school to the ninth grade . . . but when I got to the ninth grade, that was the first time that I had failed. Not because I couldn't do the work but mainly because of absences. I was skippin' at school a lot because I had started gettin' in the street. Like I say, I was smokin' more weed, and I started sellin' crack and all that. Basically, thuggin' . . . and started keepin' me a firearm with me and you know, just gettin' into little nonsense trouble and stuff. I went to juvenile [detention center] when I was 14. Aggravated assault. All that was senseless. About a couple of weeks after that, went to jail again for havin' a pistol. You know, I was in and out of jail for my teenage years, juvenile years . . . I kinda slowed down a little bit, goin' to jail . . . I ended up goin' to

prison and stuff a little bit down the road. I mean, a lot of things changed so far as the music . . . a lot of the other stuff pretty much stayed the same as far as people fixin' up cars, you know, slabs or whatever . . .

That's always been a part of Houston.

People fixin' up slabs and goin' to hang at MacGregor Park, hittin' different little club scenes, throwin' block parties, hittin' this and that . . . but I'ma tell you a big difference probably . . . now versus then . . . I think there was a lot more unity back then, especially so far as the DJ, MC, and stuff concerned . . . nowadays it seems like the music industry has kinda got a whole lot more politics involved. You got all these DJ pools and all these DJ clubs and such and such . . . it's kinda like the MC and the DJ on separate teams or somethin', you know? Instead of one another helpin' each other to prosper, it's kinda like a . . . almost like a gang thing . . . "If you not down with this, we not gonna help you do this." And speakin' of gang things . . . a lot of that I'm pretty sure had something to do with it too, but I'm just sayin' even people that's not in gangs have to go through some of the similar things that people have to go through in gangs, 'cuz they not a part of a certain organization or they not supportin' a certain organization or somethin' like that. You know . . . the DJs don't wanna play your music, and they don't wanna give you a chance.

How organized was gang activity back then? Not just talking about crime—I'm talking about the gang presence.

It really tripped me out because, you know, when I was growin' up . . . a lot of the LA gangs and Chicago gangs and this and that . . . they didn't really have much influence on my neighborhood or surrounding neighborhoods. And then, as time went on, that changed drastically. I mean, that's like . . . when you ride through some neighborhoods, if you don't know where you at, you might think that, you know, you in Cali or Chicago for the simple fact . . . the influence that a lot of those gangs have put upon some of the other cities or whatnot because— me personally . . . I'm not fittin' to represent nobody else's neighborhood, nobody else's street and all that. That's what be trippin' me out about a lot of people I know . . . they representin' areas and places that they not even familiar with, that they not even from, and a lot of them, where they can't even go—they won't even be accepted at! So, you know, that be trippin' me out.

We think about something like that today where we have the internet as a possible tool, where something like that could trickle down, where you could find out about gangs, but back then, how would somebody have done that from afar? How would somebody have put their influence there?

Well, for one, we already know that movie *Colors* played a big part in it because a lot of people see movies and see TV, and you know, for some reason they glamorize that stuff. You know, they get all flabbergasted and, like I say—TV, and people wantin' to be on TV—so a lot of people wanna live the lives that they see people livin' on TV. But then when you got guys from Cali and different places that come to a different region or area or whatever, you know, some of these guys be fascinated by that for some reason. And then they wanna learn about those peoples' lifestyles, the organizations they into, and the next thing you know they wanna join.

They wanna be a part of it.

Yeah, just like how the armed services—Marines, Air Force, and Army and stuff send recruiters out to different neighborhood areas to get people . . . you know, a lot of the gangs do the same thing. And you be havin' so many people eager to be a part of something and belong to something and do something that they get caught up.

How easy was it when you were growing up in South Park, when you were 13, 14 years old—well, I don't know if that's how old you were when you were selling crack, but I definitely know people who were selling crack when they were . . .

Yeah, yeah, yeah! That's how old I was when I first started.

How easy was it for you to get into that, and how easy would it have been for you to avoid that?

Well, first of all, drugs were in my house when I was growing up. My old man was a math and science teacher, but he was also a daily user of marijuana and alcohol. And you know, later on he ventured off into other drugs . . . but he also sold and grew weed. It started off bein' in my house, so when I went in the streets and saw other people gettin' high it wasn't nothin' odd to me. It was normal. So that's how easy it was for me to start gettin' high and eventually into drug peddling and stuff like that. But I didn't sell crack for as long a period of time as most people I know. For some reason, it just really didn't sit right with me. I never really . . . I don't know, there's just something about cocaine and crack, man, that just didn't . . . I just really didn't agree with it. I guess, for one—you can see what it do to people, and two—you know, they started givin' real harsh and stiff punishments for people that were bein' caught with it, and I just didn't feel that it was worth it.

So you drew the line. Do you think a lot of people did? Do you think a lot of people saw that crack is a much different thing than just smoking a blunt?

Well, I think so far as using it, I think more people probably try to separate the harshness of it . . . you know, a lot of people, when they talk about usin' it, they might say, "Cocaine is a lot different than weed," but when it comes to sellin' it, most people probably pretty much put it in the same category. Me, you know, I used to sell weed for years and years and years, and to me, it was totally different than sellin' crack. I mean, but you know, a person who don't do neither one'll probably put it all in the same category.

Did you separate that because of . . . you must have seen a difference—you sell some crack to somebody and you sell some weed to somebody, you gotta see a difference in the customer, right?

Yeah, that's true. That's true. You could see a difference because weed is something that's more manageable, whereas crack cocaine, seem like people just go all out to where they jeopardize everything. They livelihood, period. Just losin' everything from they house, they kids, they means of makin' a livin', they groomin', they self-respect. I mean everything. Weed, you know . . . you don't really see too many people lose as much behind that. I mean, it happens now—don't get me wrong. It's just very, very . . . scarce when compared to what the effects that cocaine have on people.

What about syrup? From your perspective.

Syrup . . . see, now I done did a lot of different drugs myself too, personally. Syrup is very, very addictive. You know, a lot of people get caught up with syrup because it got to a point to where it was like a social thing. Like, "You drink this syrup and kick it with us—you hip." Part of the in-crowd. That's how a lot of people was lookin' at it, but not realizin' that syrup was just as addictive as heroin and cocaine! 'Cuz I . . . I'm speakin' from experience, 'cuz I know it was real . . . it was *real* hard for me to kick the habit. I mean, real hard. And if you not sellin' drugs, or have some high payin' job, then I don't know what kind of means a person will take to try and supply that habit, because that's a real expensive high.

It's really expensive.

I was addicted to syrup for, you know, 10 years or better, and that was a hard 10 years, I tell you . . . I'm talkin' about—feel like 20, 25 or somethin' . . .

How did you kick it? How did you kick the habit?

Well, I guess it's pretty much like anything else. You know, you have to ask for help from your higher power. A lot of times, yeah, we think we can do everything by ourselves, but we end up findin' out that's not true. So we have to ask for help. You know, from God. But I don't care how many twelve-step programs you go in and this, this and that . . . ain't none of that gonna do you no good if you not gettin' help from the right source, you know what I'm sayin'? Yeah.

Some people will look in from the outside and see in rap culture an exploitation of women . . . what's your take on that now, from what you used to do, to your new outlook?

Well, first of all—not just from a pimp's perspective but just from anybody's eyes I guess, you know . . . a person is only gonna do what they are allowed to do. And a lot of times, we get so caught up in doin' what we wanna do, we forget about what we should do. And I say that to say this: when these females can dress half-naked and get all the attention that they feel they want, been missin', and feel they need or whatever to help with whatever complexes they might have or whatever . . . and they go out and do that, they get the type of responses and things that they want, then . . . they not gonna see nothing wrong with it. The same way as . . . as a pimp. The pimp don't see no problem with it either because the same attention that they gettin', a pimp know that there's gonna be guys that's willin' to pay and this and this and that, and if he can get into the chick head good enough then he knows he's gonna make that benefit him. But what I come to realize is that the pimp ain't really no better than the ho. In God's eyes. You know what I'm sayin'? But as a pimp we think, "Well this hooker ain't nothin'. She goin' out here turnin' tricks and havin' sex with all these guys, don't care about us, blah, blah blah . . ." But at the same time, in God's eyes we . . . the pimp ain't no better than the ho.

Some guys say that everything they do from the moment they wake up in the morning—the slabs, cars, jewelry—that everything they do is for the ladies.

Well, see . . . me personally, I tend to disagree. Now, you got a lot of people . . . see the main ones who say that . . . I mean, don't get me wrong—I'm pretty sure there might be some pimps that say that too, but most people who think like that are the tricks. Them the ones that wanna give the ladies all they money, see. A pimp and any man with any kind of wisdom know it's about *him*. It's about him. Because . . . you ain't gonna get nowhere runnin' behind no women, and always tryin' to please women and puttin' yourself on the back burner, know what I'm sayin'? You got to be your primary concern. Because you got to make sure that you are the foundation. You got to be solid like concrete. And anything else that you get that's worthy, you can build with that. But you can't never have nothing steady, runnin' around chasin' skirts.

How early on did you realize that? Did you learn that early on?

Oh yeah. Most definitely. Like I say in one of my books—I feel I learned more between the ages of 12 and 17 than most men probably learn in they entire life. About women.

Why is that?

Well because most boys grow up tryin' to learn how to have sex with little girls . . . tryin' to say the right phrase or right line, do the right thing. But little girls . . . most little girls are brought up and then taught how to play games and run games on little boys, you understand what I'm sayin'? So it's kind of like a cat and mouse game from the beginning. And that's how a lot of people are brought up. But somebody have to step in and tell the people, "Well, hey—the man is the head of the household. The man was here first. The woman was put here to please man." So, the man has to stand up. Be the tree. And everything else be the branches from the tree. But a lot of men feel like they can't do nothin' without no woman. And like you say—some of them feel that it's all about the woman. But a smart person'll tell you it's a man's world. A woman just helps make it complete.

You were talking about how you've been looking at things differently for the past year, year and a half. Tell me what you're seeing now that you didn't see before.

Well, for one . . . here true enough, I was pimpin' hos, but the devil was pimpin' *me*. I was pimpin' hos, but the devil was pimpin' me. I pimped hos for, like, about 15 years or so, you know, and I can't lie to you—I done had some good times and a lot of good memories and stuff like that, but

when it all boils down to it, it really was all really meaningless, and I just got tired of my life going in circles. I was feeling like I was getting the short end of the stick a little too often, you know? I was puttin' too much time, money, and effort into the things that I was doin', and I felt like my output wasn't sufficient. Once you keep doin' somethin' like that and you feel like them lil' hamsters, in a cage spinnin' all his wheels, exertin' all they energy not goin' nowhere . . . well, sooner or later reality gonna slap you in the face. I'd be like, "You know, well, if you keep doin' this, you gonna keep gettin' the same results."

How did that happen for you? What was that slap in the face?

Well . . . for one, I guess after . . . I didn't do no long bids or nothin' in jail, just like a year or so at a time, but still goin' back-and-forth to jail and then gettin' out, pretty much havin' to start over, and then a lot of the females were, you know, untrust-worthy. They had selfish intentions.

Yeah, I read your book.

[Laughs] Yeah! And so, you know, just dealin' with a lot of them day after day, week after week, month after month, you like, "Man, you know, there gotta be somethin' better for me than this. Got to be." That was one of the things I kept sayin' to myself—got to be somethin' better. But you know, I was in denial for a long time because I'd just say, "You know, maybe if I could just find me some better *women*, that would have a whole lot to do with it." Which was true, but the better women I needed to find wasn't hookers, see? That's the main thing I was really lookin' for was hookers, you know? If a female is a hooker, I don't care how good of a hooker she is, she's still a hooker, which means that somewhere in her mind or in her heart, somethin' is not right. Somethin' that she goin' through, somethin' that got a hold of her that's just not right. And whatever it is that's got a hold on her, and have her not right, is gonna also make her not be right with you. Or in my case—not be right with me. So a lot of the qualities that I was probably really lookin' for in women, I wasn't gonna find in those type of women. But as long as I was in that mind frame, it didn't matter because the main thing I was tryin' to do was get as much as I could get and split. Gain 'em, maintain 'em, and drain 'em, know what I'm sayin'? I knew they wasn't gonna stick around no way. That wasn't even my intention. I mean, if they was good enough—yeah, I would try and keep them around long as possible. But I knew that it wasn't gonna be long before they unraveled.

Do you think that your past kind of had to happen to get you where you are now? Was this all a lesson that needed to happen?

Oh yeah, oh yeah—most definitely. It's part of my testimony, you know? But it's hard for us to talk to anybody else about things, especially when we haven't went through nothin'. We have to get down and dirty and then wipe the mud and stuff off of us in order to let other people know, "Hey, you don't wanna get in this. You don't wanna get down and dirty like I did because you don't wanna suffer a lot of the consequences that I had to suffer," and then maybe there's worse than I managed to weave around and weave through, you know?

If somebody would have told you that back in the day, would you have listened?

It's hard to say. It's hard to say because like I say, experience is the best but then when you have somebody that at least try to talk to you and can warn you about some of life's pre-set traps, I'm pretty sure it'll make a difference. Now, some things, I'm pretty sure you have to experience on your own, but maybe some of the things can be avoided and maybe you won't have to go through some of those things, and if you do, then possibly you would know how to deal with them better, where you have a better outcome. Then you have some that you possibly just wouldn't do at all. But if we don't make some type of effort to pass the knowledge on to somebody else that could benefit and keep them from sufferin' some type of ill fate, we not sharin' our testimony, and then a lot of stuff that we went through is in vain.

Snapp of The Niyat

THIRD WARD/SOUTH PARK

Charles Fields first made noise on vinyl in 1992 with his group, Poetic Souls, and their 12-inch "Too Much TV." The duo (including Brooklyn native GT) was part of an early 1990s underground hip-hop movement that could loosely include K-Otix, Square Frame Garden, DJ Cipher's work behind the scenes, and an important center of hip-hop culture on Houston's Southwest side called The Shop. Later in the decade, Snapp came together with rappers D'Ology, Synato Watts, and Tabu in a group called The Niyat, bringing an altogether new level of conscious thought to Houston hip-hop. The Niyat has been mostly dormant of late, but Snapp and Synato Watts have a project together they call Synapse.

Was Poetic Souls your first group, or were you doing stuff before that?

That was my first actual group, me and GT, like the first official, "Yeah, okay, we're gonna do a group," type of situation. We came together through a crew of us that just started off doin' positive things. It was before Poetic Souls—called Wyze Tribe. It wasn't a rap group, it was just a group of us who did different things. There was a guy that designed clothing. His name was Smooth G. There a guy who did airbrushing, his name was Kid Styles. There were guys who just did different things within that group, and we kinda branched off from that. That's how I met GT, in that circle, and we built a relationship from there and decided to form Poetic Souls.

I saw Poetic Souls back then. I saw you in '93 with The Pharcyde. The Crack Hill Dealers played too, and people were booing them. You remember that?

Somebody was asking me about that show today.

At The Brass Monkey. Bushwick was with you.

Oh, *that* show! Bushwick *was* there! Crazy.

Remember y'all had to perform off of that little balcony. There was a big dance floor with a high ceiling, and then y'all were out on a little balcony one story up.

Yeah, that's how they had it designed like that there. We opened for KRS-One there too one night.

There was a whole scene around that era that y'all were a part of. Where else were you performing in town?

They had a place called Goat's Head Soup.

On Westheimer. Before they burned it down.

Before they burned it, right. And then I don't know if the Waxx Museum was still goin'. We played a few times there. In that era we performed at 9.9. It started gettin' into the mid-'90s, and then D'Ology's stepbrother opened up this store called The Shop on the Southwest side. It was on the 59 freeway and Bissonnett. Have you heard of Club Cardi's?

GT AND SNAPP OF POETIC SOULS. COURTESY OF CHARLES FIELDS

Oh yeah. The old rock club on the Southwest.

Yeah, it was like an old rock club but they had a few hip-hop events they would throw there, and quite a few rappers came there, because right next to Cardi's, that's where The Shop was. It was right next to Cardi's, so we took advantage of a lot of opportunities because a lot of hip-hop acts used to come there, and we opened up for a few acts. We actually opened up for Biggie Smalls there. We opened up for The Fugees there. We got to meet a lot of people. A lot of the groups that came through to perform there, they used to come right next door to The Shop because it was like a hip-hop shop. We sold records, we sold CDs there, we had a booth set up in the shop for the guy who did the sewing. His name was Smooth G. Larry Goodall did the booth set up for Kid Styles who did the airbrushing. And then a DJ booth set up for GT, because GT was DJin' as well. We were in *Rap Pages*! The one with Goodie Mob on the cover. They covered Houston across the board, a lot of underground hip-hop.

How long was The Shop open?

We threw a lot of events there, man. Freestyle Fellowship came through there. We were up with them all night. Redman and Method Man came through there, Tha Alkaholiks came through there.

We got to vibe with all those people. That's a whole piece of history that a lot of people don't know about. That was a whole era, early '90s to mid-'90s. That's when hip-hop in Houston was . . . that's when we had the Southside sound just getting popular too. But as far as on the underground, authentic hip-hop level, that was goin' on as well, and a lot of people didn't know about it.

I think the whole Southside thing may have sucked up all the attention, but y'all were doing things in a different direction.

Exactly. People were expecting a certain sound, which is the Southside, gangsta type of sound from Houston at that moment. People were expecting *that* sound. They didn't expect the type of vibe that we were comin' with. Some people try to categorize people who rap like that from Houston, sayin' that, "Oh, you're tryin' to sound like New York," when it wasn't. It was just—I mean just 'cuz we enunciate certain words, I don't think you have to wear spurs to say that you're from Texas. We were always a movement in the *art* of it, in terms of the lyrics prowess of rap.

I talked to Kay of The Foundation the other night, and he was saying that he met you and GT and Cipher all at the same time, but he also said that he met D'Ology back then. So were you already crossing paths back then with the people who were going to later get involved in The Niyat?

D'Ology was in the Wyze Tribe with us. We go way back, man. D'Ology and Tabu, they were in a group called The Darkside. Within the Wyze Tribe, there were several different groups. Like me and GT were Poetic Souls, Tabu and D'Ology was The Dark-side. And the third person, Khalif, from The Niyat, he was in another crew called Epilfedis. That's a whole 'nother crew.

Were they from a certain part of town?

Khalif was from Alief. He was born in Queens, New York. That's the third member of The Niyat, so it was me, Khalif, and D'Ology. And it's funny how everything came together from different crews.

How I met Khalif—like I used to dance. We used to breakdance, and me and him met on the battle floor. We battled each other when we first met, and it came to a draw. That was at The Palladium, on the Northside. That was way early.

How did you all come together as The Niyat?

Well, first of all we went through variations of names before we came to call ourselves The Niyat. The first name was 25 Square Feet. For what reason I don't know. I think we just thought it sounded dope. But we went from that to callin' ourselves *Akhi*, which means "brother" in Arabic, and then we went from that to *The Niyat*, which means "intention." We were still staying along the lines. We're Muslim—me, D'Ology, and Khalif—so we wanted to kind of stay within the realm of that. So we went from "brother," once we found out somebody already had the name, then we had to find something else, so there came The Niyat, "The Intention."

Your faith must play a role in what you all want to write about, yeah? What direction did it lead you at first?

There was a time when we just stopped rapping together, period, because of the faith. There's a word called "haram" in Islam, to get involved with certain instruments. So we contemplated, we went through an era where we put the mic down for a second, but then the urge came back to us, and it *did* affect our writing. We did touch on certain topics, but without tryin' to be too preachy. We didn't try to shove Islam down people's ear. We just stayed within the prowess of still havin' the lyrical dexterity but tryin' to still—every now and then we'll drop a jewel on certain topics. We try our best to keep it relatable to everyday situations.

Translatable, to where people who are outside of what you're talking about can understand it.

We try not to put too much emphasis on *our* beliefs.

But is there an overall message, a directive that pushes The Niyat along that all three of you are focused on?

I think it depends on the mood. I mean there's no—I don't think there's just one overall . . . "Okay, this is it right here." I think it's more—just be original. Just be you. Don't follow what's popular at the moment. Don't try to fit in too much just because everybody else is doin' that. Change up with that. You have something different to bring.

B-1

MISSOURI CITY

B-1 is a lesser-known member of the South Park Coalition who was there from the early days of the Southside scene in the late 1980s. In the early 2000s, he was in a group called Network with rapper Black Mike. B-1 went on to release three albums in the 2000s on the local Martell Music label.

So when you were growing up in Missouri City, was South Park kind of a place to go? Was it a destination?

PHOTO: TIFFANY REEDER

Shit, it was the *main* place to go! Hell yeah, because Hiram Clarke was in between South Park and Mo City. 288 wasn't even built yet, so we was takin' a ride on them backstreets through Hiram Clarke to get to South Park to get the music and to come buy weed and go to the Sokol Village and the Boomerang and all that kind of shit. So yeah, eventfully, it was the place to be.

Where was the place you would go? King's Flea Market?

King's Flea Market, Trading Fair II, and Sokol Village, before it turned into Boomerang, them was the main places—I'm talking about we got hands on steering wheels, that's what we was goin' off with. Go get some clothes from the flea market or go get some jewelry or somethin' and try to hit the club and get us some girls and catch K-Rino and Street Military and them in concert, or Too Short or MC Ren or whoever Wickett Crickett and them was bookin', we was tryin' to be there.

Trading Fair, man, that place was fucking crazy. I remember going in that place.

Hell yeah. Crazy. We'd come in there and be havin' a couple hundred dollars tryin' to getcha a b-boy chain with a fresh edge up and you was ready!

So what was Boomerang called before?

It was called Sokol Village. It was actually on Cullen and Holmes . . . Cullen and Holmes Road intersect.

I've seen the building.

They done switched that building up now. That's where it used to be, boy. The spot.

And you could get in there being underage and everything, they didn't care?

Nah, you know what? It wasn't so much that everybody could get in there underage, but it was 'cuz we knew—'cuz we knew Icey Hott and we knew K-Rino, you know, and Klondike and shit . . . they never really asked us for ID and shit. They just took us bein' down with the fam, or bein' somebody little cousin, little brother. That's how we used to get in. They didn't have a lot of underage—you had to be 18 to get in, 21 to drink.

What else were you listening to then? Mostly Houston stuff or national rap?

I was definitely listening to all rap, but I was probably more inspired by the local thing. You know, I was feelin' like if they could do it and make a way then we can do it the same way. But shit, I was listening to everything, man, Eric B. & Rakim, Big Daddy Kane, Ice Cube, N.W.A., Eazy-E, a little bit of The Dayton Family, MC Breeze, Tupac, and then pretty much when the . . . I would have to say the turning point in all that shit was when Mr. Scarface dropped the first Scarface song? Oh, it was over, bro. When Scarface dropped "Mr. Scarface," and the Geto Boys came out with "City Under Siege" on Rap-A-Lot, and Ganksta N-I-P signed to Rap-A-Lot, oh, it was over. It was all . . . it was gettin' real H-Town, baby, after that.

K-Rino told me a story that was very much like that . . . when that song broke, he said, people just freaked out, and every club you would go in every night, you would hear that song. And he said that's when it changed.

No doubt, and see that was the thing—like, you know, he might be eight years older than us, and then he was with my brother and Crazy C and them, so we wasn't feelin' too much younger, but we was younger. But because we was mature for our age and we was around, you know, we used

to get away with shit. But you know, [K-Rino] and them was doin' they thing, and [Icey Hott] and them was doin' they thing on the music industry with the tapes, and it was bumpin' and they was rockin' the parties and shit. And when that "Scarface" had dropped and Too Short and all that shit, when Scarface was down and he was talking about South Park living and was gettin' attention? It's just like everything changed, people's perspective within . . . boys started gettin' feared. Studios . . . like Crazy C was DJing parties, and him and DJ Aggravated and Lil' Troy. 'Cuz the connection . . . you know, if you go back far enough in Mo City, and Ridgemont—Ridgemont kinda turn into Hiram Clarke, and if you go back a little bit farther, you'll be on the outskirts of South Park. So that's what made our little shit connected, and Crazy C and Icey, they was DJin' parties one day, and the next thing you know they was just makin' beats. And they started makin' them beats, and them beats was jamming, and there wasn't a lot of . . . like they went straight from them goddamn mixtapes to them beats. There wasn't too many demos or none of that shit. Like, they first couple of demos, them motherfuckers was for sale shortly thereafter.

That really got people on the Southside going and really thinking and moving, huh?

Yeah, really it was the whole of H-Town because Lil' J was from Fifth Ward, so it wasn't no bias at this point. It was just all H-Town . . . Fifth Ward, Northside, because *everybody* got family on the Northside, so it wasn't no thing, you know what I'm sayin'? But that shit just sparked the fuel. The shit all happened so fast, you know? One day we listenin' to "Scarface," and them boys on the little 12-inch singles, and about a year, year and a half later, J Prince comin' through soupin' niggas up . . . hand-washing your cars and shit, know what I'm saying? Got all them dope fiends hand-washing your cars and shit. Got all them dope fiends hand-washing and hand-detailing, and they got all them trying to block the street off and make it one-way traffic to where you couldn't make U-turns or be turnin', and then by 12, one o'clock, police be sitting out there in they cars and they horses just *waitin'* to harass people.

Where was the car wash, exactly?

You know the car wash on MLK—right at MLK and Kassarine—that was the car wash that everybody used to go to and get they cars washed and floss up-and-down MLK. The slabs, all swangin', poppin' trunks and you know, whatever.

I remember for the Kappa in Galveston, there would be a line two or three miles long just waiting to get into that car wash, all night long.

You know what? The amazing shit about the car wash on MLK—that car wash ain't got but, god-damn, probably four big stalls, and there'll be a lot of dope fiends up there hand-washing your car. So that's what pretty much switched it up, and then Screw had moved from South Park to Mo City, so when he had moved and then they cracked down on a lot of them streets and them houses with the activity, that's what, you know, kinda slowed up . . .

It is a lot slower now, but do you still see an area where people go? I mean there are the record stores . . . people still go to Screw's shop, Timmy Chan, King's Flea Market. I mean, there are still places like that, right?

The Screw Shop is a fo' sho' . . . that's like a guarantee . . . if that motherfucker closes, it's gonna get ugly. Screw shop, Timmy Chan's, and people go to King's Flea Market to get they music done. People still go to BAM's. There's a lot of people still go to BAM's to get they car washed, you know, that's still a focal point. MacGregor Park has started picking up here, probably in about the last four or five years with new activities and shit, and a lot of hangin' and chillin'. But them goddamn cops, man, they come out there trying to write some tickets, and that shit keep people away. You know, it don't take but one or two times for you to come out there and get pulled over and motherfuckers ain't really comin' through, but yeah, it's still . . . it used to be poppin'! You know what I'm talking about? It used to be severely poppin'. You would have people from the Northside, Southwest just . . . ridin' to the Screw shop, ridin' to Timmy Chan's, MacGregor Park, makin' laps and shit. And now, it's more so the natives. If you born and raised out here . . . you know, Hiram Clarke or Third Ward. That immediate locale, I would say.

So when you first started working on your own rapping, putting together tracks and that sort of thing, who did you first start working with as far as producing?

My first little dude I was fuckin' with was Black Mike. You familiar with Black Mike? Black Mike was cold. Like Black Mike was ahead of his time. I had more of a relationship with Street Military and The Killa Klan and S.P.C. than Black Mike, but I was trying to put him all . . . you know, with the music, with them, and they wasn't really . . . I wouldn't really say they wasn't takin' to him as much, but he was so caught up on his self, trying to get his solo thing off that when the shit didn't start to work, that's when I start getting serious and people start likin' my rhymes. So me and him started as a group, and he was the primary producer for about the first . . . three, four years. And then we met Rakesh.

What was your group called?

The Network. We was called The Gangsta Network.

The Gangsta Network.

Yeah, we was all about networkin' with the gangstas.

Right on. And where were those guys from? Were they from South Park, or were they from Mo City?

They was from Mo City. We went to the same high school with Lil' Flea, and because everybody was linkin' up with South Park, Pharoah and Flea and [Icey Hott] and them formed Street Military, so everybody was behind Flea in the whole thing. And you know Street Military was composed of people from South Park and Mo City, so that's why I say it wasn't really a . . . you know, there wasn't really no plex or there wasn't no discrepancies, so to say.

Were all those guys from Mo City? Street Military?

Nah, KB from the Northside, Icey was from Hiram Clarke, Flea from Mo City, and Pharoah was from South Park.

What about Nutt? The one that died?

Yeah, Nutt was from Mo City. That's why it was so much connection, because they had members from all parts of the city, so you had no choice but to accept them. And then the Geto Boys had Willie D from Fifth Ward, and the Northside with Trinity Garden Cartel was comin' out, so it wasn't a Northside/Southside thang, it was a Houston thang, you know. And . . . shit, that's what it was. Me and Black Mike, we was from Mo City, and after school—right after high school we had started makin' a little noise in the hood and shit, and they was tryin' to make a movie about Fifth Ward, and we was tryin' to get on the soundtrack, and we ended up meetin' Rakesh. You know who Rakesh is? Well, I'm sayin' Rakesh but his name is Rak. He produced the first Z-Ro album and the first Guerilla Maab album. That's when we really got in the studio and got with it hard. And because we was younger, we were still honin' our craft. You know, Murder One and Dope E. and them, they was just schoolin' us on the aspects 'cuz they was already . . . you know, by that time they were celebrities. Definitely by then. They was definitely celebrities by then.

Who did you come the closest to? I mean, who had the biggest influence on you personally?

Ah man, it was . . . initially, no bullshit, Ganksta N-I-P and Point Blank. 'Cuz you know Ganksta N-I-P was doin' that writin' . . . he was doin' the writin' for the Geto—for Bushwick and shit, also on a lot of Bushwick's shit 'cuz he was on Rap-A-Lot. They had dropped so simultaneously that it just took us all . . . it took everybody by storm, and really it was Ganksta N-I-P that kinda rocked me so hard. At first. I had done already heard K-Rino on mixtapes and shit . . . but what took it for me was Ganksta N-I-P because this is the only person I've ever seen . . . I'll say this: This was the first person that I seen walk in the club, walk in the DJ booth and just rock the whole muthafuckin' club *live*. Dead in

the middle of prime time—I'm talking about 1:15 in the morning, "Well, we got Ganksta N-I-P in the house, he 'bout to do his brand new single." And man, that man mixed that record in, and it was just like he was on wax, and Ganksta N-I-P was in the booth live! I swear to God he was rockin' that bitch in living color, and that was . . . I think that was in, like, '93?

And where was that? Was that at Boomerang?

Nah, it was at Carrington's. He was promotin' his new album.

Carro's.

Carro's was the spot. And that was for the sho' 'nuf slab riders. Sokol Village and Boomerang was more of a hood spot, so to say. They was doin' a lot of shows at that motherfucker, but Carrington's was just like the regular club.

Was it a little bit more upscale?

It was the same thing, but it was more flossy and flashy. A lot of parkin' lot pimpin', you know, and it was 21 to get in. You had to be 21 to get into Carro's. You could be 18 and get into Boomerang and shit. That was pretty much the difference. Probably more big-time dope dealers as opposed to hood dealers.

Cl'Che

SOUTH PARK

Cl'Che emerged in 1998 with her debut album *Clasyfyd Lady* and has released several albums and mixtapes since, including a number of collaborative efforts with fellow Southside denizens Mr. 3-2, Big Pokey, Billy Cook, and the late Big Hawk. Cl'Che also worked with DJ Screw, is a member of K-Rino's South Park Coalition, and is known for her philanthropic endeavors around the city as founder of the women's organization S.H.E. Movement.

PHOTO: RICO KING

How different is South Park now from when you were growing up there?

I guess it's different as far as like how the world is different now. Because, I mean, like a lot of things that were happening that we could do back then in the neighborhood—in the world it's a lot different now. The crime rate now is more advanced. As the generations change, more things change in the neighborhood, and it changed more for the worse than better. Just as the world changes, the neighborhood changes, and adapts the same way. The world, the neighborhood, we can say it's worse than before. Things that wasn't so bad back then, it's really bad—and tremendously bad—right now. So, the neighborhood where I'm from is just like the world today. Back then, it wasn't as bad, even though things happened back then, but now it's worse. Because we're losing a lot more people, the crime rate is up, more businesses are failing, and a lot of people are losing their homes, things like that. So it's starting to change with a different environment now.

You mean in the last few years?

Yeah, I could say even within the last two years, because since the recession, a lot of things changed on this earth and in the neighborhood. Because like I said, people are losing their homes. That's makin' the crime rate go up because people don't *have*. A lot of younger children are now kind of roaming the streets, or taking any vacant houses and running their dope houses. Even though these things were done back then, they wasn't done in the aspect that it is today that's really killin' people and hurting people a lot more.

When people think about the recession, they think so much about the middle-class, and about people who have mortgages and homes and that sort of thing. I don't think people really think about how that trickles down to really poor neighborhoods—and South Park isn't a really poor neighborhood, but it's not upper middle-class like what you always hear the examples of.

Right, that's what I was about to tell you—that South Park really used to be a middle-class neighborhood. You know, at one point, a majority of whites had lived there. Years ago. When my grandmother had first moved in the South Park area, my grandmother and my grandfather, it was predominantly . . . a majority of it was all white people years ago. You know, as more black people had moved in and—saying this, just as it's being said—more black people start moving in, a lot of more things in that environment changed once again. The environment started having more drug affiliations, more robberies, burglaries, killings, and more children that are roaming the streets, doing things they gotta do as far as prostitution and so forth. You know, from being hooked on all types of drugs and stuff . . . and because it's a minority neighborhood, and I'm not just saying just blacks or whites or Mexicans or whomever. Whatever ethnicity you are, it can happen in your neighborhood. But I'm speaking on South Park right now . . . that . . . it's a lot of work in that minority neighborhood, a lot of blacks tend to kind of get into the dope dealing scene because that's all they hear about as they growing up. Like, that's the thing to be or to do when they're listening to our culture of music such as hip-hop, rap, and these rappers are talking about it. So, they're constantly seeing it from family members that they were kids to . . . I mean, just growing up. You know, you see your aunts and uncles smokin' they weed and doing they thing. It seems like it's nothing, but it's already instilled in the values of doing those things is not bad to that child because they've seen it done all they life. So they grow up and they do it. Now they're

dope-selling, and they still in South Park years from now, with their kids and so forth, so now it starts spreading. It starts spreading. It starts kind of putting neighborhoods, as far as statistics, saying that we have the highest crime rates and that we have the highest drug rates and incarcerations and deaths and things that are going on. Because within the last three years, the people that have died in the South Park area alone or that were found dead in the South Park area has risen—a lot! Half the people that were here two or three years ago is not standing here today! Every year I have someone that . . . the next year, they're not living. And it's people that I know. It's not happening just . . . it used to be happenin' every now and then, then it started being in our own backyards, now it's being right next to us. The person that was sitting right next to us disappears now. It's that close, and it's happening that often. So, as far as me involved in the South Park community, that's something that I try to work on every year to just try to bring unity there. And because I do music, I know that hip-hop has a lot to do with it. I'm from South Park. This is where I was born, this is where I was raised, and my family still lives there. I'm always there. So I chose the place to start where I was from first. I hope that, in the future that I can take it to other neighborhoods and start building unity in their neighborhoods. I know it won't change the world but definitely will instill something for them to think about and hopefully change someone's life to choose another direction.

How do you feel about the new generation of kids coming up in South Park?

The newer generation of kids coming up out of South Park, which is . . . I have a little brother. So . . . looking at it right now, my little brother is incarcerated again. And I'm saying *again*, you know what I mean? Because the new generation feels like the only way to survive is to sell drugs to make it. Or to rob someone to make it out of South Park. I mean, I'm, like, amazed every day seeing someone that I grew up with or that I remember was a kid from South Park . . . to hear something or be looking at the news and see my people on there, and it's like, "Oh my god, I couldn't believe that they did this!" Because it's somebody that we know. But it was happening like all the time, in our neighborhood. This new generation is coming up and they are learning the wrong things and it's killing them. So many, every year. I know it's most definitely over one, two, or three that dies every year from South Park alone—people that I know for myself. And they're kids. They're probably not even to the age of 25 yet. The value . . . the value of life, throughout the world but most definitely in South Park, those kids there . . . they have a whole different perception of life. Like, the value of it is zero to them. There's no value no more so they have no standards. They don't have anything. They think what these rappers rap about, as far as the . . . sippin' syrup and smokin' weed and selling they rocks, sellin' pounds or ounces or whatever, is . . . what it is. But it is not. I feel like the new generation from the South Park community is kind of growin' up in the era where it just seems like . . . because knowin' the parents that have been there, like my grandparents or the other people that live in this neighborhood, they're well-rounded people. It was a middle-class neighborhood, like I said, back then. So I would say that they raise their kids up the right way, but once they step out, the kids step outside of the door, the kids got lost. So I feel like there was a *community* loss. Because now, even just so I know it happens in more places than South Park, it's a community loss where the community is not taking initiative and trying helping each other. As far as back then, your next-door neighbor could whoop you, you know what I'm saying? You can't do that now. It's like nobody will take the initiative of seein' some of the crowd doin' something wrong, like in the new generation, and correct them . . . to correct them! But no one takes the initiative to stand up and do that, and say, "Hey man—that's not what it is," and this and that. You know, you might get some of the older people—if they're out—but they don't be outside hearin' people like that. So they're not . . . I feel like they're missing something. They're missing something as far as when they go up out of their parents' door, they get lost. They start learning a whole new teaching that's not of good health. Or wealth.

You have a sense of history there and a sense of what a bright future for South Park would be. Are there advantages and disadvantages to being a female voice in that movement?

I most definitely think it is different. The advantage is . . . that I'm a female. [Laughs] And for one, guys like pretty females. I feel that God blessed me to where I'm pretty. I feel like . . . I got your attention already. Right there. But to be able to deliver something positive into your life because now I got your attention . . . now I've got you looking at me another way as well. Before you ever hear me. At the same time, the disadvantages are . . . some people feel like if you a woman and, as far as the guys . . . or some of the women, or . . . if you a woman and you don't sell dope or you ain't did this, "You don't know, so you can't tell me," and, "Man, man, you don't know." Basically, they feel like the drug dealers, and the people think they're the only one that know what they do and how they do and, "Don't nobody else understand." But that's not true. Because you don't know what this woman has been through in her life that's tryin' to tell nobody that, "You don't know." It's hard just to fight in the battle as far as a man and woman. Because the man, of course, should be the head, but even when they're not, they wanna be the head in the wrong manner. You know? So, it's that battle we're kind of fighting, and I feel like through-out the years, because I'm in a male-dominated industry in this rap game, I've always had to really physically, mentally fight my way through, because I was always underestimated some kind of way. So I always had a big voice. Me, being 14 and in high school, I had a big voice. That was my defense right there. I thought the world was right in that voice, but I didn't care if they liked it or they didn't. So, you know, that's what made me a stronger individual. That kind of pushed me to have the power to take someone's attention, as a woman, when I'm trying to deliver something. The perfect words that I'm trying to give them.

Do you see the industry adapting to stronger female presences?

No. I don't see that, so Lance, I'm not gonna tell you that. I don't see that as changing. Because I feel like, as we know, the industry has been one way. The business is built one way, and that's the way they're gonna operate music. I mean, they can care less if you've got talent, as far as the industry goes, you know what I mean? They wanna know if they market you, are you gonna make some money? It's the strategy of how they make money. That's why you can have Lil' Kim come out and then Nicki Minaj comes behind her and they use the same marketing strategy, because they know it's gonna work. It's just to make money. That's their purpose, to make money. I don't feel like there is still a voice for the female in hip-hop. I don't feel like they are respected. I feel like our voices are more being heard than they were back then, but they ain't opened that door yet. They ain't gonna do that yet. They ain't did that yet. They still hold us back. That's why you still get more rap to come out in the game that's only one rapper, or one female rapper, period, in the game. Why every time one female rapper come out, that's the only one that they let through the industry? Other than that, they let Rick Ross or Ludacris or whoever else. They'll drop a whole buncha dudes per year, but . . .

Like they're rationing them out.

Yeah! They give you one female every six, seven years or 10 years. That way it's easy, and the woman they do put out don't have no competition. I know that's how they've did the industry, and they still rockin' the industry like that, because it's the pattern that they've been running off for years.

What influenced you when you were younger . . . did you have somebody or something that just hit you early on, that made you really want this?

I think it's something that's in you, and then you be learnin' what's in you, so it wasn't nothin' like I was livin' and from practice I learned how to do it. I learned from something that was already within me, *how* to use it. And back then, I didn't have anyone that was in the music industry in my family that could help me, so it wasn't that. God kind of directed me on my own. I didn't have nobody to push me, but I brought along people who had any new pieces of information that would move me forward in my career and in my life. Some people grow up in a family, and they can put them in a place. I didn't have that. I came straight from scratch. Just on my own. Even though my mom respected what I did and they liked the mixes and they would tell me things . . . they enjoyed ideas, but I mean, they wasn't in the music industry, so they didn't know how to take me and put me somewhere, you know? That wasn't their field. So I feel like I was influenced by my mom listening to the music that she was always listening to. That's what I would always hear. I used to sing those songs and to this day I still remember those songs . . . Stephanie Mills and Teena Marie, because those were the songs that . . . my mom loved music, so she used to jam it all the time. And my dad. I can't forget my dad because he was really the entertainer, but he just liked to dance and act a fool. I heard that my grandmother on my dad's side . . . she sounded really good and she played piano, but I didn't meet her. She died right before I was born, so I never met her. So that's the closest thing to me that I had in my family oriented towards music. And I'm still learning it. I'm learning how to use it. You're using for God. And using it, not saying that it has to be a holier-than-thou album or song or whatever, but as I'm growing and maturing in life, of course the music is going to mature. It's gonna get wiser of course because these are the things I'm learning, and these are the things I'm talking about.

What about the guys who talk about God, and their love for God, and they're still out there doing the bad things. What role do you think God plays in their lives? They're talking the talk, but aren't necessarily walking the walk.

That's something that I've been evaluating myself . . . even though you're just speaking, your words are powerful. 'Cuz if you're speaking, you're believing some of it, somewhere. The faithful must believe, and God got you. I know he got you. All of us got God in us. I don't care how hard they're lost. They're lost in that aspect. Ain't nobody that hard, though. Everybody has God in they heart because God created you. God is the air that's in us. Every one of us is breathing that breath of air through God. You're not that hard. So when you talk that other talk, on the other side, you're doin' something else, you're gonna go through that to where God is going to bring you to your lowest point, so you have no choice but to accept him. Some may lose they life before they're able to get saved. That's why it's always said that you better get saved and you better get the knowledge about who G-O-D is. Regardless of what you're doing. I don't care if you're the biggest dope dealer, the biggest killer in the world or something like that—you cut your time short when you keep going against God's will. I didn't know until I'd been studying in my Bible as effectively as I have this year, that literally, it is said in the Bible that we cut our time short. We can die before our time. Because you die, and God had that time set for you. God wants us to live fulfilled lives, and only we can shorten our life span. By choice. By going against God's will, by having a choice. God allows us to have a choice to make the decisions about that. And that distinguishes my life. God wants to fulfill us, but we cut it short by the things we do.

Anything else you want to throw in there in closing?

Let me say it like this: People wonder why all the negative stuff goes before all of the positive stuff. The industry is set up that way. That's the way it's structured. People are out there fighting—and it's not just me, it's not just K-Rino that's been fighting this fight—there's people that have been fighting for decades before us that's been fighting the fight to defend substance in music. At the same time, the negatives get exposed so dramatically. But what about if we expose the positives as much as we expose the negatives? We can change the mindsets of the people. I feel like hip-hop is the biggest marketing tool ever—*hip-hop* is. Music, entertainment, video outlets, movies, and music, all of that, is one of the biggest outlets that brainwashes people. If everything we hear or we see on television is negative, the mindset of the world is gonna be negative. Now, if that gets changed around, and there's more positive things on television and more positive things on the radio, and more positive things in any type of media outlet . . . if it's more positive there, I feel that the mindset of the people will be more positive. More technology allows more to be seen. With the internet, and giving people the ability of people to put anything on the internet, the freedom of it is hurting our mindset.

Justice Allah

FIFTH WARD

Justice Allah surfaced in the mid-2000s as a powerful and intelligent voice amongst that era's movement of politically awakened rap music in Houston, and was a member of the group 144 ELiTE along with K-Rino, Dope E., and Ashlei Maya-dia. In 2010, he started the "Friday Eve" radio program on Optimo Radio, on which he discussed the New World Order, health, politics, and current affairs with radio personality Optimo Ram. As of 2014, after many endeavors to further the culture of hip-hop as an educational tool, Justice Allah dropped off of the map to, as he told me, "live happily ever after away from the systems of control and belief."

We talk about bigger things than just the hood, and bigger things than just South Park. We talked about vaccines, fluoride being pumped into our drinking water. You had some thoughts on how something like that directly relates to a community like South Park.

The whole condition of the hood in general is poor. If we was to get a checkup, it would just really be a poor grade because there's no type of health education goin' on, and then the very little education that people do have in regards to, you know, general eatin' habits and exercise and, you know, they knowledge of medicines and doctor's visits and the whole health care industry in general is so small that most people don't even bother with it. We lead the numbers in all of the bad statistics, you know, the heart disease, the high blood pressure, all the cancers. There's just nothing really in the neighborhood to make it convenient to have good health. It's not a good food supply in the neighborhood. It's mostly just fast-food, fried chicken, and burgers, and it's just like they turned that chicken into our number one enemy. You can't go to a neighborhood, an urban area, whatever, and not, you know, have five or six chicken places that specialize in serving just fried chicken only! You can't even get it in any kind of form, you know—just fried. With fries, and a side of rice and fried biscuits and fried everything. Then, it's so cheap that it makes it real feasible to go and buy this fried food rather than just make groceries because, you know, the groceries cost more than just paying $2.99, or in some cases just $1.99, and getting what's perceived to be a whole meal. If people would ever analyze, there's no way possible that they can give you a whole meal for $1.99, or $2.99 like that when you can't go to the grocery store and do it. How can they possibly do it? And then, you mix that in with, you know, just not having the top-notch foods. There's only one or two grocery stores—if that many—in the average black or Hispanic community, which is known as the hood. In most cases, there's just one grocery store, and if you're not close to it, then you're forced to do business, like most people, at the corner store—what they call the convenience store—and there's one on almost every other corner where they can go in and, you know, rather than buy green-leafed vegetables, you can just, you know, buy chips and noodle ramens they're sellin' where you can just eat that air and basically chemicals and stuff and kill your body up, man. Even when you

PHOTO: PETER BESTE

look at these noodles you think it would say just "noodles" on the back or something, but they have 25 different ingredients just to make up a pack of noodle ramens, man, and it's one of the staples of the neighborhood. One of the main things people eat—noodles and chips and cereal. And little tidbits just to get 'em by.

Even the real food that's there is just starch.

Just straight carbohydrates . . . if that much. I've been doing research on chicken, seeing that it's not even chicken anymore. They pump it up 30 percent with water and then fill in the rest of it with pork powders to try to hold it together. So wherever you go, you're getting poisons with the fast-food places. There's little beef, if any, in the burgers, and you compound that with there being a liquor store on every corner . . . not literally, but figuratively . . . you know, per capita, I'm pretty sure that there's more liquor stores in the neighborhoods than there is in any other community environment. You know, in most communities, they zoning laws and stuff against that. But, like I said, not in the neighborhood, the so-called hood. You know, fast-food place, convenience store, liquor store . . . they all go hand in hand, and the health is bad. Most people just . . . doin' very little exercise and, you know, it's just a deadly combination when you're putting that garbage in your body and not doin' anything to maintain or exercise your muscles and organs. It's just a death trap, man, and most people end up with diseases before they 40 years old that end up killin' them before they're 50. If they make it over 50, it's just a few years, you know. I don't know what the actual life expectancy is, but I'm hearing more and more of people just dying out now at 40, and 50, and just recently one of my rap colleagues died at 30 years old, man. It was sad, you know? Heavy D . . . Erick Sermon had a heart attack . . . it's just sad, people not being aware. But you *should* be aware of your health, you know? It's all good when it's good, but when it go bad, it's already too late, damn near.

Because people think if there's no alarms going off, then everything must be fine. "I drink the way that I do and I smoke the way that I do and I feel fine, so be it." But that stuff takes a long time to show up in the way that you feel it . . . trying to deal with those poisons being inside of you that your body doesn't know how to process.

It can't process it, because it's unnatural, and your body is a natural organism that has no way of dealing with these toxins, and foreign substances, you know. It's just not equipped. There's nothing to put inside the body to deal with these chemicals and stuff that mankind has put together in just an effort to save money, and maybe a more concerted effort to just kill more people off. When you look at the health care system, man, it's not real geared towards cures. It's more geared towards treatments, and there's not a cure for anything. There's only treatments that help you to deal with the suffering or the diseases. Mainly just pain suppressants and stuff like that, and nothing really geared towards helping your health. Your health is really controlled by the intake that you put in your body, and not the disease itself. You wouldn't get these diseases, and nobody would have them, if we just ate the right foods and avoided the toxins.

You know, we're not born with these diseases like they try to fool us into thinking. When you go to the doctor and they have you fill out all this paperwork, and the main part of the paperwork is your family medical history, they wanna know, "Did your grandmother have this, did your mother have that, your father . . ." As soon as you check the box that says "Yes," then they just simply go back and tell you, "Yeah, it's hereditary!" And that's the reason that you have it, is because they had it. And I mean, if you wouldn't have checked the box then they wouldn't have been able to go to that conclusion, and even if it is the same disease that your grandfather or your mother and father had, you might wanna just analyze. Are you two people exercising the same eating habits? Are you eating bad foods and goin' through a bad life experience, not getting the proper amount of exercise and the balanced diet that your parents didn't do? Most times, we just follow what we was trained! If we grew up in a house eating starches and not drinkin' the proper amount of water or getting the right vitamins in, then we're gonna really maintain that same status quo in our homes . . . you know, it's just going to keep on propagating throughout our generations, and it's going to keep looking like these diseases are hereditary, when the only thing that's hereditary is the habits. The bad habits.

And there seems to be that so many of the things that are available feed bad habits. I mean, you think about the sugary snacks, sugary candy and everything like that that's right up front in the stores, and then the alcohol, cigarettes, all that kind of stuff. These are all habitually addictive things that bring people back, that take away from the person . . . the intake doesn't fuel the person's being.

I know personally the makers of these products you don't see other places. They're geared for the neighborhood, and I'm speaking of all these energy drinks, they probably got about seven or eight different brands of energy drink out with more and more chemicals in them besides just caffeine. But then you have the other drinks that's real popular here now, the so-called slow-down drinks, the simulated Promethazine and simulated syrup drinks

that's really geared towards getting the children on this stuff so they can experience what it feels like and then graduate towards the real drug. You know, they call it "Sippin Syrup," and one is called "Purple Stuff," and "slowdown." They got all kind of fancy names for it.

I think part of it in Houston with drank, codeine, is that it's never really been stigmatized in ways, even like smoking weed. It seems to be such a natural thing. That's not necessarily a good thing when you're talking about kids and you're talking about a product that they can have available to them when they're young. Maybe that is a "natural" thing and maybe it's not demonized within their family, but it's still too young for them to be partaking in even a fake drug.

Yep. It's just a training program. So they can imitate what they hear and what they're seeing about it. And people think codeine is safe. They think that, you know, this is safe, and it's a fruity, fun type of drug, but they don't understand what happens to they bodies once codeine is processed through the liver and everything. It turns into heroin, and it's the same effects, you know, because it's from the heroin family. That's why they have that ending of "i-n-e," just like all the derivatives of heroin do. It's highly addictive. People are not just doing it for fun. It starts out as a certain thing, but then it ends up bein' something that you have to go through withdrawals and everything to try to get off of it. And most people just supplement with different type of pills, with alcohol and more drugs and weed or whatever else they can supplement they desires for that drug for. It's definitely not a joke, and you'd think after all these years, and after all the major Houston rap artists and other people that have died from it, somebody would finally stand up and finally say, "Hey, man, this stuff here is a drug!" It's not just a fruity drink that you po'ing it up in sodas and stuff. It is killing people, it got 'em strung out, got 'em stealin' and really incapacitated. Shuttin' . . . shuttin' down their kidneys and all the kind of different things it does to your organs. You know, and nobody's speakin' on it. Nobody's speakin' against it. It's just a fun, "reppin' in H-Town" type of drug.

Well part of that rationale is that you can't overdose on codeine. You just can't drink enough of it, you can't process enough of it to take you to that limit in one sitting, but when somebody is using over and over and over again and they're having their bodies have to process that all of the time, it slows down their metabolism and starts messing with other systems in their bodies. And like you said, for so many people, it's a cocktail, and so they're drinking codeine and they're smoking Sherm, which is a hallucinogen, so you've got all of this stuff going on in your body at the same time. It's wearing down people.

Yep. All the different chemicals, man. That's where they come with the examination and tell you about your chemical imbalance. And that's what we're really doing to ourselves, is imbalancing ourselves chemically when we start taking in all these different type of, you know, whether it's drugs or it's food, it's still the same chemicals now. You turn it on the back, you can't even pronounce some of this stuff that's on the face of a gum wrapper or something. I mean, it's no different to me than somebody cookin' up some crack or something in the lab. You still don't know what the ingredients is, and you can't say a 100 percent what effect it's gonna have on each individual. You know, we're not like cars or boats or machines where we can just take this cog off and replace it with another and it's gonna run the same. We're all individually tuned and different. The makeup is different. Despite being the same species, we're all different, and it's just hard to say what one thing will do to one person and what it'll do for another. But in the neighborhood, the awareness level is just . . . it's way, way down. It's to a point it's so far down that it's taboo to even talk about this stuff. Myself, I stopped eatin' meat thanks to the help of K-Rino and Dope E. educating me on what this processed meat was doin' to me and what that really was. And, you know, it's taboo for me to talk about this kind of stuff. It's always a stigma behind it, and people just can't understand it, to the point where they don't even wanna hear about it.

I think they'd just rather not believe it. It's about their options. They know the stores they go to in the neighborhood, and they know what's on those shelves. And they know that basically that if they wanted to make a big change in their lives, it would have to involve a lot more than just the hood, you know? It would be a huge step for a lot of people.

It's just fear of the unknown. People who don't have any type of idea of what the alternative would be. Because there's nothing else presented. It's just like the health issue goes across the board. More prevalent than the physical health is the mental health and everything that's tied in with that also. It's not just the bad food. It's the environment. The stress and just everything involved with living in a situation where you're just not number one on the list of priorities. It wears you down, so the general consensus for the health in the hood is . . . on a scale from one to five, I would say we're close to being on one. Trying to work our way to one. It's just . . . it's poor. You know, we need more awareness, and we need somebody that people in the neighborhood respect . . . any one of these athletes or one of the . . . I hate to keep puttin' it on entertainers and stuff because it's such a petty feeling of work, to keep puttin' all the pressure and blame on for uplifting people and makin' people do the right thing. There's way too much credit given to entertainers, and way too much emphasis put on they opinions and what they do. But, unfortunately, we gonna have to use these entertainers or use the athletes and people that, you know, can be looked upon as "prestigious" by the people in the neighborhood, and somebody amongst them gonna have to speak out against this stuff and be an example, you know? Be an example. Be an example of the guy that says, "Hey, look at me—I'm rich and I got this and I got that, and one thing I don't do is I don't abuse my health," you know? "I'm rich. I do this and that and I don't sip syrup, man. I know syrup is heroin, man." And just say it, you know? If people speak, eventually, future generations will know the truth, and they can make a decision if they wanna try it or not. Based on the truth. Some people might wanna try heroin. It's no big deal. They just didn't wanna shoot up. It's the same thing, but you're shootin' up with that white cup.

Do you think for a lot of people that the prestige you were talking about, the idea of prestige just distills down to money?

Well, unfortunately, it does. It shouldn't, because I know some pretty prestigious people that don't have a lot of money—people that I have way more respect for than people that I know have money. But in the general consensus that the public has, it's all based on financials and objects that they can see. You know, they can't see into the heart of a man, and they don't know all his good accomplishments because they don't recognize his good accomplishments. They just keep a record of everything he done bad. So they base a person's worth on what they can actually see with they eyes. "Okay, this guy's got a Bentley, this guy dress in $500–$600 suits, his jewelry and all this, your women." You know, they associate that with being successful and somehow bein' smart and bein' powerful. You don't have material objects and financial wealth. So, unfortunately, it's the wrong assertation to have, but human nature tends to lead people towards the celebrity, and you're not really a celebrity if you don't have money. That's the way people feel, man. Even the celebrities who get to that status without having money, they end up gettin' money once they get to that level. And for all the people that sneak their way into celebrityhood, they end up with money, and bein' set apart from the rest of society. So people really look towards that, you know, and judgin' you by it. A lot of people might have respect for what you do, or they might look up to you as an artist or athlete or whatever you have to say, but at the end of the day, don't consider you to be prestigious, because you don't have any money. You just another guy.

What about the things that really compound this too? We talk about vaccinations, flu shots, that sort of thing, things that are introduced in the hood that you don't see introduced in River Oaks, and in the Montrose, white neighborhoods . . .

The neighborhoods is mainly controlled by fear. Everybody would hate to admit it, but that's the main emotion that's goin' through most people's minds that live in the neighborhood, is fear. You know, they scared of the police, they scared of the government, they scared of what's gonna happen if they don't maintain they jobs or whatever they do for income. They scared of crime. You know, it's just a lot of fear goin' around, so most of this stuff is forced on us. You don't get your child immunized, then they're not gonna be able to attend school. If they not able to attend school, then the police is gonna come and get you. After a certain amount of time, you're gonna be in trouble and end up dealin' with that. And plus, your child gonna miss the opportunity to go to school, and be able to do their job and be a productive citizen. So it's all based on fear—something somebody said you have to do, and if you don't do it, then there's gonna be a consequence—a negative consequence—to you. And in neighborhoods, most people know. They've lived their whole life goin' through negative consequences, and they're gonna try to avoid it if at all possible. According to what people feel, the neighborhood is a place that's crime-ridden, everybody just swabbed out, it's a concrete jungle they call it, and people do whatever. But I've lived in the neighborhood most of my life, and I can tell you the people there, mostly all the people, follow the rules, man, and they do what they're told, and they productive citizens because they know what the alternative's gonna be. They live in fear of breaking the rules, and it's misconstrued that these are people that are not following the rules, and they're one of the only groups of people that *is* followin' all the rules. They're still being victimized with the forced immunizations and all the thoughts of, "You can go to the doctor and get a medicine, a pill or something, that's gonna cure your ailments," and all it does is cause you more ailments. More side effects that end up doing you in faster than the disease that you went to get treatment for.

And then you've got, on the other end of it, you talk about how people who do follow the rules and how people are trying to lead productive lives, and that's because the reality is a lot of those people know intimately, have a friend or a loved one or family member who has gone to prison, been locked up, and so that's something that hangs over the heads of everyone. It's almost like a correlative industry with what we're talking

about—things that lead you to crime and then the prison-industrial complex just waiting right there. It's a business.

Yeah. It's all a design. I'm not gonna say most of it—all of it is a design. Just like cause and effect. You know, you put out poor health, bad education, poor mental health, lack of knowledge, lack of job opportunities, poor economy, and just a general consensus of not caring about a group of people, and the rest is very natural. You know, you can just put it out there. You put the drugs right there in the mix, you put the guns right out there in the mix, the alcohol out in the mix, and you take everything else but that element away, and naturally, you know, crime's gonna exist. So you'll be able to go in and lock people up every day. It's an open pool that they've got to keep up. It's not a day that the police don't go into the neighborhood and fish people out. Each individual officer goes into the neighborhood. There's not one day that an individual officer is not able to fish somebody out and take them to jail. That leads us to believe that the whole neighborhood, the whole community is full of nothing but criminals, and that can't be the case, because how could it exist? How could it be going on this strong, this long, each individual neighborhood and community, if it was full of nothing but criminals like that? It would be total anarchy. It's just ridiculous, man. I went online and saw that the Correctional Corporation of America, one of the leading providers of prison facilities in America, is headed by Dick Cheney. They sellin' they shares for $10.42 a share last time I checked. That's how much these people payin' to keep folks locked up—$10.42. It might have went up or down since that time, but it's okay. It's so trivial. But that's what you really payin' for, the worth of a human being, just to make sure this system keeps going—$10.42. Each time you buy your share, you guarantee that you're going to get another prison built, and keep more and more people locked up. Around the world, man, this country leadin' . . . I mean, other nations throughout the world, in prison populations . . . it's ridiculous . . . more black men locked up in prison right now than ever was involved in the whole slave trade! The height of it, in the 1830s and stuff. Now, you know, it's the same thing. You locked up, you

don't have any rights. Your Thirteenth Amendment right is refused when you're convicted of a felony and locked up like that. So, you're not even a free individual. You're back in slavery again. And they say now that the numbers is even higher than they was when there was actually slavery. So what's that tell us about how far we've advanced as a nation, and all the freedoms and everything that we go and fight wars for other people about, when you've got this segment of your own population that's not even free citizens of your country? You're lockin' them up for $10.42 a share, so the stockholders and the chairmen and CEOs can get rich off of making sure that human beings stay behind bars and live like animals. There's just so many different things. I mean, even with the youth, they got so many different ordinances and laws they've passed now. Curfew violations and truancies and, you know, all kind of different things that we shouldn't be doing. They do the same things that I did or my father done or somebody else would do in school. Played hooky or kissin' a girl or somethin'—now you're convicted for sexual assault for that. So you end up with a record. Then you have to deal with deferred adjudication and stuff that you have to have expunged from your record. It takes years if you *can* get it expunged. Most cases, it won't come off, and you end up with a record before you even get out of school, and it's just a stairstep thing. Once you get convicted, the court system looks at that and they quickly convict you for the next, add on to the sentencing, and get you more time, and a more lengthy, felonious record.

They use it for a basis for everything else. Anything to get you on the books.

You're worthless out here, man, you know. I used to myself . . . I worked with the Houston Independent School District for 13, 14 years. I was doing $3 million, $4 million budgets every quarter, balancing everything off, but then I ended up gettin' myself into some trouble, and once that happened, it was over, you know? It was over for me. I was convicted, never ever been to prison, never even had a felony, but it's just enough to where I'm unemployable. And it's turned into a lifetime sentence now. Something that happened 15, 12 years ago has changed into a lifetime sentence for me. You know, and I could be a weak person, like most of the people are, and say, "Well, you know, I can't be employed . . . or I can't be adequately employed, so maybe I can turn to sellin' drugs or doin' crime in order to supplement my income." It just so happens that I'm not that weak as a person, and I know other ways about gettin' money, but that's not to say that I'm greater than anybody else, because another person is gonna go to what they know how to do to get money . . . so maybe they would be smarter than I am. But needless to say, the prison-industrial system is waiting on both of us to slip and fall, and still be sold on the US Mercantile Stock Exchange for $10.42 a share, no matter what crime we committed—rape, drug dealin', simple theft, or whatever. It's still the same amount of money, and a lot of times no disparagement in the sentencing. Just keeping you locked up so the average person, they're generating $600 a day for these prison systems, man. Just the amount of money that the federal and state and municipality governments pay to keep these people locked up. Averages out to about $600 a day to pay the corrections officers and all these people to watch them, the health people, and employ all the people involved in this system. You gotta keep people locked up now because somebody's gotta feed the system.

It's a business.

It's an industry.

Z-Ro

MISSOURI CITY

From some of the hardest voices in Houston—
K-Rino, Klondike Kat, Pharoah—you will hear
the most soulful singing. Z-Ro came up listening
to all of those rappers, developing his own big
pipes through the low register into a swagger and
delivery that exudes all manners of confidence and
vulnerability at the same time. He invented "Pain
Rap," be that its own genre, and he's recorded
enough music to establish it as such with over 20
albums of Southern classics under his belt. Z-Ro
first gained notoriety with his 1998 album *Look
What You Did To Me*, and was involved early in his
career with the multi-neighborhood group Street
Military. He later became part of The Screwed Up
Click and the groups ABN and Guerilla Maab.

PHOTO: PETER BESTE

**You were going over [to the Street Military house]
early on, right?**

Yeah, yeah. I was over there damn near . . . I ain't
gonna say the beginning, but in *my* beginning, I
was like, yeah, I was over there. Like '93, '94. I
started fuckin' with Flea first. You know Flea from
Ridgemont, from Mo City. I ain't know who the
fuck they was. I was just like, "Man, who is them
niggas always come over here every day whoopin'
. . . beatin' people up and shit? Who these niggas
is?" And they was like, "Man, you know, that's, you
know . . . Street Military. Flea." So shit, man, I slid
'em a CD. I ain't even . . . you know, way back then,
I wasn't . . . I was tryin' to do beats and shit, and I
. . . I was good, but like I say, I can't mix. I couldn't
at all back then, so I gave 'em some shit, and they
was on some . . . just on some smokin' weed shit.
And you know, Flea, out of the group, to me, he
gonna get the deepest on the round. He gonna
really make you think about what he sayin'. That's
where I got that, tellin' real good stories from, was
from Flea. So when I gave him some shit about just
smokin' some weed, e'rebody was talkin' about
candy paint, swangers, smokin' weed, tryin' to fuck
a bitch or some shit like that. I had to switch that
shit up. I gave him some gangsta shit, and he was
like, "Yeah, okay. I feel this." He brought me to the
studio, I mean . . . it was a wrap from there. We
started gettin' it in from there. It was cool.

You went out to the Northside?

Nah, we went to . . . where the fuck we went to . . . at that time, man, they was on like Braeswood. Nah, not Braeswood . . . Farm Park. . . . it's down the street from here. It's on the West. Yeah, they in Farm Park in some apartments over there, man, and that's just where they little headquarters was at. We'd go over to that bitch, get fucked up, cut on the instrumental, and just . . . everybody would go off. And whoever had the best shit to say, that's who was gonna go to the studio that night type shit. That was right around the time when they had Bam and shit like that, so . . . you know, Bam, Water Boy, all them motherfuckers from The Fakkulty and shit. So I mean, you know, it was a long-ass time ago.

So what year was that, when you first started hanging out with those guys?

Shit, hell if I know. Shit, it was a long-ass time ago, that's all I know. I was high all the time, so I just know it happened, you know what I'm saying? It was something like . . . it had to be like '94, '95.

Okay, so they already had records out, and they were already . . .

Yeah, they had "Tears Came From Making This Dream," all that shit. You know, they already had all that shit out. And then, like, Fakkulty was fittin' to get ready to release they record with X-Bam, signed with X-Bam. That shit ain't do nothin' for me. That's when KB and Flea came together to do they duet album with each other and shit, and I mean, that's when the shit really started professionally for me. So it was pretty cool. There wasn't no money involved because I was too new to the shit, but it was cool, though. Got me a chance to, you know, fuck with other people who rap like how I was rappin'. Because I was listenin' to everybody else with that . . . you know, no disrespect, 'cuz I'm Screwed Up Click, but a lot of that was like, "Man, hold up, syrup in my cup," shit. You know, I jam that shit, but I ain't wanna *be* that. I wanted to be on some . . . man, look, I want my shit to go everywhere. You know, and even though that shit went everywhere, I was wantin' my shit to be more realistic on the shit I was talking about. So, you know, just fuckin' with Flea, even though they was

rappin' different, there was a lot of tongue-flippin' . . . there wasn't really too much singin', unless Klondike was on that motherfucker . . .

Klondike was practically the sixth member.

Yeah, he was, he was the sixth man. He was the sixth man like a motherfucker, so I mean, it was cool. That's where I got a lot of my game from. It was like mid-'90s with that shit. Mid-'90s. I was still younger than a motherfucker. I was doin' my thang.

Street Military really inspired a lot of people because of the group aesthetic, with all these people throwing their voices into one thing.

Hell yeah, because I mean, like, when you do a solo record, it's more . . . I ain't gonna say *pressure* because this shit is easy, but I mean there's more work for you to do. And you know . . . when you're doing a group project, it's simple to just be like, "Alright, *bam*!" You doin' a verse, so I mean, you gonna put your hardest shit in the one verse, and then when you gotta do like a bunch of solo shit, it's like, "Okay, *bam*," now you gotta sit here and write three verses. You gotta make sure all that shit is on. That shit hard for some people, when they ain't really got nothin' to say. So even if you got somethin' . . . it's better for you to get your shine on features and shit. Like when a nigga get on a feature I kill everybody because . . . okay, I only gotta do it once. So this one time, I'm gonna make sure I stick the dick all the way up in you and fuck your whole shit up. So I mean, that's . . . I mean, even if it's your homeboy, it ain't . . . it's just a healthy competition.

Well, also there's kind of a different aesthetic to it too, though, right? I mean when you go in, and you know you're working on an ABN record versus working on a Guerilla Maab or another project like that, they all kind of have their own thing going on, right?

Yeah, everybody got, they all got their own thing going on, but I mean, at the end of the day it's the same shit.

It's chemistry too, though.

Yeah, the chemistry. I mean, it's who you workin' with. But I mean, like, very seldom do mother-fuckers bring shit out of me. I'ma bring something out of you before you bring something out of me, because by the time . . . I'm gonna be thinkin' music from when I walk in the door. Like when I go in the motherfuckin' lab, everybody wait on me to come up with the hook first. Motherfucker might tell me, "We wanna talk about this," so once I get my shit down, that's when y'all gonna start vibin' off of me. I'm not fittin' to wait on y'all. Fittin' to go ahead and get this shit . . . you know, I'ma get it crackin' so we can blow this motherfucker up. I mean, I know my role. I'm the front man.

You say "seldom," which means that sometimes, there's exceptions. Can you name those? Can you remember times that you went the studio and somebody just really . . . just pulled it out of you, the first time that you worked with somebody?

The only motherfucker that ever pulled anything out of me was K-Rino. That's the only mother-fucker, and even on them times, I come up with the hook first. He pulled something out of me just because of the respect I got for him, and he was like, "I want you to do a song." I'm like, "Nigga, you want me to do a song with you?" I'm like, "Nigga, you the greatest in the world." Like, "I'm not fittin' to fuck with you on no song. You not fittin' to *kill* me, nigga." Like, naw . . . naw, fuck that shit.

How long did it take?

About three days! Man, that's like . . . I'm not fittin' to slit my wrists. I ain't made like that. I can't . . . fuck that shit. I can't do that type of shit, you know what I'm sayin'? But then I was like, "Fuck it." They played the motherfuckin' song, and I started listen-ing to it. I was like . . . so I just started comin' up . . . I'm like, "The game goes on . . ." I just started just thinkin' about some shit. "Okay, yeah, we gonna talk about gettin' some money, tired of bein' broke, the shit everybody always talk about in our circle, and we're gonna make this shit melodious. That's what we're going to do." And that's what we

did. And I kind of just, like, fell in play, because it wasn't one of them type of songs where, "Okay, bam—we fittin' to prove our lyrical skills." It wasn't no shit like that where like, "Okay, we can be on some . . . *talkin' about* some type of shit." Because back then, man, I was like . . . man, please . . . I'm listening to what this man is sayin' on CDs about sending motherfuckers' spirit to hell in neck braces and slappin' you so hard you can see your facial expression in his palm and shit. I'm not fuckin' with that shit! I was like—back then I was like, "I'm not . . . I'm not crazy."

You gotta listen to it five times before you get it, before you soak it in.

I listened to that shit once and I know what it mean. It mean don't fuck with him! That's what that shit mean. It means . . . it mean don't cross this man, 'cuz he gonna whoop your ass without touchin' you type shit. But I was a big-ass fan, so it just . . . it took a while, but when a man . . . when he was like, "Say man, you talenteder than a moth-erfucker," that's kind of like Jordan tellin' a mother-fucker in high school ball, "Man, you talented." Like . . . *That* motherfucker told me I'm talented? I'm fittin' to dunk on *everybody* now." That's how I took that shit, and that's when I started kinda goin' crazy with this shit.

11 years later now, we think about Screw's legacy and how in Houston, the history really gets handed down. The stories really get told. People coming up really learn about the important fig-ures and the important people in the time line of rap music in Houston. How do you think his legacy has sort of evolved in the last . . . even maybe in the last five years?

I mean, it's obvious, man. Everybody doin' chopped and screwed now. And that shit really should be chopped and *slowed*, but I mean . . . it's evident. You got a lot of people on the East Coast slowin' they shit down or double-beatin'. A lot of people try to pay respect and double-beat forward. But you got a lot of people that's double-beatin' backwards and all these artists releasin' two CDs per one album. Regular version and screwed and chopped version type shit, so it's obvious what it does. I mean, you even had motherfuckin' Erykah Badu slow her shit down, and [Lil'] Flip came on that motherfucker. And I mean, even today, with the new motherfuckers with the Kirko Bangz, with the new "Drank In My Cup" song, he slow that shit down. And I mean, "Drank in my cup," that is a Screwed Up Click saying within itself. But I mean, like . . . a lot of motherfuckers that's doin' this shit right now, they wouldn't be doin' this shit right now. It wouldn't be possible at all for them to do this shit unless Screw dubbed them worthy of the rap game. And it probably woulda took me a little bit longer just because I was . . . Screw was fuckin' with me because I was different. I was the only one in that bitch that wasn't talkin' about how, you know . . . how everybody else was doin' they style. The different motherfuckers you had in there, were like E—like E.S.G.—when he freestyled, it was like . . . it was *real* rap. Like . . . all this shit was real rap, but he was actually gettin' in that bitch, and he was talkin' about shit that was goin' on. He could look around the room and rap about your shirt, your shoes was too tight . . . you know what I'm sayin' . . . your haircut didn't quite just . . . blend right . . . he was gonna rap. And like me . . . I was gonna rap. Big Moe was different because he was gonna come in that motherfucker and *sing*. You got all this real shit around, so it was kinda like, "Man, I need you in my Click. You kinda like, complete the gumbo. We got boys who freestyle rap, we got boys who really rap, and then we got people who really rap. We got people who sing, and then we just got homeboys . . ." I mean, it was like . . . it was just a whole lot of different genres, and that shit was cool for me because I got to be around all that shit. And I got to create my own lane outta that shit. I created the Pain Rap for this Texas shit. I created this shit.

Those became moments on a Screwtape . . . he kinda takes you through a story when you're hearing those different voices, they've all got different things to say.

And that's what make it cool. It go back to that feature shit we was talkin' about. He'd very seldom have too many people come back and rap on the same song unless it was just a few people. Like on "G Love," you got Shorty Mac, Al-D, me, Grace, Screw . . . I mean, like, we all got to get on that bitch one good time and say what the fuck we wanted to say. And I mean . . . when you know you got one time, you fittin' to pile all of the shit you got to say at one time and you gonna do it at one time. And get it off your chest and do it at your best. That was real good practice for the real career that was comin' along shortly. So, you know, man, it was a blessing for me. I ain't . . . we ain't even fuck with music like that. I met Screw, of course, to do music, but you look at most motherfuckers that's musical . . . "Motherfucker fake, he don't do none of the shit he talk about." But Screw wasn't like one of them people because he didn't talk. His hands did it. So it was just like a dream to get in that motherfucker and actually witness him go in that bitch and do all that shit you heard on them Screwtapes. And after that, I forgot I was rappin'. I was just like a fan. Like, man, you know, I'm fuckin' with DJs, but he doin' his shit? I'm like, "Yeah." I was fuckin' with that. When them turntables go off, we just ride and talk about shit. Like . . . fuck a *song*. He'd have to ask me, "Hey, you did anything new?" "Oh yeah, I got this motherfucker. Check it out." And that was it. Very seldom put a new song on a Screwtape, unless it was some Guerilla Maab shit. We was always fuckin' around, just on some . . . we goin' to the beach, we goin' to somebody concert, we fittin' to go to Hartz Chicken or some shit like that. I mean, that's what that shit was.

And he took you through that too because in that broadcast, during the times he would speak, he'd take you around the room . . . he'd tell you who was there . . .

Yeah. He gonna make sure everybody get recognized, and he was doin' that for a purpose. A lot of people was there to do tapes, but a lot of people was there to build they career. That's why he always made sure, he was like, "Yeah, Z-Ro, Screwed Up Click . . . get ready, keep watchin' me." Or Yungstar . . . E.S.G., Lil' Keke, Fat Pat, Hawk, Big Steve. Enjoli, Sherro . . . you know, Grace, LOS . . . even to the people that was just rappin' and not tryin' to do it as a career but as a pass . . . I mean, he ain't pass over nobody. The man was real humble. He knew he was the shit, but he would never tell you that. That's why I fucked with him. Because if you walked in the room and didn't know who the man was, he wasn't gonna tell you that. That's why I don't do that shit. 'Cuz I mean, that's just some . . . a real form of humility to me. That shit is important right now. A lot of motherfuckers let this royalty name that they got go to they head, and they forget who the fuck they really are, and it's hard when you fall on your ass to go back to who the fuck you really are when everybody like, "Oh, naw, nigga, I thought you was such and such . . . oh, now you back over here fuckin' with me?" So it's kinda like, naw, you better stay grounded. Even when you get off the motherfuckin' ground, you gotta stay grounded. You might be flyin', but it ain't really smart to pull your landing gear up, because you gonna come down one day. I don't give a fuck. That's how I look at that shit. Right now, I'm soaring. I *know* I'm soaring, but if I was to crash immediately, my motherfuckin' landing gear is out. I ain't never pulled that shit back in, 11 years later. My shit still out. Every day is different.

You'd been rapping for several years before you'd ever worked with Screw.

Yeah.

I know he didn't change anything about what you did, but what did the experience of working with him add to you?

Being grown. Looking at shit through a man's eyes versus lookin' at that shit through a warrior's eyes all the time. My whole shit before that was, "Oh motherfucker, you stepped on my shoe. I fittin' to beat your motherfuckin' ass." Or, "You bumped into me at the club. I'm fittin' to beat your motherfuckin' ass." "Fuck me? I'ma beat your motherfuckin' ass." Okay, for nothin', you just walk in here and you look like somebody I'm fittin' to beat they motherfuckin' ass, and just beat your motherfuckin' ass. Like . . . you would never know how to be a man until you hold the hand of a man and see what that shit feel like. When they tell you, "This what you do, this not what you do, and this is why."

Like a lot of motherfuckers will fuss at you and be like, "You don't do that shit," and they don't tell you why not to do it. So you look at them motherfuckers like, "Bitch, you just hatin'. You just hatin' 'cuz I'll knock that nigga out in a style and a fashion that you could never do." But Screw would be like, "Aight, when that motherfucker wake up, and go get a gun and come back, what you gonna do then? You ain't even got a slingshot, nigga. What you gonna do when he get up and go home and come back. Nigga, you gonna get me shot 'cuz I'm fuckin' with you. Since you my boy, I'm not gonna leave you, so if you not gonna leave, I'm not gonna leave, but when he come back with a gun, we both gonna get killed. He gonna kill both our legacies before the motherfuckers even really start." So then you like, "Damn . . . that nigga right. My bad. I'm trippin' . . . Say dude—yeah, fuck me. Yeah, you right . . . yeah, gon' ahead." And that's probably the same dude today buyin' all my CDs and some shit. Just lookin' at some shit through some grown eyes versus some adolescent shit.

He really cooled people off, didn't he?

Hell yeah. I ain't never been in Screw's house and there was no . . . like Hawk said, there wasn't never no trippin' over there.

And he just quietly demanded that.

He wouldn't demand it. It just kinda like . . . you know you're not gonna go into church and light up a blunt. It was just some shit that was automatically . . . you know not to go in Screw house with no bullshit. 'Cuz for one, when you walk in there, you gonna be trapped in that bitch for three days *anyway*. So if you do fight somebody, you gonna be fightin' for three days. You can't get out. Once he lock them doors, and he go to sleep, you fucked up. You in here for the next 72 hours. But at the same time, you can't come around somebody that's showin' even the motherfucker you beefin' with love . . . and there was a lot of times, man, you go in there and there's motherfuckers that were beefin', but when they walked in Screw house, they had to shake hands, 'cuz it was kinda like . . . almost an embarrassment to be like, "Man, Screw, you know I don't fuck with that nigga." Screw would be like, "Y'all take that shit . . . wherever y'all started that shit at, get that shit right, then y'all come back in here together," type shit. But he ain't never have to do that because it was automatically understood. 'Cuz he showin' you love, he lettin' you get on a dub, he lettin' *you* get on a dub. Why you gonna go in this bitch and fuck your blessing and your chance off at the same time? It don't make no sense. So even damn fools that was in there, you didn't know they was damn fools if they was in Screw house. You would walk in that bitch, "Hey what's up?" "Hey, how you doin'?" But you might see the motherfuckers at the club, "Hey, how you doin', remember Screw house?" "Nigga, fuck you and your mama." But you wasn't gonna do that shit at Screw house, though. It was just gonna be a mutual respect for everybody.

380 Dat Lady

THE SOUTHWEST

Carmen Ruth started working in music when she was 13 years old, making her debut on the Crime Boss album *All In The Game* in 1995. She recorded under the name YellaBone back then, changing it to Skanless 3 before settling on the name given to her by Memphis transplants 8Ball & MJG. She started out working with Tony Draper's Suave House label, but recorded her debut, *Day In The Life Of 380 Vol. 1* for Cartel Records in 1996, when she was 16 years old. She appeared on releases alongside other Houston artists including D of Trinity Garden Cartel, Ace Deuce, and Da Herb Man before picking up and leaving Houston—two short years after her debut—to pursue an education in Georgia.

PHOTO COURTESY OF CARMEN RUTH

Did you start making music in Atlanta when you got there, or did you kind of get out of music for a while?

I actually got out of music. I'm currently working on a master's degree, concentrating on television and film. Ultimately, I'm probably going to work for a news broadcasting network. But you know, I still work on material. I'm 34 years old at this point, so I'm doing more writing and trying to solicit music to the younger generation. You know, there's been such a shift in music from when we were younger and listening to music that I don't even really listen to the radio or . . . it's so different.

It's hard to even know where to start or what you're even hearing.

When I was younger, listening to the stuff that our parents listened to—by all means, don't get me wrong, don't take this the wrong way—the subject matter is still the same, it's just the context in the way it's being presented now. Nothing's taboo anymore. You had Al Green, those kind of guys, that had the same type of material that the Ushers and the R. Kellys are singing, but it was more tactful and tasteful.

They were just as nasty, but they were just saying it in a different way.

Exactly, and I think that's what we're so far removed from, that the tact, and the class and the poise and the elegance of the industry. And so for me nowadays it's rather disappointing. We've dumbed down the music so much. You know, I was reading an article—an interview that Scarface had done, and he made some pretty interesting statements, and essentially what he was sayin' was that now we're being told what we should like instead of *feeling* the music. Instead of us *feeling* the music, *feeling* good music, we're being programmed by saturation to say, "This is what we like." Or what we *should* like. And so I think that's the big shift that took place—everybody's under the illusion that something happened after the death of Tupac and Biggie, but this transition had been in place long before then.

Well, a lot of people hypothesize that it was an industry-wide goal to dumb down the music into candy so that everybody would keep consuming it in regular doses.

To a certain extent I totally agree. Like I said, I'm 34. When I became most impressionable was when *my* group became most impressionable—early '90s—and we were *huge* fans of *The Cosby Show*, huge fans of *A Different World*. Leaders of the New School, KRS-One, Public Enemy. You know, music that meant something, that sent a message. Yeah, you heard them rappin' about drugs, you heard them rappin' about guns, but there was a *moral* to the story. But now, they're rappin' about guns, drugs, sex, and violence, and it's just because, "That's what makes you a man." And so it's the same *content*, but the message is different. It kills me when I hear people say, "Oh, Jay-Z is Illuminati. These people are part of the Illuminati." But if you're a history buff you know the Illuminati disbanded in the early 15th century, and not to mention they wouldn't let a black man be part of the Illuminati *anyway*. No matter how much money you give a black man, he'll never have that same amount of power.

That's a common theme that comes up, talk about the New World Order and the Illuminati. I always found it an interesting dichotomy that that language and those concepts come out of the most oppressed area of the city.

You know, growing up my mother had been involved with the National Black United Front Center and the Black Panther Youth Coalition, so we were very exposed to Pan-African culture and a sense of self and self-awareness, but I think what we as individuals oughtta do is *read*. And study on our own. Just take a concept and we run with it. And so while I totally agree, there is a grand design for a New World Order, I don't think it's as transparent and black and white as people would like to assume it is. I grew up with a white stepmother who was very aware, not to be mean, but raising black children, being a white woman, she made it a point to say, "Listen, I'm gonna be real with you guys—this is what it is." And she confirmed what was being—she broke it down to where, "Read—history, history, history." So it's funny, are we targeted as black females and black men—with two strikes against us, black and female. I mean, absolutely. But I think what we're failing to realize, it's not so much about a race thing, to emphasize race thing. It's more becoming a *class* thing. Who has the money? Who has the power? And who has the *education*? You know, the price of education is consistently rising because they figured, "Okay, we gave them this leeway in music and sports and 'cooning,' as they say. They mastered that! What happens if we take their ability and avenues to educate themselves?" And it gets more and more deeper, so I just find it fascinating that we put ourselves in a box where we really go in about the Illuminati—and I totally agree—one thing I totally agree with Scarface on is—Scarface is an interesting story. Scarface, when he came down here to Atlanta to be the CEO of Def Jam South, he came down here with the intention of really making that brand grow really big, and almost separating Def Jam South completely—creating a differential avenue. I brought my project, Ludacris brought his project, and a few more local talents from Houston he wanted to sign, and he really had no control. And so when you hear him—I can bear witness to this—he really had no control. They were basically tryin' to use him as a figurehead. And so when you hear him say the things that he's saying, he's not saying it because he doesn't know what he's talking about. He's saying it because he's experienced it firsthand. I mean, these people really told him, "Listen, this is what we're looking for you to bring to the table. This is what we want you to go seek out." In that sense, they were using him more as an A&R instead of the President and allowing him to have the creative control he needed to take it in a direction in which they entrusted him just by giving him his title. And it was really interesting.

How did you get into rap?

It's funny. I had no intentions on getting into the music industry whatsoever. I was 13 years old and it was '93, you know, Snoop and all these people out, and it was battle rappin', and I was a kid that was bullied in school. My mother's an English major, we spoke proper grammar, we enunciated—what you hear is the result of Trinity Garden Cartel and Alief. That country twang. So I was bullied, and I said, "You know what? I'm gonna write a diss rap. I'm gonna talk about this girl . . ." And I didn't even have a formula. I just wrote a long rap one day, and my cousin happened to be dating Thorough of South Circle on Suave House at the time. And she called me one time and she was like, "Rap for him!" And I rapped for him, he sent me to 8Ball & MJG—8Ball and MJG liked me, they introduced me to Tony Draper, I got on Crime Boss's album *All In The Game*, on the two last songs. They had me listed as "YellaBone." That was my rap name at the time. And the rest is history. I was signed to them for a while, ended up leaving *them* because my mom wasn't willing to sign the parental rights for them to take me on the road and everything. She wasn't a manager—she didn't know everything about the industry—so I transitioned over to D of Trinity Garden Cartel at about 15, and the rest is history. But the person who actually taught me how to rap was Ricky Robinson, a.k.a. Thorough of South Circle. He sat me down, told me how to format a rap. He taught me that you think of a title, a concept, and you write to it. But did I aspire to be a rap artist? Absolutely not.

But did you feel like—once you got in there and you write that first rap, it's so cathartic and you're getting it out. Is that what you were feeling, and those years of being bullied and growing up that you felt like were growing through your writing?

Exactly. I felt empowered. I felt like being bullied in school, you know, and being associated with big names in the industry at the time, I felt empowered through my lyrics. I wasn't gettin' bullied anymore! Because, you know, kids don't know that 8Ball & MJG aren't going to come to the school and shoot the school up and beat 'em up if they mess with me. All they know is 8Ball & MJG made "9 Little Millimeta Boys!" So it was a feeling of empowerment, and as I grew and got to listen to myself and listen to the talent that I had, I just kept writing and going and going. It wasn't until D of Trinity Garden actually got arrested in 1998 and had to serve like a 5-year sentence—it made me really sit back and reflect on life. I'm 18 at the time, and I'm like, "Whoa—wait a minute. Now what? What happens from here?" I needed to educate myself because I wasn't fortunate enough like Bow Wow and Brat to get signed to legitimate businessmen. They've been indicted. On drug charges. I don't want—both of my parents have several degrees. You know, I can honestly say I didn't *come* from a background where my mom was a drug addict and my dad was a drug addict and there was abuse in the home. I don't have that story, so I'm not that cliché artist that you talk to, "Oh, life was so *hard*." No, it was not hard. I grew up in Alief, and I lived in the suburbs.

But that didn't mean you didn't have feelings and stories that you could pour into music.

Exactly. Of course, the early rap that you hear me rap about is again—keep in mind I was between the ages of 13 and 17—it would be my observation of what I saw. Let's be honest. Am I walking down—what if there are other people my ages with pockets full of money and a mouthful of crack and a pistol? Absolutely. Was I one of 'em? Absolutely not.

Well what was the dynamic of being a young female rapper amongst more seasoned guys that had been making music for a while?

It was great! I don't have any horror stories with Suave House. Like I said, when I was under Tony Draper's direction, I was treated with respect. I saw a lot of things that I probably shouldn't have *seen* at that age, but I was *very* well-protected. And being in that industry, you *have* those predators that say, "Okay, she's hungry. Let's try and take advantage of her." *Those* type of people were kept away from me, and if they did slip through the cracks, well, of course you know what happened if they tried it. Tony Draper and even Trinity Garden Cartel always encouraged me to finish my education, get educated, but at the same time hone my craft. You know, always write. Always take it seriously. If you're going to do it, *do* it. So I never had a bad experience dealing with Suave House. *Cartel Records* on the other hand, [Laughs] that was quite a . . . I can remember one of the best lessons I ever learned dealing in the industry—when we dropped an album at the same time. Which is, he dropped *Game Done Changed*, and I dropped *Day In The Life Of 380 Vol. 1*.

1996.

Yeah. And at the time, his mentality about the record label—I remember us sittin' down one day. We were on Tidwell and we were having a meeting, and he announced, "I'm not puttin' my money in—I'll pay you guys all day to feature, and I'll even drop some more albums on you—but I'll never put the money and effort behind you guys as an artist that I'll put behind myself. If I don't make it first, nobody's makin' it." And so his partner, who actually got indicted along with him, said, "That is just a poor attitude to have as a businessman." So what *he* ended up doin' was takin' his money and investing in *Day In The Life Of 380 Vol. 1*. He got the posters printed up, got Darryl Mencken and Robert Guillerman over at Southwest to front him the product, and we took it to 97.9 The Box and later found out that D had called Robert Scorpio, Madd Hatta, and all these different people, these DJs and remote personalities on the radio, and told them, "Play the record." Because it was such a commercial appeal. He knew once I got that radio play, it solidified me as an artist. He knew it was going to take off. So I remember we met at the liquor store on Lockwood, and I had done an interview, and I was always taught that family business is family business, so I gave a shout-out on the radio some kinda way, playin' with the

telephone game, and it got back to him, and dude came up there and *slapped* me! And that's when I knew. That's when I knew that I wanted to be different. I didn't want to *do* business with the drug dealers. I didn't wanna do business. I wanted to do business legitimately. I didn't want to bring the streets into my business in the industry. That's not what I'm about. So that was a turning point for me, and shortly thereafter, like I said, two years and maybe a little under two years later he got indicted, he went to prison, and ever since I've just . . . you know, I still have a good relationship with him. I've talked to him before, from prison. You know, I still have a good relationship with Mike D, Irv . . . I talked to Jamie Foster not too long ago. You know, we're good, but as far as doing business, if it's not legitimate business there's no room for it.

Did that feel like an uphill climb in Houston, where so many of the labels were started with street money?

Absolutely. And I don't knock these individuals, because their effort—their valiant effort to try and go legit, I commend them, but the thing is that you can't be daytime executive, nighttime street thug, you know, organized crime drug lord. I mean the only person who pulled it off successfully—allegedly—we're all going to use the word "allegedly"—was J Prince. And so I think, again that's where the shift comes in the industry. It's so violent, it's so saturated with thugs and these wannabe gangsters that it's almost a turnoff for the people who really love the art and the craft. Now the old-school people—we're not saying . . . you know, these old-school guys who are "split ditch" and the new people—we're not saying . . . we're not hatin', we're just sayin', you know, we've lost so many artists, when is enough enough? People are dying over lyrics. It's not a game. And not to mention—you wonder why white people look at us in a particular light? Hip-hop has crossed over! You have their children speaking our vernacular, which is . . . they don't like! Their kids are saggin' pants, they have earrings and jewelry draped everywhere. They're taking their allowance, and instead of investing in schoolbooks and cars to get back-and-forth to school and stocks and bonds, they're gettin' grills by Paul Wall, which, there's nothing wrong with it. But there are so many . . . hip-hop is so much *broader* now. There's so many different genres under the *umbrella* of hip-hop . . . but it's so tainted with BS now that it's hard for people like myself, who are not rappin' about guns and hos and drugs and all that stuff, to even get airplay because now the trend is to be dumb! Sell drugs. Not be educated. Be a whore. You know, it's just crazy.

Well that's the stuff that people see when they're flippin' channels and they go past the rap videos, that's what they see is the cars and the girls in bikinis and the guns and drugs and everything like that, but even when you're talking about gangsta rap there's still so much more beneath that. There's more going on, even with music that you might completely hate, and I say this for people who maybe don't listen to rap or are turned off by it, that sort of thing.

And you know what was so interesting? While I was home, it was so disappointing—my heart goes out to Trae, who recently got signed to Grand Hustle, something happened down there. I don't know the full story, but something happened at one of his shows, one of his community events, a young lady from Clear Channel—

Oh yeah. That was a mess.

I'm like—so, he didn't *threaten* her! He stood up for himself. He defended himself, and he got *banned*, and it was so . . . I also think of that because, like . . . yeah, does this music send a message that you want your children or impressionable ones to listen to? Absolutely not. But that's when you step in as a parent, and you don't allow them to listen to it. But at the end of the day, he was hosting a community event to say, "Hey, thanks for supportin' me and allowing me to get to this level." And for the sake of the drama that society has embraced with reality TV and everything, you target this man for radio ratings—*I* think it was because nobody listens to the radio anymore! And so it was so disappointing—I'm like, "Gosh, this guy is a classic example of bein' a victim."

Well, I think the most unfortunate thing about that whole incident was that it was such an opportunity to become a learning experience. It was so much a high profile event that just blew up in everybody's face, and I think it was such an opportunity for them to extend some olive branches and then go on the air and talk about what happened, and that just didn't happen. When you ban somebody, you're telling them that you don't want to talk to them. You don't want to talk about them. You can't even mention Trae on the air there. And so I think it's such a lost opportunity. It's not to say that it couldn't happen, but that opportunity is so much further away now than if they would have taken it by the horns.

And use it as a platform to start the conversation of, "Is the shift that has taken place in the music industry taking us in a dark direction?" But you're absolutely right—it was a teachable and a coachable and a learning moment where we should have opened up dialogue. Until we address some of the issues surrounding hip-hop, it's gonna be this vicious cycle of what you're getting. Rappers are *not* responsible for raising your children. At the same time, we *are* responsible for the message that we put out there. We *are* responsible for what we personally say as individuals, and I think that's what a lot of rappers wanna stray away from. Yes, it's up to the parents not to allow their children to listen *to* us. No, we're not claiming ourselves as role models, and I think that's pressure the parents shouldn't put on us, but at the same time you know the power of your words. Use your power wisely. Realize that people are listening to that, and that you're teaching people whether you realize that or not. It's so funny because Ganksta N-I-P is a pretty good friend of mine, and even then, when I was a younger child, I used to go out and just kinda hang with him, and these were the same conversations that we would have! I was like, "If you *believe* that, why do you make the music that you make?" And he's like, "Listen, at the end of the day, I'm a victim of my circumstances, and this is how I feed my family and pay my bills." So unfortunately, it kinda is what it is. You have a lot of brothers out there that rap what they—see, this is another thing that I think we're also responsible for saying as artists—you guys know me as 380. I am here to entertain you. It's entertainment! When I go home, I'm Carmen Ruth. When I go home, I gotta wash my dishes, wash my clothes, take my dog out. You know, I go home and I am who I am. My rap name is a character, and I'm entertaining you. There's a fine line. Everybody wants to top their words, and it's cool to say, "I went to prison." Like, dude—you can't even vote!

KB Da Kidnappa

TRINITY GARDENS

An original member of Street Military, KB was touring the country with the group (also consisting of Pharoah, Lil' Flea, Icey Hott, and Nutt) while still in high school. After Pharoah's imprisonment and the group's disbanding in the early 2000s, KB went on to pursue a solo career and has released a number of albums on his own label, Spitting Venom. KB is also considered part of the South Park Coalition, and over the years he has been a frequent sight (and guest on the mic) at the annual S.P.C. Picnic gatherings at MacGregor Park.

KB AND DOPE E. PHOTO: PETER BESTE

We were talking a little last time about Rap-A-Lot.

It's a hell of a blueprint been laid out here, man, by people like Rap-A-Lot. That was one of my favorite record labels, was Rap-A-Lot. They can say what they wanna say, but Rap-A-Lot is the bread and butter of Houston, and really showed a lot of artists from Houston that it could be done. And then when Houston picked up on the DIY, the do-it-yourself method, so far as pushing your own music, whether it be in the stores or out the trunk, that's when a lot of CEOs was created, during that situation. And to this day, I still keep that CEO mentality.

The real ones are out there with their trunks open.

The real ones will always stay out there with their trunks open. The real ones are always gonna be on that sale, man. I love what I do. I'ma tell you the truth: I love what I do, and it's not all about money, man. It's just . . . it's really like a passion, a love. When you love something, and you have passion for something, man, it ain't about the money. The money comes and goes. Love for something—it's all about the passion and the love. I love doing music without receiving no money, but I like to get paid from it, and I like to make a living out of it, but even if I didn't make a living out of it, I would still be doing it. Because that's my love. That's my passion. If you in it just for the money, then . . . ain't no drive if the money ain't there. In this music situation, there ain't no guarantees. Money can be there and the money could be gone. And then money could come back and money could be gone.

If your drive consists of money, and the money ain't there, then your music is . . . you can't create good music because you've got no drive!

How did Street Military come together originally?

Street Military consists of me, Pharoah Tha Thuggish King from South Park, Lil' Flea from Missouri City, Icey Hott from Hiram Clarke, and Nutt . . . was the fifth member of the group, was also from Missouri City, and the group consisted of five members, all from different parts of the Houston area. It's kind of funny how we came together. I mean, after it was all said and done, we sat down, and none of us . . . knew our fathers. There was five ghetto bastards in the group. Now, that was kind of crazy, man. It was like we all vibrated to each other. It was like it was destined for us to be together. When we started, there was three members already in the group. Icey Hott, Lil' Flea, and Pharoah was already clicked up. And they were coming out to this club called Charlemagne. It was a club on the Northside, not too far from my hood. It was off of Homestead.

You're from Trinity Garden, right?

Yeah, I'm from Trinity Garden. I heard about them coming to this club and winning these rap contests. They was having rap battles, you know, and guys from my neighborhood was pushin' me on to go get in it. Because I was a threat in the neighborhood—I was like a rap threat in the neighborhood. Man, that's when it was just so fun. Where I could see a guy coming down the street, walkin' my way, and he see me walkin' his way, and he got his little crew with him, I got my little crew with me. It's almost like a Western showdown or something, you know what I'm sayin'? We was goin' around the neighborhood battlin' like that. It was fun, man. So I end up getting convinced to go get in these rap contests with Flea, Pharoah—which Icey was shinin' it up for—and I got in there, and man, I end up winning this rap battle. Because there was a lot of people in there from my neighborhood, and I had got a lot of support from my neighborhood. So I end up winning, and then when it was all said and done, we went outside and I found out that . . .

Icey Hott was my cousin. I didn't even know Icey was my cousin. That's where I met them guys, and that's where we first bonded at. At that rap battle.

What neighborhood was that?

That was in Scenic Woods. It wasn't in my neighborhood. The club wasn't in my neighborhood. It was in another neighborhood, but it was a popular club.

And this was '90, '91?

This was '90. We really came out with our first record in '91. So, after that, you know, we went to that studio out there in South Park. Called Jeriod Records. I would go up there, and the first executive that we started messin' with was Keith Babin. To make a long story short, you know, they wanted me to join the group. So I was the last member to really join, because like I say, there's five members, but Nutt . . . the guy that was the fifth member was this guy named Antoine. And he wasn't a rapper, he was just a guy that was with us.

Like Bushwick—but kind of like a fool, right?

Yeah, yeah, he was part of our clique, man. He was a part of our clique whenever we'd do shows. He would do all kinds of crazy shit like jump off the stage or jump off a speaker and land on his side. I mean, he was just . . . he was a crowd hyper.

You must have picked that up from him, then.

Yeah, yeah. So that's when we formed Street Military, I was really the last rapper to join the group.

Where did you grow up?

I was born in Galveston, and my mother was from Port Arthur so . . . I stayed in Port Arthur from like birth to three or four years old. Then we went to St. Louis with my dad, my original father, and then my mother ran off from my original father, and came back to Port Arthur, and ended up meetin' a man in the service, and that's when we moved to Germany. So I started school in Butzbach, Germany, because my stepfather was in the military. It's so crazy because I ended up bein' in a group called Street Military, and I was like a little military brat around in Germany, playing in tanks and on army bases, shootin' machine guns on Field Day . . . it's crazy, man. Whenever I think over it, I'm like, "Damn, I end up bein' in a group called Street Military," and a lot of people don't really know the background that I came from.

And so how old were you when you came to Houston?

When I came back to Houston, I was, like, 7. I was down there four years.

A lot of people lump together Fifth Ward and Trinity Garden because of their proximity on a map, but they're really very different neighborhoods, aren't they?

Yeah, yeah, they're different neighborhoods. Matter of fact, let me correct that—we stayed in Fifth Ward before I stayed in Trinity Garden, so I stayed in Fifth Ward too. I was a resident of Fifth Ward. And they're right on the side, man. I mean, it's like they're two, three minutes apart. Same thing that goes down in Fifth Ward goes down in Trinity Garden. No difference but the name, man. And that it's recognized as separate areas, man. That's it.

Coming up, were there clubs in Trinity Garden and Fifth Ward, where people would rap?

Me myself, coming up, I never went to clubs. I got in the club when I was 14 years old. That same club I mentioned where Street Military was at, my uncle used to get me in there. You know, I wasn't old enough, but that's where I first started going to clubs at age 14.

Street Military did a lot of work with Klondike Kat back in the day.

Man, you might as well go ahead and document this: Klondike Kat is probably really the sixth member of Street Military, man. We had so much love for Klondike, man. Whenever we needed singing,

he would sing. Klondike was def, and he was a soldier too. My first time seein' Klondike, he was in an R&B group, like a singing group. I forgot the name of the group, but a lot of people don't know—Klondike Kat, he just don't rap, man. That boy can blow. I'm talkin' about he can really sing his ass off. That was one of things I really admired about him, how he was able to go back-and-forth between the singin' and the rappin'. And during those early Street Military years, we really bonded, man. Them were some beautiful years. Money don't determine the happiness or the friendship of a group. When we wasn't makin' money and we was doin' it for the love and passion, it was such a more harmonious situation. We was a true group, man. Without money, or none of that, we was true. Like when we was on tour, I'm tellin' you—there's some places that we can't even go back to, man. Shit, we tore up the fuckin' rooms! From wrestlin' and shit, like we was WWF or some shit. We was doin' pranks on each other, man. I mean, that's how we played on tour, man. It would probably be me and Icey teamin' up on Flea, Pharoah, and Nutt. When we were out somewhere, we would probably sneak back to the room and get their key, and go in their room and fuck that room up! Pour water everywhere, I'm talkin' 'bout, man . . . we would fuck around and piss on they bed. They'd come back and see they room all fucked up, we laughin' and gigglin'. And then, whenever we slip, we not payin' attention, they'd get our motherfuckin' ass. We'd come back inside that room—man, I can't even sleep in my motherfuckin' bed.

Icey Hott

HIRAM CLARKE

The DJ and producer for Street Military appears all over the Houston rap lexicon, with production and feature credits on numerous albums and singles, all the way back to Willie D's 1992 album *I'm Goin' Out Lika Soldier*, on which he makes an uncredited appearance alongside Sho, Rasir X, and Klondike Kat. Icey Hott has recorded several albums as a rapper, but he's really known as a producer, collaborating over the years with artists like Filero, Mafia Genie, and Komodo DBX. He has also produced tracks for Galveston's World Wide Riders and all of his Street Military brethren. Icey Hott released an album with Mr. Baldhead in 2011 called *Supa Jammin* and records for his own label Snotrag Music.

That lane y'all cut sure is holding up.

I done seen it go wild out there. We like heavy rap, you know what I'm sayin'? Hardcore. Hardcore from the heart, you know what I'm sayin'? We had so much heart, they dare to come and mess with us while we doin' our thang, and some of 'em had heart too. So you whilin' in clubs sometimes and there's people on beer in them olden days, man, fightin', shit, they got some good-ass hard music and get round in there, they like, "Mann!" But don't nobody *kill* nobody or nothin'. They just like . . . they was waitin' for that, and when it hit 'em, it hit 'em like a spear or somethin'. That's how it was, and it was that era where everybody was so aggravated and *mad* that they ain't even have no song that'll please the . . . satisfy they appetite, so shit . . . we came with that agg shit back in the day because

we were mad, too! So when we hit that spot where a lot of people *mad* at, shit, they was like, "Shit, we love that shit!" And that was it. It was like . . . like a pressure in the pipe. Like a volcano blowin' *big*, straight like that. But that's how it was back with Nutt. Nutt'd jump offstage, dive on the floor like it's water. Treat the hard ground like it was *water*. Like, *aah!* How he hit the ground like that and ain't hurt, he had it *together*. That was his talent. He'll come dropkick us while we rappin' on the mic—*bam!* Some people, they ain't even care, we ain't even get to finish our raps, shit! Hell yeah. Man, we breakin' it off right now. Everything can't come out the ghetto. I can just say right now.

I heard y'all's tours were crazy, man. The hotels.

Oh yeah, it went down back in the day. We hit some spots, and then they had me in that newspaper. I think that was in Memphis or somethin'. Everybody was gone all night. Shit, it was like an old-school classic on the rap side, but you know if it'd been on the rock side that probably'd have been an old-school classic rock comin' through. You know, like some classic stars comin' through.

Where all did you go?

All through the South. I mean, it was so many clubs and spots we hit. I mean, we carved a way through where there wasn't no rap music at. We went where wasn't no rap was around. That's what we did for the East Coast right there, for Wild Pitch. Because they ain't know the South, so we dug

DOPE E AND ICEY HOTT. PHOTO: PETER BESTE

Yeah! And where it was, we still promoted and, bam! Bam! Bam! We showed love as far as buyin' a lot of product, and even if they know us, they could make somethin' happen with that music. Had our CDs and all of that, and if you don't like the music you still could sell it. You ain't gonna get that much in your hand. Not if you ain't paid for it.

Did you get a good response? I know in some of the towns you had some rough experiences, but by and large, do you think people were feeling the music when you were coming through?

Yeah, we were feelin' it! Because we were rappin' and dropkickin'. One time we went through Dallas, and Dallas was booin' everybody. I'm talkin' about all the top-of-the-line rappers from everywhere. Shit would start—I ain't gonna say nothin' agg 'cuz I'll put that on they record. It *was* on they record, though. I remember the dude that owned that club that we went to called The Venue, and we was in there in '93. And they booed *everything* that came *through* that motherfucker! I'm talkin' 'bout *everything*. They booed *everything*. And when we came in town and they told us the ropes, they said, "Okay, everybody on this shit, they madder'n a motherfucker. They booin' *every*thing come in the club, so fellas, if y'all get out there, y'all just do y'all show, and then if it don't work out too well, we still do business and we got security," such and such, this and that, and that is like that. And they was just givin' us the ropes, like, "Damn! Like we fittin' to do a Tyson fight!" Watch out for that uppercut. That's what they was, like that. From that club. So okay, then, we parked up anyway. We gonna get parked up anyway! Like, "Sheeeet, they better be ready for *us*!" Because we was already comin' through clubs that were wilder than a mug. They were wild as fuck. So when we came in and, bam! We came out there onstage, the music came on, Nutt start burnin' chicks with them cigarettes, "Ah!" Lit cigarettes on 'em. They shut the hell up from that point right there. We were G'd up and it was just a—we were crunk. We already been in mo' clubs and been wild so we already ready for that. But as soon as Nutt did that, me and Nutt was on top of the speakers and that "Crank This Bitch Up!" came on, Nutt jumped up off that speaker, that

through the South a certain lil' route, and through that route it wasn't friendly. And you probably could find somebody at Wild Pitch who was on the road with us, they might could tell you better. [Laughs] When they came through the ghetto and turned up ways, they thought we was prolly mean dudes, we had guns and stuff, they thought we was mean dudes 'til after we hit the road for a while and came through certain lil' spots, and people walkin' with guns, and they not expectin' it! Except it was better that we had some when we was ridin' through. I said, "Now you see why we got them motherfuckers." 'Cuz *shit*, we pulled up in the projects, in a spot, and next thing I know, I seen about eight full shotguns pass by. It's like, "Whew! They packin' in here!" We were strapped, though. We were strapped with automatics, and we wasn't playin' that shit. There wasn't no plex. There wasn't no plex. It was just people in they own world. Don't mess with nothin' runnin' around and make 'em pay attention to you much.

Gotta have that protection.

high speaker, and hit that stage monitor, you know the stage monitor sits low. The big speaker on the side—on either side like that—and they sittin' up high, so he like about, what, 8, 10 feet in the air. He—*uhh*!—he jumps up off that speaker—*huh*!—he hit those monitors—*pow*!—the wire broke up off that mug—*uhh*!—he threw it in the crowd. Soon as he threw it, that thing in the crowd—*bah*!—the crowd start fightin' like they slam dancin', like they *boxin'* up in that bitch. In Dallas, man. They was *that* agg in there. They ain't had nothin' come through there, and when they did that, everybody kinda shit calmed down and they was just crunk. Man! And then a lot of the OGs and stuff in Dallas start brangin' that liquor—whole bottles to us. Onstage. While we bustin', we gettin' them bottles sent to us. Wham—*wham*! They was sendin' 'em. Everybody was sayin' they was lookin' for that right there. They ain't had that in Dallas, and we came with that gangsta shit, comin' up in there. They just wanted to hear somethin'! It's like there wasn't nothin' pleasin'! Motherfucker mad, ain't too much gonna make 'em happy! We hit 'em like that. That juice hit 'em! They got that juice. We already was on that juice. There ain't no more comin'. They just already knew the name so they was wired up, probably wanted to fight us for a second. We were ready to fight everybody too! We were fucked up. Don't get embarrassed! We gonna come on that mic—don't get embarrassed up in your town, now! We comin' through this mug with real shit. We wasn't dissin', though. You better not diss in Dallas. Motherfuckers'll take some heat off. You can talk shit, but don't diss. Don't diss in that motherfucker, that's all. Niggas ain't trippin'. Everybody was in that motherfucker there. They jumped out hard, though. They jumped out hard. That was in one spot. One time we was—I can't tell you who it was in the South 'cuz I get mixed up on exactly some of the spots, but I remember the event at the club one time we was at a spot they wasn't used to that shit. We were rappin' hard, and we came out of Texas for that, though. But when we was in Texas, Texas was crazy. Texas, we were fightin' up in that mug and then we went to some other towns, we was like, "We ain't doin' no fightin' with anybody else out of state. No knuckles." We was talkin' about layin' a motherfucker out. We ironed!

We got that heat, baby. But we ain't here for that. And they was like, "Man, they got that heat! But they ain't there for that. So just let everybody know." But anyway, shit, we came through. That's all I'm sayin'. It was harder in the South. Motherfuckers mad.

DJ Gold

SUNNYSIDE

Gold is a member of the Screwed Up Click who has been close to Screw's brother Al-D since the early '90s and early on worked with Jam Down Records as a DJ and producer, traveling with Lil' Keke in his Jam Down days to play shows around Texas and Louisiana. He became close to Screw, and was a traveling member of the Screwed Up Click (Gold was usually the one back there selling tapes). In recent years, he has been DJing at a strip club on the Southside, and when you see him out, he's still usually out with Al-D.

PHOTO: ATIBA CADDELL

One of the things I want to talk about is the connection between the strip clubs in Houston and the rap scene in Houston because it really is connected. You're producing, you're playing tracks [at the strip clubs]—we heard some of the gangsta stuff that you were playing there . . . how long has that been going on?

I mean . . . really, that's where it's at. I mean, the connection is so serious that if it wasn't goin' on, a lot of artists wouldn't even get *heard* in the city, you know what I'm saying? Opposed to, you know, grinding out in the streets. It's all about your grind ethic too. It's a serious connection because when you play that, and you instantly get a response, then you know that's something you can work with. You can keep on pushing it. But you have to try it in the strip clubs first because the girls are always—that's one thing—the girls are always gonna promote good music. If they feelin' the song, and they request that when they wanna dance or anything . . . they wanna hear the song, you in, you feel me? And when they go dance in another club, then they gonna say, "Well, do you have this song? 'Cuz I danced at the other spot to this song. I wanna know if you have it." And then that DJ gonna be like, "Okay," especially if the girl, you know, is a looker. Then he gonna respond quicker, and he gonna be like, "Okay, alright . . ." Then it goes around. It's a chain . . . a domino effect. It goes from each club to each club, and that's how it gets started right there.

So why is it strip clubs as opposed to the regular clubs? In the strip clubs they kind of test things out?

Well, yeah, you have more leeway to test things out, Lance, you dig what I'm sayin'? Because it's not an intense set like a club. Most . . . me being a DJ, you know, since I was 12 . . . in a *club* club, dance club, it's intense because . . . if you go up to a DJ—even if you can get up to the DJ—and you ask him, "Hey, man, my song jammin'—can you play it for me?" See, there's a lot of things that these young cats don't know about, and it's called DJ etiquette, you know what I'm sayin'? You cannot just go up to a DJ, I don't give a damn how good you think you're jammin'. DJ etiquette is this: You do not go up to a DJ, man, and say, "I'm jammin', man, play my song." No, no, no. You don't do that. You go up to a DJ, man, and you say, "What's your name?" Nine times out of ten you already know who he is, especially at a hot club.

Yeah, you always know who's up there.

Yeah, and you approach him and say, "DJ such and such, man, I have a song . . . if there could be any time, you know, for me, man, here goes twenty dollars." Or, "You want something to drink with that? If you could just listen to my song . . ." Just the gesture of that money, it always wins you, man. I'm just tellin' you from experience. You know, I been doin' this too many years, man, and I've seen it done with my boys. You know, 'cuz I'm in the DJ pool, man. I have a camaraderie with DJs across the nation because I've worked with them or I've done shows at their clubs. And it don't have to be me—I've seen it done. Because there's been guys out there that have been taught DJ etiquette. But it *is* DJ etiquette. I should write a book on that. In a nutshell, I get a lot more guys in the game quicker, man, because they'll know what to do. It is what it is. A DJ starts it off. Not the rapper. I mean, from the beginning, when it started in New York, you didn't . . . it was just cats out there rappin' a cappella. They didn't have no kind of beats until the DJs came and was beat matchin' and makin' these songs, catchin' these beats in between four bars or eight bars here and keepin' that shit continuously goin' so a cat could rap.

Kool Herc was rapping himself.

Yeah, that was the first beat machine. I don't give a damn what anybody talk about. Two turntables was the first beat machine because cats was doin' that . . . when I first seen that, in the, what . . . that was late '70s, early '80s, I was sprung. I mean, I knew, workin' or not, that's what I was gonna do all my life. But I mean, my role ain't over. I done had a beautiful journey so far. If I go tomorrow, I wouldn't complain about nothin'. I couldn't complain about nothin'.

When did you meet Screw? What year was that?

Oh, man. That was in . . . that was '92? Yeah, '92, because I was back-and-forth from California, and then I was DJin' for a group called Double Trouble in California. Kurtis Blow's group, as a matter of fact. I was back-and-forth, like I said, and then I would start workin' for Jam Down . . . Jam Down Records. That's the first label that put Al-D out.

Oh right, right. Way back.

Jam Down. Patrick, yeah. I was DJin' and doin' some production with G411. We had got a crib in Third Ward, man, and we just . . . we was at Jam Down and Screw was messin' with . . . we was just doin' a lot of stuff, man. It was when Filero and them was doin' it back then too. It was a Spanish group of rappers . . . with Triple Threat and all them, yeah, Filero and all them. So it was a lot goin' on, man, and Screw was DJin' and I was doin' sound too, 'cuz that's what I did. I mean, anything dealin' with music, sound, you know . . . DJin' . . . I was there, I was doin' it. You feel me? So I kept runnin' into Screw, man, and I hadn't even met Al yet—you know what I'm sayin'?—until I was runnin' into Screw. But I didn't know how connected they were until I start seein' Al come to the studio at Jam Down, and come to find out he was they main artist! Yeah, yeah! So Screw was like, "Yeah, man, I heard you doin' . . . you over there at Jam Down, man. You know, my brother over there, man." He was like, "Man, look, you know, you a real cat," this and that, and it was just on the DJ camaraderie, you know what I'm sayin'? And he was like, "I want you to look out for my brother, man. He got skills, you know, you gonna hear his album. You over there at Jam Down with Pat, so I know you gonna be workin' with him and everything, so look out for my brother, man. We fittin' to get it in." So, man, it was on from there, man. Me and Al hooked up and we been brothers ever since. We just connected, like, right off the bat. There ain't been nothin' else but that, man.

Were you around when he started experimenting with slowing stuff down?

He was already doing that. Like I said, it was early '90, '91, '92 and then I had . . . like I said, he was doing his thing, so I didn't really grasp what was goin' on until I started hearing it and hearing it. He had told me, but naw, I didn't . . . we didn't link up 'til Al dropped, and then that's when it was, like, *on* for us. He was like, "Man, you doin' this, Gold . . . you a good dude, I get a good vibe from you. You stay sucka-free." It was like, "I just . . . you know, you're lookin' out for Al." Like, "Man, I want you to rock with me, man." So it was on from there, man, and then that's when I start learning the process and seein' it. I'd be in and out checkin' it, and that's when I start just bein' around all the time and cats started droppin' CDs . . . I mean, droppin' tapes—and this was when there was digital recorders, man, 12 and 16-track digital recorders. Well, he started off on the little 4-track tape . . .

Tascam.

Yeah! You damn right, Lance. You damn right. He started off, he went to the 8, then he went to that 12, that 12 digital and went to that 16 . . . well, you had an 8, then it was 12. Yeah man, I remember like yesterday. Them fuckin' grey tapes, that was the master.

So what did you pick up from him? Not even as a DJ, but as a producer or a listener of music, I mean what kind of things did you . . .

Aw, man—why you think my shit sound original like that? You heard it. It ain't no carbon copy, man. It's from that era, man.

Old-school.

That's why I can produce that sound. A lot of cats wanna produce that kind of sound. I'm a cold motherfuckin' DJ, you hear what I'm sayin'? But he thought outside of the box. You view this Screwed Up shit like he did, and the way that he did, you knew he thought outside the box anyway. I mean, man, just to see him . . . because, if anybody knew the process, it wouldn't really mess 'em up, but it would really . . . they think that he's doin' this all slowed all the time. Naw, he was a regular speed DJ, and he would eat your ass up in any competition or anything like that, tricks and everything. Behind the back . . . we used to play . . . the only thing me and him had a problem with . . . [Laughs] he had . . . I would have to go around the other side of the fuckin' box because Screw was backwards. Like, if I'm right, he left, so it's goin' the other way. He always set his fader like that, you feel what I'm sayin'?

Some percentage of DJs do that, right?

Yeah! So I'd have to go around the other side to even, you know, fuck with the shit. It was crazy, man! You got me laughing thinkin' about that shit right now, man, but I remember . . . we had a show, man, I'll never forget this shit. We had a show in San Marcos, man. At Gordo's. It's a club in San Marcos, and I think it might be like a historical spot because they been open for many years, man. It has a balcony and everything, man. It's called Gordo's. Everybody was there, man, and Screw had an attack, man . . . and passed out. So everybody . . . Tommie, he was like our road manager at the time. He was the one . . . Tommie Langston. He was the one that handled all the road trip business. I got all the info from him to get everybody straight before we got on the road. So we was jokin' and trippin' and shit, and Screw, I guess he had him like a four [ounces of syrup]. I thought it was a deuce! Back then, drank was so plentiful that it just wasn't nothin' to have it, you know what I mean? So we get to San Marcos, man. Everything cool, man. Screw got hot. He had a hot spell, man, so he was like . . . you know, we tryin' to wake him up, wake him up . . . showtime . . . because that was the thing—we had come in, like, damn near right in the showtime a lot of times. Remember I was tellin' you about I'd have to call him early? To get at him ready, before we leave? Man, when we got there, Screw was passed out!

At his house or at the club?

Naw, naw! At the club! We was all in the same van! We never went . . . we all rode together, man. That's why Pokey and them called me "Gold Patrol," 'cuz I used to be in their . . . I had to be in their ass, bro! I had to stay in they ass, man. You know, they was just slowpokin' and doin' all that kind of shit.

So how'd you get him up?

Ah, man, you know. Like I said, I called him early, man. I called him early, bugged the hell out of him. Let him know, you know, what time we gettin' on the road, man. Pokey, man, he wasn't too much a problem, man, 'cuz you know, I used to love goin' over there off of Yellowstone anyway. 'Cuz that's where his grandmother stayed, and she always have some throwed breakfast, especially if we leavin' in the morning, you know what I'm sayin'? Yeah, man, his grandmother used to hook a nigga up with that breakfast. Big Moe mama was the same too. She always used to feed us before we left.

What would they make?

Ah, man. Pokey's grandmother, man, would have the grits and eggs and sausage and the bacon. Pokey a big cat, man, so you know, he eat up some shit. Yeah, he was on that football still back then. Yeah, back then he was still playin' that ball. Yeah, but back to that—man, so we in San Marcos, man, goin' on, this place fuckin' off-the-chain packed, man . . . so, they tryin' to wake Screw up, and we . . . the dude, the promoter is all like, "Oh, they here? We need to get the show started," this and that. So, we like, "Hold the fuck on, man, we just gettin' here . . . and we still fittin' to wake Screw up." So Tommie was like, "Hey, man—Gold, you gonna have to go out there, man, and start this shit off." I'm like, "What?" I done rocked it in front of 20

or better, man, in a couple of venues, bro. I think that was the most nervous night I've ever had as a DJ.

Because you had to go before Screw?

I mean, because I had to start off his show! You feel me? *His* show! You dig what I'm sayin', man? He already started bein' the main man, man. I mean, you know, he sellin' tapes, man. He sellin' tapes like crazy, man. This was when they was in the white boxes. A hundred in the fuckin' box. You know, I remember all this shit because I was the one sellin' the shit. So like I say, it was a long time, man, but you had . . . you seen Screw, you seen me. When Al was locked up, and when we was all together, Screw . . . I mean, you seen me, him and Al. And a lot of times, Shorty Mac.

So how many tapes—he would take tapes out on the road with him whenever he'd go out and DJ?

Oh yeah! That was our first thing. We had to pack the van and load it with boxes of tapes, man.

And you'd sell 'em all?

Man, we would never came back with no fuckin' tapes.

10 bucks a pop?

10 bucks a pop. That's what I'm tellin' you, man. That night in Austin, this was . . . man, I'ma tell you somethin'. The last shows that Pat had was in Austin at this club called the Red fuckin' Barn, man. In Austin, Texas. Man, lemme tell you . . . man, we had such a great time, but did you know . . . yeah, because I remember we had like maybe 1,500, maybe 1,500 tapes, man. That's why I say he made like 15 grand that night. Do you know I had . . . the money box, it was a grey money box. I remember this shit like yesterday. Man, I couldn't hardly close that motherfucker, man. I sold . . . I had to start stuffin' money in my shoes, in my back pocket, man . . . every pocket was—you understand what I'm sayin'? I never seen shit like that in my life, man. Never, man. Al could tell you that shit,

man. Real talk, man. I wish he was here, man . . . that's when I knew . . . man, this dude is like . . . it's crazy, man. We never came back with tapes. Bottom-line. All them nights, man, we never came back with tapes. Not one. It was amazing to me, bro. I'm serious.

What was it like watching Fat Pat perform? Or being in the studio with him?

Aw, man . . . that was my heart right there, man. I mention him, but what makes me laugh, just like I'm smilin' right now—all the memories are good with Pat. You know why? Because, man that dude was so talented—I was just talkin' about this on the radio, on Optimo [Radio], man, Sunday night—this dude was so talented, man, fuck rap. He could go onstage and be an A-1 comedian like it was nothin', man. He could go and work the crowd and have everybody in there rollin'. The dude was that funny. He was a clown, man! That's all I'm tellin' you, man. That's all he like, man, baggin' on cats, man, and talkin' shit. That's what he was like. I said, "Man, you got a stupid slick mouth, man." And he would always bust out laughin'.

He had a real good sense of humor. You could hear that on the tapes because you'd hear Pat laughing all the time.

You'd hear Pat laughin' and jokin'! That's him, bro! That's all I remember about Pat, man. Anywhere we went, man . . . he was like, "Gold, man—what's up baby?" 'Cuz that's how Pat talked, you know what I'm sayin'? He was like, "What you think, man, you think my CD gonna *sell*?" I was like, "Man, is you motherfuckin' crazy?" 'Cuz I told him, I was like, "Pat, man, you can't be rockin' all your songs like that." But he was so crunk 'cuz he was promotin' his album. He was so crunk, man, he did like, man, fuckin' . . . eight songs a night, man. And we were tellin' Pat, "Man, you can't be doin' all your shit like that, bro!" He was like, "Fuck it—we comin' out the gate!"

Klondike Kat

SOUTH PARK

Known as the Gangsta of the South Park Coalition, Kat is one of the original members of the S.P.C. and appears on nearly every record by the influential Houston group Street Military. Originally cutting his teeth as a battle rapper in the late '80s, he developed as a solo artist in the early '90s and has continued to release well-received underground records on which he does all of the writing, rapping, singing, and production himself. He also records R&B music under the name Diamond Dre. This interview was conducted after his release from prison in 2012.

How long exactly have you been out?

Maybe . . . since April 10.

It's been kind of a whirlwind, huh?

Yeah, yeah. I mean, well . . . you know, it's all about picking up this bike and ridin' it again.

How long were you in?

Three years.

That's a big gulf. What happens to your creative process when you're in there?

Well, I mean, it's probably more in-depth, really, because you don't have all the obstacles in the way. It depends on your mind frame. You know, a lot of guys get caught up in sorrow, dwellin' on,

"Aw, man, this is goin' on," and what's goin' on out there. But me, myself, I did a lot of . . . more than music, because I did a lot of music, and that's like secondary. You know, it's like walkin'. I can do that without thinkin' about it. So, in the midst of makin' a lot of songs, I just did a lot of studying different things. A lot of self-evaluation, you know what I'm sayin'? Yeah, so I did a lot more than that. Studyin' a couple of languages . . .

Really? What did you study?

French and Spanish.

Where was the prison?

Well, they had me—I went three places. First they had me in Garza East, which is in Beeville, Texas, right close to the border, about 15 minutes from the border. Then they moved me to Hondo, Texas, which is close to San Antonio, and then where I did most of my stay was at Ramsey 1, which is like maybe 30 minutes from Houston, in Rosharon, Texas.

Fuck man, they had you on a tour.

Yeah, yeah. But when you first get in the system, they'll do that, and shift you around and move you around, and then they'll get you one place, and that's where you'll mostly do your time. So, the first couple of months, they'll move you a couple of times.

PHOTO: PETER BESTE

The way that people are cycled through there. It's become just . . . big business.

Yeah. It's big business.

And then you see it from the inside, and I'm sure it seems even more like a gigantic machine.

It's definitely that. It's nothing but modern-day cattle . . . modern-day slavery. It's all of the above. It's not about *who*. The individual person doesn't mean anything. It's just to get that number.

Did you keep in touch with a lot of people when you were in there?

A few, yeah, you know, mostly my real comrades. [Point] Blank, K-Rino, Shan-No . . . I kept in touch with a lot of them, and then a lot of my close family. So I kept in touch with a lot of people.

Did you have any perception of what was going on kind of in—you know, there's been some changes, since you've been gone, in the scene and just in the music that's being made and kind of the movement.

Well, I'ma tell you. [Laughs] Dudes used to call me "The Library" because I ordered every *XXL*, *Rolling Stone* . . . I had music magazines, *PC World* . . . aw, man . . . fashion magazines . . . anything . . . clothes design, all kind of stuff. So I would get 13 different, 14 different subscriptions every month, so I was kinda tuned in, man, to everything that was goin' on. And you know, we got radios and stuff, so I would hear things that's goin' on, and I mean, I was on all the radio dials and I just . . . I was already startin' to check out, man . . . dubstep, the pop scene, because, you know, other than the rap, I'm a writer. I'ma try to publish some songs out too. So I been studyin' all the genres.

Wow, so you were on top while you were in there.

Yeah, yeah. On it. 100 percent. I ain't miss a beat.

When did you start doing production?

Well, you know, I've always done all my own. From my very first CD, I've done all my own music.

From the EP—"The Lyrical Lion"—so you were producing way back then?

Yeah, on "The Lyrical Lion," I did all of those on there except for the last one Dope E. did—"Brain Matter." And then on my second one, *Mobbin' Muzik Melodies*, I did all them except one. Icey Hott did one called "Material Life." Yeah, Icey did that, and then on the last one, I did all of them.

Did you ever do any producing with Icey, with Street Military?

I did "Gasta Get Paid." I actually did that track, "Gasta Get Paid" and then . . . "Next Episode," me and Icey did that together.

Well, of course that one's kind of yours, really. I mean that hook is so totally that song. You were really the sixth man for them, right?

Anything Street did, I'm on it. Anything I'm on . . . anything that I make, as Klondike Kat, you'll always see some of them guys on there. Just not all together.

Did you do shows with Street Military, back in the day?

Yeah, always. Every time they did a show.

Do you remember any crazy stories from any of those shows?

Without a doubt. I remember a time when we used to have Nutt—Nutt used to be our stage . . . like a propster. He would do all the tricks. He would get the crowd hype while we rappin', man, and he would crowd surf and everything. And he always had a thing where they used to have this old break-dance move—they called it the "Donkey Kick." You know, when you go down, touch your hands on the floor, and kick back with your feet. And Nutt used to take cereal and throw it all on the crowd. He used to take some Cap'n Crunch and just throw it all out in the crowd. They'd be lovin' it, and you might have two—you had an HPD officer that was on the side of the stage, so Nutt was, like, messin' with him, you know, goin' in his face, "Ahhh!" Just messin' with him. He'd go around, mess with the crowd, he'd come back and mess with the law, you know. And the crowd was getting crunk 'cuz he was doin' it—and he turned around and Donkey Kicked him, man. And I'm talkin' about, was like a centimeter away from the man's face. Kicked dirt in the man's face and everything. The law got mad! He pulled his handcuffs like, "If y'all don't do something with this fool, I'm fittin' to arrest him right now." We was like, "Man, Nutt, leave the man alone!" The law tried to grab him, he just jumped in the crowd and just crowd-surfed. We had to hide him because the law was lookin' for him after the show. You know, like, "I'ma get him." Man, he gonna put him in the car, y'all take him off. Yeah, man.

Icey was telling me that Nutt used to dropkick members of the group!

Yeah, yeah! That was just part of his thing. He gonna do all kind of crazy stuff, man.

Icey told me this story about this show in Dallas— some club up there where they just . . . it didn't matter how good they were, they booed everybody . . . Were you at that show?

Yep.

You were there!

As a matter of fact, I went back to that club myself and did the same thing!

They were booing.

They was like, "Man, we can't never enjoy no shows, man. These dudes always comin' in here dissin'." Half the crowd was, like, pissed off, you know what I'm sayin'? 'Cuz this same group of cats would always crank it up, man.

And so you handled them alright when you went back?

I did, like, three songs, and I basically just told the crowd, "Hey, man, I know y'all got a few people out here that's trippin', man. But for the ones who really came to embrace us, man, we love y'all. 'Preciate it." So, you know, we had some "Yeahs," to mix with the boos. They was like, "Man, they always do this shit. Every time somebody come here they do that. They don't never let us enjoy no show."

That was during Street Military time, so mid-'90s? Were you doing a lot of touring around that time? Just as Klondike Kat?

Yeah, I stayed on the road. I would be gone, like, three months at a time. Man, shoot—all over Texas, of course. Shreveport, Louisiana . . . Jackson, Mississippi . . . ah man, . . . man, Tennessee . . . I been to Brooklyn, I been to Albany, New York, way up there.

How was your show in Brooklyn?

It was good! It was good, surprisingly. Man, I even battled a few rappers on the streets and stuff. Yeah, me and Blank went out there, man, and man . . . ah man, it's like they was trippin' that we was—"Y'all can't be from Houston, man. Y'all really from Houston?" You know, they thought we was some old country, cowboy ridin' boys. They was like, "Man, these dudes got some skills."

And they'd never heard that style before—that Southern style.

Yeah, and they was trippin' off it, like . . . we had the girls gathered around, and man . . . these niggas went and did they little thing, and I murdered him! He was like, "Man . . . you got the CD with you?" I'm like, "Yeah, I got some in the car." It was a lot of love and respect, man.

And would you experience that same enthusiasm when you brought the Houston style to other cities? I mean, you got booked, so there must have been somebody there that was into it.

Yeah, yeah. I got a lot of shows—I did a tour. A nine-city tour with . . . it was me, Scarface, Bam, Big Mike, Too Short . . . Goldy that used to rap with Too Short. We did nine cities together.

Those must have been big.

Yeah, they was in, like, coliseums and stuff like that. Too Short was the headliner. And Scarface was with him—did I say Scarface?

Scarface would have been huge at that point too.

Yeah, at that time, Scarface and Too Short was huge, together like that.

When you talk about battling, you were also battling back in the day, like, on The Battleground, with K-Rino? Were you a battle rapper back then?

That's how me and K-Rino met.

You were battling?

Yeah. See, when I was in junior high, my rap name was not even . . . when I was in middle school, my rap name was not Klondike Kat. It was something else. It was Devious D. And K-Rino went to a school in my neighborhood that was further down, and I went to my school, so I'd always be battling dudes in my school, and then they was like, "Man, there's this dude at Thomas, man . . . man, he cool—he tearin' up all the high schoolers." I was like, "I need to meet him. I want his crown." [Laughs] So I traveled about 30-deep, you know 30 of my boys, we went to K-Rino school and waited on him outside. We set it up. So I'm thinkin'—the whole school let out . . . there was no K-Rino . . . So, you know, I'm cocky and confident. I was like, "Man, this dude must be scared. He ain't came out. I ain't seen him. He must ain't even come to school." Next thing I know, here come K-Rino. He come out the door with about 40 of his boys behind him, and he got the black book in his hand. I said, "Oh, he got somethin'!" I told 'em, "Yeah, he got somethin'." And me and K-Rino battled 'til the sun came down. Kids was like, "Man, I gotta go home, man, my mom lookin' for me, man! Man, y'all need to finish this another time!" Years later . . . years later . . . I told K that too. This was, like, maybe 2006, I told K, I said, "K, you remember a guy, when you was at Thomas, man, and you came out with a bunch of dudes from your school, and there was a dude waitin' outside and he had a bunch of his homies with him? Man, y'all battled 'til the sun came down, man!" He said, "Yeah, man! That little sucker was hard! " I said, "Man, that was me!" I said, "Yeah, my name was Devious D." Boy, he bust out laughin'. He said, "Damn, that's crazy! Now I remember that!" He said, "Ah, man—that's cold, man!"

He never knew it was you.

Nah, he didn't know it was me. And then we met again—we met again battlin' when we was in high school, and we met at a school over here by my house, in a park, so there was some people from Sterling High School and a lot of people from my high school, and at that point I had been battlin' for money. I wasn't battlin' for free no more. "We goin' fifty dollars a round." I was, like, serious about it. I be goin' all over the place, battlin' whoever had juice. Me and N-I-P was startin' doin' that. And me and N-I-P kinda got into a disagreement or whatever, because like . . . I was feelin' like rap was goin' more towards reality than battle rappin'. I always still wrote my battle rhymes for battles, but as far as when I wanted to make songs—this was before we even got deals—I still was like, "Well, I'm gonna make my songs talkin' about what's goin' on," you know what I'm sayin'? But N-I-P was rappin' psycho. 'Cuz we used to be a group called the Forever Def Crew, me and N-I-P, and our styles started to clash. I was like, "Man, you talkin' about feedin' babies with unleaded gas and . . ." you know what I'm sayin'? And I'm talkin' about life situations. As far as a group, it's not gonna come together that way. So we split ways. He was kinda bitter about it, but you know, we still homies. We still cool. We stayed cool. He realized what I was talkin' about once he did his own thing because that put him in his own lane. That put him in his own lane. Nobody was doin' what N-I-P did, and it ended up workin' for him. Yeah, it worked out for him.

Yeah, because then he could make that his whole thing at that point. He didn't have to make a concession.

He wouldn't have been the full Psycho with me addin' my part to 'em, and then I wouldn't have been the full, like, lyricist that I was and wouldn't have been able to incorporate my singin' melodies with the Psycho stuff.

The Psycho stuff is not looking for those melodies.

Yeah, yeah! You know what I'm sayin'.

That stuff's just gotta drive hard.

Yeah, so me and K-Rino met to battle then, and I was like, "K, man, I don't do this for free, man." K was humble, man. He was like, "Man, I do it for the love of the art." I was like, "Man, I love the

art too, or I wouldn't be serious about my craft." When I found a dude that wanted to battle me, I made 10 raps with his name in it, and then I had 50 raps just to battle with, and I used the last 10 just to murder him off with. Find out his business, find out anything goin' on with his family, whatever! I did my research, man. I took that serious. So, I was like, "Look, man—I don't do this for free. We can go fifty dollars a line." He was like, "Man, I don't do this for money." I was like, "Well, tell your homeboys to patch up, you know? We gonna patch up, we do this for money." He was like, "Man, I do it for the art." He kept sayin' it. They was like, "C'mon K, go on and do it. Go on and do it." So, we went best two out of three. K wins and I win, K wins and I win it, and then they say, "Kat won." You know, K. He was humble. He called me back about two weeks later, said, "Man, I wanna do this battle again off of either one of our turfs. I don't wanna do it on your turf or my turf. I wanna do it somewhere neutral. And we do it again." I say, "Cool." So we met up this time, I was like . . . K was like, "Go ahead, man—go." I said, "Well, man, I'ma do this for money. How much y'all wanna do it for?" He was like, "Man, I told you—I just do it for the art. Man, I don't do it like that." So I was like, "Alright, man, well look—I'm fittin' to go on and spit." And then, you know, so I said some little bullshit, low-grade rhymes, and K was like, "Man, that ain't even your caliber. I'm not battlin' that. You just chunked somethin' out there." He said, "I came to battle you." And I was like, "Man, that's all I got." I started to walk off. So K was like, "Come here, man." He said, "Man, I'm startin' this crew called the S.P.C., man, and we gonna form together, man, try to come together, man, and get our music out. Just be a crew and a clique, man." He say, "I like your rhyme style and how you put it down, man. I wanna, you know, get together with you." I said, "Alright, well, cool then! That's what's up!" He gave me his address, the next day I was over there. Shit, I been S.P.C. ever since.

That was kind of the birth of it, then. Right at that time.

Yeah, that was the very beginning of it, 'cuz there was just a few people, you know, that was S.P.C.

Rapper K . . . N-I-P had just kinda got with him too, a few months before that.

And they had a real legendary battle that brought them together.

Yeah! See, that's . . . and that's how we all really came together. Me, K, and N-I-P, that's how we all came together. And I know—I gotta say this too: I know that second time, he was ready for me! 'Cuz he saw my craftiness. I saw him bein' crafty, he's like, "Oh, okay." I said, "I have to do my homework on this sucker. I'ma get him this time." I had a lot more stuff ready, but I was like, "Man, this dude hard to handle." I tried to—I always said that, "Hey, man, I'm winnin'. I've never lost battling nobody, so if a dude take me out, he gonna really take me out. He gonna have confidence in himself." So, I would use theatrics and everything. I'm movin' around, doin' my—animated and everything. It just turned out to be a beautiful thing because we all came together, man, and all that energy, all those raw MCs together, bein' around each other on a daily basis, man, that created some classics.

So there was an instant chemistry with y'all, once you all got together.

And what I like about us all—even though we were all similar, we still had our own unique way of delivering. Our own unique styles. Like nobody just copied each other.

Not only that, but the voices were all really distinct. It was real easy on those early recordings— it's real easy to tell who everybody is immediately. You're all very, very different.

I used to hear—and still today you hear a lot of crews, one dude come in and you don't even know when the next dude came. "Who was that? Who was that?" They all sound alike.

But there's something about the music that makes it S.P.C., more so than just your voices together. There's kind of a musical direction isn't there? What would you say it is?

It's just . . . subliminally, we all know where each others' mind frame is, and we feed off of each other, and at the same time, we feed off bein' individual in the midst of each other. So it's just like playin' piano keys, playin' the same key over and over. There's a high, there's a low, there's a minor, there's a major. We kind of blend them all together like that, and then we still all in the same mind frame, or within the same realm of doin' this music thing, and it comes out like that.

You got some future collaborations coming up? Anybody you're going to do an album or a song with that you've never worked with before?

Yeah, I just did two songs with Z-Ro, a song with Z-Ro and Mike-D from the Screwed Up Click. My son is puttin' it down now. He's nice now. He's 18. Him and my little brother is doin' something together. They call him "Brick," so I'm workin' with his stuff too. Others like—I got a few features lined up with different people, man. I know Z-Ro talkin' about me, him, and Slim Thug doin' something. I talked to Pokey, I talked to E.S.G., I talked to Trae— they already, "Kat, when you need me, you know what it is." So there will be songs with these guys as well.

It's really one big Houston now. Everybody's collaborating with everybody else in a way that it's never happened.

Yep. Yeah, it's like Screwed Up Click and S.P.C., doin' a lot more stuff together, cats from Northside—because, you know, it used to be kind of divided, North and South—cats from the Northside and South gettin' it in, you know. Every-body just tryin' to collab and meet, man. It's just . . . it's less plex, less turmoil as far as, "Ooh, I ain't gonna mess with . . ." All that's kind of blown over now, so everybody just tryin' to network. This is the information era, so everybody tryin' to network with each other.

Russell Washington

BIGTYME RECORDZ

Founder of Bigtyme Recordz, located at King's Flea Market in South Park since the late 1980s. His first signing to the label was UGK, and he went on to release records by Point Blank, PSK-13, 20-2-Life, and some of DJ Screw's only label releases, including the landmark Houston albums *All Screwed Up*, *3 'N The Mornin' Part One,* and *3 'N The Mornin' Part Two.*

Did you open the shop before you started the label?

I opened the shop when I was 19 years old.

What was King's like back then? The same sort of gathering area that it is now, with everybody coming in?

Oh, back then it was the wild, wild West. I mean, now, back then it was incredible. Back then there might have been four or five times the traffic. It was a hot commodity. When we did the UGK record, we sold like 4,000 copies out of my shop in a month. You know, that's a lot of copies of a cassette for a small record label. Man, it was unbelievable. Now I think they just don't market the Flea Market like they used to.

So they marketed it back then? Did they do radio commercials and that kind of stuff?

Haha, no. It was a lot more . . . it was a different time, man. You know, you had a lot more street money, you had a lot more people workin', it was

just . . . man, people used to just come in there . . . you know, it was nothing for somebody to walk in and spend $300 on CDs. Now you won't see $200–$300 in a day. Occasionally, you'll get maybe one wholesale customer come and spend that amount, but most of the customers now . . . you've got a whole generation of people that's conditioned themselves not to buy music out of stores. They either look for it free on the web and buy a song from iTunes . . . check a guy on the street—three, four, five discs for ten dollars, something like that.

Yeah. Or guys out hustling, popping trunks, and selling CDs that way.

Yeah! I mean, you know, it became a . . . it's sad to say it'll probably be a while before it recycles to what it used to be.

Well, it becomes kind of a boutique thing, where a lot of people seek that out. Because a lot of old-school people—like me and I'm sure like you—you like to have the record. You want to have it and be able to look at the artwork and actually have the physical record.

Yeah. I wanna reintroduce tracks, adjust the publishing company and things like that, and the new generation . . . they just wanna listen to a couple of songs, see if they like it or, you know . . . do what they do with it. Put it on the phone . . . a thousand songs for free on the iPod. That's just the nature of our game now.

PHOTO: PETER BESTE

When you started out, were you just doing tapes, did you start off with tapes or records?

I started with tapes and records.

Because you started before CDs even existed, really.

Yeah, I was there for like the beginning, when they started coming and they was in those . . . what they call those . . .

Those longboxes.

Longboxes, yeah. All that paper wastin', you know . . . but I like those boxes. Those would have been a great piece these days.

Well, they were cool because it just gave you more artwork . . .

Yeah, it was cool back then. Them are the days I miss, especially the checks. Seems we gotta live with iTunes. It's no great thing for me to get a third less on a record, wholesale, but then sell it for retail. I'm not excited about that, you know. I can't project when it comes, but it's really . . . when you think about that you sell thousands and thousands of records on iTunes, and, you know, they sellin' for $6.99, $5.99, whatever . . . and you can get more than that on wholesale, sellin' it yourself, but . . . you know, that's the medium everybody's using right now, so we have to take it.

Right. How much . . . did you ever depend really heavily on Southwest?

Uh . . . very heavily! [Laughs] I mean . . . not as far as runnin' Bigtyme, but just . . . it was great to have a place that you could go and trust that . . . it's your one stop, and then that stuff is taken care of. I hated to see them go because the expansion they was makin', I think in the long run woulda been great, you know, as far as their distribution. I just think they took some shots that they shouldn't have took. And I think it added to the downfall, because . . . the things they never gave to the locals and the locals addressed that . . . ultimately just didn't work out like it should have.

Yeah, because it was really . . . I mean, they were really reaching some people there for a while. Point Blank told me he used to go over there and get five-figure checks all the time. A couple times a month.

Yeah. I mean, when he did the project that was good, you know . . . *3 'N The Mornin'*, we shipped out just under 59,000 in the first day. And it definitely rose from the humble beginnings of me with UGK, with them taking a hundred CDs. So, it was a definite kind of . . . weird feelin' for me. I just felt like it was losing a part of your family. You know, I was over there . . . what, 1992 to 2003 it closed, I think?

Yeah, 2003.

Eleven years with them, and I had some good times, you know? They had me under some bad times, and we definitely rose to some good times together.

So how did it change your business plan? What did you have to do at that point?

Basically, you was lookin' at a guy, in my case . . . I was like the don, period, when they closed. And I actually gave it a shot a couple months out . . . I had got heavy into, like, doing my own little sales and kind of wholesales, and I was trying that, but I think the big problem that hurt me was just . . . I held on to too much of the staff, you know? My income had dropped—severely—but I still was employing about seven people all the way up to, like, 2005 or '06. You know, I just went too many years holdin' on to some of the staff. I always felt like it was gonna change a little bit, but, you know . . . it didn't.

Well, the thing was that Southwest crashed in 2003, and then a couple of years later was when record sales really started dropping off . . . there was no way of knowing that was going to happen the way it did, where people just stopped buying records.

And the big thing, too, is that generation basically made DJs more powerful than they should be. You know, I've always been a fan of DJs, but there's not too much originality to a DJ no more, and especially the modern DJ. What do they do? They download songs on their computer, and they play records at a club. I mean, okay . . . half of them don't scratch, they're not . . . you know . . . you buy your Mac and you play records!

Copy and paste out of your iTunes.

Yeah, and then just get some little fake turntables that scratch, and you do that and you're a DJ now. But they all do mixtapes, and then when everybody does mixtapes, who wants a real record when I can get 10 or 15 of the major hits on one CD? And it's everywhere now. There's more DJs than artists . . . or mixologists . . . whatever they call it. I just think it's a bad thing because I feel like a lot of people who . . . you got people who probably would never in their lifetime see $1 million that was makin' $1 million from the music business. And that's all been wiped out. I mean, even in Houston—when was the last "next star" we've heard from in Houston to blow up? In how long? A new guy—not an old guy getting a little resurgence, but somebody new? It's been a long time.

It's been a long time.

It's been a real long time, and you know, back in the day, we used to hear about the next great guy, I mean . . . weeks before that guy was like . . . you know . . . the only mixer I think that was really makin' an impact was Screw. The guys that rapped on a Screwtape, many of them, they at least got to do one or two records. *Now*, it's not happening that way. Everything's just flooded. It's just flooded out, and guys giving away 30 burned CDs for 10, 15 bucks, and I'm like, "What are you doing?" That's just too much music. All these sites just give it away free. It's just terrible.

Talking about Screw, and back when he was selling lots and lots of tapes—when you guys came together, that was his first real release, right?

No. Uh-uh. He did *Bigtyme Vol. 2, All Screwed Up* for us. That was . . . they got that history wrong. Everybody say, "Oh Screw was sellin' a bunch of tapes in his house before he met Bigtyme." No way, José. Screw didn't even have a car when he met Bigtyme. He was sellin' some tapes, but in between that '95 to '96, '97, he started sellin' a lot of tapes, and that's based on Bigtyme because we put . . . you know, *3 'N The Mornin'* was incredible records. One of the best records of the South.

Fantastic.

You think about *All Screwed Up*—65,000 [units] on that compilation, which was all Bigtyme people. I went to Screw, I said, "Hey, it's a down period. I wanna do the least expensive record I can do. I been hearin' about you, you know, your Screwtapes. People like you on the streets. I want you to Screw an album." He said "Bet." His manager at the time said "Give him $400." I pulled that right out and gave him $400. I think I gave him, like, 2 percent on the record or something. You know, I was looking for a record to do maybe two or three thousand, something . . . the record, it started off with a little slow movement, but that record went on to sell 65,000 units. I asked him, I said, "Hey, I want you to do one that's yours. All you." And that's when we started the *3 'N The Mornin'* thing. But in that process of doin' *3 'N The*

Mornin', we ran *Rap Pages* ads, we ran *Murder Dog* ads, we probably put out . . . I don't know, maybe two or three hundred thousand black-and-yellow flyers. We had posters—"DJ Screw"—and then for people just to write it out and say, "Oh, man. He just was sellin' tapes out of his house and it just blew up." They left out a very big point: That for almost two years, six people worked day and night for this man. I have no doubt he woulda been pretty much the same thing or even more with the right atmosphere, but to say that Bigtyme didn't work as a major force in the sellin' of that record is ridiculous. Or those . . . even the tapes at his house, because if there's no Bigtyme, they don't know about Screw all over where they knew about him. We put him everywhere. You know, he's in *Rap Pages* ads, he's in *Murder Dog* ads, you know? That's . . . from your first record, I think 2,000 or 3,000 goin' out 'til your next record. 58,000-something going out? That is a huge, huge thing, and that's a big step. Major label artists might not even make a jump like that. When you're a dude that don't rap, or do nothing, and they're giving you $5,000 to do a show? There's a lot of things, but it was . . . it was a great thing because he had a lot of people supporting him, and they just always believed in him, and I'm not that guy that . . . I don't make no big deal about it, but I know for a fact what we did.

Did both parts come out at the same time?

What parts? Of *3 'N The Mornin'*?

Yeah, because you had the West Coast version and you had the Houston version. Did they both come out at the same time?

No, we actually . . . the *3 'N The Mornin' 1 and 2* was actually gonna be the record, and at the time when we submitted, we did the onesheets and submitted it, we had got probably 100,000 orders. But what happened was, we hadn't cleared all the samples and the licensing of the songs. After meeting with the legal team, it was just unfeasible to try and do it without clearing it, and it was unfeasible to try and clear it, being such a small company. So, we started workin', and we actually did the whole license deal with all Houston people.

And the only reason the other one came out is because the Soundwaves guy made us an offer we couldn't refuse, so we released . . . we basically just pressed up enough for him.

Oh, just kind of, like, on the underground level?

Yeah, the guy from Soundwaves blew us up about it and we basically just sold it to him, and he distributed it a little bit and then he kind of sold it through the mail, but it was never . . . those two records were never distributed. We just, like . . . you could call and order it.

What was it like working with Screw on the creative end?

I think Screw was an artist that didn't get to see what he was truly supposed to be, just what he could have been. I mean, he had just got in to tryin' to play, you know, the keys a little bit, maybe do some rappin' . . . I mean . . . I think Screw was definitely a turntable genius, because to make beats from clips and pieces of songs, and to make something that you could listen to and be hypnotic like that . . . *damn*, he was good. Screw had people who don't even like music—Screw music—like *3 'N The Mornin'*. I don't know what they said about the best Houston records. I think we was number . . . I forgot the number, but at least we got acknowl-edged, for bein' on there, because it was definitely one of the best Houston records.

Especially with the way that mix flows, it's got a nice sort of patchwork to it. It wasn't just a mix-tape. That's why *3 'N The Mornin'* is such a good introduction for people.

Yeah, and I mean even . . . I think even his ability to take a vocal track, and find that right beat that make that track just all the way different. I mean, even with, like, with "My Mind Went Blank," and they come in with Aaliyah or whatever . . . he mixed it with . . . changed the whole focus of that song. It was on *All Screwed Up*. I mean, man, he definitely had a . . . I think if he'd had just been a little bit more . . . better on the business side, he would have definitely had a big, big career. If he was really pushing for that.

Well, it's amazing considering the framework around him and such, that he did as well as he did. It all kind of snuck up on him, you know?

Yeah, I think that too. To me, sometimes life can take you. I mean the life just was . . . music was different for a lot of people. You know, you hear that story over and over again. They get in music, and your whole life change. I mean, it's like me. I had my shop, so I had tasted the experience of makin' money, and then to go—within two months I'm signing my first group to a major label contract, a pretty decent one. But I also got the experience of the . . . [Laughs] the bitter side of it, at a real early point in my career.

How long did you have the store open before you started releasing tapes?

I had it open a couple of years, and I actually had, like, two stores, and one of them had sales real bad, and I just basically was payin' off my debts. And then after I got those taken care of, I hung up a sign that said, "Would like to produce a rap record?" And the first person that came was Pimp C. I consider myself one of the luckiest producers of the '90s.

They just happened to come into King's?

Yeah. They had been in King's before, but then when he saw the sign looking for a record, they came and brought me a demo. They were the first demo that I got. It was UGK's demo, and when I heard it I was real nervous. The second demo I got was the Sexx Fiends, but they wasn't called the Sexx Fiends then. They was Twice As Nice, and I was workin' with them and UGK at the same time. And after starting, you know, I realized that was a little too much for me to take on, and I . . . me and my wife at the time said, "These boys are the best," so we went with them. I think Pimp C was a musical genius too.

Yeah. He really was.

He started doin' that recordin', tryin' to get that record done in '91 . . . then, February of '92, we

dropped the EP, and I think it was out two weeks and we got a contract offer from Nastymix. I remember that, thinkin' it was like . . . I forgot if it was like $15,000 to sign with them . . . and I was like, "I think we gonna make that." We hadn't even really started doin' . . . but they saw something, and within two weeks, we hadn't even sold a lot of records. In that first two weeks, records would count. We were sellin' some in my store. I don't think anybody even ordered one in the first two weeks. But I think that was back in the day when all the record companies had interest in the city, and somebody must've gave 'em a tape, and they was like, "Yeah, they faxed a contract." I remember just sittin' there when that contract came over the fax, and I was like, "What the heck?" And I actually was a big Nastymix fan because I was in love with Sir Mix-A-Lot . . . I knew a lot of the records because I sold the records.

Right, right. I guess you knew just about everything back then.

Yeah, I was really on top of my music. [Laughs] But the only thing is with UGK, I wish I woulda got along . . . and I mean, before Pimp passed, we actually was . . . I think we was . . . I think me and Pimp would actually have mended our relationship a lot more if he wouldn't have passed, because we had a lot of communication goin' on before he passed.

He was really changed, don't you think, after coming out of prison?

Oh yeah, man. He was a different person. I think he was kinda a little bit more temperamental at first, but me and him . . . from a conversation we had, it was like I could feel like he was a changed person. As far as what he was doin' . . . the conversation we was havin', and I had gave him a lot of words because when he passed, they had Chris Young mix his song, and I was like, "That's the last record I'ma do. That's the record I wanna make my last. That's how I came in, that's how I wanna leave." I was just like, "He gonna do it, he gonna do it." But, you know . . . he just passed, and it was really upsetting.

DJ Chill

SOUTH PARK

Andrew Hatton grew up in South Park, befriending a young DJ Screw in the late 1980s. Between the two of them they owned enough good equipment to get DJ gigs, and they played parties and dances together all over the Southside, getting a lot of those gigs once Chill started working at Magic 102 and was the one who answered the phone when people called the radio station looking to hire DJs for their parties. He went on to become the featured DJ on Matt Sonzala's long-running Pacifica Radio show, "Damage Control," and is still an active DJ as well as a clothing designer with a line of T-shirts he prints himself.

PHOTO: PETER BESTE

If Screw were around today, how do you think what he was doing would survive in this economy?

He would survive in this economy because he was on the forefront of the situation. So you have to feel value in his music. They would still value him. They would still value going out and listening to his music. People will still go out and buy Jordans. They believe in that, they'll still hold onto that. They believed in him, so they still hold on to Screwtapes. That's the only the reason the Screw shop is still alive, because cats value listening to his music. They grew up with it, they wanna keep it. That's like cats right now, they still buyin' elbows even though they look different. People still buy 'em because they remember when they wanted them when they were a kid, and now that they got that money they're gonna go get 'em. Which is stupid, but . . .

What do you think it was about Screw that made people so dedicated to him in that respect?

Man, it's like . . . a lot of cats really don't know how dedicated he was to the music. And you can hear it in how the production was. So that's how you knew how dedicated he was to it. He was a rare commodity. That was kind of exotic.

When you were holding a Screwtape in your hand, you were holding something really special.

Oh yeah! Man, I remember times when we would make a list and he would make that tape, that was like having a personalized shirt! You know what I'm saying? Nobody had that shirt on but you! Nobody was shoutin' out nobody else name but you. Unless you had somebody you had you wanted him to shout out. But other than that, that was your personal relation right there. That was like you havin' your own slab, your own car, your own car the way you want it to be. The way you wanna look it. Your own paint job.

So it was a reflection of you, but it was also a reflection of somebody you believed in, Screw.

Yeah! The way he put it down, and there was more to it. There was an art to it too, because the way he put it down. He put so much energy into it. He put a lot of *him* in it. Cats couldn't duplicate.

What were the sessions like at his house? Did time just sort of get . . . lost? Stand still?

The first sessions he was doin' at the apartment was different than the ones he was doin' at his house. The ones at the apartments, there wasn't any sessions. Cats would just drop off a list, and he was in his own world doin' 'em. When he came down to the microphone and, you know, all that started when he had his crib. So those sessions right there were kinda crazy because it was dark—it was dark and you couldn't see what time of day it was outside. So, once you got in there, you was in another world.

That's the way he liked it, being a different little universe, huh?

Yeah, that was crazy. That was totally different right there. You'd come out the next morning and damn . . .

So he would just mix and people would step up to the mic?

You'd step up to the mic and just go, know what I'm sayin'? If you was there that evening, you might not come out 'til that next morning, so there wasn't no time . . . time wasn't of the essence to him, know what I mean? Time was just time.

Shorty Mac

SMITHVILLE

One of DJ Screw's oldest friends, Shorty Mac is symbolic of the juggernaut that was the Screwed Up Click in the late 1990s. He moved on from hustling to become Screw's tape distributor in Austin—a second home to the Screwed Up Click starting in the mid-'90s all the way through to today. He appeared on a number of Screwtapes over the years, many of them with Al-D Tha Lion, whom Screw called his little brother. Photo taken at a 2012 conference at the University of Houston discussing Screw's legacy and its impact on hip-hop culture and the world, where Shorty Mac appeared onstage along with Lil' Keke, E.S.G, Big Pokey, and Meshah Hawkins.

PHOTO: ANNE MARIE D'ARCY

So are you from Austin or from Houston?

Well, me and Screw grew up together in Smithville. He moved to Houston, and then after I got out of school I moved to Austin, and then I moved to Houston with Screw, maybe two, three years before he died. Probably, like, a year after he died I moved to Austin.

Did you appear on a lot of his tapes?

A few of them. I was on *Austin 2 Houston Pt. II*, *The Final Chapter*, *Off the Head*, *Playaz Nite*, *G Love*, *Only the Real*. Some I'm on, I don't even know the name of them. I never heard them after I rapped on them.

Did you live with Screw?

Yeah, when I moved down there, I lived with Screw. I was actually just . . . he wanted me to come down there, and it was me, him, Al-D—this was after he was on Greenstone. He was leaving Greenstone and going to the Southwest side. Mo City. And I just stayed there, and then after I got there I started workin' in the shop. Helpin' him in the shop. So I was working in the shop 'til, like, maybe 2001, and then I moved back to Austin. All the Screwtapes we ever done was in Houston, and the majority of them was done on Greenstone. We had a few that we did at the new house, well, you know, it was just a different thing, a different situation, always going to court behind his music. They was after him in Mo City.

He was in a trouble for using other people's tracks on his mixtapes?

Nah, nah, nah. It was this lady next door—she kept calling the police on him, saying different stuff about us, saying we was harassing her kids and all this different kind of funny stuff. Then when the kids' mama go to work, they'll come knock on the door and tell us that they were sorry, and Screw used to give 'em CDs and stuff, and they used to tell him that they loved his music and all this. It was all just one little situation.

He also got into a lot of trouble at the old house, right?

Well, they kicked his door in 'cuz they thought he was sellin' drugs. And he was just selling music. But that's the only—I mean, as far as police coming in and harassing him or whatever, that was the only main time. We was in a lot of situations where they would pull up and take pictures of us and all kind of shit like that, but just . . . when they kicked his door in, that's the only time they really came in there trippin' like that. That I seen. Or was closer to. You know, you may have had people leave his house and get pulled over. Or something like that. 'Cuz they tryin' to figure out what he doing.

Papa Screw told me that that happened at least two or three times, that someone kicked the door in, and that each time, they'd search the house and they wouldn't find anything and then they'd just leave. They just thought something was going on.

I only know about the one time. That was when he was on Greenstone, but as far as I know, I remember the one time because of the way they done the house. They tore the gate off, the front gate—I don't know if the house is still the same—they had a gate, like, by the front door, like burglar bar gates. They tore that gate off, and they knocked the front door down and came on in. And then they messed up a couple of his tapes too. They crushed maybe about 40 or 50 tapes. Because they was pissed off. Wasn't no drugs in there. It was records and tapes.

Were you in there?

Naw, I wasn't there when they kicked the door in. I was actually in Austin. Because me and his deal was, I mean, we grew up together, so I just seen a lot from the start because me and him started rappin' together. When they did kick his door in, he called me and told me what was goin' on 'cuz he'd actually just set me up in Austin to start sellin' music and shit because the life that I was livin' at that time, you know . . . he just didn't wanna see me doin' it no more. So he started givin' me boxes of tapes to come to Austin and sell, and I think maybe . . . I think we started in, like, '94. By the middle of '95, I would come to Houston every two days, pickin' up boxes of tapes, bringing 'em back down here to Austin to sell 'em and shit. It just jumped off that quick! I mean, you know, ain't nobody really on the music except me and the people I hang around. I think when I first brought a Screwtape to Austin was in, like, '92. And it was called *3 'N Da Mornin'*, and everybody used to think that my tape deck was messed up. I used to tell 'em, "Naw, that's the way the tape goes!" So then I put some music in my car, and I used to just ride around and bump these tapes and I would go see him, and every time I would go up there he would give me a different tape to listen to. But, then he eventually got me to start sellin' tapes too. I was out here hustlin', so he kept tellin' me, "Man, the only thing you gonna do is do time if you keep doin' what you doin'."

How did the people in Austin react to it? You lived in Houston for a while and so you understand the environment in Houston and how the weather and the way the city moves is really reflected in Screw's music. Did people in Austin pick up on that?

Yeah. And it actually . . . it kinda changed the pace of Austin, because Austin was on kind of a different pace. They was like . . . for instance, there was a lot of dudes down here ridin' Daytons, you know, but in Houston, they main thing was ridin' swangers. So, once I came with it, I had to deal with . . . really, like, gangs. You had to deal with that shit, and there was some people that

. . . listenin' to music, say, "Well, this is a Crip," or, "This is a Blood on this tape," so I switched tapes with them. Then, you tell me something you wanna hear, I call Screw, I say, "Okay, I'm dealin' with this type of crowd. They wanna hear this." So I come back with what they wanna hear, and then it went from there to them hearin' the freestylin', and when they start hearin' the whole combination together, I'd say it took it less than a year before . . . I was sellin'—you're literally sellin' out. I could go to a club on a Friday night with over 100, 200 tapes, and I won't have one tape in my pocket by the time I leave the parking lot. That's how serious it got.

The clubs in Austin back then—they weren't as big as the ones in Houston.

Nah. But see, I just had a different area to deal with. I was dealin' with Austin and the little country towns around here, and then there's people comin' through Austin, like maybe from Killeen and just different little areas around here. Everybody just got connected on there, and it got to be kind of the same thing for me, because every time you look up at my house, you seen a whole bunch of fixed up cars at my house with people comin' to get these CDs. And all these tapes—they was tapes then— they comin' to get these tapes. So they was like . . . people used to tell me all the time, man, "If the law pass by here, they think you sellin' drugs, anytime there's slabs over here."

Blocks of them.

Yeah, yeah, and I even had . . . I came from Houston one night, and I walked up to my door, and there was a cell phone in a box sittin' at my door. And I picked it up, took it in the house, plugged it in, and it was on. So I put it back in the box and put it outside because it scared me at that time. Because I know—it was right . . . it may have been right before Screw got his door kicked in or right after he got his door kicked in, so it just scared me, and I called him and I told him, I said, "Man there's a cell phone at my door, and it's already on. I ain't order no cell phones." And he said, "Man, it might be them people." And then, I was . . . at that time,

me and my sister was stayin' together, with her kid, and she said—when I had went to Houston and came back and she said some agents came by the house askin' questions and they went to all the neighbors askin' questions. But all the neighbors knew I wasn't doin' nothing but sellin' music, so, I mean . . . that never got our door kicked in or nothin'. They was just tryin' to figure out, I guess, what was goin' on because of all the activity that was goin' on in the neighborhood.

And that was in Austin.

Yeah, this was in Austin. Yeah, it got serious—when Screw had his first concert in Austin, after . . . I wanna say . . . it wasn't *All Screwed Up* . . . it may have been *3 'N The Mornin'* 'cuz Keke and Big Moe and, I wanna say, Point Blank was with him, and we was pullin' up to the club, we got out at the club and all these cars start comin' down the street, bangin' Screw. And Keke turned around and said, "Screw! They jammin' you in Austin like this!" And me and Screw looked at each other and started laughin'. I mean . . . didn't nobody know . . . I guess they didn't know I was down here sellin' tapes and just trying to push the issue, tryin' to . . . I don't know, I just . . . once I started doin' it, I just got into it, and it was just like a job to me.

What was your impression of Houston when you got there?

Well, I used to come to Houston, but the only part I really knew of Houston, after I started coming down there just hanging out with Screw, was Screw's part of it. Like, now I feel a little different about Houston than I did back then, but it was just like, it seemed like there wasn't nothin' but love everywhere. I guess it's just . . . I wanna say it's the way . . . the type of person Screw was, because he had different neighborhoods hangin' out with each other that didn't like each other, and I just thought, "This is cool." I really thought it was cool. But now that he not here, it just don't seem the same to me no more, you know? Like, I go to Houston, I'll go see Al-D . . . you know, I don't stay in Houston too long no more. I don't get the same feelin' about Houston, because I know from back then that it's some good people around, and there's some people that ain't too friendly around there, so you just gotta watch out who you deal with, man, when you're in Houston. But like Al, I know he a good person, so I know ain't nothin' gonna happen to me when I go see him or whoever he with. I know everything gonna be all good.

So what was the first year that you went to Houston? Do you remember?

When I first went to Houston was '91.

This was to see Screw?

Yeah, yeah, yeah. He actually . . . it was like my senior year in high school, and for some reason his sister drove up to the school . . . his sister came up to the school to tell me that Screw wanted me to come to Houston to see him. It was, like, almost graduation time. Yeah, I think it was like September of '90, '91 . . . and I drove to Houston, like when I got out of school, and me and him sat around and we made a little tape, we hung out, like all day long, and then when I was leaving, he handed me—it had to be '91 because he handed me *3 'N Da Mornin'*—the first tape he slowed down, and he mixed it with four turntables.

So the original *3 'N Da Mornin'* was in '91?

Yeah, that was '91, and he told me to listen to this tape and tell him what I thought. So I said the first thing that everybody else said, on my way back! I'm listenin' to the tape, and I kept takin' it out, putting it back in, and I called him, and I said, "Hey, man—I think you gave me a messed up tape," and he started laughin'. He say, "Naw, it's supposed to sound like that." I said, "Okay," and I just let it play. Then I say, "Okay, yeah! Okay!" All these different songs coming in, and him mixing—yeah! So I called him back after I got to Austin, and I said, "Yeah, that motherfucker jammin'!" He say, "Yeah, appreciate it." And that's when he told me right then . . . I don't know, he just had something in his eye, he said, "Man, we got us a way out." And I said, "Okay," but at the same time, I was still doin'

what I was doin', so I would just go up there every other weekend and stay three, four days and . . . at one point in time, it was like I was hustlin' just to go to Houston so I could jump in the mix or . . . a lot of times—I done been to Screw house so many times, a lot of times, I would just come just to kick it. It wasn't about makin' no tape, it wasn't about goin' to no studio, it wasn't about none of that, because we was always best friends before everything really jumped off. Before the music jumped off, all this, I would go up there, ride up there, we'd just go to the movies. Or we'll go somewhere and chill, go play pool. But then a lot of times I would be in there when he makin' tapes, and wouldn't be *on* them. Because if he said something like, "Man, just chill and just pay attention," I know that means whoever fittin' to come in and make this tape, keep your eye on them, *'cuz I don't really know 'em like that*. So, a lot of times, you know, that may have been my position or what I was doin' at that time, payin' attention to see . . . make sure that don't nobody get out of line. Or something like that, you know. Not like I'm just the biggest dude in the world, but at the same time, we all grew up together, so we was all gonna stick together.

He knows that you know how to feel out a situation.

Yeah, yeah. And you know . . . but he would let me know who he felt that was cool or who he felt like . . . 'cuz I was from Austin, so even though somebody would tell me, "Okay, this your partner from Austin," and then they'll say, "Come ride with me to the store, come ride with me here," and he would give me a look to tell me, "Naw, don't ride with this dude," or, you know, "It's cool." So it was pretty picked out, who he would pick and choose to deal with. People who he really, really felt in his heart was good people, he would let me know who they was. Or people just comin' in to make a tape and just . . . he would let me know who they are too. He was the same with everybody, though. He wasn't no different with me, Al, or anybody else. He was that same person. He didn't change or act a different way in front of nobody. He was the same person at all times.

But what I understand is that a lot of times people would get around him, and he would affect the way that people would act. Like people would be really, really cool around him, people maybe who might have had some beef with each other . . . dudes like that would get around Screw and all of the sudden they were really cool.

Yeah! Yeah! Yeah! That's true! I mean, there was just something about him that had—he had that in him, to do that. I don't know if I'm saying it right. You might have to ask Al, but like, when he really just jumped in the mix, the crime rate in Houston dropped like 20 percent.

Yeah, somebody said that to me one time. They say the crime rate *around* Screw dropped like 20 percent.

Yeah! So that was . . . that was kind of big, and I seen . . . I don't know. I guess it was just him, though, because he never really had no problems at his house or his studio. He didn't have no problems with people. If they didn't like each other, they didn't act like they didn't like each other. They was cool with each other that night.

I was talking to Al-D about this. I said, "So nobody ever fucked with Screw, huh?" And he said, "Man, if you did, where would you go? Do you think you could ever actually get around Houston? So many people had that guy's back, where would you go afterward, if you fucked with Screw?"

He right. I remember *3 'N The Mornin'* dropped . . . back then I had a slab, and I came to Houston, and we was goin' to, I think, the album release party or something. We pulled up in this neighborhood, and I think about 30 dudes walked up to the car. Screw said, "Hey man, this my kinfolk, Shorty Mac. He from Austin." Them dudes looked at me and told him, "Okay, he good. Ain't nobody gonna mess with him around here." And I was just sittin' in the car, and I was just trippin'. I was like, "Damn! It's like that?" But you know, I really . . . I knew Screw had some power, but I didn't know how big his power was until after he died. That's when I just

started seein', like, a lot of stuff. I said, "Man, this dude was like . . . he was serious." He was serious, man. That dude had power like . . . I don't know. I can't even put a name on it, but I just start seein' different stuff, how the reaction of people . . . the people and different people comin' around. And I mean, you seein' gangstas cry, and I say, "Man, this dude was very effective on people's lives, man!" And not even that—this dude *changed* a lot of people's lives. By listenin' to his tapes. I mean, I done seen dudes come up there that's been hustlin', and they goin', "Man, I'm fittin' to go to college . . ." and like, "Man, I'm listenin' to this tape, man, Screw, you got me thinkin' . . ." I'm like, "Wow, this is serious." But Al is right, man, if you was to do somethin', or try to do somethin' to this man, you not gonna get away with it. They had that much love for him, because he was a respectful dude, so he ain't never disrespect nobody. He was a humble dude, he showed a lot of love, so I mean, you know, that's what he really got back. I ain't gonna say now, people didn't hate him, because there may have been a lot of people hated him, but there wasn't nothin' they could do about it.

So how would you describe the energy that was going on in Houston at that point? You were sort of an outsider because you didn't grow up in Houston, but you knew some of these prime characters who really helped to create it—like if you had to go back to Austin and say, "Hey, man—you know what's going on in Houston is . . ." What? What would you tell them?

Well . . . I don't know because they didn't treat me like that. Especially the people in the Click, you know? They didn't treat me like I was an outsider. It was like a . . . it was different, because they treated me like I was, like some kind of star or something in Houston.

Yeah?

I was doin' music with Al, and I had jumped on a couple of Al's albums, and I was with Screw, doin' Screwtapes, but I mean . . . I was like . . . I guess I was like the speaker of the house for Austin. I was comin' down here lettin' 'em know everything that was goin' on, and whatever I said, "Man, you need to get this—it's fittin' to come out," everybody was jumpin' on it. And then, after so long, I didn't have to tell 'em nothin'! Because albums was steady droppin', and they knew these people was who was with Screw. After a while, it just went on affiliation. If you in the Click, and you done a song with somebody, then they gonna get that song, because there's somebody from the Screwed Up Click on there or somebody . . . Wreckshop or whatever. So I mean, it wasn't hard, really. It wasn't hard to come back to Austin and say, "Man, this dude here is jammin'," because a lot of the dudes, they had already heard 'em on Screwtapes.

So they already had reference points for a lot of stuff . . . they knew who Lil' Keke was, and you can say, "Okay, man, there's this guy Big Pokey . . . you gotta hear this guy. He did a track with Lil' Keke," and it just kind of passes on that way, huh?

Yeah, yeah. Like . . . Austin is like a second home for the Screwed Up Click. They still come down here and still get a lot of love. You say somebody from the Screwed Up Click comin' to Austin, and it'll be people that ain't came out in two years come out because these cats are comin' down here. It's just like a second home for 'em, man, and a lot of 'em will say that. E.S.G.'ll call me, let me know when he havin' a concert down here, and we'll kick it. I don't know, man . . . it's amazing, because I never thought . . . until I went through it—if I wouldn't have went through it, I wouldn't have believed it, you know what I'm sayin'? I don't know, man . . . it wasn't hard. After '95 hit, it wasn't hard for nothin', because everybody in Austin was lookin' for a Screwtape with either Keke, Fat Pat . . . and then as it went on Pokey, E.S.G.—E.S.G. went in Screw house and just used to do 100-minute tapes. He'd just freestyle. And they knew who it was, with "Swangin' & Bangin'," and all that. So, it just got easier, and anybody that came in and done somethin' with Screw really got them a fan base in Austin from that.

You were talking about Screw's first concert in Austin. Do you remember when that was?

That was in '96.

What do you remember about Screw's skills?

The dude was just good with his hands, period. I mean turntables, he used to cut hair . . . I remember, like when he first start DJing, we used to walk around Smithville with jamboxes. We was walkin' one day, and his handle on his jambox broke. He picked up his jambox—it was still playin'—had it under his arm . . . his mama was gone to work, he took his jambox loose, went in the living room, took his mama turntable, brought it in the room, and hooked it into his jambox some kinda way. And the thing that used to switch it from radio to tape? On the jambox? He made it into a fader. And I was like, "Damn!" He was like 13 years old when he done this.

This was in Smithville?

This was in Smithville. And there was a guy that stayed across the street from us named DJ Butts. He would go over there—this is how we would make our little tapes—he would go over there and borrow a turntable from him. The jambox he had had RCA plugs on it too. So he had this one turntable—his mama turntable—playin' on the inside of the jambox, and he had the other turntable plugged in with the RCA jack. No headphones. And he put six by nines all around his room for music and one little old stereo speaker right in the middle, and he just start . . . he started mixin' from there, with no headphones. I wish I had some of the tapes that he made back then. They wouldn't have been great quality, because he had one of them little black tape recorders sittin' up by the speaker recordin' the tapes. Or we would get in front, or lay down and freestyle in front of the tape recorder with the music playin', but the mixes was just . . . I mean they were just off-the-chain, even to us back then, and we was just like 13 . . . he was 13, I was 12. We used to take these home and jam 'em, but we could only make . . . every tape was different. Because we could only record one tape

. . . and we never thought about, you know, dubbin' back then. They was just . . . we would be at his house at, like, two in the morning—at this young age! At two in the morning, talkin' like we got a radio station . . .

Well, you did.

Yeah! And we just be in there just makin' little tapes. We might do two or three tapes in one night! Just different songs, mixing different songs. You know, you had 60-minute tapes back then, and they wasn't really long. They was some cheap tapes. And then he just . . . I don't know, that was just what we liked to do! We'd get out of school and we'd go to his house . . . I mean, I got in trouble a lot of nights! Going over there and just sittin' in, but we wasn't in no trouble, though! If it just came down to it and my t-lady, my old man was lookin' for me, they would know exactly where to come. You didn't have to worry about me bein' too much of no other place, and if I wasn't there, then we was all gone somewhere. It got to a point where his mama started putting a time limit on the door. We used to do it so much, you know what I'm sayin'? You'd walk up to the door and the piece of paper might . . . today it might say, "No coming until after three." Tomorrow it might say, "After four," the next day it might say, "After five." Then you knew not to knock on the door. Turn around, and at that time, you could come over there, and it's all good. She never had no problem with us. I think it was more just gettin' a peace of mind. She was workin' two or three jobs. She was workin' like two or three jobs, and she wrote her own blueprints out, got 'em a house. When somebody do that, and we understand this now that we grown, sometimes they just want peace. For a few minutes, you know. She never had no problems with it. Because a lot of . . . I'm not sayin' nothin' was wrong with nothin' . . . I didn't find out actually what happened 'til later on, when we grew up, that . . . okay, I came to Screw's house one day and he was gone. And his mama looked at me and said, "Baby, he moved to Houston." This was, like, in the middle of the night. I was just with him yesterday! He ain't tell me nothin' about he was movin' to Houston. And then, it's like, through the middle of the night, he was

gone. But then, after me and her was sittin' down, and the words came out of her mouth that it was either that Pops gonna have to pay child support . . . so instead of him payin' child support, he came and picked Screw up, to move him to Houston. So, it wasn't . . . I guess he didn't wanna come up with the money to pay child support. He just . . . "It's my son, let him come stay with me." So, I mean, you know . . . it was rough for Screw either way. He used to still come home like Christmas, Thanksgiving, you know, holidays like that.

So what family did he still have out there? He had his mom, did he have some aunts and uncles?

His mom, his sister, his grandma, his cousin . . . Screw was the only person that left. He was the only person that shot out. He was . . . and I guess it was under them situations, you know what I'm sayin'? He can't pay child support . . . "I'm not gonna pay child support. My son can come stay with me." So he was gone, you know. And I can't say that that wasn't the best thing for him as far as his music, because Houston is a big city, and I believe it never woulda gotten that far just doin' it in Smithville.

You would think so, thinking about the influences and just everything he's hearing, that he was able to get to, everything like that.

But under other conditions, the things he had to go through, I just . . . I didn't kinda understand that, you know. Or even the way he was even treated when he got there. That made Screw strong. I can just say that made Screw strong.

You can see that [Al-D] gets a lot of it from his mama [with whom Screw was close]. I've never met Al's dad, but you can see that's where he gets it from, and that trickled down to Screw.

Yeah, yeah, yeah. You're sure right. Screw introduced me and Al . . . he got off of lock, and Screw house . . . no, I came to Houston, and him and Screw was sittin' in the house—he introduced us—and me and Al been cool ever since. I'm talkin' about outta everybody out of the Click, that's the person I clicked with the most. Like, say now, Screw ain't around . . . I know I ain't gonna have no problems dealin' with Al. Because of just the type of person he was, man. That dude, man . . . that dude done taught me a lot, man . . . that dude really taught me a lot, and he really filled my spirit up to be the person that I am now. And that's one of the main reasons why I came back to Austin after Screw died, because I was hurtin' so bad, and I was like . . . I just wanted to come back and be around my kids. I didn't wanna . . . I didn't wanna take them trips like that no more. For one, Screw wasn't there, and everything wasn't bein' done the same, but . . . losin' Screw . . . I just . . . got to a point where I felt like I couldn't take it, man. I was so stressed out when I got back here that . . . I say, I just wanna be around my kids. I wanna, you know, watch them and when they need me, I'm right here, and stuff like that. But at the same time, like when Screw was livin', my son . . . in the summertime, my son and Screw nephew would come stay with us. So I still had dinner with my kids when I was livin' in Houston. I would come home, like, every other weekend, every two or three weekends I'd come home, see them, you know, and kick it with them. I was still comin' back, but just . . . losin' Screw, I just felt like I was just . . . I don't know. I ain't wanna see anybody else leave, and I ain't gonna say that didn't happen, 'cuz we lost a lot of more people after Screw done died, but it got to that point where I wasn't as focused because he's . . . he's missing, you know what I'm saying? And when you tryin' to do a lot of stuff, and there ain't too many people in your corner . . . the only people in your corner is Al-D and . . . shit, that was probably it. Everybody else was just hopin' something else go wrong, so they would have a reason to do other shit. But Al-D was always there. Me and Al-D actually moved in together after Screw died. We moved into a little duplex together, and we stayed there for a while. And then I just got to the point where I just said, "Man, I'ma move back to Smithville," I mean to Austin . . . and I actually moved to Smithville first, and then I came back to Austin. But I just . . . I don't know, I just . . . it's been 10 years, and it still seems like it just happened. And it's like that feelin' still ain't went away. I done got a lot better, though. I know we all done

got a lot better. It used to be real hard on a lot of people at first, you know. And we still . . . we all still do music, but I mean . . . that was like the best dude to do music *with*, man. I mean, for real. You know he wasn't fittin' to try to screw over you, but now you gotta take a chance on somebody tryin' to screw over you.

When you talk about that feeling, you're talking about the feeling that you had once he was gone or the feeling that you had while he was around?

I mean, it was a totally different feelin' when he was around because we always knew things was . . . everything was gonna be good. You don't get that feelin' dealin' with people now. You gotta watch 'em. Like . . . I wanna take my album up to this place . . . I got a 50/50 chance of me gettin' my money off of it. And I even went through that dealin' with this dude in California. You know, he talk real good . . . for a couple of years. I done an album, and then me and Keke done a little album together. Got a little change off of it, but then he disappeared, so . . . it's just . . . Screw never tried to get over on nobody. That's just the type of person he was. And I told him . . . maybe a couple years before he died, I told him, "Man, I really don't wanna do music with nobody else but you. That's the only person I would ever do music with, is you."

What did he say to that?

He said one of his number one words, was, "Man, that's real." And it was like, I ain't gotta worry about no contracts, none of that. I just had that feelin'. I don't have to worry about none of that. I don't . . . I know you ain't fittin' to try to get over on me, you know?

That wasn't just because you knew him from back in the day, though.

No, that's just the type of person he was. That's just like he done everybody else, you know what I'm sayin'? Only thing I didn't really get was . . . I mean, you know, I believe it was everybody got they own destiny, even when there's a Click, you got . . . everybody got they own destiny. I just think a lot of times . . . I sit up and I still think about this . . . sometimes, I think some people move too fast. Because I think if people woulda done just small things a little different, it would have been a different reaction as a whole game plan of doin' tapes or even doin' albums. I know everybody got they own best plan, everybody wanna do they own thing and everything. I think if people woulda clenched around Screw a little better than what they did, then as soon as he gettin' them in the limelight, they takin' off tryin' to do they thing . . . because I sit in the car and listen to this dude talk to different major labels tryin' to sign him, and him not takin' it because he's trying to make sure everybody eat. He coulda signed with a major label back in '97, '98, but he didn't take it because he was tryin' to make sure everybody got on. Or the people that he really thought could, you know, could really do something and bring somethin' off the top. He was tryin' to make sure all these people ate, and I'm listenin' to the dude tell 'em, "Man, I got a check for you right now, you can go buy you a Benz and take your girl out to a nice restaurant," and he tell the dude, "Man, I'm already takin' my girl to a nice restaurant. I want everybody to be comfortable." And that's just the type of dude he was. If they woulda came with the right . . . you wanna call it the right "price," or gave him the right situation, he woulda went and let everybody know what was goin' on. But I guess his thing was, you know, until they get right, I can't . . . I'm not gonna tell nobody, "Okay, this person wanna sign us," and then we start jumpin' the gun. He wanted to make sure everything was right.

When you think about the direction he took with his career and his tapes and his shop, it couldn't possibly have been about money.

Nah, nah, nah. Because he was actually . . . I mean, even before he got the shop he was helpin' people pay they rent, pay they light bill, you know.

There's that part of it, and then he was making stars out of people. Rapping on his tapes, they were becoming stars. They were becoming huge. Careers were born out of his tapes.

And you know, I would guarantee . . . I ain't gonna say everybody, but a few of them was probably doin' it for fun, and then the . . . in a matter of months, a couple of years, it turned into a career. "Okay, hey man, I need to make a Screwtape tonight. We gonna go over there, we gonna freestyle on a tape," and then . . . "Hold up! Hold on! People are listenin' to me, man! This is for real! I can do this!" You get 50,000 fans to buy your tape, and you put it out yourself, you got you a nice check.

That's all you need.

Yeah! Hell yeah. I used to always look at that. I was like, "Man, if it wasn't for Screw . . ." I ain't gonna say I just got a big name, but I'm well-known, and I can pretty much do something and get a good response out of it, you know, and it's all because of him. I mean, God first at all times with me, but it's because of him, what he did on them turntables, and puttin' me out there . . . I'da never got myself out there that far in the manner of time that I got out there, in the short time span that got me to where I'm at. It woulda took me a little longer—a lot longer—if I was to do it on my own.

Well you were part of a broadcast. I mean, wouldn't you consider what he did like a broadcast?

Like an underground radio station or somethin'! And that was the . . . that was crazy, man, because when he stayed on Greenstone, major labels would send him CDs, records, to put on his tapes to promote they shit.

Far be it from him getting in trouble, it was like, "I'm gonna go ahead and send you this."

Yeah. Yeah! I mean, because he was makin' . . . by him puttin' a song off of somebody album, the South found out about who you was, and then they would go buy your album. They wasn't just listenin' to it from the Screwtape. They wanted to go hear what else you had to offer, and that was one thing about it—he didn't never slow down somebody whole album. That wasn't on his agenda. His agenda was to help you the best way he knew how, and that was with the turntables set up with his style of slowin' it down, and that's what he did. And he got a lot of love from a lot of rappers. I met a lot of rappers from different states from that. I met the Outlaws . . . I was up there one night, he got a phone call . . . I'm just fittin' to leave, he said, "Man, I'm fittin' to go to dinner with Ice-T." I'm gettin' ready to leave, Ice-T pull up in a limo! Pick him up. They leave and go to dinner! I mean, this dude was . . . he met them because he was Screw, but he met a lot more people than me . . . I mean there was literally rappers that walked up to his door, like Master P. He never got to meet C-Bo, which was one of the rappers he used to love, but C-Bo even came to his house one day. He was asleep, and his cousin didn't wake him up. I think he was mad for about a week behind that.

Was it Big Bubb?

Nah, I wanna say it was D-Ray. So after Screw woke up, he said, "Man, this dude came over here," and he said, "What was the dude name?" And he said "C-Bo." "You ain't wake me up?" So he never got to meet C-Bo, but the crazy thing about it, we was readin' a magazine, and Screw was one of the people C-Bo always wanted to meet. And back in the day, these dudes used to look like brothers to me.

Screw and C-Bo?

Yeah! So Screw went into his studio, grabbed a C-Bo album, and came back out and showed . . . it was either D-Ray or Lil' D, and said, "Is this the dude that came to the door?" And he said, "Yeah." And [Screw] got so mad because it was somebody he always wanted to meet. I'm tryin' to think of who else I done seen come through there . . . E-40, D-Shot came, and there was another cat with them.

He never got Mac Dre through there, did he?

No, he got Spice 1. He got Spice 1 on a tape! Those are just some of the names . . . we pulled up to a concert in Bryan–College Station. B-Legit and

Richie Rich walked up to us. That's the first time I heard somebody say something about they had supposed to've smoked [2]'Pac ashes. I don't know how true it is! But then I heard people start rappin' about that shit, after maybe a year after they said it. They said, "Man, we put some of 'Pac ashes in a blunt, and smoked it." And I was like, "For real?"

Well, you gotta pack something in there.

Yeah, man. Screw said, "Would you smoke my ashes?" I told him, "Naw, man. I respect you too much for that. That just wouldn't seem right."

Lil' Keke

HERSCHELWOOD

The original Screwed Up Click rapper has had many junctures in a career that started in the early 1990s with his introduction to DJ Screw, and Keke's subsequent breakthrough as a freestyle rapper alongside the late Fat Pat on dozens of Screwtapes. Lil' Keke is noted by countless artists as a major influence on their style and has recorded some of Houston rap's biggest hits over the years. This interview was conducted at one of those aforementioned junctures, when he had just signed with Swishahouse subsidiary TF Records, run by Swishahouse producer T. Farris. It was a big move because it was a Southside icon signing with a Northside label, but Don Ke had his reasons.

PHOTO: PETER BESTE

What made you decide you wanted to go with T. Farris?

I had a few other things I coulda did, but I already knew it was a retooling situation. It wasn't really about no money no mo'. I was really just ready to get where I belonged as far as my career, you know what I'm sayin'? And each situation was gonna be a retooling situation of goin' through it, so I basically wanted to get back to my fans, the same type of fan base . . . I basically just wanted to get back to bein' a rapper, period. I was wearin' a lot of hats and doin' a lot of shit on my own.

Were you producing and everything on your own?

I was puttin' out my own albums, I was puttin' out all kinda albums. I wasn't doin' the producing, but goin' to the radio and all of that, I got tired of all that. My best years were when all I had to do was get up and concentrate on music. So T. Farris was really makin' that closer to happenin'.

He was willing to handle all of that.

Not only that, man . . . really, but also the resume of what he had done, giving me the opportunity just to come after Mike and Paul and then me. Which, Mike and Paul are already my fans.

They grew up listening to you.

Yeah, so it was all about that, man. It was really about gettin' with the right people. I been with all type of people, man. Koch and Polygram, different things in the game, but none of them know South music, and I wanted to get with someone who was already winning with my type and just to get me back to a comfortable atmosphere of just bein' a rapper the way I was, get me to those fans. For every company that wanted to do something, that was still the deal that looked the best. It's been nine months now—we're just now gettin' to the video, just now gettin' to the single . . . it was all the work that I thought it was gonna be, but I don't think I'd be at the same place if I was with somebody else right now.

You wouldn't be doing the same kind of work.

Nuh-uh. Because of the *interest* that they got in me, the confidence, the work that they wanted to do and their previous success with my type of rap, period.

Some people theorize that there should be static, or even a squelching of static seeing as you're a Southside rapper coming to a Northside label. How do you see that?

It was gonna take a person like me to bridge the gap, because the Southside believes in me. They know I got talent. There's really a lot of people on the Southside. You're goin' to have mixed results, but one thing they know about me, man . . . business is always business. This wasn't about the North or the Southside, this really was good for Houston. Because, man I sold a lot of records on the Northside. I sold over 150,000 albums in Houston, Texas. A lot of those albums are on the Northside.

They can't all be on the Southside.

Naw, and I just felt like I could bridge the gap 'cuz they wasn't doin' this out of spite. They was doin' it because they said, "We feel like Keke one of the best talents in the city, and we want a chance to give him an opportunity." It was strict on that. I knew there was gonna be some ups and downs, but I also know once time passes and heals, once

the movement hits, man, the Southside, they gonna follow.

You're always from the Southside.

It's business. And opportunity. So I had to make a choice. It's been nine months now. Just imagine if I had waited to do it. Imagine if I had waited 'til January or somethin' . . . it would be *still* next December, and one of the things that was goin' through my mind was . . . what Houston was goin' through, this buzz and it's goin' through this wave, and I'm a big reason for it . . . I needed to make sure that I tapped into it.

Since you were a large part of the reason for that sound, you almost couldn't miss.

It was a matter of straight confidence. All I gotta do is go to the studio. I ain't gotta talk to the DJs, really, unless I'm doin' drops or somethin for 'em. I ain't gotta go to the radio. I ain't gotta talk to the promoters. All I gotta do is concentrate on the music. Since I been doin' that it's just . . . it's rollin' perfect. It never was about money, man . . . I been had money.

You probably could have gotten a better deal money-wise, at least at first, but it wouldn't have been as good for you as an artist.

One thing, man, artists need to understand, and I didn't understand this early in my career—all money ain't good money. You got to realize that. Some people don't. It wasn't about money at all. Structure. It wasn't our fault, man. We was so wrapped up in the independent game, makin' so much money, when these people came on . . . the new generation, Slim Thug, Chamillionaire, they came in more really about gettin' a deal, TV. When we was comin' up we wasn't even thinkin' about that. I was makin' $250,000 a year without doin' *nothin'*. None of that. Videos, nothin'. So that's what it's about.

It's really permanently changed the game in Houston, hasn't it?

It's changed the game. You gotta come on with it now. With me, man, I could really say that. Texas really had the biggest independent game as far as breakin' artists and makin' money. The game has changed, man. It really struck me once I seen these boys goin' platinum, and I know this my style, I know this what they grew up on, and I noticed they sayin' everything I said. It really pushed me to just take it all the way, man. Way more than I ever thought.

All it became at that point was a business decision. You weren't changing your style.

When I was with Koch they tried to *get* me to change my style, turn this down, turn that down, tried to get me to be . . . have my fans sayin' I needed to go back to the old 'Ke. They took a year tryin' to turn me into this whole 'nother rapper, so it felt good just to get back in this atmosphere, and T. Farris pushed me out of that so hard.

You've been able to support yourself here for so many years. How involved have you been on the national scale?

I haven't done less than $7,000 to $10,000 on shows in years. And those were bad years. On good years, man, you could pull 30 and 40 in months, man. I could live off Texas. I don't never have to leave.

That's why I was asking about your national involvement, because that's set to change now.

When I was with Koch, they were an East Coast company, so they promoted more in Midwestern states, so I sold big volumes in places like St. Louis, Kansas City . . . these people already know Lil' Keke. When I was with Polygram in '98, I was all over California, all up-and-down Sunset Boulevard because they promoted mostly in the West. So the biggest advantage with Swishahouse is that all these people already know Keke, but now I'm bein' promoted from Houston, from where I'm from, and from this new game.

Koch never even had to mess with the South, did they?

They didn't know *how* to do it. They didn't even know how, man. There was a point in time when I was with Koch where I was tryin' to change my style, but now with this new generation, it'll be an easy transition for me, man, 'cuz they know this. All Swishahouse got to do is just reach out to the fans that's already there, and pull them in. And *then* you go and get the ones you didn't have before.

And a lot of the fans of this new generation are going to start learning about where these cats came from, going back and reading and finding out that you're part of the background, part of the fire. That they need to hear you.

It's gonna come out, man, it's gonna come out. To say all that, man, Swishahouse gave me the best opportunity. Even with Universal and the Chamillionaire situation, man. Look where he's at now. Chamillionaire was with Universal so, so long before he turned. But for me, I didn't have that type of time. I'm ready to do this now. Nobody was waitin'. I wanted to be in a situation where I could go ahead now. That's what T. Farris done gave me. We're movin' right along.

Big DeMo

LONG DRIVE

Best known as the inspiration for DJ Screw's legendary June 27th mixtape (1996), as it was his birthday tape. Demo Sherman grew up on South Park's Long Drive and is part of the group Vetranz. His sister Tashia introduced him to DJ Screw.

Do you remember the first time you ever went over Screw's house? Did you meet him before you ever went to his house, or did you just get taken to his house by somebody?

My sister always was a popular girl, and she knew Screw. She had been tellin' me about this guy because she knows I'm a hip-hop head to the fullest. KYOK had the radio station "1590 Raps." That's what we was listening to back then on the AM dial. And she was tellin' me, "DeMo, I got this homeboy, and he a DJ. I want you to meet him." She said, "You need to meet him, DeMo, you gonna like this dude. I'm tellin' you, man. He remind me of you. He be makin' mixtapes, and he don't do nothin' but old school D.M.C., Fat Boys, stuff like that." I was like, "Well, I don't care. I can make my own tapes, you know?" She was like, "Man, I'm tellin' you, you need to meet him." So one day I go over to her house, and she playin' this tape with Run–D.M.C. on it. It's mixed up real good, and I'm like, "Why is the pitch of it so slow like that?" And she's like, "Man, that's my homeboy I been tellin' you about! That's why I put it on! I just put it on when you came in." And I was like, "Well, whoever he is, he is a DJ for real. He mixin' his ass off. It's slow, but I like it like that. It sound pretty good to me." And she like, "I'm tellin'

you he a good DJ, man. You need to see him." I was like, "Well, maybe I will meet him one day." So about a week later I'm at the house, and my sister call me. She says, "DeMo, I need you to go pick up my tape, from my homeboy I was tellin' you about." And I was like, "Now you fittin' to send me to this man house?" I was like, "I don't wanna go over this man house, man, it's a different time of night. You don't just go over somebody house that you don't know. You say he got all this equipment and stuff, he gonna think I'm tryin' to get him or something." She like, "Man, I done paid for this tape, DeMo. He stay right down the street. Go over there, please." I went over there. She had paged him. Cell phones weren't a popular thing back then, and he came out and I came out and he talkin' about, "So you Tasha brother?" I was like, "Yeah, I'm Tasha brother, man." He's like, "Man, your sister don't never stop talkin' about you. She been wantin' me to meet you for months, man. She always been tellin' me about you." I was like, "She done the same thing with you!" I'm kinda low key, man. I don't always wanna be poppin' up on people. He say, "So what you do, you a DJ, you rap or whatever?" I said, "Man, I been rappin' since the Sugarhill Gang. When I heard that, I knew that was me." And I say, "Nobody ever wanted to help me, so I had to become my own DJ and learn how to make beats, and when I started improvin', they really wasn't helpin' me, so I was just always on my own." He like, "Well, man, I DJ, I get down." And man, we talked for hours, just right in his driveway. And that day was the same day I met Fat Pat, I met Hawk, I met a bunch of more other people,

AL-D AND DEMO. UNIVERSITY OF HOUSTON LIBRARIES SPECIAL COLLECTIONS.

but I can remember him tellin' me how much he had love for Fat Pat and Hawk, that's what made it stick with me. And we just . . . I'm talkin' about, man, we talked for hours. It was daylight, and I can remember my sister kept pagin' me 'cuz she wanted her tape! And I was like, "Man, I'm out here talkin' with this dude, you know . . ." And we just talked. I remember people comin' over to his house and people that was callin' and he was like, "Well, I'm talkin' to my homeboy right now." He just disregarded everybody when me and him was talkin'. And from that moment on, me and Screw was just tight, tight, tight. He was like, "Well, come over here tomorrow man! And I'll show you what I do." And I came over there . . . and man, I was just amazed, so amazed by what he did. I was like, "I been lookin' for you for years and didn't know it, man. I'm a hip-hop head." So the next time I went over there, I gave him all my records. Every record I owned, I gave it to Screw. I said, "I know you got a lot of records, but maybe I got something you don't have." And I can remember one of the first Screwtapes I did, it was alternative music. It wasn't really actually alternative music, but it wasn't rap. It had Queen on there, and Boy George, stuff like that, because I listened to everything, you know? I wasn't just prejudiced with music. I respect any good music no matter what it is. And we made that tape, and I was surprised he had those records. I

was like, "You got Queen 'We Will Rock You' and 'Another One Bites The Dust'?" You could just throw songs out, and he would go to his library, "I got it right here!" And we made a tape on the fly without a . . . I think that's the only tape he made without a list. And we made that tape, man, and I was like. "The next one, I'ma just go hood with it! We gonna jam." And, you know, we just started pushin' our tapes. I was makin' a tape . . . at least once a week I was makin' a tape. Sometimes twice a week. You know, Screw was 24/7, man. He hardly got any rest. You know, he'd work and go hard all day, and you'd leave Screw house at 8, 9, 10 in the morning, and you'd be back over there about 1. He got very little sleep, and it was really kinda amazin', especially due to the fact that he was sippin' codeine all day! And I can remember . . . you know, I knew about codeine and cough syrup, stuff like that already because I'm from that kind of family that always hustled, you know. My grandpa, you know . . . so I knew about that stuff, man. I used to always ask, "Man, what you drinkin' in them wine coolers?" He'd have a four-pack of wine coolers, and he'd put an ounce of cough syrup in each one of them. He was like, "Man, I'm drinkin' syrup." I was like, "Syrup? Like cough syrup?" He like, "Yeah, man. It taste alright.'" I'm like, "Man, that ain't my party, but you mixin' it with something . . ." I say, "Man, I see people drink that stuff straight! You . . . you mixin' it up!" He was like, "Man, I can't take it like that. It's too strong. I just wanna . . . sip it and relax a little bit." I was like, "Okay, whatever." And it got popularized, you know, it just . . . everybody just started doin' it because, I guess . . . you talk about it on a Screw-tape . . . whatever was happenin' on a Screwtape, everybody was emulating whatever was happenin'. And that's what—it was crazy how this stuff took off, man! It seemed like overnight it just took off, you know. If you wasn't jammin' Screw, you wasn't jammin'. If you was a rap artist in this country, you wasn't sellin' in Houston unless you touched one of those Screwtapes. 'Cuz we didn't know about you, man! We didn't know about you. Guys don't buy records anyway, but if you that good, there was a respect thing where you gotta go buy the 8Ball & MJG because it's *that* jammin'. You ain't gonna listen to it, but you gonna buy it because you gonna get yours slowed down by Screw. So we . . . you'd buy a cassette or a CD, and just put it up and, "Screw, man, I need you to slow down this whole thing for me." And Screw will have it for you, the same day it come out. He'd go and slow it down and, you know, the rest is history, man. That stuff took off. I mean, people were jammin' Screw, but it was, you know . . . a few people in the neighborhood. Maybe a bunch of big-time dudes that knew Screw knew how to get in touch with . . . because people still didn't know where Screw *was*. When I met him, he had just moved on Greenstone. Just moved there. And that's known as the Screw house. You know, "That's Screw's house!"

Off Reveille, right?

Yes, yes, that's it. Well, really off Poplar, but we say Reveille because that's the major street. Everybody knew about that. Like some people knew where he stayed, but you couldn't get in . . . you know, you'd have to get in to Screw's house. A lot of people came, knocked on the door, "I wanna get a tape." You know, like a little candy store. They could do that, but to get inside was a major deal, and I remember it started blowin' up, blowin' up, and he got the gate. And you know, "Aw, man. Screw done put up a fence! Man, aw man . . ." It was like he had to get through the fence 'cuz you know, you had to knock on the side door. The front door was enclosed by burglar bars, so you couldn't ring the doorbell. So if you didn't have his number, and now you can't knock on the side door, you couldn't get to Screw. And Screw loved it just like that. Because he wanted just people he trusted to be able to get him. So if you didn't have that pager number, you wasn't gettin' to him. And then, you know, people would pass by . . . people would pass by and wait for a car to pull up, wait to catch that gate open or a line formin' at that gate, and that was . . . boom! That was they chance, man. And it was just people in the know. It was people from the Northside and the Southside. Let me repeat that: It was people from the Northside and the Southside. It was never just a Southside thing, but more people on the South knew about it because it was on the Southside. Houston always been Northside/Southside, and it just turned it into a plex thing because, you

know, people would hear Herschelwood this and Martin Luther King [Boulevard] that, and on the Northside, they want to hear you say Homestead! But we wasn't from Homestead, so we wasn't saying Homestead. And then with the event of people startin' to jack for cars and . . . you know, you got people stealin' cars and sayin', you know, somebody from the Southside steal somebody from the Southside car, they'll leave a note: "YEAH, THE NORTHSIDE RUN THIS." Knowin' good and damn well it wasn't nobody from the Northside. The Northside did the same thing. So they was buildin' stuff up and, you know, makin' the Northside hate the Southside more, making the Southside hate the Northside more until you got your spin-off, like your Michael Watts and all of that. And that's how all of that came about, because they wanted they own Screw too! They had rappers, they had MCs, they wanted to stress they skills, but they knew they couldn't get in Screw house. That was a no-no. They knew it wouldn't happen. That's what made all of the enemy stuff happen, and it really wasn't really that bad as people think, but when you listen to Screw all day and you hearin' people say this and that about the Northside . . . if you an outsider, you diggin' all the way into it, this and that. It wasn't really as bad as people made it out to be.

It was really an echo of what was going on in LA too. The West Coast/East Coast thing that was happening in rap at that point. A lot of people got attached to that. A lot of people kind of romanticized that, you know, East Coast versus West Coast. And that just kind of fostered its own little reflection in Houston.

That's exactly what it was. Especially with the East Coast/West Coast thing because we feel like we in the middle lane. We down South, so we wasn't with nobody. But the prominent music was coming from the West Coast, so a lot of people down here was like, "I like Snoop, I like Dre. Dre be jammin', Eazy-E be jammin', man. I'm not likin' no Wu-Tang." You know, a lot of guys down South, we wasn't likin' that East Coast because of the beats. They had more of a hip-hop-rooted beats, more to the roots of hip-hop, but the beats wasn't . . . you know, we love our cars down South, and if it couldn't bang in the car and sound rhythmatic and sounded real good, we wasn't likin' it. Because it wouldn't sound good in our car.

The East Coast stuff was too fast.

And then, you know, East Coast rappers were still rappin' about rappin'. You know, they would rap about rappin', and people down South didn't care about Farmers Boulevard. They ain't seen Farmers Boulevard. They ain't even seen the Eastern Time Zone, so they didn't care about that. They just wanted a good beat to ride to and say somethin' they could relate to. So that made a lot of people down South—and in other areas, I imagine too—say, "Well, we like the West Coast rap." But down here in Houston, we always had our own little hip-hop scene. And people around the country wasn't feelin' us, we never felt—we've had this discussion before—it wasn't cool to be from H-Town. And Screw made it cool to be from H-Town. He made it cool to say "H-Town," "Southside, that's where I'm from." By trade, I do hazardous material handling, so I was travelin' all over the country, and I was seein' all kinds of hip-hop and rap acts, you know. And so I had a lot to choose from. I had a lot of different styles from a lot of different coasts, and I liked nothin' but West Coast and down South, so that's what we gravitated to. And when the movement really started happenin' down here, people were like, "You like the East Coast or West Coast?" "Nah, I like the South. I like anything from the South." But these people had a harder time fittin' in with the South! Because when people think of the South, they think Florida, they think Atlanta, they think New Orleans . . . they were leavin' us out because we were in Texas. Well, it wasn't our fault that Texas is so big it can be in the South and the Midwest, you know? Dallas is, you know, Dallas is a totally different beast from Houston. Totally different. They got different kinds of food and everything. Like I told a lot of people that I knew from New Orleans that Louisiana is the Bayou State—Houston is the Bayou City. We had so many bayous we had to cement 'em. So we had our own crisis goin' on just bein' accepted as the South, but the people in Houston knew that a lot of the music from the South was still just a copy off

what we did in Houston. And a lot of people that's not ignorant to the facts realize a lot of the hip-hop today is originated off what Houston did. You know, Screw made it like that because you got the guys from New Orleans that come over, and they come to Screw house, and they'd buy a hundred Screwtapes, and they'd hear what we flow about, like diamond grills, candy paint, drank in our cup, and then you got guys like Master P that went to U of H (University of Houston), that was a Houston/ New Orleans/LA—well, I ain't gonna say LA—we'll say Richmond . . . and then come the Hot Boys. And those guys just rapped about what we rapped about, you know, on the Screwtapes. And it just blew up for them, and they made it seem like we were copyin' them! When actually, we'd been doin' this since '91, man, c'mon! And so a lot of people was like, "Well, you know, we know that's our style, you know we did the diamonds and drank." I've had diamonds in my grill since 1991, man. I mean, '91. You don't realize how far back that was, and I got the idea from Slick Rick, you know, because Slick Rick was a flashy guy. Slick Rick was from England, so he was about royalty and bein' the king and, you know, like people live in England. That's why he was Slick Rick The Ruler. It was crazy about Slick Rick because we didn't know studio magic. We didn't know about 24-track or 48-track . . . we would hear somebody . . . you hear Rakim say, "48-track." I had no idea what that was, you know? But when we found out—because there's a lot of studios in Houston, but they didn't let us in. You know, they ain't lettin' us in. We beatboxin' and spittin' on the mic. They don't wanna hear that. And so when we start findin' out more about it and learnin' more about it, you know, you had people that knew some stuff. What helped it was these band guys. The guys that were in the band. These guys that played the piano. These guys helped music down here in Houston—helped hip-hop grow, because they knew about tracks. They knew about musical notes. They knew how to read music. They knew how to play anything with keys. They knew that stuff. So, you grab those guys, you grab the dude that played the piano or the organ in the church, 'cuz you say, "Oh, I think I need them." So you grab him, and you put him on your team, and then you take the guy that plays that one drum in the band. You grab him, and you pull him with you, and now you got you a production crew. Well, let's find out what this 808 is. "Well, I can't get an 808." "Well, let's get a 505." I remember the first drum machine I had was a 505, and *you couldn't tell me nothin'*! I thought I was Davy DMX Mantronix, man! Because, you know, in the early days, there wasn't no tunes in rap music. It was just raw drums. And so we take these drums, and we program them to . . . well, the first thing I did with my drum machine was try to recreate every beat I heard. I was like, "Okay, I gotta do the Run–D.M.C. beat, I gotta do that." So we learned those beats and then, you know, you start tampering with it: "Well, I want my own beat ain't nobody heard," you know. But you don't know how to play, so in come the guy that plays the one drum. And then you be like, "Man, you gotta, we gotta get these beats, and we gotta get these tunes, you know." You go through all your records, and you get Stevie Wonder . . . and you put that over a beat you, "Aw man, I just made—aw man, I made me a beat! I'm good!" Well, all of the sudden, hip-hop start changin'. People start seein' money in it. Well, you can't just sample people records no more. Now they wanna get paid. So that's where the guy that play the piano in the church come in. "Man, can you come up with my own tune?" "Yeah, I can do it!" "Uh-oh. Now I got my own tune and my own beat. You can't tell me *nothin'*!" And then, you know, that's where it go. You just start from there, and just . . . it got better and better and better. By the time you really in a real studio—'cuz everybody had a pro studio in their houses by then. We had 4-track machines—you know, you couldn't tell us nothin' with them little 4-tracks. We were so happy. "I got one disc for the beat, I got one disc for the tune, and I got two tracks to rap on! Aw man!" It was incredible to us, you know? It was so amateur, but it was so *necessary* at the time.

Wood

THIRD WARD

Already an established artist by the time he met up with DJ Screw in the late 1990s, Wood saw a rebirth in his career virtually overnight when he became part of a new wave of rappers appearing on Screw's legendary mixtapes, joining the original tide of Screwed Up Click rappers Fat Pat, Lil' Keke, Big Pokey, E.S.G., Hawk, Big Moe, and Botany Boys. He continues to make records today as Wood Of The Screwed Up Click.

Where did you come up in Houston?

BIG BUBB AND WOOD. PHOTO: LANCE SCOTT WALKER

In the bottom part of Third Ward, close to 45 and Scott.

How old are you?

Man, I'm 34 years old.

What year would you say that crack came into that neighborhood?

Actually at about 10, I had my first look at it. I actually touched it and sold it at that age. Man, it got real hectic between '84 and '86. It was a real fast transformation from an alright neighborhood to a war zone.

And crack was the main proponent of that.

Correct. Of course you had your marijuana and the same amount . . . you know, the pills and all that stuff. But what really took a toll on the neighborhood and the lifestyles of people was the crack.

Why do you think the crack trade was so different than, say, somebody who sold weed or even cocaine?

Actually, because of the being able to get intoxicated anywhere and the amount of time that it hits your bloodstream, the amount of time that you begin the peaking at the high. I think that made a difference 'cuz, you know, with cocaine you had to go indoors somewhere and do it, get out of peoples' sight and do it. But with the crack,

I mean . . . they do it on the street corner, they do it in abandoned houses. The cocaine was more of a party drug, and you had to live the lifestyle, you had to have the wine or the expensive liquor, and you had to be at an inside party somewhere. You know, with the upper echelon of people. And crack was more of the lower echelon. And you had them anywhere. I mean you could sell it anywhere. In the alleyways . . .

Some say that the reason you had such a problem with crack in neighborhoods like that is because it just kind of went uncontested. That it wasn't really policed.

Of course a lot of people didn't know what it was, or know what was going on. It was kind of like a secret society thing. It spread around like wildfire because of that. I mean, everybody knew of the cocaine, everybody knew of . . . I guess you would call it freebase at that point in time, but once it got around for a normal person to create it, man, it was ridiculous.

So what was the economy like in the neighborhood at that time?

Actually if it wasn't for the crack, I probably never would have seen the downside of the neighborhood. I never woulda lived in the bad part of that neighborhood. We went from maybe a $265,000 home off of North MacGregor, minutes . . . maybe 45 seconds away from Carl Lewis's mansion. And a couple of more . . . you look at people like Debbie Allen and Phylicia Allen—or Phylicia Rashad—they grew up in Third Ward, they grew up in my neighborhood, and they ended up buying mansions off of North MacGregor. So, coming from that side of the neighborhood to our house burning down and having to move to the ghetto side of the neighborhood, it was real. You know, for a kid, I didn't really understand what was going on. It was a real stunning event, and as I grew older I was able to see what it was. I actually thought we just foreclosed on our house—our home got burnt up and we had to foreclose on it—but it was actually due to my mother starting a hectic drug habit. A $300 to $400-a-day habit, and me being a 10-year-old kid

. . . I went from the kid that everybody wanted to play with my toys and visit my house to being the kid who doesn't have any toys, who don't have any food. It was widespread. Nobody cared. I mean, it was actually like the police policed for neighborhood crime such as burglary, rape, car theft, stuff of that sort, because the drug peddlin' was always . . . it was like they policed it, but they watched . . . they just kept on goin'. They kept their nose out of everybody's business.

But it wasn't just something that was on the streets. By your own contention with the story about your mother . . . it was trickling into the households.

Oh, it was into the households! Now, don't get me wrong—we went from a $265,000 house, and my mom was running my grandmother . . . my grandmother had a funeral home that was in Third Ward called Jackson Funeral Home, that was in the Third Ward area since 1911. So it's been passed down from generation to generation, and my mom was actually the owner and she did the embalming and the directing. You know, you had the funeral director, she did the directing, and no one in their right mind believed that . . . "Oh, she own her own business." She has this predominantly black-owned business that's been here for almost a hundred years at this point. For her to be on drugs, it was like, "Nah, she not on drugs—she has this business, they have limousines, they have a nice car, nice house." But some way, somehow, some fashion—I don't know if it was one of my mom's new boyfriends or what . . . a party, I don't know what happened, but it changed drastically. And of course—it was ridiculous, because as I went from 10 to 15, me and my friends were actually . . . I would sell one of my friends's mom drugs and he would sell my mom drugs, so we wouldn't do it to our own parents. It was ridiculous. And . . . you know, after . . . that was 10 to 15, you know, we're kinda young, we're gettin' used to what's really . . . we're catchin' up with reality and after 15, 16, 17, 18, I was like, "Okay, I have this guy in my mom's house because my mom owes him money—he's runnin' my house." And at that point in time I took a drastic step. I actually said, "Okay, well, this guy's not runnin' my mom's house—this is not a crack house, but my mom does have friends that come to smoke, so I'm gonna get me enough crack and this guy has to leave and I'm gonna run this crack house." It was ridiculous. It made me who I am, but it also hindered me, you know? Because I took a step, and I read the Bible, I read the Qur'an and stuff like that, and I was actually dealin' death in my own house, you know? But it was just so I could have a little control in my household. And me and my friends, man, I mean, we crack jokes about it now today, but we were so young, and we did have feelings. We tried to act hard because of the streets, but we were so sentimental—I would sell his mom dope and he would sell my mom dope, but at that time we did not step across that line and do it to ourselves. After a while, you know, after we grown up and we got hardened by . . . the crack hardened us because we got to see good households broke down, and after a while everybody's like, "Fuck it, I don't give a fuck. Fuck this shit. My life's fucked up, fuck it." Once we got to that point it was like, "Shit, I'm gonna sell my momma crack—fuck it." I don't want nobody else in my house, I don't want my mom suckin' somebody else's dick for no rock, you know what I'm sayin'? That's the low that it got to.

And it makes you realize how powerful that drug is. It can get my mama. It can get anybody.

Man . . . and of course, I have her in a nice . . . she lives in a mansion in Kingwood now, but I mean it took 20 years to break that fuckin' habit, man—20 years. Now, of course, I didn't . . . I actually took her—they had a SHIC (State Health Insurance Counseling) program in Galveston—I actually drove her to Galveston, got her to sign up. Now, during the crack age, my father moved me. When I was 12 or 13, he seen what was goin' on, and I moved to the Almeda Mall area. I ended up goin' to Beverly Hills and Dobie High School instead of goin' in Third Ward. He pulled me out that circle, was tryin' to get me out of that circle 'cuz he seen what was goin' on, but at that point in time, man, we went from a $265,000 house to my mom movin' into a shotgun house. To the funeral home closing down.

So how did the habit eventually break? For her.

I didn't have anything to do with it. I actually drove her to the SHIC and before I got to Almeda Mall . . . I drove her to Galveston, I stopped, I got to Almeda Mall, I grabbed me some clothes outta Almeda Mall, and before I made it back to Third Ward, you would not believe it, but my mom was already back home. I had just dropped her off in Galveston. So, you know, me, bein' from Third Ward, I'm like, "I'ma stop off at Almeda Mall. I used to live out here, lemme go shopping. I wanna feel good about myself. I just dropped my mom off." And I go into the mall and grab me a lil' something, come back and drive back to my neighborhood and there she is—she's sittin' on the front porch. I took her keys, I took everything from her to try and make her not get home, and she just hitched a ride. At the SHIC, she signed herself in and she signed herself out. And she end up beatin' me home. And I was like, "Whoa." But what made her change was actually—I didn't have anything to do with it, man. It was her pastor of her church. He actually came to my weddin', and he was a good man, man. It was all the church. It was all him. He got her straight. He put her in a hotel for about two months. And then found her a home and I helped put up money for a home and now we got her a nice mansion in Kingwood. I mean, she's not my same mom because you cannot wash away what drugs do to people. I don't care if it's marijuana—I don't care what it is—alcohol. You cannot wash away what it does to people. She's not the mom that I used to have, but she's a better person. She maybe smokes cigarettes now, maybe drink a beer here and there, but no drugs. It wasn't my power. It was the power of the Lord, man, and her pastor. She's been to SHIC three or four times, she's been to the penitentiary before . . . all behind crack. And it's changed now because, you know, I don't know too many 60-year-olds doin' drugs, but you know . . . I don't know if it's her getting old or the pastor or a combination of things, but I got her in a mansion, and I'm proud of her now. We grew up. And I'm good with that.

What perspective did that give you, seeing that from such a young age? Did you ever get hooked yourself?

No. No, never.

Why do you think you didn't? I mean, did you try it?

Nope, nope. Never. I actually . . . now, during my heyday . . . she taught me how to cook it myself. Of course she taught me the right way, to cook the best—so she taught me how to cook it and cook it and cook it, and during all the chaos, maybe there's a time or another I'd do the Tony Montana—I'd try to inhale me some. And I didn't get hooked. Man, it was just something I was doin' because I was buyin' a lot of powder and I had to cook it up and I'd just . . . I'd sniff me some and then go ahead and cook it, but it never became a habit. I never did it more than three or four times. Of course I smoke weed, sip syrup, but other than that . . . cocaine—I seen what it done to my family so I couldn't do it.

So in Third Ward at that time, when you were coming up in '84, '85, '86 as a young teenager— were there options for jobs at that point, or was it kind of understood that selling was a way out? Or a way in?

It was the thing to do, man. If you was a young teen and your household didn't have income, you had no choice.

No other options.

No other options. I had no other options. I mean, I tried sackin' groceries early. They let me sack groceries early. You know, I got a job at Kroger when I was like 14, sackin' groceries. But that was only just to get me started in the dope game. So I worked there two or three weeks, get my check, take that check, go buy me some drugs. Now of course, mind you—I could have actually tried another route, but me bein' an average inner city kid, I said, "Okay, this is the route I'm gonna take because it's the easiest route right now, and nobody's makin' $1,200 a day."

Is that how much you made selling?

Yeah, when I was a kid I was makin' like $1,200 a day. Of course, I wasn't doin' anything with it. I would end up having to right the shit with my mama's rent man. Other than payin' bills and keeping the lights and stuff on . . . I mean, it taught me a lot of responsibility. I'm 34 years old now, but I been livin' at home since I was, like, 19, I had an apartment at 17. It taught me payin' bills. It taught me responsibility. As well as a whole lot of negative shit.

So when did rap come into it for you?

Now, of course, me bein' the kid that I was, I went from havin' a mother and father in the house-hold—my father was probably makin' a hundred or better, my mother was probably makin' a hundred or better—I was spoiled. So before my teens, I really had nothing to trigger me to write poetry or to write my feelings on paper. Now, when all of this came in, that was when I was like, "I need to write some of this shit down because I've seen enough," you know? I watched my mom and my dad get divorced. I watched the home that I grew up in—I'm supposed to be comin' home from college to visit—I watched that get washed away. I watched my brothers who played sports lose chances of havin' scholarships and that type of thing because of my mama's not bein' able to be a parent, you know? My father had to come kidnap me and my brothers from my mother to come and raise us in the Pasadena School District area. That actually helped, but it always made me run back to Third Ward, run back to Third Ward. And it just got ridiculous. At 13, I got introduced to poetry through school, right? So I broke the stanzas down to bars, I broke the bridges down to the hooks, you know, I used the whole of poetry to learn how to do my rap. I actually . . . in sixth grade or seventh grade we had a talent show, and I actually used something that I got . . . a poem out of a book, I actually revised it, or what we call a remix, and actually made it into a rap and performed it at a talent show, and every-body went crazy, and I was like . . . "Either I have a gift or I'm pretty good at this thing or . . . everybody just wants somebody to entertain them." So at 10 years old, I had on my Run–D.M.C. Adidas sweat suit, my Adidas shoes, and I did a talent show at school. And then following school, the school talent show, I did a talent show at a summer camp at the YMCA on Wheeler next to TSU. And after those two talent shows—I actually won—I said, "Okay, well, maybe I caught something. I learned how to write raps through poetry here," and now I'm in seventh and eighth grade in English class, and I'm not doin' English. I'm writin' raps. It became habit. From, like, seventh to ninth grade I was just writin' raps. Just writin' raps, writin' raps, now in the ninth grade. Because I was still in a nice area. Now if I was still in Third Ward, I maybe never woulda seen a studio, you know?

What area were you in at this point? You're talking about down by Almeda?

Yeah, I lived off Sagemont in the Kirkwood area. I lived, like, off of Beamer and Blackhawk. Now, bein' in that area, in that neck of the woods, I happened to run across the wife of a Hispanic friend named Noah, and he has a whole fuckin' studio in his house. He's in high school, he's the drum major of Dobie High School, and of course he knows music—he's the drum major—he actually plays some instruments, but he was so talented that he didn't need an instrument. He was the drum major. He had a studio in his house. And then I met this other kid who lived in Deer Park, and he was, like, maybe . . . I was in ninth grade, he was maybe in seventh grade. And this guy was a fuckin' . . . he was a musical wiz, but he kinda screwed up his life. He went to jail and stuff like that. But I had the chance to actually work in studios as a kid and to start payin' for studio time with the money I was makin' at my mom's house. I was spending twenty dollars here, studio time, fifteen dollars here, studio time. And it helped me become who I am now. I learned a lot about the music business as a kid. I managed my own group at 15 years old. We had the club called Metronome that was behind Almeda Mall. They had one behind Almeda Mall and one on Gessner. They was teen clubs then. I would walk in a teen club, find the owner/ manager, tell 'em I had a group, tell 'em I wanted to perform. And it was crazy 'cuz I was a kid, and I used my grandmother's funeral home limousine. [Laughs] I used the limousine from the funeral home, I used the music we got from the studio, and then we'd go to the lil' small teen clubs, perform, we'd have a limo outside waitin', I'd get 33 percent of the door. And as a fuckin' kid, I'm negotiatin' with the manager of a club and I'm getting 33 percent of the door. It created somethin'. My little brother, a lot of our friends came to our first concert, and they were like, "Man, it almost looked like you guys were performin' for real!" I'm like, "We *were* performin' for real." But because they know me and we're young, you know, they actually were like, "Okay, you guys look like somebody other than yourself." And that was like the start, man. Ninth grade triggered it, tenth grade it was over. I was spending all my money on studio time. People lookin' at me like, "You're a fuckin' kid—where you gettin' all this money from, and why are you spendin' it on music? Shouldn't you be buyin' a bike? Or somethin' of that sort? A remote control car?" But I seen so much as a kid, and I lost what I had, that I felt like I had to give my story and tell a story about how your life can change or how you should keep your head up or, you know, this is how it is as a kid comin' up without a parent. And my father actually passed away at that time.

Wow. Right at that same time, huh?

At that same time, so my mom was on drugs, my father passed away, and I was like . . . I already started my little music venture, but it was like . . . there was no light at the end of the tunnel at that point.

You take a deep breath and say, "I gotta do this."

What do I gotta do, you know? My father passed away two weeks before Christmas. And there it was. I had—like some pastors and some reverends—now I have testimony. I've lost everything. I was the spoiledest kid I've ever known. I've lost everything that had me in that position. My father's gone, my mother's smokin' crack. I will never be that spoiled kid again. I feel like I had a story. I talked about my dad passin' away. I talked about my mom bein' on drugs. I talked about me livin' in the street, sleepin' at bus stops, sleepin' in my potnah Grace's dad's car. And then I actually . . .

this is when the trouble starts, because when I lost my father, I was angry at the world. Because he was a genuine man. He had a lot of money, he had a good heart, and he would take me to the mall and buy my friends tennis shoes. That's the type of money he had. If you accidentally got in the car with us and we were goin' to Toys "R" Us or somethin', you would get somethin'. That's the type of person he was, and I lost that. I lost him and I was mad at the world and I was a dumbass lil' kid. I was mad at the world. So 15, 16, 17 . . . here comes . . . now I'm grabbin' the pistols, now I'm takin' the knives, now I'm at the mall stealin' cars, now I'm shootin' up parks. The clubs that I was performin' in, I'm just goin' to the club now to start fights and shootin' up, havin' fights outside of the club. Man, it got ridiculous at that point. I felt like I didn't have anything to live for because my dad was like my best friend, you know? Mom's smokin', dad gone, my little brother passed away—within two months I had a drastic change. My father passed away December 15, my grandmother passed away January 20, my youngest brother passed away January 19. All this is 1989 . . . well, this is December '89 and January of '90. And at that point I went ridiculously crazy. I ended up bein' on probation. I ended up goin' to jail. I mean, a lot of crimes I was doin', I actually got away with, but when my father passed away that's when the erratic side came out of me, and I didn't give a . . . it was like I wanted to get caught, you know? I actually had $900 in my pocket, and I'm at Baybrook Mall and these kids come out and they're happy, and I'm tryin' to rob them of their happiness. I actually wasn't tryin' to take their . . . whatever they bought out of the mall out of their hands. I was tryin' to rob them of their happiness 'cuz I felt so unhappy, because I was livin' with my stepmom. My mom was on crack. My dad was dead. I felt like nobody understood me. I stole some bags from somebody at the mall. They came to my school, took me to jail, and that beginned my criminal career because without that small lil'—me catchin' the theft case and bein' put on proba-tion—I probably woulda never went to jail. But at that age, I was 17, and, "Okay, now I'm goin' to jail, I'm writin' raps in jail." They sent me to boot camp. I'm on probation and now I'm the crack man, the weed man, and it just got ridiculous.

How long were you on lock?

The first time I went to jail I was 17. I ended up doin' 90 days in boot camp and getting out on probation. After that, of course, bein' on probation, I still didn't learn my lesson. I still was runnin' the streets. My head was hard. I moved to the South-west side. I'm a teenager now. I was 17. Nobody wants to take care of me. I was livin' with my aunt. She was like, "Your parents are dead, and you've moved in with me, you're goin' to jail. I caught you with this pound of weed." My aunt actually thought a pound of weed was like a kilo of cocaine, [laughs] and she said everybody was gonna break into her house and come kill everybody for a pound of weed. I said, "Aunt, this is a pound of weed. I paid for this. It's paid for. Nobody fronted it to me and nobody's comin' to kill me." But in her mind she'd never seen that amount of weed in her life. Of course, my dad and his brothers—they went to Vietnam, so they mingled with weed. They probably mingled with heroin and none of us ever knew about it. But they mingled with weed and my grandparents and all their brothers and sisters knew about it. But she seen me with a pound of weed, and she's like, "Oh, you gotta get out." So I got out and got me an apartment at 17. I supposed to've played on the state team for Willowridge. I'm playin' basketball. I go to jail two weeks before the state basketball game. And shit, there it was. They sent me to the pen that time.

LOS

MISSOURI CITY

The brother of the late Macc Grace (once known as Dat Boy Grace), and a close friend of DJ Screw, he and his brother were part of a wave of younger rappers who joined the Screwed Up Click in the years before Screw's death, with both brothers appearing on a number of Screwtapes (often on the same song). Grace, whose career was inter-rupted by multiple prison stints, is best known for his 2000 album *From Crumbs To Bricks*, while LOS (whose name means Loc'ed Out Soldier) released an album called *Certified* in 2012. This interview took place the year before that, after a basketball game. Grace passed away in August 2017.

LOS AND MACC GRACE. PHOTO: PETER BESTE

So you're the basketball coach?

Yeah, I'm the head coach. See, I used to go to school for basketball. This is what I did, this was my thing. Then when I start havin' my boy—you know, I was fittin' to go to the NBA and all that, man, but my last year of college, I didn't go because I had my wife pregnant. So I came home to be a dad, take care of my business, know what I'm sayin'? Then when I came home, they tried to get me to go overseas and go to the Globetrotters, but I was like, "That's just like the NBA too—I'm gonna be on the road all the time." So I ended up coming on back.

Where did you go to school?

I went to San Jac and then I went on to Colorado. I was All-American. McDonald's Second Team All-American. Basketball was my thing, bro. Music was just my fallback. I love music, but basketball was my first love, man. I've been playin' ball ever since I could walk right.

What neighborhood are you from, you and Grace?

We're from the Southwest. I played ball at Willow-ridge in Missouri City. Yeah, we from Mo City. We did our groundwork in Mo City and then we moved to the Southwest. My brother was fittin' to go to the MLB in baseball, man. Yeah, he blew his knee out. He had blew his knee out and came back home. He was fittin' to go to the Cubs. Grace was a top-notch baseball player, man. He was fittin' to go to the Cubs because his roommate was a pitcher too. He was going to the Cubs to pitch, and my brother was going to play outfield. Yeah, Grace was a beast, man.

So what year was that, that you guys were in college? You guys are pretty close in age, right?

Yeah, we about three years apart. I graduated in '94 and my brother graduated in '91. We both graduated from Willowridge.

Growing up in Missouri City, were there a lot of resources like that, to keep kids out of trouble?

You know what our resource was? Our mom and dad, man. On everything. My mom and dad been married since . . . forever. They was our coaches. That's why we do what we do now, because they gave back and gave us they time. That's all I know is family, man, so I felt like it was my responsibility to do the same thing they did for my boys. That's why my boys play on the team and my brother's boys play on the team. We're giving it back, doing this. A lot of people talk—say they do this, they do this . . . but man, if you spend time and help these kids out, bro, it's more of a high than you can get on any type of drug when you helpin' some kids, man. It's like a natural high. It's just like a good, good feelin', man, to help these kids out. Because lot of these kids are a lot of have-nots. They don't have shit, they ain't got no daddy, they . . . it's hard, but it's fair. And I just be tryin' to be there for them and show 'em a better way, you know what I'm sayin'? Show 'em a better way, man.

When did you start coaching?

I've been coaching for about the last six years. Yeah! This where all my time be, man. I coach football and basketball . . .

What age are your boys right now?

One is my stepson, but I done had him since he was two, and he just graduated. He 18. 12, nine, and my other son just turned three.

You mentioned coming up in Mo City, and it sounds like you had some time in the streets here and there. What measures do you take to make sure that doesn't happen with them? It's gotta be a careful hand, right?

Yeah, it do, man. That's why I be so into it. People like, "Man, how you ever make time for yourself?" I say, "Man, this is myself makin' time. This my kids. That's the problem y'all not doin'. Y'all don't make no time." You know, everybody wanna do what they wanna do—go out, do this . . . If I ain't in the studio or doin' a concert . . . I don't even go to clubs no more unless I have a concert, because I don't have time. All my time go to this basketball, man. This is where it's at because I'm trying to show these kids. You can tell 'em, but when you doin' it with them . . . you know, you can tell anything, but when you show 'em, it's different. That's why all these kids respect me, a lot of these people respect me and what I'm doin', man. It's hard. You know, all this shit costs money. Your money and your time, and your time is one thing you can't get back. I practice Monday, Tuesday, Wednesday, Thursday, Friday, games on Saturday and games on Sunday. Two weeks ago, we had games in Beaumont. Just so happened we had a concert that same night. Me and my brother went and coached Friday, coached Saturday, concert Saturday night, then had a game Sunday morning. It's a nonstop grind, man.

Grace was locked up two years?

Grace was locked up five years.

Five years, man. Did you talk to [your sons] about that? Did that become kind of a lesson for them, things for them to learn?

Yeah, it did, man. It made 'em stronger, 'cuz they love they uncle. Our family is, like, tight, you know what I'm sayin'? My boys and my brother's boys call each other brothers. They don't call each other cousins. They always together. So, when he was locked up, I was doing what he woulda did for me—I had his boys with me. So, when my brother get locked up, they just learned. It made us even tighter and bond even tighter. Like, "We gotta get it." 'Cuz it's like—you not gettin' locked up for stupid shit. We just gettin' locked up to try to take care of our families and better ourselves. It's not to go try to—you know, some people do what they do tryin' to shine and make theyself look good, but man, we givin' back to these kids. And I try to shoot out to some of the homies, man, say, "Hey man—help out. You ain't doin' nothin' for your own kids. Help out these kids, man, I'm tryin' to help them out. Help me out. Help me help these kids." Some of them do. Some of them—a lot of them—say they gonna do something, they don't do shit, man. So I get to the phone. I just gotta make it happen, man, you know? I try my best to make it happen, man. It's a building block, but we make it work. We make it work.

It's huge, because you're building your community. You're building up things just beyond your family.

You feel me? Exactly, man. I'm tellin' you. I got one kid, man, this kid mama just drops him off and leaves him at the gym. If that gym wasn't there, I don't know where this kid would be, you know what I'm sayin'? It's stuff like that that make me just wanna keep on doin' what I'm doin', because I'm helping. Not only am I helping my kids, and my nephews, but I'm helping the kids out in the community that ain't got nothin' else. Mama don't care, daddy—he don't even know where his daddy at, mama just droppin' him off and she do what she do, be gone all day. She don't pay for shit, she don't help out . . . I know she have food stamps, she don't even try to go buy no Gatorade for the team. She don't do nothin' . . . but my mom and dad, to this day, they still helpin' me and my brother out with this coachin' stuff. If I'm on the road and I need something, they got me. If I need some help for the players there, they got me. It's a trip, but that's how it is. I wouldn't change it—because I hear a lot of these rappers, my potnahs, they be a little better just because circumstances . . . they had one hot song or one hot verse here or there, buy they not doin' nothing to help give back!

How different do you think it would be if Screw was still around?

It would be so much different because there was one thing he did, man: He didn't talk it, he walked it. His heart is how he treated everyone. He treated everyone with love. There wasn't no jealous bone in his body, there wasn't none of that, man. It was nothin' but love. That's how me and my brother was raised up, and that's why Screw loved us like he did and called us his brothers. That's why he came to our house every Sunday with our mom and dad, and we would have dinner. He wouldn't even do nothin' on Sundays but just chill as a family. We was tryin' to reach that out to everybody. Some people got it, some people did it for the moment, and once he gone people just started goin' here, there . . . know what I'm sayin'? People say, "Why did Swishahouse do it but the Screwed Up Click didn't?" Because Swishahouse stayed together and they did the business part of it. We didn't do the business part. It's not like they better than us or we better than them—I don't even like to do that no more because people say you hatin'. It's not hatin', it's just the facts, man. Screwed Up Click is what built Houston, besides Rap-A-Lot Records. We was the next thing coming. We was everything everybody was mimicking . . . but we didn't take care of our business right. We wasn't on the internet like Paul Wall and them. Of course, we had a lot of people gettin' incarcerated. Because we wasn't just rappin' just to be rappin' it. Most of the time what we was rappin' about was our real lives. Living that life situation, that's what happens. We would lose someone for two or three years here . . . someone would get killed. That's just how it went, man, but it wouldn't be like it is now, man. Half of these people you wouldn't have never heard of. They'd probably be somewhere cuttin' grass or something. I don't know what they woulda been doin', they just wouldn't have been doin' no rappin'.

When you talk about losing somebody for two or three years here and there, and then you have the experience with your brother . . . I'm curious about your thoughts on the prison-industrial complex.

That's all it is, is a business. They plan is to lock you up and keep you there as long as they can so they can make money. It's all it is, is a business.

Just think of my brother being incarcerated for a five-year stretch. That ain't just nothin' you can just do on top of your head. That's a long damn time. Five years. You know, you can't get back time. You can't get that time back. So, it's just hard, man. Now Mike-D, he been gone for about two years. He and my brother, they ain't seen each other in about seven or eight years. It just be crazy, man. When my brother was locked up, Moe died, Hawk died, Pimp C died . . . all these people died when he was locked up. Pimp C was locked up when my brother was free, and so my brother got locked up, Pimp C got free.

And it hangs over people's heads.

No doubt, man. And I don't mean to be hatin', but the few people that did make it, they didn't reach out. Like right now, ain't nothin' goin' on in Houston really, as far as the big scene. They not really talkin' about us no more. But, if the people that was in the right position woulda said, "Hey . . ." introducing you to the right—it's all about who you know, and when you know the right people, you get into that mix. Because we've got talent, man. You know that. It ain't no way it's still not supposed to be . . . you know how it was three, four years ago, right when my brother got locked up, Houston got real hot. And he was gone. That loss right there—that really hurt me. I was emotionally like, "I don't even wanna mess with music no more." But when he came back, he lit the fire back under me. Because I was working on an album when he was locked up, but it was deep. I was like, "This album might be too deep for these people to even be able to relate to me." I get people to this day be like, "Man, why ain't you drop that?" I'll be like, "I don't know, man." I need to put it out there, though, man. I need to put it out there. But when my brother came home, everything he dropped, I was in there. In there. In the music, and just lovin' everything about music. Z-Ro had me in there workin' a little bit. Mike-D had me in there workin' a little bit, but there's nothing like working with my brother, you know what I'm sayin'?

When your brother got out of prison, I'd never seen anybody work that hard, like with Pimp C.

Yeah, man, workin' nonstop. Nonstop, man. Nonstop. I wish Pimp C woulda been here. Because if Pimp C woulda been here when my brother came out, it woulda been different for us right now. It'd have been different right now. They was reachin' out to each other when my brother was locked up. He told my brother, when he got out he ain't got nothin' to worry about, man. There just be so much goin' on that the world don't know. It just be crazy. The opportunities just got shut down. When Pimp C died, a lot of stuff died with him. When Screw died, a whole bunch of shit died with him. It's just a trip. It's just a trip, man. I just keep believin' in that man upstairs and just keep on pushin', man. Just keep on pushin', and just know it's gonna happen for us because we got it in this light. People who don't even know us be like, "Man, why are y'all not where y'all supposed to be?" I say, "Man, it's coming." Opportunities. It's just opportunities, man.

Southside Playaz

SOUTH PARK/THIRD WARD/HIRAM CLARKE

Southside Playaz were a group that formed in the late '90s and featured rappers Fat Pat, Mike-D (a.k.a. Bosshog Corleone), and Mr. 3-2 (a.k.a. Lord 3-2, formerly of Convicts and Blac Monks). After Fat Pat's death in 1998, Clay Doe took his place in the group. Southside Playaz released albums in 1998 and 2000 and were an integral part of DJ Screw's Screwed Up Click. Mr. 3-2 was murdered on the Southside of Houston in November 2016. He was 44. This interview was conducted on Cullen Boulevard in South Park, across from Screwed Up Records & Tapes, with the members of Southside Playaz standing in the street.

MR 3-2, CLAY DOE, MIKE-D. PHOTO: PETER BESTE

When did you first start out?

Mike-D: Man, since the beginnin'. Day one! Michael Price! Thing about it, see . . . Screw didn't start the shit, you feel what I'm sayin'? It was Michael Price and Darryl Scott kicked it off, and Michael Price screwed—Screw used to do his music *fast*, you feel me? We been down since the Broadway days 'cuz Michael Price was like a brother to me. He was a DJ, Screw was a DJ. *Snap*. That's when dancin' and all that shit was in. Parties and shit. But what Michael Price would do, he would slow down the *party*. You feel what I'm sayin'? The whole party. Not doin' it for tapes and . . . you'd just come to the house party and the music slow and you tryin' to figure out what's goin' on, why you like this shit. And then they would be on the corner—one day they was on the corner and the batteries went dead. On Calumet. Muthafucka was playin' slow.

His tape recorder.

Mike-D: Yeah, and when they heard that, e're-body was just goin' crazy like, "Man, we gotta get *enough* of it." You know, Michael Price got killed at a dice game by a mutual friend that he lost some money from. And since then, Screw just took it and ran with it, man. And we took it to the next level. I been there since day one. But the boldest . . . the boldest shit was screwed, you know? When it was just DJ Screw on a clear tape, no rappers, no nothin', you know? For real.

What was it like, the first time you went over [to Screw's] house?

Mike-D: Man . . . like a natural event. Because see . . . Screw used to always come to my brother's detail shop. I *been* knowin' him. It was just natural, know what I'm sayin'? It was always a proud moment to be amongst, you know, your peers or whatever, but we wasn't *tryin'* to rap. That wasn't . . . it wasn't the big record deal shit, you know what I'm sayin'? It was just, "Let me make a tape for my car." I go back into the '90s with the music shit with Lil' Troy, when Scarface was doin' this shit—when he was doin' this shit—'89! This dude here too, Pimp Money. This nigga here [Clay Doe], this nigga here [Mr. 3-2] . . . I'm talkin' about '89, '88! You know? But goin' to Screw house, it was just about gettin' your tape done. Some kinda ways . . . God has this way of workin' shit out that . . . it just became a phenomenon. We still don't know how. That "Hellraiser" song? That's a mixtape that's a straight flow. We walked in there . . . Screw doin' a beat and just . . . start flowin' on the motherfucker, [Laughs] and before you know it, we listenin' . . . me and Clay listenin' to the tape all the way to the . . . when we get back the tape done made it all the way across the city, all across the country. One copy turn into 10, 10 copies turn into 20—just like that. Another time, when me and [Fat] Pat and 3-2 was first doin' this thing, we start recognizing the thing we was gettin' out the tapes, so we started goin' to the studio, doin' our thing. So, goin' to the studio, we ridin' around, we let one of my homeboys listen to it. I left the tape in his car. Six songs on it. "Money Over Bitches," "Turnin' Lane," "Superstar," "Young In The Game," and two other songs—maybe "Hard To Survive" or some shit. That's some old shit. I left the tape in his car, he went right around the corner to Darryl Scott, pressed up about 20 copies, 20 copies turned into 40 copies—before the week was out that shit was 400 copies. Man, this shit was like it was meant from God. This shit is just something else. I guess that's why people be like, "Why y'all haven't done this, why y'all haven't done this?" Because we wasn't dealin' with rappers in the first place. We was just dealin' with street dudes that was just doin' music, was just goin' to make a tape.

They didn't know any different.

Mike-D: Didn't care no different! We had money already. It wasn't no big deal, but the shit came later, and then that's when the division . . . that's the . . . anytime you put money in a pack of rats, it's gonna scatter. That's just how it is, you know what I'm sayin'? You get the money in the equation and everybody get dumb. Screw . . . this shit is gonna be forever. What I have seen is that this shit has changed the culture of Houston. I've seen from the time when people say the people on Suave House Records . . . even Lil' Troy in his earlier days . . . Street Military, the forefathers of the game . . . these guys were really Screwed Up Click haters, you feel me? Not *haters*, but they didn't believe in it, you feel me? There was no belief in it. Shit, we didn't have belief in ourself! Let alone somebody else believin' in us. But you know, you get the, "Y'all ain't gonna make it past [Highway] 288—you ain't gonna make it past 610 Loop with that music," you know what I'm sayin'? And you look at 'em all now, and they have to come back and embrace the music that has influenced the culture. This whole generation. People talkin' like Fat Pat now. People raise the roof all around the world like Fat Pat did when he rode with Corey Blount down the street in that car, you know what I'm sayin'? And that shit has influenced a whole lotta shit, man, and I just want it to continue and grow, bein' the next generation—let them be young entrepreneurs like we were and find somethin' to learn from our mistakes and capitalize, because there's no way that every individual in the Screwed Up Click or has somethin' to do with the Screwed Up Click shouldn't be millionaires. Not to say it ain't comin', but we should already be there. That's our own mistakes.

Where do you think it's going? I mean, you've seen the culture of Houston change, you've seen the rap landscape of Houston change just over the past couple of years . . .

Mike-D: Yeah! It's changin' now! The youth involved. They gangbangin' now, you know? I'm watchin' it change and evolve into the gangbangin' . . . shit don't do nothing but go in a circle. The same shit we doin', our fathers' fathers were doin', you feel what I'm sayin'? All they doin' now is goin' back to the—stick together, without the black pride, without the gang shit. I'm sayin' this shit, though . . . people tryin' to get together because of the economy, and certain drugs ain't on the streets no more. It's not like how it used to be in the '80s. You can't just walk out no more and fuckin' make $4,000, $5,000 on the block no mo'. So they turn it to this gang shit, and that's where I'm seein' the change. I don't know if that's for the good or for the bad, but there's some good in everything and there's some bad in everything. I just hope they find something. And stick with it. And fuckin' capitalize off this shit.

Seems like even the young kids that come up here understand the work ethic that's gotta go into it.

Mike-D: Yeah. Exactly. It's a grind. You got to. That's never gonna change. The struggle got to come before any success, you understand? If they want to jump in the game and be Lil' Keke . . . shit, Lil' Keke . . . it took him 10, 15 years before he got himself to his status he is now. He had to deal with it too. If we'd have known 10, 15 years ago, we'd be in a whole different position now. We had to go the hard way to learn.

You become a different person through it—how different do you see things now from when you started?

Mike-D: I didn't really see too much too different, I just woulda been more . . . I wasn't serious. I knew what to do. Me and Pat—I was the first person to have Fat Pat on—but we were friends, so it didn't matter. When he came and D-Red wanted to do a solo album, I'd do it. Because we'll be right back to doin' Southside Playaz. If it's a move that's better for you, that's okay. Actual contract. I knew what the fuck to do because my big brother Bamino— BAM's Auto and Detailing—he always gave me the intellect part of this game, you feel what I'm sayin'? To have sense with spendin' your money. I was spendin' my money in the studio, buyin' these beats, doin' this here—man, get your paperwork

done. We knew what to do, we was just like . . . when the tape come up missin' incident. Instead of us takin' that publicity and droppin' the album, we take it and try and you know, hold it and not really knowin' what you're doin', scared to release it. You know, I wouldn'ta been as scary as I was back then. I know right now me and Clay came to form LafTex Records—we knew what we was doin', but we *didn't* know what we was doin'. Experience was our teacher. There's no way around that. So, the young generation gonna have to put in they work, man, you know what I'm sayin'? And we're doin' a hell of a lot for 'em right now. We've laid some bricks, because there was a time when a Houston rapper couldn't get heard in a damn juke joint, let alone a coliseum. Oh yeah. For real. Street Military is some of the hardest individuals, let alone as a group in the rap game, and they wasn't getting they respect due. They was sellin' 10,000, 15,000 bullshit records, you know what I'm sayin' . . . when they shoulda been sellin' millions.

They really were ahead of their time.

Mike-D: Yeah, Street Military was ahead of they time. That's who gave us the rap part of it. Street Military, like Z-Ro say, "The South Park Coalition is our fathers." That's the beginning of us, but we had to deal with them same niggas hatin' when we was tryin' to get in the game too.

That's part of the game, though, isn't it?

Mike-D: Yeah, it is! Nobody wanna see the young bull come and take over. You know? That's just life. Nobody wanna see that. But, that's where the shit gotta change right now. The young . . . y'all been all, "I'ma come down, I'ma come through," in your rap, but you gonna have to find *you*, and then let us co-sign that, and then that's gonna be okay.

Clay Doe: Street niggas, real niggas . . .

Mike-D: There's dudes that got in the industry pretendin' to be street.

Clay Doe: Street cats know the laws of the street. They know you can't just slide up . . .

Mike-D: Without acknowledgin' the muthafuckas who blazed that path.

Clay Doe: If you're a street cat, you know how to maneuver in the streets. Some of these dudes ain't street cats, 'cuz they don't know how to maneuver in the streets. And they know if you put some real street cats on, they gonna roll they ass over, and that's just all there is to it. Muthafuckas don't wanna see they shine get whooped. Now, don't get me wrong—there's some muthafuckas look out—like some of them South Park Coalition and fuckin', Kay-K, Lil' Flea. Some of them muthafuckas looked out for us.

Mike-D: Street Military! They came back when we was startin' to get on—Southside Playaz—they knew what it was. There was no stoppin' the bowlin' ball anyway. We was mo' than honored to have the niggas on there, but they was so proud that they ran to the opportunity to come and get on it.

Clay Doe: They knew street movement, and they was street niggas knowin' the street movement.

You can't learn it in reverse.

Clay Doe: You can't *learn* that shit in reverse. There's motherfuckas tryin' to be gangstas after they became rappers. You can't do shit like that. If you's a gangsta, you can turn a rapper, but you can't be a rapper and turn a gangsta. Because, if you dig, motherfuckas gonna be touchin' your ass on the street like a bunch of these rappers be gettin' dunked. 'Cuz the motherfuckas that's turned rappers, they done got an image behind 'em and a coupla million, and now all the sudden they dressed up in costume tryin' to be gangsta. That shit is weak, and real street niggas can recognize that off the top. That's for real. The Southside Playaz—Mike-D, 3-2—we street cats. I met Mike-D in the streets. That motherfucker happened to rap, and I just happened to fuck around with rap. I wanted to be a CEO, he wanted to be a rapper and a CEO, that's how we just end up fuckin' around with each other. But that motherfucker knew me from doin' shit in the streets and was askin', "What the fuck is he doin'?" And vice versa. And we end

up linkin' like that. Some of these cats, man, they groups put together by the executives or the PR people . . . that shit ain't gonna work with straight down day one niggas. We down day one niggas. In the street, if we didn't make one rap or we ain't write one line, we still was gonna be every day linked together, you know what I'm sayin'? And that's why all these years, we still fuckin' with each other.

When was it that you met Mike-D?

Clay Doe: Shit, man, I couldn't even tell you. All I know is probably it was before '95. We met through a mutual friend of ours. And we end up just kickin' and shit or whatever, you know what I'm sayin'? And both of us was young dudes . . . you know, young bosses in the hood. Third Ward. He heard I was certified in the hood. I heard he was certified in the hood. We was leery about fuckin' with each other 'cuz that's how street cats is. But eventually we end up linkin' up, and next thing you know we every day fuckin' with each other. 'Cuz I recognize him bein' a real cat, he recognize. So then I end up meetin' cats like 3-2 through him, I end up meetin' Pimp Money through him, Fat Pat through him. But I already knew people like Big Moe, Pokey, and Screw. So we end up just fuckin' with each other 'cuz we was all just associatin' with the same people. Eventually that was gonna happen anyway.

What's a memory that you have of Screw?

Clay Doe: Man . . . Screw. I met Screw through a potnah of mine and his. They used to live together way back in middle school or whatever. We didn't even know that Screw was *Screw*, you know. *He* didn't even know that Screw was Screw. But we end up meetin' him one day. We was all together in a meetin', we got to kickin' it, he got to kickin' it with me, Screw got to noticin' that everybody knew me and a few people knew me from Third Ward, like all the S.U.C., Third Ward people. And then I was tellin' him that I wanted to, you know, be an executive in the rap industry. So he start givin' me pointers, publishin' pointers, lettin' me know what points was. Eventually he was seein' I was serious with it, so eventually he just wanted me around him, so he just start pullin' me in every time I go over maybe just to get a tape. He would sit me down, lock me in the house and wouldn't let me leave. And that's how we end up havin' a friendship. He was always just serious about it, and I was just like a pupil. I was his pupil. If he knew that you was serious about it, he was gonna give you all the information he had, whereas a bunch of bullshit muthafuckas keep it for theyself.

Mike-D: For free!

Clay Doe: He kept it so 100 off the top that he saw I was serious about it and he brought me in, he taught me stuff, and then every opportunity he had to work with me, he worked with me. And then Fat Pat and Mike-D, just every time they wanted to come in Screw house, they got to come in Screw house. So I'm ridin' with them, and eventually I'm in Screw house every day. But we street cats runnin' in and outta Screw house, know what I'm sayin'? He wanted us to stay still—we runnin' in and out his house, bein' street cats. He kinda had a love for us like that, for the fact that he was tryin' to look out for his little brothers. He was tryin' to show us.

Mike-D: And people say like . . . even I be mad at him sometimes, I be like, "Man, we'd be so far if we'd just been mo' *business*," but that wasn't him. It wasn't about that with him. He wanted to show you another way so you can do it. *You* do it! You can do it! I got your radio station right here. This is a fuckin' radio station right here: 97.9 Screw . . . The Box. Any time you drop a tape it's like a fuckin' Monday night, you feel me? On the radio. Friday night on the radio, man. There was no better way to promote than the way he had it.

It was like a broadcast.

Mike-D: It was a broadcast. It's just like FM radio is now, or underground radio like that, that's how Screw shit was. I tell you what—you ask C-Note who showed him what to do. Ask C-Note who showed him what to do. When I seen C-Note do it?! We seen C-Note?! I was like we fittin' to *do* this shit!

3-2: I just got him down live at five with it. Kickin' it, havin' fun, makin' a CD. You know what I'm sayin'? Getting down behind the gates. After hours.

How long would you guys stay in for a session?

3-2: We'd stay all night. 'Til the break of dawn. Then sometimes up through the mornin'.

Mike-D: You gotta remember back then when beepers and shit . . . there wasn't cell phones and all that shit. Toward the end we had cell phones and shit.

So you could get lost in there.

Mike-D: You keep a roll of quarters in your pocket. So you get locked in that house, you in that bitch. There ain't no goin' out . . . if you leave, he be lookin' at you like, "Where you goin', muthafucka?" You don't just fuck with . . . you gotta be somebody. You gotta be a Clay Doe or a Mike-D, 3-2. You gotta be somebody that's somebody to run in and out this door. If you bullshittin', you fittin' to get out there . . .

3-2: Bullshit niggas get kicked to the wayside . . .

So he would lock you all in?

Mike-D: He fuck with street cats, and he ain't want cats runnin' in and out his house. He was straight like that.

3-2: Write your list down, all the songs you wantin' . . . and you kick it with Screw all night long 'til the break of dawn, 'til the mornin' come. Get your tape made. Then you move around, go get you some breakfast and lay down . . .

Get up and make another tape.

3-2: Make another tape next week, next month. Same ol' thang. Pretty much. To sum it up. Sum it up.

Clay Doe: A lot of the motherfuckas you talk to don't know half the story. They gonna know how shit is, but they don't know *why* shit is. We could tell you everything.

When did you get started? It was in the '80s, right? Convicts was early '90s, but . . .

3-2: It was like '88 . . . I think it was '86.

What were you listening to back then?

3-2: EPMD, Rakim, KRS-One, Big Daddy Kane. Ghetto Boys, Raheem, Royal Flush, and other groups that Rap-A-Lot made.

That would have been the original Ghetto Boys too, with Raheem?

3-2: Raheem. *The Vigilante*. Ready Red.

Jukebox.

3-2: Jukebox, Ready Red.

What were the Ghetto Boys like live when you saw them back then?

3-2: They played at the Rhinestone Wrangler.

What was that like?

3-2: Rhinestone Wrangler? That was the club. Where everybody performed.

What do you remember about it, when you would go in there?

3-2: Me and Scarface, know what I'm sayin' . . .

He was Akshen back then, right?

3-2: DJ Akshen. We used to go to the club, kick it all night long. We was really lookin' up to them guys. Lookin' up to them guys.

What's your memory of Face from that era?

3-2: Me and Face grew up together. Briargate. Missouri City. We used to play with lil' race cars. Drive dirt bikes. Mongooses and dirt bikes.

Did you start rapping together?

3-2: We started rappin' then, havin' battles at Willowridge, know what I'm sayin'. Had battles at Willowridge. I was skippin' school. That's when I first got in the Convicts, me and Big Mike. Me and Big Mike made the Convicts album here in Houston, then we moved to California. Went out there to Death Row.

You were working on a deal with them, weren't you?

3-2: Yeah. We was messin' with Dr. Dre and Suge Knight. We never put the album out. We came back to Houston, I did the Blac Monks . . . Awol, Da. *Secrets of The Hidden Temple*.

So what happened to the Convicts at that point?

3-2: We broke up and I did my solo project. 1995. Did a video, "Comin' Down." '95, '96. Later on I got off Rap-A-Lot and got with the South—Screwed Up Click, DJ Screw.

So what did you think about those guys when they came around? You had already been around a while.

3-2: I met DJ Screw at Club Boomerang. Tony Randle and Victor Bass. Victor Bass was our manager in the Blac Monks. Victor Bass took us to Boomerang to hear DJ Screw, Robert Davis. He had a flattop then.

He was spinning?

3-2: Yeah, he was spinnin'. He was supposed to be our DJ, but he was real busy doin' work in the clubs so we end up pickin' DJ Aggravated, of the Convicts. He's still workin' at 97.9 to this day. DJ Aggravated. That was our DJ. And I had—William Ross was my DJ in high school. Def Jam Blaster. He also works at 97.9, know what I'm sayin'? Good guy.

Boomerang was open, like, '92, right? DJ Chill was out there.

3-2: Yeah, yeah. We was doin' the Convicts album, we went on the road from here all the way up to the Midwest doin' promotional shows.

How did those go? Did you prefer playing in Houston?

3-2: Went very well. You know, you blow up on the road, and then you come back to Houston, to H-Town. Do it up on the road first.

DJ DMD

Rapper and producer DJ DMD split time between his hometown of Port Arthur, Texas and Houston throughout the '90s, and was close to fellow PA transplants Pimp C and Bun B of UGK. He also worked with DJ Screw and is best known for his 1998 hit "25 Lighters," which was based around an Al B. Sure! melody and featured Lil' Keke and Fat Pat. It was a huge hit, in Houston and beyond, and a breakthrough moment because an entirely independent song was being played on the radio. The Houston rock band ZZ Top recorded an interpretation in 2012, and DMD recorded a response track to his own song called "25 Bibles," reflecting his conversion to Christianity in 2002.

You said you came to South Park in 1992. What was it like? What were your impressions of South Park as a community?

I mean, it was ghetto. Where we stayed in, we were with some street cats, and they put us up in an apartment—if I'm not mistaken we started out in Truxillo near U of H, and then we end off in some apartments . . . you know, it was projects! Low-budget, roach-infested. But I didn't care. I was young, not long out of high school, and I just wanted to make music. And I've always been the type of person where I could get along with just about anybody. That's one of the reasons that I was able to hang with street cats and be around them and not be worried. I just loved making music, so no matter where I was gonna be, I was gonna be happy. As long as I'm doing music, I'm gonna be happy. But the people . . . it was gritty.

It took projects—the area, the community, the low . . . the whole street side of town, street life of things—it was multiplied compared to what I had experienced in Port Arthur. It was a whole 'nother level coming to Houston. I got, I guess, a chance to experience that side of life, on that level. And in hindsight, of course, none of that stuff is good for anybody. I wouldn't condone it, I wouldn't encourage anybody to get involved in that lifestyle, but it was good people, just like there are good ghetto people in Port Arthur, good ghetto people all over the world. But the ghettoness was to another level, and the deepness of their *activity* was to another level. And, as I said, eventually led to their downfall. And unfortunately, their falls are harder than the falls of the guys in Port Arthur, so . . . they on another level, you know what I mean? And that sent us back to Port Arthur. That's on the list of things, I guess, that my conscience was using when I made the decision in 2002, because I saw FBI agents bust open my door, and they raided my record company's clique, all at the same time. So here I am with DEA agents with shotguns in the back of my head, thinkin' that I'm some part of somethin', dope rings. The game was another level! It's a bigger city, there's a whole bunch of other stuff to get involved into out here, and that's exactly what I remembered. The people were cool, but the street life was to another level. And when we went back to Port Arthur, one of the things was that I didn't wanna be involved in that, that deep. Unfortunately, I wound up makin' the same mistakes, years later, and gettin' involved in that stuff, that deep, again.

PHOTO: PETER BESTE

Why do you think it's so easy for people to get dragged back into it?

For me, I was just chasing my music. Anybody who would help me finance my musical dreams . . . that's how I remained involved with people like that. And as you said, earlier in the game, that was really the only way that people in the ghetto could get records made—they have to link up with the dope boys, you know? They'd have to link up with the street cats to have the money to fund studio time, to fund manufacturing, to fund all this . . . 'cuz we were little kids in the ghetto! We can't go to the bank and get a loan to finance. You know, the bank isn't gonna loan businesses for entertainment purposes right now at all. They didn't do it then, they're probably not doin' it now because it's such a speculative industry. But we couldn't find financing, so back then the only way that I could continue my dream was to yoke up with dope dealers. People who wanted to get out of the dope game, per se, but didn't have a legal way to do it—the music was

the option that people used. You know, Master P, Cash Money . . . everybody started off in the street money. And the same thing was in Houston! That's how every label got started back then. That's how every label got started unfortunately, with street money, with dirty money, and then they wound up finding a way to clean it up. That's why I was in it. Now, the cats who were in the street life, while they kept staying in the street life . . . well, unfortunately, they fell victim to the mentality that they had no other way. And when you around that for years and years and generations and that stuff get passed . . . you get to think that there *is* no other way. As big as America is and as opportunistic as this country is, you can be whatever you want to be if you put your mind to it, and there's a whole bunch of ways where you can do things legally. But these cats in the street, in the ghettos, they are bred like that, to just believe that they can't do nothing without doing it the wrong way. And that winds up trickling off into people's music and creativity, that whole mind frame that, "I gotta do the street life in order to be big," and that's why they stay in it. Fortunately for me, I never grew up like that. I was a nerd, single mama. I didn't get involved with the street cats until I was into music in my 20s. So I grew up knowing that—*believing* that I could do anything I wanted to do. I went to college, I was a magna cum laude graduate . . . I didn't grow up like that. So when I would hang out with the street cats, it was, "Hey man, we doin' business—you using me to get out the streets, I'm using you to blow up my music career." But it wasn't about me bein' enraptured with the street life, per se. Not me. But a lot of the cats got involved—some of the hot rappers were actually dope boys who just wanted to get out of the street life using their skills. But problem is, once you start experiencing some success in the music business, they couldn't leave the street mentality alone. And I believe that's still going on a little bit today. They don't know how to separate, "I'm an artist now—I'm all about music now . . ." and, "I'm involved in the street life, I've gotta do this." Man, you can't—you gotta be one or the other. You gonna be a music man or you gonna be a dope man? One of the two, but you can't be both or you gonna split yourself up.

In our last interview I asked you about some guys' faith in God and how some of them talk the talk but they're still acting bad, not walking the walk. You had some thoughts on that.

Well, as a born believer, having been walking with Jesus for eight years now, just my personal faith, and, well . . . that's the faith that we're instructed to, according to scripture. I mean, I understand now why there are people like that out there in the world. I mean, the word of God itself talks about the different levels of growth. We are all growing at a different level, and even if you profess the name of Christ as your savior, you're on a journey as well. And, what I've learned is when people are walking—or talking but not walking—that's either suggesting two things: either they're not really a believer or, number two, that they are just "baby believers," as the scripture defines them, and there's room for them to grow. And this could be a part of their growth process. A person has to understand ultimately that they are responsible for their own actions, and that it's up to them to get their words and their lifestyles to match up. All I know is, I've grown to know that I should definitely not be judgmental towards anybody as far as how they portray their faith. You know, ultimately, we all have to stand in front of the Lord one day, and we all have to be accountable for what we've done and said in our bodies, especially after professing Jesus as Lord. So, if you are a person out there saying one thing, doing another thing, I just wanna encourage people to get close in the faith, learn what it means. There's power in your words and your life matching up. We paint a bad picture for Christ, for God the Father, when we say one thing and we do another thing. That only comes with growth . . . trusting him and learning how powerful, how good he . . . how much he has your back. And I've had to learn that, maybe even in the last couple of months from talking to you. And I just wanna encourage people just to take your faith seriously. You can trust God, you can trust his word, and that's what I'm learning to do, so I'm very careful now of being too hard or judgmental on anybody in that particular walk. It does pain me to see someone saying one thing and doing another. It does pain me to see someone to say, "I love the Lord," and then got B's & H's and negatively influencing other people. It pains me, but it doesn't surprise me anymore, and it doesn't trip me out or offend me anymore, because that's what the Bible tells us—there are people like that in the world. So I just have compassion and understanding, and if I ever get a chance to minister to somebody who is in that predicament, it's just to encourage them to continue growing, growing, growing. Keep growing. And if they real, they will grow. If they won't, well, they'll be exposed later on, and the Bible has a whole lot to say about what happens to a person who's fakin' a front. I just want somebody to know that. You might could fool me, you might could fool Lance, but you can't fool the Almighty. You can't fool him.

Talk about UGK's relationship to Houston.

A lot of people know they're from Port Arthur, but of course they blew up and got . . . people register them on the national or global scale with bein' from Houston. And that's always been fine with them. People in Port Arthur have never really had an issue with it, but they made a huge impact, I guess more so in Houston than in any other part of the country. I been knowin' Chad since ninth grade—in Lincoln High School. Bun graduated from the school that my wife graduated from, Thomas Jefferson in Port Arthur. So, I didn't really know Bun, but Chad and I had a real close relationship from the time he was 15 to the time he really broke out and started really hanging with Bigtyme and Russell and their career blew up. It was the summer that went down. Right before "Tell Me Something Good" blew up, we kinda had gone our separate ways because I was older, I was in college, and Pimp C was still in high school. I remember the time he came back with the music from "Tell Me Something Good." He let us hear it in my bedroom, in a house full of people, and I remember listening—because we're talking about Chad Butler now, not Pimp C—and I remember that, "Man, what are you doing?" you know? Not knowing what was about to happen to this young man's life, "You pretty out there with these lyrics, you know?" At the time, N.W.A. was heavily influencing us. We both were starting to fall in love with Dr. Dre's production. I remember hearing it, not knowing, "Man, I don't know if the world is ready for this, coming from the South. I know N.W.A.'s having success on LA, but I don't know if the South is ready for some . . . some dirty mouth rappers, you know?" Lo and behold, "Tell Me Something Good" hit the scene and the rest is history. I got to watch him transform the Houston scene, man. Before that, nobody was using the 808s he was using, and before Chad there wasn't anybody getting that soulful and singing on their songs—even gangsta stuff. Nobody was doin' that stuff, so it was amazing to see a cat that I grew up with bloom as a musician, do something on a national scale. And then for him to always represent Houston. He was always Pimp C behind-the-scenes and onstage or whatever, but he tried his very best to represent Port Arthur and Houston in a positive light every time he got a chance to—you know, nationally speaking. And Houston . . . I don't know if they ever really appreciated him . . . Houston owe a lot of success to Chad and them opening doors. If it wasn't for UGK, "25 Lighters" never would have had a chance. At the time, they weren't playing independent records on the radio. Rap-A-Lot was the biggest indie, but by that time, they were already blowing up. They were already blown up and their records were on the radio all the time . . . They didn't have no independent underground records playin' on the radio until "Tell Me Something Good" hit, and that was the first big record that really opened the door and made Houston radio pay attention to what was going on in the underground. And that's the real deal. "Tell Me Something Good," when it came on the radio, became 97.9 The Box's number one requested song of all-time to that point. That blew it away. It forced them to have to pay attention to what was going on in the streets, what was going on in Screw's house, what they were already cooking in Screw's bedroom. It made them pay attention, so that by the time "25 Lighters" came, it was difficult compared to the majors, but it wasn't as difficult as it was pre-"Tell Me Something Good." For me to walk that record into the radio station, give my . . . "25 Lighters" came straight from the studio. The version that the song that it's known for wasn't even finished. I was able to take a demo

of the mix of the song, bring it to the radio station, had some guys that were friends of mine and I just left it with them to get some opinions. On my way driving home from the radio station, it's on the radio. And by the end of the weekend, it was in full heavy rotation. That's how supernatural that song was, but it wouldn't have been possible if not for the pioneering efforts of UGK, what they did for Houston music. And they represented South Park. Pimp and Bun B loved Screw and the whole North and Southside cliques to death. They never had beef with anybody. Those boys was adored by Northside *and* Southside cliques. UGK was really instrumental in squashing the beef that we had in the city. You hear about the dirty mouths and the hard-hittin' bass, but they don't get props as beef squashers, and pioneers in the radio market. We never would have had a chance to get our records played on the radio had it not been for Chad and them doing what they did with their music.

Bun B

PORT ARTHUR

As one-half of the duo UGK (along with the late Pimp C), Bun has become an ambassador for both Port Arthur and his second hometown of Houston. UGK was the original signee on Bigtyme Recordz in the early '90s, later inking a deal with Jive and gaining national recognition which exploded years later when Jay-Z asked them to appear on his summer 2000 hit "Big Pimpin'." Upon Pimp C's incarceration in 2002, Bun forged on as a solo artist while "Free Pimp C" became a battle cry for the city. UGK reformed to great critical acclaim upon Pimp C's release in December of 2005 and remained active until his untimely death two years later. Interview conducted at Timmy Chan in South Park for the *Vice* documentary "Screwed In Houston."

What do you think makes Houston such a hustle town?

I think the fact of the placement of the city itself . . . being that it's basically, like, as far as the South is, we're dead center in America, and I think with us being just as far from LA as we are from New York . . . to even think of trying to achieve in those regions, or at least making and taking what you do here that far, it's almost like a pipe dream. For years, nobody ever had an outlet for this type of thing, so the grind was already there. None of these guys ever thought they'd ever get a major recording deal. Most of them had seen people try before them, most of them had tried themselves, and it just wasn't going to happen. So a lot of these cats learned to make what they needed to make happen outside of the system, and by the time the system came into play, they weren't just a new artist looking for a deal—they were businessmen, looking for joint venture deals and distributions. These cats came in—whereas most kids 19, 20 years old come in pretty blind to the game, never having sold a contract, never having dealt with a wholesaler, never having dealt with retail, never having dealt with radio or video or magazines and so forth—a lot of these cats learned how to deal with these things on their own, without help from anyone. No publicists, no A&R, no marketing, promotion department. So that when these things come into play, they know exactly not only what they want to do, but how they want to do it. These cats are going to the promotion department and being able to say, "Well, look . . . this is how we've been promoting this company and the image of this product for the past four years, so if you're gonna come onboard, then this is what we're doing. You need to just play along with it," as opposed to just going to the promotion department of a label and saying, "How are we gonna sell this?" Artists in Houston, more than most other regions—I won't say *any* other region, but more than most other regions—are primarily businessmen first. They took all the fun out of this shit for us here. All the . . . making a record, going somewhere and giving them your demo, hope you get a deal—we did that shit. We tried that shit for years. Got turned down . . . every door slammed in your face. So we just said, "Fuck it," and it's that "fuck it" mentality that gets these cats these great deals, and they can take advantage of the game like they want to.

PHOTO: PETER BESTE

Why do you think it was turned down so long? Do you think that because of the geography nobody took Houston seriously, or the quality of the music?

Well, for one . . . I'm not going to say the quality of the music because we've been making good music out here for years, capable to stand on any level. I think the problem is that when you have a record label based in New York, the majority of your employees are probably going to be New Yorkers. And with them not really understanding the South—the scene, the area, the people, or the music—they're going to be less adept to want to grab onto it and take a chance on it because they don't know what it is. So, it was a lot easier for a lot of these A&Rs and VPs or whatever to sign New York people or to sign LA people, somebody they knew from their area, like, "I'm from Brooklyn, he from Brooklyn, he got Brooklyn hot right now so we'll just sign him. It's easier." For us to sign a deal, every time we have a problem with the label we gotta get on a plane and fly 1200–1500 miles, 3,000 miles just to deal with the issues. So I think geography and how far we were away from the companies, but also just a lot of lazy A&Rs and shit. Just taking the easiest thing, the closest thing to them. Nobody wanted to take a chance on the music down here.

What finally woke them up?

I think the Screw sound. First of all, they knew that Rap-A-Lot Records was putting out good music, but everybody down here wasn't able to sign with Rap-A-Lot. I think the Screw sound and the fact that somebody like Screw was selling these thousands of mixtapes and people were getting all of this big local fame and were starting to get radio fame and shit off of mixtape songs. Guys started to put albums out without really . . . in the beginning most of them didn't really know what they were doing, but they took chances and were selling 40 to 50,000 units based on this type of stuff. Any major label can see that if these guys can sell 40,000 or 50,000 on their own with no real promotion, then imagine what they can do if we put our force behind them. I think the Screwed Up sound probably was the first thing . . . and I tried to tell my label years ago—even with *Ridin' Dirty*, we tried to convince them to put out a screwed and chopped version of *Ridin' Dirty*, and they didn't understand. Shit just took a little time, and I think with the internet . . . the age of the internet made the world a lot smaller and made these distances minute. Literally, there is no 3,000 miles between me and New York now. With e-mail, the internet, and shit like that, it's instantaneous, it's automatic.

Because of what's happened with our city in the last year, and with the fact that a lot of these artists are businessmen, do you think the game has changed for them?

Yeah, definitely. I think the approach is, "You know what? They probably don't like us, they probably don't really feel our music, they probably don't understand what we're saying, and not because they can't but because they don't want to. I'm not even gonna concern myself with it. I'm gonna make my music strictly for the people that I know wanna hear it, make my money and get up outta there." If they wanna try to come down here and use us to latch on to the Southern music buying market, it's gonna cost them, because we're already tied into the market, and we don't need them to get our music to the people.

The artists are wise to it.

Absolutely. Been wise to it. To a certain extent, we had no other choice *but* to get wise to it. If we wanted to make a living off of music then we had to go out there, make relationships with retail stores, and had to make relationships with one-stop wholesalers and shit just to get this shit heard, man. A lot of this shit was done on faith and from the heart . . . just believing what you were doing.

There's been a lot of bleed-over from the newer Houston artists—people hearing one and then checking out the others. Do you think that's going to bleed over backwards and renew interest in the generations of Houston artists that came before them like Klondike Kat and K-Rino?

I would hope so. But you know, these artists, like the K-Rinos, the Klondikes, the PSKs, the Point Blanks . . . a lot of people that I know that are coming back into the game, they've got to do the best that they can to tie themselves in to the younger cats. A lot of these younger cats look up to all of us, so all I did was to go to the cats that I knew respected me as an artist and as a person, and asked them to make music with me and get on their stuff. Everybody's not going to be that easy, everybody's not going to be that receptive to it, but I think the possibility is there. I think being from Houston right now and saying you're a Houston rap artist and if you can get one good co-sign from somebody that pretty much everybody knows is from Houston, reppin' Houston right now, you can sell easily 40 or 50,000 units. Worldwide. And you're an independent artist, all that money yours, man. That's good money, man.

How do you maintain a sense of social responsibility in your lyrics and still retain street credibility?

Well, even in the streets there's codes that you have to go by. And we tend to stick to that script. We honor the streets, honor the code of the streets, and we honor the people in the streets. And the people in the streets change but the streets don't change, and the rules in the streets don't change. So as long as we go by the rules in the street and respect the people in the street doing what they do, they will always stand up for us. UGK has always represented the underdog. There's always going to be more underdogs than top dogs. UGK has always spoken for those who can't speak for themselves. The silent majority. That's who we represent. So we will always be heard, and there will always be this force behind that. A lot of people don't understand, but it's always going to be there because these people are sittin' here, they're hurtin', they're tired, and they're misrepresented, and they want somebody to stand up for it. And that's usually what we try to do. There's a lot of . . . people talk about the candy paint, the cars, the lifestyle, or whatever, but they don't talk about the hardships of the people living the lifestyle, then even people inside the lifestyle that can't live it to the fullest. Like everybody out here doesn't have a candy car, everybody out here doesn't have swangers. Everybody can't afford it. I can afford it, but there's shit I want that I can't afford, so I constantly let people know, "I'm doing alright, but I'm still not where I wanna be." Everybody can relate to that. That's the struggle of the common man, and that's what UGK tries to represent. And the common man, nine times out of ten, is always getting fucked over. So we'll always have that class of people to represent.

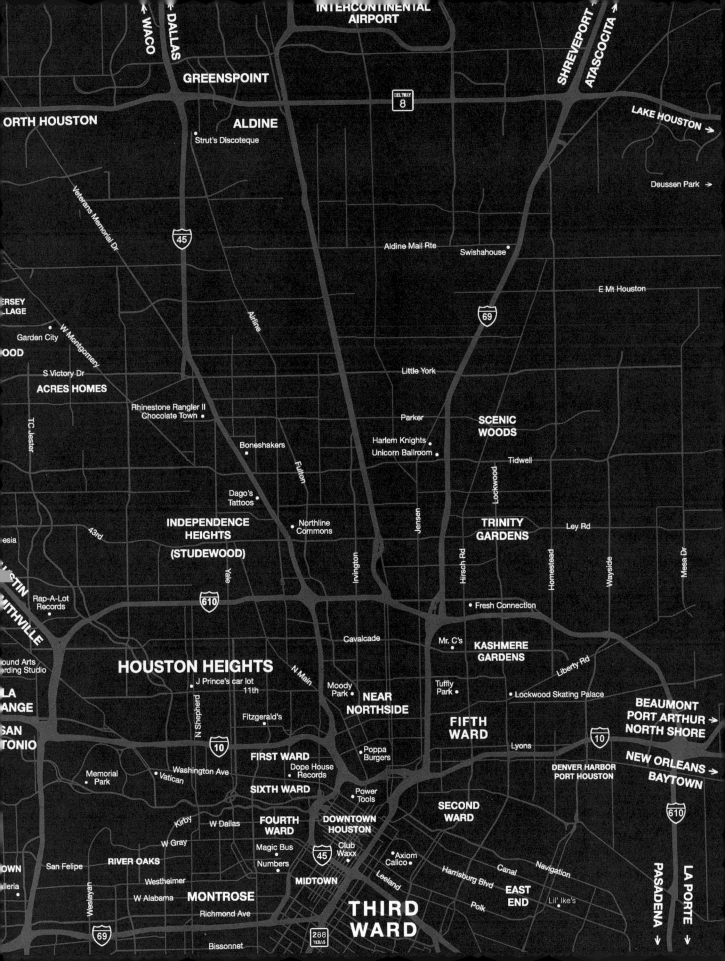

NORTHSIDE

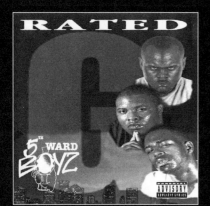

When the 2000s rolled around, great records were still coming out of the Southside. That never stopped. What did happen in the new millennium was that the Northside/Southside beef was finally put out of its misery, and a movement that had been brewing in north Houston for years swept into the mainstream and put the Bayou City back on the map in a way the city had never experienced. And it benefitted every side of town. In the past, records by artists from Houston had made a splash here and there, but this was the first time mainstream hip-hop was interested in the whole *city*.

Swishahouse had built a juggernaut on the Northside, slowing down records like DJ Screw had on the Southside, but DJ Michael '5000' Watts and OG Ron C took a different approach. Their stuff wasn't just available on cassette. It was on CD. It was on the radio. It was for sale on the internet. This brought an entirely new audience to the music. Because for all the dozens of voices coming out of Screw's house, each of them painted a picture only of the streets of the Southside. The Northside was hungry for that sound, too, because it was the sound of the whole city anyway, and their voices soon rose to the surface. For years Swishahouse had been riding its mixtapes to fame through the hands of interns who had come up by running their product primarily on Northside streets. Turned out some of those interns could rap, and they soon started getting *on* those mixtapes. The Northside was making a new kind of noise.

The death of DJ Screw in November of 2000 set off a shockwave that sent the city reeling and the whole world around Screw scrambling. His death would signal the end of an era in that the Screwed Up Click scattered, but it also forced the S.U.C. to define themselves as individual artists in a new light. Life was not the same for them without Screw. The game was different. And then, a few years later, Southwest Wholesale shuttered, closing the loophole that had been such a robust source of income for so many Houston artists.

But something bigger was coming. Northside and Southside artists had already begun to collaborate, but it was the Northside that finally broke through when Mike Jones, Slim Thug, and Paul Wall released the single "Still Tippin'" in 2004, catapulting Houston back onto the national hip-hop radar the next year. A full head of steam had built up for the entire city behind the promise opened up by that song, and Mike Jones's album cashed in on it by debuting at #3 on the *Billboard* charts, followed by Slim Thug at #2, and in the fall of 2005, Paul Wall became the first rapper from Houston to debut at #1 on the *Billboard 200*.

Paul's former partner Chamillionaire followed with his first major label album, and then artists who had been around for years rode the wave, all of them having been in business for themselves long enough to know it was just a wave. When the attention went elsewhere, as it always does, and Houston was no longer the place in which people were looking for the next hot thing, most of them rebounded and remained independent.

On the Southside, Screwed Up Records & Tapes stayed open after Screw's death. It's still open. They had to move in 2013, but suffice to say DJ Screw's sound outlived him. The proof was in the new millennium, when Houston held tight to its roots while reinventing itself over and over, and there arrived a whole bunch of new definitions for the Houston "sound." ✖

G-Dash

SWISHAHOUSE

This interview with the president of the Swisha-house label was conducted for a magazine article on the business side of the label back in 2006. The piece never did run, but this is that conversation in its entirety, recorded after Paul Wall's *The People's Champ* debuted at #1 and just before the planned release of the second album by Swishahouse rapper Mike Jones, who was then in the process of attempting to jump ship for another label. Interview conducted at the home of longtime Swishahouse Art Director Mike Frost.

What did you do before you were with Swishahouse?

I was working for the penitentiary. For, like, eight years.

In Houston, Huntsville?

Nah, I worked at Rosharon, a unit in Dayton, and a unit in Atascocita. That was like a state jail. But you know, I was always doin' this music on the side.

You worked in the industry or were you producing, rapping, what?

At one point I was rappin', like, early in the game. When Watts had regular speed mixtapes I was rappin'.

Under the name G-Dash?

Yeah. I wasn't one of these dudes—you see dudes now, like, 35, 36 years old, been rappin' since they was 18 and had a deal since they was 18. I started sayin', "Damn, I'ma jump on this business side." 'Cuz I'm just not connected to the streets like I used to be 'cuz I'm not a youngster no more. I got priorities and family to take care of, so I needed to start gettin' on the business end.

You already felt like you had a good business sense.

Yeah, most definitely. So I started kinda readin' up on it, and I really got my experience with dealin' with this label shit, dealin' with Southwest Wholesale. We was an indie label at the time, distributed through Southwest, 'cuz you know Southwest was the biggest thing goin' as far as distributorships back then. So that's how I got my game, and you know I did a lot of stuff that other guys wasn't doin'. You had other labels in Houston that might've been lettin' Southwest press up they product? I wasn't lettin' 'em do it. I was pressing up my own product and I was givin' it to 'em.

You wanted to keep everything in-house.

Yeah, 'cuz I heard so many rumors about the bootleggin' and them overpressing, you know what I'm sayin'? I was hearing all kinda shit.

They can do whatever they want.

PHOTO: MIKE FROST

So you first worked with him in the late '80s, when he was doing regular speed mixtapes, then you worked for the penitentiary for about eight years—when did you retire from there?

I retired from the penitentiary in about . . . '99.

And you came straight into Swishahouse from that?

Yeah, and actually, I believe the whole year during '99, I was, like, actually helping Watts out, but then I start . . . like I say, I was already studyin' the game as far as the business aspect of it, so I just put my money in it and we came together.

You did a lot of housecleaning when you came in, didn't you?

Yeah, I guess you could say that. You could say that.

Well, by all contentions, you came in and straightened a lot of things out that others may not have had the foresight to correct.

Really, I'm not the type of person . . . I won't necessarily hang you—I'll let you hang yourself. Everybody kinda, like, was weedin' theyself out. I was coming through, moving forward, just continuing the work no matter who was down or who wasn't, and worked with the people that wanted to continue to work. But a lot of those guys just dropped off. And Slim Thug—he was never signed. So we've always worked good together even after that 'cuz he was always basically like . . . he was an artist on the mixtape scene with Swishahouse, but he was not signed to the label.

So he was paid for his appearances on the mixtapes, just not signed as an artist.

Yeah, and he sort of branched out . . . Chamillionaire, Paul, and Slim branched off and did they own thing, but we still had a working relationship, where they're still featured on our projects. But there was a point, man . . . where we didn't have *no* artists.

Exactly, exactly. They got your masters! So I was like, "Nah, we gonna press up our own shit." And that's why a lot of guys was complainin' about gettin' paid out there. We was gettin' our money 'cuz before I would fill another order, I'd need a check.

So you came in first as a rapper. How early on was that with Swishahouse?

Man, Swishahouse wasn't even formed then. Watts was doin' just regular speed mixtapes. I wanna say that was, like, '87, '88. Watts was like a senior in high school at the time, I think.

He was just DJing. There wasn't a company involved.

Nah, there wasn't a company involved, and actually in the beginning I had more of the company aspect of the game, so I was thinking more of the label at the time when I did come back and Watts was doin' his mixtapes. My original plan was to take the artists that Watts was makin' hot on his mixtapes, but shit blew up so big that we just came together—did the company together.

At which point?

I wanna say it's the point right before we signed Mike Jones and Magnificent. We didn't have no artists.

Because everybody was involved with the label, but not signed.

Yeah.

Had you released an album at that point?

We had released several albums. We had released *The Day Hell Broke Loose*, *Mista Masta Archie Lee*, and we also had another artist by the name of Big Tiger. We released Big Tiger *I Came To Wreck*. T. Farris was just a youngsta up under my wing, actually just helping us out with everything we needed help with. But everybody just stepped they game up to another notch, and he took it upon hisself to go out there and find Mike Jones and Magnificent. I believe they was goin' to college together.

How did T. Farris begin to show you he had an ear?

I guess by him takin' his own initiative and recording Mike Jones and Magnificent, bringin' back the freestyles to Watts, and then he started beat shoppin'. He picked good tracks. I mean he had an ear for pickin' good tracks. We realized that because the first project he really A&Red was *First Round Draft Picks*, the Mike Jones and Magnificent album.

He credits a lot of developing his ear to just being around the label, hearing everything you guys were doing.

And at the time, Watts was more, like, into puttin' his mixtapes out, but I more or less focused on gettin' the projects out, like three, four albums out back to back. Archie Lee and Big Tiger, I was A&Ring them projects.

How did you make the transition from mixtapes to albums? I mean, that's a totally different approach.

That was my focus from the beginning. We gotta get these albums out. If we plan to ever break as a label, we can't have a hundred mixtapes and no albums out. We gotta have albums out to make the transition to a record label. You not a record label if you just puttin' out mixtapes.

Which was the first album? Archie Lee?

The first album was *The Day Hell Broke Loose Part One*. That was '99, Archie Lee was 2000, Big Tiger was 2001. First Round Draft Picks came out in . . . I wanna say the beginning of 2003.

So what differentiated *The Day Hell Broke Loose* from the mixtapes? That you marketed it differently?

Yeah, it was a real commercial project. It wasn't underground. It was a real commercial project with real tracks, distribution.

You were working with Southwest at that point?

Yeah.

What year was it . . . 2003 that Southwest closed?

2003 I believe, because I had to go back and get all our product from 'em, and I believe they had got a little piece of *First Round Draft Picks*, if I'm not mistaken.

Looking back on it now is different because back then it was so devastating that they closed, since a lot of labels had only worked with them as a distribution point, but some now see it as a blessing because they can work with multiple distributors.

I'ma show you . . . this is what's so different about my situation: I was still workin' with other distributors . . . we was workin' with Southwest, and then we was workin' with independent distributors.

You know, you got these out the trunk distribution companies where these guys, they get 400, 500 pieces from you, and they go workin' the streets, the stores, they got an internet set up. You know, the internet is the biggest thing happenin' right now as far as gettin' your product out there.

So it wasn't until after Southwest folded that you began to work with Select-O and Gonzalez?

Yeah.

Because Southwest wanted exclusivity, didn't they?

The thing is, they knew our following, so I told them I wasn't gonna do exclusive with them, and I didn't do exclusive with Select-O or Gonzalez. So I was dealin' with both of them direct.

They didn't allow that of a lot of labels.

Nah, if it woulda been a new label comin' out they probably wouldn'ta let them do it. But we had a track record. We sold records, and you know, that's what they do. They move these independent projects.

Once you started marketing *The Day Hell Broke Loose*, that outsold the mixtapes, didn't it?

Most definitely, but you know, as the years went by, our mixtapes was growin' and growin' because of the colleges and military. You know these kids leave to go to school in California, New York, whatever. They from Texas, they take Swishahouse, Screwtapes, whatever's happenin' in they country. Same way like somebody from New York, they go to school down here in Houston, they gonna bring what they used to listenin' to.

When you came in and became CEO, you took a lot off of Watts's shoulders . . .

Me and Watts both CEOs, but Watts handle more of the creative side, you know what I'm sayin'? I'm more of a business type. I get stuff done and don't let people bamboozle us, that kind of thing.

So what's the structure of the company now?

I got Michael Clarke doin' marketing and promotions, and then we got several people that assist us around the office also. They help us out with the shipping. We still got a small staff, but we tight.

When did the Asylum deal come through? Was that 2005?

I'm trying to think . . . we dropped *First Round Draft Picks*, we dropped *Freestyles 5*, and we dropped *The Day Hell Broke Loose 2*.

That was the first time "Still Tippin'" appeared, right?

Yeah, that was the first compilation "Still Tippin'" was on, and we had also shot that video and got that video up and runnin' before we signed that deal. I mean, we had it runnin' on BET and MTV2. That was before the deal.

That was what sparked the deal then, wasn't it?

Yeah, 'cuz that caused the whole world to start lookin' at Houston, when they seen our culture on film.

It was a very accurate snapshot. When did that video drop—late 2004?

It might have been late 2004.

I know the song was like a year old . . .

Yeah, it was old, it was old. But it wasn't old to the rest of the world.

It was a different beat, even, by the time it was released on that compilation, right?

What it was . . . it was a producer named Bigg Tyme we was workin' with that did a track up under it, but we ended up using the track that Salih [Williams] produced. The one with the violins.

So what all did the Asylum deal entail? I mean, I know it puts you under the canopy of Warner and Atlantic, with the option to upstream artists to those labels—which is what you did with Mike and Paul . . .

It's basically like a P&D situation with an upstream agreement in it also.

So did it mean at that point that you retained control of the mixtapes, and they just took over the albums?

Well, the mixtapes is in the streets. They don't have nothin' to do with those.

They couldn't control them if they wanted to.

Exactly, so they basically just deal with our artists, which are Mike Jones and Paul Wall.

But you're still cut in.

Yeah, on the P&D side, there's so many units it's gotta sell before it's upstreamed. We get paid on the P&D side for so many units, then after that it's upstreamed, and you know, the numbers change.

They upstreamed it right away, though.

Yeah, they upstreamed both our projects out the gate. I mean, because it was hot. We'd been dealin' with these guys for years.

There hasn't been an album released on Swisha-house since *The Peoples Champ*, right?

No, that was the last project we dropped. We got *The Day Hell Broke Loose 3* that's about to drop, and then we supportin' T. Farris with the TF Records thing, licensing our logo to TF Records, and we supporting this whole Lil' Keke situation, and you got other artists such as Yung Redd and E-Class comin' out under that umbrella.

Besides Archie Lee and Coota Bang, are you actively looking for other new artists to bring in? Your roster's pretty short now, isn't it?

I think we good now, man. 'Cuz we got Mike Jones, Paul Wall, Archie Lee, Coota Bang, Michael Watts, and then our extended family . . . Lil' Keke, Yung Redd, E-Class.

Has Asylum tried to exercise any control over who you're signing?

Nah. We don't use their A&Rs. We don't listen to their A&Rs. They can't tell us nothin' about our music 'cuz they don't know this music, man. They sittin' out there in New York in big, tall skyscrapers, you know what I'm sayin'? They don't know what's goin' on down here, so when it comes to this music and our sound, I don't even take their opinions into consideration.

That was never a part of the deal, was it?

No it wasn't. 'Cuz we got a proven track record. We know what we doin'.

What really is the Swishahouse aesthetic? What do you hear in an artist that tells you they're a Swishahouse artist?

Individuality. Don't sound like everybody else. Have his own unique sound. I get artists all the time run up on me, "Man, I sound like this person, I sound like that person." Man, we lookin' for *individuals*. That's what made the whole Houston scene stand out this past year, because it was something different. We wasn't rappin' over the same beats that was goin' around the industry from the same producers. We came in with a new formula, a new sound, and everybody gravitated toward that because they was hearin' somethin' new and fresh, that was original. So it made people key in on that and not pay attention to these people that was doin' what everybody else was doin'.

Houston didn't come to the mainstream—the mainstream came to Houston. What was missing from mainstream hip-hop that Houston was able to replace?

Something different, man. You see the same kinda girls all the time and then a beautiful Hawaiian girl walk into the crowd of them same girls, the Hawaiian girl gonna stand out, you know? 'Cuz she look different, her beauty, her skin tone, her hair. So you gonna focus on her. Everybody else . . . they just beautiful women, but they all look alike.

It's also almost in a way that, because of the fact that Houston was ignored for so long, that the artists here had an advantage, because they had time to perfect something so totally different while nobody was paying attention. By the time anybody else paid attention, everyone had been self-sufficient for years.

But really it's a second time coming for Houston, though, 'cuz Rap-A-Lot did it back in the early '80s, mid-'80s. Really, I feel like we brought Houston back to having a second chance in the game. Houston already been on the map before, with the Geto Boys. That was a platinum group.

There's always been a sort of gentleman's agreement or relationship between Swishahouse and Rap-A-Lot. Does the fact that Mike Jones has purportedly signed a management deal with them change anything, or is that just business?

Oh, nah. It's business with us.

But he's still on the label.

Mike Jones is still signed to Swishahouse, and we supportin' him 100 percent. As far as the business is concerned, if he don't drop an album, nobody makes money. Nobody's gonna benefit from it.

Were you surprised when he wanted to break ranks?

I wasn't surprised, but we don't have no ill feelings towards Mike Jones. He make money, we make money. It's business. This game is 95 percent business.

In the same way it's happened in Atlanta, do you think that a part of the hip-hop industry will begin to permanently root itself in Houston?

It's hard to say, you know, 'cuz if we don't keep hot shit out there, pretty soon somebody else . . . maybe in Wyoming, they culture might step up and all the limelight go to them. You know, this hip-hop thing jumps around, man. I remember one time when New York was hot, I remember one time when West Coast was hot, I remember one time when Miami was hot . . . the Midwest, St. Louis was hot. So to me, it just jumps around.

Do you think that if that national attention goes away, it'll just snap back to the way it was?

Yeah, 'cuz I honestly . . . and other artists will probably tell you this . . . deals have been comin' across our tables for a minute. We didn't jump at the first deal 'cuz, like you say, this whole hip-hop thing was supportin' itself, guys down here moving mixtapes and get eight dollars a unit, whereas up on the East Coast they might get like two dollars or three dollars for a mixtape. But I mean these guys was wholesalin' mixtapes for eight dollars. They wasn't thinkin' about no deal. That's why it took Slim Thug so long to sign a deal. We was already makin' money.

That said, do you think the landscape here has changed now? Do you think that the kids coming up are going to view the game differently than even this generation that came right before them?

I think so because you know what? Actually, now it's flooded. To me, it's flooded right now. There's about a million kids handing you a demo or a mixtape that they done put out. It's just saturated now.

Do you think that's a good thing, that it's going to bring out more talent that you wouldn't otherwise hear?

It's gonna be hard to find it now 'cuz now instead of listenin' to maybe a hundred mixtapes, I gotta listen to about five hundred mixtapes before I come across *that* guy. But usually we like to look at the guys that's out here hustlin' and building a buzz on they own, sorta how the majors do it. They don't just go and pick a label 'cuz they wanna sign a label. They lookin' for a label that's workin' and hustlin' and is buildin' its own buzz and its own movement. So them the kinda guys we lookin' for.

Because every once in a while, those guys could actually be really good at what they're doing—Paul and Cham could have been hustling the way they were and still not have been good at what they were doing.

Yeah, but they was good at what they was doin' and they built a buzz, a fanbase, which caused people to be interested in 'em. 'Cuz you got guys walk up to you nowadays just off the streets and say, "Hey, man, I rap, man. I want a record deal." They ain't been in no studio, ain't made no demo. They don't wanna pass out a flyer with they own picture on it, right?

You gotta have some . . .

Self-motivation.

Do you think that the passion and the work ethic are greater or less now?

I think with some of the kids it is 'cuz I see them every weekend in the club, passin' out they CDs. I see some of the same ones comin' up to me sayin', "Hey G, I'm out here workin'. I'm out here workin'." So some of them, they tryin' to grind it out. But like I say, you got some that—they want you to hand it to 'em.

Mike Moe

THIRD WARD

Mike Moe is the founder and owner of Beltway 8 Records, which he shut down in 2008 after a decade in business. No, he's not from the Northside, but his label came alive in this era and was an active beneficiary of the production and distribution deal with Southwest Wholesale that propelled so many Houston labels to success in the 1990s and early 2000s. Mike now operates a restaurant on the Southside featuring his family's recipes and is a published author. Photo taken next to the Astrodome at the Houston Livestock Show & Rodeo.

Straight to it—are you really retiring?

Yep. I spent 10 years in it, and I just realized I need to build a foundation business-wise on my

PHOTO: LANCE SCOTT WALKER

own back—not on an artist's back. Because artists, pretty much, they're fickle. One day they're like this, one day they're like that, I mean . . . I can't base my future on how another person feels. So I decided to go into two different businesses. One of them is Moe's Family Smoked Ribs and another one, I wrote a book called *Cheat 2 Save Your Marriage*.

What's Moe's Family Ribs? Is that a family recipe?

Well, I been cookin' ribs for a long time, and somebody asked me, "Man, you need to sell those." And I had been lookin' for something else to do to get out the music business, and the light went off, "You know what? I can sell these ribs!" And that's what I did, I started sellin' ribs and packaging up my family secret sauce, started sellin' them, started catering folks, and then people just started ordering up slabs, and I bought a pit. I had a big pit custom-made. It's been going pretty good. I haven't opened up an actual restaurant yet, but I'm about to buy some property on the main drag on the Northwest side and hope to have a spot up there.

So it's a Houston recipe? Your family's from Houston?

Yeah, they're all from Houston.

Barbecue recipes are different in all parts of Texas.

Yeah—of course, traveling on the road, I done tried 'em all. So I kind of know where I fit at when it comes to my barbecue. But basically it's concentrating on ribs, and I got four or five different sauces.

So do you have anything planned for your sort of going away from music? Are you going to exit music completely, you think?

I don't . . . I know eventually I wanna come back. I know right now what I really wanna do is kind of consulting, and I'll still sell my catalog stuff, but the only way I'll come back is . . . I do it as a hobby and not as a living. I want to do it just for a hobby. I think for the most part my whole reason for gettin' in the business was to help young guys get into business for themselves, whether they be rappers or whatever the case is. It worked out, and then there was ups and downs with it pretty much, but you know, after doin' it for so long and then a lot of people didn't just get the idea and the concept. It's like, "Damn, what am I really in this for?"

Do you feel like 10, 11 years ago—did you get into it then as a hobby, or did you have that business sense in mind already?

I got into it . . . I mean, I intentionally got into it as a business. I was laid off in '99 . . .

You had, like, a serious longtime job, right?

Back then I was working at Bettis Actuator Control Valve Company. I was a warehouse manager. I had been there for six, seven years or so. And they laid me off, and I took the unemployment money and built a studio and bought a record store.

And that was in Prairie View?

That was in Prairie View.

So were the artists you were working with then located in Prairie View? Obviously some of the artists were in Houston . . .

Yeah, for the most part when we was in Prairie View, we was strictly dealin' with the Beltway 8 Boyz. And then . . . but we were doing a bunch of production stuff as far as slowed and chopped albums for pretty much everybody in Houston. And so that was kind of my connection. But the Prairie View situation, it was great because I've always been the kind of person . . . I like the music industry, but I don't wanna be *in* it. I don't want to be in the fast lane or whatever the case is. I want to run at my pace, and Prairie View's kind of like the ideal spot where . . . if you come up to Prairie View, that means you wanted to do business. If you didn't come, you wasn't tryin' to do any business. It was kind of out of Houston, you know, 45 miles out of Houston.

Do you feel like there was a certain point when it sort of got out of your hands and you *were* in the music business?

Yeah, I mean, when Southwest Wholesale was open, I was in there maybe four days out of the week, makin' sure . . . because I didn't know anything about the music industry, so I had to actually put in more time to understand it fast. Within probably a year, I was really entrenched in a business I knew nothing about.

Which is exactly the way that most everybody comes into it.

It was cool. I had a smart team around me. I had the things I excelled in and the areas where I was weak, my partner, he picked up on that end. I mean, it really worked out.

So as far as getting your stuff into full swing, it took you two years? That's pretty quick.

When I came into the business, I started makin' money right away. I describe it this way: At the time, you had DJ Screw, you had Swishahouse, and it was like the door was closing, and right at the last minute, Beltway 8 just kind of squeezed through there. We started putting out albums, and like I said, instantly I started makin' money. So that's why I had to learn so fast, it was like, "Okay, I got some money comin' in . . . what do I do?" You say you wanna make money, and then when you start making money, it's like, "Damn, you know, I didn't plan for this . . ."

So you didn't plan for it in what sense . . ."I don't know what to do with all this money?" Or like . . ."I don't know how to plan for what's next?"

Well, it was shocking to me at first, if you will. I mean, you think about it, I'm getting 10, $18,000 checks a month. And I wasn't used to seein' that kind of money from a job perspective, so next it's like, "What do you do?" One of the most important things I did was to invest money in a recording studio, so the studio could continue to make music, and the register would continue to make money. Everything else kind of followed. Okay, we need vehicles to travel in, so we get wrapped vans. So everything that was spent was well spent as far as investment-wise. Back then, what we was doing—we was pressin' up our own CDs, so we needed a CD machine, so we did . . . I pretty much took the whole "independent" aspect and stretched our company to where the only thing I needed to get from outside sources was print paper. Eventually you end up spending the money.

Everyone talks about Rap-A-Lot as a template for things in Houston, for the way in which a label should be run, but do you feel like that, as time went on, Screw and Swishahouse each ended up becoming their own sort of template?

Swishahouse did a smart thing, and their thing was that they made it an organized business. They went at it and they were successful at it. It's just one of those type things that it worked for them, and I look at it this way: the first great idea's great, but it's always normally the second or third person that comes in and makes that product better. I've heard stories of Screw as far as not wanting to be in the distribution sector, and Swishahouse did. And so, okay, well there's a . . . "Well, if Screw don't wanna do it, we'll do it." 'Cuz Screw music was sellin', and Swishahouse was available. Beltway was available.

I've always thought about it this way too—you look at those three examples, with Rap-A-Lot included, and you have three very different hustles. You have three very successful organizations, but they were successful in three very different ways. What do you feel like made Beltway successful in that respect? I mean, you had to have been different than those three . . .

Well, one thing we did was we did a survey before we even started makin' the slowed down music, if you will. And a lot of the complaints that we got was, "We don't like the Screw music, it's too slow." Or, "They don't play the whole song—they just play parts of the song and go on to the next one." So, that's what . . . we gonna speed up things a little bit, and we gonna play the whole song. So we grabbed that market, and what a lot of people don't know is Beltway 8 was more of a production company, promotion company than anything, than a record company. Because there were times when we were on the road for months from here to Canada, and of course our mixtapes got everybody songs on there, so at the time we was pretty much just mixin' the South. But we kind of took the Southern market up to Toledo, Ohio—Cleveland, Ohio and all those places . . . all those areas in between. So that was our niche. I mean, of course we couldn't compete with Rap-A-Lot. Rap-A-Lot had a big history. Of course. They built the template here, and you honor that system, you honor that template. It's like, "Okay, let me just take a piece of the Rap-A-Lot," or, "Let me just take a piece of Swishahouse," "Let me take a piece of Wreckshop," or, "Lemme take a piece of this . . ." You know, you kind of make your own way with it.

You talk about going outside of Houston, venturing outside of Houston—you talk about Ohio and such—how did you reflect on Houston once you began to see the scenes and systems in other cities?

Houston was the mecca. When it came to Southern music, Houston was it. Everybody from out of state—Oklahoma City, Oklahoma. Kansas City, Kansas. Kansas City, Missouri. Omaha, Nebraska.

Des Moines, Iowa. All those routes we traveled—they wanted all of Houston. I mean they loved it. It made me feel good. I remember one time we were at a record store in Kansas City, Missouri—Seventh Heaven, that's what it was. They had a whole row with nothing but Houston music, you know? It was something you didn't get at home. I mean, you know how they say, "At home, you don't get the just due," because everybody knows you. But I remember one time we pulled up in Toledo, Ohio and everybody just going crazy and I was like, "Man, I never seen nothing like this before." You don't know the impact of your music because . . . I mean, we're shipping music across the country, but we'd never actually seen it from . . . a person, hand-to-hand, who wants to buy your music. And then we got home, and it was this awesome thing. It gave me a little bit more fire up under your ass to get out there and do it again, and let's do it better this time. Because they really appreciated the Southern sound.

Why do you think that Houston developed the way it was? I think there are a lot of ways that people think about it, and certainly being in the industry, you can probably speak to this, but maybe less so about the generation you're talking about—part of the reason that J Prince started his label is because Houston was ignored for so many years, but I think being off the radar was what forced Houston to develop its own sound, don't you think?

That, of course, and then at the same time, Houston had an independent spirit. It was one of those can-do attitudes where, like you said, J Prince—people didn't respect us, so, "Let's do our own thing, let's build our own foundation." And that's what happened. I mean, we had no one to say thank you to outside of Houston because we did it ourselves. You develop that sense of pride about your city, and of course the music reflected that. I mean, it's one of those situations where you really take each other's sound—and people really loved our sound, so they started mimicking our sound, and that made us even hungrier and more willing to go out and sell our own music. That was one thing about the Houston market, is that we would go get in the car and sell our music. And that was great—you'd

go out and make cash and come back home and make more music. It's just a different time of day out here now.

Do you think that the idea of the record label as we know it is gone? We grew up during a time where record labels were important because they found artists, developed artists, and curated artists. They are so much less a part of the process now—do you think the idea of the record label as we knew it even 10 years ago is dissolving?

Definitely, and one aspect I believe is that record labels are not developing artists anymore. And pretty much they want you ready to come in and start selling records, and in this case, ringtones or whatever the case may be. Downloads. To me, that takes away the fun of being in the music business. It has turned into a machine. Make the music, put it out, let's see what happens. I went into meetings with distribution companies, and they would say, "We don't care how many records come in, we're going to push them all out." They didn't care how it sounded or whatever, and I think that was one of the most different things to me, it was like, "Man, they don't even care no more." They just wanted to get the music out there and hope it sticks. Just hope one of them sticks. And that wasn't the way I seen it. That wasn't the way I was brought up in the music business. The artists that are coming up, the young guys, they don't have the independent spirit. They want a major deal. And I'm like, "A major deal is cool, you know, for lip service, but at the end of the day, you're not going to make your money." An independent artist that really goes out there and works his project, I mean, he'll make more money than that guy with the major deal. I've never had a major record, I never had a major deal, and I been in this business 10 years, and lemme tell you, my stomach is fat. And I never chased after a major record deal. At the end of the day, I wouldn't want one, no way.

Maybe it's all them ribs.

Man, it was before the ribs. The independent spirit is gone here, and the other thing is that we don't have strong distribution in Houston anymore. We don't have a major record store here and an outlet to sell our music, so we make the music. Understand this: everybody don't have the hustle to go out and sell CDs on the street corner. Before I did it, I used to sit in the office all day, and street teams would go out there and sell it. I didn't know what was going on until one day Southwest Wholesale filed bankruptcy, lost a lot of money.

When was that, 2003?

January 31, 2003. I remember it to this day. I had to go out there and see how to sell CDs, and I loved it. I could sell a CD, get cash right there, and at the same time meet a great bunch of people that enjoyed our music. So you build a rapport with those people, and every time you come back to that city, it's like open arms for you. You can't buy that. A major record label can't give you that.

When we think about where rap music in Houston comes from, we think about South Park, Fifth Ward, Third Ward—you're from Third Ward, aren't you?

Yeah.

One common theme that you find amongst several of those neighborhoods—these are neighborhoods that, in the geography of Houston, may seem sort of abandoned, ignored. Police stay away, municipalities suck. We're interested in some commentary on those areas. You grew up in Third Ward?

I grew up in Third Ward, Sunnyside, and South Park, and Southwest Houston. When you say "abandoned," I think for the most part I go by this theory: Squeaking wheel gets oiled. If no one's calling in to the city about whatever the problem is in that area, then no one's going to come give you some oil. In those communities, when I lived there, if there was a pothole in the street, that pothole was going to tear up a bunch of tires. We never thought about calling the city to come plug that pothole up, so after a while you just get kind of down into survival. I mean, most times, when you're in Third Ward, South Park, Sunnyside, Southwest—you're in survival mode. So a lot of

issues that you would like to see taken care of, I mean, I can't be bothered with that. I gotta figure out how I'm gonna try and eat. Those things come second, third, if that. It's home, regardless of how it looks, it's still home.

You gotta make the best for yourselves in that community, because it's not like the city's giving you any help.

Don't get me wrong, it's nothing against the city, it's just that some things aren't on our radar to fix first. My first thing is to fix the table, with some food on it.

Houston is a series of communities on the outskirts of . . . nothing, really. Do you think that plays into the music too?

When I lived in Third Ward, Third Ward was a community. Third Ward was a city. That's why they called it "Third Ward, Texas." And South Park was "South Park, Texas." Southwest was "Southwest," you know, Hiram Clarke was "Hiram Clarke." Missouri City, "Missouri City." For a prime example, Missouri City and Hiram Clarke is one street across from each other, but you wouldn't dare catch someone from Hiram Clarke claim Missouri City, or vice versa. We're in the same city, but at the same time, you claim your part of town as your city. And collectively, you go somewhere outside of Houston, Texas, of course you scream "Houston," because hey—everybody knows Houston. And at the end of the day, regardless of what it is, Third Ward is home to me. I mean, that's what made me the person I am today. So no matter how far I go away from Third Ward, I still have Third Ward in me. In some of my daily routines I have to go through Third Ward. I been getting a haircut at the barbershop in Third Ward for 30 years. There's just certain things, it's like when you go to Third Ward, it's like, "Oh, I'm home!" And don't get me wrong, I've lived on the Southwest all my life also, but Third Ward is where I was born, until I was 12 years old and moved to Sunnyside. Houston is home for everybody, but we're in our city, we don't claim Houston. We claim Fifth Ward, Third Ward, Sunnyside, South Park. That's just it.

It seems like a lot of Third Ward hasn't changed, either. I worked there for years when I first got to Houston and kept a studio there for years. It seems like maybe that's a part of it too, for Third Ward and maybe the other neighborhoods . . .

Some things, you know, you don't want to change. I mean, some parts of Third Ward are being split into Midtown now, and I'm the kind of person—I'm for growth—but what I found myself doing one time, I was going around Third Ward just taking pictures of Third Ward before Midtown took over. I know economically, in order for Third Ward to grow, there's gonna have to be some money come in because there's going to be some opportunity for people in Third Ward to get jobs, but there's certain aspects of Third Ward that some of us don't ever want to change. I mean Jack Yates [High School] is a monument. I dare you to try to change Jack Yates' name to something else. You couldn't close Jack Yates. The little guys, back in the days, that's where they came from. Their crews, those streets, that's memory lane for them. So you just can't touch it.

But Fourth Ward is almost completely gone through gentrification . . . that's part of the commentary, though, how Houston eats itself and destroys its own history. That's sort of what you mean in a way, but I think certain parts of Third Ward and almost all of Fifth Ward, have retained what they had, and in some cases areas haven't even been touched.

I used to tell folks that back in the days when I lived in Third Ward, I called it the "flight of black" from Third Ward, because you lived in Third Ward because economically, it was affordable. And Third Ward was a black community, and it was a city, you know, and as you begin to make a little bit more money, you had the opportunity to move to Sunny-side. But you moved to Sunnyside, and if you made a little bit more money, and you didn't own a house in Sunnyside, then you moved to South Park. And then from South Park, if you was lucky, you moved to the Southwest. I remember we moved to the Southwest, man, back in late '70s, early '80s, I thought we were *rich*.

Salih Williams

AUSTIN

As the producer of the Mike Jones/Slim Thug/ Paul Wall breakthrough hit "Still Tippin'," Paul Wall and Big Pokey's "Sittin' Sidewayz," and Bun B's "Draped Up," Salih will forever be connected to the H-town juggernaut of 2005. But he is also known for his extensive work with Wreckshop Records, where he produced "Barre Baby" for Big Moe well before Houston broke through to the mainstream. Salih long ago expanded his music and production work beyond the genre of hip-hop, and more recently has turned front man, making blues records under the name Dirty Water. He continues to record and produce at his studio near Austin under the name Carnival Beats.

COURTESY OF SALIH WILLIAMS

When you were coming to Houston in '99, 2000, that's when you were working with Big Moe. Were you ever working with Pat too?

Actually, I never did get a chance to work with Pat. I kinda . . . we did some remixes towards the end, but I came right when Pat had passed away. Moe was over there. Moe had just got signed over to Wreckshop. He was coming basically from the S.U.C.. He was freestylin' on a lot of they stuff, singin'. And I actually got in contact with Reck—D-Reck, Wreckshop CEO—when I was here in San Marcos. I met them at a show and basically, you know, let 'em hear some tracks, and he was like, "Man, why don't you come up?" So I came up one night, actually one night they had a show, and I just kinda got in the studio with them and . . . man, they had just signed Moe over there at Wreckshop, so it was perfect timin'. Actually, Moe was new to Wreckshop and then I was new, you know what I'm sayin'? So that was like the first project we attacked, was Big Moe.

How did you approach that? I mean you had been working with rappers before, and Moe is a rapper, but he's so different, you know?

Moe always looked at himself as a singer, you know. Moe woulda did a Luther Vandross album if he could've. But we were like, "No, Moe, you still gotta rap. You still gotta be street. Gutter." We used to approach it basically just like an R&B project with more of a street edge to it. And then a lot of writers came in, you know, Z-Ro wrote some stuff, a bunch of people just came in to help make his little sound. But Moe pretty much had that style anyway. That sang/rap kinda style. He just came out, you know?! We did a lot of remakes, remakes of just old-school remakes, just changed up the lyrics, kept the melody the same, changed up the lyrics. Pretty cool, man. Worked out, though.

Growing up so close by, you had to have known what was going on in Houston over the years. How much did that history affect how you looked at it—did you feel like there was a Houston sound you had to shoot for?

Well I was out on the West Coast doin' a lot of tracks in Phoenix and LA and everything, so when I came to Houston I kinda brought, like, a little of the West Coast . . . some of the songs that I was presentin' to 'em . . . the way I felt like, why should I come to Houston and try and do what Houston is doin'? I felt like I should bring a new element. So I never really got caught up in the Houston sound, even though it was jumpin'. I was just bringin' something that I felt like I would like. And it was a mix between some West Coast type flavors . . . like when I did [Big Moe's] "Purple Stuff," it had that little bounce. That, plus the carnival kind of symbolizes fun music. That's what I was doin' back then. I would consider us, like, havin' fun. The carnival . . . I don't know why I came up with it, but it just fit. Because some of the licks I used to do on the keyboard just . . .

That's how you got the name, Carnival Beats?

I grew up playing jazz all my life on keyboards, so I've been playin' since I was seven. And I studied different jazz licks. Some of the licks that I really did like had that little bow-bow, and I started to integrate that into my tracks. And it worked out, though! And like I said, I never really got caught up in the Houston sound. I loved it, though. But I didn't feel like I was just gonna come up there and take over. That's not what I was tryin' to do. I was just tryin' to add another element.

And they were open to that, then. It wasn't like they were trying to get you to do one thing.

Yeah, nah, and they respected that this is what this producer brings, and that's what he brings, you know. That's the good thing, you know, a lot of people will want you to bring a certain sound based on . . . because this is what's goin' on, "Man, you gotta do this. You gotta do this because this is what's happenin'." Wreckshop wasn't like that. D-Reck already was takin' a chance on just bringin' in Big Moe and putting out a kind of R&B rap record. Everything was straight hardcore rap then. So he was takin' a chance, you know. He was a chance taker. So we tried different stuff and it happened. That's the key about a label. If you look at radio now, everything startin' to sound the same, you know? Everybody usin' this T-Pain voice, I mean, Lil' Wayne . . . come on, man, let Lil' Wayne do his thing. All the other elements, man. I would blame it also on the labels too, because they're afraid of steppin' out too far in case they don't get a hit.

And people coming out with some really thin tracks.

Yeah. Exactly. Let me tell you, dude. It's gotten to a point where . . . when I signed my deal over at Universal as a songwriter . . . right now I've been doin' a lot of pop stuff, man. R&B. I just signed . . . I started my label, I just signed a guy named Evan Phelps. Even Phelps is like the next John Mayer. This little kid is 22 years old, man. White kid. Phenomenal. Plays guitar, sings, songwriter. So right now I'm not sayin' I'm steppin' back from rap, but I've started seein' that . . . people need to get out there and try something different. I mean just like when I did "Still Tippin'" and some of the Mike Jones stuff back then, a bunch of the record labels would call me and say like, "Could we get a beat like 'Still Tippin'?'" and I'm like "That's 'Still Tippin'. That's that beat. That's that beat, man. Leave me alone." And that's what happenin' with a lot of these labels, man. Take for instance . . . T-Pain come out with a hit. What's gonna happen is that everything that comes out now, all these labels are gonna say, "Well, we need a song like this. T-Pain, he's killin' the airwaves." You know, so everybody out there sound like T-Pain. It's not growin', man. There's no growth right now.

Why do you think people connected so much with that beat?

At the time when I did that track, Lil' Jon was really big. You know, all his stuff was bassy, bassy and in a real club . . . I think at the time Houston was at a point where it was at that level like, "Either we gonna follow this Atlanta sound, or we gonna follow this . . ." you know, whatever sound it was they were looking for. But I think that came at a time, when I did "Still Tippin'," I was definitely not tryin' to make a Lil' Jon track, or whoever was hot at the time . . . it just worked, man. It may have not been the tightest track, it don't necessarily have to be the tightest track, but it has to just stand out. There has to be something unique about it. And I think that's the key, you know, the strings . . . and it just worked. It was cool timin', man. And I always tell people . . . I don't never stand back and say I got the tightest track, you know. I just think that I tried to do somethin' a little gimmicky for rap that people can identify with. Kinda repetitious. But it just was good timin'. The track came at a good time and like I said, Houston was at a level of tryin' to figure out where the rap game fittin' to go. Mike [Jones] had just signed his deal, and Mike was like . . . I was turnin' in records to Swishahouse, and they was like, "Damn, it's cool, though. But we need somethin' like this . . ." And I knew what they was talkin' about. They wanted some Lil' Jon, basically. I was like, "Yeah, man, but I don't . . . I don't do them beats." Lil' Jon . . . every drum he has loaded up on his pad, that's catered to his sound. The drums that I load up on my pad are catered to my sound, you know what I mean? So I have to go in and start jackin' sounds and kicks, and that's not what I wanna do. But what happened, they had turned in the record, and they had, like, two tracks of mine on the Mike Jones record. But they turned it in to Warner Brothers, and they had heard "Still Tippin'," Warner Brothers had heard it, and from what I heard, they told me Warner Brothers was like . . . 'cuz they had got some tracks from Lil' Jon, they had some Atlanta producers . . . so the record sounded like Houston rappers with Atlanta music, basically. And Warner Brothers was like, "Man . . . no, no, no, no, no, no. We want Atlanta groups, we gonna sign Atlanta groups!" You know what I'm

sayin'? And that's what it was. They was like, "Well, what's up with this song? Why does this song sound so different from the rest of the record? We like this. We like 'Still Tippin'.' We like 'Back Then.'" So that's when they had called me. They said, "You know, Salih, we gonna have to go more with your sound." I said, "Man . . . *our* sound." This was for us, you know?

It was an interesting time, Houston exploding in 2005, but don't you think that Houston had its own sort of national stage within Houston before that?

Yeah, the underground. We've always had a solid underground market. Face and them came and was blowin' up at one point, you know, Geto Boys. They had time to really shine, but it kind of died out after Face and Geto Boys really stopped just putting out a bunch of records. But the good thing is that we always had an underground. We always had people that supported the local rappers even if we weren't sellin' nationally or didn't have a major video out or anything. We always felt like we were on top of our game. As far as we were concerned, we were on top of our game based on the underground level. We were makin' money . . . Slim Thug was makin' big money and didn't even have a video out on BET, didn't have no type of major deal. So, cats always felt like we was on our game, but nationally, we were lackin'. And I think Mike Jones, Paul Wall, will always—definitely with Bun and Scarface, who basically paved the way—that gave us a national look. And I think Mike Jones at the time, Mike was like the first platinum-selling young, new rapper who really didn't have a lot of history in them streets. Mike didn't have a big name prior to that, you know, he was just doin' a lot of underground stuff, but he really wasn't big, man. And it kinda made people look at him like, "Damn, man, what the hell? This kid wasn't really . . . he wasn't payin' dues." But he had the right song at the right time, and he had a new energy. He had a nice little gimmick, and he could sell. He could sell.

Going back to the Wreckshop days . . . Screw was still alive when you were with Wreckshop.

Oh yeah. Definitely, man.

Did he chop and screw any of the beats that you did?

You know, it was crazy because I'm sure he touched a lot of stuff, man, because I would come up and do tracks . . . and it was like a job, man, pretty much. I would come up on weekends, and I would stay the whole weekend and just work, man. And Screw would be there and he would have CDs and I'm sure . . . I just never really . . . it was like we never really hashed, man, because he was always there. I don't know, man! I'm sure he touched some stuff, I just could never tell you which ones he done. But I'm sure he came through and touched up a couple of things for us.

Well, did he chop and screw versions of them, though?

Ah, you know, I never really heard nothin'. I never really knew. I'm sure he grabbed some stuff. Screw would grab anything, you know? I mean, I'd have to go back and get those CDs and search all the crates. I'm sure he did, though. Knowin' Screw, I know he did.

Did you ever go over to one of the sessions at his house?

Never, man. Actually, when I came to Wreckshop, Screw music was kind of . . . everybody was bootleggin' it, so Screw was kinda gettin' to a point where he was wantin' to just get more into doin' records, doin' Screw CDs. So Screw was comin' to Wreckshop a bunch, man, and I was kind of around showin' him a lot of little things on MPC. I showed him a lot of things on MPC because he was wantin' to actually get into *producin'* producing. Instead of doin' turntables. So I think at the time when I came, Screw was just trying to pretty much transition himself as well, and that's what I saw. So the sessions at his house were weird, man. His sessions . . . I think they was pretty much kinda dyin' out, but he was still doin' it. It just wasn't really big at the time.

He had moved out to Mo City at that point too, right?

Yeah, yeah he had moved. When I would come up there I would pretty much just hang out . . . Pokey, and everybody would come through. Hawk. Everybody came here, you know? We never really had to leave the shop. 'Cuz Wreckshop was real hot then, man. Wreckshop was hot.

Who really stood out to you at that time?

I always took a liking to Pokey, really. Pokey would come through, man, he was always jolly, had a good attitude, crazy. Moe too, man, 'cuz if you knew Moe, man . . . Moe had a real . . . just a good attitude, man. He would have you laughin' up under the table by the time you walked out of the room with him.

He was really smart too.

Yeah! Moe was smart! Lemme tell you one thing about Moe: The good thing about Moe, the reason why I think Moe kept a lot of people that really loved him is 'cuz Moe was one of those artists that . . . he would talk to anybody. He stood outside of the club, stood outside of the show . . . we used to have to tell him, "Moe, come on, get onstage!" He out there talkin' to somebody . . . you know, somebody had a CD. He wanna hear it. He gonna try and play it. "Moe, you gotta get onstage!" He was real sincere, man. But everybody, man . . . like I said, I had came during a time . . . I had a real good time when I was over there, man. They had a lot of good people who came through, but the ones that really stayed around are the ones you pretty much hear about now . . . the Pokeys, the Hawks, Moe . . . Slim, Flip. I ain't never . . . I never seen Mike [Jones] over at Wreckshop, but Mike wasn't really doin' nothing . . .

Yeah he wasn't really around yet.

He wasn't around. I had seen him once before . . . he was a little short guy. I'm 35 years old, see. Back then those cats was 23 years old. Right now

. . . you go back eight years, that takes a chunk off they life right there . . . they were like 13, 14 years old.

When you and I graduated high school, those dudes weren't even in school yet.

Nah, they wasn't even in school! They wasn't into rappin', they was into kids' stuff. But you know, everybody really kinda had a chance to gel over there. It was a cool session. I had a great time over there. Came from there, started doin' work with Swishahouse, and I kinda, like, started surfin' around. I went over to Freestyle Kingz and was doin' some stuff with Chalie Boy.

Isn't Chalie Boy from up near Dallas?

Actually they were in Huntsville at the time. And then I went from there . . . from Huntsville, that's when Bull, the owner of Dirty Third . . . they connected me with Swishahouse, and that's when I met Watts. He came down to Huntsville one time and I met Watts . . . Watts was like, "Hey, we got this poppin', got this boy Mike and Paul." I was like, "Cool, man, I'll shoot y'all some tracks." I shot 'em some tracks, "Still Tippin'" was on that beat CD I gave 'em, along with some other tracks. And they put out *The Day Hell Broke Loose*, and it took off underground . . . before you know it, "Still Tippin'" just went there and went there and before you knew it, it got added to where it became one of Mike's biggest singles, Slim's biggest single, Paul Wall's biggest single. It really jump-started they careers, man. It started their careers, man. People still send me texts, "Man, you bust 'em over with that one." It was different, though! And trust me, Lance, I got a lotta heat still that can bring back that same element like that, but right now I'm just kinda waitin' to see what's gonna happen with this Houston and Texas rap. I think what we need to try and do is stop bein' hit-chasers and start bein' hit-makers. A lot of us chasin' hits, man. Someone will make a beat, we chase that. And then we not . . . we not really tryin' to create a sound down here, man. We gotta create that movement. Like we did back then, man! We had a movement back then, man. Right now, people . . . they not even sellin' underground CDs like they used to down here, man. It's not even jumpin' off like that anymore man. But it's comin' back.

Paul Wall

NORTHSIDE

The first rapper in Houston to debutat a #1 album on the *Billboard* charts, Paul Slayton was a big part of the explosion of national recognition that Houston was feeling in the fall of 2005 with his breakthrough album *The Peoples Champ*. He started out as an intern of sorts with Swishahouse, working his way up through the street team to appearances on mixtapes in the group The Color Changin' Click with his partner Chamillionaire (Hakeem Seriki), with whom he would release multiple albums and then have a quiet but public falling out (the two later reconciled). Paul Wall made headlines in the rap world again in 2010 when he underwent gastric bypass surgery and lost over 100 pounds.

I was reading about your surgery—I guess you got it in 2010?

Actually I got it on New Year's . . . on New Year's Eve, 2009, so like, January . . . I got out the hospital January 1, 2010.

I was reading some of the interviews you did after that, and you're real open about it, in explaining it to people—did you experience some fans connecting with you on that? Some people who got inspired to go the same route?

Yeah, definitely. Fans and also other entertainers, too. For me, the reason I wanted to be so open about it was because of all the . . . the way it was perceived, to get surgery like that, as being vain. And for me, it wasn't for that purpose solely. You know, part of it is I wanna look good, but it wasn't like I'm gettin' a thousand plastic surgeries on my face, and you walk around looking like a fish. For me, I'm trying to save my life here, but at the same time better my life and feel good about myself. And . . . I don't know, I just wanted other people to feel like . . . shit, because anytime I see people who have the surgery, they're always real quiet about it or kinda seem ashamed of it. And they don't want people to know. But I feel completely the opposite. Like, I'm *proud* that I got the surgery. Shit, if you see how I look before and how I look now, I look like a million bucks. That's how I'm feelin' too. So I'm proud that I got the surgery, because of the results of how I feel as a person, but also, I would hope to inspire somebody else to know that there's another side to it. It's not just the embarrassed, the shamed side people get, because people will be like, "Oh, he got surgery—that don't count." Not talking about me, but talking about people that had surgery like that. There's always something negative that goes along with it. But me, I want to portray it in a positive light, to let people know that you can have surgery too. And if it wasn't for a good friend of mine that helped motivate me to wanna—because I wanted to make a change, and I was doing everything in my power to try to lose weight, but where I was at it was . . . if I wouldn't have had the surgery by now, I would have probably been another hundred pounds heavier, just 'cuz the lifestyle I was livin'. And even though I made dramatic lifestyle changes, I wasn't losing any weight. So, I don't know . . . I just wanted people to know there's more to it than that. There's another side to it. You know, I don't feel like there's nothin' wrong with gettin' the surgery. I was 320 pounds!

PHOTO: PETER BESTE

Wow.

Yeah! I just wanted people to—I was just hoping that I could shed a different light on it, and I'm proud that I had the surgery. Because like I said, if I wouldn't have had the surgery, man I don't know if I would be alive today, because I was morbidly obese.

I didn't realize 320 pounds. That's wild.

Yeah, and the doctor told me that if you're 50 pounds overweight, it takes 15 years off your life. I was over a hundred. I was like 120, 130 pounds overweight. Overweight. So you just think of all the other stuff that comes along with it: diabetes—which . . . I was borderline diabetic—I had hypertension, high blood pressure, my metabolism's fucked up . . .

All that sneaking up on you before you're even 30.

Shit, hell yeah! Gettin' on planes feelin' dizzy, performin', feelin' like I'm about to pass out. You know, as I'm performing, praying, "Man, I hope I don't pass out because I'm gonna be so

embarrassed if I fall down onstage." Stuff like that. So I mean, it was . . . for me, if it wasn't for my homeboy motivating me to do it, it kinda . . . he was tellin' me, "Man, ain't nothin' wrong with that surgery. Don't be thinkin' you should be embarrassed by that," you know, that I'm gettin' that surgery. If it wasn't for him encouraging me to do it, then I probably wouldn'ta did it, and I might not be here! And everybody woulda been talkin' about me, "Aw, man, Paul shoulda . . . man, he was too big—why didn't he get surgery?" That's bullshit. They don't say that 'til you die.

Yeah. Look at Big Moe.

Yeah, yeah. Exactly, man. Exactly.

But you're not the only one, and we look at people like Slim, he's also trimming up, and then [Killa] Kyleon—do you feel like it's an overall thing, do you feel like there's kind of a movement towards a health consciousness in rap music or in Houston in particular?

I think yeah, definitely, and some of that comes from watchin' our heroes fall. First from DJ Screw, and Pimp C, and then Big Moe, and all of them are health-related. Drug-kinda-related.

Lifestyle-related.

Yeah, just lifestyle-related. I was living that same lifestyle that they're livin', even though some of us might be doin' the drugs a little more than others, some of us might be eatin' unhealthily a little more than others, some of us might be exercising a little less than others, but we're all livin' the same lifestyle, and it just has an affect on you, where any of us are vulnerable to that, and you don't realize it until it's too late. Or until it's damn near too late.

And then it's a real uphill climb.

Yeah, exactly, man, and part of—you know, when you get your health together, a lot of it has to do with momentum, the momentum you have with it. And if you feel like the battle is lost already, and you don't have any hope for it, it just makes it that much tougher to overcome.

Because you're depressed about it.

Yeah—exactly! Oh hell yeah, and then the stress and the depression that goes along with it just adds to everything else—adds to the lower metabolism, it adds to anxiety, you know, strokes, heart attacks, things like that. And then plus the fact that we all have kids makes us wanna live much longer for, not just for ourselves but for our kids, and not just so we can be around our kids, but so that our kids can be around us. Because, being that my wife—she lost her dad a few years ago. I guess it was about four years ago now, you know, she lost her dad. And I'm sure he would love to be here, to be with her, but on the other side, she wants *him*! She wanted him to be here for *her*. So, you know, I don't want my kids thinkin', "Damn, man, what the hell is my dad doin'? You know, why he couldn't he get his shit together? Why he ain't just go get the surgery, why he ain't just do whatever he had to do to lose this weight?" So I could be there with them. And that's something that we're doin' right now, me and Slim, I think Kyleon doin' it too. And my wife's doin' it, too. She's got a whole health blog, recipes, everything. She does Zumba classes. But we're doing it with this company . . . where they're basically just tryin' to make some kind of . . . just, like, some kind of urban initiative to show that people who you look up to, who you might not necessarily perceive as "all around American guys" . . . you know, if you listen to our music, it's not the most G-rated. We don't live a G-rated lifestyle. But at the same time, we're still getting healthy and trying to be an inspiration to other people. To let them know that you can be yourself but also make changes in your life. And part of that, for me, too, was when we moved to California—we lived in California for the last two years, and in the summer we moved back to Houston, this past summer. So, bein' out there, man, I was—me and my boy Travis Barker, we'd go do M.A. training together, so he would exercise every week, a few times a week, and I'd go with him. And that's just motivating, him being a vegan, and a lot of my other friends being vegans and vegetarians, and, you know, it just— part of me bein' a Texan makes me wanna, you know, tell jokes about vegans and vegetarians, but the other side of it is me wantin' to be healthy. It's

actually me bein' a thinker, asking, "Why are you a vegan? Why are you a vegetarian? What's up, why you eatin' all this organic food, man, when they chargin' three times as much for a carton of milk?" And it's the same thing. But then they explain to you all of the benefits of it, and the things that we're eatin', and all the unhealthy things that we're eatin', from fast food and processed food, meat fillers and stuff like that, and all the corn syrup and all that kinda stuff that's just killing your body and killing our generation after generation, it's . . . man, it's incredible that it's allowed to go on like this. It's incredible to me that there's no laws, preventative laws that's makin' it happen. But, me bein' in California, though, it just really made me change my lifestyle because, man, nowhere in California has a drive-thru, except In-N-Out, and even all the In-N-Outs don't have drive-thrus. But the Starbucks don't have drive-thrus, the banks don't have drive-thrus, the restaurants don't have drive-thrus, nothin'. Man, in Houston, you can go to the bank . . . I mean, shit, you know, you can go to any restaurant—any restaurant, period—you can go to Ruth's Chris and call in an order and they'll bring it out to you. You don't even have to get out of your car. You pay for it from the window of your car.

For real.

And that just promotes a lazy lifestyle. It's convenient, but it's also lazy as a motherfucker. I mean, shit, liquor stores have drive-thrus. It's just so lazy. But the girls are thicker, and we want a thick girl, because that's fine to us. The girls want a thick dude. If you boney, then they talk about, "I don't want his boney ass." That's what girls say. They want somebody that's got a little meat on they bones. I mean, it's just a cultural thing, I guess.

What has it done for your creativity, as an artist? Has it unlocked things that weren't there before?

Oh definitely, man, because my delivery is—I have much more breath. So I don't have to take as many breaths, so it's helped my swag and my delivery. But also, onstage, like my boys that I perform with, they say too, "Man, you can tell a big difference," in how it was and how I am now. Because, shit, before, I'd need all kind of hype men backin' me up in the background. I'd be out of breath, sweatin' hard as motherfucker. But now, I can go longer. I don't need to take as many breaths, you know what I'm sayin'. And in the studio too, it helps with my delivery. My confidence is a lot better because my delivery can be there, because I can hold more breath. But . . . one thing I was curious about, though, was, "Damn, I wonder if I have this surgery, am I gonna have a super high-pitched voice or some shit?" You know, "Am I gonna sound different? I know I'm gonna look different, but am I gonna sound different too?"

And you don't.

And then, with the creativity too, I mean, I think a lot of it is mental. So since I have a different type of confidence now, shit, I feel like since I have the confidence there it's helping me be more creative. I don't know, I just have a better confidence, so shit, it's helpin' me be creative, to have that confidence that I mighta didn't have before.

And then your energy is better too, so you work more, you create more. When you create more, you get better at it.

Definitely.

You've been married for six years now?

Yep. This'll be our—October will be our seventh year.

And two kids. How does the hustle mentality evolve as you evolve as a family man?

Man, it changes completely, because I'm not the same person I was seven years ago. I have different priorities, different goals, different wants. The things that—a lot of that comes from exhaustion, from like hustle exhaustion. But also, just because shit, man, I been doin' this so long, you know, it used to be funner'n a motherfucker to go out and get fucked up and party, but now, it's like . . . it don't really amuse me anymore like it used to because I been doin' it for so long. It's like,

"Shit, I gotta find something else." And then, as you get older, you learn, you grow, so I've become a smarter individual. I know more about things. When you young, you don't give a fuck. So you can get fucked up, you know, and it's funny. "Man, we were throwin' up! Man, I drunk so much my throw up smelled like vodka!" But then, shit, you get older, your body and your organs don't work the same, and it's like, "I can't . . . damn, I can't be doin' that, man, 'cuz I'ma feel it for three or four days."

Yeah.

And I gotta get up to take my son to school, and shit, I can't pull up to school smellin' like vodka and throw up. I was pullin' up to school smellin' like weed smoke, droppin' my son off at school, man, all that kind of stuff. 'Cuz you think about things that are bigger than you. Not just about me, it's about me bein' a leader for my family. And so my kids look to me, and I don't want them growin' up rememberin' the times—I watch a lot of those "Behind the Music" or "Driven" type of shows, where you see artists and you see their families— even the old, legendary artists, where they have passed on and they interview their kids, and I don't want my kids to be growin' up talkin' about, "Man, I remember the time my daddy used to come home . . . he'd be smokin' this and that, he'd be drinkin', all . . . be leaned out," and all this kind of stuff. So it just makes me wanna separate that from my family, from my kids. Because even though I don't perceive myself as a . . . of course I'm a role model, but you don't even think of that. You don't look at yourself as a role model, you just look at yourself as livin' life and havin' fun and enjoyin' yourself. But, I think havin' kids makes you realize, like, "Damn, I really am a role model," and whereas before, "Yeah, I'm a role model, but I don't give a fuck." Now, damn—the life I live is gonna directly affect how my children live their life. Because most kids'll either wanna be like their parents or wanna be the exact opposite of their parents. Shit, my biological dad was a junkie and he was abusive, so I wanted to be exactly the opposite of him. But shit, I turned into a codeine fiend. A codeine junkie. You know, so I damn near turned into the same as him.

And he was addicted to heroin. Heroin and codeine are the same thing. They come from—not exactly the same, but they come from opiates.

Synthetic.

Yeah, so it's like—and a lot of that was scary to me. Like, growing up, my father, he was also an alcoholic, so I grew up in Alateen, going to meetings like that and all the AA-type meetings for kids. Alateen, you know, when your relative or someone who's an alcoholic or abusive. So, I was conscious and aware of addiction, and aware of the effects, so I didn't drink for a long time. I didn't do any drugs or anything for a long time, 'cuz I was afraid. I was afraid that I was gonna turn into him. I didn't wanna be the dope fiend and the junkie. I didn't wanna be the alcoholic and beat on my wife and beat on my kids like that. So, shit, that was a big motivating force for me to not do that. I wanna be the exact opposite of him. But then as I get older, you know, the shit starts to be a little more temptin'. You know, you wanna try it. The next thing you know, shit, I *love* the shit, and it's hard to say no. But also, that's a big motivating force for me to stop too, so . . . the benefit of me havin' surgery too, is that my stomach is a lot smaller, so I can't drink nowhere near as much as I could before, because a couple of drinks will have me fucked up. Same with lean, everything. Except for smoking—I can smoke like a chimney and it don't affect me. But everything else, shit . . . man, I don't need to po' up a whole bunch of syrup. I can just drink just a little bit. Even though I don't. Every now and then I do, but not on the regular like I was every day—wake up out of bed and roll over and the cup would already be there and I'd be drinkin' it!

Do you think that's still the case with a lot of people? Are a lot of people you know still hitting it pretty hard?

Hell yeah! Hell yeah. No question. No doubt in my mind. Only reason why a lot of people aren't is because it's harder to get, and it's so much more expensive. And a different company makes it now, so it tastes a little bit different.

Is that right?

Yeah, other than that, man, shit, there's no doubt in my mind everybody would be doin' it just as much. Only reason—everybody I know who stopped only stopped because they can't afford it anymore, or there's too much hassle, or it don't taste—something like that. And there's only a few that don't drink it for like the health, beneficial reasons, like, you know, because it makes you lazy and it fucks up your health and that kinda shit. There's only a small few. And man, the people who stop, it's just because it costs too much. They can't afford it, or it's harder to get, or . . . you know, shit like that.

The repercussions are a lot greater now too.

Yeah—oh, hell yeah. Hell yeah. Shit, especially if you get caught with some of it? Like with the police, shit . . .

It's a felony, isn't it?

Yeah, because it's a C-2 level street, the penalty is greater than if you get caught with cocaine. It's the same as if you get caught with heroin. So shit . . . man, that's crazy.

You went to Iraq in 2007.

Yeah.

And Afghanistan in the same trip?

Nah, I went to Iraq and Kuwait, and then went back again the same year and then back again the next year, and then to Afghanistan after that. I went four times total, and then actually next week I'm going again. I'm actually goin' to Africa and Kuwait.

Are you gonna perform in Africa?

Yeah, I'm doin' five shows. I don't know where. I'm goin' to some other countries too, but they didn't tell me 'cuz the places I'm goin' this time is all super classified, like . . . people don't even know there's bases there, so I'm not allowed to talk about it after I went, I'm not allowed to say where I went, and they won't even tell me where I'm goin' until I get there.

So it's all military stuff, all the shows that you're playing.

Yeah, they're all military.

When you went over there, what was the biggest eye-opener for you? The thing that you found that people misunderstood the most about what was going on over there?

I don't know, man, it just . . . goin' over there, there was so many people from Texas. They told a statistic that 80 percent of the people over there were either from Texas or stationed in Texas. I don't know if that's still true today, but when I went there, people had Texas flags, they were holdin' them up. Texas tattoos, Texas shirts . . . they were pullin' out Texas—Cowboys jerseys, Texans jerseys, Oilers stuff. Like lookin' at little things that reminded them of home, things like that. And there were people that ranged in ages from 18 to in their 40s and 50s, and probably older than that. So there was like a—it was like a whole different world. Like, the military world is a different world than the civilian world. And it takes a hell of a person to do that, and the people that have wives and hus- bands, it takes a hell of a spouse to support them too because your spouse is gone for so long. Shit, it's hard to do shit on your own when your spouse is gone, because you miss them, you stress about them. You have needs, you have emotional needs, you have also physical needs, but shit . . . it's just hard to not be there because you feel alone when they're gone. I was gone—you know, every trip I'm gone is about two weeks, a week and a half . . . I miss my family like a motherfucker. Shit, and these people are gone—some of these people are gone six, eight months, a year. There was a dude over there, he was gone for two years. He was only supposed to be gone six months— he was over there for two years. And he was supposed to come home. He had a child at home he had never seen. He was supposed to come home, and he had just got the notice that he was gonna be—that he was needed for another six months. And I think some of

it is . . . they wanna come home—by all means, they wanna come home—but it's a recession. It's hard to find jobs, and when you get stayed like that, when they make you stay for another six months, a lot of these people are gettin' pay raises, pay bumps, they might get—some of them are gettin' promoted in their ranks . . . so it's like, shit, as much as you wanna go home, you have to sacrifice it because it's really—you can't go home, 'cuz the opportunity to stay there is . . . man, it's a hell of an opportunity to get that pay bump, and all that extra stuff that come along with it.

My brother has been over there multiple times, and the more dangerous the situation you're in, the more you get paid . . .there's an incentive.

Especially—like when we went over there, Bush was still president. So, it was a . . . man, the country was kinda . . . I wouldn't even say it was torn, it was just all anti—it seemed like it was a lot, not all, but a majority of the country, especially the younger generation, was anti-war. "We don't need to be over there, we're fightin' somebody else's war . . ." You know, people hated Bush. I'm from Texas, so I didn't really—I don't know if it's that Texas pride where you kinda support people from Texas, even though I didn't all the way like Bush. But I also feel like, "Damn, he's from Texas," so I closed my mind to the negativity because I didn't wanna believe it. You know what I'm sayin'? And then as I started lookin', watchin' all the documen- taries like *Loose Change*, *Zeitgeist*, and all that kind of shit, it made me be like, "Damn, man, you know what? Damn! What the hell we got goin' on over here?" But when you go over there, like to do the USO trips, you can't talk about none of that shit. I asked people because people are open, and they want to talk about it. Some people wanna talk about certain things, but shit, they ain't never seen Bush. They just over there doin' they job, you know what I'm sayin'? And a lot of them would be like, "Man, if Bush cancels the war, that means we goin' home and we out a job." So it was a different type of perception from a lot of the people over there. But, you know, our generation—shit, our generation is, "Ah, man, we're fightin' somebody else's war, it's bullshit," all that kind of stuff. So, I don't know, man, it was wild goin' over there just to experience that in the middle of all of that goin' on. And you see, too, that these people have families just like I do. The same age as me. They're younger than me. Some of them are older than me, but I don't know, man, they live in—it's a different type of world that they live in.

You mentioned, kind of dipped in there for a second talking about *Loose Change* and kind of venturing over into conspiracy theory territory, and that's a broad term that's used to blanket that, but it really is more the idea of questioning the government and questioning the foundations of what we've always believed. How far do you lean in that direction? I know that the belief in the Illuminati is very, very widespread throughout the rap community in Houston. Is that the same for you?

Man, I think that it's so hard, man, because there's a lot of loony people out there that, if you question the government, people group you in with them. And it shouldn't be like that, because there's some crazy people out there who believe some crazy things, but some of those things they believe are true. And there's some general things that are truc too, but people—like especially some of the media outlets— will perceive . . . they'll paint a picture of people that question the government as, "Aw, he's a conspiracy theorist, he's a crazy, he's loony." But that's not the case at all. It's just that we're questioning our government, and that's what we're supposed to do as a people. We're not supposed to just accept what people tell us. We're not just supposed to accept what they tell us and what they say, because a lot of times, you know, all the smoke screens that they give off is bullshit. And if we just accept it . . . they're not here, they shouldn't have the power. You know, it's of the people, by the people, for the people. So, you know, it's *our* government. They're supposed to be serving *us*. We're not supposed to serve them, you know what I'm sayin'? And too many times it becomes . . . since they're in power, and people feel powerless, we just accept it. We accept what they tell us and what they do, and we feel like there's nothing we can do about it. And if we

ask questions, people get blackballed, they lose their jobs, they get—people look at 'em like they're crazy. You know, people look at you like you're loony. So I don't know, man. But I love all that, all the conspiracy theory—you know, like you said, it's a broad term, but I love all those documentaries. All the documentaries, man. I love documentaries. Because it's mind-blowing, and you don't even . . . in some of them, you don't know if it's true or if it's not, but it just shows a completely different side of the story, a completely different perspective than what you see when you turn the news on. When you turn on the news, no matter what news outlet you watch, it's gonna be the same thing. It's gonna be the same story, and this is just tellin' it from a whole different perspective.

You went to Africa before, for the *Bling: A Planet Rock* documentary.

Yeah, yeah. Man, that was wild too.

Tell me about that.

This lady named Raquel Cepeda, she put together this documentary, and basically, she just wanted to . . . it was diamond mines and the diamond conflict, the war that had went on from 1991 and ended in 2001. And Kanye West's song "Diamonds from Sierra Leone," "diamonds are forever," that really just opened up a lot of people to asking about, you know, "What is this?" It just kind of familiarized people with what was goin' on. Because people didn't know. I didn't know. I had no idea, no clue.

Yeah, it's crazy, man.

I had never even heard of Sierra Leone. You know, "Where the hell is that?" I never heard of that, but she got me, Raekwon, Tego Calderón, and we, just basically three rappers—you know, Tego Calderón does Reggaeton, but he's a rapper too, though. So three rappers from three different parts of the country—he's from Puerto Rico, and me from Texas, and Raekwon from New York. So we had kinda three different perspectives, but still . . . she just took us to the diamond . . . to Sierra Leone. We went to the diamond mines. There's two different kind of diamond mines. There's the big, industrial diamond mine, kind of looks like a Fred Flintstone gravel pit, where they go to work. And then there's the one that's in the river, where they got kids out there naked or in they underwear. Even though just butt-ass naked, siftin' through muddy water, tryin' to find diamonds, getting paid a cup of rice a day to do that. Even if they find a diamond, all they get is a cup of rice. So it's just like . . . it just shows that you know how people are bein'—it's modern-day slavery because people bein' taken advantage of, and they have no options, no opportunities, no ways to fight back. No ways to make a livin' for their family, no ways to make a change for they government. We go in there, we sat down with the vice president of the country and the head council. So shit, picture it: You come over here, and you sit with Joe Biden and Hillary Clinton and all kind of other big name people, and we sittin' with them, and we're tryin' to ask questions, how we can help shed light on this and how we can help make a change and what can we do, and they're sittin' there tryin' to get us to invest and buy hotels and stuff like that. They didn't care! You know, they had nothing goin' on. It was wild. And then we went to this place—in the documentary we went to this one place—we went to a lot of different places, but one of the spots was right on the water where . . . it was an open, outside market, and it was also the public city dump. There was just trash piled up. And right there, there was shackles . . . it was like, where the wall was, it was all shackled up where . . . from 200-plus years ago, where the slaves were shipped off from there to North Carolina. The shackles on the wall were still here. So it was just a haunting experience. It was just a real wild, haunting experience. And when we go through there, we have the UN as our security, and they were—I think they were Nigerian, or something like that, I'm not sure, I'm just bein' real broad about it, but I think they were Nigerian, but they were—wherever they were from had some kind of beef, like some tribal beef or somethin', shit goin' on with the Sierra Leone people. So, since they're the security and they're the UN Police, they was in there bogartin', pushin' people around, bein' rude, pushin' people down, cussin' people out. And it's like, "Damn, man, when you come through like that, naturally the people there are gonna hate us, because they're . . ." You know? And I was embarrassed. I was feelin' bad, like, "Damn, man, you can't be doin' that, man." It's just like if I have a concert somewhere and my security guards, like I go somewhere and I got fans and my security is pushin' people around, bullyin' people, it's just gonna make the fans be like, "Man, well, fuck Paul Wall." It's just how it was, and we were over there, and there was some . . . there was some young Sierra Leone thugs that was there that just kind of got fed up, wasn't takin' it no more, and one of 'em kept tryin' to talk, man. And everybody, they got so spooked, and they got the hell up outta there. But he just wanted to talk. He wanted somebody to listen to him. And nobody would listen to him. Everybody was kinda scared. And I just went up to him, gave him a hug, like, "What's up, bro? I feel your pain. I don't know what you goin' through 'cuz I ain't from here, but shit, I feel your pain, you know what I'm sayin'? It's fucked up." And he was like, "Man, it's fucked up, man. We ain't got no government, no jobs, no opportunities," was basically what he was sayin'. But it just reminded me of one of the stories in the Bible, where there was a man on the side of the road and everybody passed him by and nobody would stop to talk to him. And then Jesus stopped and talked to him, and blessed him . . . or something along that line . . . I don't remember the story, it just reminded me of one of the stories in the Bible. And it made me wanna talk to him, 'cuz I was like, "Damn, man, why is everybody runnin' away?" 'Cuz the guns are banned from the country, so you can't have no guns in the whole country. So I didn't feel threatened, like my life—I didn't feel, like, threatened. Like what's the worst he can do? Whoop my ass? I can fight pretty good, it's alright, shit . . . I don't know. I thought I was straight, you know what I'm sayin', so I wasn't, like, afraid. "What's up?" But it was just a wild experience, man, the whole time over there, and the whole thing really was just to use us to draw attention to the whole conflict that was goin' on and everything, spread and raise awareness to that. Because there's something called the Kimberley Process, where diamonds are found and they get registered through the Kimberley Process, and if they don't—see, some people don't do that. Some stores buy their diamonds not from the—they aren't registered through the Kimberley Process, but it's just to help encourage people to wanna buy . . . to ask questions. You know, "Is this certified? This isn't a blood diamond, is it?" It's to ensure that the diamonds aren't illegally smuggled or traded. Because that's what was goin' on. People would—when the rebels took over, they took over the diamond mines and were tradin' the diamonds for guns, or trading the diamonds for drugs that they used to—on the child soldiers to take over to not train but . . . influence their minds . . .

Assimilate.

Yeah, yeah, there you go. Man, shit, so the diamonds—it's a very valuable commodity, and what we look at is, we wear diamonds for show, like a status of success. You know, you got diamonds, shit—this is a diamond ring, it signifies that you got married. The bigger the diamond, the more your husband loves you. That's how some women feel. Or the bigger the diamond, the more money you got. Or just . . . as a rapper, shit, if you got diamonds around your neck that means you ain't broke. So if you ain't broke, shit, you got something goin' on. But if you walkin' around here lookin' broke, then people—it don't matter what your music sounds like, people gonna be, "Man, look at the way he look, how he lookin'. He look broke." In rap, image is everything. Shit, if you look broke, then people think you broke.

It really turned stuff around, though, for you and [business partner TV Johnny]. You changed your distributors, and you kind of changed your approach.

Yeah, and shit, that's why I was like, "I gotta bring Johnny," 'cuz Johnny run everything. I'm just like the promoter. I'm just like the face of the company. I don't know none of that other shit in the background, all the . . . man, I don't handle none of that paperwork or none of that office, administrative . . . I don't know none of that shit. Johnny handles all that. So it was like, man, Johnny has to come. So

he could see it too. So he could feel the same feelings I'm having, see the same things I'm seeing. That's a once in a lifetime opportunity, anyway, to go to Africa—how many people get to go to Africa? Yeah, so, immediately, the day we came back, we fired our diamond distributor, our diamond wholesaler, hired somebody else that was abiding by the Kimberley Process—not to say that the diamonds we were selling before were blood diamonds or conflict diamonds . . .

But you wanted to be sure.

Yeah, we wanted to be sure, and we wanted to be able to . . . you know, it's just like, "How can I tell someone to vote if I'm not votin'?"

Do you feel like it's brought awareness? Just speaking in hip-hop terms, really, with the materialism and everything. Do you think it's opened a lot of eyes?

Nah. It did when it came out. You know, it did at the time, but not really. The people that are buyin' the jewelry, they don't give a damn. They want the cheapest diamonds they can find. They don't care where it came from. They just wanna look good. Honestly. 'Cuz, shit, honestly somebody from Fifth Ward who wants a diamond grill—man, you think they give a damn where the diamonds came from? About the diamond conflict? Hell no! They just wanna look good. They want a good lookin' grill, and they ain't tryin' to spend extra money for anything. But the benefit of it is, shit—it's not like if a diamond is Kimberley-certified that it costs more, 'cuz it doesn't. It costs the same thing. It's just a motivatin' force to get the jewelry stores to subscribe to the Kimberley Process. But I don't think the actual general public, the general consumer, don't give a damn. There's some people that care about it, like, "Oh, those are blood diamonds," this and that, but them people don't even buy diamonds. Those people don't buy diamonds anyway, the people that care. Because some people will be like, "Oh, that's why I don't wear diamonds, that's why I only wear this and that." See, they not even buyin' diamonds, so it don't even matter.

Right, they're not in the market.

They're not even in the market. The people that are buyin' diamonds and buyin' jewelry? Man, they wouldn't give a damn, 'cuz they have their own family members who lost their lives. They livin' in their own modern-day slavery, where they don't have opportunities, and all they can do, all they feel like they can do is sell dope or hustle or doin' those type of things. So, they don't care what's goin' on in Africa. Man, a lot of these people that buy diamonds never even left their neighborhood except for once in their life to go downtown to go to court! So they never even went to the other side of town, so they really . . . you know, as much as they . . . maybe in the back of their head might care what's goin' on in Africa, a lot of these people don't give a damn because they got their own problems goin' on. And then the recession came. When the recession came, shit . . . people wanted to look good, wanted to feel good, and how you feel has a lot to do with how you look. Not 100 percent, but it has a lot to do with it. When you look good, you feel good. Not 100 percent, but shit . . . if you look bad . . .

It reflects.

Yeah, it reflects on how you feel.

That was gonna be kind of the next direction I was going to go, talking about materialism and all of that. Do you feel like the recession hit hip-hop in any way that affected it for the long term?

It definitely changed it. Definitely changed it. It definitely changed a lot of things. It also gave people an excuse to not spend money on jewelry. Because a lot of people couldn't afford jewelry, but they were . . . you know, it's all about image, so people would do what they had to do. A lot of people were buyin' fake jewelry, people were borrowing jewelry, or had their little starter jewelry kits. Like the "baller on a budget" jewelry, 'cuz they couldn't afford the real thing. Then the recession hit, and you had people like Diddy, other people sayin' they don't wanna wear jewelry 'cuz they don't wanna be shittin' on everybody, makin' people feel bad 'cuz

they got money and they don't. But I don't know, I always look at it from a different perspective 'cuz I was always motivated when I saw somebody shinin'. When I see somebody lookin' good driving a Bentley, with a bunch of diamonds and chains around their neck, that makes me wanna work even harder so that I can get it. You know, like as inspiration, to make me wanna work harder. So I just . . . I never toned down on it. I never wanted to tone down on it because I wanted to inspire other people that, "Shit—yeah, it's a recession, and I'm still lookin' like this, so that means you can look like this too." But I don't know, man, I think it gave a lot of people an excuse—not that Diddy didn't have money or couldn't afford the jewelry by any means—but a lot of people saw what he did and was like, "Oh, thank god. Now . . . okay, yeah, now I'm not gonna wear jewelry either." When really, at the end of the day, they just couldn't afford it, or . . . not for the same reasons why he stopped wearin' his jewelry 'cuz shit, I bet he got a thousand Rolexes, Patek Philippe, Franck Muller, any watch you can name, I'm sure he got it!

You mentioned Fifth Ward a minute ago. When you were coming up and learning about what was going on in Houston . . . South Park, Third Ward, Fifth Ward, were those kind of mythical places to you?

Definitely South Park was. Not really Fifth Ward because it was around my . . . you know, it wasn't too far from where I live. But South Park—the Southside was kind of like a legendary place, like mythical place. Like a fantasy world because it was so far away. And so many people in my neighborhood, growing up, had never ever been to this other side of town. Never even left their neighborhood. And still to this day haven't! Except to go to jail. So . . . and I forget that. You forget that sometimes, because I've traveled the world—man, I'm goin' to Africa next week, shit . . . but there's people that I know that I grew up with my whole life who've never even been to the other side of town. And if you've never been to the other side of town, then how can you, in your mind, strive to go worldwide? How can you, in your mind, believe that, "I can make it worldwide, and I can go to

Paris, Italy, wherever I wanna go in the whole world," you know what I'm sayin'? And I think it's sad that it's like that, because people get stuck in the neighborhood mind frame, and they accept it. My mom, she marched with the Freedom Fighters and all kind of stuff like that. She did sit-ins and protests. She traveled the world, like she lived in Jerusalem, Germany, so she would always tell me stories of these different places, and me . . . I don't know . . . I always loved *Indiana Jones*, like those type of movies, because I always wanted to see something different. It just was exciting to me. My wife always calls me the "Crocodile Hunter of Hip-Hop" because I always be doin' crazy shit like goin' to Afghanistan. I was in Afghanistan the deadliest month in the history of the war for American soldiers. I was over there that month. So shit, she always calls me the "Crocodile Hunter of Hip-Hop," where I be doin' this crazy shit. And I'm not like an adrenaline junkie at all, man. I'm scared of heights, man. I can't ski or snow ski or none of that. I mean ski or water ski, none of that. Man, I'm not an adrenaline junkie, it's just that, I don't know, I like those adventurous type of things, and shit, as a rapper, comin' from where I come, who woulda thought that I could have done it? But I feel like, shit, if I can do it, they can do it, too. But these fools have never even left the neighborhood. So, growing up, I would go to AstroWorld, you know, I had a grandmother that lived in Meyerland, so when I'd go over there sometimes, it'd be like, "Damn, I can't believe I'm over there on the Southside." One of my best friends, he went to . . . I can't remember the high school . . .

Jones? Sterling?

Nah, nah . . . it was off of 288 and Yellowstone. 288 and OST right there. It's like . . . not HSPVA, but . . . man, what is that high school? It's like a magnet school too. Like a performin' school, some shit . . . gonna text my homeboy and ask him right now. So yeah, we go there, we like, "Damn, man, how far are we from . . . where the Screw shop at, man?" "Where this and that at, man? Let's go to that South Park—where's Herschelwood at?" All that kind of stuff. And it was funny growing up, you know, me and my homeboy were undercover

Screwheads. Because livin' on the Northside, shit . . . they were talkin' shit, dissin' the Northside. But as much as we were like Northside soldiers, we loved . . . we would get in *fights*. We would always go to Club Oasis, Jamaica Jamaica, all the time, and we would wear Northside shirts . . . all kind of stuff, get in fights all the time. But at the same time, we just loved the Screw music. We loved DJ Screw, Keke, Fat Pat. They were my favorite rappers. So it just . . . one of my homeboys, I remember . . . my homeboy was playin' some Screwtape where they were sayin' something about the Northside on it, and I was just listenin' from a fan, like, "Damn, man, he goin' off!" But my homeboy was like, "Man, get that shit out my car!" He threw it out the window, "Man, that shit gonna get no play in my car!" He was gettin' pissed. So we were undercover Screwheads. Needless to say, when Slim Thug and E.S.G. did "Braids 'N Fades," man, we were a lil' happy that, "Okay, now the beef is over." We would always joke around, "Okay, now the beef is over, we can listen to Screw in public now."

If you had to sum that beef up for somebody who kind of knew some of the artists involved [with Houston's Northside/Southside beef in the 1990s], what would you tell them?

It was the equivalent to gang violence. You know, because even on the Northside, there was a lot of Northside beef where, you know, Acres Homes and Fifth Ward would always get into it at Chocolate Town. All my homeboys from Acres Homes would get into it. All my homeboys from Fifth Ward . . . well, not necessarily *my* homeboys . . . but people from Acres Homes and Fifth Ward would always get into it at Chocolate Town. Always be fightin', people getting shot, losin' they life over that, and then, so . . . the Southside against the Northside was more like . . . it was like straight up gang violence. It was just exactly what it was. Bloods versus Crips. Or the perception of Bloods versus Crips, because really, Bloods versus Crips . . . shit, there's just as many Bloods versus Bloods and Crips versus Crips, you know, but just the general perception of Blood versus Crip, that's what it was.

Well the East Coast/West Coast thing is kind of what inspired/touched it off in Houston anyway, right?

Yeah. Oh yeah, because a lot of us in Texas felt like we were bein' overlooked. This was all pre-internet, so shit . . . people still thought people in Texas rode on horses . . . and shit, my uncle, he have a trail ride every year! But we don't ride on horses to go to our job. And I know just as many people in California ride on horses. I know more people in California got horses than I do in Texas! But the perception back then was everybody in Texas is a hick, cowboy, you know, we slow, we don't know nothin' . . . 'cuz we got a country slang—we got a country twang to our voice. We talk with different slang, so since they don't understand what we say, we're dumb and ignorant. But really, they got people from different—people from every city and state have their own slang, their own twang, and their own little culture that makes them their own. And instead of getting to understand it, people just wrote it off. It was all East Coast/West Coast, and that just motivated us in Texas—and this is in the Dirty South in general—to wanna just . . . shit, come up and work harder 'cuz we felt like we weren't gettin' our just due. I'm sayin' "we," but they were doin' that long before me. The roads were paved way before me.

And now the Texas slang, the Texas vernacular is global. It's all over the place.

Hell yeah! People are sayin' "what it do," sayin' "I'm throwed," stuff like that. Shit . . . syrup. Look how big syrup is! Man, syrup is so huge in Atlanta right now, in Florida—oh my God, it's incredible!

"Awready."

Yeah! "Awready," shit . . . everything, man, it's just amazing to see that. And some people get upset behind that. Some people feel like, "Aw, they stealin' our culture." And they have every right to feel that way, but me, as a fan of the culture, and me as someone who always was a champion for the underdog, and a champion for our culture, fightin' for it, shit . . . I'm *proud* of that. When Usher

got a song sayin' he "throwed," and Drake talkin' about bein' "throwed" and stuff like that, shit . . . Lil' Wayne, Drake . . . the two biggest rappers right now. Sippin' syrup, talkin' about sippin' syrup, everywhere they go they got two white cups. Talkin' about Screw. Shit, Drake got a song with E.S.G. with "Swangin' & Bangin'" on it! Shit—1992 was when it came out! 1992, 1993, so this is almost 20 years later.

That's crazy.

So as a fan of that, man, that's amazin', and it just puts a smile on my face to see that people are finally gettin' their just due and just recognition that they deserve, who paved the way for me and who also paved the way for others. It's incredible to see that. I'm happy to . . . but there's a lot of people that feel the exact opposite. They're mad, upset, "Man, they stealin' our culture, they stealin' this and that." You know, they have every right to feel that way if that's how they feel, it's just . . . they're not right and I'm wrong, or I'm right and they wrong. It's just two different opinions and two different ways to look at it.

Well, you know, part of it, though, in Houston in particular—the history really gets handed down. People talk about the history and the artists in Houston who have really laid the groundwork. Those stories still get passed down. Look at *The Peoples Champ* . . . for some people, when they listen to that, it's like a table of contents. It brought a lot of things to light. That's part of it, is that there was this entire vernacular, this entire history. When it blew up, people were able to learn about that stuff.

And you know what? The whole theme of that album was that: "They Don't Know." The song "They Don't Know" was . . . the whole theme of the album was: People don't know about our culture. Well, let me explain it. Let me talk about it, and let me promote it, and let me, you know, explain the best I can . . . especially with the visuals, the videos and stuff. And then gettin' other artists, and me having that same "show love" mentality, and bein' a fan just of hip-hop in general, when I had the opportunities to work with other mainstream artists or other top-of-the-game artists, man, I tried to seize every one of those opportunities and do songs with these people. Because, for one, it's not just me doin' a song with them. I try to make it be them doing a song with *Houston*. Just to help put our city and our state on the map, and keep it—not that it wasn't on the map already, but just put it in the forefront, put it in the light, and just to show that, man, we're not just some hicks that are ignorant and dumb and don't know what we talkin' about down here. You know, we might talk a little different. We might talk a little slower, but that don't mean we're dumb, and that don't mean we have . . . you know, there's not real lyricists down here. That don't mean we don't have talent. That don't mean the music ain't good, that we don't have a live culture.

What do you think it would be like if Screw had lived, if he were alive today?

Man, it's hard to say. I don't think it would be the same necessarily. Same with Pimp C. When Pimp C went to jail, that gave us something to rally behind. It gave us a rally cry. You know, he was our hero . . . Oh! This is what I was going to tell you: One time I was doin' an interview in New York, on Hot 97, and we were talkin' about things, and I said, you know, "Hey, I know it's a little different because you're from the mecca of hip-hop, you know, you're from the home and the origination where it all started, but I'm not from here, I'm from Houston. And I'm from a different generation than a lot of older people. I'm from a whole different generation than the founders of hip-hop, and I'm from a different generation than the generation after that. My old-school isn't KRS-One. It isn't Afrika Bambaataa and Kool Herc. And those are heroes and legends, but my old-school growin' up, the people who influenced me, who I listened to who inspired me to want to rap were DJ Screw, Fat Pat, Lil' Keke." People don't understand that. Since they're not from where we're from, they don't understand how a lot of that music didn't trickle down here. Man, everything I know about KRS-One and Afrika Bambaataa and Kool Herc, I learned after I had fell in love with hip-hop from listening to Screwtapes. And that offends

a lot of people. Sayin' that in general, that offends a lot of people, but shit, man . . . the culture . . . they weren't talkin' in the language that I spoke. Lil' Keke and Fat Pat and UGK were talkin' in the language that I spoke. You know, they were talkin' about things that I saw, they were talkin' with slang, with the same slang that I spoke, and that I grew up around. So shit, they influenced me a lot more and a lot different. That's what made me fall in love with hip-hop, not the originators of hip-hop. I mean, that offends a lot of people. People get upset behind that. There's a lot of people that feel that way. Shit, my old-school was somethin' different. The people that made me fall in love with hip-hop was different, you know?

Slim Thug

NORTHSIDE

Slim was part of the Swishahouse movement in the late '90s, mostly appearing on mixtapes before he shook up the Northside/Southside beef with a pair of collaborative efforts with Southside icons—first with E.S.G. in 2001 ("Getchya Hands Up" was their hit), and then with Lil' Keke. In 2005, Slim's mixtape hustle paid off as the release of his major label debut, *Already Platinum*, went straight to #2 and catapulted the already popular rapper to the mainstream, going global the next year with his feature on Beyoncé's "Check On It." When his second solo album came along four years later, Slim was away from the majors and back to his own label Boss Hogg Outlawz, where he's remained since.

PHOTO: MIKE FROST

What's the dynamic like between you and Z-Ro? You guys had a beef for a while but then obviously you reconciled, and when you come together, you create a different bond and a different dynamic in the music.

Right, man. And it's like . . . even through all that, we so much alike in a lot of ways with the way we do our music. We don't really do *commercial* music or *try* to do commercial music. We kinda, like, keep it real gritty and grimy and underground, like we been doin' for all these years. So, you know, it's gonna be that type of record. We ain't really just go into it like, "Oh we tryin' to make a million dollars and drop 10 singles." Nah, we wasn't on that. We wanted it to have that ridin' dirty kinda feel like that, you know, that real street type of record, type of album. And we actually get in the studio together every time. We don't do stuff where he do a verse and then he send it to me. Naw, we get in the studio together and start from scratch, so it ain't no shit we just kinda throwin' together. It's a real album.

So you get that vibe, that real dynamic of working with each other. That chemistry.

Right. And workin' with him, it's been crazy, man. That dude a genius. That's really—that's all he *do* is work, basically. All he do is make music. But he *sing*, and to see him do all that—sing, rap, then he a *producer* also, man. He got a lot of talent, man. He definitely love what he doin'.

It's incredible that he makes as much music as he does.

That's what I'm sayin'. And I'm sure he got 200 songs nobody ever heard in his fuckin' computer at least.

You know he does!

That's all he do is make music, so yeah, man, I enjoy workin' with Z-Ro.

Speaking of beefs and ironing them out, when you first started working with E.S.G., what was y'all's conversation about that? Did he come to you and say, "Let's do this," or was it a thing that you guys thought, "Well, this is going to help to kinda squash the North/South thing" that was going on then?

Yeah, that's what his thought process was. He was the one that reached out to me. He just got out of jail, and he was sayin' that, "Man, I heard about you in jail. I been hearin' a lot about you in jail. Let's get on a record together." And you know, we went to the studio and we came up with the concept. I think it was him that came up with the concept of doin' the North and South thing or whatever. And you know, it seemed like after that, you saw a lot of other artists follow the lead and do a lot of Northside/Southside collaborations to the point where it's not even no big deal no more after we did that record. Nobody ain't trippin' on that. You know, I'm sure there's a few knuckleheads, you know, who probably still trippin', or was back then. But for the most part, it kinda brought the city together in a lot of ways. That's one record I'm definitely proud of doin', you know what I'm sayin'? I feel like it helped the city.

Part of it was that the spirit of that record was so good that it kind of needed to be a record like that to break through and just kind of put everything aside.

Right, and when we did that, not only for the fans or whatever—it was also the rappers who began to

reach out and understand that, you know, shit—we *all* Houston. It don't make sense, we trippin' over this bullshit. So, you know, we all began to work together, and now look, man—even me and Z-Ro's doin' shit together. It's all good. It was all good, man, so I'm happy I did that.

I just talked to Domo about this, and I had a long conversation with Paul about this, and I don't know if it's something that you really talk about, but I know you really got your health together in the past few years and made some changes in your life, lost some weight. Was there a catalyst, and what did you do differently?

I have high blood pressure—from my family. It's from my mama—she got high blood pressure. It's inherited through the family. But in the beginning, when they first put me on the *pill*, I was like, "Hold up—I don't wanna take no pill for the rest of my life." So I got a friend that's a personal trainer—his name is Milton Harris—and me and few of my potnahs, we all began to start workin' out, goin' to Memorial [Park], runnin' every day. I do it every—I ran today. I still do it. But, you know, I began to run three miles and then try to get the—because the doctor said if I can lose the weight and change my diet, I probably can get off the pill. But, I *did* lose a lot of weight, and I didn't ever get off the pill. Usually it's just like, man, some people just gotta take it or whatever. So, you know, it didn't actually work for me—well, it probably did because I don't take a higher dosage. I'm still on a kinda low dosage of it. I still gotta take it every day, but at the same time, I developed that habit of workin' out and beginning to like how I look better, and after that I got all the fat off me so it just make me, you know, wanna continue and do it. Sometimes, I might go back and eat up a storm and gain that weight back, but, you know, like right now, I'm on a diet right now, like a liquid diet, tryin' to get this gut off. It's just . . . it go back-and-forth, man. I feel like sometimes I wanna do this shit, and sometimes I might shift for a month or two doin' all this travelin', shows and shit, it's kinda hard to keep it up on the road, but for the most part I try to stay healthy and be out there.

Well, you know, one of the things I talked to Paul about too—a lot of it is about momentum. When you start going in that direction, and you're getting your health together, you don't wanna let it slide.

Right, right. So—like I say, I ran today. I try to run, still do three miles at Memorial. I don't do a lot of weight liftin'—like I train with boxing and that type of stuff. But I don't wanna get all swole up and shit. I don't wanna get all big.

When 2004 came around and the spotlight really started focusing on Houston, one of the things I noticed that was happening around that time, 2004, 2005, was that we had a lot of really, really big events that were coming to Houston around that time. We had the Super Bowl, we had the World Series come here, the NBA . . .

All-Star. Yeah, all that.

I was writing for the *Houston Chronicle* then, and one of the things that I remember the most was that all of the parties that were happening back then were hosted by rappers. Were you involved in a lot of that?

Oh yeah, I was definitely involved. Around All-Star and the Super Bowl and shit—hell yeah, I was definitely a part of that. Even this year—even last year. I mean, this year—the one that just passed. That definitely brought a lot more attention, for them to come down here and witness the city theyself and get a feelin' of how it is out here. That all played a part to it, and you know, to hear "Still Tippin'" on the radio when they all got out here and be able to be able to bring it back home, wherever they was from, and share it. So it all worked out for us.

It was sort of a window to Houston for a lot of people. Don't you think? For that couple of years?

We had a lot of attention, man. It was real good for us. It was really the *movement*, man. It was like four or five of us at that time, and when you have a movement, it demands that attention. When it's

one person, that's something else. It's hard for one person to demand all that attention, but when your movement is good and everybody can feed off of each other, that's what make people recognize and see what's goin' on faster, when you got a movement goin'. And that was a movement—me, Paul Wall, Mike Jones, Chamillionaire, you know what I'm sayin'—a bunch of people at one time.

Well, with a really solid foundation, because you guys had already had things going.

Right, we already had covered the grounds of the streets. We had the streets on lock at that time, doin' the mixtapes and stuff like that. But, it felt like, to me, rather, the reason why I went and got a deal is stuff like, we was in the same circle. I started in '98—'04 is like six years in the game, and I felt like I'm goin' to the same clubs and doin' the same venues over and over again and goin' in the same circle, like I'm on 610 or somethin'. And it's like, I wanted to go further than that, so that's why I ended up goin' with the majors. And at that time, that's when I think the mixtapes—you know, the Best Buys was killin' a lot of the independent stores or whatever, so that played a part into it too. You know, so it was harder—we dealt with stores, you know, hand to hand—and we went to a lot of these mom-and-pop stores and did everything from the bottom—from makin' a CD to deliverin' it— everything, distributin' it everywhere. We did that. We used to do it hands-on like that, and I think that was what had a lot to do with our success, when we was underground or whatever.

But Houston's always been a long game, though, hasn't it?

Right, right. That's what—a lot of people don't understand that outside of Texas. Like, motherfuckers out of town think the last thing I did was "Still Tippin'" or some shit sometimes, you know? I go to a lot of places and perform a lot of shit, but there's some people, like, that think that we really ain't been doin' nothin' out here. But it's kinda like Texas is its own fuckin' country, man. This state so big, and there's so many big cities in it, that we really don't *have to* go outside of Texas to be successful, and eat good or whatever. I definitely would want that and love that, but at the same time, I don't have to have that. And a lot of artists out of Houston and Texas got the same type of fan base and can do the same thing, have they own little circle of where they go and get money. All these years. I been doin' it since '98.

But that's an entire world down in Houston, and it really always has—I'm not going to say it always has been, but it has been for a long time.

Right, right. That's what people don't understand, but, you know, like I say, we do good, man. We still doin' shows and gettin' money to this day, and still puttin' out new music and havin' that on the radio, and it's sellin' on iTunes, still doin' good. So it's like, we good out here. We really . . . it's really a wonderful place to be as far as bein' a rapper, you know what I'm sayin'. There's a lot of spots I go to, and they don't get that same type of love, man, or that same type of loyalty or treatment from their fans. It's something special. I mean, we stay real to our culture for the most part, and that's what keep them fans loyal like that. People who chase trends end up fadin' away with the trend. So, you know, we do It lIke that, man.

That said, do you do a lot of out of town shows, do you do a lot of shows out of state and around?

Yeah, I do end up doin' a lot of shows out of town, man. Like, out of state too. Like I got a show this weekend in Arkansas. I stay doin' shows all the time, but I'm just sayin', like, the core of the fan base where it's real crazy is out here, man. But I be surprisin' myself, man. I went on tour with K.R.I.T., and, you know, I feel like we got a different type of fan base or whatever, but at the same time, everywhere we went, people was rockin', man. You know, they *knew* it. It wasn't just I was on the stage and they was listenin'. They knew the words.

Meshah Hawkins

THIRD WARD

Meshah attended Jack Yates high school with Big Pokey and Big Moe in the early '90s and later became the longtime girlfriend of Fat Pat's older brother Big Hawk, who was known as the "Five Star General" of the S.U.C. and was regarded as a leader, especially when the Northside and Southside were warring in the 1990s. Hawk was murdered on May 1, 2006 when going to a friend's house to play dominoes in South Park, less than a month after he and Meshah had married. In the aftermath of his death, Meshah became a prominent voice in Houston's rap community and still maintains Hawk's recorded catalog while leading the effort to find his killer. She is the mother of Hawk's two young sons.

PHOTO: PETER BESTE

Hawk had a regular job before he ever rapped, didn't he? Didn't he work at an insurance company?

Yes! He was at American General for 10 years. And when DEA [Dead End Alliance] came out, all of that, he was working at American General. He was one of the only guys doing that. All these guys was out here just partying, going out of control. But he would get up . . . he would be with them, all night, and he would get up and go to work. And he would come home and do it all over again. I don't know how he did that. I don't know how he did it, but he did. He did. He got up every morning and went to work.

So did it kind of sneak up—because he was the older brother, he was older than Pat, right? But he started rapping after Pat.

Yep. Him and Pat . . . you know, siblings are always in competition. So Pat come home, he raps. Hawk was like, "Nah, nah, you sound good, you sound good, but I can rap too." Of course they competin'! [Laughs] Hawk really . . . I think he was more of a gifted writer . . . you know, just some things he's written to me, and I have just books and books and books of all his lyrics and tablets, and I just really feel like he was a gifted writer, and I used to tell him that all the time. And I used to encourage him to write for other people, write for other rappers and everything. Because he was really, really a gifted writer. He used to write all kind of poetry and, you know, he could just write a letter to you and it would just be so endearing, you know?

Just from the heart.

Yes, the *words* he would use. And he wasn't afraid to show that side. He showed that side to everybody. He wasn't afraid to show that side to people.

What's your personal relationship to music? From your perspective?

You know, it's really been something for me, because it's been such a big part of my life. Because I grew up in Third Ward, and I've always been, you know, just . . . my mom was married to a musician, so it's like my mom had kinda . . . I always grew up in music, around music. Different genres of music. So it was only natural for me to gravitate toward somebody that was in that career. Because of my love for music. And then, so I grew up in Third Ward and then I went to Yates, and the culture . . . it started there, you know, the creativity, like Moe would be singing in the hallway. And then Pokey played football at that time, but like [we were with] one of the first DJs [that] was doin' all of our parties that started slowin' down records too. His name was Michael Price. He got killed. Yeah. Pretty early. But he was one of the first, first ones to actually slow down the record—like he had a screw in the radio, and it made the tape go slow. And so that kind of made him come up with the concept, but Screw actually took it to another level. Michael Price wasn't doin' it nowhere near—he had like stumbled upon puttin' the screw in the radio. Screw actually started . . . got the tempo, he did everything. He created everything, basically. I graduated in '93. Pokey and them were in '94. They were in the year behind me. My year, we went to the State Championship in football, and so every game—and this was like right, you know, this was all around, like, the birth of hip-hop I guess here in Houston, you know what I'm sayin'? It was like all durin' that time, everything, the events, everything just got blown up because it was like we had this new music that was creating and forming here, so it was like everybody gravitated to these certain places, these different events. Like they talk about the Slab Holiday with the Kappa Beach Party, Memorial Day Weekend beach party. And see, Yates would always—every football game it was

like a slab fest in front of the school. You know, it would last for hours. [Laughs] It would just be crazy, and I was just like a little teenybopper. And then we started sayin', "boppin'." It was like all of the words we started sayin', the whole slang, it just . . . all the guys started . . . you know, Pat invented a lot of those words with the slang, him and Keke. "Raising the roof," you know, "throwed." All that. That's Pat! They started sayin' the words, Keke with that "Peanut Butter & Jelly," and you know, "pancake." They just invented all this stuff. It was around the cars. Pat had a love for cars. I mean, he just loved cars ever since he was a child, and he would build model cars. So he started just like . . . gettin' all these different slabs, and then Third Ward had they set of slabs, South Park had they set of slabs . . . Fourth Ward had their set of slabs. And they would all ride in the line [Laughs] at all the different events. It was just . . . it was just so much fun. Oh my god, it was like we *had* to be there. It was like you was dyin' to get to the beach or wherever the event was, and it brought everybody together. Everybody together at that time.

It was the music bringing people together.

It was the music, yeah. It was like Screw was blowin' up . . . it really was like . . . at first it started with the slabs because there was, like, Rap-A-Lot . . . of course, they were the first ones, kind of on the Houston scene. So it started with the slabs, Rap-A-Lot, and then there was . . . you know, we had our little separate music scene . . . it was Big Mello, Rap-A-Lot, Big Mike, Wickett Crickett . . . I mean, you know, we had all that goin', right? And so then they started with the slab cars, with the slab cars with the bass, the music, right? And so then, you know, the guys [Screwed Up Click] still wasn't together then. They knew each other, but you know, we still really hadn't bonded. So then when all the guys started goin' to Screw house, and when the Screw music hit the scene, then everybody just started gettin' together, you know what I'm sayin'? All the people together. Because everybody wanted to be at events to hear the music, to hear the Screwtapes. Like the people from the Northside—they couldn't get the Screwtapes, really, so at the events, they would just sit there. We were just, like, parked and all of the cars would be out there, and you would hear the new Screw. You know, because all the slabs—see, you can't ride slab and not bang the Screw, you know what I'm sayin'? You not ridin' slab if you ain't bangin' Screw. It just goes hand in hand. You can't do one without the other. You ain't holdin'. That's what Pat would say, "You ain't holdin', you ain't comin' down if you ain't jammin' Screw!" [Laughs]

Well, and that was the way to hear Screw too. You listened to Screw in a car. Not only was that the way to listen to him, but it was kinda the _only_ way because you didn't hear it on the radio, you didn't hear it in the clubs. People played it in their cars. That's where you heard it.

They played it in their cars, that's right. That's right. You would go right to those places where you know those cars gon' be just to hear it. See the cars, hear the music, you know, then it just started the culture. Everybody started raisin' the roof and . . . you know, I wasn't even a . . . me and my girls—two of my girls—we wasn't, you know, sippin' syrup and doin' all of that. We just . . . you know, we were part of the culture. That was our culture. We were right there. We growin' up with these guys, these are our friends. Basically. We're just seeing them branch off and do different things. Next thing you know, they're superstars, you know?

Do you remember the beginnings of that—when Screw was doing his tapes early on, he was doing regular speed mixtapes and then he started slowing down stuff and then it was still a little while before he started having those guys come and freestyle on the tapes. Do you remember that, when that started?

Yeah, it started . . . okay, like C-Note, Courtney of the Botany Boys, he was actually the first one who started. And so, like, they got into music because they have . . . the Botany Boys is C-Note, Will-Lean, D-Red. But Will's father is actually . . . was in an old singing group back in the day, and they had put out an album. It was a popular album around here [Archie Bell & The Drells]. So, you know, Will grew up in music too. And so his cousin can sing

really well and somebody else in his family—both of his cousins have beautiful voices. They can sing. So that's them singin' on a lot of those old Botany Boys songs and everything. So they—so he grew up around that too. And so they started, you know, there was some . . . I don't wanna talk about all the other stuff that was goin' on! [Laughs] Because you know there was some wrongdoing as well, but I don't wanna talk about all of that . . . but they started like that, and so Courtney actually—C-Note—went over there, he flowed on the Screwtape, and so then, you know, him and Pat, all of them was from the . . . they all hung out together. So then Pat heard it, Pat ran over there, and he flowed, so it was like Courtney first, Pat second. And so then everybody else started coming in. Coming in doing the freestyles and everything.

It just kind of blew up after that, huh?

Right. Screw was just really a DJ, you know. He did some little local clubs and stuff. He just did different gigs, and it grew from there. He did different gigs and then him and—I don't know how he listened to the . . . I don't know how he actually came up with the concept. I think him and Michael Price had kinda hooked up together, or either him and Darryl Scott.

I know he learned some of it from Darryl Scott.

I know 'cuz . . . Darryl Scott was really one of the originators of the mixtape here. He had it sewed up. He was the only person here doin' mixtapes, and his mixtapes were legendary. Everybody really loved his mixtapes, and he would—I believe he would slow it down a couple of octaves . . .

I think he would do like a couple of slowed songs on a tape, but he never did a full slowed tape like Screw did, and never with the chopping and screwing at the same time.

Right, right. So then Michael Price was Darryl Scott's protégé. When Michael Price died, then Screw I guess . . . he just took it to another level. Nobody could do what Screw did. Nobody. I mean even to this day, you know, I've traveled after I put out the album, and I would run into different DJs and things from different places all over the world, and they would say to me that, to this day, they haven't ran across a DJ that could cut as sharp, you know, as he could, and that was one of the compliments that somebody told me . . . I wish I could quote him, but he . . . that stuck with me. And they were like, "Man, he was cold." And they would give him a lot of respect for how he created that music. And it took him a lot of work! That's what really killed him. You know, I've seen him over there. It was just really . . . whew! People don't understand. The guy, he would not sleep! He would not sleep. I would go over there, and I would just be like, "Wow . . ."

Fall asleep on the turntables.

Yeah! There would just be crates all over. Did you get a chance to go over there?

No, I didn't. We started the project in 2004, so he was already gone by that time. Did you go over there a lot?

Well, I went over there enough. [Laughs] I went from a child . . . I remember goin' when he lived with his Dad, I don't know what street it was on, in Southeast Houston, with the gate in the front . . . when the line would be down the street. Okay, we would just ride by there because we would see all the guys, you know? We were tryin' to see all the guys, so we would just drive through there, and then we would go get our tapes from there, and then I remember when he was in the . . . the next time I went to his house—went over there a couple of times as a child, and then the next time I went when he was out in Missouri City.

I know they got kicked out of a bunch of places.

When I went to that house . . . I went out to that house several times, and it was just . . . oh gosh . . . it would be all night! He would literally . . . he would be in there for days workin' on something. And he would not sleep! We'd be over there—we wouldn't get over there until about three! In the morning! And he'd just be goin'. He'd just be goin',

goin', goin'. I said, "Oh gosh . . . this dude . . . this dude here . . ." I mean, you'd just be like, "What can I *do* for you?" We'd be sittin' there, you know, and come over there to entertain him or just to hang out with him or whatever, but he could not—he would just be workin' the whole time. He'd be runnin' from room to room, putting albums on from different crates. He'd be lookin' through his different crates, you know, and he'd just be goin' from—we'd be sittin' there chillin', and then he'll get an inspiration, he'll just take off and go in another room and he'd be lookin' through some crate, and he'll come back and he'll put somethin' on, and we'll be, "Yeah!" And we'll start talkin' and this, this and that, and he'd be gone. He got the headphones on, he over here doin' this and he . . . I mean, he worked himself to death. He worked himself to death. I wanted to step in and help him so bad. I was like, "Well, who am I?" But I really wanted to step in and help him. Him and Hawk too, because they really just did not know the business side. You know, a lot of the guys got into it that, unfortunately, used to sell drugs, and so they just put that business savvy over to the music game basically.

Which really works for some people.

Yeah! It does, it works for some people, but it doesn't work on a large scale, you know what I'm sayin'? If you want to be mainstream—if you really wanna make it and you wanna be mainstream and really have a celebrity status, you know, like the Paul Walls and the Chamillionaires did—then you can't go that route. You gotta really have some-thing reputable, you've gotta have some reputable business people workin' with you . . .

Gotta clean your money up.

Right. You know, go through the proper channels, and hire an attorney and publicist and this and that. Basically, not *you* doin' everything. And so they were really self-taught. You know, they had—they went through a lot of different experiences where they got screwed, and they just kept gettin' screwed through different experiences, and some of them took it like, "Okay, it's a learning thing. I can flip this, I can do this." But some of them got bitter. Some people were makin' money, some people were not. Screw was makin' money off of the guys' tapes—he was sellin' the guys' tapes, but the guys wasn't necessarily makin' any money off of the Screwtapes, you know what I'm sayin'? So that's what happened, and that's the difference between . . . the guys, that's what kind of led them to break apart. Because they were not makin' any money off of the Screwtapes or anything like that that they were makin', so they had to go out and get other deals, and do other stuff on their own, and work with other people. Whereas, Swishahouse would allow their people that did the mixtapes, Slim Thug and them, they would allow them to make some money off of their tapes. So . . . they were not organized, I guess, you know, at first. And so it just kind of got a bitter . . . it just didn't turn out, I guess, the way it was supposed to turn—everything didn't turn out.

It sort of snuck up on everybody too, the whole success of it.

It really did, and Screw—I say, "Hawk, why Screw don't just have his label, have all y'all on his label, and . . . you know, why he just not doin' that?" So I would sit down and talk to Hawk all the time about this, and he's like, "Babe, Screw really wanna be a DJ. He don't really wanna have his own . . . get into, you know, runnin' a company and this and that. He still wanna be able to make his tapes and do his music and this and that . . . he really don't wanna have a record label. He really just kinda wanna DJ." And I was like, "Well, you know, he can DJ. Somebody just run it for him." So, basically . . . because I was in college at the time, and I was, "Okay, maybe I can go into this as a career."

Run a label.

I mean, I grew up with all of them, so it was like . . . I wanted to see everybody make it. I thought it was really fascinating that what had came out of the culture, just from us kickin' it, hangin' . . . you know what I'm sayin'? Hangin' out and kickin' it, to see the talent. Because we had made a business, we had did this . . . we had this whole little swagger

goin' on, and we didn't even know what was goin' on, you know, the creativity that we really had. Because I was in the communications [department] at Yates. We were doin' music, we were doin' music videos in the studio and everything. I mean, we were doin' all kind of stuff at that school. We were emulating everything we were seeing on *A Different World*, *In Living Color* . . . everything. We were acting all that stuff out.

All the dances and everything.

Yeah, and the music videos and everything. And so then it was sparking all of our creativity, and all of our culture—our Houston culture—started coming out. That's how it went down.

So that was an idea you had around that time, running a label. I mean, that was an aspiration that you had kind of early on.

Well, I saw the need. I just saw the need. I really didn't wanna be in the limelight. But I saw that there was a lot of confusion and chaos with the Screwed Up Click, and I saw that . . . you know, because I would see the stress, I guess, and everything that my husband had to endure. And trying to . . . well, he was cool with everybody. Everybody loved him, and he was friends with them, and they always called him first for everything. And he was always there for them, and he was like a father figure to them. A lot of them would call him Daddy. 'Cuz they know that he was gonna get on them if they were messin' up . . . you know, he wasn't gonna sugarcoat anything. He was gonna tell them real, straight up, and be honest with them.

That's a big brother.

Right, and look out for them. At the same time, look out for 'em and have they back. And so they would always call him for everything.

It's coming out a lot more that there are ladies working behind the scenes, yeah?

It is, and I'm glad. Now it's coming out because a lot of the rappers are in monogamous relationships. They are, and it's really bein' publicized now, because they're really in wonderful, devoted relationships. And I was in one of 'em. Paul Wall and Crystal . . . they have a wonderful relationship. Bun and Queenie, and you know . . . there's some other rappers out here that really are devoted to they women, and we've been there with them, all that they've endured, you know, we've supported them. And I did that every step of the way. I didn't wanna get too involved in his business and feel like I wasn't there for him. But I wanted to support him, so I went on and did my thing, did my career. I wanted to show him that, "Hey, I got my own career." You know, I graduated and started teachin' school. Graduated from college and started teaching school. And I was waiting, basically, for him to say, "Babe, you know, I think you could help me and be beneficial in this." And then he had did that right in '05. Finally he was like, "You know what? We need to turn this into more of a family operation." Because it comes to that point where you're young, you're with your guys, y'all hangin', you're doin' this, you're doin' that, and then when all that's gone, said and done, you go home to your family, and those are the people, the closest people with you, and you start havin' children. And everybody's life *did* start changin'. And so then it became more family oriented. At the time, when we were . . . when I saw the need for somebody to step in and help them and this, this and that, I was in college, and they were all just young and hangin' and . . . you know, they were just kids! They were just kids. And they had no sense of responsibility. They had no responsibility to step in, to be like, "Let me get something stable goin' on and get my family involved and really work this business." We're lookin' at that more so now. It's bein' publicized . . . as you look at the reality shows now with the celebrities, you see that all of the people in their family are basically around them doin' everything. So it's givin' you an example. It's giving you that example, whereas that wasn't even thought of or heard of, what, 20 years ago when these guys started out. They didn't know what to do. They really didn't know—they were clueless. They was just happy to have money in they pocket, ride around in a nice car . . . they were just clueless! They didn't know. They were kids.

Didn't know how long it would last or what made it work anyway.

No! And then the guys . . . the pressure came. It was all this peer pressure and egos start kickin' in . . . and whew, that can be ugly. [Laughs]

Well, it's a really interesting point that you bring up about them being in longer, monogamous relationships, because people read the lyrics and they might not think that. But they are just lyrics . . .

Right, right! Music is an outlet of expression, so you're able to vent. So you get all that stuff out, and you're venting. Some of it is what you see . . . it's therapy! So you know, once you're gettin' it out, you're able to go on about your business, right? After you express yourself and get it off your chest, and then you recognize and you're aware, to talk about it . . . it makes you . . . you can't do the same thing that you're talkin' about. You gotta do something different. I hope.

You're aware. And just hope that people connect with it.

Right, right. But you know, the people—like Hawk and all of his stuff was changin'. You know, his life had changed. We had gotten married, we had kids, you know . . . the boys were the love of his life. All of his stuff, his whole mind-set started changing. And his music—his lyrics—you know, he made some stuff real gutter, raunchy, and then he made some stuff where you could tell the maturity in him, and people really wanted him to be the same way that he was when he first started! And he struggled with that because he was evolving and changing. And he wasn't on the corner sippin' syrup, you know, rollin' in the 'Burb, on the vogues and the elbows . . . I mean, he wasn't necessarily doin' that anymore because he was a grown man, gettin' married and all that. So, it was hard for him to kind of transition his music as you mature. You had that one audience, and then, you know, you have to start putting more substance into your music. And that's what he started doin'. He started putting more spiritual, more of a . . . you know, just really started tryin' to educate.

There was competition within the Screwed Up Click. Did you see that?

They were competin' on those Screwtapes. They were competin'. It was a *big* competition goin' on too. On them Screwtapes. If Pokey was on there, E.S.G. was on there, whatever . . . they'd be kind of like battlin' on the cool.

Well, you hear stories about guys—one guy's in the corner writing his lyrics, another guy's in the corner writing his lyrics looking over his shoulder.

Yeah, yeah, yeah! Like I say, the egos took over. When they really saw that this was what it was doin', that they was gettin' the hood, the street popularity . . . what do they call it . . .

Street cred?

Hood celebrity? Neighborhood superstar? When they saw that they was becoming that from these tapes? Oh, baby—the testosterone kicked out. They started battlin'. I mean, it started becoming like . . . that's how the Click developed, because the weak didn't even step up, you know what I'm sayin'? It become a battle of the different hoods. The top dudes in each hood just started battlin', and whoever was on top, that was the hood that was kinda on top too. And so the guys start—the traffic, people would gravitate toward the hood. To those hoods.

South Park was the place to go back then, huh?

It was popular! We used to just ride—I used to steal my mom's car just so I could ride either down Martin Luther King or Cullen. And we would just ride down those streets! And that was it. You would see somebody you know, you would see some car you recognize or somethin', you know. The car wash back then—all the car washes would have cars.

Be a line down the street.

Yep. It would be so fun.

How often do you drive back through South Park now?

It's rough. It's hard for me to go down Cullen. 'Cuz, you know, his mom lived there. I lived there, too, at one point with them. Down there on Cullen. And you know, that's where he got killed too, so that whole area just reminds me of him, so much. Every time I get on Cullen, it's just . . . South Park, period—everything over there reminds me of him. Everything. So I don't really go to that area. And then, that area is . . . you know, it's janky. It's crime, it's raunchy over there. I don't fool around over there.

It's for real.

It's for real. It's raunchy over there. They'll get you in a minute. If you tryin' to get got. You gotta be careful over there. Even as a child, when I was hangin' out over there, or gettin' my mom's car, ridin' down there, I'd be scared to death. It was a thrill. It was a thrill just to ride down there and make it and ride back! [Laughs] It was a thrill. And I'm from Third Ward. I grew up in Third Ward, but it's like, in Third Ward, if you know everybody on your street, you feel comfortable. They don't really mess with you too much. But you still have your suspect people walkin' down the street. You gotta be careful. Well, not really, I guess, where I lived. You know, like I say, I grew up in this house. I really feel safe here. There's a lot of older people here on my street. I'm not down in the bottom. But, you know, they're cleaning that up even!

They're gentrifying, yeah. Entire blocks that are just townhomes there.

Yeah! You see all those lofts and townhomes and stuff now? Yes!

You don't recognize it.

I know! And they're sellin' them for like $300,000.

It's happening to Fifth Ward too. Fourth Ward's gone.

Yep. It's gone. It sure is. It's gonna change. And you know what? It's due for a change.

I guess so, some parts of it for sure.

But it's up to the people to keep the culture going. And that's what is hard with Screw because, to be very honest, with me and Papa Screw, we're really fightin', trying to keep our family's legacy and uphold their legacy. Because it's no road but this. And that's why I was so excited about the collection at U of H, because this is going to solidify their name in the history of the hip-hop, the creation of hip-hop culture here in Houston. It's going to solidify their names, and the legends that they were—and instrumental pieces that they were in the hip-hop history here in Houston, Texas. So it's gonna do that! And give 'em that credit, that recognition. And it's just not that type of respect here in Houston for their names. Because of their deaths, the way . . . whatever type of hidden agenda or conspiracy that it looks like, you know what I'm sayin'? The way that all of the guys died, everything was just really crazy to me. It's really, like, surreal. It's like some type of crazy conspiracy story. You know, novel or something.

Their deaths really are all very bizarre.

The way everything plotted out, you know what I mean? And then it's like . . . so it's just really something. So, they don't get the recognition.

When would you pinpoint when you felt that Screw culture had really come to life?

You know, every region, I guess, had their birth of their own culture. Of course the birth of hip-hop was from New York, but then there was other births in different regions, and so our birth . . . we developed a whole sound. It's like the sound from Texas. It's like our soundtrack for Texas, like the West Coast developed their sound with Dr. Dre, and the East Coast developed their sound, you know, with Russell and Rick Rubin, and so then we developed our own sound. And in that culture, with the birth of Screw culture came a slang, a whole new glossary of Ebonics. A whole new glossary of Ebonics came out of our culture. That, the cars, the slang, and the influence is so great that every record that damn near comes out of Houston or Texas has some type of influence, some little bit and piece in there. It's something that they have taken from the Screwtapes. The influence is just that great. That's how you know it's a record almost—you can almost spot a Texas artist anywhere, because of maybe a word they say or something they say that's associated with Screw, that's associated with the Screw movement. And like I say, Fat Pat really created a lot of those slang words. You know, his creativity was unreal. His swag was just unreal. Him and Keke and Hawk, they would joke and rank on each other and just say things, and then just turn it into the whole culture. And then the clubs, it was the clubs, the events, the slang . . . because they would make Screwtapes for the events. They would make the Bayou Classic Screwtapes. So, you know, you had to go to the Bayou [Bucket] Classic to hear the new one. You know, everybody who was there would be jammin' that tape. After the Kappa, or before the Kappa. So it was the events, the slang . . . I just wanna make sure the culture is really represented. From the guys' perspective, they gonna tell you about everything else, but from the woman's perspective, I wanna make sure that the culture is represented in its entirety, so that no element of the culture is left out.

Part of it with Pat, with that slang and that creativity— part of that was that he was just really funny, wasn't he?

He was funny. All of 'em! Keke is a comedian! Keke is a . . . Pat—they would have you in tears, laughing. Hawk, all of—when they got together, they would play "the Dozens" 'til six in the morning. All day. They would rank on each other, and it was hilarious. You would be in stitches. And they'd have some skits too. On some of these Screwtapes, where they laughing, you hear Hawk in the background just crackin' up. You know, laughin' and this and that. Pat was just ridiculous. He would dance and stuff, all of that. He made up the Southside dance! He made the dance up!

I didn't realize that.

Yeah, and then Keke did the song for it, and then Pat was like, "I gotta make me a dance song!" So then he did "Body Rock." They were just entertainers. They were funny. It was just the gift of gab.

That's what I've always heard, that Pat could have just got up on stage and talked and made everybody laugh.

Yep. He was. He was hilarious. A personality. They're raising the roof, you know how they hit the roof? That was him.

Where did that come from?

It came from . . . I think it came from . . . at first, I think the guys would just speak in the slabs, right? A lot of the slabs would just be stickin' to each other, but some of the slabs, I think you couldn't roll down the windows, so they would just put they hand up in the air. And then, it started . . . they would hit the roof when they'd be rockin' from side to side. Like Pat would do that, roll his arms from side to side, when he was bangin', when he was jammin', in the groove . . . just jammin' some music. And he would just be groovin' and dancin', and he would start hittin' the roof. When he saw somebody in another slab—he'd be ridin' in his slab, he'd see another slab or somethin', and he'd be jammin', and he would start hittin' the roof.

Kay of The Foundation

The number of artists working in Houston makes it so that some folks can appear to be working on the perimeters when really they are centers of activity themselves, focal points from which other artists draw inspiration and energy. Such is the case with Kay of The Foundation—Kevin Jackson—who is also sometimes known as Dekay, or K of The Example, and whose name appears on a broad range of projects across disparate connections of Houston's scene. Part of that may be because for a few years there, Kay was nowhere to be found on the Houston scene. In a rare interview, he talks about the ups and downs of an MC's career.

So I heard of Kay of The Foundation long before I knew about The Foundation.

So there was a time—you know about The Foundation?

I know it's a group that did have five members. I don't know if it changes . . .

So initially . . . the stuff I did with DJ Cipher—the whole Example days—that's when I first got started MCin'. I learned to produce from him and The ARE. I got my lil' first ASR, and we worked on *Impulses* together and *Progressions* . . .

This is '90s?

I first started around '94. I played college football—and this is goin' back a little bit further, but I mention it in some of my songs—I played in

Missouri, I came back to Texas, and there was this hip-hop cipher that I went to. I was invited by Elliott Ness, and I met Snapp, D'Ology, GT, and all those guys were there. My first lil' cipher battle was me, Elliott Ness, Snapp . . .

Snapp and GT must have still been making music together at that point, Poetic Souls, right?

Yeah, it was at that time. I met all of those guys in '94. When I met Cipher, we just hit it off, and then he heard me freestyle, so he had me go up to KPFT when him and Sincere was doin' the show up there. So I did, like, a little battle on the air and, you know, I just fell in and they were my kinda people, and we still like brothers now. So at that point, I just kinda start hangin' out with him, and we'd go over there and it'd be me, Cipher, and Rico—I don't know if you know Rico—Sincere, and just random cats. I saw the ASR, got excited about it, and Cipher showed me how to sample records. I just kept goin' over there, just learnin' more and more about music. There was a Parliament concert at KTSU, and at that time just from the neighborhood I was from, I had a curfew, but I was like, "Yeah, I'ma gon' take the chance and watch the Parliament concert." So I got kicked out the house. I showed up, got home about four in the morning, my dad had my suitcases ready. You know, because I was just *doin'* it. There was other stuff, but you know when you get into hip-hop, and you're like, "I'm not doin' the whole school thing, you know, I'm a *musician*," he wasn't really feelin' that. So me and Cipher became roommates, and

PHOTO: ANGELA TELLEZ

the beat farm, Fresh Produce, is basically our first spot that we lived together, and that's when I met K-Otix and we all had our little crew, and that was, like, the Example time. And you're gonna laugh about this—remember when computers only had like a gig hard drive?

Maybe a gigabyte.

So, they used to have this thing called a Windows Recorder, where you could import wav sounds. And so what I would do, is I would loop jazz CDs that my dad had, like The Crusaders, and I would make little songs that would loop for like a minute, and I would just listen to 'em. And that's all I would do, but it would *kill* like all the memory on my parents' computer. Like they wouldn't be able to do *nothin'*. Like, "Why is the computer not workin'?" And you got this 15 minute Crusaders loop with a wav file *that* big . . . [Laughs] So when I go over there I didn't really understand how stuff worked. Cipher had been doin' stuff for a while, so he kinda broke it down, explained programmin', and a lot of the music that we did when we started diggin' for wax, you know, I grew up with it. Some dudes would dig for wax and not really get what they're diggin' for, but when I started it was a lot of the music I knew from my family, I guess, and it expanded from there. But yeah, I've always liked production,

but I was an MC as well, so I never really spoke on . . . like me and Cipher split all the production on that Example record, but I'm just like, "I'm a rapper, so I don't really have to talk about that." I'm gonna be in the front anyway. So I never really mentioned it. From there, after Cipher and I did the *Progressions* . . . record, there was this album called *Ethos* that I was doin' with the K-Otix, and I didn't really . . . we start workin' on it, and I just felt like I kinda was evolvin' as a producer, and one of my friends, Michele Thibeaux—she's a singer in the city—she was like, "Well, you need to meet this guy. He's a drummer. His name is Chris 'Daddy' Dave. He's the drummer for Mint Condition." I liked Mint Condition. I didn't really realize what I was gettin' into. So I go over there, and of course Chris is more of a jazz guy. All we start talkin' about is jazz records. I think he liked the fact that I really like jazz. A *lot*. And so we just kinda start messin' around, and lo and behold—you know, we just start recordin' songs and the music that he had—that was the beginning of The Foundation. You would have these musicians that would come through, and so I would chop up a sample, and *kinda* program drums on it, and I would leave it. And then he would have all these guys come over and play on the top of it.

Use what you did for a backbone.

Yeah! But you know, I didn't realize that, say, Robert Glasper was one of the guys. Luke Austin, he's one of the guys. That's a full band. Cleo "Pookie" Sample, he's in The Vanguard with D'Angelo. Jon Jon did stuff with Beyoncé.

So Chris was already playing with people outside of Houston. He was just still based in Houston.

Well when we met, he was still doin' stuff with Mint, but he had started with the whole *Comfort Woman* time we were already formed as a group. So we worked on music, and from there we did the first album that didn't get released. We sat on it because we were like . . . we probably shouldn't have, but we were tryin' to get a bigger deal because of the caliber of musicians that we had, it didn't make sense for them to *not* be on tour. So basically it was supposed to be the Robert Glasper Experiment *before* The Experiment. The Robert Glasper Experiment, before the Experiment, was The Foundation. From there I did a song called "Tight," and I didn't know, but Chris sent it to Ali Shaheed Muhammad.

From A Tribe Called Quest.

Yeah, so when he sent it to him, I'm in the room, you know, just jokin' around, and he's like, "Yo, Ali's on the phone. He wants to talk to you." So I'm like, "Ali who?" And he's like, "Ali from Tribe." So I'm like, "Man? Really?" Because I'm a Tribehead. So I pick up the phone, and he's like, "Man, I like your music, and what you talkin' about and how you come across." We had a cool lil' vibe, so he was like, "I wanna sign you. Come to New York, come hang out with me." So he wanted to sign the band. Chris didn't wanna sign. But I'm like, "Dude, this is Ali Shaheed Muhammad. I'm from Houston, Texas, and I'm talkin' to Ali Shaheed? You're not tellin' me no. Uh-uh." So I get on the plane, go to New York . . . a lot of this stuff ain't gon' seem real, but I go into the studio—I sit in the studio with Ali—I'm already freaked out. You go in there, you see the Zulu beads and it's like . . .

They got their shit down.

Yeah! I go in the room, there's an EPS there. I'm excited about that, because I was like, "I can work on that." And he was like, "Well, it shorts out. It don't really work." He was like, "That's the EPS that we made D'Angelo's first album with."

Wow.

Exactly. So I'm sittin' there like, "This is crazy, I'm excited." So he was like, "Well, basically, the company is gonna be called Garden Seeker." And this is around 2005 at that point. We had The Foundation record done. I complete that, go up there, sign to this label, and it's me, Chip Fu from Fu Schnickens, Sy Smith, and Stokley, and Ali. So I'm sittin' in there, gettin' all the production that I want, so I go up to the door. At this time, you know, it was, like, the Okay Player time? So me and S1, Symbolyc One from Strange Fruit Project. S1 is

from Dallas. So basically I'm friends with all these producers that haven't blown up yet. So The ARE, me, S1—you know Kanye's "Power," he produced that. Nicolay, Illmind, all these guys. I pretty much go to New York with an album done. So Ali's listenin' to it, and he's like, "Well, what do you—I mean, what can I get you?" I was like, "Well, I want a track from *you*." And then I was like, "If you can get me some tracks from J. Dilla, and Pete Rock, I'd be happy." I knew it was a crazy ask, but I'm like, "Man, might as well ask."

Why not.

So he gives me all these Dilla tracks.

That was before Dilla passed too, right? He was still alive.

Right. I actually have sessions that I recorded with him, but then he passed away and I didn't use them. So this is in that time frame, so in Garden Seeker I go and do this record called *The Talk Show* that released late.

Just a few years ago.

Yeah. I was annoyed about that record. They made me release it. Cipher made me release it. When I was on—I finished that like 2005. I was totally done in '06. And so I kinda sat on it. And this is where things kinda get, kinda go downhill a bit. So I'm sittin' there, you know the *Beats, Rhymes & Life* documentary? I was up there with them durin' that whole time frame, so the plan was, "Kay, your record is done. People like it, but they don't know you. So then you just kinda hang with Tribe and roll with us." They were gonna do the Tribe reunion when they first started tourin' the first time around. Ali was gonna release *his* record, and then my record was gonna be the next record.

Which would have had some of his tracks on it.

Yeah, which . . . you know, if you heard *The Talk Show* at that time, like I was in *Billboard*, *The Source*, *XXL*. And it was kinda weird because I was from Houston and people didn't really put two and two together.

Because there was a totally different Houston movement going on at the same time.

Yeah. So I'm like, "Man, this is happenin'! I'm on the road with Tribe!" And then his record didn't do nothin', and then he start havin' issues with gettin' distribution, so I'm just kinda sittin' there waitin'. Just imagine, like, they hear my album, I get interviewed in *Billboard*, they say I'm like the next Mos Def, and then I just . . . I can't say nothin', I can't release the record. I'm just sittin' on the album. And out of respect, I ain't wanna go nowhere because I'm like, "This is Ali from A Tribe Called Quest."

I'm ridin' with him.

Yeah, I'm ridin' with him, and ultimately I end up gettin' annoyed, and we start gettin' in arguments with his manager. And then on top of that, I had all these producers give me all this music.

On spec.

For free. They were just lookin' out. They were like, "Yeah, we can do this!" So I'm like, "*Ali* . . ." See, nobody really blew up. Nicolay—it was, like, really before he was doin' the Foreign Exchange stuff. Like, all of that was *pre*-that. And it didn't jump off, so I was like, "Well, I can't do nothin' with this record," so I got upset and I just left. At that point I was like, "Man, I don't know what I wanna do, this is like a big waste of time." I was frustrated. So then Nicolay called me and is like, "Yo, you got that 'My Story' song?" Because I just gave it back to 'em. So he put it on his *Here* album. We did the *Time:Line* record and we toured it.

That was the first record you did since being kinda blue-balled for a couple of years? That must have been nice to get out.

Yeah, it felt better, and just like, "Okay, I'm not stuck." I still like *The Talk Show* better, but you know, I couldn't release it. But *Time:Line* was a great album for me. That was '08, so you'd moved to New York by that time! [Laughs]

Late 2006 I did, yeah. Wait but you released something else too because you released "Together Brothers" with The ARE before I left Houston.

Yeah, that was before. At that point, me and Russel would go to New York together. That was right before he started doin' the Trackmasters stuff. You know, and he starts poppin'. We had been doin' a lot of work together. I known Russel since I was 14, 15, just seein' him at the mall at Brother's Pizza in Greenspoint.

Oh, you're from . . .

I'm on the Northside. I'm not from Greenspoint. My wife's from Greenspoint. I'm from a neighborhood called Audubon. I grew up in the same neighborhood as Wine-O. "Pop My Trunk." We're actually friends. Sound crazy! Audubon Park.

Where is it in relationship to Trinity Garden?

It's at the intersection of Beltway 8 and 59. Northeast Houston. I used to go to Greenspoint back in the day, and he worked at Brother's Pizza. Greenspoint back in the day was like . . . that was, like, the cool mall when I was young. Now, it's closed down.

Man that's way up there. There's a whole city up there.

Homestead, Mesa Drive, all those neighborhoods. Audubon is like the *last* neighborhood.

Before you get to Humble!

Yeah, so you got Audubon and then you go down Homestead and then you start goin' through Scenic Woods. Trinity Garden is closer to 610.

Kashmere Gardens, Fifth Ward.

And then you're in the city, but when you drive down Homestead past 610, on the other side of 610 . . . Kashmere Gardens is within 610, but then Kashmere High School is on the other side, like Rosewood. Everybody—they all joke with me because in the whole underground crew, for what we all do . . . and I guess it's because we're older, but in the history of people that do what we do, I'm, like, one of the only dudes from the Northside. Everybody else . . . like they all went to school together, Snapp and them stay, like, Southwest. Well, Cozmos went to North Shore.

Far east side, kinda like Baytown area.

Yeah, they Eastside. You know Russell Guess? Anonymous? That was an underground group. They're from the northwest side.

Did they record anything?

Yeah! Me and Cipher kinda mentored them. Russell Guess produces out of SugarHill now. So *Time:Line* I did there. I did a record called "Fly Guys" with Donwill from Tanya Morgan. I did the Nicolay thing. I was workin' on my new solo, and I was gonna release it myself, and then my wife end up gettin' pregnant, and I wasn't . . . I ain't have a degree, and I was, you know, an older MC. So I'm like, "Man, I don't wanna be the rapper that can't pay his bills." When I was on Garden Seeker—me and Chip Fu are really close friends to this day—we was out shoppin' in New York and I walk in the store and they playin' *Time:Line* stuff! I'm like, "How come I don't get no checks?" It was on a store system. You know when you play your stuff on Muzak or whatever, that means it's playin' in multiple stores all at the same time. So he said, "Well, you need to get an accountant to audit the record label to figure out where your money is so you can get paid." I was like, "I need to *be* an accountant, so I can get my own money. I ain't payin' nobody to do that." I was just jokin' about it, but I end up goin' to school and becomin' an accountant and gettin' a Masters in Finance.

"I'm gonna do this!"

I got a job and I kinda stopped doin' music. People called me "The Unicorn," because I basically did all these records, had all this influence as far as I helped a lot of people out in the city musically,

and I kinda broke—for what *we* do, I made a lot of headway—and then I kinda stopped, and then, you know, they were like, "Well, why you stop?" And I'm like, "Well, if I wanna get a new keyboard, it's a struggle. Everything's a struggle." Because I just didn't have the means to do it. And so I did well in my job, I got hired on as an accountant, and they paid for me to get my Master's Degree. So I'm, like, pretty much a controller/director of finance in oil and gas now, and I actually hide the fact that I'm a rapper. Nobody—one of my coworkers found me on Discogs this week. He was like, "You're Kay of The Foundation!" And I was like, "Huh?" "I saw you online. I had no idea you had this much music."

Being Kay of The Foundation doesn't pay your bills.

A lot of us go through that. I guess this is the new chapter. I talked to Russel about this all the time. After he did his whole Trackmasters thing, and now you back in the city, it's kinda like, "Okay, well, what am I gonna do now? I spent all these years investing all of my energy into this, shiftin' . . ." And so my wife was happy 'cuz I'm able to pay bills and stuff like that. Because she really sacrificed a lot. We been married since '98, so she was with me the whole way.

Through all of that.

Yeah, through all of the ups and downs and, "No, it's *happenin'* this time! I'm up here with A Tribe Called Quest! I got Stokley Williams on my record! Phife is my homeboy." So from her eyes, it's like, "Okay, all this stuff is happenin', but when you gonna get *paid*, though?" And it didn't jump off. I was so frustrated. I graduated, but I just didn't talk to people. So, Cipher and my wife bought me a machine. Like, he gave her everything. When I graduated, they bought me a machine and Pro-Tools. They were just like, "You need to be *you*."

FUTURE

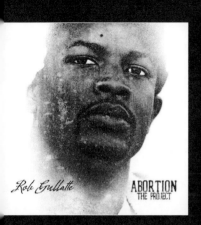

Role Gullatte
ABORTION
THE PROJECT

HOLLYWOOD FLOSS
GODS FORGOTTEN ANGEL

STEAKXSHRIMP 2

THE HUE
Heat Gamma

KIRKO BANGZ
DRANK IN MY CUP

PARADIME

PROPAIN
DANGEROUS MINDS

DEEP

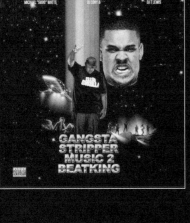

No one ever really *leaves* the neighborhood. There are always new generations taking shape, running in the same streets as older brothers and sisters, uncles and aunts, maybe even having grown up hearing them rap. A lot of the rappers that young Houstonians grew up listening to *still* rap, and still rap about the same neighborhood, even if they no longer recognize it. The churches are still there—some of them—and plenty of businesses. The street names haven't all changed—Homestead, Selinsky, Long Drive, Cullen, Blodgett, Dowling—even if rows of neighbors along those streets are gone.

New voices continue to emerge at street level, building on H-Town's hip-hop identity. Houston rap becomes more diverse as does the city, growing from the inside out in a metropolis full of people investing themselves in their communities. Hurricane Harvey put that to the test, when the world bore witness to the citizens of Houston going to work for one another in a crisis. Screwed Up Click rapper Trae Tha Truth was in the thick of those efforts, as were DJ Mr. Rogers, Bun B, Paul Wall, Z-Ro, Slim Thug, Killa Kyleon, and J. J. Watt of the Houston Texans. Beyoncé came home to help, too. The Bayou City rose up where others could only see wreckage.

That is the story of Houston, left for dead and more full of life each time because of it, its history becoming more vivid all the while. Future generations won't arrive with lessons from the past. Their eyes will only see the streets as they are. But through the music, they'll hear stories, and the stories of our neighborhoods are how we learn about ourselves.

The flame is being kept alive in a way that is distinctly Houston in its attitude, character, tempo, and tone. Rob Gullatte, Fat Tony, Candi Redd, Rosewood Thievz, Seano Phresh. They all arrive decades after Houston's foundation was built, full of new stories to tell. There's the promise of the late Big Gerb (at bottom right, by Anthony Rathbun), the faith of Lecrae, the space of The Hue, or the continuing lessons of H.I.S.D. and The Niyat.

The past is easy to let slip away. Records come out at a breakneck speed, new slangs take root with a quickness, songs travel around the world in minutes. Whole movements fade away under the light. Everything arrives so fast, we forget how it got there. Nowhere is this more apparent than in hip-hop. That has always been the beauty of the culture, that it was ahead of everything else. It is a genre of immediacy. *Now* is what matters, even when things are at their most fleeting, most exhaustive, or seemingly most pointless. Sometimes, that's the point.

Maybe *now* was what mattered in the Rap Attack Contests at Rhinestone Wrangler. Maybe *now* was what mattered in those sessions at DJ Screw's house, or in the rounds of the Dozens they'd play before passing the mic. Maybe it was in the moment—in that *now*—that some of the most seminal decisions by Houston artists were made over the years.

It's harder today to look towards the future because it's already here. Everything is saturated, and sifting the past has become a window into the present because the context of the world around us has evaporated. Hip-hop has always given us that context, making the messages of its past even more crucial now because those messages were never filtered in the first place. We look over our shoulders not to gaze back at our pasts, but to find the truths contained in those moments, and learn something about where we're going. ✖

Big Gerb (1983–2016)

EASTSIDE/NEAR NORTHSIDE

The late Hongree Mobb don Big Gerb (pronounced "jerb") always struck people at first sight by the size of his heft, but it was the size of his heart that overwhelmed when you met Gerardo Elias Martinez, Jr. in person. For his record release show in 2012, he bought Poppa Burgers [*author cosigns*] for the first 100 people who came into the club—one of numerous recollections of his generosity over the years. Hongree Mobb grew to include Surreal, U-Neek, DJ Meshak, Astrid, Young Dough 281, Spiktakula, and Gerb's brother, Swisha Man—who was in prison when we spoke, and to whom he wanted to give a shout-out. Gerb died of a heart attack in January 2016. He was 32.

When did your brother go to prison?

He went in, I wanna say it was 2010. August, 2010. He got sentenced to five years, and he should be out hopefully sometime this year. Well, he got sentenced to five and a half years, so if he doesn't make parole, he should be out sometime next year.

What was he convicted of?

He already had several felony cases, and he was already out on probation on an assault case—he had shot at somebody. And he got real bad on them Xanax pills, man. I seen them pills destroy him, man. This dude had the gold chains, the Versaces, the nice rims on the car . . . he had it all, man, and I seen them pills destroy him in a matter of time, man, you know?

Had you had anything like that in your family before, where somebody that close to you got locked up?

Yeah, man. All my uncles are in and out of prison. I had one uncle that did a couple of years in [a] Tijuana prison for bringing cocaine over here—well, attempting to bring cocaine over here to the US. So crime is no stranger in my family. Actually, my mom's side of the family—they're no strangers to prison. On the other hand, my dad's side of the family—they all went to law enforcement high school, they all went to U of H, took criminal justice classes, so it's like . . . opposite ends, you know? My dad's a bad boy, but all his family's good. My mom's a good girl, all her family's bad. I like to think I fall in the middle, you know?

You grew up on the Northside, yeah? What was your neighborhood like—where were you?

To give you a general idea, like North Main and Quitman, like minutes from Downtown.

Close to Fifth Ward then too.

Oh yeah, man. Fifth Ward is just over the train tracks. So, you know, I grew up listening to all the Geto Boys and all that local stuff, you know? We weren't like bottom of the barrel poor, but we weren't nowhere near rich or average. There were times when my mom had to go to, like, local churches, and they would help us out with groceries 'cuz it was a family of five in a one-bedroom

PHOTO: PETER BESTE

and that's about when I started fuckin' around with it. My homeboy had a karaoke machine, and we would chill out in his little garage, drink MD 20/20, and just freestyle and shit. We were just joking about it, man. We weren't taking it seriously back then. But that's about the time I got introduced to picking up a mic or tryin' to record. I used to be in a group, and we would save up our money—seven of us—enough to get an hour of studio time. That was a big deal, you know?

You started out freestyling, but do you remember the first time you took pen to paper and wrote something?

Yeah, a buddy of ours got killed back in 2000, and like I said, that was around the time I started rapping. Senior year of high school we lost a good buddy of ours. He was killed, and we made a little song in tribute to him, and I just let my feelings out, like, "I'll see you again one day, buddy." That was the realest shit I wrote back then.

That gave you the fever, yeah?

Really what gave me the . . . after just trying at it so many times, I realized I was just a natural, man, and everybody was like, "Man, you got it. There's no doubt. It's just a matter of time before some-body recognizes you or your skills get polished." That's all I've been doing over the years, man, is polishing my skills.

How did you get the Hongree Records crew together? When did that come to life?

That happened around 2007, when I was on the run. I was a fugitive, and my buddy, man, he lived in Humble, his name is Spiktakula and my brother that's currently in prison, his name is Swisha Man. At that time, I had just shot my way out of my little . . . I guess you could call it little record deal with the neighborhood drug dealer, so I was like, "You know what? We got ourself on the bottom, you know? I'ma put something together with my little weed money, without this big-time money." We were just joking around, and we were like, "It could be a half-bitten cheeseburger, man, and we'll just

garage apartment, man. So, yeah, there was a lot of tension, man. You know, my mom and dad constantly at each other's throats, me and my sister—my brother was a newborn baby—so my dad, finally, he was like, "Man, I gotta get us out of this." In 2000, he purchased the home we're in now, so we moved on up to the Eastside like *The Jeffersons*.

You're not that far from where you grew up, I guess, but it's a different feel over there, right?

It's the same shit, dude. It's actually a little nicer looking, but it's an optical illusion, man, because there's a lot of drugs bein' moved around here. To the untrained eye, you'll miss it, you know? But trouble's everywhere, man. If you look for it, you'll find it.

Were you rapping when you were still on the Northside, or did you start on the East End?

I think I started on the Eastside. When we moved over here, I was in my senior year of high school, call it *Hongree*, and we'll spell 'hongree' with an 'o' because we're from the South." So it started kind of as a joke, to pay homage to fat people. Like, you know, you got the Apple logo, it's a little apple—well this is a silhouette of a cheeseburger with a bite mark.

Were you a big guy when you were younger?

My whole life, bro. My whole life, man. Ever since I was a baby. I got some old-ass pictures, man. I been big my whole life. You know what's funny, man? I never see myself. Recently, just recently, man, just the last few days I realized how big I was. I never realized that I was that massive of a guy. I always knew that I was bigger than a lot of people, but when I saw 8Ball perform, and I got real close to him—and 8Ball's a big guy, man—he's a big dude, but when I got next to him, man, he looked small. Compared to me. So, I was like, "Damn, Big Gerb, you're a pretty big guy, you know. If you make 8Ball look little, you're a pretty big guy." It was a humbling experience, you know?

Well, you're pretty open about it—you talk about it in your rap and in your stand-up comedy.

Yeah, it doesn't bother me none, man. It only made me a better person. I believe that if I was able to jump fences, you know, if I was in good shape, I think I'd be robbing people, having sex with even more girls, and my dick would probably fall off by now, so I work with what God gave me, man. I still get pussy, man, and I'm still having a good time. You can't sit there and cry. Some people gotta be fat, man, and some people gotta be skinny. We're supposed to be different. You know, people say it's unhealthy. You know what? It may be, man, but I'm happy. I'm doin' it. There are people that are skinny that have never got a piece of vagina, and you know, I feel bad for *them*. It's like what God gave to man, and you're missing out on it, you know?

Part of what rap music is about is celebrating who you are, right?

I love being sexual, man. It's not so much that I'm being perverted, it's just . . . man, there's just nothing better than a young, attractive woman showing you her body, like what the fuck is better than that? You could have the worst day and that shit'll brighten your day. I love it. I love women.

What would you say it means to be a Latino rapper in Houston in 2014?

I feel like we go unnoticed a lot, man. You know, back in the SPM [South Park Mexican] heyday, there was a whole little Latino craze for a little while when I was growing up in high school, man. You had Dope House, you had Salty Water Records, you know, there was a couple of local cats that were makin' a buzz, and then it all just fell off, man. When SPM went away, it was like a whole Latino rap culture died with him, you know, got locked up with him. We just need somebody to speak for the people. I don't know that I'm ready to carry that burden, but I'm up for the challenge. I don't wanna be famous, man. I wanna be a voice for my people because too many times we go unnoticed, man. We go unrecognized for our work, man. And that's what I wanna do. Black people have Quanell X ready to stand up for them. Mexicans—we don't have somebody like Quanell X that we can call for help, and I feel a lot of it has to do with the language barrier. I don't even speak the best Spanish, bro. I've never been to Mexico. But these are still my people.

Cal Wayne

THIRD WARD

Some folks in Houston call him their "Tupac," but he can shrug that off because Cal Wayne doesn't sound like any other rapper, Houston or elsewhere. Wayne grew up in Cuney Homes in Third Ward, a public housing complex near Texas Southern University named for Norris Wright Cuney, a prominent black politician and civil rights leader from Galveston who fought for equal rights across Texas. Wayne grew up singing in church, but the hard-living at Cuney, the fact that both of his parents went to jail when he was young, and his brother's murder made the streets the subject of his lyricism once he became a rapper, debuting in 2008 with the mixtape *About My Brother's Business*.

PHOTO: JOBREA NEAL

You come from a neighborhood with a lot of history.

It's a jungle out here right now.

Did you get hit by the hurricane at all? Did you get flooded?

Nah, I did well. That's why people like Bloodbath and me stayin' on the phone. They wanna call Third Ward "Midtown." Everybody want the land because see they built them sewers and everything, in the ghetto you got the drainage sewers and all that . . .

They've gobbled up entire blocks over there. You don't even recognize them anymore.

Well, see Third Ward put up a fight when they were doin' that . . . Third Ward, the original name was Emancipation Park. That first park dedicated to Juneteenth. But Third Ward and Fifth Ward were the original neighborhoods. Freedman's Town, Bucktown, and Emancipation Park. So all the culture really come from where we a part of, Third Ward. It's just like we've always been outcasts. I mean like we to the Southside like Fifth Ward is to the Northside. You can't come to the South and not come through Third Ward, same way you can't get to the Northside without goin' to Fifth Ward. But through music, that kind of stopped the Northside/Southside beef. It's real.

Do you think it's because Third Ward is so big? I mean it goes all the way through South Park, the whole Southside, that's all Third Ward.

Yeah, a lot of people don't know that. A lot of people call Enyart and all that South Park, but they're really Third Ward. But we a big-time ward with a bunch of neighborhoods. A lot of people don't know that. I'm surprised you heard that. See, on the Southside, Yates is where we're divided, like by my mama's time, then they came from South OST to my zone at Yates. I was chillin' like they wasn't from Third Ward. I'm like, "Y'all ain't really Third Ward." But that's where it came from, that just goin' on, goin' on, and the new generation, they went all the way up. What they call that generation, that generation we a part of?

You're kind of a millennial, I think. I'm Generation X.

When Generation X?

I was born in '73.

Well, that'd be about right. We the fuck-ups, and they the *super* fuck-ups.

Well we hand it off. We teach each other.

You know, even musically, Third Ward's never really had a voice. Like we had Big Moe, but Moe wasn't Third Ward like that. So I didn't have somebody to come teach me how. Trae, Z-Ro, Lil' O, and all them, they rappin' about the streets, and they'll do somethin' with you, and you know, we come from where I came from, and Moe died, so we really got to get out there and *earn* it, but it's like that naturalness, that genuineness is what is kinda our strong point.

Well you got Darryl Scott. That's some voice.

Yeah. That's my boy. I loved when Darryl Scott used to make tapes. That's a throwback right there. We were younger than dirt.

Were you going to Blast when that was open?

Nah, I never did swish through there. I was super Southside. I mean, I was a Swishahouse hater. I just . . . the first person on Swishahouse that's

been, like, one of my best homies right now, J-Dawg, I told my guy in prison, I say, "Man, I never seen nobody get play on the Southside like *that*. And after that point, well, you can understand the CD in they car, and they be jammin', and you can tell it was authentic and it was actually jammin'. I never seen a Slim Thug CD growin' up, I never seen a Paul Wall CD growin' up, Mike Jones . . . you know what I'm sayin'? It's not knockin' 'em, I just never! And for them to be able to cross that boundary, to do stuff on both sides of town and get the love, you know what I mean?

Now it's all mixed together, right?

Well, yeah. Yeah, basically, but you're just talkin' about culture. Northside, Southside, it's like, we all cool with the dudes that's on the Northside rappin'. The Southside was already cool with them, but the Southside boys can't get along with each other right now. And still, by the end of the day, you'll still have that feelin', no, this my whip. And boys on the Northside can always say they always stuck together more. I feel like Swishahouse looked at Screwed Up Click like, "Damn, they don't really realize what they got over there." And they capitalized on it, made it a business. And same thing now, a lot of things that we didn't get the credit for, it's like we ain't trippin', but a lot of people don't realize we started like this. That's how Bloodbath out here. Southside got all the flavor. Like I say, everybody'll tell you that. The swag comes from the South. Comin' down, know'm talkin' 'bout, that was all Southside. Them Southside fools.

Northside just did it a different way.

The thing is, Paul Wall, Mike Jones, and all of them, they my age, right? And what it was, they grew up in the area I was growin' up in over there. Like I was *on* the Southside, so I enjoyed it. *They* had to listen to Keke and Pokey and them dissin' 'em on Screwtapes and all that. So they went and said, "We gonna go on and make our *own* stuff." And they lookin' at Screwed Up Click on everybody that done *died*. So many of them died or went to jail or somethin', and even when I was with Lil' Keke, for the time when we had the label we was doin' together, it's like I learned a lot *from* Ke because Ke really pioneered the whole thing, but Ke really got fucked, you know what I'm sayin'? The whole city rode off of his style. The whole city rode off of . . . I ain't even gonna say rode off it, but the whole city embraced his . . . Ke was the don of the city. Scarface from the South too, but Scarface was bigger than Ke outside of Houston. But in Houston, when I was growin' up, when they had the "Top 5 at 5" on the radio, all five songs were Ke. You wanted to be like him. Keke kicked everybody on a Screwtape, Lil' Flip sayin' he the freestyle king. Nobody on the Southside.

Keke can freestyle for a half hour, no problem.

Every Screwtape he was ever on, whoever was on the tape with him, Ke mashed 'em. He kilt 'em. Flip ain't never been on no Screwtape with no Ke and no Fat Pat, no Pokey. He couldn't stay in the water. Screw gained a plaque, you know, somebody stood behind it, but Screw had a bunch of lil' homies that didn't take it serious. In the streets, we never felt that way. You walk around on the Southside, ask anybody on the Southside who it is, and they'll say Ke and Pat. And my potnah E.S.G. You know, I'm the misfit. I'm an outcast. But in the streets I'm the people's champ right now.

Tell me about that. You started in Third Ward—you were in Cuney Homes?

Yeah, I was born and raised in Cuney Homes. Cuney Homes is the largest real project in Houston. Like, you know you got a lot of low income parts of town, but these owned by the government, like the real projects, like the Magnolia in New Orleans, Queensbridge in New York, and Pork & Beans in Miami. It's the real projects. We born and raised here, and shit . . . it's the same story as everybody else, but we had all our other lil' kids, me and my brothers. My brother Qball went to prison in '07. And my mom went to jail when I was like, maybe 12. I was homeless at, like, 12. My homeboys—I used to come sleep on they bed and everything. I ain't have no bed. But I been doin' music since I was little bitty boy. I was singin' in the choir and we did all kinda stuff while I was in school, but we just

the dirty kids, you know what I'm sayin'? It ain't in my mind. I didn't really think, "I better make it." Because, man, people where I'm from don't make it, you know what I'm sayin'? That's for the *other* side, you know what I'm sayin'?

It always seems like that, right?

Yeah! But I always say in my heart, I'm talkin' about Third Ward has always been known for havin' heart. We known for bein' ratchet, we known for bein' wild, you know what I'm sayin'? But it's like—I had heart. I always said anything I put my mind to—it took a while for people to start to take to it, but I just think, like, people in Houston are scared of change. They kinda for a long time, like, they mean to my folks. They ain't know you already. Houston is a biased city. I say all the time the H in the Astros hats stands for "Hatin', hold your nuts." You'll be killin' a motherfucker and they so syruped out and chilled out and they ain't groovin'. Just lookin' at you. Like you fucked up or somethin'. Naw, you gotta stay there, find your direction. One thing about Houston—if you can win the streets over, you'll never die. I done been to prison four times, man, to the penitentiary, and I met every one of these niggas out here, and at the end of the day, I still survive, you know what I'm sayin'? This is what I do. No support, no backin'. The whole crew that I done put together, me, Junebug, Bloodbath . . . all this come from my story. And Scarface—I was the first artist he really wanted to cosign, but I ended up goin' to prison. I end up goin' to prison, and every time I get it goin' I go to prison. Even when I was with Lil' Keke for a while I end up goin' to prison. I never reached out to him or he never reached out to me, and that was the crazy part. I thought that he wasn't *hearin'* it. And then out of the blue I started gettin' them calls, man. "Hey man, Scarface wanna meet ya." I done hooked up with everybody in the city, but it's different for Cal Wayne. Cal Wayne can't get no radio play, but you can hardly post up in the neighborhood without hearin' e'rebody jammin' Cal Wayne. But it's like, if you can survive here, you can survive anywhere, man.

How long was the last time, when you were locked up?

I did like three years four months last time. I been out like a year and a half, but I done caught three more cases on three bonds, on parole, I just did the last two like a month ago. I done had a five-year sentence, a three-year sentence, and another five-year sentence. I been back-and-forth. But man, if you ain't comin' out of the right side of town now, knowin' somebody who know somebody, you gotta beat the streets up! You get a lot of experience. A lot of experience in this shit.

But that's what you do.

Yeah! See, I'm like, "Shit . . . that ain't gonna hurt these niggas." That's what I'm used to! That's where I come from. If anything, to me, it's an accomplishment. I'm out of prison now like I told you, a year and some change, and even though I had to fight some more cases and get my paper, I'm still nominated for every award so far as bein' the people's champ. I'm just tryin' to stay home, you know, wherever you go, they know your name. *People* root for you. That's what means the most for me, because *people* are rootin' for Wayne out there. Bloodbath, Junebug. As we speakin', I'm on the block in the car, know what I'm sayin'? It's like my brother J-Dawg. J-Dawg call himself the "Northside Cal Wayne," and that's a compliment because he been there.

I was watching the video for "48 Bars Of Power." That's really street level, everything that you're saying in that track, and you shot it at street level, like on the corner.

Yeah, and look at the numbers versus the people that's on the radio. And that song is like 10 years old! I recorded that song on an old, old, album I did, and this dude wanted to do that for a video. He loved that song and wanted to do a video. That song was old. I been to prison twice since I did "48 Bars Of Power." I been two times.

And the video is from years ago?

No, the video was from this summer that just passed. Right before I went to jail. I went to jail 30 minutes after I shot the video. I had a $250,000 bond because my name is Cal Wayne. I walked out that store in the video, went down the street, and went to jail.

Dr. Robert S. Muhammad

MOSQUE NO. 45

Dr. Muhammad earned his PhD in urban planning and environmental policy from Texas Southern University in 2016 and is a longtime advisor to some of the subjects interviewed in this book. He has been an advocate for the marginalized from a number of different perspectives during his lifetime, pairing a deep background in city planning and community activism with an understanding of the money and politics involving decisions that disproportionally affect Houston's minority communities. He is the Southwest Regional Representative of Minister Louis Farrakhan and hosts a radio show on KPFT each Wednesday afternoon called "Connect The Dots."

PHOTO COURTESY OF DR. ROBERT S. MUHAMMAD

I know that you've had a lot of contact with K-Rino, Justice Allah, and figures like that over the years. How did you come together?

I became a student minister here in Houston, Texas on July 1, 1987, and the first building that we used for our meeting place was on Brandon and Scott, right there in Sunnyside. We moved from there in 1990 to Cullen Boulevard, right there in what's called Foster Place—what some would consider Sunnyside. So it has always been the place I hold my ministry to because that's where I got started. That being said, what middle schools and high schools are in that area? You of course have got Cullen Middle School, which is over there on Scott, you've got Worthing, you've got Sterling further down MLK, Jones High School, St. Lo off of MLK. So, being that I'm in that community, I know these children. I would run into them as I would be speaking at different schools, or different events, or vigils. In fact, that's where I met Quanell X. He was a high school student at Worthing. So it was a natural environment that I would know people from the South Park Coalition, from South Acres, from Sunnyside, and from Third Ward. So that's how I come to know them, and they come to know me.

I know that you've got a background in urban planning . . . your association with MTZ and your consulting firm, you know a great deal about city planning. As far as the history of South Park—why was it planned where it was?

Well if you look at actually outside of the 610 Loop, at one time everything outside of the 610 Loop was considered suburbs. [Laughs] When you go over 610 between Cullen and MLK, and you look at that street or that subdivision over there, you'll find it has a lot of World War I names—places or cities that are associated with World War I. So that community actually has little to do with, really, black people. These places that we consider the suburbs once were where Caucasians and Jews lived. I'll give you an example: Ezekiel Cullen Junior High School was a place—that area actually was where a lot of Jewish people lived. Riverside. Along North and South MacGregor. Jewish people were not allowed to live in River Oaks. They lived there first, because you'll find some old churches, even in Third Ward were actually old synagogues! In fact, the church right across the street from—I don't know what they call it now, but it used to be called the Contemporary Learning Center—right there at, I wanna say Blodgett and Almeda. There's a high school there, with a park that's next to it. Right there, there's a church, right in the middle of the block, or down the street from Almeda, one block east of Almeda, right there on Blodgett. Look at it and you'll see the Star of David right up in the entrance. It used to be a synagogue. So what I'm saying to you is, is that there was a time when black people couldn't be caught south of Alabama [Street] past sundown. It was a white area, South Park was. That was considered the suburb. We moved out that way, and when we moved out, others moved out. They went further out. Then Jewish people began moving out on Braeswood, and other places. When we began to integrate, they moved out.

And what era was that during?

This was like the late '70s, early '80s . . . all of the '70s and the '80s they began leaving out of—what you think is in the city, really used to be the suburbs. I'll give you another example. Where you find 45? The Pierce Elevated? Particularly over there by U of H? Actually, that's Third Ward.

Yeah!

[Laughs] There's no way to cut it in half. In fact, I-45 in the '60s used to be at Polk and Scott, right across the street from the Latino Learning Center, right down where the light rail is being built. Where 288 is cut off what you consider Third Ward, over to the west. The point I'm making is that the 288 cut off a whole . . . took about, I dunno, about 20,000 to 30,000 residents out of what used to be Third Ward! Cut right through. To the west. So, we done coughed up a highway, and by a purposeful *disinvestment* of public infrastructure dollars—particularly when this city had at-large elections, and didn't have single-member districts—our city was cut up. And our money was spent elsewhere. It was spent out in the suburbs, and as the public infrastructure dollars went out, so, too, did the private infrastructure dollars, and so, too, did the middle-class population. And on and on and on . . . I mean, I could give you the history . . . for instance, southwest Houston. Look at how, at one point, you looked and you saw how all of the sudden Willowridge, in the early '80s, was a powerhouse. How was that? That's because your middle-class blacks and whatnot start moving out there. And then, when they built Lawrence Elkins High School—then the blacks started moving from where Willowridge was—Briargate, Ridgegate and all of that, and start moving out towards Elkins, and Elkins—they moved out to Hightower, those subdivisions out there. There was a time when Aldine was like—off-the-chain. That's because many of the students went out north. And those who went out north, the further north they went, they went out to those suburbs, and then middle schools became powerhouses there. Like they are—these West-fields and other ones, the further out you go, you find all of this beautiful black talent out there, just like what integration did to our historically black colleges and universities. Prairie View was the Notre Dame of the South at one time. That arena named after Billy Nicks? That's because you had All-Pros that were coming out of Prairie View, man. You couldn't beat Prairie View! This is true! Then integration came, and then they could go to those other schools. They didn't want us punishing their talent out there, kickin' they tail. Even Bear Bryant woke up, sooner or later, and made Alabama—now you look out there, all the great talent . . . there's brothers out there runnin' that ball, dunkin' that basketball, and doin' all of that. I'm way off track, brother . . .

Do you think that Third Ward and Fifth Ward and South Park have had similar issues, similar problems, circumstances that have put them where they are now?

Absolutely. The biggest danger we have to our community is not light rail, or eminent domain by government. It's tax foreclosures. It's moving control of the land. If our mama or auntie or grandmama owns some property in South Park, instead of us holding on to it, fixing it up, and renting it out, what we do is sometimes is . . . siblings begin fighting, and because the siblings are fighting, they don't pay the taxes. So we're losing all of our property at tax foreclosures. And it's not all because the taxes got too high and we couldn't pay 'em. We just moved away! Our middle-class, our black intellectual and intelligentsia, in some cases have moved away. And so now we're seeing a gentrification . . . I should say a *regentrification* of certain parts of Third Ward and Fifth Ward. Look at Fourth Ward! Fourth Ward is gone.

Fourth Ward is *gone*.

Freedmen's Town is gone. Freedmen's Town is just a byword. It's just something we say. But it's gone.

Are the bricks still even there, in the street?

Yeah, in some cases, and then they tear them up if they have a chance.

Yeah, they'd take them right out. If somebody gave them a green light, they'd have them out of there tomorrow.

That's a fact. Already know that. If it wasn't for the work of Gladys House, and others there in that area—Lynwood Johnson with the Allen Parkway Village people—that place would've been bulldozed a long time ago. But see, what has happened is you have had a generation go out to the suburbs, raise their children . . . it was white flight. It was one of the reasons they created the magnet programs in HISD. That's another story for another time. But white flight—they went out to suburbs . . . once they raise their children, put their children through college, then they're tired of cutting grass and driving back-and-forth into the city, so they come back in to the city because we have now the best arenas and stadiums Downtown. Think about it: We've expanded the George R. Brown Convention Center, we have a large convention hotel, we have light-rail now, we have one of the greatest museum districts in the world. We have the greatest medical center in the world. We have all four of the performing arts: stage, opera, symphony, and ballet. What more do you need?

So when a developer comes around and starts plucking away the outer fringes of Fifth Ward, putting condos there, that's fine for some people, "Yeah, I'll take it."

See, we don't mind having new neighbors. See, your neighborhood doesn't change. It's your neighbors that do. We don't mind it, but when we change a demographic, sometimes the politics change. Economics change. So, it's something that they had . . . again, a purposeful public disinvestment, and when there's public infrastructure investment, then what happens is that private dollars follow that. Or, private dollars will be invested with the promise of public infrastructure investment. Either way, there's a nexus between the two.

So that gets pretty complicated in areas like Fifth Ward and Third Ward, when it comes to the allotment of tax dollars to fix up streets that they haven't looked at in 30 years.

That's correct because those streets need more work than the other streets. Bringing a neighborhood up to standard, as [former Houston mayor] Bob Lanier called it, which really was his way of fixing up—was fixing up certain neighborhoods, and giving his developer friends a wink and a nod that, "I'm getting ready to fix up this area with public infrastructure dollars. If I were you, I'd make sure I come in there and do some developing."

Because now the water lines are going to have the capacity to support multi-family and commercial use, instead of just single family housing. See, the waterline capacity and the larger wastewater capacity, the ability to have different kinds of structures other than a single family shotgun house. Or a ranch-style home. So the infrastructure is important. Without the infrastructure . . . look where the public works dollars are going, and you have a good idea of where development's gonna go. A good idea. South Park and Sunnyside . . . see, here's where it has happened. The same pattern. It's really not complicated. I wouldn't even use that word. It appears to be complicated, but it's not. It's pretty simple. When you look at the Native American, and what was done to him . . . they came and they caught, fought, or killed all of the braves. And the only thing left was the elders, the children, and the women. Look at our community! Brothers gettin' locked up like 45 goin' north, and look where they all come from. Look at where the cases of HIV/AIDS are. You don't have to be no conspirator, no conspiracy theory nut. Just look at it. And what's left in our community: women, grandmothers raising their grandchildren, babies, and elders. That's all. Where are the brothers?

Locked up.

Yeah! So now, what happens is you become a renter, and when you're a renter, you don't have no property or ownership rights, and what happens is they come in . . . since there's no zoning, you can build whatever you want to on your own property. Unless there's a deed restriction, and if there's no deed restriction, brother, you can build whatever you wanna build. So, after a while, these subdivisions—which once were peopled by Caucasians or by middle-class blacks, before they moved out further—now these deed restrictions have expired. And so now next to my new ranch-style home, now you look and all of the sudden there's a condominium, a big monstrous condominium built right next to my home. That drives my property taxes up.

And drives you out.

But he was able to build it because my deed restriction expired, which would have precluded him from building such a house, or such a structure next to me.

We talk about those sorts of things and the regentrification of those neighborhoods, with issues in the educational system, the health system, vaccines, and everything like that in the neighborhoods, how do those things get rearranged? Do you see those things improving?

Only if we wake up. We have to wake up, brother. We have to wake up. Our problem is that we know the truth and we ignore it, so we're paying the price for that. I mean, since I've been a student minister of Houston, Texas, I can honestly say, brother, I've put literally—not I but *we*—have put literally a hundred thousand people in front of Minister Farrakhan in this city. It's not like they don't know the truth, brother. Once you hear what I'm telling you, brother Lance, it's not like they don't know the truth. But we choose to ignore the truth. Anyone's opposition—I'm gonna say from the establishment and from different preachers in this city—to the rise and the influence of Islam in this city . . . and I own some things we did. We shot our own selves in the foot. But what I want you to know is that when you ignore divine words, brother, it's like ignoring this pain you've got in your chest. "Aight, I'ma go with it. Lemme take two aspirin, and hell, that's gonna be it." The next thing you know, you got a damn heart attack or a stroke. Why? Because you ignored the warning signs. We were already told this day was coming. When there wouldn't be no jobs for us. We was already told! That the day was coming. That the day was coming, man. Not to take these . . . end these vaccines. We were already told that land was the basis of freedom, you know? And we need to own some of this Earth we can call our own. We were already told all this. So why didn't we heed, when we were told this? By Minister Muhammad, and his servant Minister Farrakhan? Why didn't we heed this? So now, we're suffering. We're reaping what we've sown. And it's not all our fault, but at some point in time, you've got to mature enough to be able to say, "We can't be sittin' around here just blamin' the white man." It ain't the man's fault.

He gonna do what he gonna do. He did it to the Indians, he'll do it to you and me again and again and again, and of course, if we didn't learn the first time, what the hell's gonna make us learn the second time?

One of the things I was talking to Justice [Allah] about is when you talk about the health problems in an area like South Park. Drive around—what do you see? There's no grocery store where people can go to and buy healthy foods. They can go to the convenience store or they can go to Timmy Chan's, or Tammy Chin's if it's on the other side of the neighborhood . . . but where do you start?

Well, you start, brother, with teaching, from my perspective, from our perspective, you gotta teach people how to eat to live. If you know better, you'll *do* better. You teach people how to eat to live. You change their diet, then what they'll do is they'll say, "You know something? I do believe in economics and the law of supply and demand." If there is no demand, you will look to supply the people with what they're demanding. If we were taught better, or would listen to good teaching, we would demand better food. There's no way we would be eating that garbage. And they would slowly but surely go out of business. And the people who supplied our better needs would be the ones that we would go to. You know, it's like that in the street. If a man got some dope that's stepped on, you understand, or got some wacky weed he growing in his backyard, but there's another cat here who's bringing in some red bud Sensimilla, or he got some cocaine that ain't stepped on, so when you smoke it, it goes right straight to your knot? Well, word gets down the street! "Man, he has got some bomb!" "Nah, here you go—shoot—you need to eat some of this!" Well, that cat's the hottest cat in town! They on the same block. You got a dope house on the same block he got a dope house, but everybody come to your dope house. Why? 'Cuz you got the best stuff. Supply and demand, brother. If you got the best food, if you teach people—if you give the people what they want, or teach the people what they should want and need, and they will heed that teaching. Then you'll find, brother, that when you supply their needs, that's how you make money. So

I'm not angry at the immigrants for coming in the country and making money off of us. I'm not angry at them at all. Because the truth of the matter is, brother, if there's somebody that supplies your needs, then they deserve to make some money.

That's on you. It's your needs.

Right. Right. So we gotta learn to supply our own needs.

Third Ward and Fifth Ward are obviously different situations because of the gentrification that's happening on the fringes of those neighborhoods, but as far as providing a strong economic base in an area like South Park, what do you think are the keys?

The keys are to learn the lesson from Third, Fourth Ward, Fifth Ward, and look at what happened to them. It is to have a sense of community once again. To stop wasting our money, and to begin to pool our resources and buy up property in South Park and Sunnyside. Until and unless we do that, all the conversations really are a waste of time. That's the first thing, is to pool our resources and begin to buy up the community where we live. Second thing we've got to do, is that we've got to supply our own needs. Instead of complaining about Timmy Chan's, open up your own restaurant that feeds your people a more healthy style of food, and ask your people, and your people should have enough sense to support you. Be a good businessman. Be a good businessman to them, and let them become good customers so we may circulate our own dollars.

That kind of thing is contagious.

Absolutely. The third thing is make your own neighborhood a decent place to live. Get with your neighbors and clean up your neighborhood. Get rid of the junk cars. Cut your grass, fix your fence, paint your house. You know, there's no excuse to live like that. When we can all pool together and clean up, when we can cut down the weeded lots. The city will come help you, but you've got to work the political apparatus so that you can tap into the resources that you already put down for. Whether you rent or you buy, you're still—the taxes the homeowner has to pay at the end of the year get wrapped up in your rent payment. You've already paid for the property taxes, even though you're a rental.

You're paying them for the landlord.

Right, so you can just demand of the city that they come out, whether you own or rent, come out and cut these weeded lots and help clean up your neighborhood! Pick up the heavy trash, stop dumping, illegal dumping. This isn't in any particular priority or order, I'm just givin' it to you off the top of my head. And then get involved with the local schools! But don't wait 'til high school! Get in the elementary schools and the middle schools, and straighten these children out before they go further and get caught up in the madness.

Part of the problem is that the city ignores those neighborhoods until they want to start coming in and giving areas to developers.

Well, the day after someone gets elected to represent me is the day I'll be knocking on their door. This is what I need, and if you don't have this done in two years, then don't come back to me for no vote. They only come to us when they want us to vote for them. But what you should demand is for them to help you clean up your own neighborhood. "We gonna have a neighborhood cleanup on this block—will you come out and help us?" Call your city councilwoman or city councilman and say, "We wanna clean up this area, this subdivision. We wanna clean up these lots, clean off this old garbage, pick up this stuff, pick up that." And they can pool together all of the public works and heavy trash pickup, neighborhood protection, to get all that done. They can help you! Every Saturday you can have a community cleanup.

Who is the city councilperson that represents the area of South Park?

I wanna say it's Wanda Adams, because they've redrawn District D, but I'm not really sure because they might—Cohen might cover that. I'm not sure. But I'm thinking—I'm about 80 percent sure that District D is now . . . is Wanda Adams, but you'd have to ask City Council . . . call down to her office.

Right. I could just see about getting a map of the redistricting lines.

Right. Should be online. Let me get this point across before we do close this interview, brother Lance. In the '90s, Minister Farrakhan came to Houston, and there was a meeting between myself, Quanell X, and J Prince of Rap-A-Lot. And Minister Farrakhan, he told J Prince, he said, "Brother, one of your rap songs will reach more of our youth than all of my speeches." That's heavy. For a man that has given thousands of speeches, has spoken millions of words, has spoken all over this world, all over this planet, brother. For him to say something like that . . . and yet, he *said* it. So, the power of hip-hop has yet to be unleashed to change our condition from bad to good. It *has* been manipulated to change our condition from bad to worse. But now there's a rise of conscious rap all over the world as a result of social networks, social media—also over in the Middle East—and it's hip-hop music. You've got the youth of Occupy Houston and Occupy Wall Street. All of them have been affected by the hip-hop generation. Now it's time for them to get down for they crown, brother. And to rap, and to put some words of wisdom in their heads about a new world. It's okay to rap about what's going on in your city, about syrup, and "25 lighters on the dresser," and smokin' on hay, and the "City Of Syrup," and all of that. All that's fine. But you gotta tell 'em it's time to rise. They gotta get ready for the revolution, and they have to seize the time. And this is what we are attempting to do by just teaching them the truth, and then letting them put it in the hip-hop music, and then circulate it among the children, so you can then plant seeds of wisdom going forward. There's nothing wrong with rapping about the realities that you face, the poverty and the poor education and all of that, but they need to preach a new world that's fair. That's equitable. That's just. That's free—what kind of world they would like to see.

Do you feel like those seeds are taking root?

Yes. Because this thing is . . . how much lower can we go? We can't go any lower. We can't get any more low down than we are right now. We'll just look silly before the world. But we're settin' ourselves up for genocide, for slaughter. Because should the enemy decide to turn on us and slaughter us, nobody would cry out because we're being portrayed as the clowns and buffoons and the degenerative factor throughout the United States! That's being projected around the world. So if they came and mowed us down with tanks and machine guns like the Chinese did their youth in Tiananmen Square, wouldn't nobody say anything. Because we're seen as just being so totally out of the box that somebody needs to put us back and put us in a garbage bag and put us out on the curb. That's the way the world is beginning to look at us. But we've allowed our enemy to do that. We've played into his hands. So what must be done is what the Minister showed us in the Million Man March. He showed the world another picture of the black male like they had never seen him before. Sixteen hours—we occupied Washington, DC for sixteen hours! The Supreme Court didn't meet that day, that Monday. The Congress didn't meet that day, and the President was here in Austin giving a speech on race! DC first! And look over there—go right on MSNBC website and look up any of those stories about Egypt. What do they call for Friday? They call for a Million Man March on Friday! Where is the paradigm? Who started that paradigm of "you can't even have a march if you don't call for a million people?" It ain't even a march if it ain't a million. After that, it was the Million Woman March, Million Children March, Millions for Reparations, Million Fat People March, Million . . . Million Latino March. Man, please. You can't have a march unless you put "million" in front of it now. We're at the root of world revolution, or I'd rather say—in spiritual terms—that global resurrection. The resurrection of the righteous is taking place, all over the planet, regardless of class, creed, or color. The dead are rising around the world, and now's the time for our hip-hop artists, for their consciousness to rise. And whether they get played on 97.9 The Box or not, whether they're on the *Billboard* 100 for hip-hop music or not, they need to seed the minds of the youth to be ready for the new world yet to come, because the new world is for them. And the enemy of us all would like to take us to hell with him, but our children are the Joshua generation that will lead us into the promised land, and the hip-hop artists are the ones that can put the idea in their head. And when the time comes, that seed will germinate, and they will lead us to the promised land.

OMB Bloodbath

THIRD WARD

The first part of her name means "Only My Brothers," and it refers to a whole movement of artists with which she rides, including fellow Third Ward rappers Junebug and Cal Wayne. The Bloodbath part of the name becomes evident in the music. Born in 1993, OMB Bloodbath's career started in earnest upon her release from a two-year prison stint, but she had been writing for years by then. Growing up in Third Ward, what she saw in the neighborhood was what she reported in her songs, and she took that message into the clubs, first appearing on most folks' radars in 2015 with her video and single "Shootston." She had Third Ward behind her way before that.

How long have you been making music?

I started writing poetry when I was nine years old, and I recorded my first song when I was 11, called "Tre's Finest." You know, "The Tre" is another way of sayin' Third Ward. That was my first song. I started around nine to 11.

And was music a part of your life early on? Were you listening to a lot of music when you were growing up?

Yeah, my mama is a singer, so I just . . . I don't know. In school, I was really into activism. Like Angela Davis, and I was into a lot of poets like Langston Hughes. And this was in elementary. This was before I even really knew about rap. The first song that ever really just caught my eye with rap was Cash Money "Back Dat Ass Up." [Laughs]

When I first seen that "Back Dat Ass Up," I was like, "Man, I wanna live like *them* dudes." So I just mixed that, what they do, in between the poetry I was readin' and just made it my own way.

What was it about that song that you connected with?

I don't know! They just looked like they was havin' fun! Gold, diamonds, nice cars—it was just live. I was like, "Man, I wanna be like *them* niggas."

But that's totally not what ended up in your lyrics. You stay away from that stuff. You're rapping about a lot more real stuff.

Yeah, see—the way I always thought about music, like breakin' into the industry-wise—I been havin' a business mind since I was—I got tattoos on my hands at 14. Everybody was like, "You don't want a job?" I was like, "Man, I'ma be a rapper when I get older." Like, it's *been* in play, you know what I'm sayin'? I just think if you come with somethin' turnt up—like my first video was "Shootston." There's nothing positive at all about that song, but it caught the peoples' eye. So I always thought if I just get they attention, *then* I can give 'em the message. Because a lot of young people, you know, they feel like people preachin' to 'em and all that shit. Lemme get they attention first, then I'ma let 'em know what's really goin' on. It's the best of both worlds. Like I make turnt up music too, I just feel like there's too much goin' on in the world for you not to be touchin' on what's really happenin'.

If you just talk about all that other shit, you livin' in la-la land.

Well the preaching part is a matter of you figuring out a way to say it where it doesn't come off as preaching, but they just take it in.

I gotta do it to where they can feel it, where they can say, "Man, I been through this too," you know what I'm sayin'? And not you *tellin'* me what to do. I'm givin' you the ultimatum—you can do this and you can live and be free, or you can end up like my homeboy or some nigga that grew up in my hood. So I be lettin' 'em know that it's all about the choices you make.

What part of Third Ward did you grow up in?

I'm from Blodgett. Almeda, dog. Over by MacGregor and all that. Shit, I started comin' to The Bottom real young, so I really done traveled all over The Tre. I get love everywhere, but it started on Blodgett.

I saw an interview with you where you talked about how rappers rap about how they live and it's not really how they live—when did you realize that? Were you already making music, or did you learn that pretty early on?

Nah, you know, as a kid you're lookin' at cats like, "Man, I want that to be me one day." But shit, they probably was renting cars and makin' shit look good too! It's just, as a kid, you grow up and certain shit look good, but once you start living in the real world, you come in the door and you payin' bills and seein' how life really works, a lot of that shit, it's not what it is. I remember when I was comin' up, it was like a group of friends I had, they was always "Polo Down, Polo Down," all the time. I was like, "Man, I need to get my money right so I could . . ." And come to find out they was runnin' out the stores with the shit! So everything good ain't gold. You gotta learn it. 'Cuz like I said, comin' up you not gonna know it 'til you experience it and know for sure with your own eyes.

Well you were saying earlier you were reading Angela Davis and Langston Hughes, and I would imagine Dick Gregory and all kinds of other important black writers—when you started writing lyrics where you knew they were going to be rap songs, did you automatically start putting that stuff in or did that come a little bit later?

Nah, I remember around the time when I first start tryin' to rap—'cuz I started rappin' when I was 11. I had wrote a little rap, and I was like, "A crust of bread and a corner to sleep in / A minute to smile and an hour to weep in." The first line of that is from a Paul Laurence Dunbar poem. To be honest, the older I got, the more I dumbed my songs down for people. Because when I say I used to be—a person can hear my song now and be like, "Man, she speakin' on street, she speakin' on real." But back *then*, it was like *lyrics* with me. I wanted to make motherfuckers be like, "Damn!" So I had to dumb my shit down a lot just so people could get they ears to it. Like I said, most people want it turnt up. They don't wanna really hear no real shit.

But do you feel like it's dumbing down or it's just making the language simpler and keeping the message real?

Yeah, yeah! I'ma put it like that. I ain't gonna say dumbed down. Yeah. It's makin' it easier for *everybody* to understand. 'Cuz back then I was readin' a thesaurus every day, learning different words, like, "Okay . . . friend. That could be comrade, that could be . . ." You know what I'm sayin'? I wasn't tryin' to be stuck on one thing because one thing—I love Houston music, don't get me wrong. I love my city, and I love the impact that our music and our culture made on the world still to this day, but one thing that I hate is that when you hear "Houston rap," the first thing you know they're gonna say, "Sittin' on fours / fuckin' bad hos / ridin' candy doors . . ."

Comin' down.

Yeah, comin' dyne! Like I never could get with that shit. I always wanted my shit soundin' different. That's why a lot of people will hear me and be like, "You don't *sound* like you're from Houston."

The thing is also when you're from Houston you know a lot more Houston music, and you know that not all of Houston sounds alike. That's just what the mainstream hears.

Exactly. That's exactly so. I just wanted to show a different side, because if you listen to somebody like *Hawk*, Hawk wasn't doin' no . . . you know what I'm sayin'? Hawk wasn't playin' with these niggas. Bro was spinnin' *lyrics*, you know what I'm sayin'?

Real songs, real messages.

Yeah, man, but I feel like to each his own. And I feel like K-Rino, these people that really just . . .

Well K-Rino made a lot of people realize there was a spot for them to do that kind of thing. It's a big city.

It's a *real* big city.

You've been cutting your own lane. Seems like you're bringing some people to hip-hop and to Houston rap that might not have found it otherwise, right?

Yeah, yeah. It's like sometimes it get overwhelming, like, my people be havin' to tell me, "You don't

even understand—what you doin'," like, 'cuz to *me*, it's not as big as it really is 'cuz I ain't . . . I'm still independent. I'ma *stay* independent. What I'm sayin' is I'm still damn near just rockin' out in the streets, you feel me? So it's like, when people like, "Man, they jammin' you in Atlanta. They *love* you in Atlanta. They love you in Dallas . . ." Some lady came to buy a CD from me when I was on tour, and she was like, "I'm from Iraq. Man, we love y'all music down there. 'Same Boat' got me through a lot of hard times." And it's fuckin' my head up because I'm like, "Man, this lady said she from Iraq." Like I've never even breathed that air before. I wouldn't even think to ever go there one day. And you sayin' I'm gettin' you through hard times? That was gratifying. It's way bigger than me. It's way bigger than I think, but I feel like I have brought love, and a little light to the city on another note.

Also maybe people haven't heard a rapper speaking from your perspective, right?

And see, one thing about that is like, I'm all about bein' myself to the fullest, so it's like, a lot of people expect, "Oh, alright—it's a girl. She 'bout to come and spit some extra hard shit," but when I sing, I don't have . . . I'm not ashamed to sing a love song, sing a song and really put my . . . you know, because I love music as a whole. I'm not tryin' to be extra tough, but I ain't a ho neither, you know what I'm sayin'? But it's like . . . I feel like a lot of people be tryin' to categorize me. Like I see a lot of people get out there, "Man, that's the hottest female rapper in Houston." But in my eyes, shit, I'm the hardest in Houston, *period*. But you know, that's just how certain people perceive it and how they mind work. Some people just give me my just due and be like, "Shit, she cold, *period*. Ain't nobody fuckin' with her." I really think I be fuckin' their head up how I'll do a mean-ass drill song, then come with a love song, like you'll be like, "Damn, this motherfucker will do *anything*."

Who were the first artists that you met and started fucking with on a musical level?

You know, niggas rap in my hood. Like I been . . . to me, I ain't gonna lie . . . I really been, like, for a minute I was doin' that shit on my own. Like I was on an ankle monitor, recording songs in my house. Whole CDs, just passin' 'em out in the hood, like, I never was really on some cliqued up shit, you know what I'm sayin'? But there's niggas from my *hood* that been rappin' for a minute before I . . . because, you know, I was passin' CDs out and shit, but I wasn't doin' no *videos*. These were like Junebug, Cal Wayne, they was already doin' videos, doin' shows, like, a nigga lookin' up to them niggas! Now I got a chance to rap with 'em, and they believin' in me! Like when people be askin' me who my favorite rapper is, I always say Cal Wayne. He's our Tupac. He tellin' the story like Tupac, but he tellin' it for The Tre, like the whole Tre. That's really the main people. But as far as, like, rap, just fuckin' around, like I been fuckin' around with everybody from like . . . I got songs from Philly, Dallas, New York, everywhere. I even got a song with somebody from the U.K. I just be networkin'.

I know that you have some people that you're not necessarily cliqued up with, but you have a movement around you. Did those people just come around in the last couple of years? A lot of them are from Third Ward, though, right? You must have known some of them since y'all were kids.

Yeah, yeah. That's the thing I'm sayin' is that we been growin' up together, but we fuck with each other—it ain't have to do with the music. When I first came home from jail, that's when I started takin' my music serious, shootin' videos and doin' shows. Like, I was never doin' that shit. It was just, e'rebody knew I could rap. I always used to be in school rappin'. It was what I wanted to do, but I didn't know *how* to do it at the time, you know what I'm sayin'? When I came home—I did two years in TDC—so, when I came home, that was all that was on my mind, like, *I'ma be a rapper.* You feel me? I went here first.

How long ago was that?

I got out in 2014.

So that kind of focused you, like, "I'm gonna leave that behind, and I'm gonna do this work."

For real.

And that's when stuff started kinda coming together. That's when I heard about you, probably 2015.

Yeah, man, it start gettin' wicked. I ain't gonna lie. My first year home, I was really just tryin' to get adjusted. I may have dropped a mixtape, but I hadn't shot no videos. In 2015 I had shot that "Shootston," and it just took off from there. "Shootston" got me so much like . . . that song did a lot for me.

What are your future plans? What are you working on now, and what do you see coming up in the future for you and for Houston in general?

Shit, man . . . shit is lookin' good right now. I don't know. You know how they always say, like, "Houston, we just hate each other and don't support each other," and all that? It was like niggas were so focused on the hate that they wasn't realizin', like, all you gotta do is stop talkin' about the hate and just start working. They can't deny you! You work hard enough, they can't deny you. It's just that niggas be worried about the wrong thing in competition with each other, but now that that shit has died down, niggas actually out here workin'. Like you got niggas that's actually from the H gettin' played on 97.9 The Box. We ain't had that shit in years, know what I'm sayin'? It's lookin' up for the city, like niggas just gotta work. Niggas gotta stop complainin', stop worryin' about what they not gettin' and start makin' it happen. Shit, if they don't wanna stay in Houston, keep goin' somewhere else until they *forced* to listen to you.

BLACKIE

LA PORTE

In the early 2000s a figure emerged on Houston's punk scene, or its noise scene, or really at any venue or parking lot that would allow him to haul in his sound system, scream into his microphone, and shake everything off of the walls. If there was a stage, B L A C K I E . . . All Caps, With Spaces (as his full performer name goes) would build his tower of speakers in front of it, push a button, and then thrash and shriek down to the feet of anyone who could endure the volume. There was no dividing line between audience and performer, and even though nobody could tell what Michael LaCour was saying, everybody knew what he was feeling.

Do the limitations of technology factor into your sound at all? Was there any kind of old technology sound that you got out of that you may have not gotten out of nice new gear?

Sometimes I use even older computers. Like I have a laptop from the '90s, and it can barely run anything. I like using that. I think if I go back to makin' more electronic sounding stuff, programming beats or whatever, I had been usin' that thing, because that thing, it's got like a real chunky sound, like reducin' the sample rate, and just doin' all the little weird things you can do with it.

Things that it does because it doesn't really have the power to process things the right way, so it kinda simplifies it or breaks it down in a way that you might not even know how to do if you had the equipment to do it, right?

Yeah. Or just like . . . you can't save nothin' on it. Like that really old one? I couldn't save anything, so I would have to write down presets so that every time I start a new session, I would automatically just go back to the presets I wrote down and put 'em in every time. It just had me workin' totally different.

So what did that mean when you started playing live? Did you bring like an ADAT with you or something like that? How did you do it playing live?

For a long time I had used an MPC500. I was makin' everything on the MPC500. But that thing broke 'cuz I was playin' too many shows with it, I guess. When I went to Europe the first time I couldn't bring too much stuff, so I just started usin' all these weird phones and just stupid shit like that. I don't like playin' off a phone, but I couldn't bring anything serious over there.

What did you bring? Were you able to bring any kind of speakers or did you get some over there?

The first time I went out over there they had the stuff backlined for me, and that was cool. They had a lot of gear and a van and everything. The next time I went out there I was just goin' through the little club systems everywhere.

Where all did you go?

All those tours were like—there was just two of them, but they were mostly in France. I played in

PHOTO: MICHAEL CRAFT

Amsterdam, I played in Belgium, but most of 'em were like all over France. Like a whole bunch of France. They really hold it down in France.

How did they react to it?

A lot of it was part of these art festivals, some of it was in like museums, so the people were kinda just like standin' back, like, "What the hell is goin' on?" But at the end of it they would come up to me and talk to me about it. It wasn't like playin' in America. When I got to the South of France, though, it was more punk rock clubs, and yeah, people would start headbangin' and mosh pits kinda, but for the most part they were just reserved.

Were they open to the fact that you're a bunch of styles mixed up and you can't really be pigeonholed?

I think they try to put you more in a box over here. I think they were just kinda more just like, "Oh, he's from America," or "He's from Texas—what's this guy doin'?" I played with some pretty weird bands, though. Some noise bands and stuff. Sometimes some rappers. It was pretty diverse.

What about the subject matter, what you're writing about? How do you source that kind of stuff, does it come to you naturally, do you keep up on current events?

Yeah, it'll come out naturally. It'll come out naturally in a way that later, when I play it back, I'm surprised—I'm like, "Whoa—that was . . ." I wasn't even thinkin' to take it that way, but now that I'm listenin' back to it, I'm like, "Whoa—that actually was relevant to some things maybe personal, maybe out in the world, *somethin'*." But yeah, it's very just tryin' to be—not think too much—because if you think too much about it, I think sometimes it'll come out kinda corny or kinda like you thought about it before. The stuff I've been writing lately, I'm trying to get back to not totally even thinkin' about it. It's just comin' out how it's gonna come out.

Not too literal.

Yeah, not on purpose. Not too literal on purpose. Maybe later when I play it back I'll be like, "Okay, damn—yeah." Lookin' at the news headlines or lookin' at somethin' that happened to me in the past year I might be able later to be like, "Aw, man—I musta meant it that way," or whatever. But at the time it was just like comin' out how it needed to come out.

Do you go back and revise lyrics a lot? Do you keep drafts?

Not too much. I kinda like to keep it real in the moment, like whatever recording session I'm in, I like to just go all the way through it, and as long as I didn't, like, mess up a take—technically mess up or somethin'—I'll just keep it. I don't really like to go back and change too many things.

So you got a setup at the house?

Yeah, yeah. Everything's just kinda pieced together. Just puttin' up like a lot of blankets, doin' a lot of, like, sound down—keepin' the sound in the room. Dampenin' the room.

Do you perform in La Porte sometimes? Is there a place out there?

Early on, when we were younger, playin' in some of those bands, yeah, we would perform here, and they had little, like, venues, but I think everybody kinda got older, everybody moved into the city. Some of the stuff I was doin' early on, because I couldn't find anywhere to play, I would just get a generator and set up at this little skatepark out here. And I would try to throw my own little shows at the skatepark. Some of those were cool.

The kids loved it?

Yeah, I was surprised because I didn't really put up fliers, but people just found out. "There's all these weird bands playin' at the skatepark tonight. We don't even know if it's legal," or whatever. And I had just—because of some personal events, I had run into this police officer, and he actually came to check on me when I was in the hospital or whatever. I was cool with him to a degree, and I just stopped by the police station and told him, like, "Yeah, man, I'm out the hospital. I think I'ma rent a generator and play some of my music down here at the skatepark." And he was like, "Well, I can't let you do that, but since it's one night, I'll try to keep it—as long as y'all don't get too loud, I'll try to keep it happenin'." And it *worked*—like it went down, it went on, and eventually at a certain point he stopped by and he was just kinda like, "Yo, it's time to cut it." He was cool, man. That was a cool cop.

I guess only you could have a generator right next to you and not have your sound affected, huh?

[Laughs] Yeah, yeah. Back then I had more speakers than I do now!

How long did that take—when you first started doing shows as B L A C K I E did you already have that whole big speaker setup? Was that part of the very first incarnation of what you were doing?

Yeah. Yeah, because even when I was playin' in some of those bands, those punk bands early on, I had already started stackin' speakers up and building crap out of crap because I just couldn't afford no real gear. And my dad would help me build some of the stuff early on, so yeah, I think I was just like . . . I just liked building the speakers. Like, I think I was just more on some kinda nerd thing. I just liked puttin' the wires together and cuttin' the wood, and I was just into just like, "Aw, man. I can build this. This is cool."

So you were building your own cabinets and everything.

Yeah early on my dad helped me build a few. Took some amplifiers apart. Nothing too technical, but I just liked takin' the stuff apart, seein' how it worked, seein' how loud you could turn it up.

Seeing what you could do to tweak the sound, bend the sound a little bit.

Yeah, yeah. There's even like a really old picture of me from back when I was a teenager, and I had a bunch of—because I was playin' bass in those punk bands—I had a bunch of bass amps stacked up even back then when I was like 13. They were all just wired into each other, distorting it. I was just plugging everything into everything!

Did stuff blow up on you sometimes?

Yeah, yeah. Whatever amp was at the end of the chain, I guess because of all the gain, the level of turning everything up and not knowin' what I was doin', usually, like, the little top speaker, it would fry out just because of running too many pre-amps into each other.

When did you start playing shows in general?

I was probably like 13 years old, playin' in a punk band. Just around town, just anywhere, churches

. . . there's a festival here called Strawberry Festival. That was like, the first show we ever played was at that thing.

And what was the band called?

It was called Mike and The Whiteys actually, because I was the only black kid in the band. We were just kids and we couldn't think of a real name that everybody liked and I was just goofin'. I was just like, "Man, Mike and The Whiteys. I'm the only black motherfucker." And they just could not stop laughin', and they were like, "Yeah, that's it! That's it! That's ridiculous." And then, all them years later, you ended up bein' called B L A C K I E. I was like, "That's fuckin' silly, man." Life is silly.

That was late '90s?

That was like 2000, 2001.

So it was really only a few years later that you started doin' what you're doing now, huh?

Yeah, yeah. Because I had been rappin' just for fun. And when all those bands broke up, those guys were just like, "Aw, you should keep rappin'." I tried to join other bands, but they would hear me rappin', and they'd be like, "Man, you should just *rap*, dude." And then once I realized like, "Yeah, all these bands keep breakin' up, nobody really wants to practice. I can just rap on my own and not have to rely on anybody," that's when I was just like, "Alright, I guess I'll just rap now."

It opens up things for you creatively too, right? "Now I don't have to run this by anybody."

I was always cool with bein' in the background! Because I played bass with those bands, and I'm kinda like a pretty quiet person, so I kinda liked bein' in the background and somebody else write the songs, and then I come in with just a weird bassline. That was more my personality to be honest. Startin' off rappin', it was just by accident. Like on two ways, 'cuz like, I just wanted to be in a band, and then once I started rappin', per se, I

wasn't really *rappin'*, I was more concerned with makin' the beats, but I couldn't find anybody to *rap* on 'em, so then I was like, "Oh, I guess I gotta start rappin' now." But bein' out front was never really something I intended to do. It was just because nobody wanted to rap on these weird beats I was makin'.

Did it take a while before you got used to that, bein' out in front?

Yeah, yeah—I'm still not used to it. *Still.* Like I was just lookin' at my social media—it keeps givin' me notifications, "You haven't posted in 12 weeks." I don't think I've posted on Instagram in like a month or something. Like, I'm *still* not really a forefront kinda person.

Well that's a hard energy to keep up too, though, right?

I'm never doin' nothin' cool, man! It's like everybody's doin' cool shit, parties or at the bar doin' this and that. I'm just like, "I'm never doing anything that cool that I could document!"

I remember you coming to New York, 2009, something like that, and I met you before the show and [you] were like, "I'm so nervous for this show." And it occurred to me that night that when you're performing live, I can't tell if you're blissed out and don't give a fuck, or if you're totally nervous and that's where the energy is coming from. Your show straddles that edge, so nobody can tell, so they kinda throw themselves into it.

Yeah, I definitely get hella nervous before I play. A lot of that is just crazy energy from just not really wantin' to be in front of everybody but knowin' that my fate or whatever, "I can do this." I can still perform in a manner that's gonna captivate people. So I just like, yeah, just tune everything out and just go for it.

But it gets easier, right? You can't possibly get as nervous as you used to.

What I learned now is that if I *don't* get nervous before I play, then usually the show sucks. That's kinda what I figured out. Like if it's a real kinda, like, bigger show where it's going to be a memorable show, sometimes I can't even put my equipment together because I'll be so nervous just like—the electricity will just be runnin' through my arms to where I can't feel my fingers. Like, "Shit I'm nervous! Maybe this show will be crazy." But the shows where I'm just totally relaxed, I realize later, "Man, that show was kind of a bummer."

So you're just channeling all of that energy each time.

Yeah, I guess I'm pickin' up on whatever's goin' on in the room or somethin.'

When does that fade away—as soon as you start playing or is it a couple songs in? Does it ever really go away?

Oh yeah, as soon as I hit the button, and the beats start blastin' out, it's goin' down. It's automatic. Everything up until I start the music, I'm hella nervous, but once the music starts, I'm just gone. I'm just flyin' out my body.

Acknowledgments

First thanks goes to Peter Beste, whose dedication to this history and passion for these subjects have given this project (and me) direction and life from the start.

For helping us make connections over the years, a huge debt goes out to Willie D, Bun B, K-Rino, Devin the Dude, Murder One, Jugg Mugg, Big Bubb, Matt Sonzala, Cl'Che, Papa Screw, Meshah Hawkins, Shorty Mac, Mike Frost, G-Dash, T. Farris, Michael '5000' Watts, Petey Wheatstra, Pimp C, DJ Chill, Justice Allah, Optimo Ram, Freeze, Big Tho, DJ Domo, Captain Jack, AI-D, DJ Gold, Dope E., Script, Mike-D, Bamino, Kyu Boi, Darryl Scott, Mean Green, DJ Good Grief, Craig (BBC) Long, Rad Richard, Rashad Al-Amin, Dominique Turner, Bird, and everyone else who went out of their way for us (especially Orian "Lump" Lumpkin).

Thanks to Julie Grob at the University of Houston, Dr. Anthony Pinn at Rice University, and Matt Carter and Dennis Brandner at City College of New York for bringing our work into the academic world, and to the Houston Museum of African American Culture and The Association for Recorded Sound Collections (ARSC) for help preserving the legacy. Also thanks to Rob Semmer, Trace Crutchfield, and Mike Washlesky with VBS, and to the *Houston Chronicle*, *Houston Press*, *Free Press Houston*, *Local Houston*, *Fader*, *Vice*, *Dazed & Confused*, *RBMA*, and other publications in which our work has been published together in the past.

Many thanks to our hosts Screwed Up Records & Tapes, Cactus Music, Brazos Bookstore, MATCH, and Sig's Lagoon in Houston, Farewell Books in Austin, Ghost Pizza (San Antonio), Red Emma's (Baltimore), Joint Custody (Washington, DC), UGHH (Boston), Type Books (Toronto), Rough Trade (NYC), Powerhouse Arena (Brooklyn), The Owl Music Parlor (Brooklyn), Record Grouch (Brooklyn), The Last Bookstore (LA), and Marfa Book Co.

Thank you Michael P. Daley, Sheila Browers, Sirena Guenther, Todd Burns, Harley Brown, Jamie Saft, Elliott Goldkind, Dave Tompkins, Lawrence Burney, Gonzo 247, Brian Coleman, Joan LeMay, Anna Godbersen, Kaiama L. Glover, Kim Barker, Stefanie Sobelle, Magus Magnus, Liesl Schillinger, Omar Columbus, Eddy Machtinger, Peter Spagnuolo, Oren Bloedow, Dana Scott, James Torres and Darwin Lopez, Bobby Phats and K. Dubb Watson, Optimo Ram, Sean Setaro, Tim Johnson, Verda Carr, Craig Lindsey, Shea Serrano, Maco L. Faniel, and Flash Gordon Parks for your support.

Hats off to everyone at Boo-Hooray in New York and Now Again Records in Los Angeles. Together, you are Sinecure Books, and it is an honor to have produced the First Edition of this work in such good company. Thank you Eothen and Johan.

At University of Texas Press, immeasurable thanks to acquiring editor Casey Kittrell for believing that this was worth a new edition and that this and the forthcoming *DJ Screw* are as important to Texas history as they are to Houston's history. Also thanks to Angelica, Nancy, Amanda, Cameron, Kathryn, Bailey, and Leyla at UT, and to Houston blues historian Roger Wood for introducing me to the gang.

Deepest gratitude to everyone I interviewed both for this book and *Houston Rap*, whether or not your voices ended up in print. Every word helped paint the picture. I'm grateful for your truths. Some of the folks in this book are no longer with us: Big Gerb (1983–2016), MC Wickett Crickett (1957–2016), Macc Grace (1973–2017), and the artist in the original cover photo, Mr. 3-2 (1974–2016), making their histories that much more important.

Cheers to the 2017 Houston Astros for bringing such joy to a city that needed it so badly.

Special blessings to my family in Texas, DC, Louisiana, Colorado, Michigan, New York, and Canada, with a lifetime of gratitude to my wife JC.

Thank you H-Town. Stay strong.

Index